걸프 사태

유엔안전보장이사회 동향 6

걸프 사태

유엔안전보장이사회 동향 6

한국학술정보

| 머리말

걸프 전쟁은 미국의 주도하에 34개국 연합군 병력이 수행한 전쟁으로, 1990년 8월 이라크의 쿠웨이트 침공 및 합병에 반대하며 발발했다. 미국은 초기부터 파병 외교에 나섰고, 1990년 9월 서울 등에 고위 관리를 파견하며 한국의 동참을 요청했다. 88올림픽 이후 동구권 국교 수립과 유엔 가입 추진 등 적극적인 외교 활동을 펼치는 당시 한국에 있어 이는 미국과 국제 사회의 지지를 얻기 위해서라도 피할 수 없는 일이었다. 결국 정부는 91년 1월부터 약 3개월에 걸쳐 국군의료지원단과 공군수송단을 사우디아라비아 및 아랍 에미리트 연합 등에 파병하였고, 군·민간 의료 활동, 병력 수송 임무를 수행했다. 동시에 당시 걸프 지역 8개국에 살던 5천여 명의 교민에게 방독면 등 물자를 제공하고, 특별기 파견 등으로 비상시 대피할 수 있도록 지원했다. 비록 전쟁 부담금과 유가 상승 등 어려움도 있었지만, 걸프전 파병과 군사 외교를 통해 한국은 유엔 가입에 박차를 가할 수 있었고 미국 등 선진 우방국, 아랍권 국가 등과 밀접한 외교 관계를 유지하며 여러 국익을 창출할 수 있었다.

본 총서는 외교부에서 작성하여 30여 년간 유지한 걸프 사태 관련 자료를 담고 있다. 미국을 비롯한 여러 국가와의 군사 외교 과정, 일일 보고 자료와 기타 정부의 대응 및 조치, 재외동포 철수와 보호, 의료지원단과 수송단 파견 및 지원 과정, 유엔을 포함해 세계 각국에서 수집한 관련 동향 자료, 주변국 지원과 전후복구사업 참여 등 총 48권으로 구성되었다. 전체 분량은 약 2만 4천여 쪽에 이른다.

2024년 3월
한국학술정보(주)

| 일러두기

· 본 총서에 실린 자료는 2022년 4월과 2023년 4월에 각각 공개한 외교문서 4,827권, 76만 여 쪽 가운데 일부를 발췌한 것이다.

· 각 권의 제목과 순서는 공개된 원본을 최대한 반영하였으나, 주제에 따라 일부는 적절히 변경하였다.

· 원본 자료는 A4 판형에 맞게 축소하거나 원본 비율을 유지한 채 A4 페이지 안에 삽입 하였다. 또한 현재 시점에선 공개되지 않아 '공란'이란 표기만 있는 페이지 역시 그대로 실었다.

· 외교부가 공개한 문서 각 권의 첫 페이지에는 '정리 보존 문서 목록'이란 이름으로 기록물 종류, 일자, 명칭, 간단한 내용 등의 정보가 수록되어 있으며, 이를 기준으로 0001번부터 번호가 매겨져 있다. 이는 삭제하지 않고 총서에 그대로 수록하였다.

· 보고서 내용에 관한 더 자세한 정보가 필요하다면, 외교부가 온라인상에 제공하는 『대한 민국 외교사료요약집』 1991년과 1992년 자료를 참조할 수 있다.

| 차례

머리말 4

일러두기 5

유엔안전보장이사회 이라크 대량살상무기 폐기 특별위원회, 1991.
전3권 (V.2 8-9월) 7

유엔안전보장이사회 이라크 대량살상무기 폐기 특별위원회, 1991.
전3권 (V.3 10-12월) 367

	정 리 보 존 문 서 목 록

기록물종류	일반공문서철	등록번호	2020010147	등록일자	2020-01-28
분류번호	731.33	국가코드	IQ	보존기간	30년
명 칭		유엔안전보장이사회 이라크 대량살상무기 폐기 특별위원회, 1991. 전3권
생 산 과	국제연합1과/중동1과	생산년도	1991~1991	담당그룹	
권 차 명		V.2 8-9월

내용목차		* 8.15 이라크의 무기 폐기 이행 위반 규탄 결의안 채택(안보리 결의 707호)
		
		  10.11 이라크 대량살상무기통제 검증을 위한 유엔사무총장 및 IAEA 사무총장 계획안 승인 결의안 채택(안보리 결의 715호)
		
		  10.21-23 제2차 본회의(New York)
		
		* WHO 의 이라크 내 생화학 무기 사찰 폐기 활동 포함
		
		* 유엔 핵 조사단의 핵 사찰 실시 포함

0001

주 국 련 대 표 부

주국련 20313- **618**   1991. 8 . 1 .

수신 : 장관

참조 : 국제기구조약국장, 중동아프리카국장

제목 : 대이락 무기공급금지(2)

　　　　　　연 : UNW － 1872, 주국련 20313-574(91.7.18)

　　　각국이 안보리 결의700호에 의거하여 유엔사무총장에게 통보해온
표제관련 조치내용을 별첨송부합니다.

　　첨 부 : 상기문서.　　끝.

주		국		련		대		사
선 결					결재(공람)			
접수일시	1991. 8. 5							
처리과		43747						

0002

**UNITED
NATIONS**

S

Security Council

Distr.
GENERAL

S/22835
25 July 1991

ORIGINAL: ENGLISH

NOTE VERBALE DATED 24 JULY 1991 FROM THE PERMANENT MISSION OF JAPAN
TO THE UNITED NATIONS ADDRESSED TO THE SECRETARY-GENERAL

The Permanent Representative of Japan to the United Nations presents his compliments to the Secretary-General of the United Nations and has the honour to refer to the latter's note SCPC/7/91/91 (4-1) of 3 July 1991, requesting information regarding the application of the provisions in paragraph 4 of Security Council resolution 700 (1991) of 17 June 1991.

The Permanent Representative is pleased to inform the Secretary-General of the following:

1.   The Government of Japan, in accordance with the Three Principles on Arms Exports adopted in 1967 and the Policy Guideline on Arms Exports adopted in 1976 (see annex), takes a very strict position with respect to the exportation of arms and equipment related to arms production, and virtually prohibits such exportation to all regions of the world.

2.   In addition, in August 1990, the Government of Japan took the following measures in order to comply strictly with Security Council resolution 661 (1990) of 6 August 1990:

(1)   Exports of all goods to Iraq became subject to approval by the Minister of International Trade and Industry; trade activity is thus virtually prohibited (with the exception, on humanitarian grounds, of medical and related services, and basic foodstuffs);

(2)   Transactions of service with Iraq became subject to approval by the Minister of International Trade and Industry and/or the Minister of Finance; such activity is virtually prohibited;

(3)   Any engagement by Japanese nationals and vessels flying the Japanese flag in cargo transactions originating in or destined for Iraq is prohibited.

3.   In consequence of the above, the Government of Japan strictly fulfils all obligations contained in paragraph 24 of resolution 687 (1991) of 3 April 1991; therefore, any additional measures to carry out the above-mentioned obligations are not necessary.

91-23979 2577j (E)   /...

0003

Annex

1. Three Principles on Arms Exports

On 21 April 1967, Prime Minister Eisaku Sato declared the Three Principles on Arms Exports at the Diet Session:

Arms Exports to the following countries shall not in principle be allowed:

(1) Communist bloc countries;

(2) Countries subject to embargoes on arms exports under the United Nations Security Council's resolutions; and

(3) Countries engaged or likely to be engaged in an international conflict.

2. Policy Guideline on Arms Exports

On 27 February 1976, Prime Minister Takeo Miki announced the Government Policy Guideline on Arms Exports at the Diet Session:

(1) The Government, in keeping with Japan's position as a peace-loving nation, has been dealing carefully with arms exports so as to avoid any possible contribution to international conflict. The Government will continue to do so in accordance with the following Policy Guideline and shall not promote arms exports;

    (i) Arms exports to areas specified in the Three Principles shall not be allowed;

    (ii) Arms exports to other areas shall be avoided, in conformity with the spirit of the Constitution and the Foreign Exchange and Foreign Trade Control Law; and

    (iii) Export of arms production-related equipment shall be dealt with in the same way as "arms" are.

(2) "Arms" as referred to in the Three Principles are defined as "goods which are used by military forces, and which are directly employed in combat".

0004

UNITED
NATIONS

Security Council

Distr.
GENERAL

S/22840
26 July 1991
ENGLISH
ORIGINAL: FRENCH

NOTE VERBALE DATED 25 JULY 1991 FROM THE PERMANENT MISSION
OF BELGIUM TO THE UNITED NATIONS ADDRESSED TO THE
SECRETARY-GENERAL

The Permanent Mission of Belgium to the United Nations presents its compliments to the Secretary-General and has the honour, with reference to paragraph 4 of Security Council resolution 700 (1991), to provide him with the following information:

The export of arms and munitions to Iraq has been subject to sanctions in Belgium since 1980; the sanctions were, furthermore, confirmed at the beginning of 1990 by the Ministerial External Relations Committee. As of 8 August 1990, Belgium took the necessary measures to implement the commercial and financial sanctions adopted by the Security Council in its resolution 661 (1990) (see document S/AC.25/1990/2, entitled "Measures taken by Belgium in application of Security Council resolution 661 (1990)").

It has thus been possible to ensure compliance with the provisions of article 24 of resolution 687 (1991) without the creation of any additional legal instruments.

Legislation

Belgian laws and regulations are fully consistent with the obligations set out in resolution 687 (1991), as well as with the previous binding decisions of the Council. The export of arms and military matériel is subject to the provisions of the Act of 11 September 1962 on the import, export and transit of goods, of the Royal Enforcement Decree of 24 October 1962 and of the Ministerial Decree of 8 August 1990, requiring the production of a licence for the export to Iraq of any products originating in or coming from the European Community.

Belgium also applies the regulations formulated by the European Community to govern exports to Iraq in accordance with the resolutions of the Security Council (such as Regulation (EEC) 2340-90).

91-24077 2493h (E)

0005

/...

Apart from these provisions, which cover all types of exports, Belgium also has legislation that dictates a very strict procedure for the export of nuclear materials and equipment (Act of 9 February 1991 and Royal Decree of 12 May 1989).

In addition, Belgium points out that, under the Act of 10 July 1978, it has prohibited the development, production, stockpiling or transfer of bacteriological (biological) and toxin weapons and has acceded to the related Convention of London, Moscow and Washington of 14 April 1972.

Implementation

The competent authorities are the Customs and Excise Administration within the Ministry of Finance and the Central Office for Quotas and Licences within the Ministry of Economic Affairs.

Documentation and goods are monitored by the Economic Inspectorate and the Customs Administration. There is a clause prohibiting the re-export of such goods.

The only permits granted by Belgium for exports to Iraq have related to food products and urgent requirements in accordance with the rules set out in resolution 661 (1990) and in resolution 687 (1991), in the light of the report of Mr. M. Ahtisaari (document S/22366).

In addition, with a view to ensuring strict compliance with the decisions of the Security Council, Belgium has ensured that these decisions are made known to the institutions and establishments concerned.

Note

Belgium points out that a draft act on the import, export and transit of arms, munitions and equipment for specifically military use and of related technology has just been approved by the Belgian Parliament. The fact that a specific act should govern international trade in such products is an innovation. The intention of the Belgian legislator is more effectively to combat the illicit traffic in weapons and thus to ensure the attainment of the objectives established by the United Nations in that regard.

0006

Security Council

Distr.
GENERAL

S/22841
26 July 1991

ORIGINAL: ENGLISH

LETTER DATED 25 JULY 1991 FROM THE PERMANENT REPRESENTATIVE OF
THE UNITED KINGDOM OF GREAT BRITAIN AND NORTHERN IRELAND TO
THE UNITED NATIONS ADDRESSED TO THE SECRETARY-GENERAL

In response to your Note SCPC/7/91(4-1) of 3 July 1991, I am writing to inform you about the measures undertaken by the United Kingdom to implement Security Council resolution 700 (1991).

Current United Kingdom laws and regulations already meet the obligations and requirements of resolution 687 (1991) as regards the sale, supply, or the promotion or facilitation of the sale or supply of goods to Iraq, including those items specified in paragraph 24 of resolution 687 (1991). The Guidelines adopted by Security Council resolution 700 (1991) fall largely within the scope of existing United Kingdom legislation. This includes the following Orders in Council:

-       The Hong Kong (Control of Gold, Securities, Payments and Credits: Kuwait and Republic of Iraq) Order 1990 (6 August 1990);

-       The Caribbean Territories (Control of Gold, Securities, Payments and Credits: Kuwait and Republic of Iraq) Order 1990: SI No. 1625 (6 August 1990);

-       The Iraq and Kuwait (United Nations Sanctions) Order 1990; SI No. 1651 (8 August 1990);

-       The Iraq and Kuwait (United Nations Sanctions) (Dependent Territories) Order 1990: SI No. 1652 (8 August 1990);

-       The Export of Goods (Control) (Iraq and Kuwait Sanctions) Order 1990: SI No. 1640 (8 August 1990);

-       The Iraq and Kuwait (United Nations Sanctions) (Amendment) Order 1990: SI No. 1768 (29 August 1990);

-       The Iraq and Kuwait (United Nations Sanctions) (Bermuda) Order 1990: SI No. 1769 (29 August 1990);

91-24083   2598d (E)

0007   /...

- The Iraq and Kuwait (United Nations Sanctions) (Dependent
  Territories) (Amendment) Order 1990: SI No. 1770 (29 August 1990);

- The Iraq and Kuwait (United Nations Sanctions) (Channel Islands)
  Order 1990: SI No. 1771 (29 August 1990);

- The Iraq and Kuwait (United Nations Sanctions) (No. 2) Order 1990
  (5 October 1990);

- The Iraq and Kuwait (United Nations Sanctions) (Dependent
  Territories) (No. 2) Order 1990 (5 October 1990);

- The Iraq and Kuwait (United Nations Sanctions) (Second Amendment)
  Order 1990: SI No. 2144 (31 October 1990).

Her Majesty's Treasury issued a separate legal direction - the Control of
Gold, Securities, Payments and Credits (Republic of Iraq) Directions 1990: SI
No. 1616 - on 4 August 1990. The Bank of England issued a notice - Emergency
Laws (Re-enactments and Appeals) Act 1964: Iraq - on 7 August 1990.

In addition, the European Community has enacted the following legislation
preventing trade by Community members with Iraq:

- EEC regulation 2340/90 extended and amended by EEC regulation
  3155/90.

- ECSC decision 90/414.

These regulations and decisions have direct effect in the United Kingdom.

The controls on the sale or supply of technology and personnel or
materials referred to in subparagraphs (c) and (d) of paragraph 24 of
resolution 687 (1991) will be reinforced by a new Order in Council. This will
be self-contained and will fully implement all the requirements of
paragraph 24, and the Guidelines adopted by Security Council resolution
700 (1991). A copy of the new Order in Council will be made available to the
United Nations when it has been promulgated. The legislation will provide for
criminal sanctions in the form of imprisonment or fines. Responsibilities for
enforcement of the new legislation will fall largely to the Department of
Trade and Industry and Her Majesty's Customs and Excise.

I should be grateful if you would arrange for this letter to be
circulated as a document of the Security Council.

(Signed) D. H. A. HANNAY

0008

Security Council

Distr.
GENERAL

S/22842
26 July 1991
ENGLISH
ORIGINAL: SPANISH

NOTE VERBALE DATED 25 JULY 1991 FROM THE PERMANENT MISSION OF
SPAIN TO THE UNITED NATIONS ADDRESSED TO THE SECRETARY-GENERAL

The Permanent Representative of Spain to the United Nations presents his
compliments to the Secretary-General and has the honour to refer to his note
verbale SCPC/7/91(4-1), which draws attention to paragraphs 2, 3, 4 and 5 of
Security Council resolution 700 (1991).

In this connection, and in accordance with paragraph 4 of resolution
700 (1991), the Permanent Representative of Spain is pleased to transmit the
following information concerning measures adopted by the Government of Spain
to fulfil the obligations set out in paragraph 24 of Security Council
resolution 687 (1991).

Following the invasion of Kuwait by Iraqi troops, the Spanish Government
in August 1990 adopted a series of measures (Ministerial Orders of 4 and
6 August, pursuant to Regulations (EEC) 2340/90 and 3155/90), imposing general
sanctions on the export of defence matériel to Iraq, immediately suspending
the issuance of export licences and instructing all Spanish customs units to
freeze any operation which might already be under way.

Since August 1990, the Interministerial Board with responsibility for
monitoring external trade in defence matériel and in products and technologies
susceptible to dual use (a body comprising representatives of the Ministry of
Industry and Trade, the Ministry of Defence and the Ministry of Foreign
Affairs whose responsibility it is to authorize or to refuse export licences
for defence matériel and which monitors implementation of and compliance with
the sanctions) has granted no new licences for exports to Iraq; any permits
relating to contracts authorized prior to the imposition of the sanctions have
been cancelled.

The ban on exports or imports of defence matériel to or from Iraq applies
to all types of equipment, including spare parts, and also covers the transit,
temporary import and export and deposit in a free-trade zone of such matériel.

91-24118 2457i (E)   0009

UNITED NATIONS

Security Council

S

Distr.
GENERAL

S/22848
29 July 1991

ORIGINAL: ENGLISH

NOTE VERBALE DATED 29 JULY 1991 FROM THE PERMANENT
REPRESENTATIVE OF SRI LANKA TO THE UNITED NATIONS
ADDRESSED TO THE SECRETARY-GENERAL

The Permanent Representative of the Democratic Socialist Republic of
Sri Lanka to the United Nations presents his compliments to the
Secretary-General and, with reference to latter's note No. SCPC/7/91 (4-1)
dated 3 July 1991, has the honour to state that, in accordance with guidelines
contained in Security Council document S/22660 of 2 June 1991, the Government
of Sri Lanka has complied fully with Security Council resolution 687 (1991),
in particular paragraph 24.

0010

91-24264 2533e (E)

Security Council

Distr.
GENERAL

S/22849
29 July 1991

ORIGINAL: ENGLISH

NOTE VERBALE DATED 29 JULY 1991 FROM THE PERMANENT
REPRESENTATIVE OF SINGAPORE TO THE UNITED NATIONS
ADDRESSED TO THE SECRETARY-GENERAL

The Permanent Representative of the Republic of Singapore to the United
Nations presents his compliments to the Secretary-General and, with reference
to his note SCPC/7/91/4-1 of 3 July 1991, has the honour to inform the
Secretary-General that the Republic of Singapore, in full conformity with the
spirit and letter of Security Council resolution 700 (1991), strictly abides
by the prohibitions against the sale or supply of arms to Iraq. The Republic
of Singapore has imposed comprehensive economic sanctions on Iraq since
August 1990 via the Prohibition of Imports and Exports (Iraq) Order 1990 which
prohibits the imports and exports of all goods, including arms, from and to
Iraq. Singapore continues to strictly enforce these sanctions.

91-24270 3161a (E)

0011

UNITED NATIONS

S

Security Council

Distr.
GENERAL

S/22851
29 July 1991
ENGLISH
ORIGINAL: SPANISH

NOTE VERBALE DATED 23 JULY 1991 FROM THE PERMANENT MISSION
OF ECUADOR TO THE UNITED NATIONS ADDRESSED TO THE
SECRETARY-GENERAL

The Permanent Mission of Ecuador to the United Nations presents its
compliments to the Secretary-General and, with reference to note
SCPC/7/91(4-1) of 3 July 1991, has the honour to inform him that the
Government of Ecuador, in keeping with the principles of international law,
observes and respects all decisions legally adopted by the United Nations and
its bodies. Ecuador strictly observes all resolutions of the Security
Council, including the prohibitions contained in paragraph 24 of resolution
687 (1991).

Accordingly, the competent national authorities and organizations have
been specifically instructed to ensure compliance with and implementation of
those prohibitions, in accordance with the Ecuadorian legislation in force.

0012

91-24252 2459i (E)

UNITED NATIONS

S

Security Council

Distr.
GENERAL

S/22852
29 July 1991

ORIGINAL: ENGLISH

NOTE VERBALE DATED 26 JULY 1991 FROM THE CHARGE D'AFFAIRES A.I.
OF THE PERMANENT MISSION OF MALTA TO THE UNITED NATIONS
ADDRESSED TO THE SECRETARY-GENERAL

The Acting Permanent Representative of Malta to the United Nations presents his compliments to the Secretary-General of the United Nations and, with reference to his note SCPC/7/91/4-1 of 3 July 1991 has the honour to inform that Malta strictly abides by the prohibition against the sale or supply of arms to Iraq, in accordance with the relevant Security Council resolutions.

91-24258 2458i (E)

0013

UNITED NATIONS

Security Council

S

Distr.
GENERAL

S/22858
30 July 1991

ORIGINAL: ENGLISH

NOTE VERBALE DATED 26 JULY 1991 FROM THE CHARGE D'AFFAIRES A.I.
OF THE PERMANENT MISSION OF GREECE TO THE UNITED NATIONS
ADDRESSED TO THE SECRETARY-GENERAL

The Chargé d'affaires a.i. of Greece to the United Nations presents his compliments to the Secretary-General of the United Nations and with reference to His Excellency's Note No. SCPC/F/91(4-1) of 3 July 1991 has the honour to inform him of the following:

The Greek Government immediately after the invasion of Kuwait by Iraqi troops adopted a series of measures enumerated in Doc. S/21613 of 23.8.90 and has also been implementing EEC regulations 2340/90 and 3155/90.

All exports of arms and of any kind of military equipment from Greece are under governmental control and subject to a licence issued on a case-by-case basis by the Ministries of Foreign Affairs, Defence and Trade.

The competent authorities involved in the export of military equipment have been informed of and strictly comply with the pertinent Security Council resolutions, namely resolutions 661 (1990), 687 (1991) and with the Guidelines annexed to the Secretary-General's report (S/22660) approved by the Security Council in resolution 700 (1991).

Consequently Greece does not sell or supply any kind of military equipment to Iraq.

91-24388 2461i (E)

0014

Security Council

Distr.
GENERAL

S/22859
30 July 1991
ENGLISH
ORIGINAL: SPANISH

NOTE VERBALE DATED 29 JULY 1991 FROM THE PERMANENT MISSION OF
CHILE TO THE UNITED NATIONS ADDRESSED TO THE SECRETARY-GENERAL

The Permanent Mission of Chile to the United Nations presents its compliments to the Secretary-General of the United Nations and has the honour to refer to his note SCPC/7/91(4-1) of 3 July, relating to Security Council resolution 700 (1991), which reiterates "the prohibitions against the sale or supply of arms to Iraq and related sanctions established in paragraph 24 of resolution 687 (1991)".

In this connection, the Permanent Mission of Chile informs the Secretary-General that the Government of Chile is maintaining in force Supreme Foreign Affairs Decrees No. 808 of 8 August 1990, which orders full compliance with Security Council resolution 661 (1990) imposing sanctions on the Republic of Iraq, and No. 1139 of 30 October 1990, ordering compliance with Security Council resolution 670 (1990) which supplements resolution 661 (1990).

91-24394 2538e (E)

0015

UNITED NATIONS

S

Security Council

Distr.
GENERAL

S/22860
30 July 1991

ORIGINAL: ENGLISH

NOTE VERBALE DATED 29 JULY 1991 FROM THE CHARGE D'AFFAIRES OF THE
PERMANENT MISSION OF FINLAND TO THE UNITED NATIONS ADDRESSED TO
THE SECRETARY-GENERAL

The Acting Permanent Representative of Finland to the United Nations presents her compliments to His Excellency the Secretary-General of the United Nations, and with reference to his note SCPC/7/91/4-1 of 3 July 1991, has the honour to transmit to the Secretary-General the following information on the implementation of paragraph 4 of Security Council resolution 700 (1991).

All exportation of defence material from Finland as well as the transport of such material through the Finnish territory to a third country are regulated in the conventions and agreements binding upon Finland and the relevant domestic laws.

According to Act 659/67 Concerning the Implementation of Certain Obligations incumbent upon Finland as a Member of the United Nations, mandatory decisions of the Security Council, including e.g. a prohibition to export military equipment to certain areas, are binding upon Finland.

It is an established policy that Finland does not supply arms to belligerent States or crisis areas or areas where hostilities are likely to break out.

Since Iraq invaded Kuwait no authorizations for licences to export defence material to Iraq have been granted by the Government of Finland.

New York, 29 July 1991

91-24400   3162a (E)

0016

Security Council

Distr.
GENERAL

S/22861
31 July 1991

ORIGINAL: ENGLISH

NOTE VERBALE DATED 30 JULY 1991 FROM THE PERMANENT
REPRESENTATIVE OF MYANMAR TO THE UNITED NATIONS
ADDRESSED TO THE SECRETARY-GENERAL

The Permament Representative of the Union of Myanmar to the United
Nations presents his compliments to the Secretary-General of the United
Nations and in reply to the Secretary-General's note dated 3 July 1991
requesting information, in pursuance of paragraph 4 of Security Council
resolution 700 (1991), on the measures instituted by the Government of Myanmar
for meeting the obligations set out in paragraph 24 of resolution 687 (1991),
has the honour to state as follows:

Following the adoption by the Security Council of resolution 661 (1990),
the Government of Myanmar on 15 August 1990 decided to take neccesary measures
for the full implementation of the provisions of the said resolution. To give
effect to this decision the Ministry of Trade of the Government of Myanmar
issued directives to all ministries and government departments concerned as
well as to non-governmental organizations, private enterprises and Myanmar
nationals prohibiting them from engaging in any trade directly or indirectly
with Iraq.

In conjunction with the laws and regulations in force in the country
those directives that the Myanmar Government is continuing to enforce fully
meet the obligations set out in paragraph 24 of resolution 687 (1991) and will
also enable the Myanmar authorities to act in a manner consistent with the
relevant parts of the guidelines approved by the Security Council in
resolution 700 (1991).

91-24416   2490g (E)

0017

주 국 련 대 표 부

주국련20313-

619

수신 : 장관

참조 : 국제기구조약국장, 중동아프리카국장

제목 : 걸프사태(안보리)

91. 8. 1.

표제관련 안보리 문서를 별첨과 같이 송부합니다.

첨 부 : 상기 문서. 끝.

주   국   련   대   사

선 결			결재(공람)	
접수일시	1991. 8. 5	번호	0h	
처리과	43746			

0018

UNITED NATIONS

Security Council

Distr.
GENERAL

S/22837
25 July 1991

ORIGINAL: ENGLISH

NOTE BY THE SECRETARY-GENERAL

The Secretary-General has the honour to transmit to the members of the Security Council the attached communication which he has received from the Director-General of the International Atomic Energy Agency (IAEA).

91-24018 2453i (E)   /...

0019

Annex

Letter dated 25 July 1991 from the Director-General of the International Atomic Energy addressed to the Secretary-General

Please find attached the report of the third IAEA Inspection in Iraq under Security Council resolution 687 (1991). You may deem it appropriate to transmit the report to the members of the Security Council. I remain of course available with the Chief Inspector, Mr. Demetrius Perricos, for any consultations you or the Council may wish to have. I am planning to go to the United States on 28 July.

(Signed) Hans BLIX

/...

0020

Enclosure

REPORT ON THE THIRD IAEA ON-SITE INSPECTION IN IRAQ UNDER
SECURITY COUNCIL RESOLUTION 687 (1991)

7-18 July 1991

Salient points

The IAEA team, which arrived on the eve of the day when the Government of
Iraq disclosed its enrichment programme, devoted most of its time to
performing inspections in order to verify the Government's declaration and
fill gaps in it and to seeking explanations.

Although the Iraqi side was cooperative in facilitating the team's
efforts and provided many clarifications about the declared enrichment
programme, the team considers it likely that the full extent of the centrifuge
enrichment work has not yet been disclosed; the possibility also exists that
there are still undeclared locations with sensitive equipment and material.

The leader of Iraq's enrichment programme, Dr. J. Jaffar, Deputy Chairman
of the Iraqi Atomic Energy Commission and Deputy Minister for Industry and
Minerals, denied that any political decision had been taken to use the
enrichment programme to develop nuclear weapons. The primary aims were stated
to be development of the country's technological and industrial infrastructure
and the production of fuel for research reactors and a future nuclear power
programme. The team noted that the possibility of combining separators with
high capacity/modest separation factor and separators with low capacity/high
separation factor suggests a specific intention to produce highly enriched
uranium.

Through imports and indigenous production, Iraq had accumulated a large
inventory of natural uranium.

Uranium tetrachloride - feed material for the electromagnetic isotope
separation (EMIS) enrichment method - was produced in a factory outside Mosul
and at Tuwaitha. The buildings were severely damaged.

The Iraqi side confirmed earlier inspectors' suspicions that Tarmiya was
the main production site for the enrichment of uranium by the EMIS method. A
layer of concrete which had been poured over a key component of the separators
in order to conceal it was removed at the request of the team, which was then
able to confirm that the installation in question had indeed been constructed
for enrichment purposes.

The Iraqi side gave the team videotapes showing the inauguration of the
Tarmiya plant (in February 1990) and what the plant looked like after the
bombing; it had been extensively damaged. The team made a tape of what it
looks like now.

0021   /...

On the basis of the design data provided by the Iraqi side, the team considers that Tarmiya, if fully operational, with 90 separators running at design capacity, could have produced up to 15 kilograms of highly enriched (93 per cent) uranium a year, or proportionally more uranium at a lower enrichment.

It was confirmed that, as surmised, the facility at Ash Sharqat had been built as a replica of Tarmiya and was not, as alleged during the inspection, a factory for the plastic coating of equipment. Most of the facility was destroyed by bombing, at which time it was about 85 per cent completed; no separators had yet been installed.

Milligram quantities of uranium enriched to a level of 40-45 per cent and other quantities enriched to lower levels at Tuwaitha were declared. At Tarmiya, batches of uranium with enrichment levels ranging up to 10 per cent were declared, giving together 0.6 kilograms with an average enrichment level of 4 per cent.

It was confirmed that the Research Centre at Tuwaitha was the site of all the research and development work on uranium enrichment, including EMIS, centrifuge enrichment and chemical enrichment. The relevant facilities at Tuwaitha were completely destroyed.

0022   /...

INTRODUCTION

1.   The present report summarizes findings of the third inspection carried
out by IAEA under the terms of Security Council resolution 687 (1991) with the
assistance and cooperation of the Special Commission of the United Nations.
The team consisted of 26 inspectors and 11 supporting staff, comprising
22 nationalities. It was headed by Mr. Demetrius Perricos of IAEA as Chief
Inspector. The team arrived in Iraq on 6 July 1991 and started the inspection
on 7 July. The original schedule was for the inspection to end on 12 July
but, owing to a new declaration of the Iraqi authorities dated 7 July which
provided additional information on Iraq's nuclear programme, it was necessary
to extend the inspection to 19 July. The team was reduced to 20 inspectors as
from 13 July.

2.   The inspection team verified, to a large extent, the information
contained in the Iraqi declaration of 7 July regarding Iraq's enrichment
programme, which was supplemented by information presented to the team at its
request on 14 July. A number of follow-up actions have been identified and
will have to be performed during subsequent inspection missions. It was not
possible for the inspection team to verify the extent of the centrifuge
enrichment programme, nor could the team exclude the possibility that there
are still undeclared locations with sensitive equipment or material installed,
in use or stored. In addition, the industrial and technological
infrastructure which has been built in connection with this programme has to
be assessed, and the information provided to the team regarding the industrial
establishments involved in this effort has to be verified.

3.   The process of additional clarification by Iraq and subsequent
verification and further questioning by the inspection team went on throughout
the two-week inspection period, and it will continue during subsequent
inspections. A large number of samples were collected, but they have not yet
been analysed; also, many documents, some provided by Iraq and others
collected at various sites by the inspection team, have still to be fully
evaluated. No access problems were encountered and the attitude of the Iraqi
authorities to the team was one of cooperation throughout the period of the
inspection.

I. THE IRAQI ENRICHMENT PROGRAMME

4.   According to a statement by Dr. J. Jaffar, leader of the enrichment
programme, Vice-Chairman of the Iraqi Atomic Energy Commission and Deputy
Minister for Industry and Minerals, the primary motive for proceeding with a
uranium enrichment programme was the expected contribution to the
technological and industrial infrastructure of the country regardless of
whether the programme was successful. The need for uranium enrichment was
ascribed to the need to fuel research reactors and possibly, at some point in
the future, power reactors. Dr. Jaffar noted that a capability to produce
highly enriched uranium may create, in his words, a "political option" for the

0023   /...

development of nuclear weapons. However, he steadfastly denied that a decision to develop nuclear weapons had been taken or that any weapons development work had been done.

5.   At one time or another, gaseous diffusion, electromagnetic isotope separation (EMIS), gas centrifuge and chemical exchange technologies were examined by Iraq. The commitment to EMIS for production-scale development and deployment followed early successes with the method and, more importantly, the demonstration that the separator units and magnets could be made in Iraq.

6.   According to the disclosures made to date, efforts comparable to that devoted to EMIS were not made as regards other separation technologies. Iraqi declarations indicate that research on gas centrifuge technology was second in priority and that some promising results were recently achieved, including successful single-machine trials with UF_6 gas. Operating data from some of these trials were presented to the inspection team on the last day of the inspection period, but it seems likely that the full extent of the centrifuge work has not been disclosed. There is no doubt that Iraq has developed the technological and industrial infrastructure necessary for EMIS. As far as centrifuge enrichment is concerned, Iraq was developing an indigenous technology even if they were dependent on foreign suppliers for key components and materials.

A.   Uranium enrichment research and development at Tuwaitha

7.   Research, development and testing of EMIS components were carried out in the Nuclear Physics Building (80).* Reviews of an Iraqi-provided videotape showing the EMIS facilities in the building, together with examinations of components of the 1,000-millimetre separators (this number refers to the radius of the ion beam in the separator tank) and the model 106 ion source test stand are consistent with Iraq's declaration. In the opinion of the inspection team, the facility was not designed for - nor was it capable of - producing enriched uranium in quantity. The Iraqi statement that the only real obstacle remaining in the development of an efficient EMIS system was an improved ion source is consistent with experience elsewhere in the world. Work on graphite collectors and on the configuration of ion sources and collectors was also carried out in this building. Research on EMIS chemistry was carried out in the nearby Chemical Research Building (85). A small pilot line for the production of UCl_4 was also contained in this building. Both buildings, 80 and 85, have been levelled and the rubble removed. Experiments with gas centrifuge enrichment were declared by Iraq to have occurred in the Cold Material Testing Building (63).

---

    *   The numbers in parentheses refer to the locations indicated on the Tuwaitha site map in annex I to the present report.

0024   /...

B. Acquisition of natural uranium (Al Qaim and Akashat)

8.   Iraq has accumulated, through imports and indigenous production, a large inventory of natural uranium. The indigenous material is largely from an uranium extraction facility (producing yellow cake) associated with a superphosphate plant at Al Qaim. The facility was extensively damaged during the bombing. There is no evidence that the facility served any purpose beyond that declared. The operator stated that a total of 168 metric tons have been produced since the facility was commissioned in 1984. This amount is considerably below the production capacity of 103 metric tons a year. The operator's explanation was that the uranium content of the phosphate ore was far lower than expected. Samples of the ore were taken to investigate this issue.

9.   Akashat is an open-cast mine which feeds Al Qaim. No other activities were detected during the inspection.

C. UO_2 conversion and UCl_4 production (Mosul Production Facility)

10. The team founded that UCl_4 production had been carried out at a facility outside Mosul. A standard production process with UO_2 feed and CCl_4 as the chlorination reagent was used. The facility included a UO_2 conversion capability. It was stated that the UCl_4 plant had gone into production in August 1990 and operated for about six months. The plant manager indicated that production had been limited for most of that time because of corrosion problems. The inspection team found no evidence contradicting those statements. The UCl_4 production building had suffered substantial damage, and the UO_2 building had completely collapsed and was covered with debris. There was also an Iraqi statement that the UCl_4 used for EMIS development and testing at Tuwaitha and Tarmiya had been produced in Building 85 at Tuwaitha.

D. EMIS; the facilities at Tarmiya and Ash Sharqat

11. The Tarmiya site has been described in previous inspection reports (see S/22788). The third inspection team visited the site again following Iraqi confirmation that the site had been used for EMIS and further declarations regarding the extent of the EMIS installations and operations. The team found evidence confirming statements about the number and type (1,200 mm) of EMIS units installed in Building 33. The process building contained two areas (A and B) for EMIS installations. An eight-separator system (nine magnets) had been installed in area A during January and February 1990. A 17-separator system was in the process of being installed (three magnets were in place) in area B at the time operations ceased.

12. In an attempt to conceal the EMIS equipment from the inspection teams, the return irons and rails for the separators had been covered with concrete. This was removed at the team's request. The length of the installed return

0025

/...

iron in both area A and area B conformed to system specifications provided by Iraq and to independent separator component measurements made by the inspection team.

13. An Iraqi video film made at the time when the installation of magnets, vacuum chambers and end pieces for the eight-separator system was completed (February 1990) and one made in February 1991, after the bombing, were provided to the inspection team. The latter video film appeared to confirm that only three magnets had been installed, without vacuum chambers, and that area B had therefore not yet been operational. A computer printout showing the performance of one of the separators during a run late in December 1990 was provided. The data have not been examined in detail, but it appears that the ion beam current was not up to the design value. The number of separators ultimately intended for Building 33 has not been determined. The facility design provides for a maximum of 70 separators, but Iraqi authorities indicated that no decision had been taken beyond those concerning the 25 separators installed or being installed. Facility specifications indicate that Building 245 was designed to accommodate 20 of the smaller (600 mm) units, which have a higher separation factor. Uranium recovery, the construction and configuration of ion sources and collectors and the construction of separator tank liners were all done at the Tarmiya site.

14. A second facility, a replica of Tarmiya, was being constructed at Ash Sharqat. According to information provided during the inspection, construction at Ash Sharqat started shortly after that at Tarmiya but none of the major buildings had been commissioned. The overall state of completeness was about 85 per cent at the time when most of the facility was destroyed. There was no sign that installed equipment had been removed, as had happened at other sites. The electric power supply to the site is very substantial and, while installation was not complete, the substation serving the site would certainly provide power at a level equivalent to that at Tarmiya. At the time when this site was inspected, the Iraqi authorities had not declared it as a nuclear facility; they stated the purposes of the installations at Ash Sharqat to be the protective coating of large pipes and containers and the production of machine tools. The Iraqi authorities have since stated that the Ash Sharqat facility was constructed from the plans used at Tarmiya. Further, they have indicated that the replication of important buildings had become a policy of the Iraqi Government. It is not clear whether Iraq intended to utilize the Ash Sharqat facility for uranium enrichment as long as the Tarmiya facility continued to function.

0026

/...

E. Material and equipment declarations*

15. Declarations of material directly associated with the operation of EMIS development units in Building 80 at Tuwaitha were provided to the team on the last day of the inspection period. Milligram quantities of uranium enriched up to a level of 40-45 per cent and a few kilograms of uranium depleted down to a level of .02 per cent were included. Material in five enrichment ranges (up to 10 wt. per cent U-235) resulting from the testing of EMIS production units at Tarmiya was declared, and samples were taken. Again, only small amounts of material were involved. This material was declared on 7 July as about 0.5 kg with an average enrichment of 4 per cent.

16. All tell-tale equipment at Tuwaitha, Tarmiya and the Mosul Production Facility had been removed and turned over to the Iraqi Army for destruction and concealment. The Army proceeded to transport the equipment to remote locations where much of it was destroyed and buried. Equipment from Tuwaitha and Tarmiya was distributed among locations 1-5 and 8, and equipment from the Mosul Production Facility was taken to locations 6 and 7 (near Mosul). Much of the equipment was destroyed to the point where it was no longer recognizable. The inspection team tried to concentrate on major EMIS components identified as end pieces, double-pole magnets with coils, vacuum chambers, liners, ion sources and collectors. The end pieces, magnets and vacuum chambers could not be destroyed completely and, given the circumstances, the inventory was reasonably consistent with Iraqi declarations. However, no collectors and only one ion source were found. Several pieces of a collector were eventually provided, but the locating of ion sources and collectors will have to be a major follow-up activity. Iraq's clarification dated 18 July included components (but no ion sources or collectors) for six 600-mm separators intended for installation at Tarmiya. With the exception of one dipole and several coils, this equipment has not been found by the inspection team. The equipment inventories at locations 6 and 7 are consistent with the declared purpose of the Mosul Production Facility. Facilities where EMIS components were fabricated were identified by Iraq. Some of these facilities had been inspected before the declaration, during the second IAEA on-site inspection, as a result of designation by the Special Commission.

17. In the opinion of the inspection team, the broad goals cited by the Vice-Chairman of the Iraqi Atomic Energy Commission neither require nor justify the construction of a facility the size of Tarmiya, much less two such facilities. Design drawings of Building 33 and Building 245 show a combination of high-capacity/modest separation factor units and low-capacity/high separation factor units. This is the type of arrangement that would be configured if the goal was to produce highly enriched uranium. Design data provided by Iraq indicate that if Tarmiya had become fully

---

    *   For the area of Tuwaitha and Tarmiya and equipment locations 1-8, see the map contained in annex II to the present report.

0027   /...

operational, with 90 separators running at design capacity, up to 15 kilograms a year of highly enriched uranium or proportionally more uranium at lower enrichments could have been produced using natural uranium as the feed.

F. Gas centrifuge enrichment

18. In the 7 July declaration, Iraq listed certain gas centrifuge activities, equipment and components. Additional data were also made available, including information about a planned project to build a 100-machine gas centrifuge cascade. Iraq claimed that it had not progressed beyond the point of conducting single-machine trials with UF_6 gas and that the technical specifications for its gas centrifuge had not yet been fully determined. It was also claimed that it had had only very limited capabilities for centrifuge component manufacturing and no significant stockpiles of special materials (e.g., 350-grade maraging steel). In addition, it was claimed that there had been only very limited, laboratory-scale activities with UF_6.

19. On the basis of the evidence available to date, the inspection team cannot draw conclusions as to whether Iraq's gas centrifuge declarations are complete. A statement made regarding the technical status of machine operations and performance which had been achieved appears plausible, though its accuracy cannot be verified. The precise status of the "planned" project to build a 100-machine gas centrifuge cascade remains a question mark. Furthermore, it appears probable to the team that the full extent (material, equipment and locations) of Iraq's gas centrifuge component manufacturing infrastructure has yet to be revealed.

II. NUCLEAR MATERIAL VERIFICATION

20. In addition to the reverification activities performed on the nuclear material presented to the first inspection team, the following quantities of nuclear material stated in the declaration of 7 July were verified:

(kilograms)

Yellow cake	331 368 (corrected value)
UO_2	116 173
UCl_4	2 577
UF_6	0.465
ADU	1 850
UO_3	2 050
UF_4	310 (corrected value)
UO_4	2 255

0028   /...

Also, one drum of scrap material and two drums of UO_4 sample bottles which had not been included in the 7 July declaration were brought to the Tuwaitha site and verified. The weights of this material were not provided and, owing to its late arrival, it was not possible to determine them. Furthermore, 235 kg of natural uranium in U_3O_8 form and four natural uranium fuel elements, which had previously been under safeguards and which were recovered from the rubble after the first inspection, were brought to the storage area at Tuwaitha and verified. The irradiated heavily enriched uranium (HEU) fuel elements in the IRT 5000 reactor were fully verified during the inspection.

21. <u>Hot cells and glove boxes</u>. The hot cells and glove boxes present at Tuwaitha were all inspected, and all the manipulators of the hot cells which had not been severely damaged were sealed for unique identification purposes.

22. <u>Removal of fuel items</u>. The conditions for removal and transportation of both fresh and irradiated highly enriched fuel elements were examined and discussed with the Iraqi authorities. In order to minimize the costs, the Iraqi authorities expressed the wish to perform as many of the activities as possible involved in the removal of fresh fuel and the loading of irradiated fuel into transport containers. Further discussions on this matter will take place in the near future.

III. OTHER INSPECTIONS

23. <u>Facility near Tuwaitha</u>. The third inspection team examined a facility which the Iraqi side had identified as the Engineering Research Centre under the Ministry of Higher Education. The facility was surrounded by a low berm and a fence and had guard towers at each fence corner. Most of the equipment had been removed but some evidence found in the buildings suggested that the facility was a forensic laboratory of the Ministry of the Interior. The team is confident that no nuclear activities were conducted at the facility.

24. <u>Al Qa Qaa Facility</u>. At the invitation of the Iraqi authorities, inspectors visited this facility, which was declared to be a high-explosive testing facility. It did not appear to the inspectors that the facility possessed the diagnostic capability to support other than conventional explosive and ordnance production.

0029

/...

Annex I

TUWAITHA SITE MAP

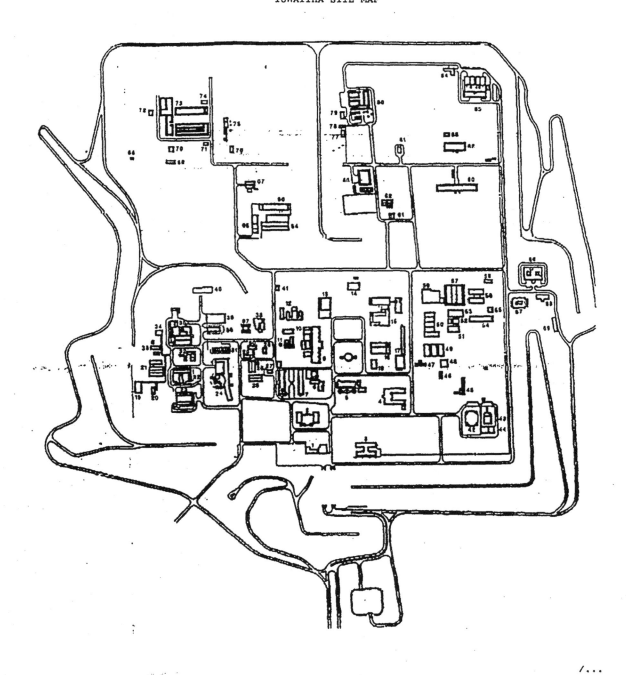

/...

0030

Annex II

MAP OF LOCATIONS

**UNITED
NATIONS**

General Assembly   Security Council

Distr.
GENERAL

A/45/1042
S/22853
30 July 1991
ENGLISH
ORIGINAL: ARABIC

GENERAL ASSEMBLY
Forty-fifth session
Agenda item 153
IRAQI AGGRESSION AND THE CONTINUED
  OCCUPATION OF KUWAIT IN FLAGRANT
  VIOLATION OF THE CHARTER OF THE
  UNITED NATIONS

SECURITY COUNCIL
Forty-sixth year

Letter dated 29 July 1991 from the Chargé d'affaires a.i. of the
Permanent Mission of Kuwait to the United Nations addressed to
the Secretary-General

On instructions from my Government, I should like to inform you that Iraq
has deployed Hawk anti-aircraft missile batteries which are the property of
the Kuwaiti Army in the areas surrounding the city of Baghdad. Since these
missile batteries were seized by the Iraqi regime during its aggression
against Kuwait and its brutal occupation of the country, it is obligated in
accordance with Security Council resolution 686 (1991) and 687 (1991) to
return them immediately and without delay.

Iraq's deployment of these weapons in such a provocative manner is a
flagrant contravention of its obligations under the relevant Security Council
resolutions, and it reveals a calculated intention to retain possession of
these weapons.

We request you to make every possible effort to compel Iraq to withdraw
and dismantle the aforesaid missile batteries and to return them immediately
to the State of Kuwait.

I should be grateful if you would have this letter circulated as a
document of the General Assembly, under agenda item 153, and of the Security
Council.

(Signed)   Mohammad Saad AL SALLAL
Chargé d'affaires a.i.

0032

91-24304   2537e (E)

Security Council

Distr.
GENERAL

S/22844
29 July 1991
ENGLISH
ORIGINAL: ARABIC

LETTER DATED 29 JULY 1991 FROM THE CHARGE D'AFFAIRES A.I. OF
THE PERMANENT MISSION OF SAUDI ARABIA TO THE UNITED NATIONS
ADDRESSED TO THE SECRETARY-GENERAL

I refer to the letter addressed to you on 22 July 1991 by the Permanent
Representative of Iraq to the United Nations (S/22821) and to its two annexes,
dated 17 April and 6 May, in which mention is made of sorties carried out by
the Saudi Air Force over Iraqi territory after the entry into force of the
cease-fire.

I also refer to our letter of 9 May 1991 (S/22584) and, on instructions
from my Government, should like to inform you that, following the necessary
inquiries by the competent authorities in the Kingdom, it has been established
that the statements made in the letters of the Permanent Representative of ·
Iraq relating to the Saudi Air Force bear no resemblance to reality and
constitute an allegation that has absolutely no truth. The Kingdom is
involved in no air activity in Iraqi airspace and has been involved in no such
activity since the moment the cease-fire went into effect.

I should be grateful if you would have this letter circulated as a
document of the Security Council.

(Signed) Mohammed H. Mirdass AL-KAHTANY
Chargé d'affaires a.i.

UNITED NATIONS

S

Security Council

Distr.
GENERAL

S/22845
29 July 1991
ENGLISH
ORIGINAL: ARABIC

LETTER DATED 29 JULY 1991 FROM THE PERMANENT REPRESENTATIVE OF
IRAQ TO THE UNITED NATIONS ADDRESSED TO THE SECRETARY-GENERAL

On instructions from my Government, I have the honour to inform you that
the massive destruction wrought by the United States and its allies on Iraq's
civilian facilities and infrastructure in the course of their military
operations, which lasted from the night of 16/17 January 1991 until
28 February 1991, clearly demonstrated the iniquitous character of the United
States and its unlawful use of the cover of international legitimacy and
Security Council resolutions in order to destroy an entire people.

Not content with the more than 90,000 tons of bombs which they dropped
during over 100,000 air raids on Iraqi cities and installations, United States
aircraft continued - even after the cessation of hostilities and on the
pretext of conducting reconnaissance - to carry out intensive air activity in
Iraqi airspace, to shoot down unarmed aircraft, to destroy tanks, to drop
airborne troops onto roads inside Iraq and to intercept Iraqi helicopters
which were performing civilian duties and carrying civilian officials,
political figures and relief agency delegations inside Iraq because military
operations had destroyed and cut most of the country's land transportation
routes.

The following are details of these acts of provocation:

Date	Details
1/2 July	Twelve sorties flown by six formations at speeds of 600 to 700 km/h and at low and medium altitudes over Arbil and Mosul, for the purpose of observation and provocation
2/3 July	Ten sorties flown by five formations at speeds of 600 to 700 km/h and at low and medium altitudes over Mosul, Arbil, Dohuk and Tall 'Afar, for the purpose of observation and provocation
3/4 July	Twenty-two sorties flown by 11 formations at speeds of 600 to 900 km/h and at low and medium altitudes over Arbil, Mosul, Zakho, Dohuk and Amadiyah, for the purpose of observation and provocation, achieved when the American aircraft ejected flares north of Sadd al-Mawsil at 2040 hours

91-24223   2607d (E)

0034   /...

Date	Details
4/5 July	Twenty-two sorties flown by 11 formations at speeds of 600 to 900 km/h and at low and medium altitudes over Mosul, Arbil, Dohuk, Zakho, Tall 'Afar and Sadd al-Mawsil, for the purpose of observation and provocation
5/6 July	Three sorties flown by one two-aircraft formation and one single aircraft over Dohuk, Amadiyah and north of Mosul, for the purpose of observation and provocation
6/7 July	Twelve sorties flown by six formations at speeds of 600 to 720 km/h and at medium and low altitudes over Mosul, Dohuk, Zakho and Tall 'Afar, for the purpose of observation and provocation
7/8 July	Seventeen sorties flown by eight two-aircraft formations and one single aircraft at speeds of 600 to 900 km/h and at low and medium altitudes over Mosul, Arbil and Dohuk, for the purpose of observation and provocation, achieved by low-altitude flights over Sadd al-Mawsil
8/9 July	Thirty-three sorties flown by 16 two-aircraft formations and one single aircraft at speeds of 700 to 900 km/h and at medium altitudes over Arbil, Mosul and Rawanduz, for the purpose of observation and provocation
9/10 July	Thirty-one sorties flown by 13 two-aircraft formations and five single aircraft at speeds of 600 to 900 km/h and at low and medium altitudes over Mosul, Arbil, Tall 'Afar, Sinjar, Dohuk, Zakho and Dukan, for the purpose of observation and provocation
10/11 July	Thirty-seven sorties flown by 18 formations and one single aircraft at speeds of 600 to 800 km/h and at low and medium altitudes over Mosul, Dohuk and Arbil, for the purpose of observation and provocation
11/12 July	Nineteen sorties flown by nine formations and one single aircraft at speeds of 600 to 720 km/h and at low and medium altitudes (4,000-5,000 metres) over Dohuk, Arbil, the area north of Mosul and Amadiyah, for the purpose of observation and provocation
12/13 July	Twenty-nine sorties flown by 12 two-aircraft formations and five single aircraft at speeds of 700 to 900 km/h and at altitudes ranging from 2,000 to 8,500 metres over Mosul, Dohuk, Arbil, Amadiyah, Rawanduz and Zakho, for the purpose of observation and provocation

/...

Date	Details
13/14 July	Thirty-two sorties flown by 15 two-aircraft formations and two single aircraft at speeds of 600 to 900 km/h and at low and medium altitudes over Arbil, Mosul, Dohuk and Rawanduz, for the purpose of observation and provocation
14/15 July	Twenty-three sorties flown by 11 formations and one single aircraft at speeds of 600 to 720 km/h and at low and medium altitudes over Arbil, Mosul and Dohuk, for the purpose of observation and provocation
15/16 July	Twenty-seven sorties flown by 13 formations and one single aircraft at speeds of 700 to 900 km/h and at altitudes ranging from 500 to 4,000 metres over Dohuk, Arbil, Mosul, Tall 'Afar and Amadiyah, for the purpose of observation and provocation
16/17 July	Twelve sorties flown by six formations at speeds of 600 to 800 km/h and at low and medium altitudes over Mosul, Dohuk and north of Arbil, for the purpose of observation and provocation
17/18 July	Eighteen sorties flown by five two-aircraft formations, one four-aircraft formation and four single aircraft at speeds of 600 to 720 km/h and at low and medium altitudes over Mosul and Arbil, for the purpose of observation and provocation
18/19 July	Twenty-five sorties flown by 12 formations and one single aircraft at speeds of 700 to 900 km/h and at low and medium altitudes over Mosul, Arbil, Dohuk, Amadiyah and Tall 'Afar, for the purpose of observation and provocation
19/20 July	Sixteen sorties flown by eight formations at speeds of 600 to 700 km/h and at altitudes ranging from 4,000 to 5,000 metres over Mosul, Arbil and Dohuk, for the purpose of observation and provocation
20/21 July	Six sorties flown by three two-aircraft formations at speeds of 600 to 700 km/h and at medium altitudes over Dohuk and north of Mosul, for the purpose of observation and provocation
21/22 July	Twenty sorties flown by nine two-aircraft formations and two single aircraft at speeds of 700 to 900 km/h and at low and medium altitudes over the area north of Mosul, Dohuk and the areas north and west of Arbil, for the purpose of observation and provocation
22/23 July	Nineteen sorties flown by nine formations and one single aircraft at speeds of 650 to 720 km/h and at altitudes ranging from 4,000 to 5,000 metres over Mosul, Arbil and Dohuk, for the purpose of observation and provocation

0036

/...

Date	Details
23/24 July	Thirty-four sorties flown by 12 two-aircraft formations, two three-aircraft formations and four single aircraft at speeds of 600 to 950 km/h and at altitudes ranging from 3,000 to 8,500 metres over Arbil, Mosul, Dohuk, Amadiyah and north of Rawanduz, for the purpose of observation and provocation, achieved when the aircraft ejected flares and broke the sound barrier over the areas east and north of Mosul
24/25 July	Eight sorties flown by one four-aircraft formation and two two-aircraft formations at speeds of 700 to 900 km/h and at altitudes ranging from 2,000 to 4,000 metres over Arbil, Amadiyah, north of Mosul and Dohuk, for the purpose of observation and provocation

In placing these facts before the Secretary-General of the United Nations, members of the Security Council and all the nations, peoples and organizations of the world, we hope that the world will appreciate the length to which America has gone in its excessive and unjustified use of force, thus violating Security Council resolutions, showing contempt for the feelings of Iraqi citizens and disturbing their tranquillity and security.

I should be grateful if you would have this letter circulated as a document of the Security Council.

(Signed) Abdul Amir A. AL-ANBARI
Ambassador
Permanent Representative

0037

UNITED NATIONS

Security Council

S

Distr.
GENERAL

S/22846
29 July 1991
ENGLISH
ORIGINAL: ARABIC

LETTER DATED 29 JULY 1991 FROM THE PERMANENT REPRESENTATIVE OF
IRAQ TO THE UNITED NATIONS ADDRESSED TO THE SECRETARY-GENERAL

On instructions from my Government and with reference to the letter from the Chargé d'affaires a.i. of the Permanent Mission of Kuwait to the United Nations contained in document A/45/1040-S/22833, I have the honour to inform you that the Kuwaiti violations of the provisions of the cease-fire between the two countries under Security Council resolution 687 (1991) which are mentioned in our letters contained in documents S/22719 and S/22755 were not a mere hypothesis on the part of Iraq but one that was confirmed to us by the United Nations Iraq-Kuwait Observation Mission (UNIKOM) and one that it communicated to the Kuwaiti authorities at the time.

In informing you of this fact, I should like to point out to you that any violation of Iraqi airspace by warplanes coming from Kuwaiti airspace after the entry into force of the cease-fire is regarded as a Kuwaiti breach under the rules of international law whether such aircraft are Kuwaiti or not.

I should be grateful if you would have this letter circulated as a document of the Security Council.

(Signed) Abdul Amir A. AL-ANBARI
Ambassador
Permanent Representative

91-24229 2581j (E)

0038

**UNITED
NATIONS**

S

Security Council

Distr.
GENERAL

S/22809
18 July 1991

ORIGINAL: ENGLISH

LETTER DATED 17 JULY 1991 FROM THE PERMANENT REPRESENTATIVE
OF KUWAIT TO THE UNITED NATIONS ADDRESSED TO THE PRESIDENT
OF THE SECURITY COUNCIL

On instructions from my Government I should like to draw your attention
to the failure by Iraq to abide by the terms of relevant Security Council
resolutions, in particular those pertaining to the urgent humanitarian demand
that Iraq <u>immediately</u> release under the auspices of the ICRC <u>all</u> Kuwaiti and
third country nationals and arrange for the ICRC <u>immediate</u> access to all POWs
and detainees. In this regard, I should like to convey the following:

First, there are around 1,890 Kuwaiti POWs and detainees still held by
Iraq, in addition to 1,990 non-Kuwaiti POWs and detainees.

Second, a number of the above were detained at a restricted area in
Baghdad, Al-Rahwaniya, near the International Airport. Others were detained
at General Intelligence (Al-Mukhabarat) building in Al-Athimiya district in
Baghdad.

Third, the ICRC confirmed our information on some locations of POWs and
detainees, a matter which was brought to the attention of the members of the
Council on 20 May 1991.

Fourth, POWs and detainees have recently been transferred to undisclosed
locations. The ICRC have been denied information of, let alone access to,
these new locations.

Fifth, since the cease-fire formally came into effect on 11 April 1991
only 68 POWs and detainees of different nationalities have been repatriated in
five phases, on 15 and 25 May, 12 and 27 June and 14 July.

Sixth, it is noteworthy that before the cease-fire formally came into
effect on 11 April 1991, Iraq had released through the ICRC 5,060 POWs and
detainees of different nationalities. Around 1,498 more persons of different
nationalities have escaped Iraq through various routes.

91-23331 2688b (E)

0039 /···

Seventh, Iraq includes those returned under family reunion in the total number of POWs and detainees thus inflating the number of repatriated POWs and detainees. To illustrate, 56 persons were released to Kuwaiti authorities on 14 July 1991, of which 53 persons qualified for family reunion, 2 were Kuwaiti POWs and the last was a Syrian detainee.

While bringing the above to your attention, Kuwait wishes to emphasize its deep concern at the fate of those still held by Iraq. Our concern is compounded due to the recent transfer of POWs and detainees to undisclosed locations. Lastly, the Iraqi pattern of release of POWs and detainees puts into question the credibility and motives of the regime vis-à-vis a humanitarian matter of no apparent strategic asset to it.

I should appreciate it if you would bring this letter to the immediate attention of the members of the Security Council, and arrange for its circulation as an official document of the Security Council.

(Signed) Mohammad A. ABULHASAN
Ambassador
Permanent Representative

0040

UNITED
NATIONS

A S

General Assembly   **Security Council**

Distr.
GENERAL

A/45/1037
S/22812
19 July 1991

ORIGINAL: ENGLISH

GENERAL ASSEMBLY
Forty-fifth session
Agenda item 153
IRAQI AGGRESSION AND THE CONTINUED OCCUPATION
  OF KUWAIT IN FLAGRANT VIOLATION OF THE
  CHARTER OF THE UNITED NATIONS

SECURITY COUNCIL
Forty-sixth year

<u>Note by the Secretary-General</u>

The Secretary-General has the honour to transmit to the members of the
General Assembly and of the Security Council a letter dated 19 July 1991
addressed to him by the Director-General of the International Atomic Energy
Agency concerning the resolution adopted on 18 July 1991 by the Board of
Governors of the Agency entitled "Iraq's non-compliance with its safeguards
obligations" (see annex).

91-23434 2515e (E)

/...

0041

ANNEX

**Letter dated 19 July 1991 from the Director-General of
the International Atomic Energy Agency addressed to
the Secretary-General**

At its meeting on 18 July 1991 the Board of Governors of the International Atomic Energy Agency found that the Government of Iraq had not complied with its obligations under its safeguards agreement with the Agency. The resolution of the Board, adopted by 29 votes to 1, with 3 abstentions, is attached (see appendix).

Article XII.C of the Agency's Statute and Article III.2 of the Agreement Governing the Relationship Agreement between the United Nations and the International Atomic Energy Agency require the Board to report non-compliance with safeguards obligations to the Security Council and General Assembly of the United Nations. I would, therefore, appreciate it if you could bring the Board's finding to the urgent attention of the Security Council and of the General Assembly. A copy of the records of the Board's meeting will be sent to you as soon as they are available.

In accordance with Article VII of the Relationship Agreement, I am at the disposal of the Security Council should the Council so desire.

(Signed) Hans BLIX
Director-General

0042

/...

APPENDIX

Iraq's non-compliance with its safeguards obligations

Resolution adopted by the Board of Governors of the
International Atomic Energy Agency on 18 July 1991

The Board of Governors,

(a) Stressing the importance of non-proliferation of nuclear weapons to international and regional peace and security,

(b) Expressing grave concern about the conclusion of the report of the Director-General (GOV/2530) that the Government of Iraq has failed to comply with its obligations under its safeguards agreement with the International Atomic Energy Agency (INFCIRC/172),

(c) Recalling United Nations Security Council resolution 687 (1991), which, inter alia, called upon Iraq to declare all its nuclear activities to the International Atomic Energy Agency,

(d) Noting with appreciation the efforts of the Director-General and his staff to implement the tasks assigned to the Agency by that resolution, and the diligent and effective conduct of the Agency's inspections of Iraqi nuclear activities,

(e) Expressing grave concern about the evident deception and obstruction of the International Atomic Energy Agency inspectors in their efforts to carry out the Security Council's mandate in resolution 687 (1991) in violation of that resolution and the undertakings by Iraq governing the status, privileges and immunities of the Agency and the inspection teams mandated under Security Council resolution 687 (1991),

1. Finds, on the basis of the report of the Director-General in GOV/2530, that the Government of Iraq has not complied with its obligations under its safeguards agreement with the Agency (INFCIRC/172);

2. Condemns this non-compliance by the Government of Iraq with its safeguards agreement;

3. Calls upon the Government of Iraq to remedy this non-compliance forthwith, including placing any and all additional source and special fissionable material within Iraq's territory, under its jurisdiction or its control, regardless of quantity or location, under Agency safeguards in accordance with the relevant provisions of INFCIRC/172 and in accordance with relevant technical determinations of the Agency;

0043   /...

4.   <u>Decides</u>, in accordance with Article XII.C of the Statute, to report this non-compliance to all members of the Agency and to the Security Council and General Assembly of the United Nations;

5.   <u>Calls upon</u> Iraq to cease all obstruction or interference with the International Atomic Energy Agency inspection teams in their efforts to implement Security Council resolution 687 (1991);

6.   <u>Requests</u> the Director-General to keep the Board and the General Conference informed of progress in the implementation of this resolution so that they may consider appropriate action in accordance with Article XII.C and XIX.B of the Statute in the event of the Government of Iraq's failing to take fully corrective action;

7.   <u>Decides</u> to inscribe an item entitled "Iraq's non-compliance with its safeguards obligations" on the agenda of the September Board of Governors and requests the Director-General to include such an item in the provisional agenda for the thirty-fifth regular session of the General Conference.

0044

Security Council

Distr.
GENERAL

S/22815
19 July 1991

ORIGINAL: ENGLISH

NOTE VERBALE DATED 18 JULY 1991 FROM THE CHARGE D'AFFAIRES A.I.
OF THE PERMANENT MISSION OF TURKEY TO THE UNITED NATIONS
ADDRESSED TO THE SECRETARY-GENERAL

The Chargé d'affaires, a.i. of Turkey to the United Nations presents his
compliments to the Secretary-General of the United Nations and, with reference
to his note SCPC/7/91/4-1 of 3 July 1991, has the honour to inform the
Secretary-General of the following:

All exportation of arms, ammunition, military equipment and related
technology from Turkey lies under the control and administration of the
Turkish Government.

The Turkish Government has informed its competent authorities of the
mandatory nature of the relevant United Nations Security Council resolutions
which prohibit countries to sell, supply or convey weapons or other military
equipment as well as technology and services which can be used for military
purposes to Iraq. The report of the Secretary-General (S/22660) and its annex
on the guidelines to facilitate full implementation of paragraphs 24, 25
and 27 of Security Council resolution 687 (1991) have also been brought to the
attention of all concerned. Hence, Turkey does not sell or supply any
material listed in paragraph 24 of resolution 687 (1991) nor does it promote
or facilitate such sales.

91-23453 2582d (E)

0045

UNITED NATIONS

S

Security Council

Distr.
GENERAL

S/22825
23 July 1991

ORIGINAL: ENGLISH

IDENTICAL LETTERS DATED 23 JULY 1991 FROM THE CHARGE D'AFFAIRES A.I.
OF THE PERMANENT MISSION OF THE FEDERAL REPUBLIC OF GERMANY TO THE
UNITED NATIONS ADDRESSED RESPECTIVELY TO THE SECRETARY-GENERAL AND
THE PRESIDENT OF THE SECURITY COUNCIL

In my capacity as Acting Chairman of the Western European Union, I have the honour to transmit to you on behalf of the member States of the Western European Union the annexed declaration with reference to paragraphs 3 (d) and 6 of Security Council resolution 686 (1991).

I should be grateful if this letter and its annex could be circulated as a document of the Security Council.

(Signed) Hans-Joachim VERGAU
Ambassador
Acting Permanent Representative

91-23723 2589d (E)

/...

0046

Annex I

In compliance with United Nations Security Council resolution 686's call for action to cooperate in the reconstruction of, and to ensure safe shipping to, Kuwait, the undersigning Nations conducted mine countermeasures operations within the boundaries defined in annex II until 20 July 1991 and declare:

1. The routes and areas specified in annex III have been searched as far as practically possible and, although a residual mine danger cannot be discounted, are considered safe for navigation. It is recommended that these areas be marked in accordance with IMCO standards.

2. Known minefields within the boundaries defined in annex II have been cleared as far as practically possible. However this area, with the exception of routes and areas delineated in annex III, should be avoided because a remaining risk cannot be excluded.

3. In addition there remains a risk of drifting mines in the Northern Gulf.

    Belgium, France, Germany, Italy, Netherlands, United Kingdom of Great Britain and Northern Ireland.

0047   /...

<u>Annex II</u>

The navigation within the boundaries of the line defined hereafter with the exception of the routes and areas defined in annex III should be avoided because a remaining risk cannot be excluded.

Reference: WGS 84.

	Latitude	Longitude
AA	29°35'N	048°15'E
AB	29°35'N	048°40'E
AC	29°44'N	048°55'E
AD	29°21'N	049°15'E
AE	29°00'N	049°07'E
AF	28°43'N	048°55'E
AG	28°32'N	048°42'E
AH	28°32'N	048°27,5'E

Note:

There is a known Mine Area (MDA 10) bounded by the following coordinates

AI	29°51'30.000"N	048°46'18.000"E
AJ	29°51'30.000"N	048°48'00.000"E
AK	29°40'18.000"N	018°18'00.000"E
AL	29°37'15.000"N	048°39'36.000"E
AM	29°37'15.000"N	048°32'30.000"E

which lies outside the area delineated above and is outside the remit of United Nations Security Council resolution 686 (1991). MCM operations in this area are ongoing.

/...

0048

Annex III

1. Routes considered safe for navigation

Width of the routes: 1000 yards left and right from the axis.
Reference: WGS 84.

QCR 301

Point (Axis)	Latitude	Longitude
A	28°52.0000'N	049°25.1000'E
B	29°07.9000'N	049°13.4000'E
C	29°07.9000'N	048°46.8333'E
D	29°09.5000'N	048°38.2500'E
E	29°09.5000'N	048°15.1000'E
F	29°08.2000'N	048°11.4000'E

QCR 302

Point (Axis)	Latitude	Longitude
A	29°09.7500'N	048°29.8000'E
B	29°06.4000'N	048°20.3000'E
C	29°02.9000'N	048°10.7000'E

QCR 303

Point (Axis)	Latitude	Longitude
A	28°52.7500'N	049°03.7000'E
B	29°57.5000'N	048°54.1000'E
C	29°06.6000'N	048°28.5000'E
D	29°09.5000'N	048°15.1000'E

QCR 305

Point (Axis)	Latitude	Longitude
A	28°57.5000'N	048°54.1000'E
B	28°57.1000'N	048°46.3000'E
C	28°57.2500'N	048°41.3500'E
D	28°58.3000'N	048°37.8000'E
E	29°00.8167'N	048°32.4333'E
F	29°00.5667'N	048°31.1000'E

0049

/...

Point (Axis)	Latitude	Longitude
G	29°02.0333'N	048°26.6167'E
H	29°02.2200'N	048°25.2833'E
I	29°05.3500'N	048°21.0000'E
J	29°06.4000'N	048°20.3000'E
K	29°07.5000'N	048°19.7000'E
L	29°09.5000'N	048°15.1000'E
M	29°23.2500'N	048°07.3000'E
N	29°25.6000'N	047°59.8500'E
O	29°25.6000'N	047°51.2500'E
P	29°23.4000'N	047°46.9500'E
Q	29°22.6000'N	047°47.2000'E

QCR 306

Point (Axis)	Latitude	Longitude
A	29°05.0000'N	048°10.7000'E
B	29°07.0000'N	048°10.7000'E

QCR 307

Point (Axis)	Latitude	Longitude
A	28°31.0000'N	049°26.0000'E
B	28°37.0000'N	049°00.0000'E
C	28°42.0000'N	048°49.4000'E
D	28°45.6000'N	048°43.8000'E
E	28°55.0000'N	048°23.1000'E

QCR 308

Point (Axis)	Latitude	Longitude
A	29°05.3500'N	048°21.0000'E
B	28°55.0000'N	048°23.1000'E
C	28°52.2000'N	048°18.5000'E

QCR 309

Point (Axis)	Latitude	Longitude
A	28°45.6000'N	048°43.8000'E
B	28°44.9000'N	048°30.0000'E

0050

/...

QCR 310

Point (Axis)	Latitude	Longitude
A	28°31.0000'N	048°40.0000'E
B	28°44.9000'N	048°30.0000'E
C	28°52.2000'N	048°29.3000'E

QCR 102

Point (Axis)	Latitude	Longitude
A	27°20.2000'N	050°39.8000'E
B	27°50.7000'N	049°50.9000'E
C	27°58.1000'N	049°50.5000'E
D	28°10.1000'N	049°41.4000'E
E	28°11.6000'N	049°22.6000'E
F	28°31.0000'N	049°26.0000'E
G	28°52.7500'N	049°03.7000'E

NORTH MINA AL AHMADI PIER HOLDING AREA

Point	Latitude	Longitude
A	29°08.5500'N	048°08.8500'E
B	29°09.2100'N	048°11.0400'E
C	29°07.2800'N	048°11.7700'E
D	29°06.6800'N	048°09.5600'E

MINA SAUD HOLDING AREA

Point	Latitude	Longitude
A	28°44.8000'N	048°34.0000'E
B	28°45.0000'N	048°36.4000'E
C	28°42.8000'N	048°34.0000'E
D	28°43.0000'N	048°36.4000'E

AL-FAO AREA

Point	Latitude	Longitude
A	29°02.0900'N	048°10.6800'E
B	29°09.4800'N	048°11.7300'E
C	29°01.2600'N	048°12.3200'E
D	29°00.8700'N	048°11.2700'E

0051

/...

ABU JEZZA AREA

Point	Latitude	Longitude
A	29°10.0000'N	048°15.8000'E
B	29°10.0000'N	048°38.2500'E
C	29°06.5000'N	048°38.2500'E
D	29°06.5000'N	048°20.6700'E

MINA ASH SHUAYBAH ANCHORAGE AREA

Point	Latitude	Longitude
A	29°02.1000'N	048°10.7000'E
B	29°02.1000'N	048°15.0000'E
C	29°05.0000'N	048°15.0000'E
D	29°05.0000'N	048°09.4000'E

0052

UNITED NATIONS

Security Council

S

Distr.
GENERAL

S/22826
24 July 1991
ENGLISH
ORIGINAL: ARABIC

LETTER DATED 23 JULY 1991 FROM THE PERMANENT REPRESENTATIVE OF
IRAQ TO THE UNITED NATIONS ADDRESSED TO THE SECRETARY-GENERAL

On instructions from my Government, I have the honour to transmit
herewith a letter dated 23 July 1991 from Mr. Ahmad Hussein, Minister for
Foreign Affairs of Iraq, concerning the resolution adopted by the Board of
Governors of the International Atomic Energy Agency on 18 July 1991.

I should be grateful if you would have this letter circulated as a
document of the Security Council.

(Signed) Abdul Amir A. AL-ANBARI
Ambassador
Permanent Representative

91-23783 2593d (E)

0053 /...

<u>Annex</u>

<u>Letter dated 23 July 1991 from the Minister for Foreign Affairs
of Iraq addressed to the Secretary-General</u>

We have examined the resolution of the Board of Governors of the
International Atomic Energy Agency, adopted on 18 July 1991 on the basis of
the report of the Director-General of the Agency (document GOV/2530).

We should like to set out our official position on the aforementioned
resolution, as follows:

1.   We have carefully studied the contents of this document and find that it
takes as its fundamental premise article 34, paragraphs (b) and (c), of the
safeguards agreement concluded between Iraq and the Agency (INFCIRC/172).

We have already expressed our views with respect to these two paragraphs
of article 34 in our two letters to the Director-General of the International
Atomic Energy Agency dated 10 and 12 July 1991. Whereas the Agency could have
considered our point of view and taken some time to reach a joint
understanding with us of the sense of this article, the Director-General
instead hastened to pronounce judgements against Iraq on the grounds that it
had not provided the Agency with information on certain nuclear materials.
The Director-General did not, however, bear in mind the following points:

(a)   Iraq did in fact officially provide information on the nuclear
materials to the Agency, as set out in our letter of 7 July 1991.

(b)   The said materials were subjected to inspection by the third
international team, which left Iraq on 19 July 1991: that information is now
in the Agency's possession.

Accordingly, it was entirely possible for the Director-General of the
Agency to treat those developments as constituting a corrective measure in
accordance with article 19 of the agreement, to be dealt with in the same way
as previous similar cases addressed by the Agency. We should like to draw
attention to a similar case, as mentioned in the 1984 report on safeguards
implementation (document GOV/2201), which referred to the export by Luxembourg
of 41 tons of enriched uranium to Israel. Or are we not entitled to inquire
why the 11,000 tons of enriched uranium produced each year at power stations
which are not subject to the Agency's safeguard system do not attract the same
attention as do the tiny quantities of yellow cake and uranium compounds
present in Iraq?

It is our belief that the submission to the Board of Governors of the
International Atomic Energy Agency did not conform to the criteria applied by
the Agency in previous cases, nor did it have adequate legal justification.

0054 /...

2.   We were not expecting such a meeting to be convened before the Agency's inspection teams had finished their last round of inspections and submitted their final report and conclusions, in accordance with the provisions of article XII.C of the Agency's Statute. We believe that the results of the teams' work are of direct relevance to the discussion of an item of this nature, and we also believe that it is improper to take results of the teams' work in isolation, without awaiting the amalgamation of all such results and the drawing of overall conclusions.

3.   In adopting its resolution, including preambular paragraph (d) and operative paragraph 5, the Board of Governors chose entirely to ignore the following truths and facts:

     (a) Iraq has so far been visited by three nuclear inspection teams and three teams with responsibilities in other fields. They all received full cooperation from Iraq, except for one team which encountered some confusion. This we have already explained to the President of the Security Council and to the high-level mission which visited Iraq and of which the Director-General of the International Atomic Energy Agency was a member. Iraqi officials at the highest levels gave firm assurances of Iraq's absolute willingness to provide every facility to all teams and to cooperate with them in the performance of their duties.

     (b) The high-level mission submitted its report to the Security Council and clearly mentioned the assurances provided by Iraqi officials. It noted that the teams' future visits would demonstrate the extent of Iraq's cooperation.

     It would have been more appropriate if the Director-General of the International Atomic Energy Agency - as a member of the high-level mission - had explained this to the Board of Governors and if the Board had postponed the inclusion in its resolution of preambular paragraph (d) and operative paragraph 5 until such time as at least one of the inspection teams had completed its work subsequent to Iraq's explanation of the reasons for the confusion which had occurred with the second inspection team and to the expression of Iraq's clear and confirmed commitments.

     (c) The Board of Governors of the International Atomic Energy Agency held its meeting concerning the resolution on 18 July 1991, i.e. the last day of the third inspection team's stay in Iraq. The leader of the team and all its members expressed their great satisfaction with the full cooperation shown by Iraq, yet the Board of Governors did not take this into account and adopted its resolution before examining the team's report. Does this not give rise to some questions?

     We are confronted with an incomprehensible situation. While Iraqi technicians and the technicians of the inspection teams are cooperating and working together on a scientific level, we find the Board of Governors insisting on condemnation of Iraq for its lack of cooperation.

0055

/...

We are consequently alarmed and dissatisfied and conclude that the resolution was adopted on the basis of predetermined political concepts and motives, the intention being to bestow technical legitimacy through a specialized agency in preparation for a fresh act of military aggression against Iraq, following the full revelation by Iraq of its nuclear programme. Neither is it a secret to anyone that the same parties which induced the Board of Governors to adopt this resolution are endeavouring to maintain the embargo and sanctions imposed on Iraq, without any legal or moral grounds, in the hope of starving the Iraqi people and thus creating a pretext for intervention in Iraq's internal affairs and an attempt to subject it to the will of foreign Powers.

In affirming Iraq's official position with respect to the unjust and unbalanced resolution adopted by the Board of Governors of the International Atomic Energy Agency, we wish to emphasize our profound concern at the absence of a spirit of fairness and justice in the dealings of certain parties in this regard, despite Iraq's undertaking to fulfil its obligations under Security Council resolution 687 (1991). We also request that you have this letter circulated as a document of the Security Council.

(Signed) Ahmad HUSSEIN
Minister for Foreign Affairs
of the Republic of Iraq

0056

어 왕

주 국 련 대 표 부

주국련20313- 1991. 8. 1.

수신 : 장관 623

참조 : 국제기구조약국장, 중동아프리카국장

제목 : 이락핵사찰(안보리)

당관에서 입수한 표제관련 IAEA 사무총장의 91.7.30 안보리 비공식 협의시 발언문을 별첨과 같이 송부합니다.

첨 부 : 상기 발언문 (91.7.30). 끝.

주 국 련 대

선 결			결재 (공람)		
접수일시	1991. 8.	번호			
처리과	43709				

0057

IAEA

INTERNATIONAL ATOMIC ENERGY AGENCY
WAGRAMERSTRASSE 5, P.O. BOX 100, A-1400 VIENNA, AUSTRIA,
TELEPHONE: 1 2360, TELEX: 1-12645, CABLE: INATOM VIENNA,
TELEFAX: 431 234564

25 July 1991
PR 91/26
FOR IMMEDIATE RELEASE

PRESS RELEASE FOR USE OF INFORMATION MEDIA • NOT AN OFFICIAL RECORD

FOURTH IAEA INSPECTION TEAM IS LEAVING TODAY FOR IRAQ

An inspection team of the International Atomic Energy Agency (IAEA) is leaving today to carry out the fourth nuclear inspection in Iraq under the terms of Security Council resolution 687. The team has fifteen members.

The report of the third team is being readied for submission to the Security Council through the UN Secretary-General.

The third team inspected nuclear material and facilities which formed part of the enrichment programme which was declared by Iraq on 7 July. It received supplementary information and explanations regarding this programme. Nevertheless, the team felt that there may be more that should be declared and that it is premature to draw conclusions as to the full extent of the Iraqi nuclear programme. Further sites to be inspected may be designated by the Special Commission appointed under Security Council resolution 687 (1991) and a number of follow-up actions have been identified by the third team and will be performed during subsequent inspection missions. In particular, the extent of the programme in the area of centrifuge enrichment needs to be clarified. It also needs to be investigated whether more locations exist where sensitive equipment or material might be installed, used or stored. In addition, the industrial and technological infrastructure which has been built in connection with the nuclear programme has to be assessed.

During the three inspection visits carried out so far, more than 30 sites have been visited, most of which had many buildings. In particular, the Tuwaitha Nuclear Research Centre had more than 90 buildings, all of which were inspected. More than 300 samples of nuclear material and environmental samples have been taken and 950 inspection days have been spent. The sites covered have been spread throughout the country.

* * * * *

0058

INTERNATIONAL ATOMIC ENERGY AGENCY
AGENCE INTERNATIONALE DE L'ENERGIE ATOMIQUE
МЕЖДУНАРОДНОЕ АГЕНТСТВО ПО АТОМНОЙ ЭНЕРГИИ
ORGANISMO INTERNACIONAL DE ENERGIA ATOMICA

WAGRAMERSTRASSE 5, P.O. BOX 100, A-1400 VIENNA, AUSTRIA
TELEX: 1-12645, CABLE: INATOM VIENNA, FACSIMILE: 43 1 234564, TELEPHONE: 43 1 2360

IN REPLY PLEASE REFER TO:
PRIERE DE RAPPELER LA REFERENCE:　　N4.21.0 Circ.

DIAL DIRECTLY TO EXTENSION:
COMPOSER DIRECTEMENT LE NUMERO DE POSTE:

29 July 1991

Sir,

Article XII.C of the Agency's Statute requires the Board of Governors to report non-compliance with safeguards obligations to all Agency Member States and to the Security Council and General Assembly of the United Nations.

I accordingly have the honour to inform your Government that on 18 July 1991 the Board of Governors found that the Government of Iraq had not complied with its obligations under its safeguards agreement with the Agency. The Board resolution, adopted by 29 votes to one with three abstentions, is attached.

I transmitted a copy of the resolution to the Secretary-General of the United Nations on 19 July 1991, in order that it might be brought to the attention of the Security Council and the General Assembly.

Accept, Sir, the assurances of my highest esteem.

Hans Blix
Director General

Attachment

His Excellency
The Minister for Foreign Affairs
Ministry of Foreign Affairs
Seoul
Republic of Korea

COPY : COPIE : COPY : COPIE : COPY : COPIE : COPY : COPIE : COPY : COPIE : COPY

0059

International Atomic Energy Agency

BOARD OF GOVERNORS

For official use only

GOV/2532
18 July 1991

RESTRICTED Distr.
Original: ENGLISH

IRAQ'S NON-COMPLIANCE WITH ITS SAFEGUARDS OBLIGATIONS

<u>Resolution adopted by the Board of Governors</u>

<u>on 18 July 1991</u>

<u>The Board of Governors</u>,

(a) <u>Stressing</u> the importance of non-proliferation of nuclear weapons to international and regional peace and security,

(b) <u>Expressing</u> grave concern about the conclusion of the report of the Director General (GOV/2530) that the Government of Iraq has failed to comply with its obligations under its safeguards agreement with the IAEA (INFCIRC/172),

(c) <u>Recalling</u> United Nations Security Council resolution 687 which, inter alia, called upon Iraq to declare all its nuclear activities to the International Atomic Energy Agency,

(d) <u>Noting</u> with appreciation the efforts of the Director General and his staff to implement the tasks assigned to the Agency by that resolution, and the diligent and effective conduct of the Agency's inspections of Iraqi nuclear activities, and

(e) <u>Expressing</u> grave concern about the evident deception and obstruction of IAEA inspectors in their efforts to carry out the Security Council's mandate in resolution 687, in violation of that resolution and the undertakings by Iraq governing the status, privileges and immunities of the IAEA and the inspection teams mandated under Security Council resolution 687,

1. <u>Finds</u>, on the basis of the report of the Director General in GOV/2530, that the Government of Iraq has not complied with its obligations under its safeguards agreement with the Agency (INFCIRC/172);

4010292
91-2978

0060

2. Condemns this non-compliance by the Government of Iraq with its safeguards agreement;

3. Calls upon the Government of Iraq to remedy this non-compliance forthwith, including placing any and all additional source and special fissionable material within Iraq's territory, under its jurisdiction or its control, regardless of quantity or location under Agency safeguards in accordance with the relevant provisions of INFCIRC/172 and in accordance with relevant technical determinations of the Agency;

4. Decides, in accordance with Article XII.C of the Statute, to report this non-compliance to all members of the Agency and to the Security Council and General Assembly of the United Nations;

5. Calls upon Iraq to cease all obstruction or interference with the IAEA inspection teams in their efforts to implement Security Council resolution 687;

6. Requests the Director General to keep the Board and the General Conference informed of progress in the implementation of this resolution so that they may consider appropriate action in accordance with Article XII.C and XIX.B of the Statute in the event of the Government of Iraq's failing to take fully corrective action; and

7. Decides to inscribe an item entitled "Iraq's non-compliance with its safeguards obligations" on the agenda of the September Board of Governors and requests the Director General to include such an item in the provisional agenda for the thirty-fifth regular session of the General Conference.

0061

STATEMENT BY DIRECTOR GENERAL, HANS BLIX, IAEA,

IN INFORMAL MEETING OF THE SECURITY COUNCIL

30 JULY 1991

I APPRECIATE THE OPPORTUNITY AGAIN INFORMALLY TO PROVIDE THE SECURITY
COUNCIL WITH SOME INFORMATION CONCERNING THE FULFILLMENT BY THE IAEA OF
TASKS GIVEN TO IT BY THE COUNCIL UNDER RES. 687 (1991).

ON 15 JULY, PROFESSOR ZIFFERERO, THE LEADER OF THE AGENCY'S ACTION TEAM
REPORTED TO THE COUNCIL ON WHAT WE HAD LEARNT ABOUT THE IRAQI NUCLEAR
CAPABILITY THROUGH OUR FIRST TWO INSPECTION MISSIONS. TODAY, MR.
PERRICOS, WILL TELL YOU ABOUT THE CONSIDERABLE AMOUNT OF KNOWLEDGE WHICH
WAS GAINED BY THE THIRD TEAM, WHICH HE HEADED AND WHICH CAME TO BAGHDAD
ONE DAY BEFORE THE IRAQI DECLARATION OF 7 JULY. WITH MR. PERRICOS TODAY
IS MR. THORNE, WHO HAS BEEN ON SEVERAL MISSIONS TO BAGHDAD AND WHO WAS
ONE OF THE INSPECTORS INVOLVED IN THE SHOOTING INCIDENT. THE FOURTH
MEMBER OF THE IAEA ACTION TEAM IS MR. KAY, WHO HEADED THE TEAM WHICH WAS
DENIED ACCESS AT THE FALLUJA SITE AND WHICH IDENTIFIED THE CARAVAN OF
TRUCKS. HE IS AGAIN IN BAGHDAD NOW, LEADING THE FOURTH INSPECTION
MISSION.

THE ACTION TEAM OF THE IAEA FOR ACTIVITIES UNDER RES. 687 (1991) CONSISTS
OF ONLY THESE FOUR FULL-TIME PROFESSIONALS AND TWO SECRETARIES. HOWEVER,
OUR SAFEGUARDS DEPARTMENT PROVIDES MANY INSPECTORS TO THE TEAMS AND THE
PARTICIPATION OF SOME EXPERTS IS ARRANGED THROUGH THE SPECIAL

0062

COMMISSION IN NEW YORK OR THROUGH GOVERNMENTS. TO-DATE WE HAVE
PERFORMED ALTOGETHER AROUND 1000 INSPECTION MAN-DAYS.

THE FOURTH TEAM IS EXPECTING TO STAY ABOUT TWO WEEKS, FOLLOWING-UP ON
THE FINDINGS OF THE THIRD TEAM AND INSPECTING FURTHER SITES DESIGNATED
BY THE SPECIAL COMMISSION. A LIST, WHICH WAS PROMISED IN A LETTER TO
MR. PERRICOS ON 24 JULY AND WHICH HAS NOW BEEN GIVEN TO MR. KAY, OF
NUCLEAR MATERIAL AND EQUIPMENT, SOME OF WHICH WAS FOUND AFTER MR.
PERRICOS' DEPARTURE, DOES NOT SEEM TO PROVIDE ANYTHING DRAMATICALLY
NEW, BUT ADDS TO THE PICTURE THAT MR. PERRICOS WILL GIVE YOU.

I THINK YOU WILL FIND THAT THE PICTURE OF THE EMIS PROGRAM IS NOW A
RATHER DETAILED ONE. THIS, OF COURSE, IS NOT TO SAY THAT IT IS A FULL
PICTURE. WE ARE NOT, FOR INSTANCE, IN A POSITION TO CONFIRM IRAQ'S
STATEMENTS THAT ONLY ABOUT HALF A KILOGRAM OF URANIUM AT AN AVERAGE
ENRICHMENT LEVEL OF 4% HAD BEEN PRODUCED.

AT THE INFORMAL MEETING OF THE SECURITY COUNCIL ON 15 JULY I SAID I
COULD NOT SEE ANY PEACEFUL PURPOSE IN IRAQ'S ENRICHMENT PROGRAMME. THE
METHOD USED FOR ENRICHMENT, EMIS, WAS EXTREMELY EXPENSIVE AND IT WOULD
BE UNECONOMIC TO PRODUCE ENRICHED URANIUM BY THIS METHOD, WHEN ENRICHED
MATERIAL FOR PEACEFUL PURPOSES IS ABUNDANT IN THE WORLD MARKET.
MOREOVER, IRAQ'S NUCLEAR POWER PROGRAM WAS NOT VERY ADVANCED.

0063

IN THE REPORT OF THE THIRD INSPECTION TEAM, IT IS RECORDED THAT THE
LEADER OF THE IRAQI ENRICHMENT PROGRAMME, DR. JAFFAR, EXPLAINED THAT
THE PRIMARY AIM OF THE PROGRAMME WAS TO DEVELOP A TECHNOLOGICAL AND
INDUSTRIAL INFRASTRUCTURE. SECONDLY, IT WAS SUGGESTED, ENRICHED
URANIUM WAS NEEDED FOR THE RESEARCH REACTORS AND FOR A FUTURE NUCLEAR
POWER PROGRAMME. NEITHER EXPLANATION IS CONVINCING. A TECHNOLOGICAL
AND INDUSTRIAL INFRASTRUCTURE MAY BE A SPIN-OFF OF A PROGRAMME OF
ENRICHMENT BUT HARDLY THE PRIMARY AIM OF IT. AS REGARDS FUEL FOR
RESEARCH REACTORS AND A FUTURE POWER PROGRAMME I MUST REITERATE THE
COMMENT THAT LOW ENRICHED URANIUM IS AVAILABLE AT A MUCH LOWER
PRODUCTION COST THAN THAT WHICH COULD HAVE BEEN ACHIEVED IN IRAQ. THE
THIRD INSPECTION TEAM REPORT NOTES ANOTHER DETAIL THAT SEEMS OF
INTEREST IN THIS CONTEXT, NAMELY THAT THE COMBINATION IN THE IRAQI EMIS
PROGRAMME OF HIGH CAPACITY/MODEST SEPARATION AND LOW CAPACITY/HIGH
SEPARATION WOULD BE PARTICULARLY USEFUL IF THE GOAL WAS TO PRODUCE
HIGHLY ENRICHED URANIUM.

WITH YOUR PERMISSION, I SHALL REPORT TODAY ON TWO IMPORTANT MATTERS.
FIRST, THE ACTION BY THE BOARD OF GOVERNORS OF THE IAEA ON 18 JULY TO
DECLARE IRAQ IN NON-COMPLIANCE WITH THE SAFEGUARDS OBLIGATIONS OF THE
COUNTRY. SECONDLY, THE PLAN WHICH HAS JUST BEEN SUBMITTED BY THE IAEA
CONCERNING THE FUTURE ON-GOING MONITORING AND VERIFICATION IN IRAQ AS
REQUIRED IN PARAGRAPH 13 OF SECURITY COUNCIL RES. 687 (1991).

AN EXAMINATION BY THE IAEA OF THE LISTS THAT WERE ATTACHED TO IRAQ'S

0064

DECLARATION OF 7 JULY SHOWED THAT SOME OF THE NUCLEAR MATERIAL SHOULD
HAVE BEEN REPORTED TO THE AGENCY UNDER THE SAFEGUARDS AGREEMENT
CONCLUDED BY IRAQ PURSUANT TO THE COUNTRY'S ADHERENCE TO THE
NON-PROLIFERATION TREATY. THIS CONCLUSION WAS COMMUNICATED BY ME TO
IRAQ, WHICH MADE TWO PRINCIPAL POINTS IN REPLY. FIRST, THAT THE
QUANTITIES OF MATERIAL WHICH SHOULD HAVE BEEN DECLARED WERE
INSIGNIFICANT. SECONDLY, THAT HAVING NOW DECLARED THEM, IRAQ WAS NO
LONGER IN NON-COMPLIANCE WITH ITS SAFEGUARDS AGREEMENT BUT HAD TAKEN
REQUISITE CORRECTIVE ACTION.

THIS CORRESPONDENCE WAS REPORTED TO THE BOARD OF GOVERNORS OF THE IAEA
WITH THE COMMENT THAT THE DUTY TO REPORT NUCLEAR MATERIALS EXISTS
REGARDLESS OF WHAT THE QUANTITIES ARE. WHEN THE BOARD MET, IT HAD
FURTHER BEEN MADE CLEAR THAT THE TARMIYA SITE HAD BEEN IN OPERATION AND
THAT SOME URANIUM HAD, IN FACT, BEEN ENRICHED THERE. ACCORDINGLY,
DESIGN INFORMATION ABOUT TARMIYA SHOULD HAVE BEEN GIVEN TO THE AGENCY.

AS REPORTED TO THE SECURITY COUNCIL, IN ACCORDANCE WITH ARTICLE XII C
OF THE AGENCY'S STATUTE AND ART. III:2 OF THE AGREEMENT GOVERNING THE
RELATIONSHIP BETWEEN THE UNITED NATIONS AND THE AGENCY, THE BOARD OF
GOVERNORS OF THE IAEA FOUND THAT IRAQ HAD NOT COMPLIED WITH ITS
OBLIGATIONS UNDER ITS SAFEGUARDS AGREEMENT WITH THE AGENCY. IT
CONDEMNED THIS NON-COMPLIANCE AND CALLED ON THE GOVERNMENT OF IRAQ TO
REMEDY ITS NON-COMPLIANCE AND TO PLACE ALL NUCLEAR MATERIAL, REGARDLESS
OF QUANTITY AND LOCATION, UNDER AGENCY SAFEGUARDS.

0065

SUBSEQUENT TO THE ACTION BY THE IAEA BOARD, THE FOREIGN MINISTER OF
IRAQ, IN A LETTER ADDRESSED TO THE SECRETARY-GENERAL OF THE UNITED
NATIONS, AGAIN EXPRESSED THE VIEW THAT THE DECLARATION OF 7 JULY BY
IRAQ AND IRAQ'S COOPERATION WITH THE THIRD AGENCY INSPECTION TEAM
CONSTITUTED SUFFICIENT CORRECTIVE MEASURES AND THAT IT SHOULD NOT HAVE
BEEN NECESSARY TO TAKE THE MATTER TO THE BOARD SO SOON. IN PARTICULAR,
HE SUBMITTED THAT THAT RESULTS OF ALL INSPECTION TEAMS SHOULD HAVE BEEN
AWAITED BEFORE CONCLUSIONS WERE DRAWN.

I HAVE REPLIED TO THIS COMPLAINT BY REFERRING TO A STATEMENT WHICH I
MADE IN THE BOARD MEETING ON 18 JULY. I POINTED OUT THAT THE
DIRECTOR-GENERAL'S DUTY TO REPORT IRAQ'S NON-COMPLIANCE WITH ITS
SAFEGUARDS AGREEMENT TO THE BOARD EXISTED REGARDLESS OF ANY CORRECTIVE
ACTIONS BY IRAQ. FURTHER, THAT THE FAILURE OF IRAQ TO REPORT HAD
REGARD NOT JUST TO A TECHNICAL MATTER INVOLVING SMALL QUANTITIES OF
NUCLEAR MATERIAL, BUT AMOUNTED TO AN ATTEMPT TO CONCEAL A MAJOR PROGRAM
FOR THE ENRICHMENT OF URANIUM. THE BOARD HAD TO REACT TO THIS ATTEMPT,
IRRESPECTIVE OF WHETHER IT WAS UNCOVERED AS A RESULT OF INSPECTIONS OR
OF A DECLARATION MADE BELATEDLY BY IRAQ. A NON-COMPLIANCE WITH A LEGAL
OBLIGATION, WHETHER DISCLOSED BY A DECLARATION, OR DISCOVERED BY
INSPECTORS, IS NOT UNMADE SIMPLY BY BEING ADMITTED. THIS
NON-COMPLIANCE IS NOW REPORTED TO THE SECURITY COUNCIL BY THE BOARD OF
GOVERNORS OF THE IAEA.

THE SECOND ITEM ON WHICH I SHOULD LIKE TO MAKE SOME COMMENTS IS THE

0066

PLAN NOW SUBMITTED BY THE AGENCY TO THE SECURITY COUNCIL FOR FUTURE
ON-GOING MONITORING AND VERIFICATION OF IRAQ'S COMPLIANCE WITH RES. 687
(1991). REGRETTABLY WE DO NOT YET KNOW THE FULL EXTENT OF IRAQ'S NUCLEAR
CAPABILITY AND DO NOT YET HAVE AN INVENTORY OF ALL NUCLEAR MATERIAL IN
IRAQ SUBJECT TO THE AGENCY'S VERIFICATION AND INSPECTIONS. ACCORDINGLY,
THE PHASE OF IMMEDIATE ON-SITE INSPECTION CONTINUES AND IT WOULD BE
PREMATURE TO SUBMIT ANY FINAL PROPOSAL FOR FUTURE ONGOING MONITORING AND
VERIFICATION.

THE PRESENT SITUATION IS CHARACTERIZED BY THE SECURITY COUNCIL'S VERY
CLOSE ATTENTION TO IRAQ, THE CONTINUED APPLICATION OF SANCTIONS AND THE
CHARTING OF IRAQ'S CAPACITY IN THE FIELD OF WEAPONS OF MASS DESTRUCTION
AS WELL AS THE NEUTRALIZATION OR PREPARATIONS FOR THE NEUTRALIZATION OF
THIS CAPACITY. WE HAVE CONCLUDED THAT SO LONG AS THIS PHASE LASTS, AND
SUBJECT TO ANY OTHER DIRECTIVE BY THE COUNCIL, THE PRESENT ARRANGEMENTS
FOR MONITORING AND VERIFICATION MUST CONTINUE.

THE SECURITY COUNCIL HAS DETERMINED WHAT ACTIVITIES IRAQ IS FORBIDDEN TO
UNDERTAKE IN THE NUCLEAR FIELD. THESE HAVE BEEN INDICATED IN PARAGRAPH
12 OF RESOLUTION 687(1991) TO BE THE ACQUISITION OR DEVELOPMENT OF
NUCLEAR WEAPONS OR WEAPONS-USABLE MATERIAL AND VARIOUS ACTIVITIES LEADING
TO THE PRODUCTION OF SUCH MATERIAL. WHILE THE PROSCRIBED RANGE OF
ACTIVITIES IS THUS DETERMINED BY THE COUNCIL, THE AGENCY CAN BE GIVEN THE
RESPONSIBILITY TO DEFINE THESE ACTIVITIES IN DETAIL AND TO MONITOR

0067

AND VERIFY THAT THE LIMITATION DECIDED BY THE COUNCIL IS RESPECTED.

THE PLAN FOR FUTURE ONGOING MONITORING AND VERIFICATION THAT THE AGENCY IS PROPOSING DRAWS INSPIRATION FROM THE ARRANGEMENTS WHICH GOVERN THE PRESENT PHASE, IN PARTICULAR, THE EXCHANGE OF LETTERS OF 6 AND 17 MAY BETWEEN THE SECRETARY-GENERAL AND THE GOVERNMENT OF IRAQ. IF FULL CERTAINTY WERE NOT TO BE ATTAINED IN THE PRESENT PHASE, THAT ALL IRAQ'S NUCLEAR CAPABILITIES HAVE BEEN CHARTED, AND THAT ALL PROHIBITED ITEMS HAVE BEEN DESTROYED, REMOVED OR RENDERED HARMLESS, THEN A CLOSE FUTURE ONGOING MONITORING AND VERIFICATION WOULD BECOME EVEN MORE CRUCIAL, AND WOULD PERHAPS REQUIRE A PERMANENT INSPECTION PRESENCE IN THE COUNTRY TO ALLOW, INTER-ALIA, INSPECTIONS ON SHORT NOTICE.

IT IS TOO EARLY TO DRAW WIDERLESSONS FROM THE PRESENT INSPECTION ACTIVITIES IN IRAQ. YET A FEW REFLECTIONS MAY BE APPROPRIATE. THE DISCLOSURE THAT IRAQ, A PARTY TO THE NPT AND TO A SAFEGUARDS AGREEMENT CONCLUDED PURSUANT TO IT, WAS ABLE TO CONDUCT, SINCE THE EARLY 1980'S, A PROGRAM FOR THE ENRICHMENT OF URANIUM BY THE EMIS METHOD, WHICH WAS ONLY UNCOVERED THROUGH RECENT INSPECTIONS UNDER RES. 687 (1991), MUST LEAD TO MEASURES TO STRENGTHEN THE EFFECTIVENESS OF THE VERIFICATION REGIME UNDER THE NPT. THIS VERIFICATION REGIME WOULD HAVE MUCH SHARPER TEETH IF THREE ELEMENTS WERE ALLOWED TO INTERACT, AS THEY HAVE INTERACTED IN THE CASE OF IRAQ.

0068

FIRST, THAT THERE IS ACCESS TO INFORMATION FROM ALL SOURCES, INCLUDING NATIONAL TECHNICAL MEANS, REGARDING LOCATIONS THAT MIGHT HAVE UNDECLARED NUCLEAR ITEMS OR FACILITIES, DESERVING INSPECTION.

SECOND, THAT THERE IS AN UNLIMITED RIGHT OF ACCESS FOR THE INSPECTORATE TO LOCATIONS WHICH IT WISHES TO VISIT, EVEN AT SHORT NOTICE, AND

THIRD, THAT THERE IS A READINESS IN THE SECURITY COUNCIL TO SUPPORT THIS RIGHT OF ACCESS.

0069

International Atomic Energy Agency

INFORMATION CIRCULAR

INFCIRC/392
31 July 1991

GENERAL Distr.
Original: ARABIC

STATEMENT OF THE GOVERNMENT OF
THE KINGDOM OF SAUDI ARABIA

The attached text of a statement issued by the Government of Saudi
Arabia is being circulated for the information of Member States at the request
of the Saudi Arabian Resident Representative.

4023225

91-03094

0070

STATEMENT OF THE GOVERNMENT OF THE KINGDOM OF SAUDI ARABIA

In pursuance of the firm policy of the Kingdom of Saudi Arabia to promote peace throughout the world, so that mankind may enjoy peace itself and its positive effects on human well-being and socio-economic development, the Government of the Kingdom of Saudi Arabia has always supported and continues to support all efforts aimed at curbing the proliferation of destructive weapons in the world as a whole as well as in every region of the world.

It has likewise always supported and continues to support the establishment of zones free from such weapons in every part of the globe.

In implementing this constructive, peace-loving policy, the Kingdom of Saudi Arabia acceded to the Treaty on the Non-Proliferation of Nuclear Weapons, has been complying with its provisions and has been supporting in various international forums efforts to ban chemical and bacteriological weapons.

The Government of the Kingdom of Saudi Arabia is firmly convinced that the region of the Middle East, which has suffered from numerous wars and has been weighed down by the burden of producing and importing various weapons of mass destruction — nuclear, chemical and bacteriological — needs, more than any other region in the world, to be free from such destructive weapons so that it can solve its problems peacefully without resort to war and destruction.

In line with its policy of supporting peace everywhere in the world, the Government of the Kingdom of Saudi Arabia wishes to express its sincere desire and complete willingness to comply with any ban (quantitative or qualitative) on weapons of mass destruction in the region of the Middle East — provided that the prohibition is equally binding on all the countries of the region — whether it applies to production or to the import of such weapons or aims at achieving a balance of military power. The Kingdom also expresses its readiness, should any elements of such a ban apply to any of the weapons available in the Kingdom, to be among the first countries in the region to get rid of such weapons.

0071

The Government of the Kingdom of Saudi Arabia is also willing to contribute positively and constructively to any study aimed at decisions of an international framework for a regime banning such weapons in the region, to the establishment of appropriate principles for such a regime, and to specifying its stages of implementation.

Moreover, in line with its earnest desire for peace in the region of the Middle East and its persistent efforts in that direction with a view to creating confidence among the countries in the region and thereby achieving the elimination of weapons of mass destruction and removing the cause for the arms race in this region, the Government of the Kingdom of Saudi Arabia once more emphasizes its support, in this area, for the initiative of President George Bush of the United States aimed at banning weapons of mass destruction in the Middle East. It appeals to all the countries in the region to respond earnestly to this noble objective and calls upon all countries in the world to urge those in the region to realize this objective.

In expressing its support for the American initiative and for every initiative directed to the same goal, and in declaring its sincere desire and full willingness to comply with such a ban, the Government of the Kingdom of Saudi Arabia looks forward to the time when the Kingdom, together with the other countries in the region, will be able to implement this ban so that peace, security, stability and prosperity may reign in the Middle East for the benefit of the peoples in the region and of mankind as a whole.

0072

외 무 부

종 별 :

번 호 : UNW-2036   일 시 : 91 0805 2100

수 신 : 장 관(국연,국기,중동일,기정)

발 신 : 주 유엔대사

제 목 : 안보리 동향(비공식협의)

연: UNW-2020

1. 안보리는 금 8.5 비공식협의를 갖고 연호 대이락 제재조치 시행관련 정기심사문제 (결의687 호 21,28 항, 700 호 6항)를 토의한 바, 당관에서 탐문한 바에 의하면 대부분의 이사국들이 인도적목적을 위한 잠정적 예외조치(UNW-1970참조)를 제외하고는 현재의 제재조치들을 그대로 유지해야한다는 입장을 표명하였다고 함.

2. 금일 협의시 현행 제재조치를 유지키로 하는 경우 별도의 안보리 결정이 필요한 지의 여부, 동 결정 발표형태(예컨데 ,의장성명 형태)에 관해 의견이 일치되지 않음에 따라 안보리는 본건 토의를 위해 8.7 비공식 협의예정임.

3. 한편 유엔측이 금일 발표한바에 의하면, 이락당국은 유엔 생물무기 사찰반에게 지난 86년부터 90.8 까지 군사용(방어목적 주장)세균실험을 SALMAN PAK (바그다드동 남방 약 35 KM 소재)에서 실시한바 있음을 시인하였다고 함.

4. 연호 IAEA 측이 작성한 이락의 핵관련 의무이행 검증 계획안이 금일 안보리문서(S/22872)로 배포된바 동 내용 별첨송부함.

첨부:.이락 생물무기 관련 유엔측 발표내용 및 핵검증 계획안: UNW(F)-387 끝 (대사 노창희-국장)

국기국   1차보   중아국   국기국   외정실   안기부

PAGE 1   91.08.06   10:51 WH
                                            외신 1과 통제관

0073

유엔안전보장이사회 이라크 대량살상무기 폐기 특별위원회, 1991. 전3권 (V.2 8-9월)   79

UNW(Fr)-387 10805 2100
(국연. 국기. 중동원. 기정)   *총 80여*

UN BIOLOGICAL WEAPON INSPECTION TEAM IN IRAQ

Iraq has informed a UN inspection team that it has carried out biological research for defensive military purposes. According to the Iraqi authorities, this research, which began in 1986 at Salman Pak, a facility some 35 km to the south-east of Baghdad, was terminated in August 1990 and the agents on which the research was being carried out were destroyed.

Iraqi officials further told the team that this declaration had been withheld until now because it would have been misconstrued by the world at large. They said that no production or weaponisation of biological agents had taken place.

The Iraqi Government had previously notified the Special Commission that the purpose of the Salman Pak facility was the inspection and analysis of foods and liquids for human consumption, and for identifying chemical and biological contamination by laboratory diagnosis.

The inspection team is from the United Nations Special Commission. It is in Iraq as part of the Special Commission's program of inspections to verify Iraq's declarations that it does not possess a biological warfare capability.

The 28-person team, which includes 24 experts from nine countries - Australia, Canada, Czechoslovakia, France, Germany, Sweden, UK, USA and USSR - and four UN support personnel, has been in Iraq since 2 August.

The team has now visited Salman Pak on a number of occasions over the past few days. The inspection of the site has been hampered by the large amounts on unexploded ordnance present on the site. The Chief Inspector has said that the Iraqi authorities are extending excellent cooperation to the team.

The inspection is continuing.

5 August 1991

#UNW-2036
첨부물

8-1

외 무 부

종 별 :

번 호 : UNW-2053　　　　　　　　　　　일　시 : 91 0806 1930

수 신 : 장 관(국연,중동,기정)

발 신 : 주 유엔대사

제 목 : 안보리(이락 특정무기 폐기 검증계획)

　　　연: UNW-2036

　　　연호 대이락 핵관련 검증계획안에 이어 유엔사무총장이 안보리에 제출한 이락화학,생물무기, 탄도미사일 관련 이행 검증계획안이 금일 안보리문서로 배포된 바, 동주요부분을 별첨 송부함.

　　　첨부:장기문서: UNW(F)-394 끝

　　　(대사 노창희-국장)

국기국　1차보　중아국　외정실　안기부

UNW(F)-394, 10806 1930
(국연.중동.기정)   총 9아

II. THE PLAN

A. Scope

13.   In accepting unconditionally Security Council resolution 687 (1991), Iraq has undertaken not to use, retain, possess, develop, construct or otherwise acquire:

    (a) Any chemical or biological weapons or any stocks of agents or any related subsystems or components or any research, development, support or manufacturing facilities;

    (b) Any ballistic missiles with a range greater than 150 kilometres or any related major parts, including launchers, or any repair or production facilities.

14.   In order to ensure Iraq's compliance with these undertakings, the Special Commission shall, through inspections and through aerial overflights, as well as through the provision of information by Iraq, monitor and verify that activities, sites, facilities, material and other items, both military and civilian, are not used by Iraq in contravention of its obligations under Security Council resolution 687 (1991).

15.   To this end, the provisions set forth in the Plan and its annexes, which constitute an integral part of the Plan, shall apply.

B. General provisions

1. Information

16.   Iraq shall:

    (a) Provide to the Special Commission, on a regular basis, full, correct and timely information on activities, sites, facilities, material and other items, both military and civilian, that might be used for purposes prohibited under paragraph 10 of resolution 687 (1991);

    (b) Provide to the Special Commission full, correct and timely information on any additional activities, sites, facilities, material or other items that the Commission may designate for provision of information on a regular basis;

    (c) Provide to the Special Commission, promptly and fully, any additional information or clarification that the Commission may request.

Further provisions related to the submission of information are set forth in sections C, D and E and in annexes II, III and IV of the Plan.

INW-2653
첨부물

9-1

/...

2. Inspections and aerial overflights

17. The Special Commission shall have the right:

    (a) To designate for inspection any site, facility, activity, material or other item in Iraq;

    (b) To inspect, at any time and without hindrance, any site or facility declared by Iraq or designated by the Special Commission;

    (c) To inspect, at any time and without hindrance, any activity, material or other item at any site or facility, including any material or other item in movement;

    (d) To inspect any number of declared or designated sites or facilities simultaneously or sequentially;

    (e) To designate for aerial overflight any area, location, site or facility in Iraq;

    (f) To carry out, at any time and without hindrance, aerial overflight by fixed- or rotary-wing aircraft with appropriate sensors as necessary, of any area, location, site or facility designated by the Special Commission;

    (g) To carry out, at any time and without hindrance, all such other flights, by fixed- or rotary-wing aircraft, as it deems necessary.

18. Iraq shall:

    (a) Accept unconditionally the inspection of any site, facility, activity, material or other item declared by Iraq or designated by the Special Commission;

    (b) Accept unconditionally aerial overflight of any area, location, site or facility designated by the Special Commission or any other flight, by fixed- or rotary-wing aircraft used by the Special Commission;

    (c) Provide immediate and unimpeded access to any site, facility, activity, material or other item to be inspected;

    (d) Not obstruct aerial overflights or take concealment measures at any area, location, site or facility designated by the Special Commission for overflight;

    (e) Accept unconditionally the inspectors and all other personnel designated by the Special Commission;

    (f) Cooperate fully with the Special Commission and facilitate its inspections and overflights;

9-2

/...

0077

S/22871
English
Page 6

    (g) Designate its inspection representative for each inspection to accompany the inspection team in Iraq.

19. Further provisions related to inspections and aerial overflights are set forth in annex I.

3. National implementation measures

20. Iraq shall adopt the necessary measures to implement its obligations under section C of resolution 687 (1991) and the present Plan, in particular:

    (a) To prohibit all natural and legal persons under Iraq's jurisdiction or control from undertaking anywhere any activity that is prohibited for Iraq by resolution 687 (1991), by subsequent related Security Council resolutions or by the present Plan;

    (b) To enact penal legislation which, in conformity with international law, shall extend to the activities referred to under subparagraph (a) above undertaken anywhere by any natural or legal persons under Iraq's jurisdiction or control.

21. Iraq shall inform the Special Commission of legislative and administrative measures taken to implement resolution 687 (1991), not later than 30 days after the approval by the Security Council of the Plan and thereafter as determined by the Special Commission.

4. Non-compliance

22. In case the Special Commission discovers any item that Iraq, under resolution 687 (1991), is obliged to destroy or to yield to the Special Commission for destruction, removal or rendering harmless, the Special Commission shall have the right to take it into custody and shall provide for its disposal, as appropriate.

23. In case the Special Commission discovers any activity taking place in contravention of resolution 687 (1991), it shall have the right to call upon Iraq to halt the activity and to prevent its recurrence. The Special Commission shall also have the right to take any prohibited item involved into custody and shall provide for its disposal, as appropriate.

24. Findings by the Special Commission that indicate that Iraq is not in compliance with its obligations under resolution 687 (1991) shall be brought to the attention of the Security Council.

9-3

/...

0078

5. Reports

25. The Special Commission shall, through the Secretary-General, report to the Security Council every six months on the implementation of the Plan and at any other time the Security Council may request.

6. Revisions

26. The Special Commission may, after informing the Security Council, revise the technical and procedural provisions in annexes II, III and IV, including the lists of material, equipment and other items, in the light of information and experience gained in the course of the implementation of resolution 687 (1991) and the Plan. The Special Commission shall inform Iraq of any such change.

27. The present Plan shall enter into force immediately upon its approval by the Security Council. The duration of the Plan shall be determined by the Security Council.

C. Provisions related to chemical items

28. Chemicals, equipment and facilities set forth herein and in annex II could be used for purposes related to chemical weapons. They shall therefore be subject to monitoring and verification in accordance with the following additional provisions in order to ensure that Iraq does not use, develop, produce or otherwise acquire chemical weapons or related items prohibited under resolution 687 (1991).

29. Chemicals that could be used for the development, production or acquisition of chemical weapons but which also have significant uses for purposes not prohibited by resolution 687 (1991) are set forth in list A in annex II. These chemicals may be used, developed, produced, stored or acquired solely for purposes not prohibited by resolution 687 (1991), subject to the provisions under paragraphs 30 and 31 below, and annex II.

30. Iraq shall, not later than 30 days after the adoption of the Plan by the Security Council, and on a regular basis thereafter, provide to the Special Commission information in accordance with annex II regarding:

    (a) The total national quantity of the production, processing or consumption of any chemical specified in list A of annex II and of the import and export of any of these chemicals specifying the countries involved;

    (b) Any site or facility that is involved in production, processing, consumption, storage, import or export of one tonne or more per year of any chemical specified in list A of annex II or which at any time has been

/...

9-4

0079

S/22871
English
Page 8

involved in activities with any of these chemicals for chemical weapons
purposes;

(c) Any site or facility that is involved in production or processing of
organophosphorus chemicals or which is involved in production of organic
chemicals by chlorination;

(d) Any site or facility where production, processing, consumption,
storage, import or export of one tonne or more per year of any chemical
specified in list A of annex II, or where production or processing of
organophosphorus chemicals or where production of organic chemicals by
chlorination is planned;

(e) Any import or any other acquisition of equipment or technologies
intended for production and processing of any chemical specified in list A of
annex II, of any organophosphorus chemical or for production of organic
chemicals by chlorination.

31. Should Iraq plan any production, processing, consumption, storage, import
or export not notified under paragraph 18 (d) above, it may begin such an
activity only after providing to the Special Commission a special notification
not later than one month in advance.

32. Chemicals that have little or no use except as chemical warfare agents or
for the development, production or acquisition of chemical weapons or which
have been used by Iraq as essential precursors for chemical weapons are set
forth in list B of annex II. Iraq shall not retain, use, transfer, develop,
produce, store, import or otherwise acquire these chemicals. Should Iraq
require any chemical specified in list B of annex II, it shall submit a
request to the Special Commission specifying precisely the chemical and the
quantities required, the facility where it is to be used and the purpose of
its use. The Special Commission will examine and decide on the request and
establish the special arrangements it considers consistent with resolution
687 (1991).

33. Further provisions related to chemical items are set forth in annex II.

D. Provisions related to biological items

34. Micro-organisms and toxins, equipment and facilities set forth herein and
in annex III could be used for purposes related to biological and toxin
weapons affecting humans, animals or plants. They shall therefore be subject
to monitoring and verification in accordance with the following additional
provisions in order to ensure that Iraq does not use, develop, produce or
otherwise acquire biological and toxin weapons or related items prohibited
under resolution 687 (1991).

9-5

/...

0080

35. Iraq shall, not later than 30 days after the adoption of the present Plan by the Security Council, and on a regular basis thereafter, provide to the Special Commission information in accordance with annex III regarding:

(a) Any site or facility, except purely diagnostic facilities, at which work with toxins or with micro-organisms meeting the criteria for risk groups IV, III or II according to the classification in the 1983 World Health Organization (WHO) Laboratory Biosafety Manual is carried out, or any facilities at which work with genetic material coding for toxins or genes derived from the aforementioned micro-organisms is carried out;

(b) Any site or facility having a laboratory meeting the criteria for a "maximum containment laboratory" or "containment laboratory" as specified in the 1983 WHO Laboratory Biosafety Manual, such as those designated as biosafety level 4 (BL4) or P4, biosafety level 3 (BL3) or P3 or equivalent standards;

(c) Any site or facility at which production or other means for the production of micro-organisms or toxins using vessels of 50 litres individually or 200 litres in the aggregate is carried out;

(d) Any site or facility for the bulk storage of toxins or of micro-organisms meeting the criteria for risk groups IV, III or II;

(e) Any site or facility for the production of vaccines;

(f) Any research, development, testing or other support or manufacturing facility for items and equipment specified in paragraph 1 of annex III;

(g) Any imports, other acquisition or exports of micro-organisms meeting the criteria for risk groups IV, III and II, toxins and vaccines, as well as related equipment and facilities.

36. Iraq shall, no later than 30 days after the adoption of the present Plan by the Security Council, and on a regular basis thereafter, provide to the Special Commission:

(a) A list of all documents of a scientific and technical nature published or prepared by any site or facility engaged in work relating to toxins or micro-organisms meeting the criteria for risk groups IV, III and II, including those of a theoretical nature. Documents of a purely diagnostic nature relating to risk group II micro-organisms are excepted;

(b) A description of any kind of work being conducted on the dissemination of micro-organisms or toxins into the environment or on processes that would lead to such dissemination, specifying the site or facility involved.

37. Iraq shall provide to the Special Commission information on all cases of infectious diseases affecting humans, animals or plants, that deviate, or seem

/...

9-6

0081

S/22871
English
Page 10

to deviate, from the normal pattern or are caused by any micro-organism meeting the criteria for risk groups IV and III and on all cases of similar occurrences caused by toxins. The information shall be provided within one week of the occurrence and the standardized form contained in document BWC/CONF.II/EX/2 should be utilized as appropriate.

38. Iraq shall not:

(a) Import items referred to in paragraph 23 (g) above without giving prior notice to the Special Commission not later than 30 days in advance in accordance with annex III. As an exception, the emergency import of vaccines may take place with simultaneous notification to the Special Commission;

(b) Conduct any activities in the field of micro-organisms and toxins except by civilian personnel not in the employ of any military organization. Such activities shall be conducted openly; no classified or secret programmes or activities shall be permitted. The facilities engaged in such activities shall not be under the control of, or owned by, any military organization. Should any military organization need to be involved in such activities for prophylactic or therapeutic purposes, Iraq shall submit a request to the Special Commission specifying precisely the toxins, micro-organisms and the quantities required, the facility where they are to be used and the purpose of their use. The Special Commission will examine and decide on the request and establish the special arrangements it considers consistent with resolution 687 (1991);

(c) Conduct activities on diseases other than those indigenous to or immediately expected to break out in its environment;

(d) Conduct any breeding of vectors of human, animal or plant diseases. Should Iraq need to conduct any such activity, Iraq shall submit a request to the Special Commission specifying precisely its requirements, the facility where the activity is to take place and the purpose of the activity. The Special Commission will examine and decide on the request and establish the special arrangements it considers consistent with resolution 687 (1991);

(e) Possess at any one time more than one facility having a laboratory meeting the criteria for a "maximum containment laboratory" as specified in the 1983 WHO Laboratory Biosafety Manual, such as those designated as biosafety level 4 (BL4) or P4 or equivalent standard. Iraq shall not possess at any one time more than two facilities having a laboratory meeting the criteria for a "containment laboratory", such as those designated as BL3 or P3 or equivalent standard. Should Iraq require any additional such facilities, Iraq shall submit a request to the Special Commission specifying the precise requirement. The Special Commission will examine and decide on the request and establish the special arrangements it considers consistent with resolution 687 (1991).

39. Further provisions related to biological items are set forth in annex III.

/...

9-7

0082

E. Provisions related to missiles

40. Facilities, equipment, other items and technologies set forth herein and in annex IV could be used for the development, construction or acquisition of ballistic missiles with a range greater than 150 kilometres. They shall therefore be subject to monitoring and verification in accordance with the following additional provisions in order to ensure that Iraq does not use, develop, construct or acquire any ballistic missiles with a range greater than 150 kilometres or related items prohibited under resolution 687 (1991).

41. The range of missiles that are prohibited for Iraq shall be determined on the basis of the maximum distance that a missile is capable of flying over a ballistic trajectory with a zero delivery payload. The prohibition applies to any missiles, whether or not flying a ballistic trajectory, or delivery system, capable of such a range and to any related major parts of such missiles, which include missile/rocket stages, re-entry vehicles, solid- or liquid-fuel motors, guidance sets, thrust vector controls, warheads and fusing systems, launchers capable of launching ballistic missiles with a range greater than 150 kilometres and related principal launch equipment and transporters for such missiles. The prohibition also applies to any missiles not in themselves capable of such a range, but which are capable of such a range in combination with technologies such as tube- or gun-type launchers.

42. Iraq shall, not later than 30 days after the adoption of the present Plan by the Security Council and on a regular basis thereafter, provide to the Special Commission the following:

    (a) A list of all its missiles designed for use, or capable of being modified for use, in a surface-to-surface role with a range greater than 75 kilometres, specifying their name and type, type of propulsion, number of stages and/or boosters, guidance systems, warhead and re-entry vehicle types, launcher types, airframe and warhead transporters and the sites or facilities where these items or equipment are located;

    (b) Information on any site or facility for such missiles, including sites or facilities for production, assembly, repair and maintenance, storage and operational bases, specifying their locations;

    (c) Information on any site or facility for missile research, development and testing, specifying their locations;

    (d) Information on the development, production or acquisition of the items, equipment and technologies listed in annex IV, specifying sites or facilities where such items, equipment and technologies are located, and the purposes for which they are being used.

43. Iraq shall notify the Special Commission of the developmental or test launch of any missiles not later than 14 days prior to the date of launch, specifying where and when the launch is to take place.

/...

9-8

0083

S/22871
English
Page 12

44.   Iraq shall not construct, otherwise acquire or operate facilities for the
use, development and production of ballistic missiles capable of a range
greater than 150 kilometres, including facilities for research, development,
manufacture, assembly, testing, storage, repair, training, flight simulating
and operational use of such missiles, nor acquire related major parts
specified in paragraph 29 and the items listed in annex IV for such missiles.

45.   Further provisions related to missiles are set forth in annex 4.

9-9

/...

0084

외 무 부

종 별 :

번 호 : UNW-2041

수 신 : 장 관(중동일,국연)

발 신 : 주 유엔대사

제 목 : 대이락 무기류 공급금지(안보리결의 700 호)

일 시 : 91 0805 2100

연: UNW-1872 , 주국련 20313-574,618

8.1 자로 유엔사무총장이 안보리에 보고한바에 의하면 32개국이 표제관련 자국관련 조치현황을 제출했었다고 하는 바, 연호 문안 회시바람.

첨부:상기 각국제출현황: UNW(F)-388 끝

(대사 노창희-국장)

중아국   1차보   국기국   외정실   안기부

UNW(F)-388 /0A05 2/ㅇㅓ
(중동일. 국연) 총2매

S

UNITED NATIONS

Security Council

Distr.
GENERAL

S/22884
1 August 1991

ORIGINAL: ENGLISH

REPORT OF THE SECRETARY-GENERAL ON THE IMPLEMENTATION OF PARAGRAPH 4 OF SECURITY COUNCIL RESOLUTION 700 (1991)

1.   On 17 June 1991, the Security Council adopted resolution 700 (1991) in connection with its consideration of the item entitled "The situation between Iraq and Kuwait". By that resolution the Security Council approved the Guidelines for facilitating full international implementation of paragraphs 24, 25 and 27 of resolution 687 (1991), which had been developed by the Secretary-General pursuant to paragraph 26 of the same resolution. 1/

2.   Paragraph 4 of resolution 700 (1991) reads as follows:

> "The Security Council,
>
>   ...
>
>   "4. Requests all States, in accordance with paragraph 8 of the Guidelines, to report to the Secretary-General within 45 days on the measures they have instituted for meeting the obligations set out in paragraph 24 of resolution 687 (1991);".

3.   Immediately following the adoption of resolution 700 (1991) on 17 June 1991, the Secretary-General transmitted the text of the resolution by telegram to the Minister for Foreign Affairs of Iraq.

4.   By a note verbale dated 3 July 1991 the Secretary-General transmitted the text of resolution 700 (1991) as well as the text of his report (S/22660) to all other States, drawing their particular attention, inter alia, to paragraph 4 of the resolution and requesting them to submit by 1 August 1991 at the latest information on the measures instituted by their Governments for meeting the obligations set out in paragraph 24 of resolution 687 (1991). On the same day the Secretary-General also transmitted copies of resolution 700 (1991) and of his report (S/22660) to all international organizations.

5.   As of 1 August 1991, replies have been received from 32 States, pursuant to paragraph 4 of resolution 700 (1991). Each of the replies has been issued as a document of the Security Council in the chronological order of receipt, as indicated below:

91-24829   2596j (E)   2--1   /....

#UNW-2041
청와대

0086

S/22884
English
Page 2

Norway	8 July	(S/22783)	Finland	29 July	(S/22860)
Israel	9 July	(S/22784)	China	29 July	(S/22866)
The Holy See	9 July	(S/22802)	Myanmar	30 July	(S/22861)
Hungary	12 July	(S/22801)	Australia	30 July	(S/22867)
France	16 July	(S/22800)	Austria	30 July	(S/22868)
Turkey	18 July	(S/22815)	Czechoslovakia	31 July	(S/22869)
Ecuador	23 July	(S/22851)	New Zealand	31 July	(S/22874)
Japan	24 July	(S/22835)	Italy	31 July	(S/22880)
Belgium	25 July	(S/22840)	Thailand	31 July	(S/22882)
United Kingdom	25 July	(S/22841)	Brazil	1 August	(S/22875)
Spain	25 July	(S/22842)	Ireland	1 August	(S/22876)
Malta	26 July	(S/22852)	Liechtenstein	1 August	(S/22877)
Greece	26 July	(S/22858)	Netherlands	1 August	(S/22878)
Sri Lanka	29 July	(S/22848)	Yugoslavia	1 August	(S/22879)
Singapore	29 July	(S/22849)	Argentina	1 August	(S/22881)
Chile	29 July	(S/22859)	Sweden	1 August	(S/22883)

Notes

1/   See the Secretary-General's report of 2 June 1991 (S/22660).

2-2

0087

외 무 부

종 별 :

번 호 : UNW-2053　　　　　　　　　　일　시 : 91 0806 1930

수 신 : 장 관(국연,중동,기정)

발 신 : 주 유엔대사

제 목 : 안보리(이락 특정무기 폐기 검증계획)

연: UNW-2036

　　연호 대이락 핵관련 검증계획안에 이어 유엔사무총장이 안보리에 제출한 이락화학.생물무기, 탄도미사일 관련 이행 검증계획안이 금일 안보리문서로 배포된 바, 동주요부분을 별첨 송부함.

　　첨부:상기문서: UNW(F)-394 끝

　　(대사 노창희-국장)

국기국　1차보　　중아국　외정실　안기부

PAGE 1

S/22871
English
Page 4

UNW(F)-394, 10806 1930
(국연·중동·기청)

총 90h

II. THE PLAN

A. Scope

13. In accepting unconditionally Security Council resolution 687 (1991), Iraq has undertaken not to use, retain, possess, develop, construct or otherwise acquire:

(a) Any chemical or biological weapons or any stocks of agents or any related subsystems or components or any research, development, support or manufacturing facilities;

(b) Any ballistic missiles with a range greater than 150 kilometres or any related major parts, including launchers, or any repair or production facilities.

14. In order to ensure Iraq's compliance with these undertakings, the Special Commission shall, through inspections and through aerial overflights, as well as through the provision of information by Iraq, monitor and verify that activities, sites, facilities, material and other items, both military and civilian, are not used by Iraq in contravention of its obligations under Security Council resolution 687 (1991).

15. To this end, the provisions set forth in the Plan and its annexes, which constitute an integral part of the Plan, shall apply.

B. General provisions

1. Information

16. Iraq shall:

(a) Provide to the Special Commission, on a regular basis, full, correct and timely information on activities, sites, facilities, material and other items, both military and civilian, that might be used for purposes prohibited under paragraph 10 of resolution 687 (1991);

(b) Provide to the Special Commission full, correct and timely information on any additional activities, sites, facilities, material or other items that the Commission may designate for provision of information on a regular basis;

(c) Provide to the Special Commission, promptly and fully, any additional information or clarification that the Commission may request.

Further provisions related to the submission of information are set forth in sections C, D and E and in annexes II, III and IV of the Plan.

INW-2653
첨부물

9-1

/....

2. Inspections and aerial overflights

17. The Special Commission shall have the right:

(a) To designate for inspection any site, facility, activity, material or other item in Iraq;

(b) To inspect, at any time and without hindrance, any site or facility declared by Iraq or designated by the Special Commission;

(c) To inspect, at any time and without hindrance, any activity, material or other item at any site or facility, including any material or other item in movement;

(d) To inspect any number of declared or designated sites or facilities simultaneously or sequentially;

(e) To designate for aerial overflight any area, location, site or facility in Iraq;

(f) To carry out, at any time and without hindrance, aerial overflight by fixed- or rotary-wing aircraft with appropriate sensors as necessary, of any area, location, site or facility designated by the Special Commission;

(g) To carry out, at any time and without hindrance, all such other flights, by fixed- or rotary-wing aircraft, as it deems necessary.

18. Iraq shall:

(a) Accept unconditionally the inspection of any site, facility, activity, material or other item declared by Iraq or designated by the Special Commission;

(b) Accept unconditionally aerial overflight of any area, location, site or facility designated by the Special Commission or any other flight, by fixed- or rotary-wing aircraft used by the Special Commission;

(c) Provide immediate and unimpeded access to any site, facility, activity, material or other item to be inspected;

(d) Not obstruct aerial overflights or take concealment measures at any area, location, site or facility designated by the Special Commission for overflight;

(e) Accept unconditionally the inspectors and all other personnel designated by the Special Commission;

(f) Cooperate fully with the Special Commission and facilitate its inspections and overflights;

9-2

/...

0090

S/22871
English
Page 6

    (g) Designate its inspection representative for each inspection to accompany the inspection team in Iraq.

19. Further provisions related to inspections and aerial overflights are set forth in annex I.

3. National implementation measures

20. Iraq shall adopt the necessary measures to implement its obligations under section C of resolution 687 (1991) and the present Plan, in particular:

    (a) To prohibit all natural and legal persons under Iraq's jurisdiction or control from undertaking anywhere any activity that is prohibited for Iraq by resolution 687 (1991), by subsequent related Security Council resolutions or by the present Plan;

    (b) To enact penal legislation which, in conformity with international law, shall extend to the activities referred to under subparagraph (a) above undertaken anywhere by any natural or legal persons under Iraq's jurisdiction or control.

21. Iraq shall inform the Special Commission of legislative and administrative measures taken to implement resolution 687 (1991), not later than 30 days after the approval by the Security Council of the Plan and thereafter as determined by the Special Commission.

4. Non-compliance

22. In case the Special Commission discovers any item that Iraq, under resolution 687 (1991), is obliged to destroy or to yield to the Special Commission for destruction, removal or rendering harmless, the Special Commission shall have the right to take it into custody and shall provide for its disposal, as appropriate.

23. In case the Special Commission discovers any activity taking place in contravention of resolution 687 (1991), it shall have the right to call upon Iraq to halt the activity and to prevent its recurrence. The Special Commission shall also have the right to take any prohibited item involved into custody and shall provide for its disposal, as appropriate.

24. Findings by the Special Commission that indicate that Iraq is not in compliance with its obligations under resolution 687 (1991) shall be brought to the attention of the Security Council.

/...

9-3

0091

S/22871
English
Page 7

5. Reports

25. The Special Commission shall, through the Secretary-General, report to the Security Council every six months on the implementation of the Plan and at any other time the Security Council may request.

6. Revisions

26. The Special Commission may, after informing the Security Council, revise the technical and procedural provisions in annexes II, III and IV, including the lists of material, equipment and other items, in the light of information and experience gained in the course of the implementation of resolution 687 (1991) and the Plan. The Special Commission shall inform Iraq of any such change.

27. The present Plan shall enter into force immediately upon its approval by the Security Council. The duration of the Plan shall be determined by the Security Council.

C. Provisions related to chemical items

28. Chemicals, equipment and facilities set forth herein and in annex II could be used for purposes related to chemical weapons. They shall therefore be subject to monitoring and verification in accordance with the following additional provisions in order to ensure that Iraq does not use, develop, produce or otherwise acquire chemical weapons or related items prohibited under resolution 687 (1991).

29. Chemicals that could be used for the development, production or acquisition of chemical weapons but which also have significant uses for purposes not prohibited by resolution 687 (1991) are set forth in list A in annex II. These chemicals may be used, developed, produced, stored or acquired solely for purposes not prohibited by resolution 687 (1991), subject to the provisions under paragraphs 30 and 31 below, and annex II.

30. Iraq shall, not later than 30 days after the adoption of the Plan by the Security Council, and on a regular basis thereafter, provide to the Special Commission information in accordance with annex II regarding:

    (a) The total national quantity of the production, processing or consumption of any chemical specified in list A of annex II and of the import and export of any of these chemicals specifying the countries involved;

    (b) Any site or facility that is involved in production, processing, consumption, storage, import or export of one tonne or more per year of any chemical specified in list A of annex II or which at any time has been

/...

9-4

0092

S/22871
English
Page 8

involved in activities with any of these chemicals for chemical weapons
purposes;

(c) Any site or facility that is involved in production or processing of
organophosphorus chemicals or which is involved in production of organic
chemicals by chlorination;

(d) Any site or facility where production, processing, consumption,
storage, import or export of one tonne or more per year of any chemical
specified in list A of annex II, or where production or processing of
organophosphorus chemicals or where production of organic chemicals by
chlorination is planned;

(e) Any import or any other acquisition of equipment or technologies
intended for production and processing of any chemical specified in list A of
annex II, of any organophosphorus chemical or for production of organic
chemicals by chlorination.

31. Should Iraq plan any production, processing, consumption, storage, import
or export not notified under paragraph 18 (d) above, it may begin such an
activity only after providing to the Special Commission a special notification
not later than one month in advance.

32. Chemicals that have little or no use except as chemical warfare agents or
for the development, production or acquisition of chemical weapons or which
have been used by Iraq as essential precursors for chemical weapons are set
forth in list B of annex II. Iraq shall not retain, use, transfer, develop,
produce, store, import or otherwise acquire these chemicals. Should Iraq
require any chemical specified in list B of annex II, it shall submit a
request to the Special Commission specifying precisely the chemical and the
quantities required, the facility where it is to be used and the purpose of
its use. The Special Commission will examine and decide on the request and
establish the special arrangements it considers consistent with resolution
687 (1991).

33. Further provisions related to chemical items are set forth in annex II.

D. Provisions related to biological items

34. Micro-organisms and toxins, equipment and facilities set forth herein and
in annex III could be used for purposes related to biological and toxin
weapons affecting humans, animals or plants. They shall therefore be subject
to monitoring and verification in accordance with the following additional
provisions in order to ensure that Iraq does not use, develop, produce or
otherwise acquire biological and toxin weapons or related items prohibited
under resolution 687 (1991).

9-5

/...

0093

35. Iraq shall, not later than 30 days after the adoption of the present Plan by the Security Council, and on a regular basis thereafter, provide to the Special Commission information in accordance with annex III regarding:

     (a) Any site or facility, except purely diagnostic facilities, at which work with toxins or with micro-organisms meeting the criteria for risk groups IV, III or II according to the classification in the 1983 World Health Organization (WHO) Laboratory Biosafety Manual is carried out, or any facilities at which work with genetic material coding for toxins or genes derived from the aforementioned micro-organisms is carried out;

     (b) Any site or facility having a laboratory meeting the criteria for a "maximum containment laboratory" or "containment laboratory" as specified in the 1983 WHO Laboratory Biosafety Manual, such as those designated as biosafety level 4 (BL4) or P4, biosafety level 3 (BL3) or P3 or equivalent standards;

     (c) Any site or facility at which fermentation or other means for the production of micro-organisms or toxins using vessels larger than 50 litres individually or 200 litres in the aggregate is carried out;

     (d) Any site or facility for the bulk storage of toxins or of micro-organisms meeting the criteria for risk groups IV, III or II;

     (e) Any site or facility for the production of vaccines;

     (f) Any research, development, testing or other support or manufacturing facility for items and equipment specified in paragraph 1 of annex III;

     (g) Any imports, other acquisition or exports of micro-organisms meeting the criteria for risk groups IV, III and II, toxins and vaccines, as well as related equipment and facilities.

36. Iraq shall, no later than 30 days after the adoption of the present Plan by the Security Council, and on a regular basis thereafter, provide to the Special Commission:

     (a) A list of all documents of a scientific and technical nature published or prepared by any site or facility engaged in work relating to toxins or micro-organisms meeting the criteria for risk groups IV, III and II, including those of a theoretical nature. Documents of a purely diagnostic nature relating to risk group II micro-organisms are excepted;

     (b) A description of any kind of work being conducted on the dissemination of micro-organisms or toxins into the environment or on processes that would lead to such dissemination, specifying the site or facility involved.

37. Iraq shall provide to the Special Commission information on all cases of infectious diseases affecting humans, animals or plants, that deviate, or seem

                                                              /...

                         9-6

                                                    0094

S/22871
English
Page 10

to deviate, from the normal pattern or are caused by any micro-organism meeting the criteria for risk groups IV and III and on all cases of similar occurrences caused by toxins. The information shall be provided within one week of the occurrence and the standardized form contained in document BWC/CONF.II/EX/2 should be utilized as appropriate.

38. Iraq shall not:

    (a) Import items referred to in paragraph 23 (g) above without giving prior notice to the Special Commission not later than 30 days in advance in accordance with annex III. As an exception, the emergency import of vaccines may take place with simultaneous notification to the Special Commission;

    (b) Conduct any activities in the field of micro-organisms and toxins except by civilian personnel not in the employ of any military organization. Such activities shall be conducted openly; no classified or secret programmes or activities shall be permitted. The facilities engaged in such activities shall not be under the control of, or owned by, any military organization. Should any military organization need to be involved in such activities for prophylactic or therapeutic purposes, Iraq shall submit a request to the Special Commission specifying precisely the toxins, micro-organisms and the quantities required, the facility where they are to be used and the purpose of their use. The Special Commission will examine and decide on the request and establish the special arrangements it considers consistent with resolution 687 (1991);

    (c) Conduct activities on diseases other than those indigenous to or immediately expected to break out in its environment;

    (d) Conduct any breeding of vectors of human, animal or plant diseases. Should Iraq need to conduct any such activity, Iraq shall submit a request to the Special Commission specifying precisely its requirements, the facility where the activity is to take place and the purpose of the activity. The Special Commission will examine and decide on the request and establish the special arrangements it considers consistent with resolution 687 (1991);

    (e) Possess at any one time more than one facility having a laboratory meeting the criteria for a "maximum containment laboratory" as specified in the 1983 WHO Laboratory Biosafety Manual, such as those designated as biosafety level 4 (BL4) or P4 or equivalent standard. Iraq shall not possess at any one time more than two facilities having a laboratory meeting the criteria for a "containment laboratory", such as those designated as BL3 or P3 or equivalent standard. Should Iraq require any additional such facilities, Iraq shall submit a request to the Special Commission specifying the precise requirement. The Special Commission will examine and decide on the request and establish the special arrangements it considers consistent with resolution 687 (1991).

39. Further provisions related to biological items are set forth in annex III.

/...

9-7

E. Provisions related to missiles

40. Facilities, equipment, other items and technologies set forth herein and in annex IV could be used for the development, construction or acquisition of ballistic missiles with a range greater than 150 kilometres. They shall therefore be subject to monitoring and verification in accordance with the following additional provisions in order to ensure that Iraq does not use, develop, construct or acquire any ballistic missiles with a range greater than 150 kilometres or related items prohibited under resolution 687 (1991).

41. The range of missiles that are prohibited for Iraq shall be determined on the basis of the maximum distance that a missile is capable of flying over a ballistic trajectory with a zero delivery payload. The prohibition applies to any missiles, whether or not flying a ballistic trajectory, or delivery system, capable of such a range and to any related major parts of such missiles, which include missile/rocket stages, re-entry vehicles, solid- or liquid-fuel motors, guidance sets, thrust vector controls, warheads and fusing systems, launchers capable of launching ballistic missiles with a range greater than 150 kilometres and related principal launch equipment and transporters for such missiles. The prohibition also applies to any missiles not in themselves capable of such a range, but which are capable of such a range in combination with technologies such as tube- or gun-type launchers.

42. Iraq shall, not later than 30 days after the adoption of the present Plan by the Security Council and on a regular basis thereafter, provide to the Special Commission the following:

    (a) A list of all its missiles designed for use, or capable of being modified for use, in a surface-to-surface role with a range greater than 75 kilometres, specifying their name and type, type of propulsion, number of stages and/or boosters, guidance systems, warhead and re-entry vehicle types, launcher types, airframe and warhead transporters and the sites or facilities where these items or equipment are located;

    (b) Information on any site or facility for such missiles, including sites or facilities for production, assembly, repair and maintenance, storage and operational bases, specifying their locations;

    (c) Information on any site or facility for missile research, development and testing, specifying their locations;

    (d) Information on the development, production or acquisition of the items, equipment and technologies listed in annex IV, specifying sites or facilities where such items, equipment and technologies are located, and the purposes for which they are being used.

43. Iraq shall notify the Special Commission of the developmental or test launch of any missiles not later than 14 days prior to the date of launch, specifying where and when the launch is to take place.

/...

0096

S/22871
English
Page 12

44. Iraq shall not construct, otherwise acquire or operate facilities for the use, development and production of ballistic missiles capable of a range greater than 150 kilometres, including facilities for research, development, manufacture, assembly, testing, storage, repair, training, flight simulating and operational use of such missiles, nor acquire related major parts specified in paragraph 29 and the items listed in annex IV for such missiles.

45. Further provisions related to missiles are set forth in annex 4.

/...

9-9

0097

외 무 부

종 별 :

번 호 : UNW-2057
일 시 : 91 0806 2000

수 신 : 장 관(국연,국기,중동일,기정)

발 신 : 주 유엔대사

제 목 : 이락 핵사찰

　　1. 금 8.6 자 유엔발표에 의하면 , 이락당국은 유엔 핵사찰반 (제4진)에게 플루토니움 분리실험 관련사항을 추가로 통보하여 왔다고 함., (플루토니움3 그람 추출)

　　2. 본건 플루토니움 실험추진은 이락의 핵안전협정 불이행 위반으로 IAEA 이사회에 보고될것이라 함.

　　첨부 : 상기 IAEA 발표내용및 NYT 기사 : UNW(F)-397 끝

　　(대사 노창희-국장)

국기국　　1차보　　중아국　　국기국　　외정실　　안기부

PAGE 1

91.08.07　　11:10　WH

외신 1과 통제관

0098

UNW(庁)-ㅁ7 1406 2000
(국연. 국기. 중동원, 기정) 총 3매

6 August 1991
PR 91/27
FOR IMMEDIATE RELEASE

INTERNATIONAL ATOMIC ENERGY AGENCY   1991-08-06 766237
WAGRAMERSTRASSE 5, P.O. BOX 100, A-1400 VIENNA, AUSTRIA,
TELEPHONE: 1 2360, TELEX: 1-12645, CABLE: INATOM VIENNA,
TELEFAX: 431 234564

PRESS RELEASE   FOR USE OF INFORMATION MEDIA - NOT AN OFFICIAL RECORD

IRAQI SAFEGUARDS AGREEMENT NON-COMPLIANCE

Iraq has provided further information regarding nuclear activities which
should have been declared to the International Atomic Energy Agency (IAEA)
under Iraq's safeguards agreement with the Agency.

The additional information given by Iraq to the fourth IAEA inspection
team currently in Baghdad, concerns details of experimental activities that
involved the fabrication of natural uranium oxide fuel, its irradiation in one
of Iraq's research reactors (IRT-5000) at Tuwaitha, and, thereafter, the
separation of minute quantities - 3 grams - of plutonium. The ability to
separate small quantities of plutonium from irradiated fuel had already been
admitted to the IAEA by Iraq and reported in a first inspection report of
4 June 1991 in which separation of 2.26 grams of plutonium was noted.

Although these activities were on a very limited scale and the reactor
used would only have been capable of producing insignificant quantities of
plutonium, the interest of Iraq in the separation of plutonium is noteworthy.
The failure to declare them to the IAEA in timely fashion under Iraq's
safeguards agreement constitutes clear non-compliance with that agreement.
A particularly disturbing fact is that the activities could take place in
safeguarded facilities. The additional information will be reported to the
IAEA Board of Governors, which on 18 July already condemned Iraq's
non-compliance with its safeguards agreement on several other grounds. It
will also form part of the next report of the IAEA to the UN Secretary-General
and the Security Council on the inspection work of the fourth IAEA inspection
team. This team is scheduled to return from Baghdad to Vienna in mid-month.

#UNW-2057
첨부물

3 -1

0099

BAGHDAD REVEALS IT HAD PLUTONIUM OF WEAPONS GRADE

SAFEGUARDS IN QUESTION

A Small Amount of Substance Indicates Nuclear Efforts Were Underestimated

By JERRY GRAY
Special to The New York Times

UNITED NATIONS, Aug. 5 — Iraq has disclosed that its scientists were secretly able to extract a small amount of plutonium, suitable for making an atomic bomb, from spent fuel at a nuclear installation whose operations came under international safeguards, United Nations officials said today.

Officials said the disclosure was troubling new evidence that Iraq's efforts to produce a nuclear weapon were significantly more extensive than previously known, even given Baghdad's piecemeal acknowledgements to United Nations monitors since the Persian Gulf war.

The latest disclosure and a separate new admission by Iraq that it had deliberately misled United Nations inspectors about a secret biological weapons program raise new doubts about Baghdad's willingness to forswear weapons of mass destruction.

Meeting on Sanctions

Further, the disclosure about the plutonium extraction calls into question the effectiveness of international efforts to monitor ostensibly peaceful nuclear programs to prevent the spread of nuclear arms.

The disclosures came as the Security Council was meeting today on whether to lift the sanctions imposed against Iraq, a move that Baghdad insists is vital to its reconstruction. Officials said such a step was unlikely now in light of the new information.

Robert L. Gallucci, the deputy chairman of the United Nations commission charged with eliminating Iraq's weapons of mass destruction, said that the Iraqis in recent days acknowledged extracting three grams of plutonium from spent fuel in a small research reactor at Tuwaitha, an industrial town outside Baghdad. He said that the amount was far short of the quantity needed to produce a nuclear weapon and that Baghdad denied it was meant for a bomb.

'A Very Serious Matter'

Mr. Gallucci said, however, that the disclosure clearly confirmed that Iraq had been able to obtain nuclear-weapons-grade material in a laboratory that had been under United Nations scrutiny even before the gulf war. He said the plutonium extraction had begun before the war.

"This is a very serious matter," Mr. Gallucci said. "The facility was under safeguards, but the activity was not reported. It is of concern whenever practice that should be safeguarded is done outside of safeguards."

Mr. Gallucci also said United Nations inspectors now in Iraq were looking for electronic triggers necessary to detonate a nuclear bomb. Baghdad has not declared any of the devices, but is believed to have acquired them.

After the war, Iraq, which as a signer of the Nuclear Nonproliferation Treaty had already committed itself to international safeguards and inspections, at first denied having any programs to process uranium. But in recent months, as it has sought to have United Nations trade sanctions lifted, Iraq has disclosed three secret uranium processing programs. Today's disclosure about the plutonium is the fourth program that could have been meant to develop a nuclear bomb.

Even before today's new information, the United States had criticized Iraq's disclosures as inadequate, saying they concealed the true extent of its weapons programs. Washington has not ruled out new military attacks to finally destroy them, although it has had trouble achieving a consensus among its gulf war allies over any new use of force.

Paul L. Leventhal, president of the Nuclear Control Institute in Washington, said today's revelation was the clearest and strongest to date that Iraq was on the track toward developing a nuclear bomb.

"This represents fair warning," he said.

Since its defeat in the gulf war, Iraq has been required under the United Nations cease-fire resolution to list all types, amounts and locations of chemical and biological weapons, as well as all material that could be used in making nuclear weapons and ballistic missiles. In April, Iraq informed the United Nations that a substantial arsenal of chemical and ballistic weapons survived the war, but it denied having nuclear arms, nuclear-weapons-grade materials or biological weapons.

Mr. Leventhal said the acknowledgement of a plutonium-processing program was significant because, though it is extracted by a procedure "messier" than trying to build a bomb from enriched uranium, it also is one that is easier to conceal.

"In some ways plutonium is the preferable material because you don't need as much of it for a bomb," he said.

Mr. Leventhal said about eight kilograms of plutonium — which can be chemically separated from spent fuel from a research or production reactor — are needed to make an imploding nuclear device, compared with about 25 kilograms of highly enriched uranium.

"Presumably they're processing their own spent fuel," he said, which means Iraq could easily keep such a program hidden from international inspectors.

Mr. Gallucci said Iraq, as required under the nonproliferation treaty, had

3—2

0100

told the International Atomic Energy Agency about the reactor at Tuwaitha, which is just southeast of Baghdad. But it had operated the plutonium separation clandestinely.

Other officials said that Tuwaitha was one of the sites on the United Nations inspection team's list and that the Iraqis had probably decided to acknowledge operating the secret plutonium program there rather than have the inspectors learn this on their own.

Most experts agree that unless Iraq could greatly expand and improve its uranium-separation capacity, its production of uranium-fueled weapons is years away.

Plutonium has certain advantages over uranium as a bomb fuel. It is denser than uranium, and less of it is needed to achieve "critical mass," the weight above which a chain nuclear reaction begins.

Process Would Take Years

But the amount of plutonium that can be produced by treating the spent wastes of an ordinary nuclear power reactor is limited by the size and capacity of the reactor, the rate at which it is kept running and other factors. If Iraq has only purified three grams of the silvery, white metal, its production rate is presumably so low that it would take years to make one bomb.

United Nations officials said Baghdad also has admitted that it falsely stated that a plant at Salman Pak near the capital was used for food analysis when in fact it was used for biological weapons research. The Iraqis said they had withheld the information until now "because it would have been misconstrued by the world at large."

The admissions were both made within the last several days to the 28-member Special Commission team that arrived in Iraq on Friday to check the country's claims that it does not possess biological warfare capability.

'Fairly Horrific Facts'

The British representative to the Security Council, Sir David Hannay, described the new revelations as "fairly horrific facts" that once again brought suspicion on Baghdad.

"The vast majority of the council has taken the view that there's no justification for changes in the sanctions regime," Sir David told reporters as he left the council meeting today.

The Iraqi report — delivered as the first step toward the compulsory destruction of its chemical, biological and nuclear weapons sites — said it had nearly 10,000 nerve-gas warheads, 1,000 tons of nerve and mustard gas, nearly 1,500 chemical weapons bombs and shells, 52 Scud missiles and 30 chemical and conventional warheads.

The United States challenged Iraq's claims as understated, saying American intelligence reports showed that Iraq was researching and developing biological weapons at a number of sites, including the Salman Pak plant, 22 miles southeast of Baghdad.

Secretary General Reports

The United Nations Secretary General, Javier Pérez de Cuéllar, told Security Council members today that Iraq had informed the inspection team late last week that it had carried out biological research for defensive military purposes at Salman Pak. The Iraqis said the research began in 1988 and ended in August 1990, at which time all the nerve agents were destroyed.

"The Iraqi Government had previously notified the Special Commission that the purpose of the Salman Pak facility was the inspection and analysis of foods and liquids for human consumption, and for identifying chemical and biological contamination by laboratory diagnosis," Mr. Pérez de Cuéllar told Security Council members during the meeting.

3-3

BAGHDAD REVEALS IT HAD PLUTONIUM OF WEAPONS GRADE

SAFEGUARDS IN QUESTION

A Small Amount of Substance Indicates Nuclear Efforts Were Underestimated

By JERRY GRAY
Special to The New York Times

UNITED NATIONS, Aug. 5 — Iraq has disclosed that its scientists were able to extract secretly a small amount of plutonium suitable for making an atomic bomb from spent fuel at a nuclear installation whose operations came under international safeguards, United Nations officials said today.

Officials described the disclosure as troubling new evidence that Iraq's efforts to produce a nuclear weapon before the Persian Gulf war were far more extensive than previously believed, even given Baghdad's piecemeal acknowledgements to United Nations monitors since the war.

The latest disclosure coupled with a separate new admission by Iraq that it had deliberately misled United Nations inspectors about a secret biological weapons program — also raises new doubts about whether Baghdad has been fully forthcoming about its efforts to develop weapons of mass destruction. Further, the disclosure calls into question the effectiveness of international efforts to monitor extensive peaceful nuclear programs to curb the spread of nuclear arms.

Reported by U.

Robert L. Gallucci, chairman of the United Nations commission charged with eliminating Iraq's weapons of mass destruction, said today that the Iraqis in recent days acknowledged extracting three grams of plutonium from spent fuel in a small research reactor near an industrial town outside Baghdad. He said the plutonium was far short of the amount needed to produce a nuclear bomb and that Baghdad denied it was for a bomb.

Mr. Gallucci said, however, that the disclosure clearly confirmed that Iraq had been able to obtain nuclear-weapons-grade material in a laboratory that had been under United Nations' scrutiny even before the gulf war.

'A Very Serious Matter'

"This is a very serious matter," Mr. Gallucci said. "The facility was under safeguards, but the activity was not reported. It is of concern whenever practice that should be safeguarded is done outside of safeguards."

Baghdad at first denied having any programs to process uranium, but in recent months, as it has sought to have United Nations trade sanctions lifted, it disclosed three such secret programs. Today's disclosure about the plutonium is the fourth program that could have been meant to develop material for a nuclear bomb.

Even before today's admission, the United States criticized Iraq's disclosures as concealing the true extent of its weapons programs, and Washington has not ruled out the use of military action to destroy them.

Paul L. Leventhal, president of the Nuclear Control Institute in Washington, said today's revelation was the clearest and strongest to date that Iraq was on the track toward developing a nuclear bomb.

"This represents fair warning," he said.

Since its defeat in the gulf war, Iraq has been required under United Nations Resolution 687 to list all types, amounts and locations of chemical and biological weapons, as well as all material that could be used in making nuclear weapons and ballistic missiles. In April, Iraq informed the United Nations that a substantial arsenal of chemical and ballistic weapons survived the war, but it denied having nuclear arms, nuclear-weapons-grade material or biological weapons.

Mr. Leventhal said the acknowledgement of a plutonium-processing program was significant because, though it is extracted by a procedure "messier" than trying to build a bomb from enriched uranium, it also is one that is easier to conceal.

"In some ways plutonium is the preferable material because you don't need as much of it for a bomb," he said.

Mr. Leventhal said about eight kilograms of plutonium — which can be chemically separated from spent fuel from a research or production reactor — is needed to make an imploding nuclear device, compared with about 25 kilograms of highly enriched uranium.

"Presumably they're processing their own spent fuel," he said, which means Iraq could easily keep such a program hidden from international inspectors."

Iraq Reported the Reactor

Mr. Gallucci said Iraq, as required under the Nuclear Nonproliferation Treaty, had told the International Atomic Energy Agency about the reactor at Tuwaitha, which is just southeast of Baghdad. But it had operated the plutonium separation clandestinely.

Other United Nations officials said that Tuwaitha was one of the sites on the inspection team's list and that the Iraqis had probably decided to acknowledge operating the secret plutonium program there rather than have the inspectors learn this on their own.

The separation of plutonium from other chemical elements present in used reactor fuel rods can be achieved by dissolving the waste in acid and then treating the resulting fluid with chemicals. By contrast, the separation of fissionable uranium 235 from its stable isotope, uranium 238, requires an elaborate, expensive and very time-consuming process. Most experts agree that unless Iraq could greatly expand and improve its uranium-separation capacity, its production of uranium-fueled weapons is years away.

Plutonium has certain advantages over uranium as a bomb fuel. It is denser than uranium, and less of it is needed to achieve "critical mass," the weight above which a chain nuclear reaction begins

But the amount of plutonium that can be produced by treating the spent waste of an ordinary nuclear power reactor is limited by the size and capacity of the reactor, the rate at which it is kept running and other factors. If Iraq has only purified three grams of the silvery white metal, its production rate presumably was so low that it would take years to mass one bomb.

Plutonium is ordinarily detonated in implosion bombs, which are very difficult to build. A small sphere of the metal is embedded in a larger sphere of high explosive, which must be detonated uniformly over its entire surface to achieve the necessary compression of the plutonium.

END

Aug. 6, 1991
NT

외 무 부

종 별 :

번 호 : UNW-2075

일 시 : 91 0807 1900

수 신 : 장 관(국연,중동일,기정)

발 신 : 주 유엔 대사

제 목 : 안보리 동향(비공식협의)

연: UNW-2036

1. 안보리는 금 8.7 안보리 휴전결의 이행문제관련 비공식 협의를 개최한바, 당관에서 탐문한 동 협의 결과를 아래보고함.

(가) 대이락 제재조치 정기심사 (결의 687 호 21,28 항,700 호 6항)

연호와같이 다수 이사국들의 현재의 재제조치를 유지해야 한다는 입장임에 따라, 안보리의장 (에쿠아돌)은 '8.5. 비공식 협의결과 재제조치 변경을 위한 필요조건이 충족되었는데 대해 이사국들간 합의가없었다 ' 는 요지의 언론발표문 (PRESSSTATEMENT) 을 내고 동 발표문을 안보리문서로 배포하는 것으로 일단락 지어짐.

(나) 이락 대량파괴 무기 폐기 이행검증 계획안

1)핵관련 계획안 (UNW-2036), 여타대량 파괴무기 관련 계획안 (UNW-2053) 의기술적인 성격에 비추어 충분한 검토후 제토의키로함.

2)단, 조기계획 수립필요성에 대해서는 의견이 합치된바, 본건 계획을 승인하는 결의안 (단일 또는 복수결의안)이 다음주부터 교섭될 것으로 관측됨.

(다) 이락 배상기금 (석유수입공제 상한선문제) 및 이락석유수출 일부허용

1)미국은 사무총장안 (30 프로) 수락의사를 표시하여 왔으며, 이에따라 안보리 결정이 가까운 시일안에 있을 전망임.

2)단,미국은 상한선문제를 현재 상임이사국들간에 교섭중인 다음 2개 결의안타결과 연계시키고 있는 것으로 알려짐.

가)이락 석유 수출 일부허용 (UNW-1970 참조)

나)이락의 핵관련 의무이행

2.안보리는 명 8.8 신규회원국 가입신청 처리를 위한 공식회의 개최예정이며, 8.9 에는 비공식협의를 갖고 유엔사무총장의 유엔엘살바돌 옵서버단 (ONUSAL) 관련 보고

국기국 1차보 중아국 의정실 문석관 정와대 안기부

91.08.08 09:05 WG

외신 1과 통제관

0103

청취예정임.

첨부: NYT 지 사설: UNW(F)-403 끝

(대사 노창희-국장)

UNW(F)-403 10807 190
(국연. 중동외. 기천)   총 10부

Keep the Heat on Iraq to Disarm

One by one, weapons secrets are being squeezed out of Baghdad. This week, after many lies, Iraq finally acknowledged it was conducting a secret biological weapons program and pursuing yet another nuclear weapons program.

Iraq's grudging revelations confirm that Saddam Hussein intended to arm himself with weapons of mass destruction. They also confirm the need to keep the pressure on him to tell all.

International inspectors must continue to seek what he's trying to hide. Stringent economic sanctions have to remain in force to compel Iraq to submit to inspections. And for long-term security, the United Nations Security Council needs to put in place a tough plan prepared by the International Atomic Energy Agency to keep Iraq from ever acquiring nuclear arms. Similar arrangements are needed for chemical and biological arms.

●

Like nuclear age archeologists, the inspectors charged with enforcing the disarmament provisions of the U.N. cease-fire resolution are still trying to reconstruct Iraq's weapons programs. They had previously discovered three methods Iraq was using to enrich uranium so that it could be used in weapons. Iraq has now admitted trying to build the bomb a fourth way, by reprocessing plutonium from spent nuclear fuel at its Tuwaitha reactor.

But the inspectors can never be sure of what they don't know. And even if they learn everything about Iraq's present programs, they will need to keep it from rearming in the future.

Two policies are essential. One is to keep pressure on Baghdad to comply with the cease-fire resolution. That requires continued economic sanctions despite the Iraqi leader's efforts to get them lifted. No doubt the sanctions hurt ordinary Iraqis more than they hurt Saddam Hussein. But he, not the international community, is the source of their pain. The U.N. dare not let him manipulate his people's misery to escape pressure to comply.

Second, even if he does comply, what's to guarantee that he won't resume arms-making in the future? The I.A.E.A. has proposed a tough program to embargo dangerous nuclear exports to Iraq and require advance notice from states that ship other nuclear material and equipment ostensibly intended for nonmilitary use.

The new rules would allow the I.A.E.A. uninhibited access to "all locations, all persons and all information" needed to verify compliance with the cease-fire resolution. The agency could conduct on-site inspections on short notice, using its own transportation, communication and inspection equipment to avoid depending on its host.

The proposal makes some U.N. members uneasy because they don't want the precedent applied to them. But it's a serious nonproliferation policy that deserves support. If the allies take the heat off Iraq now, they will be asking for trouble from Iraqi terror weapons in the future.

UNW-2075
첨부물

/ - /

0105

주 국 련 대 표 부

주국련 20313- **629**   1991. 8. 9.

수신 장관

참조 국제기구조약국장, 중동아프리카국장

제목 대이락 무기공급 금지 (3)

연 : UNW-1872

　　　각국이 안보리결의 700호에 의거하여 유엔 사무총장에게 통보해온
표제관련 조치내용을 별첨과 같이 송부합니다.

첨부 : 상기 문서.　　　끝.

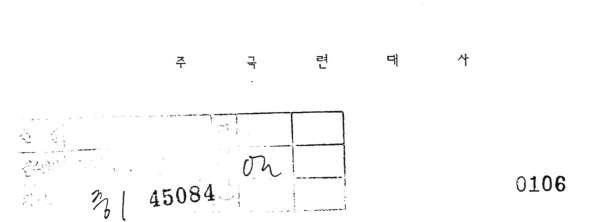

주 국 련 대 사

0106

Security Council

Distr.
GENERAL

S/22866
1 August 1991
ENGLISH
ORIGINAL: CHINESE/ENGLISH

NOTE VERBALE DATED 29 JULY 1991 FROM THE PERMANENT REPRESENTATIVE
OF CHINA TO THE UNITED NATIONS ADDRESSED TO THE SECRETARY-GENERAL

The Permanent Representative of the People's Republic of China to the
United Nations presents his compliments to the Secretary-General of the United
Nations and, with reference to paragraph 4 of Security Council resolution
700 (1991), has the honour to inform the latter of the following:

After the outbreak of the Gulf crisis last year, the Chinese Government
immediately decided to stop all military contacts with Iraq, and especially
after the adoption of Security Council resolution 661 (1990), the Chinese
Government promptly made a number of regulations with a view to implementing
that Security Council resolution to the letter. These regulations concerning
sanctions and arms embargo against Iraq are in full conformity with resolution
687 (1991) adopted later, including the obligations embodied in paragraph 24
and provisions in several other mandatory resolutions of the Security
Council.

The relevant parts of the regulations are as follows: all the Chinese
companies concerned are prohibited from delivering to Iraq any kind of
military equipments and spare parts, military supplies and police equipments,
and no new armament contracts in any form with Iraq or its agents are to be
negotiated.

Up to date, the Chinese companies concerned have strictly abided by the
Chinese Government's regulations.

91-24586   2494g (E)

0107

UNITED NATIONS

Security Council

S

Distr.
GENERAL

S/22867
1 August 1991

ORIGINAL: ENGLISH

NOTE VERBALE DATED 30 JULY 1991 FROM THE PERMANENT
REPRESENTATIVE OF AUSTRALIA TO THE UNITED NATIONS
ADDRESSED TO THE SECRETARY-GENERAL

The Permanent Representative of Australia to the United Nations presents his compliments to the Secretary-General of the United Nations and in reference to the Secretary-General's note of 3 July 1991, in which the Secretary-General drew attention to Security Council resolution 700 (1991) and specifically to paragraph 4 of this resolution, has the honour to inform the Secretary-General as follows.

Australia has complied with its obligations in relation to paragraphs 24, 25 and 27 of resolution 687 (1991), to which paragraphs 2, 3, 4 and 5 of resolution 700 (1991) refer, both through the enactment of specific regulations in relation to exports to Iraq and in the administration of existing Australian legislation and regulations relating to the export from Australia of defence and defence-related goods.

Australia established its sanctions regime against Iraq in accordance with Security Council resolution 661 (1990) through the promulgation of regulations that prohibit the export of goods to Iraq, where such export would violate Australia's international obligations, including obligations incurred under Security Council resolutions. Those regulations remain in effect. Australia advised the Secretary-General of these measures on 30 October 1990 and the note verbale was circulated as document S/AC.25/1990/24 on 5 November 1990.

The Australian Government maintains general controls on the export from Australia of defence and defence-related goods through provisions of the Customs Act 1901 and Associated Customs (Prohibited Exports) Regulations. These controls are administered by the Minister for Defence, and goods requiring the Minister's permission are specified in schedule 13 of the Customs (Prohibited Exports) Regulations. Australian Government policy, as specified in government guidelines published in 1989, is to prohibit the export of defence and defence-related goods "to countries against which the United Nations Security Council has imposed a mandatory arms embargo, or which are employing armed forces in a manner contrary to a resolution of the United

91-24592 2416c (E)   /...

0108

Nations Security Council, or contrary to the provisions on international instruments to which Australia is a party, and to countries with policies or interests that are inimical to the strategic interests of Australia its friends and allies".

The Australian Government also maintains specific controls over the export to all destinations of nuclear and related goods, toxicological agents of a biological, chemical or radioactive nature designed or adapted for warfare, and associated production and dissemination equipment, and chemical weapons precursors through the Customs Act and the Customs (Prohibited Exports) Regulations. Dual use technology is covered by the same Act and Regulations. These controls would prevent the export of the foregoing items from Australia to Iraq.

The Australian Government is opposed to private sales of defence and defence-related goods and will only approve such sales if the purchasers are acting on behalf of, or with the approval of a recognized Government and for the end-use by that Government. In the case of the controlled goods described in the two preceding paragraphs the Australian Government requires that exporters produce an end-use and non-transfer certificate or equivalent document on which the end-user Government provides an undertaking that it will use the goods for the purposes indicated and will not transfer the goods without the written permission of the Australian Minister for Defence or the Minister's delegate. The Customs Act provides for the imposition of significant financial penalties, and forfeiture of the prohibited goods and of the conveyance used for the unlawful exports.

0109

Security Council

Distr.
GENERAL

S/22868
1 August 1991

ORIGINAL: ENGLISH

NOTE VERBALE DATED 30 JULY 1991 FROM THE PERMANENT
MISSION OF AUSTRIA TO THE UNITED NATIONS ADDRESSED
TO THE SECRETARY-GENERAL

The Permanent Mission of Austria to the United Nations presents its
compliments to the Secretary-General of the United Nations and in reply to the
Secretary-General's note of 3 July 1991 concerning paragraph 4 of Security
Council resolution 700 (1991) has the honour to state the following:

Austria has instituted the following measures relating to the
implementation of the arms embargo against Iraq contained in Security Council
resolutions 661 (1990) and 687 (1991):

1.   On 21 August 1990, the Austrian Federal Government made use of the
authority granted to it by the federal law of 1977 concerning the export,
import and transit of military equipment, and adopted a decree which generally
prohibits any export of military equipment and civil arms and ammunition to
Iraq. This decree allows for additional penal sanctions in case of any
attempt to circumvent the provisions of the decree.

2.   Legal transactions or activities relating to the import or export of
weapons or other military equipment are also fully covered by the decree of
the Federal Minister for Economic Affairs of 14 August 1990 under the Foreign
Trade Act 1984. This decree declared all legal transactions or activities
relating to the import or export of commodities and products originating from
or destined for Iraq subject to prior permission by the Federal Ministry. An
export licence will not be granted if the transaction concerned has not been
approved in accordance with Security Council resolutions 661 (1990) and
687 (1991) by the Committee established by resolution 661 (1990).

The following additional measures are being prepared:

3.   A draft law containing amendments to the Foreign Trade Act 1984,
which would subject the export of various other products to export licences,
will soon be submitted to Parliament. This legislation, which is in
accordance with international non-proliferation arrangements, will relate:

(a) To precursors of chemical weapons;

91-24598 2464i (E)

0110   /...

(b) To plants and parts of plants designed to produce nuclear, biological and chemical weapons;

(c) To missiles constructed to carry such weapons.

Arms, ammunition and explosives not falling under the regulations for "military equipment" (see under 1) will continue to be covered by this legislation.

Licences will also be required for the export of related technologies and for the promotion of the sale of the goods mentioned above from outside Austria into third countries.

Legislation to further strengthen the existing non-proliferation provisions in the nuclear field by amending the Safeguards Act is currently underway.

4.   Furthermore, a proposed amendment to the Penal Code will make it a criminal offence to produce or trade with nuclear, biological and chemical weapons. The prohibition concerned will also relate to aiding and abetting.

It follows from the foregoing that Austria is committed to implement the mandatory arms embargo against Iraq adopted by the Security Council in paragraph 24 of resolution 687 (1991). As to the general position of Austria concerning the implementation of mandatory sanctions adopted by the competent organ of the United Nations, reference is made to the Austrian reply relating to the implementation of Security Council resolution 661 (1990).

0111

UNITED NATIONS

S

Security Council

Distr.
GENERAL

S/22869
1 August 1991

ORIGINAL: ENGLISH

NOTE VERBALE DATED 31 JULY 1991 FROM THE PERMANENT REPRESENTATIVE
OF CZECHOSLOVAKIA TO THE UNITED NATIONS ADDRESSED TO THE
SECRETARY-GENERAL

The Permanent Representative of the Czech and Slovak Federal Republic to
the United Nations presents his compliments to the Secretary-General of the
United Nations and, with reference to his note of 3 July 1991, has the honour
to inform the Secretary-General of the following:

In connection with commercial relations with Iraq, the decree of the
Czech and Slovak Federal Ministry of Foreign Trade on the prohibition against
trade with Iraq is still in effect. The granting of an exception to this
prohibition is possible only in accordance with the provisions of Security
Council resolution 687 (1991) for the export of foodstuff or other commodities
for humanitarian purposes.

All exports of arms <u>matériel</u> from the Czech and Slovak Federal Republic
are subject to a licence arrangement. In accordance with the above-mentioned
decree, the competent Czechoslovak authorities will not issue a licence that
is contradictory to the guidelines to facilitate full international
implementation of paragraphs 24, 25 and 27 of Security Council resolution
687 (1991) approved by the Security Council in resolution 700 (1991).

91-24604 2548e (E)

0112

Security Council

Distr.
GENERAL

S/22874
1 August 1991

ORIGINAL: ENGLISH

NOTE VERBALE DATED 31 JULY 1991 FROM THE PERMANENT
REPRESENTATIVE OF NEW ZEALAND TO THE UNITED NATIONS
ADDRESSED TO THE SECRETARY-GENERAL

The New Zealand Permanent Representative to the United Nations presents his compliments to the Secretary-General of the United Nations and has the honour to refer to his Note SCPC/7/91(4-1) of 3 July 1991 in which he sought information on measures instituted by the New Zealand Government in pursuance of paragraph 4 of Security Council resolution 700 (1991).

Following the adoption by the Security Council of resolution 687 (1991), New Zealand passed revised regulations (the United Nations Sanctions (Iraq) Regulations 1991) which maintain fully the implementation in New Zealand law of United Nations sanctions on Iraq. These new regulations, which replace those implemented in 1990 in pursuance of resolutions 661 and 670, include a new provision which implements in specific terms the prohibitions in relation to weapons technology, training and technical support services contained in paragraph 24 of resolution 687.

The prohibitions contained in these regulations, as well as the Guidelines approved in resolution 700, have been drawn to the attention of relevant New Zealand agencies.

A copy of the revised regulations is attached for the Secretary-General's reference.*

---

* The text of the revised regulations may be consulted in room S-3520.

91-24671   2723b (E)

0113

UNITED NATIONS

S

Security Council

Distr.
GENERAL

S/22875
1 August 1991

ORIGINAL: ENGLISH

NOTE VERBALE DATED 1 AUGUST 1991 FROM THE CHARGE D'AFFAIRES A.I.
OF THE PERMANENT MISSION OF BRAZIL TO THE UNITED NATIONS
ADDRESSED TO THE SECRETARY-GENERAL

The Acting Permanent Representative of Brazil to the United Nations
presents his compliments to the Secretary-General of the United Nations and,
with reference to Note SCPC/7/91(4-1) of 3 July 1991, has the honour to inform
that the Government of Brazil strictly abides by the prohibitions against the
sale or supply of arms to Iraq, in conformity with the relevant resolutions of
the Security Council.

The Government of Brazil has issued Decree No. 99441 of 7 August 1990
(document S/21476 of 9 August 1990) concerning mandatory compliance with
resolution 661 (1990) and acts strictly in accordance with the provisions of
subsequent resolutions on this subject, including in particular the
obligations set out in paragraph 24 of resolution 687 (1991). Bearing in mind
the guidelines approved by resolution 700 (1991), an interministerial
commission is currently in charge of proposing adjustments to the existing
national regulations on the export of arms and related matériel.

91-24677 2502h (E)

0114

UNITED NATIONS

Security Council

S

Distr.
GENERAL

S/22876
1 August 1991

ORIGINAL: ENGLISH

NOTE VERBALE DATED 1 AUGUST 1991 FROM THE CHARGE D'AFFAIRES A.I.
OF THE PERMANENT MISSION OF IRELAND TO THE UNITED NATIONS
ADDRESSED TO THE SECRETARY-GENERAL

The Charge d'affaires a.i. of Ireland to the United Nations presents his compliments to the Secretary-General of the United Nations, and with reference to his Note SCPC/7/91/4-1 of 3 July 1991, has the honour to transmit to the Secretary-General the following information on the implementation of paragraph 4 of Security Council resolution 700 (1991).

1.   The export from Ireland of arms and other military equipment, and related material as outlined in paragraph 24 (a) of resolution 687 is prohibited under the control of Exports Act 1983 and the Nuclear Energy Order 1977 save under licence issued by the Minister for Industry and Commerce. The Government of Ireland has determined that no such licence will be issued in respect of the export of arms and other military equipment and related "material" to Iraq. The Customs and Excise Service is responsible for ensuring that the prohibition on the exportation of these items to Iraq is fully enforced.

2.   The prohibition of the supply of non-financial services outlined in paragraph 24 (d) of resolution 687, is covered in Ireland by Statutory Instrument No. 262 of 1990 which gives full effect to Council Regulation (EEC) No. 3155/90 of 29 October 1990 which extended and amended Council Regulation (EEC) No. 2340/90 of 8 August 1990 on the prohibition of trade with Iraq, and provides penalties for infringement.

91-24683   2612d (E)

0115

Security Council

Distr.
GENERAL

S/22877
2 August 1991

ORIGINAL: ENGLISH

NOTE VERBALE DATED 1 AUGUST 1991 FROM THE PERMANENT REPRESENTATIVE
OF LIECHTENSTEIN TO THE UNITED NATIONS ADDRESSED TO THE
SECRETARY-GENERAL

The Permanent Representative of the Principality of Liechtenstein to the
United Nations presents her compliments to the Secretary-General of the United
Nations and, with reference to paragraph 4 of Security Council resolution
700 (1991), has the honour to inform the Secretary-General of the following:

Liechtenstein laws and regulations fully meet the obligations set out in
resolution 687 (1991), including paragraph 24. The guidelines adopted by
Security Council resolution 700 (1991) also fall within the scope of the
Liechtenstein legislation.

In accordance with the Princely decree of 10 August 1990, Liechtenstein
strictly abides by the prohibitions against the sale or supply of arms to Iraq.

In addition to the aforementioned decree, the Liechtenstein Diet
(parliament) recently passed legislation relating to trade with foreign
States, which entered into force on 25 July 1991. These new regulations
provide the basis upon which for reasons of external security and the
safeguarding of interests externally, legal and business transactions with
foreign States can be prohibited or limited.

91-24740 3165a (E)

0116

Security Council

Distr.
GENERAL

S/22878
2 August 1991

ORIGINAL: ENGLISH

NOTE VERBALE DATED 1 AUGUST 1991 FROM THE PERMANENT REPRESENTATIVE
OF THE NETHERLANDS TO THE UNITED NATIONS ADDRESSED TO THE
SECRETARY-GENERAL

The Permanent Representative of the Kingdom of the Netherlands to the
United Nations presents his compliments to the Secretary-General of the United
Nations and with reference to his note of 3 July 1991 has the honour to
transmit the following information on the implementation by the Government of
the Netherlands of paragraph 4 of Security Council resolution 700 (1991).

The laws and regulations of the Kingdom of the Netherlands fully meet the
obligations set out in Security Council resolution 687 (1991), including
paragraph 24, in Security Council resolution 700 (1991), as well as in the
previous relevant mandatory decisions by the Council.

The Government of the Netherlands complies strictly with the arms
embargoes agreed upon within the framework of the United Nations as adherence
to these embargoes is one of the main criteria the Government of the
Netherlands uses for its arms export policy. The legal basis for these
criteria is provided by the Import and Export Act of 1962 and the Decree of
1963 concerning the Export of Strategic Goods, which implements the
aforementioned Act. Sanctions are provided for in the event of transgression
of these statutory provisions.

Promotion of the international rule of law is a central aim of this
legislation and has been qualified by the Netherlands Constitution as a major
responsibility of the Government.

It should be noted that arms exports to Iraq have been banned by the
Government of the Netherlands since 1980, as one of the other main criteria of
the Netherlands arms export policy concerns a ban on arms exports to areas of
potential conflict.

Furthermore, the following more specific regulations were adopted, in
order to implement the Security Council resolutions and the European Community
regulations based upon these resolutions:

91-24747 2506h (E)

0117   /...

- The import and export regulation Iraq-Kuwait of 9 August 1990. This regulation was amended on 2 March 1991 and finally replaced by the Import and Export Decree concerning Iraq, of 18 March 1991.

- The sanctions decree on services Iraq-Kuwait, of 14 January 1991, which covers those elements of paragraph 24 of resolution 687 (1991) that are not covered by the other statutory provisions and regulations of the Netherlands.

0118

Security Council

Distr.
GENERAL

S/22879
2 August 1991

ORIGINAL: ENGLISH

NOTE VERBALE DATED 1 AUGUST 1991 FROM THE PERMANENT
REPRESENTATIVE OF YUGOSLAVIA TO THE UNITED NATIONS
ADDRESSED TO THE SECRETARY-GENERAL

The Permanent Mission of the Socialist Federal Republic of Yugoslavia to the United Nations presents its compliments to the Secretary-General of the United Nations and with reference to His Excellency's note of 3 July has the honour to inform him of the following.

By complying fully with the articles of Security Council resolution 661 (1990), the Yugoslav Government reached a decision on 9 August 1991 to implement strictly the sanctions contained therein. These sanctions include the cessation of arms and military equipment supplies to Iraq. This decision is still in force and encompasses the obligations under paragraph 24 of resolution 687 (1991). The decision of the Government of Yugoslavia will remain in effect until the Security Council sanctions against Iraq are abolished.

91-24756 2497g (E)

0119

Security Council

Distr.
GENERAL

S/22880
2 August 1991

ORIGINAL: ENGLISH

NOTE VERBALE DATED 31 JULY 1991 FROM THE PERMANENT MISSION OF
ITALY TO THE UNITED NATIONS ADDRESSED TO THE SECRETARY-GENERAL

The Permanent Representative of Italy to the United Nations presents his
compliments to the Secretary-General of the United Nations and, with reference
to his Note SCPC/7/91(4-1) of 3 July 1991 in which he sought information on
measures instituted by the Italian Government in pursuance of paragraph 4 of
Security Council resolution 700 (1991), has the honour to inform that
immediately after the invasion of Kuwait by Iraq, Italy passed a law
prohibiting the export of any goods to Iraq, which is still in force.

The granting of an exception to this prohibition is possible only in
accordance with the provisions of Security Council resolution 687 (1991) for
the export of foodstuff or other commodities for humanitarian purposes.
Therefore, the prohibition to provide Iraq with weapons technology, training
and technical support services is still fully in effect, in conformity with
paragraph 24 of resolution 687.

91-24794 2557e (E)

0120

Security Council

Distr.
GENERAL

S/22881
2 August 1991
ENGLISH
ORIGINAL: SPANISH

<u>Letter dated 1 August 1991 from the Chargé d'affaires a.i. of
the Permanent Mission of Argentina to the United Nations
addressed to the Secretary-General</u>

I have the honour to transmit to you herewith a letter dated 17 July 1991
addressed to you by the Minister for Foreign Affairs and Worship,
Mr. Guido Di Tella, in response to the request in paragraph 4 of Security
Council resolution 700 (1991) regarding the measures instituted for meeting
the obligations set out in paragraph 24 of Security Council resolution
687 (1991).

Furthermore, I request that the text of this letter and its annex should
be distributed as a document of the Security Council.

(<u>Signed</u>) Alfredo V. CHIARADIA
Chargé d'affaires a.i.

Annex

Letter dated 17 July 1991 from the Minister for Foreign
Affairs and Worship of Argentina addressed to the
Secretary-General

I have the honour to address you with reference to Security Council
resolution 700 (1991), which in paragraph 4 requests all States to report
within 45 days on the measures they have instituted for meeting the
obligations set out in paragraph 24 of resolution 687 (1991).

The Argentine Government wishes to report that, through Decrees Nos. 1560
and 2067 of 1990, the sanctions against the Republic of Iraq stipulated in
Security Council resolutions 661 and 670 (1990) were approved, enabling the
national executive authority and the provincial authorities to adopt the
measures required for compliance with the decisions taken in those resolutions.

In addition, it further informs you that by virtue of Acts Nos. 12,709
and 20,010 and Decree No. 1097 of 14 June 1985, legal exports of war matériel
must receive prior approval from the Coordinating Commission for the Export of
War Matériel. This Commission is composed of representatives of the Ministers
of the Economy, Defence and Foreign Affairs.

The Commission in question has not received any application for the
export of war matériel to Iraq since the arms embargo was imposed by the
United Nations. Consequently, there is no record of the sale of war matériel
to that country.

With regard to the export of nuclear materials, the policy of Argentina
is to require international safeguards on a case-by-case basis. However, no
application has been received for the export of nuclear materials to Iraq.

(Signed) Guido DI TELLA

UNITED NATIONS

Security Council

Distr.
GENERAL

S/22882
3 August 1991

ORIGINAL: ENGLISH

NOTE VERBALE DATED 31 JULY 1991 FROM THE PERMANENT
MISSION OF THAILAND TO THE UNITED NATIONS ADDRESSED
TO THE SECRETARY-GENERAL

The Permanent Mission of Thailand to the United Nations presents its compliments to the Secretary-General of the United Nations and, with reference to Note No. SCPC/7/91(4-1) of 3 July 1991, has the honour to inform the Secretary-General that Thailand strictly abides by the prohibitions against the sale or supply of arms to Iraq as contained in paragraph 24 of resolution 687 (1991).

Accordingly, the responsible authorities have been instructed to ensure the full compliance with the prohibitions, in accordance with Thai legislation in force, namely the Act on Export Control of Munition and Military Devices and the Royal Decree on Export Control of Munition and Military Devices.

91-24874   2558e (E)

0123

Security Council

Distr.
GENERAL

S/22883
3 August 1991

ORIGINAL: ENGLISH

NOTE VERBALE DATED 1 AUGUST 1991 FROM THE PERMANENT
MISSION OF SWEDEN TO THE UNITED NATIONS ADDRESSED TO
THE SECRETARY-GENERAL

The Permanent Mission of Sweden to the United Nations presents its
compliments to the Secretary-General of the United Nations and, with reference
to his note SCPC/7/91/4-1 of 3 July 1991, has the honour to transmit the
following information on the implementation of paragraph 4 of Security Council
resolution 700 (1991).

1.   The Act on Prohibition of the Exportation of Military Equipment and
Related Matters (1988:558), Section 2, prohibits export of military equipment
without the permission of the Government of Sweden. It is an established
policy that Sweden does not export arms to belligerent States or crises areas
or areas where hostilities are likely to break out. No licences for export of
military material to Iraq have been granted by the Government of Sweden since
August 1990.

2.   The Act concerning Prohibition of the Exportation of Certain
Products which can be used for the Purpose of Mass Destruction (1991:341)
gives the Government the right to control the export of equipment which can be
used for manufacturing biological and chemical weapons and chemical
precursors, as well as other dual-use items.

3.   The Act concerning International Sanctions (1971:176) provides the
Government with the authority to pass legislation based upon United Nations
Security Council decisions or recommendations.

Consequently the Ordinance on Certain Sanctions against Iraq (1990:885)
prohibits all export of commodities and products from Sweden to Iraq as well
as measures and activities to promote prohibited acts.

91-24880   3168a (E)

0124

**UNITED
NATIONS**

Security Council

Distr.
GENERAL

S/22891
6 August 1991

ORIGINAL: ENGLISH

NOTE VERBALE DATED 1 AUGUST 1991 FROM THE PERMANENT
REPRESENTATIVE OF SAUDI ARABIA TO THE UNITED NATIONS
ADDRESSED TO THE SECRETARY-GENERAL

The Permanent Representative of Saudi Arabia to the United Nations
presents his compliments to the Secretary-General and has the honour to refer
to his note SCPC/7/91 (4-1) dated 3 July 1991 concerning information on the
measures instituted by Saudi Arabia's Government for meeting the obligations
set out in paragraph 24 of Security Council resolution 687 (1991) on the
situation between Iraq and Kuwait.

The Permanent Representative of Saudi Arabia to the United Nations has
the pleasure to convey that the Kingdom of Saudi Arabia is undoubtedly intent
on continuing to prevent the selling or exporting of weapons and related
materials of all kinds to Iraq, by Saudi citizens, specifically including the
sale or transport by other means of all kinds of traditional military
equipment including what could be directed to paramilitary forces, the spare
parts and the means of producing such equipment and the items specified and
described in paragraphs 8 and 12 of Security Council resolution 687 (1991)
which are otherwise not included. Furthermore, the Kingdom of Saudi Arabia
prevents the sale and export of technology or according licensing agreements
or others, such as transport arrangements used in the production, use or
storage of items specified in subparagraphs (a) and (b) of paragraph 8 of the
above-mentioned resolution. This also applies to personnel, training items or
technical support services related to the spread, development, manufacture,
use, maintenance or support of the items specified in subparagraphs (a) and
(b) mentioned above. The Kingdom of Saudi Arabia is totally committed not to
promote or facilitate this sale, export or its completion on its territory, or
the use of ships or aircraft which carry its flag for this purpose.

91-25117 2516h (E)

0125

**UNITED
NATIONS**

S

Security Council

Distr.
GENERAL

S/22892
6 August 1991

ORIGINAL: ENGLISH

NOTE VERBALE DATED 5 AUGUST 1991 FROM THE PERMANENT
MISSION OF ROMANIA TO THE UNITED NATIONS ADDRESSED
TO THE SECRETARY-GENERAL

The Permanent Mission of Romania to the United Nations presents its
compliments to the Secretary-General and has the honour to refer to his note
verbale SCPC/7/91 (4-1), which draws attention to paragraphs 2, 3, 4 and 5 of
Security Council resolution 700 (1991).

1.   From the very beginning of the Gulf crisis Romania has committed
itself to observe strictly the sanctions imposed upon Iraq by the resolutions
of the Security Council, in spite of particularly serious consequences for the
Romanian economy. To this end, the Romanian Government adopted Decision
No. 935 of 10 August 1990 which has been immediately put into force by all
Romanian economic authorities.

Further, by Decision No. 1080/1990 of the Romanian Government, the
embargo has been extended also to air transportation. Under the same
approach, any possible delivery to Iraq of military equipment or of other
goods which could have been used for military purposes was unconditionally
banned.

Moreover, all the import-export licences valid prior to the invasion of
Kuwait by Iraq have been cancelled.

2.   The Romanian authorities have been ensuring a constant control on
the implementation of the regime of sanctions by all the Romanian companies
engaged in import-export operations or in activities of international
cooperation, including the banning of import-export licences for Iraq. Until
now no infringement of the sanctions imposed by the Security Council upon Iraq
has been registered.

3.   The provisions of the guidelines approved by Security Council
resolution 700 (1991) have been ordered immediately by the Romanian Government
to all the national authorities involved in foreign trade or in activities of
international cooperation to be fully observed.

0126

91-25123 2622d (E)

주 국 련 대 표 부

주국련 20313- **630**   1991. 8. 9.

수신 장관

참조 국제기구조약국장, 중동아프리카국장

제목 이락 특정무기 폐기 이행 검증 계획안 (안보리)

　　　표제관련 안보리 문서를 별첨과 같이 송부합니다.

첨 부 : 상기 문서. 끝.

주 　 국 　 련 　 대 　 사

45083   0127

Security Council

Distr.
GENERAL

S/22871
1 August 1991

ORIGINAL: ENGLISH

Plan for future ongoing monitoring and verification of
Iraq's compliance with relevant parts of section C of
Security Council resolution 687 (1991)

Report of the Secretary-General

I. GENERAL

A. Introduction

1.   The present report is submitted in pursuance of Security Council
resolution 687 (1991). In paragraph 10 of section C of that resolution, the
Security Council requested the Secretary-General, in consultation with the
Special Commission, to develop and submit for approval a plan for the ongoing
monitoring and verification of Iraq's compliance with its obligations under
that paragraph. The Plan is contained in section II of the present report.

2.   As outlined in my report to the Security Council of 17 May 1991
(S/22614), the provisions of section C of resolution 687 (1991) lend
themselves to a three-stage implementation procedure: gathering and
assessment of information; disposal of weapons and facilities and all other
items specified in paragraphs 8 and 12 of resolution 687 (1991); and ongoing
monitoring and verification of Iraq's compliance. The first two stages are
currently being implemented and will continue until their objectives are fully
achieved.

3.   The Plan submitted in the present report addresses the third stage, i.e.
ongoing monitoring and verification of Iraq's compliance with its
unconditional obligation not to use, retain, possess, develop, construct or
otherwise acquire any weapons or related items prohibited under paragraphs 8
and 9 of resolution 687 (1991). Thus, monitoring and verification will need
to cover not only military but also civilian sites, facilities, material and
other items that could be used or activities that could be involved in
contravention of Iraq's obligations under resolution 687 (1991).

91-24654   2550e (E)

0128

/...

4. The Plan should enter into force directly upon its approval by the Security Council, which means that the early stages of its implementation and the later stages of the disposal of existing prohibited weapons, facilities and related items would take place simultaneously. This would, at an early stage, prevent Iraq from developing new capabilities regarding the relevant weapons categories, thus already closing a potential loophole during the first stages of the implementation of section C of resolution 687 (1991). Carefully managed use of available resources would make it possible to carry out the dual tasks in parallel, to great effect. With the gradual completion of the disposal of Iraq's present weapons capabilities, resources can gradually be transformed and streamlined without therefore, at any stage, compromising the efficiency of the verification of Iraq's compliance with its obligations under resolution 687 (1991).

B. Institutional and organizational aspects

5. Bearing in mind that resolution 687 (1991) was adopted by the Security Council acting under Chapter VII of the Charter of the United Nations, it is assumed that the task of carrying out the monitoring and verification provided for under the Plan should be entrusted to an executive body under the authority of the Security Council. This is particularly important should any situation arise of non-compliance by Iraq with its obligations under section C of resolution 687 (1991).

6. The intrinsic interrelationship between paragraphs 8, 9 and 10 of resolution 687 (1991) requires that this body make direct use of the expertise, the information gathered and assessed and the experience gained by the Special Commission established pursuant to paragraph 9 of resolution 687 (1991).

7. In view of these considerations, it would appear most practical and efficient that a compliance unit be organized under the Special Commission in order to carry out the monitoring and verification tasks provided for under the Plan. The present arrangements for staffing would continue on a revised scale, with appropriate support from the Department for Disarmament Affairs. *The financing of the Plan would have to be determined by the competent United Nations organs, possibly in the same way as the arrangements agreed upon for the present phase of the Special Commission's work.*

8. The operational requirements will be similar to those now in place for the Special Commission. These include a staff at the United Nations Headquarters in New York to compile and analyse information, organize inspections and aerial overflights, prepare other field operations and provide general administrative support. A staff will be needed in the region to provide logistic, administrative and other support for field operations in Iraq.

0129

/...

C. Cooperation with the Security Council Committee established by resolution 661 (1990) concerning the situation between Iraq and Kuwait

9.   Through resolution 661 (1990) and subsequent related resolutions, including resolution 687 (1991), a comprehensive set of sanctions was established to be implemented by all States against Iraq. The prohibition of the acquisition by Iraq of any weapons and related items specified in paragraphs 8 and 12 of resolution 687 (1991) and of the sale or supply to Iraq by other States of these items is of unlimited duration. However, it cannot be excluded that the Security Council, at a future date, may wish to review the present sanctions regarding items with dual use, i.e. items that could be used for prohibited as well as non-prohibited purposes. In order to ensure that such items are not used for prohibited purposes, the Plan submitted in the present report includes specific provisions for the monitoring and verification, from within Iraq, of any eventual import by Iraq of relevant items with dual use.

10.   The efficacy of these provisions would be enhanced if they were complemented by transparency and timely information as regards any future sale or supply by other States to Iraq of relevant items with dual use. Such a comprehensive approach would call for the development of a mechanism that:

    (a) Upholds the prohibition on the sale and supply to Iraq by other States of any weapons or related items prohibited under section C of resolution 687 (1991);

    (b) Provides for timely information about any sale or supply to Iraq by other States of items that could be used not only for permitted purposes but also for purposes prohibited under resolution 687 (1991).

11.   The Plan submitted in the present report contains in its annexes lists of items relevant to the monitoring and verification, from within Iraq, of prohibited items as well as of items with dual use. These should be taken into account in the development of a mechanism related to the sale or supply of items to Iraq by other countries.

12.   Such a mechanism should be developed with the cooperation of the Special Commission and the Committee established by resolution 661 (1990) at the earliest possible date, and not later than before the lifting of sanctions covering relevant items.

0130   /...

II. THE PLAN

A. Scope

13. In accepting unconditionally Security Council resolution 687 (1991), Iraq has undertaken not to use, retain, possess, develop, construct or otherwise acquire:

(a) Any chemical or biological weapons or any stocks of agents or any related subsystems or components or any research, development, support or manufacturing facilities;

(b) Any ballistic missiles with a range greater than 150 kilometres or any related major parts, including launchers, or any repair or production facilities.

14. In order to ensure Iraq's compliance with these undertakings, the Special Commission shall, through inspections and through aerial overflights, as well as through the provision of information by Iraq, monitor and verify that activities, sites, facilities, material and other items, both military and civilian, are not used by Iraq in contravention of its obligations under Security Council resolution 687 (1991).

15. To this end, the provisions set forth in the Plan and its annexes, which constitute an integral part of the Plan, shall apply.

B. General provisions

1. Information

16. Iraq shall:

(a) Provide to the Special Commission, on a regular basis, full, correct and timely information on activities, sites, facilities, material and other items, both military and civilian, that might be used for purposes prohibited under paragraph 10 of resolution 687 (1991);

(b) Provide to the Special Commission full, correct and timely information on any additional activities, sites, facilities, material or other items that the Commission may designate for provision of information on a regular basis;

(c) Provide to the Special Commission, promptly and fully, any additional information or clarification that the Commission may request.

Further provisions related to the submission of information are set forth in sections C, D and E and in annexes II, III and IV of the Plan.

0131   /...

2. Inspections and aerial overflights

17. The Special Commission shall have the right:

(a) To designate for inspection any site, facility, activity, material or other item in Iraq;

(b) To inspect, at any time and without hindrance, any site or facility declared by Iraq or designated by the Special Commission;

(c) To inspect, at any time and without hindrance, any activity, material or other item at any site or facility, including any material or other item in movement;

(d) To inspect any number of declared or designated sites or facilities simultaneously or sequentially;

(e) To designate for aerial overflight any area, location, site or facility in Iraq;

(f) To carry out, at any time and without hindrance, aerial overflight by fixed- or rotary-wing aircraft with appropriate sensors as necessary, of any area, location, site or facility designated by the Special Commission;

(g) To carry out, at any time and without hindrance, all such other flights, by fixed- or rotary-wing aircraft, as it deems necessary.

18. Iraq shall:

(a) Accept unconditionally the inspection of any site, facility, activity, material or other item declared by Iraq or designated by the Special Commission;

(b) Accept unconditionally aerial overflight of any area, location, site or facility designated by the Special Commission or any other flight, by fixed- or rotary-wing aircraft used by the Special Commission;

(c) Provide immediate and unimpeded access to any site, facility, activity, material or other item to be inspected;

(d) Not obstruct aerial overflights or take concealment measures at any area, location, site or facility designated by the Special Commission for overflight;

(e) Accept unconditionally the inspectors and all other personnel designated by the Special Commission;

(f) Cooperate fully with the Special Commission and facilitate its inspections and overflights;

/...

0132

(g) Designate its inspection representative for each inspection to accompany the inspection team in Iraq.

19. Further provisions related to inspections and aerial overflights are set forth in annex I.

3. National implementation measures

20. Iraq shall adopt the necessary measures to implement its obligations under section C of resolution 687 (1991) and the present Plan, in particular:

(a) To prohibit all natural and legal persons under Iraq's jurisdiction or control from undertaking anywhere any activity that is prohibited for Iraq by resolution 687 (1991), by subsequent related Security Council resolutions or by the present Plan;

(b) To enact penal legislation which, in conformity with international law, shall extend to the activities referred to under subparagraph (a) above undertaken anywhere by any natural or legal persons under Iraq's jurisdiction or control.

21. Iraq shall inform the Special Commission of legislative and administrative measures taken to implement resolution 687 (1991), not later than 30 days after the approval by the Security Council of the Plan and thereafter as determined by the Special Commission.

4. Non-compliance

22. In case the Special Commission discovers any item that Iraq, under resolution 687 (1991), is obliged to destroy or to yield to the Special Commission for destruction, removal or rendering harmless, the Special Commission shall have the right to take it into custody and shall provide for its disposal, as appropriate.

23. In case the Special Commission discovers any activity taking place in contravention of resolution 687 (1991), it shall have the right to call upon Iraq to halt the activity and to prevent its recurrence. The Special Commission shall also have the right to take any prohibited item involved into custody and shall provide for its disposal, as appropriate.

24. Findings by the Special Commission that indicate that Iraq is not in compliance with its obligations under resolution 687 (1991) shall be brought to the attention of the Security Council.

0133 /...

5. Reports

25. The Special Commission shall, through the Secretary-General, report to the Security Council every six months on the implementation of the Plan and at any other time the Security Council may request.

6. Revisions

26. The Special Commission may, after informing the Security Council, revise the technical and procedural provisions in annexes II, III and IV, including the lists of material, equipment and other items, in the light of information and experience gained in the course of the implementation of resolution 687 (1991) and the Plan. The Special Commission shall inform Iraq of any such change.

27. The present Plan shall enter into force immediately upon its approval by the Security Council. The duration of the Plan shall be determined by the Security Council.

C. Provisions related to chemical items

28. Chemicals, equipment and facilities set forth herein and in annex II could be used for purposes related to chemical weapons. They shall therefore be subject to monitoring and verification in accordance with the following additional provisions in order to ensure that Iraq does not use, develop, produce or otherwise acquire chemical weapons or related items prohibited under resolution 687 (1991).

29. Chemicals that could be used for the development, production or acquisition of chemical weapons but which also have significant uses for purposes not prohibited by resolution 687 (1991) are set forth in list A in annex II. These chemicals may be used, developed, produced, stored or acquired solely for purposes not prohibited by resolution 687 (1991), subject to the provisions under paragraphs 30 and 31 below, and annex II.

30. Iraq shall, not later than 30 days after the adoption of the Plan by the Security Council, and on a regular basis thereafter, provide to the Special Commission information in accordance with annex II regarding:

  (a) The total national quantity of the production, processing or consumption of any chemical specified in list A of annex II and of the import and export of any of these chemicals specifying the countries involved;

  (b) Any site or facility that is involved in production, processing, consumption, storage, import or export of one tonne or more per year of any chemical specified in list A of annex II or which at any time has been

0134   /...

involved in activities with any of these chemicals for chemical weapons purposes;

(c) Any site or facility that is involved in production or processing of organophosphorus chemicals or which is involved in production of organic chemicals by chlorination;

(d) Any site or facility where production, processing, consumption, storage, import or export of one tonne or more per year of any chemical specified in list A of annex II, or where production or processing of organophosphorus chemicals or where production of organic chemicals by chlorination is planned;

(e) Any import or any other acquisition of equipment or technologies intended for production and processing of any chemical specified in list A of annex II, of any organophosphorus chemical or for production of organic chemicals by chlorination.

31. Should Iraq plan any production, processing, consumption, storage, import or export not notified under paragraph 18 (d) above, it may begin such an activity only after providing to the Special Commission a special notification not later than one month in advance.

32. Chemicals that have little or no use except as chemical warfare agents or for the development, production or acquisition of chemical weapons or which have been used by Iraq as essential precursors for chemical weapons are set forth in list B of annex II. Iraq shall not retain, use, transfer, develop, produce, store, import or otherwise acquire these chemicals. Should Iraq require any chemical specified in list B of annex II, it shall submit a request to the Special Commission specifying precisely the chemical and the quantities required, the facility where it is to be used and the purpose of its use. The Special Commission will examine and decide on the request and establish the special arrangements it considers consistent with resolution 687 (1991).

33. Further provisions related to chemical items are set forth in annex II.

D. Provisions related to biological items

34. Micro-organisms and toxins, equipment and facilities set forth herein and in annex III could be used for purposes related to biological and toxin weapons affecting humans, animals or plants. They shall therefore be subject to monitoring and verification in accordance with the following additional provisions in order to ensure that Iraq does not use, develop, produce or otherwise acquire biological and toxin weapons or related items prohibited under resolution 687 (1991).

0135

/...

35. Iraq shall, not later than 30 days after the adoption of the present Plan by the Security Council, and on a regular basis thereafter, provide to the Special Commission information in accordance with annex III regarding:

(a) Any site or facility, except purely diagnostic facilities, at which work with toxins or with micro-organisms meeting the criteria for risk groups IV, III or II according to the classification in the 1983 World Health Organization (WHO) Laboratory Biosafety Manual is carried out, or any facilities at which work with genetic material coding for toxins or genes derived from the aforementioned micro-organisms is carried out;

(b) Any site or facility having a laboratory meeting the criteria for a "maximum containment laboratory" or "containment laboratory" as specified in the 1983 WHO Laboratory Biosafety Manual, such as those designated as biosafety level 4 (BL4) or P4, biosafety level 3 (BL3) or P3 or equivalent standards;

(c) Any site or facility at which fermentation or other means for the production of micro-organisms or toxins using vessels larger than 50 litres individually or 200 litres in the aggregate is carried out;

(d) Any site or facility for the bulk storage of toxins or of micro-organisms meeting the criteria for risk groups IV, III or II;

(e) Any site or facility for the production of vaccines;

(f) Any research, development, testing or other support or manufacturing facility for items and equipment specified in paragraph 1 of annex III;

(g) Any imports, other acquisition or exports of micro-organisms meeting the criteria for risk groups IV, III and II, toxins and vaccines, as well as related equipment and facilities.

36. Iraq shall, no later than 30 days after the adoption of the present Plan by the Security Council, and on a regular basis thereafter, provide to the Special Commission:

(a) A list of all documents of a scientific and technical nature published or prepared by any site or facility engaged in work relating to toxins or micro-organisms meeting the criteria for risk groups IV, III and II, including those of a theoretical nature. Documents of a purely diagnostic nature relating to risk group II micro-organisms are excepted;

(b) A description of any kind of work being conducted on the dissemination of micro-organisms or toxins into the environment or on processes that would lead to such dissemination, specifying the site or facility involved.

37. Iraq shall provide to the Special Commission information on all cases of infectious diseases affecting humans, animals or plants, that deviate, or seem

0136   /...

to deviate, from the normal pattern or are caused by any micro-organism meeting the criteria for risk groups IV and III and on all cases of similar occurrences caused by toxins. The information shall be provided within one week of the occurrence and the standardized form contained in document BWC/CONF.II/EX/2 should be utilized as appropriate.

38. Iraq shall not:

    (a) Import items referred to in paragraph 23 (g) above without giving prior notice to the Special Commission not later than 30 days in advance in accordance with annex III. As an exception, the emergency import of vaccines may take place with simultaneous notification to the Special Commission;

    (b) Conduct any activities in the field of micro-organisms and toxins except by civilian personnel not in the employ of any military organization. Such activities shall be conducted openly; no classified or secret programmes or activities shall be permitted. The facilities engaged in such activities shall not be under the control of, or owned by, any military organization. Should any military organization need to be involved in such activities for prophylactic or therapeutic purposes, Iraq shall submit a request to the Special Commission specifying precisely the toxins, micro-organisms and the quantities required, the facility where they are to be used and the purpose of their use. The Special Commission will examine and decide on the request and establish the special arrangements it considers consistent with resolution 687 (1991);

    (c) Conduct activities on diseases other than those indigenous to or immediately expected to break out in its environment;

    (d) Conduct any breeding of vectors of human, animal or plant diseases. Should Iraq need to conduct any such activity, Iraq shall submit a request to the Special Commission specifying precisely its requirements, the facility where the activity is to take place and the purpose of the activity. The Special Commission will examine and decide on the request and establish the special arrangements it considers consistent with resolution 687 (1991);

    (e) Possess at any one time more than one facility having a laboratory meeting the criteria for a "maximum containment laboratory" as specified in the 1983 WHO Laboratory Biosafety Manual, such as those designated as biosafety level 4 (BL4) or P4 or equivalent standard. Iraq shall not possess at any one time more than two facilities having a laboratory meeting the criteria for a "containment laboratory", such as those designated as BL3 or P3 or equivalent standard. Should Iraq require any additional such facilities, Iraq shall submit a request to the Special Commission specifying the precise requirement. The Special Commission will examine and decide on the request and establish the special arrangements it considers consistent with resolution 687 (1991).

39. Further provisions related to biological items are set forth in annex III.

0137   /...

E. Provisions related to missiles

40. Facilities, equipment, other items and technologies set forth herein and in annex IV could be used for the development, construction or acquisition of ballistic missiles with a range greater than 150 kilometres. They shall therefore be subject to monitoring and verification in accordance with the following additional provisions in order to ensure that Iraq does not use, develop, construct or acquire any ballistic missiles with a range greater than 150 kilometres or related items prohibited under resolution 687 (1991).

41. The range of missiles that are prohibited for Iraq shall be determined on the basis of the maximum distance that a missile is capable of flying over a ballistic trajectory with a zero delivery payload. The prohibition applies to any missiles, whether or not flying a ballistic trajectory, or delivery system, capable of such a range and to any related major parts of such missiles, which include missile/rocket stages, re-entry vehicles, solid- or liquid-fuel motors, guidance sets, thrust vector controls, warheads and fusing systems, launchers capable of launching ballistic missiles with a range greater than 150 kilometres and related principal launch equipment and transporters for such missiles. The prohibition also applies to any missiles not in themselves capable of such a range, but which are capable of such a range in combination with technologies such as tube- or gun-type launchers.

42. Iraq shall, not later than 30 days after the adoption of the present Plan by the Security Council and on a regular basis thereafter, provide to the Special Commission the following:

(a) A list of all its missiles designed for use, or capable of being modified for use, in a surface-to-surface role with a range greater than 75 kilometres, specifying their name and type, type of propulsion, number of stages and/or boosters, guidance systems, warhead and re-entry vehicle types, launcher types, airframe and warhead transporters and the sites or facilities where these items or equipment are located;

(b) Information on any site or facility for such missiles, including sites or facilities for production, assembly, repair and maintenance, storage and operational bases, specifying their locations;

(c) Information on any site or facility for missile research, development and testing, specifying their locations;

(d) Information on the development, production or acquisition of the items, equipment and technologies listed in annex IV, specifying sites or facilities where such items, equipment and technologies are located, and the purposes for which they are being used.

43. Iraq shall notify the Special Commission of the developmental or test launch of any missiles not later than 14 days prior to the date of launch, specifying where and when the launch is to take place.

/...

0138

44.   Iraq shall not construct, otherwise acquire or operate facilities for the use, development and production of ballistic missiles capable of a range greater than 150 kilometres, including facilities for research, development, manufacture, assembly, testing, storage, repair, training, flight simulating and operational use of such missiles, nor acquire related major parts specified in paragraph 29 and the items listed in annex IV for such missiles.

45.   Further provisions related to missiles are set forth in annex 4.

0139

/...

Annex I

Detailed provisions related to inspections, aerial overflights, privileges and immunities

1.   In addition to the basic rights and obligations set forth in paragraphs 5 and 6 of the Plan, the provisions set out in this annex shall apply.

Scope

2.   The Special Commission shall have the right:

     (a) To secure any site to be inspected and prevent any material or other item from being taken to or from the site until the inspection is concluded;

     (b) To stop and inspect vehicles, ships, aircraft or any other means of transportation within Iraq;

     (c) To inspect imports or exports of material and other items upon arrival or departure;

     (d) To establish special modes of monitoring and inspection, including prolonged or continuous presence of inspectors or use of instruments.

Notification

3.   The Special Commission shall, at a time it considers appropriate, notify Iraq of:

     (a) The site, facility, activity, material or other item to be inspected;

     (b) The name of the head of the inspection team (the Chief Inspector) and the estimated number of personnel who will take part in the inspection;

     (c) The estimated time of departure and arrival of any flight from, to or within Iraq, and other appropriate details, by any aircraft of the Special Commission.

4.   Iraq shall, upon receipt of the name of the Chief Inspector for an inspection, immediately inform the Special Commission of the name of the individual who will be the Iraqi Inspection Representative for the inspection.

0140   /...

Conduct of inspections or aerial overflights

5.   The Special Commission shall have the right:

(a)   To request, receive, examine and copy any record, data or information;

(b)   To examine, retain, move or photograph, including by videotaping, any material or other item under inspection;

(c)   To conduct interviews with any personnel at a site or facility under inspection, or with any Iraqi official;

(d)   To install equipment or construct facilities for inspection, testing or monitoring activities;

(e)   To take samples of any kind and perform on-site analyses of the samples using its own equipment;

(f)   To remove and transfer samples outside Iraq for analysis off-site at laboratories designated by the Special Commission;

(g)   To mark, tag or otherwise identify any material or other item;

(h)   To use its own instrumentation to collect data during aerial overflights, including photographic, video, infrared and radar data.

6.   Iraq shall:

(a)   Provide clarification of any ambiguity that might arise during an inspection;

(b)   Perform, upon request by the Special Commission, analysis of samples in the presence of inspectors, including on-site;

(c)   Perform, upon request by the Special Commission, any additional task.

Travel, transport and communications

7.   The Special Commission shall have the right:

(a)   To unrestricted freedom of entry into and exit from Iraq, without delay or hindrance, for all its personnel, property, supplies, equipment, spare parts, material and other items, including means of transport;

(b)   To unrestricted freedom of movement within Iraq, without advance notice, delay or hindrance, for all its personnel, property, supplies, equipment, spare parts, material, means of transport and other items;

0141   /...

(c) To fly the United Nations flag on the Special Commission's premises and its means of transport;

(d) To use its own means of transport, including fixed- and rotary-wing aircraft;

(e) To communicate from any place within Iraq, and without any hindrance, by radio, satellite or other forms of communication, and to connect with the United Nations by its radio and satellite network, as well as by telephone, telegraph and other means;

(f) To use codes and receive papers, correspondence and other items by courier or sealed bags.

8. Iraq shall:

(a) Permit, without delay or hindrance, the Special Commission's personnel, property, supplies, equipment, spare parts, material, means of transport and other items, to enter or leave Iraq, promptly issuing entry and exit visas if required and accepting United Nations laissez-passers or United Nations certificates as valid travel documents;

(b) Accept United Nations registration of means of transport on land, sea and in the air and United Nations licensing of the operators thereof;

(c) Provide priority clearance processing for aircraft used by the Special Commission;

(d) Provide, upon the request of the Special Commission, the means of transport, maps or other information needed;

(e) Take every necessary measure to ensure that the inspection team arrives at the site or facility to be inspected by the time notified by the Special Commission;

(f) Provide, upon the request of the Special Commission, appropriate means of communication;

(g) Provide, upon request by the Special Commission, appropriate escort and/or support personnel;

(h) Not interfere with or censor any communication to or from the Special Commission or its personnel.

Security, privileges and immunities

9. The Special Commission shall have the right to make its own arrangements to ensure the safety and security of its personnel and property and to provide custody of any material or item.

/...

0142

10. Iraq shall ensure the safety and security of the personnel and property of the Special Commission and shall provide the arrangements to this end when so requested by the Special Commission.

11. In addition and without prejudice to the foregoing provisions, the Special Commission and any agency of the United Nations system participating in the carrying out of the Plan, its property, funds, assets and personnel shall enjoy the facilities, privileges and immunities provided for in the applicable convention or agreement, namely the Convention on the Privileges and Immunities of the United Nations, the Agreement on the Privileges and Immunities of the International Atomic Energy Agency (IAEA) and the Convention on the Privileges and Immunities of the Specialized Agencies.

12. Iraq shall extend to:

(a) The officers and other members of the Special Commission, whose names shall be communicated to the Government, the privileges and immunities, exemptions and facilities that are enjoyed by diplomatic envoys in accordance with international law;

(b) The officials of the United Nations, of IAEA and any of the specialized agencies of the United Nations, performing functions in connection with the implementation of the Plan, the privileges and immunities applicable to them under articles V and VII of the Convention on the Privileges and Immunities of the United Nations; or articles VI and IX of the Agreement on the Privileges and Immunities of the International Atomic Energy Agency; or articles VI and VIII of the Convention on the Privileges and Immunities of the Specialized Agencies;

(c) The technical experts and other specialists performing functions in connection with the implementation of the Plan, whose names shall be communicated to the Government upon arrival in Iraq, the privileges and immunities accorded to experts performing missions for the United Nations, for IAEA or for the specialized agencies of the United Nations under article VI of the Convention on the Privileges and Immunities of the United Nations, article VII of the Agreement on the Privileges and Immunities of the International Atomic Energy Agency, and the relevant annexes to the Convention on the Privileges and Immunities of the Specialized Agencies, respectively.

Other provisions

13. Iraq shall designate the Ministry responsible for liaison with the Special Commission and shall inform the Special Commission of the name or names of the liaison officers within that Ministry who shall have the full authority to secure for the Special Commission the effective implementation of the rights laid down in the Plan.

0143   /...

14.   The official points of contact between Iraq and the Special Commission
during the course of an inspection shall be the Chief Inspector designated by
the Special Commission and the Inspection Representative designated by Iraq.

15.   Iraq shall provide, at no cost to the Special Commission, in agreement
with the Special Commission, all such premises as may be necessary for the
accommodation and fulfilment of the functions of the Special Commission in
Iraq.   All such premises shall be inviolable and subject to the exclusive
control and authority of the Special Commission.

16.   For the purposes of the performance of the functions of the Special
Commission in implementation of the Plan under paragraph 10 of Security
Council resolution 687 (1991), the rights, facilities, privileges and
immunities conferred in this annex where necessary supplement and elaborate
upon the rights, facilities, privileges and immunities provided for in the
exchange of notes between the Secretary-General of the United Nations and the
Minister for Foreign Affairs of Iraq, which entered into force on 14 May 1991,
regarding the status, privileges and immunities of the Special Commission as
originally established pursuant to paragraph 9 of Security Council resolution
687 (1991).   To the extent of any incompatibility, the provisions of this
annex shall prevail.

0144···

Annex II

Provisions related to chemical items

1.   The following list contains chemicals that could be used for the development, production or acquisition of chemical weapons, but which also have significant uses for purposes not prohibited by resolution 687 (1991):

		Chemical Abstracts Service (CAS) registry No.
	List A	
1.	Chemicals, except for those chemicals specified in list B of this annex, containing a phosphorus atom to which is bonded one methyl, ethyl or propyl (normal or iso) group but not further carbon atoms	
2.	Dialkyl (Me, Et, n-Pr or i-Pr) N,N-dialkyl (Me, Et, n-Pr or i-Pr)-phosphoramidates	
3.	Arsenic trichloride	(7784-34-1)
4.	2,2-Diphenyl-2-hydroxyacetic acid	(76-93-7)
5.	Quinuclidin-3-ol	(1619-34-7)
6.	N,N-Dialkyl (Me, Et, n-Pr or i-Pr) aminoethyl-2-chloride and corresponding protonated salts	
7.	N,N-Dialkyl (Me, Et, n-Pr or i-Pr) aminoethane-2-ol and corresponding protonated salts	
8.	N,N-Dialkyl (Me, Et, n-Pr or i-Pr) aminoethane-2-thiol and corresponding protonated salts	
9.	Amiton: O,O-Diethyl S-(2-(diethylamino)ethyl) phosphorothiolate and corresponding alkylated and protonated salts	(78-53-5)
10.	PFIB: 1,1,3,3,3-pentafluoro-2-(trifluoromethyl)-1-propene	(382-21-8)
11.	Phosgene	(75-44-5)

0145   /...

		Chemical Abstracts Service (CAS) registry No.
12.	Cyanogen chloride	(506-77-4)
13.	Hydrogen cyanide	(74-90-8)
14.	Trichloronitromethane (chloropicrin)	(76-06-2)
15.	Phosphorus oxychloride	(10025-87-3)
16.	Phosphorus trichloride	(7719-12-2)
17.	Phosphorus pentachloride	(10026-13-8)
18.	Trimethyl phosphite	(121-45-9)
19.	Triethyl phosphite	(122-52-1)
20.	Dimethyl phosphite	(868-85-9)
21.	Diethyl phosphite	(762-04-9)
22.	Sulphur monochloride	(10025-67-9)
23.	Sulphur dichloride	(10545-99-0)
24.	Thionyl chloride	(7719-09-7)
25.	Cyclohexanol	(108-93-0)
26.	Hydrogen fluoride	(7664-39-3)
27.	Ortho-chlorobenzylidenemalononitrile (CS)	(2698-41-1)

2.   The following list contains chemicals that have little or no use except as chemical warfare agents or for the development, production or acquisition of chemical weapons, or which have been used by Iraq as essential precursors for chemical weapons:

0146   /...

List B

      CAS No.

1.   O-Alkyl ($\leq C_{10}$, incl. cycloalkyl) alkyl
      (Me, Et, n-Pr or i-Pr)-phosphonofluoridates
      e.g. Sarin: O-isopropyl methylphosphono-
               fluoridate   (107-44-8)
             Soman: O-pinacolyl methylphosphono-
               fluoridate   (96-64-0)

2.   O-Alkyl ($\leq C_{10}$, incl. cycloalkyl) N,N-dialkyl
      (Me, Et, n-Pr or i-Pr) phosphoramidocynidates
      e.g. Tabun: O-ethyl N,N-dimethylphosphora-
                midocyanidate   (77-81-6)

3.   O-Alkyl (H or $\leq C_{10}$, incl. cycloalkyl) S-2-dialkyl
      (Me, Et, n-Pr or i-Pr)-aminoethyl alkyl
      (Me, Et, n-Pr or i-Pr) phosphonothiolates and
      corresponding alkylated and protonated salts
      e.g. VX: O-ethyl S-2-diisopropylaminoethyl
                  methylphosphonothiolate   (50782-69-9)

4.   Sulphur mustards:
      2-Chloroethylchloromethylsulphide   (2625-76-5)
      bis(2-chloroethyl)sulphide:
      Mustard gas (H)   (505-60-2)
      bis(2-chloroethylthio)methane   (63869-13-6)
      1,2-bis(2-chloroethylthio)ethane:
      Sesquimustard (Q)   (3563-36-8)
      1,3-bis(2-chloroethylthio)-n-propane   (63905-10-2)
      1,4-bis(2-chloroethylthio)-n-butane
      1,5-bis(2-chloroethylthio)-n-pentane
      bis(2-chloroethylthiomethyl)ether
      bis(2-chloroethylthioethyl)ether:
      O-Mustard (T)   (63918-89-8)

5.   Lewisites:
      Lewisite 1: 2-chlorovinyldichlorarsine   (541-25-3)
      Lewisite 2: bis(2-chlorovinyl)
                     chloroarsine   (40334-69-8)
      Lewisite 3: tris(2-chlorovinyl)arsine (40334-70-1)

6.   Nitrogen mustards:
      HN1: bis(2-chloroethyl)ethylamine   (538-07-8)
      HN2: bis(2-chloroethyl)methylamine   (51-75-2)
      HN3: tris(2-chloroethyl)amine   (555-77-1)

7.   3-Quinuclidinyl benzilate (BZ)   (6581-06-2)

8.   Saxitoxin   (35523-89-8)

9.   Ricin

0147   /...

CAS No.

10. Alkyl (Me, Et, n-Pr or i-Pr)
    phosphonyldihalides
    e.g. methylphosphonyldifluoride   (676-99-3)
         methylphosphonyldichloride   (676-67-1)

11. Dimethylmethylphosphonate   (756-79-6)

12. O-Alkyl (H or $\leq C_{10}$, incl. cycloalkyl)
    O-2-dialkyl (Me, Et, n-Pr or i-Pr)-
    aminoethyl alkyl (Me, Et, n-Pr or i-Pr)
    phosphonites and corresponding
    alkylated salts and protonated salts
    e.g. QL: O-ethyl O-2-diisopropylaminoethyl
         methylphosphonite   (57856-11-8)

13. O-Alkyl ($\leq C_{10}$, incl. cycloalkyl) alkyl
    (Me, Et, n-Pr or i-Pr)-phosphonchloridates
    e.g. Chloro Sarin: O-isopropyl
         methylphosphonochloridate   (1445-76-7)
         Chloro Soman: O-pinacolyl methylphos-
         phonochloridate   (7040-57-5)

14. N,N-Dialkyl (Me, Et, n-Pr or i-Pr)
    phosphoramidic dihalides

15. Bis(2-hydroxyethyl)sulphide (thiodiglycol)   (111-48-8)

16. 3,3-Dimethylbutan-2-ol (pinacolyl alcohol)   (464-07-3)

3.   The initial information under paragraph 18 of the Plan to be submitted
not later than 30 days after the adoption of the Plan by the Security Council
shall cover the period from 1 January 1989. Subsequent information shall be
provided each 15 January and 15 July and shall cover the six-month period
prior to the provision of the information. The advance notification under
paragraph 30(d) of the Plan shall cover the subsequent six months.

4.   Whenever the information that Iraq is required to provide under section C
of the Plan and this annex is equal to nil, Iraq shall provide nil returns.

5.   The information on chemicals to be provided under section C of the Plan
shall for each chemical include:

     (a) The chemical name, common or trade name used by the site or the
facility, structural formula and Chemical Abstracts Service registry number
(if assigned);

0148   /...

(b) The purposes for which the chemical is produced, processed, consumed, stored, imported or exported;

(c) The total amount produced, processed, consumed, stored, imported or exported.

6.   The information on sites or facilities to be provided under section C of the Plan shall for each site or facility include:

(a) The name of the site or facility and of the owner, company or enterprise operating the site or facility;

(b) The location of the site or facility;

(c) A general description of all types of activities at the site or facility;

(d) The source(s) of the financing of the site or facility, and of its activities.

7.   The location of a site or facility shall be specified by means of the address and a site diagram. Each diagram shall be drawn to scale and shall indicate the boundaries of the site or facility, all road and rail entrances and exits and all structures on the site or facility, indicating their purpose. If the site or facility is located within a larger complex, the diagram shall specify the exact location of the site or facility within the complex. On each diagram, the geographic coordinates of a point within the site or facility shall be specified to the nearest second.

8.   In addition to information specified in paragraph 6 of this annex, the following information shall be provided for each facility that is or will be involved in production, processing, consumption, storage, import or export of chemicals specified in list A of this annex:

(a) A detailed description of activities related to the chemical(s) specified in list A of this annex, including, as applicable, material-flow and process-flow diagrams, chemical reactions and end-use;

(b) A list of equipment used in activities related to chemical(s) specified in list A of this annex;

(c) The production capacity for the chemical(s) specified in list A of this annex.

9.   In addition to information specified in paragraph 6 of this annex, the following information shall be provided for each site or facility that is or will be involved in production or processing of organophosphorus chemicals or involved in production of organic chemicals by chlorination:

0149   /...

(a) A detailed description of activities related to the relevant chemical(s), and the end-use(s) for which the chemicals are produced or processed;

(b) A detailed description of the processes used in the production or processing of organophosphorus chemicals or in the production of organic chemicals by chlorination, including material-flow and process-flow diagrams, chemical reactions and list of equipment involved.

10. The information on each import to be provided under section C of the Plan shall include:

(a) Specification of each item and the quantity imported and the purpose of its use in Iraq;

(b) Country from which the item is imported and the specific exporter;

(c) Point and time of entry of the item into Iraq;

(d) Site or facility where it is to be used.

0150

/...

Annex III

Provisions related to biological items

1.   The following list contains items and equipment relevant to the acquisition of biological weapons or biological weapons capability:

   (a)   Detection or assay systems for micro-organisms and toxins;

   (b)   Biohazard containment equipment;

   (c)   Equipment for the encapsulation of live micro-organisms;

   (d)   Complex media for the growth of micro-organisms;

   (e)   Bio-reactors and fermentation vessels;

   (f)   Recombinant deoxyribonucleic acid (DNA), equipment for its isolation or production and equipment for the construction of synthetic genes;

   (g)   Equipment for the release into the environment of biological material;

   (h)   Equipment for studying the aerobiological characteristics of micro-organisms or toxins;

   (i)   Equipment for breeding of vectors of human, animal or plant diseases.

2.   The initial information under paragraphs 35 and 36 of the Plan to be submitted not later than 30 days after the adoption of the Plan by the Security Council shall cover the period from 1 January 1989. Subsequent information shall be provided each 15 January and 15 July and shall cover the six-month period prior to the provision of the information.

3.   Whenever the information that Iraq is required to provide under section D and this annex is equal to nil, Iraq shall provide nil returns.

4.   The information on each site or facility to be provided under section D of the Plan shall include the following:

   (a)   The name of the site or facility and of the owner, company, or enterprise operating the facility;

   (b)   The location of the site or facility (including the address, geographic coordinates to the nearest second, location of the facility within any larger complex, including the specific building and any structure number);

   (c)   The source(s) of financing of the site or facility and of its activities;

0151 /...

(d)   The main purpose of the site or facility;

(e)   The level of protection, including, as applicable, the number and size of maximum containment or containment laboratories;

(g)   Scope and description of activities, including, as applicable, a list of types and quantities of micro-organisms, toxins or vaccines and equipment specified in paragraph 1 of this annex;

(h)   A list of micro-organisms and toxins, equipment and vaccines imported for the use of the site or facility, or exported, indicating the countries involved.

5.   The information on import to be provided under paragraphs 35(g) and 38(a) of the Plan shall cover:

(a)   Toxins and micro-organisms meeting the criteria for risk groups IV, III, and II according to the classification in the 1983 WHO Laboratory Biosafety Manual and genetic material coding for toxins or genes derived from the aforementioned micro-organisms;

(b)   Equipment and facilities for the production, utilization or storage of micro-organisms, toxins or vaccines;

(c)   Personnel or material for training or technical support services related to the design, development, use, manufacture or support of items specified in paragraph 35(a) of the Plan and paragraphs 1 and 5 (a) of this annex;

and shall for each import into Iraq specify:

(a)   Types and quantities of micro-organisms, toxins or vaccines;

(b)   Quantities of any items listed under paragraph 1 of this annex;

(c)   Country from which the micro-organisms, toxins, vaccines or items are imported and the specific exporter;

(d)   Point and time of entry into Iraq;

(e)   Site or facility where it is to be used and purpose of its use.

0152   /...

Annex IV

Provisions related to missiles

1.   The following list contains items, equipment and technologies relevant to the development and manufacture of missiles that could be used in the development and manufacture of ballistic missiles capable of a range greater than 150 kilometres:

  (a)   Subsystems usable in missile systems:

  (i)   Individual rocket stages;

  (ii)   Re-entry vehicles, and specially designed equipment therefor;

  (iii)   Solid- or liquid-fuel rocket engines;

  (iv)   Guidance sets;

  (v)   Thrust vector controls;

  (vi)   Warhead safing, arming, fuzing and firing mechanisms;

  (b)   Propulsion components and equipment:

  (i)   Lightweight turbojet and turbofan engines;

  (ii)   Ramjet/Scramjet engines and production equipment therefor;

  (iii)   Rocket-motor cases and production equipment therefor;

  (iv)   Staging mechanisms and production equipment therefor;

  (v)   Liquid-fuel control systems and components therefor, specially designed to operate in vibrating environments of more than 12g rms between 20 Hz and 2,000 Hz;

  (vi)   Propellants and constituent chemicals for propellants;

  (vii)   Production technology or production equipment for the production, handling, mixing, curing, casting, pressing, machining and acceptance testing of the liquid- or solid-missile propellants and propellent constituents;

  (c)   Guidance and control equipment:

  (i)   Gyroscopes, accelerometers and inertial equipment and software therefor;

0153

/...

(ii)   Flight control systems usable in missile systems;

(iii) Avionics equipment specially designed or modified for use in unmanned air vehicles or rocket systems and software and components therefor usable in missile systems;

(d) Equipment and technical data for the production of structural composites usable in missiles and components, accessories and software therefor;

(e) Pyrolytic deposition and densification equipment and technology;

(f) Launch and ground support equipment and facilities usable for missile systems;

(g) Analog computers, digital computers or digital differential analysers usable in air vehicles, rocket systems or missile systems;

(h) Test facilities and equipment usable for missile systems, to include vibration test equipment unsung digital control techniques, wind tunnels and test benches for solid or liquid fuel rockets;

(i) Specially designed software or components for missile design, production or operation;

(j) Materials and devices for reduced observables in missile systems;

(k) Material and devices for protecting missile systems against nuclear effects.

2.   The initial information under paragraph 30 to be submitted not later than 30 days after the adoption of the Plan by the Security Council shall cover the period from 1 January 1989. Subsequent information shall be provided each 15 January and 15 July and shall cover the six-month period prior to the provision of the information.

3.   Whenever the information which Iraq is required to provide under section E of the Plan and this annex is equal to nil, Iraq shall provide nil returns.

0154

Security Council

Distr.
GENERAL

S/22872
1 August 1991

ORIGINAL: ENGLISH

NOTE BY THE SECRETARY-GENERAL

The Secretary-General has the honour to transmit to the Security Council
the attached letter and plan, prepared by the Director-General of the
International Atomic Energy Agency pursuant to paragraph 13 of Security
Council resolution 687 (1991), for the future ongoing monitoring and
verification of Iraq's compliance with paragraph 12 of that resolution.

91-24637 2499h (E)

0155   /...

Annex

Letter dated 29 July 1991 from the Director-General
of the International Atomic Energy Agency addressed
to the Secretary-General

Pursuant to paragraph 13 of Security Council resolution 687 (1991), please find attached the plan for the future ongoing monitoring and verification of Iraq's compliance with paragraph 12 of that resolution. I would appreciate it if you would submit this plan to the Security Council.

(Signed) Hans BLIX

0156

/...

<u>Enclosure</u>

Vienna
29 July 1991

<u>Plan for future ongoing monitoring and verification of Iraq's
compliance with its undertaking under paragraph 12 of Security
Council resolution 687</u>

As provided for in paragraph 13 of Security Council resolution 687,
adopted on 3 April 1991, the Agency submits to the Security Council for its
approval this plan for future ongoing monitoring and verification of Iraq's
compliance with its undertaking under paragraph 12 of resolution 687.

In accordance with paragraph 12 of the resolution, Iraq is obliged:

- not to acquire or develop nuclear weapons or nuclear-weapons-usable
  material or any subsystems or components or any research,
  development, support or manufacturing facilities related to the
  above;

- to submit to the Secretary-General and the Director-General of the
  IAEA within 15 days of adoption of the resolution a declaration of
  the locations, amounts and types of items specified above;

- to place all of its nuclear-weapons-usable materials under the
  exclusive control, for custody and removal, of the IAEA, with the
  assistance and cooperation of the Special Commission appointed by
  the Secretary-General in accordance with paragraph 9 (b) of the
  resolution;

- to accept, in accordance with the arrangements provided for in
  paragraph 13 of the resolution, urgent on-site inspection and the
  destruction, removal or rendering harmless, as appropriate, of such
  items; and

- to accept the plan referred to in paragraph 13 for the future
  ongoing monitoring and verification of its compliance with these
  undertakings.

Pursuant to paragraph 13 of resolution 687, the Director-General of the
International Atomic Energy Agency was requested, with the assistance and
cooperation of the Special Commission:

- to carry out immediate on-site inspection of Iraq's nuclear
  capabilities based on Iraq's declarations and the designation of any
  additional locations by the Special Commission;

0157   /...

-   to develop a plan for submission to the Security Council within forty-five days following adoption of the resolution calling for the destruction, removal, or rendering harmless as appropriate of the items proscribed under in paragraph 12 of the resolution;

-   to carry out the plan within forty-five days following its approval by the Security Council; and

-   to develop a plan, taking into account the rights and obligations of Iraq under the Treaty on the Non-Proliferation of Nuclear Weapons of 1 July 1968, for the future ongoing monitoring and verification of Iraq's compliance with paragraph 12 of the resolution, including an inventory of all nuclear material in Iraq subject to the Agency's verification and inspections to confirm that Agency safeguards cover all relevant nuclear activities in Iraq, to be submitted to the Security Council for approval within 120 days of adoption of the resolution.

The plan for future ongoing monitoring and verification has had to be developed while the immediate on-site inspection is still ongoing, and while the plan for the destruction, removal or rendering harmless of proscribed items is still in an early stage of implementation. Despite nearly 1,000 inspection days and an extensive mapping of nuclear activities in Iraq, the Agency has not yet been in a position to come to a conclusion on a complete inventory of activities and items in Iraq relevant to the resolution. In view of this, the present plan is, of necessity, provisional in nature, and may need to be supplemented in the light of results of the current ongoing activities undertaken by the IAEA in Iraq. The plan consists of two phases as described below. The role of the Agency in both phases will be to monitor and verify Iraq's compliance with its obligations under resolution 687, and any other relevant obligations determined by the Security Council.

I. Current and near-term monitoring and verification

The first phase is characterized by monitoring and verification activities related to the identification of all items proscribed under the resolution and to the removal, destruction or rendering harmless of all such items. This phase continues to be governed for the purpose of monitoring and verification by the existing arrangements reflected in the exchange of letters between the Secretary-General and the Foreign Minister of Iraq dated 6 May 1991 and 17 May 1991 concerning the privileges and immunities relevant to the conduct of activities pursuant to Security Council resolution 687. It is expected that during this phase, the sanctions currently imposed on Iraq by the Security Council will continue to apply and that the Security Council will continue to closely monitor the situation. As a practical matter, Iraq's nuclear activities during this period will be limited in nature. At this time, it is not possible to determine the duration of the first phase.

0158

/...

II. Future long-term monitoring and verification

The second phase of this plan will be put into operation by decision of the Security Council upon completion of all the activities contemplated in the first phase. In accepting unconditionally Security Council resolution 687, as indicated above, the Government of Iraq undertook _inter alia_ not to acquire or develop nuclear weapons or nuclear-weapons-usable material or any subsystems or components or any research, development, support or manufacturing facilities related to the above. During this phase, it is proposed, the IAEA will monitor and verify Iraq's compliance with these obligations.

The undertakings by Iraq under the resolution necessarily limit the nuclear activities otherwise open to Iraq under the Treaty on the Non-Proliferation of Nuclear Weapons (NPT). In particular, reprocessing, enrichment and the possession of nuclear-weapons-usable material, and all related activities, are proscribed under the terms of Security Council resolution 687. The permissibility of Iraq's carrying out other nuclear activities is to a large measure dependent upon the position of the Security Council with regard to the continuation of sanctions.

The resolution does not define the term "nuclear-weapons-usable material". Nuclear-weapons-usable material or, as it is referred to in the practice of the Agency, direct-use material, is understood for the purposes of this plan to mean nuclear material which can be used for the manufacture of nuclear explosive components without transmutation or further enrichment. This includes plutonium containing less than 80 per cent plutonium-238, uranium enriched to 20 per cent or more U-235 (high-enriched uranium) and uranium-233. Chemical compounds, mixtures of direct-use materials (e.g. mixed oxide) and plutonium contained in spent nuclear fuel also fall in this category. For the purposes of the plan, and in view of the fact that Iraq will be prohibited from having reprocessing capability, the proscription against the possession of nuclear-weapons-usable material would not be interpreted as precluding the possession of plutonium in spent fuel resulting from the use of low-enriched uranium as fuel in a research or power reactor. To include such material in the proscription would necessitate the removal from Iraq of irradiated uranium enriched to 10 per cent which, in light of the small quantities of plutonium in the spent fuel, may not be cost-effective in relationship to the non-proliferation benefit.

The obligation not to acquire or develop any subsystems or components or any research, development, support or manufacturing facilities related to nuclear-weapons-usable material would preclude all activities relevant to or connected with reprocessing of irradiated fuel and isotopic enrichment of uranium. This proscription would extend to any research and development activities directed at reprocessing and isotopic enrichment technologies, as well as laboratory-, pilot- and industrial-scale facilities. This would also preclude conversion preparatory for reprocessing or for enrichment.

0159

/...

The undertaking not to acquire or develop nuclear weapons or any subsystems or components or any research, development, support or manufacturing facilities related to nuclear weapons would include items or components that could significantly contribute to or that are intended for use in the development or production of nuclear weapons. Certain dual-use items may be necessary for the conduct of permitted nuclear activities in Iraq in the future. The Agency's activities under the plan will include identification of such dual-use items and monitoring or verification of the use of such items.

General provisions

Under article II of the NPT, Iraq has an obligation not to acquire nuclear weapons or other nuclear explosive devices. The safeguards agreement with the Agency is designed to verify that nuclear material in peaceful nuclear activities is not diverted to such use. Iraq's undertakings under paragraph 12 of Security Council resolution 687 are broader in scope than any non-proliferation undertaking previously verified by the International Atomic Energy Agency. The plan for monitoring and verifying Iraq's compliance with those obligations will have to be commensurate with the scope of the undertakings and be so designed as to create confidence that the restrictions accepted by Iraq are actually complied with. This requires a more comprehensive approach than heretofore applied by the Agency.

Resolution 687 notes that the actions required of Iraq, including those relevant to nuclear weapons and nuclear-weapons-usable material, represent steps towards the goal of establishing in the Middle East a zone free from weapons of mass destruction. The terms of any such zone would have to be negotiated between the parties to such an arrangement. Nevertheless, verification features envisaged in the present plan may be found of interest in future discussions about verification in such a zone.

The plan is based on the following premises:

(a) The verification and monitoring activities contemplated in the plan will be carried out by the IAEA in accordance with detailed modalities to be developed by the Agency.

(b) All nuclear material, facilities and installations, as well as equipment and non-nuclear material which, in the judgement of the IAEA, is relevant to Iraq's undertaking under the resolution, shall be subject to monitoring and verification. The items subject to monitoring and verification will be identified to Iraq by the IAEA. This list of items may be added to or modified from time to time by the IAEA.

(c) While the approaches and techniques to be used under the plan draw upon the Agency's safeguards experience, the scope and intensity of the verification and monitoring under this plan are much greater in order to satisfy the requirements of Security Council resolution 687. These measures may be administered and operated by a special Secretariat unit.

0160 /...

(d)   The safeguards agreement concluded with Iraq pursuant to the NPT shall continue to be in force.   The verification activities pursuant to this plan will be carried out in a manner that takes into account the safeguards activities required under the safeguards agreement.

(e)   In accordance with articles IX and VII of the Agreement Governing the Relationship between the United Nations and the International Atomic Energy Agency,* the Agency will report on the implementation of the plan to the Security Council at its request, and to any subsidiary organ that the Council may designate (i.e., the Special Commission or its successor).

(f)   The activities under the plan for the future ongoing monitoring and verification of Iraq's compliance with paragraph 12 of the resolution (nuclear) will be closely coordinated with the monitoring and verification activities relevant to Iraq's compliance with paragraph 10 of the resolution (chemical, biological and missile), and with the body designated by the Security Council to carry out these activities (i.e., the Special Commission or its successor).

(g)   Financing of the verification and monitoring activities by the Agency in Iraq under the present plan will be secured by the United Nations.

Obligations of Iraq

Iraq shall provide to the Agency, and maintain current, the following:

(a)   An inventory of all nuclear material in Iraq, including nuclear material containing uranium or thorium which has not reached the composition and purity suitable for fuel fabrication or for being isotopically enriched, and notification to the Agency one month in advance of any change in the inventory; the inventory and any changes thereto shall include quantity, form, composition, location and use of such material.

(b)   An inventory of all facilities and installations, as well as equipment and non-nuclear material relevant to Iraq's undertaking, and notification one month in advance of any change in the inventory; the inventory and any changes thereto shall include quantity, form and composition of such items, where applicable, as well as the location and use of all items on the inventory.

---

*   Article IX provides that the Agency "shall cooperate with the Security Council by furnishing to it at its request such information and assistance as may be required in the exercise of its responsibility for the maintenance or restoration of international peace and security."

Article VII provides inter alia that, "At the invitation of the Security Council, the Director-General may attend its meetings to supply it with information or give it other assistance within the competence of the Agency."

/...

0161

(c) Complete design information for any planned nuclear facility or installation 180 days before the start of construction of any such facility or installation.

(d) Information on Iraq's nuclear programme one year in advance and any changes to that programme before they are made.

(e) Other information or data which the Agency requires to enable it to monitor Iraq's compliance with resolution 687 and any other relevant Security Council resolutions.

Obligations of other States

Paragraphs 24, 25 and 27 of Security Council resolution 687, inter alia, direct States not to provide to Iraq any of the items proscribed in paragraph 12 of that resolution. In addition to that proscription, all States should be required by the Security Council to provide the Agency, one month in advance, with full and complete reporting of intended exports to Iraq of nuclear material, facilities, equipment, technological information, including training, and any other relevant items, including non-nuclear materials which could be used in proscribed activities. The IAEA will submit to the Security Council a list of items the export of which should be subject to advance reporting.

Rights of the IAEA

Without prejudice to the rights which the Agency has under the safeguards agreement with Iraq and under the Agreement on the Privileges and Immunities of the IAEA, the Agency should have the following rights to the extent deemed necessary by the Agency to enable it to carry out its verification and monitoring activities under the resolution. These rights are similar to those contained in the exchange of letters between the Secretary-General of the United Nations and the Government of Iraq dated 6 May 1991 and 17 May 1991 concerning privileges and immunities relevant to the conduct of activities pursuant to Security Council resolution 687.

(a) The right, on its own initiative or at the request of the Security Council or any body established or designated by it (i.e., the Special Commission or its successor), to carry out inspections of any locations or facilities in Iraq.

(b) The right to full and free access at any time to all locations, all persons and all information which, in the Agency's judgement, may be necessary for the verification of Iraq's undertaking. This includes unimpeded access to all nuclear material, facilities and installations, as well as equipment and non-nuclear material relevant to Iraq's undertaking, and the right to conduct unannounced inspections and inspections upon short notice. This also includes the right of the Agency to restrict and/or stop movement of suspected material and equipment.

0162

/...

(c) Freedom of entry and exit to and from Iraq without delay of Agency personnel and experts, supplies and equipment. No visas shall be required of such personnel travelling on a United Nations laissez-passer and possessing an inspection assignment document.

(d) Freedom of movement within Iraq of Agency personnel and experts, supplies and equipment.

(e) The right to request, receive, examine and copy any record, data or information and examine, retain, move or photograph, including videotape, any item relevant to the Agency's monitoring and verification activities.

(f) The right to install equipment and construct facilities for observation, testing, verification or monitoring activities.

(g) The right to take and analyse samples relevant to the Agency's monitoring and verification activities, as well as to remove and export samples for off-site analysis.

(h) The right to have its own means of transport and communication and the right to unrestricted communication by telephone, telegraph, radio or other means.

(i) The right to use fixed wing and helicopter overflights throughout Iraq for the purposes of inspection, surveillance, transportation and logistics.

Duration

The duration of the verification and monitoring plan established under Security Council resolution 687 shall be decided by the Security Council.

0163

외 무 부

원 본

종 별 :

번 호 : UNW-2123   일 시 : 91 0812 1800

수 신 : 장 관(국연,중동일,기정)

발 신 : 주 유엔 대사

제 목 : 걸프사태(유엔동향)

1. 유엔 이락.쿠웨이트 옵서버단 (UNIKOM)감축추진

유엔사무총장은 본건 옵서버단측의 건의에 의거 경비절감 및 효율성제고를 위해 인력감축문제를 관련국들과 협의 예정임을 8.9 자로 안보리 의장에게 알려왔음. (S/22916)

가. 군요원: 300 명을 250 명으로 감축

나. 의료진 축소

다. 병참인력 감축및 재배치

라. 공병대 감축 (우선 293 명을 85 명으로 감축, 국경획정위 작업종료시 50 명으로 재감축)

2. 이락내 억류자 문제

쿠웨이트가 유엔측에 통보해온바에 의하면 현재이락 억류자는 총 2,479 명이며 국별현황은 다음과 같음.

가. 쿠웨이트 1,839 명

나. UAE 2, 사우디 66, 시리아 18, 애급 35, 오만 2, 레바논 14, 소말리아 1, 바레인 3, 비율빈 7, 인도 13, 파키스탄 4, 이란 12, 스리랑카 1

다. 국적불명 462 명

3. 이락 특정무기 폐기관련 고공정찰 추진

유엔이락 특정무기 폐기 특위측은 동 특위임무수행과 관련 이락에 대한 고공관측을 위해 미측으로부터 고공정찰기 1대를 협조받아 이달부터 운용예정이라고 8.7 자로 발표하였음. 한편 이락측은 유엔의 정찰비행 자체는 방해하지 않겠다는 입장을 밝혔으나, 미군기를 사용하는것에 대해 불만을 표시하였음. (S/22899) 끝

(대사 노창희-국장)

국기국   1차보   중아국   외정실   분석관   안기부

PAGE 1   91.08.13   08:53 WG

외신 1과 통제관

0164

외　무　부

종　별 :

번　호 : UNW-2159　　　　　　　　　일　시 : 91 0814 1930

수　신 : 장 관(국연,중동일,기정)

발　신 : 주 유엔 대사

제　목 : 걸프사태(유엔동향)

　　금 8.14 유엔측이 발표한 이락 특정무기폐기 관련 활동개요, 생물무기 사찰반
조사결과 내용을 별첨송부함.

　　첨부:상기자료: UNW(F)-428 끝

　　(대사 노창희-국장)

국기국　　1차보　　중아국　　외정실　　안기부

UNW(M)-428 10AM4 1930
(국연.중동일 기정)   통20여

NOTE FOR THE SPOKESMAN

Special Commission Inspection Schedule

Wednesday 14 August 1991

Here follows a comprehensive list of missions carried out by the Special Commission created by Resolution 687 to oversee the disarmament of Iraq.

Nuclear

15-21 May	1st inspection mission
22 June-3 July	2nd inspection mission
30 June-3 July	high-level mission (on denied access)
7-18 July	3rd inspection mission
27 July-10 August	4th inspection mission

Chemical

9-15 June	1st inspection mission (survey)
12-14 August	2nd mission (destruction techniques)

Biological

2-8 August	1st inspection mission

Ballistic missiles

30 June-7 July	1st inspection (and destruction)
18-20 July	2nd (surprise) inspection & destruct.
8-15 Aug	3rd mission (incl. "super gun")

Future missions

Nuclear: Will continue.

Chemical: Two more planned for August; "super" mission to Muthanna site end September involving more than 70 inspectors.

Biological: Will continue.

Ballistic missiles: Fourth mission will include a closer inspection of the "super gun".

F. Eckhard

fg3-45

UNW-2159
첨부팩   2-1

0166

14 August 1991

PRESS RELEASE

Iraq had previously declared that it had no Biological Weapons nor carried out any related activities.

In order to verify this declaration, a team of 28 personnel (UNSCOM 7) lead by the Chief Inspector, Dr. David Kelly, undertook an inspection of Iraq's Biological Warfare capability from 3rd to 7th August inclusive. The team comprised experts in microbiology and biotechnology, safety, medicine, and communication.

On the first day, Iraq declared that biological research activities for military purposes were initiated in Iraq in mid-1986 at the Salman site. Research was stated to be undertaken on Clostridium botulinum, Clostridium perfringens, and Bacillus anthracis. Military research was later explained to comprise research which could be used for both defensive and offensive purposes.

The inspection undertaken was a full inspeciton of a site near Salman Pak. It required five full days. Discussions were also held with senior representatives of the Ministries of Health and Agriculture to define a base of microbiological, especially pathogen, activities within Iraq.

At Salman site, the team discovered a capability to research, produce, test and store biological warfare agents. Fermentation, production, aerosol testing and storage existed at that site. However, no evidence of biological weapons per se was obtained and no facility for filling weapons was determined. The site had been extensively damaged by coalition force bombardment, and by the recent physical removal by the Iraqis of key buildings.

Iraq admitted to have worked on the following biological warfare agents: anthrax and botulinum toxin.

At the last day, before departure, Iraq handed over a collection of biological materials which could be developed as biological warfare agents. This material include brucellosis and tularaemia.

At the same time, Iraq stated that it would cease developing biological warfare agents.

2-2

0167

USW(가)-3263 108- 1200

경 : 편 (미미, 메인, 등~~한~~이대사

이건 보사부장관

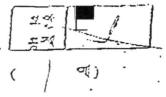

(/ 예)

U.N. Panel Describes Iraq's Anthrax Threat

No Evidence Yet That Weapons Were Built

By John M. Goshko
and Trevor Rowe
Washington Post Staff Writers

UNITED NATIONS, Aug. 14— Iraq's biological warfare research at the Salman Pak laboratory near Baghdad had the capacity to produce a little more than 50 gallons of deadly anthrax each week, an amount capable of contaminating more than 600 square miles, U.N. officials said today.

The officials stressed that while Iraq was capable of making biological weapons for offensive military purposes, U.N. investigators had found no evidence that such weapons actually had been produced.

Nevertheless, the lack of evidence of production "does not mean to say that weapons were not manufactured there," according to David Kelly, who led the U.N. team that conducted a five-day inspection of the Salman Pak complex earlier this month. He described the potential production capacity of Salman Pak as "substantial" and said: "You don't need to have a large number of biological weapons to use them as weapons of mass destruction."

Iraq's ability to manufacture vast quantities of anthrax and botulinim toxin, another virulent disease-causing agent, was described by Kelly and Rolf Ekeus, director of the U.N. commission charged with eliminating Iraq's weapons of mass destruction. In addition, the leader of a different U.N. team said they had inspected the site where Iraq was building the world's largest artillery piece, a "doomsday gun" intended to fire chemical, biological or nuclear weapons hundreds of miles.

Kelly, a British microbiologist, said Iraq's program clearly was illegal because President Saddam Hussein's government has signed and ratified the international Biological Weapons Convention, which bans signatories from producing and stockpiling such weapons.

Iraq initially had declared to the United Nations that it did not possess any biological weapons and had said its biological research was limited to peaceful purposes. However, after the U.N. team began inspecting Salman Pak, the Iraqi government admitted that its activities included biological research for "defensive military purposes."

Kelly said today that when the Iraqis were pressed, they acknowledged that their biological research also could be used for offensive purposes, as the United States had charged. Because of Washington's conviction that Iraq wanted biological weapons, U.S. planes bombed the Salman Pak complex heavily during the Persian Gulf War earlier this year.

The Iraqis said they had tried to conceal the program, as they did their separate nuclear research activities, because they feared it would be misinterpreted by the Western media and provide an excuse for U.S. attacks, Kelly said.

In addition to anthrax and botulin toxin, U.N. officials said the Iraqis had handed over to the inspection team material on other potential biological warfare agents, including brucellosis and tularaemia.

Kelly said his team still is computing the Salman Pak complex's capacity for producing botulin toxin. But, he added, the inspectors had determined that the laboratory could produce more than 50 gallons of anthrax a week.

One half that amount could "devastate" an area of 1,000 square kilometers, or 600 square miles, he said. Thus, while various scientific factors make precise measurements difficult to compute, the full 50 gallons theoretically could infect all human beings in an area twice that size, or 1,200 miles.

Kelly said that on future trips, the U.N. inspectors will look at other Iraqi sites where they suspect that biological warfare research was conducted.

Meanwhile, the Security Council began formal consultations today on a resolution that would condemn Iraq for its continued refusal to give Ekeus's commission complete information about its nuclear program and would demand that Iraq cooperate with the U.N. inspectors.

The council also is considering a parallel resolution that would permit Iraq to sell oil exports worth $1.6 billion to buy food for its war-ravaged population. Part of the proceeds also would be used to pay the costs of Ekeus's commission and another U.N. commission that must define the borders between Iraq and Kuwait.

The resolutions are expected to be voted on Thursday.

W.P
Aug.15, '91

//// // 외

/ /르

르 외

0168

외 무 부

종 별 :

번 호 : UNW-2169   일   시 : 91 0816 1800

수 신 : 장 관(국연,중동일,기정)

발 신 : 주 유엔 대사

제 목 : 안보리회의(이락문제)

연: UNW-2163

1. 안보리는 8.15 공식회의에서 연호 3개결의안을 채택함.

가. 이락 석유수출 일부허용 (S/RES/706)

- 투표결과:13-1 (쿠바)-1 (예멘)

- 6개월기간중 16억불 한도내에서 석유수출 허용

- 수출대금은 유엔사무총장 관할하의 특별구좌에 입금

- 수출대금 30 퍼센트는 유엔 보상기금에 입금

나. 석유수입공제 상한선 (S/RES/705)

- 투표결과 :전원찬성

- 30 프로 상한선 설정합의

다. 이락의 무기폐기 이행위반 규탄 (S/RES/707)

- 투표결과:전원찬성

2. 주유엔 이락대사는 결의 706 은 이락을 식민지와 같은 예속상태로 만든다고
비난하고 이런조건하에서는 석유수출을 하지 않을것이라고 반박함.

첨부: UNW(F)-433 끝

(대사 노창희-국장)

국기국   1차보   중아국   외정실   안기부

UNITED NATIONS

Security Council

S

Distr.
GENERAL

S/RES/707 (1991)
15 August 1991

RESOLUTION 707 (1991)

Adopted by the Security Council at its 3004th meeting,
on 15 August 1991

The Security Council,

Recalling its resolution 687 (1991), and its other resolutions on this matter,

Recalling the letter of 11 April 1991 from the President of the Security Council to the Permanent Representative of Iraq to the United Nations (S/22485) noting that on the basis of Iraq's written agreement (S/22456) to implement fully resolution 687 (1991) the preconditions established in paragraph 33 of that resolution for a cease-fire had been met,

Noting with grave concern the letters dated 26 June 1991 (S/22739), 28 June 1991 (S/22743) and 4 July 1991 (S/22761) from the Secretary-General, conveying information obtained from the Executive Chairman of the Special Commission and the Director-General of the IAEA which establishes Iraq's failure to comply with its obligations under resolution 687 (1991),

Recalling further the statement issued by the President of the Security Council on 28 June 1991 (S/22746) requesting that a high-level mission consisting of the Chairman of the Special Commission, the Director-General of the IAEA, and the Under-Secretary-General for Disarmament Affairs be dispatched to meet with officials at the highest levels of the Government of Iraq at the earliest opportunity to obtain written assurance that Iraq will fully and immediately cooperate in the inspection of the locations identified by the Special Commission and present for immediate inspection any of those items that may have been transported from those locations,

Dismayed by the report of the high-level mission to the Secretary-General (S/22761) on the results of its meetings with the highest levels of the Iraqi Government,

91-26595   35762 (E)

9-6

/...

0170

S/RES/707 (1991)
Page 2

   Gravely concerned by the information provided to the Council by the
Special Commission and the IAEA on 15 July 1991 (S/22788) and 25 July 1991
(S/22837) regarding the actions of the Government of Iraq in flagrant
violation of resolution 687 (1991),

   Gravely concerned also by the evidence in the letter of 7 July 1991 from
the Minister of Foreign Affairs of Iraq to the Secretary-General and in
subsequent statements and findings that Iraq's notifications of 18 and
28 April were incomplete and that it had concealed activities, which both
constituted material breaches of its obligations under resolution 687 (1991),

   Noting also from the letters dated 26 June 1991 (S/22739), 28 June 1991
(S/22743) and 4 July 1991 (S/22761) from the Secretary-General that Iraq has
not fully complied with all of its undertakings relating to the privileges,
immunities and facilities to be accorded to the Special Commission and the
IAEA inspection teams mandated under resolution 687 (1991),

   Affirming that in order for the Special Commission to carry out its
mandate under paragraph 9 (b) (i), (ii) and (iii) of resolution 687 (1991) to
inspect Iraq's chemical and biological weapons and ballistic missile
capabilites and to take possession of them for destruction, removal or
rendering harmless, full disclosure on the part of Iraq as required in
paragraph 9 (a) of resolution 687 (1991) is essential,

   Affirming that in order for the IAEA, with the assistance and cooperation
of the Special Commission, to determine what nuclear-weapons-usable material
or any subsystems or components or any research, development, support or
manufacturing facilities related to them need, in accordance with paragraph 13
of resolution 687 (1991), to be destroyed, removed or rendered harmless, Iraq
is required to make a declaration of all its nuclear programmes including any
which it claims are for purposes not related to nuclear-weapons-usable
material,

   Affirming that the aforementioned failures of Iraq to act in strict
conformity with its obligations under resolution 687 (1991) constitutes a
material breach of its acceptance of the relevant provisions of resolution
687 (1991) which established a cease-fire and provided the conditions
essential to the restoration of peace and security in the region,

   Affirming further that Iraq's failure to comply with its safeguards
agreement with the International Atomic Energy Agency, concluded pursuant to
the Treaty on the Non-Proliferation of Nuclear Weapons of 1 July 1968, as
established by the resolution of the Board of Governors of the IAEA of
18 July 1991 (GOV/2532), 1/ constitutes a breach of its international
obligations,

_____

   1/   A/45/1037; S/22812, appendix.

                                                          /...

                              9-7

— .

Determined to ensure full compliance with resolution 687 (1991) and in particular its section C,

Acting under Chapter VII of the Charter,

1. Condemns Iraq's serious violation of a number of its obligations under section C of resolution 687 (1991) and of its undertakings to cooperate with the Special Commission and the IAEA, which constitutes a material breach of the relevant provisions of resolution 687 which established a cease-fire and provided the conditions essential to the restoration of peace and security in the region;

2. Further condemns non-compliance by the Government of Iraq with its obligations under its safeguards agreement with the International Atomic Energy Agency, as established by the resolution of the Board of Governors of 18 July, which constitutes a violation of its commitments as a party to the Treaty on the Non-Proliferation of Nuclear Weapons of 1 July 1968;

3. Demands that Iraq

(i)   provide full, final and complete disclosure, as required by resolution 687 (1991), of all aspects of its programmes to develop weapons of mass destruction and ballistic missiles with a range greater than 150 km, and of all holdings of such weapons, their components and production facilities and locations, as well as all other nuclear programmes, including any which it claims are for purposes not related to nuclear-weapons-usable material, without further delay;

(ii) allow the Special Commission, the IAEA and their Inspection Teams immediate, unconditional and unrestricted access to any and all areas, facilities, equipment, records and means of transportation which they wish to inspect;

(iii) cease immediately any attempt to conceal, or any movement or destruction of any material or equipment relating to its nuclear, chemical or biological weapons or ballistic missile programmes, or material or equipment relating to its other nuclear activities without notification to and prior consent of the Special Commission;

(iv) make available immediately to the Special Commission, the IAEA and their Inspection Teams any items to which they were previously denied access;

(v)   allow the Special Commission, the IAEA and their Inspection Teams to conduct both fixed wing and helicopter flights throughout Iraq for all relevant purposes including inspection, surveillance, aerial surveys, transportation and logistics without interference of any kind and upon such terms and

/...

9-ß

0172

conditions as may be determined by the Special Commission, and
to make full use of their own aircraft and such airfields in
Iraq as they may determine are most appropriate for the work of
the Commission;

    (vi)   halt all nuclear activities of any kind, except for use of
isotopes for medical, agricultural or industrial purposes until
the Security Council determines that Iraq is in full compliance
with this resolution and paragraphs 12 and 13 of resolution
687 (1991), and the IAEA determines that Iraq is in full
compliance with its safeguards agreement with that Agency;

    (vii) ensure the complete implementation of the privileges,
immunities and facilities of the representatives of the Special
Commission and the IAEA in accordance with its previous
undertakings and their complete safety and freedom of movement;

    (viii) immediately provide or facilitate the provision of any
transportation, medical or logistical support requested by the
Special Commission, the IAEA and their Inspection Teams;

    (ix)   respond fully, completely and promptly to any questions or
requests from the Special Commission, the IAEA and their
Inspection Teams;

4.   _Determines_ that Iraq retains no ownership interest in items to be
destroyed, removed or rendered harmless pursuant to paragraph 12 of resolution
687 (1991);

5.   _Requires_ that the Government of Iraq forthwith comply fully and
without delay with all its international obligations, including those set out
in the present resolution, in resolution 687 (1991), in the Treaty on the
Non-Proliferation of Nuclear Weapons of 1 July 1968 and its safeguards
agreement with the IAEA;

6.   _Decides_ to remain seized of this matter.

9-9

0173

原油수출허용은 "후세인 목조기"

安保理결의안 배경·전망

代金30% 배상금적립등 단서로 계속制裁

이라크선 울며겨자먹기식으로 수용 전망

유엔안전보장이사회는 15일 이라크의 쿠웨이트침공 이후 단행한 對이라크 제재조치이래 처음으로 이라크에 15억달러의 원유판매를 허용하는 내용의 안을 채택했다.

이 결의안은 이미 지난달 초부터 美행정부에 의해 추진돼온 구상에 따른 것으로 당초 미국의 對이라크정책이 변한게 아니란 추측을 불러일으켰다.

그러나 15일 공개된 결의안은 유엔안전보장이사회가 이라크의 쿠웨이트 국경감시 비용으로 계상돼 있다.

게다가 원유수출간등에 따른 전후처리의 한과정의 거래와 인도절자의 수입이라는 측면이 더욱 강하다.

지난 4월 채택된 유엔의 아미르·알·안바리 한는셈이다라고 말했다.

따라서 이번결의안채택으로 이라크정부는 더욱 곤경에 몰리게된 셈이다. 알불·로 이라크정부의 관리에 대한 이라크정부의 관리에 대한 이라크정부의 파기와 한 規程하고있어 원유판매대금 께 석유수출을의 일부는 전 쟁배상에 사용할 경우은 이 신탁관치하에 두려는 것이라고 비난함만큼 이 결의안 치로 인해 앓앓의와 제재조

또 산정이 쿠웨이트로 권의 완전 배제된다. 따라서 이번 결의안은 對 라크에 유추고있다.

[南勁旭기자]

토머스·피커링 유엔주재 은 이라크정부를 당케하 가 질병과 굶주림으로 사망 美대사도 이결의안 제재 함 것으로 나쁘고 결의안 경제 조치의 해제를 의미하 조치가 이결의안이 제재 다른 「이라크정부가 이라크 율을 거부할 경우 유엔의 또 이라크정부는 이 결의안 상황이 나쁘고 결의안 이행 조치의 해제를 의미하 다른 제재조치가 있다듯게 국민들의 고통을 이용해 정 라크원유시설의 파괴라는 치적 이득을 얻는듯싶을 바 이유로 들어 93년까지 전쟁 함으로써 제재조치를 강화 배상금적립을 연기하고 배 한는셈」이라고 말했다. 상금의 상승선을 원유수입 의 19%로 해당하고 호소해 산로 이라크가 유엔의 제재 왔으나 이번 결의안채택으 로 이라크가 기아의 위험에 한데는 유엔의 제재 조치로 처 해있다는 국제적비난을 인 로 이라크 호소가 사실상 도적으로 한시적 피해보자는 거부당했기 때문이다. 산로 깔려있는 것으로 보여 진다.

이라크에 혜제조능력이 없 다는 주장이 사실상 받아들 여지고있는 상황에서도 해 정부가 對이라크제재조치를 쉽사리 완화하리라고 기대 하기는 당분간 어려워 보인다.

안보리 이라크 원유수출 일부 허용 의미

유엔 안전보장이사회가 15일 이라크의 원유수출을 일부 허용한 것은 이라크에 대한 경제제재조처의 완화를 시사하는 것이라기보다는 경제제재가 이라크 민간인들을 회생시키고 있다는 국제적 비난과 하반기 유가 급등 가능성을 우려했기 때문인 것으로 해석되고 있다.

이와 함께 이날 통과된 안보리 결의는 앞으로 6개월간의 원유수출대금 16억달러 전액을 유엔계정으로 자동입금시켜 유엔 관리하에 두도록 하는 것 외에 10억달러 상당의 긴급식량 및 의약품의 구입과 이라크 현지에

발표한 보고서에서 "걸프사태 이후 1년간의 경제제재조처에 사상 최대의 흉작까지 겹쳐 이대로 두면 많은 사람이 굶어죽게 될 것"이라고 전했다.

이 보고서는 밀가루값이 46배, 쌀값이 22배, 분유값이 16배로 뛰는 등 살인적인 인플레와 식량부족으로 특히 어린이와 임산부가 큰 고통을 받고 있다고 전하면서 다국적군의 폭격으로 파괴된 농업기반의 복구에 5억달러, 당장의 생명유지를 위해서만도 12개월간 16억달러 이상이 필요하다고 지적했다.

다른 국제구호단체들도 비슷

천3백27만배럴 수준에 머물러 있어 공급부족으로 인한 유가 앙등이 우려되고 있는 것이다. 석유전문가들은 이번 결의로 이라크산 원유 50만배럴이 오는 9월부터 시장에 나오고 지난달부터 수출을 재개한 쿠웨이트산 원유가 연말까지 50만배럴을 채울 경우 올 하반기와 내년 상반기의 유가는 현재 수준을 유지할 것으로 전망하고 있다.

서방국들은 이런 필요성에 따라 이라크의 원유수출 재개를 일부 허용했지만 후세인 대통령의 목줄을 죄기 위한 경제제재의 고삐는 늦추지 않고 있다. 이라크로서는 80% 이상이 파괴된 정유시설 복구 등 경제재건에 1백억달러 이상이 필요하고 재원은 원유수출뿐인 처지이지

대금 전액 유엔관리···경제제재는 계속

인도적 비난 모면과 유가급등 우려가 배경
이라크 '굶주림' 심각 거부 힘들듯

서의 배급까지도 유엔이 직접 관장토록 하는 등 이라크 정부의 개입을 모두 배제하고 있어 이라크로부터 주권침해라는 반발을 사고 있다.

'조건없는 원유수출 재개 허용'을 요구해온 이라크 정부는 아직 이 결의의 수락 여부를 밝히지 않고 있다. 하지만 많은 분석가들은 이라크가 결국 국가적 위신과 국민들의 굶주림을 해결해야 할 현실적 필요성 중 후자를 선택할 수밖에 없을 것이라고 보고 있다.

실제로 최근 이라크를 방문하고 돌아온 관리들이 전하는 이라크의 기아상황은 상상 이상으로 절박하다. 유엔식량농업기구(FAO)의 이라크 조사단은 지난달 이라크를 돌아보고 온 뒤

한 참상소식을 전하면서 이라크 민간인에 대한 긴급구조를 호소하고 있어 미국 등 서방으로선 이를 외면하기 어려웠던 것이다.

서방쪽이 이라크 원유수출 재개를 일부 허용한 또다른 배경인 석유수급문제는 서방선진국의 경기회복 가능성을 고려한 것이다. 경제협력개발기구(OECD)는 지난 6월 성장둔화세를 보여온 선진국의 경기가 하반기 들어서는 뚜렷한 회복세를 보일 것으로 전망했다. 이 경우 석유수출국기구(OPEC) 원유에 대한 수요는 성수기인 올 10~12월과 내년 1~3월에 각각 하루 2천4백만배럴 및 2천5백만배럴에 이를 것으로 전망되는데, 이라크와 쿠웨이트를 제외한 OPEC 국가의 생산량은 7월 현재 2

만 이번 결의는 최소한의 긴급한 기반시설 복구에 돈을 쓸 통로조차 원천봉쇄한 것이다. 더구나 원유수출대금 중 30%인 4억8천만달러는 걸프전 배상기금으로 강제적립토록 되어 있어 이라크의 목을 죄는 서방의 경제제재는 한가닥 숨쉴 통로만 남겨둔 채 계속되는 셈이다.

이라크 당국은 특히 식량과 의약품의 배급을 유엔이 담당하는 것은 정부와 국민 사이를 갈라놓으려는 서방쪽의 음모라고 주장하고 있기도 하다.

그러나 이번 유엔의 결의는 서방의 대이라크 경제제재가 경제적 이유에서건 국제사회의 약학관계에 의해서건 약화될 수밖에 없음을 보여준다는 점에서 주목된다. 〈여현호 기자〉

한겨레 8.18.

0175

외 무 부

종 별 :

번 호 : UNW-2214

수 신 : 장관(국연,중동일,기정)

발 신 : 주 유엔 대사

제 목 : 안보리동향

일 시 : 91 0820 2030

연:UNW-2169

지난 8.15 이락관련 연호 3 개 결의안 처리이후 현재 특기할 안보리의 움직임은 없는바, 당관 원참사관이 에쿠아돌 J.VALENCIA 서기관으로부터 탐문한 금월하순중 주요예상의제는 다음과같음.

1. 이락 대량파괴무기 폐기이행 검증계획안

해관련 계획안(UNW-2036) , 여타 대량파괴무기관련 계획안(UNW-2053)의 연계를 위한 사무국측 작업이 완료되는 대로 본건 토의예정

2. 사이프러스문제

유엔사무총장은 8 월말 안보리에 보고서 제출예정(UNW-1669,1678 참조)끝

(대사 노창희)

예고:91.12.31. 까지

국기국   1차보   중아국   외정실   안기부

주 국 련 대 표 부

주국련20313- **653**   91 . 8 . 21 .

수신 : 장관

참조 : 국제기구조약국장 , 중동아프리카국장

제목 : 이락 핵사찰 (안보리)

표제관련 안보리 문서를 별첨과 같이 송부합니다.

첨 부 : 상기 문서. 끝.

주 국 련 대 사

선 결			결재(공란)		
접수일시	1991. 8. 25	발송			
처리과	47645				

0177

UNITED NATIONS

S

Security Council

Distr.
GENERAL

S/22912
8 August 1991
ENGLISH
ORIGINAL: ARABIC

LETTER DATED 7 AUGUST 1991 FROM THE PERMANENT REPRESENTATIVE OF
IRAQ TO THE UNITED NATIONS ADDRESSED TO THE SECRETARY-GENERAL

On instructions from my Government, I have the honour to transmit to you
herewith the observations and comments of the Iraqi side concerning the report
on the third International Atomic Energy Agency (IAEA) on-site inspection in
Iraq, issued as Security Council document S/22837.

I should be grateful if you would arrange to have the text of this letter
and its annex circulated among the parties having an interest in the
aforementioned Security Council document.

(Signed)   Abdul Amir A. AL-ANBARI
Ambassador
Permanent Representative

91-25625 2505f (E)
()

0178

/...

<u>Annex</u>

[Original: English]

<u>Comments on the "Report on the third IAEA on-site inspection
in Iraq under Security Council resolution 687 (1991)"</u>

It is important to point out the following facts and comments relevant to the Report on the third IAEA on-site inspection in Iraq under Security Council resolution 687 (1991) document S/22837 of 25 July 1991.

1.   <u>SALIENT POINTS</u>

Para 3   The statement "The primary aims were stated to be development of ...
           nuclear power program".

           should read as follows:

               "The primary aims were stated to be to participate in the
               development of the country's scientific and technological
               infrastructure .... nuclear power program".

Para 6   The statement "A layer of concrete which had .... indeed
           been constructed for enrichment purposes".

           should read as follows:

               A layer of concrete which had been poured over a key component of
               the separators and the Iraqi side pointed it out as proof of the
               number of separators installed. The team then requested its removal
               and was able to confirm that the installation in question had indeed
               been constructed for enrichment purposes and only eight separators
               had been installed and operated in the first line whilst another 17
               were in the process of being installed in the second line and were
               never operated.

Para 8   The statement "on the basis of the design data ....
           more uranium of a lower enrichment"

           should be amended to the following:

               the design data presented by the Iraqi side showed that the average
               monthly throughput of each 1,200 mm separator would have been 2.0 kg
               of uranium. Assuming the feed material is the tetrachloride of
               natural uranium, then approximately 14.5 gm of $235U$ would be
               transported to the light receiver pocket per month. This mass would
               be contained within 121 gm of product uranium if the design
               enrichment of 12% is achieved. The separator hall could accommodate
               up to a maximum of 70 x 1,200 mm separators in two lines (each line

0179 /···

could accommodate a maximum of 35 units). If all of these separators were installed and working up to the design specifications, they would have produced 102 kg of uranium enriched to 12% per year (this product would contain 12.2 kg of the isotope 235U).

Para 9   The statement "the facility at Ash-Sharqat had .... completed, no separators had yet been installed."

should be amended to read as follows:

The facility at Ash-Sharqat had been originally intended as an alternate site to Tarmiya and since the Tarmiya site was completed first and the separators were installed at Tarmiya the Ash-Sharqat was abandoned as an EMIS site, it was later planned to utilize the site as a factory for the plastic coating of equipment. Most of the .... no separators had been installed.

2.   THE IRAQI ENRICHMENT PROGRAM

Para 4   The statement "Dr. Jafar noted .... for the development of nuclear weapons."

This statement should be amended to read as follows:

"Dr. Jafar noted that a capability to produce highly enriched uranium could be a possible option after installing both the 1,200 mm and 600 mm separators."

3.   URANIUM ENRICHMENT RESEARCH AND DEVELOPMENT AT AL-TUWAITHA

Research, development and testing of EMIS components were carried out in the Physics Building (80).

This should read as follows:

Research, development and testing of EMIS components were carried out in the Physics building (80) and in the first line of eight separator units in Tarmiya.

Please note: The title and contents of Para 7 should be changed accordingly.

Para 11   The statement "An eight separator system consisted of nine magnets had been installed in area A during January and February 1990".

This statement should read:

"An eight .... in area A between February and September 1990".

0180

/...

Para 12   The statement " .... This was removed at the team's request".

    This statement should read as in the modification suggested in Para 6 of section (1) above "Salient Points".

Para 17   The statement "A second Facility, a replica of Tarmiya" should read "a second facility as an alternate to Tarmiya ..."

    <u>Final Note</u>: Throughout the report it was mentioned that the design capacity of Tarmiya is up to 15 kg of highly enriched (93%) Uranium a year.

    We would like to point out that the design throughput, if all 70 separators, were installed, 12.2 kg 235U per year, and proportionately higher depending on the actual enrichment produced, so we would suggest that this figure should be corrected throughout the report.

0181

주 국 련 대 표 부

주국련20313-**654**   91. 8 . 21 .

수신 : 장관

참조 : 국제기구조약국장, 중동아프리카국장

제목 : 대이락 무기공급 금지 (안보리)

표제관련 안보리 문서를 별첨과 같이 송부합니다.

첨 부 : 상기 문서. 끝.

주   국   련   대   사

선 결			견재(공란)		
접수일시	1991. 8. 25	번호			
처리과	47644				

0182

UNITED NATIONS

Security Council

S

Distr.
GENERAL

S/22905
7 August 1991

ORIGINAL: ENGLISH

NOTE· VERBALE DATED 5 AUGUST 1991 FROM THE PERMANENT
REPRESENTATIVE OF TANZANIA TO THE UNITED NATIONS
ADDRESSED TO THE SECRETARY-GENERAL

The Permanent Representative of the United Republic of Tanzania to the
United Nations presents his compliments to the Secretary-General of the United
Nations and has the honour to refer to the Secretary-General's Note
SCPC/7/91 (4-1) of 3 July 1991 relating to Security Council resolution
700 (1991).

The Permanent Representative of the United Republic of Tanzania to the
United Nations has been instructed to state that before the adoption of
Security Council resolution 700 (1991), the Government of the United Republic
of Tanzania was already in full compliance with Security Council resolution
687 (1991). Following receipt of the Secretary-General's communication
referred to above and with reference to paragraph 5 of Security Council
resolution 700 (1991) and the guidelines prepared to facilitate the
implementation of paragraphs 24, 25 and 27 of Security Council resolution
687 (1991), the Government of the United Republic of Tanzania has reviewed the
measures it had instituted with a view to facilitating the implementation of
the resolution. It is satisfied that the United Republic of Tanzania remains
in full compliance with Security Council resolutions 687 (1991) and 700 (1991).

91-25429 2603j (E)

0183

UNITED NATIONS

Security Council

S

Distr.
GENERAL

S/22914
9 August 1991

ORIGINAL: ENGLISH

NOTE VERBALE DATED 8 AUGUST 1991 FROM THE PERMANENT
REPRESENTATIVE OF GERMANY TO THE UNITED NATIONS
ADDRESSED TO THE SECRETARY-GENERAL

The Permanent Representative of Germany to the United Nations presents his compliments to the Secretary-General of the United Nations and, with reference to his note SCPC/7/91 (4-1) dated 3 July 1991, has the honour to transmit the enclosed Report by the Federal Government of Germany on the Implementation of the Weapons Embargo against Iraq in accordance with paragraph 4 of Security Council resolution 700 (1991).

91-25779 2611j (E)

/...

0184

Annex

Report by the Federal Government on the implementation of the weapons embargo against Iraq in accordance with paragraph 4 of Security Council resolution 700 (1991)

In accordance with paragraph 4 of resolution 700 (1991) of the United Nations Security Council, all States are enjoined, in conjunction with section 8 of the Guidelines to Facilitate Full International Implementation of paragraphs 24, 25 and 27 of Security Council resolution 687 (1991) to report to the Secretary-General within 45 days on the measures undertaken to fulfil the commitments pursuant to paragraph 24 of Security Council resolution 687 (1991). The Federal Government submits herewith the corresponding report.

The measures called for by paragraph 24 of Security Council resolution 687 (1991) are specified in the Guidelines to Facilitate Full International Implementation of paragraphs 24, 25 and 27 of Security Council resolution 687 (1991) under nrs. 2 and 9. The following should be noted on these points in connection with German statutes on foreign trade and payments.

I. **Coverage of the various categories of prohibited items and activities under German statutes on foreign trade and payment (nr. 2 of the Guidelines)**

1. **Ad nr. 2 a), i)**

The group of products is covered by part I of the German export list, in particular by section A thereof and thus requires licensing for export.

Gaps in the list of goods cited under nr. 2 a), i) of the Guidelines are closed by means of the licensing requirement introduced in Section 5 c of the 14th Ordinance amending the Foreign Trade and Payments Ordinance of 11 March 1991. This stipulation means that the exportation of goods and documents for their production requires authorization if they are intended for construction or operation of a facility for exclusive or partial production, modernization, or maintenance of weapons, ammunition, or military equipment within the meaning of part I, section A of the export list or for installation in these items; if the purchaser, country of destination, or country in which the items are to be fitted is a country on the Country List H; and if the exporter is informed of this fact. On the Country List H are those countries which are particularly sensitive in terms of exports; Iraq is on the list.

2. **Ad nr. 2 a), II) to IV)**

As regards the group of goods cited here, it may be assumed that relevant substances, facilities, and components are fully subject to export licensing in accordance with German external economic law in keeping with the relevant international rules.

/...

0185

3.   Ad nr. 2 b)

     The extent to which the research, development and production facilities
cited under this number are to be covered by the weapons embargo is subject to
interpretation. The basic part of this equipment, however, is subject to
control by way of the position 0018* cited under part I, section A of the
German export list. A large part of the otherwise dual-use goods is subject
to controls by way of the just cited new licensing requirement pursuant to
section 5 c of the Foreign Trade and Payments Ordinance with the result that
compliance with the stipulations of the United Nations embargo is to be
expected.

4.   Ad nr. 2 c)

     In connection with this group of goods, it is to be presumed that the
embargo catalogue pursuant to paragraph 24 of Security Council resolution
687 (1991) is enacted in German legislation on foreign trade and payments
since the German provisions contain the international catalogue of goods to be
controlled.

---

     *   The following is covered under position 0018 of the German export
list:

     Facilities, parts of facilities, equipment and technology for the
production of goods cited in part I, section A of this list as follows and the
software particularly developed for such purposes:

     (a) Production facilities specially designed or reoutfitted for the
manufacture of the goods covered under part I, section A of this list as well
as specially designed components for such facilities;

     (b) Specially designed environment inspection facilities for testing the
licensing and suitability of the goods covered under part I, section A of this
list as well as the specially designed equipment for such facilities;

     (c) Specific production technologies, even if the equipment in which the
technologies is used is not covered;

     (d) Specific technologies for design, installation of components,
operation, maintenance and repair of entire production facilities, even if the
components themselves are not covered.

/...

0186

5. **Ad nr. 2 d)**

The basic technologies of relevance for the embargo are to be found on
the German export list, with the result that the exportation of such documents
is subject to licensing. In addition, section 45 of the Foreign Trade and
Payments Ordinance should be noted: subject to licensing is also the
transfer - if not occurring in the form of the exportation of documents - of
information, not generally available, on the production of certain sensitive
goods and on certain sensitive technologies, technical data, and technical
processes as well as the transfer of certain data-processing programs
(software), not generally available, to foreigners resident in a country that
is not a member of OECD.

6. **Ad nr. 2 e)**

Sensitive services are controlled in the Federal Republic of Germany on
the basis of section 45 b of the Foreign Trade and Payments Ordinance amended
by the 14th Ordinance to amend the Foreign Trade and Payments Ordinance of
11 March 1991. Subject to licensing according to the new version are services
provided by residents and non-resident Germans, that are related to goods from
part I, section A of the export list (weapons, ammunition and military
equipment) if they are provided in a country that is not a member of OECD.
Subject to licensing are further those services by residents and non-resident
Germans related to rockets, components specially designed for such rockets,
and specially developed computer programs; exceptions are projects of the
European Space Organization and services provided in a EEC member State or in
Australia, Canada, Japan, New Zealand, Norway, Turkey or in the United States
of America.

This particular licensing requirement for services thus applies to Iraq.
Services provided in its favour may be controlled in the sensitive areas.

II. **Principles for the Application of the Embargo Provisions (nr. 9 of the
     Guidelines)**

1. **Ad nr. 9 a)**

The prevention of circumvention exports has always been a particular
problem for export controls. In addition to the possibility, within the
framework of general prevention, to deter illegal exports by heavy penalties,
the only other means of preventing such circumvention exports is examination
of the final user of the exported product. This control of the final user is
provided for in German statutes on foreign trade and payments. Since a
similarity of the products to be controlled in all of the United Nations
member countries is to be assumed, the present system is basically adequate.
As a means to minimize circumvention exports, a restrictive export control
policy vis-à-vis certain countries is also worthy of consideration. This
particularly means that applications to export sensitive products to these
countries are regularly rejected.

/...

0187

2. Ad nr. 9 b)

The German export list, in addition to the already cited part I, section A (weapons, ammunition and military equipment), also has a section C, in which the special dual-use goods are covered. The embargo provisions on these dual-use goods are consequently implemented in German statutes on foreign trade and payments in so far as the respective goods are covered by section C of the export list. Furthermore, there is a control of dual-use products by way of a new statute (section 5 c of the Foreign Trade and Payments Ordinance) that was introduced in March 1991.

3. Ad nr. 9 c)

This number contains guidelines for the exportation of goods and for the transfer of know-how and services. With regard to the exportation of goods, note should be taken of the comments in the previous paragraph. As regards services, mention should again be made here of the already cited section 45 b of the Foreign Trade and Payments Ordinance. With reference to the transfer of know-how, we again call attention to the already cited section 45 of the Foreign Trade and Payments Ordinance with its licensing requirement for the transfer of specific, not generally available, information.

4. Ad nr. 9 d)

German statutes on foreign trade and payments are familiar with final user controls in connection with sensitive products (section 17 of the Foreign Trade and Payments Ordinance), in particular in the form of a control by the exporter. Incidentally, this control is supplemented by a restrictive export control policy towards certain countries and companies for which there are reasons to believe that they might continue to provide Iraq with items subject to the embargo.

5. Ad nr. 9 e)

In relevant cases, compliance with this provision is guaranteed by suitable final user controls.

6. Ad nr. 9 f)

The legal basis underlying this number of the embargo Guidelines may already be found in German statutes on foreign trade and payments. The customs authorities, who are responsible for controlling freight, post and transport, may examine goods intended for export at any time and, if necessary, seize such goods for closer inspection (sections 42, 44 and 46 of the Foreign Trade and Payments Act).

0188   /...

7.   **Ad nr. 9 g)**

The penalties corresponding to this number of the embargo Guidelines are provided for in German statutes on foreign trade and payments. Violations of the sanctions may be punished by administrative fine not to exceed 1 million DM and imprisonment of up to five years. Increasing the prison sentence to up to 15 years is planned within the context of a bill that the Federal Government has presented to the legislature.

III. Publication

The provisions of the Foreign Trade and Payments Ordinance cited above are published and explained in the Federal Gazette (Bundesanzeiger). In addition, the Federal Government maintains constant contact with the associations of German business and industry so as to inform them of the provisions and provide them with assistance in interpreting them.

IV. Conclusion

It may be concluded that German statutes on foreign trade and payments are in line with paragraph 24 of Security Council resolution 687 (1991) in conjunction with the embargo Guidelines. The Federal Government is willing to provide the committee with all of the information it might desire in this connection.

0189

UNITED
NATIONS

Security Council

S

Distr.
GENERAL

S/22915
9 August 1991

ORIGINAL: ENGLISH

NOTE VERBALE DATED 8 AUGUST 1991 FROM THE PERMANENT MISSION OF
INDIA TO THE UNITED NATIONS ADDRESSED TO THE SECRETARY-GENERAL

The Permanent Mission of India to the United Nations presents its
compliments to the Secretary-General and, with reference to the latter's note
of 3 July 1991, has the honour to state that the Government of India has been
observing the prohibitions contained in the relevant Security Council
resolutions, in particular those contained in paragraph 24 of resolution
687 (1991). The authorities concerned in India have been suitably instructed,
in accordance with Indian legislation in force, to ensure compliance with the
provisions contained in the aforementioned paragraph.

In accordance with the relevant Security Council resolutions, in
particular resolutions 661 (1990) and 687 (1991), the Government of India has
not entered into any military contracts in any form with Iraq or its agents.

0190

91-25773 2628d (E)

**UNITED
NATIONS**

Security Council

Distr.
GENERAL

S/22919
9 August 1991

ORIGINAL: ENGLISH

NOTE VERBALE DATED 8 AUGUST 1991 FROM THE PERMANENT
REPRESENTATIVE OF PAKISTAN TO THE UNITED NATIONS
ADDRESSED TO THE SECRETARY-GENERAL

The Permanent Representative of Pakistan to the United Nations presents his compliments to the Secretary-General of the United Nations and, with reference to his note No. SCPC/7/91/4-1 of 3 July 1991, has the honour to transmit herewith the response of the Government of Pakistan.

I should be grateful if this letter and its annex could be circulated as a document of the Security Council.

(Signed) Jamsheed K. A. MARKER
Ambassador and Permanent Representative

91-25846   2514g (E)

0191   /...

Annex

Response of the Government of Pakistan to Secretary-General of the United Nations note No. SCPC/7/91/4-1 of 3 July 1991

Upon adoption of Security Council resolution 687 (1991), its contents were brought, under appropriate notification, to the attention of all concerned departments of the Government of Pakistan, for full implementation of provisions contained therein.

Relating specifically to the field of defence, all organizations of the Government of Pakistan functioning under the relevant defence authorities are complying fully with the obligations set out in paragraph 24 of resolution 687 (1991).

0192

**UNITED
NATIONS**

Security Council

S

Distr.
GENERAL

S/22922
12 August 1991

ORIGINAL: ENGLISH

LETTER DATED 9 AUGUST 1991 FROM THE PERMANENT REPRESENTATIVE OF
CANADA TO THE UNITED NATIONS ADDRESSED TO THE SECRETARY-GENERAL

In response to your note SCPC/7/91(4-1) of 3 July 1991, I have the honour
to provide the following information regarding the measures taken by the
Government of Canada to implement paragraph 4 of Security Council resolution
700 (1991).

(Signed) L. Yves FORTIER, C.C., Q.C.
Ambassador and
Permanent Representative

91-25951 2778b (E)

0193   /...

Annex

Measures taken by the Government of Canada on the implementation of paragraph 24 of resolution 687 (1991)

Paragraph 4 of resolution 700 (1991) of 17 June 1991, requests all States, in accordance with paragraph 8 of the Guidelines, to report to the Secretary-General, on the measures instituted for meeting the obligations set out in paragraph 24 of Security Council resolution 687 (1991). The Government of Canada meets its international obligations pursuant to various Security Council resolutions through the provisions of the United Nations Iraq Regulations (UNIR) made pursuant to Section 2 of the United Nations Act, R.S.C.1985, c. U-2. The Export and Import Permits Act also contains provisions applicable to items identified in paragraph 24 of resolution 687 (1991) and prevents such items from being exported to Iraq.

The UNIR were put in place by Order in Council P.C. 1990-1676 of 7 August 1990 to give effect to resolution 661 (1990) of 6 August 1990. The UNIR were amended by Order in Council P.C. 1990-2158 of 1 October 1990, to give effect to resolution 670 (1990) of 25 September 1990 and further amended by Order in Council P.C. 1991-431 of 6 March 1991 to give effect to resolution 686 (1991) of 2 March 1991. Copies of the relevant legislation and of the UNIR are attached.*

The UNIR as amended:

- impose an embargo on the export of goods to Iraq;

- impose an embargo on the import of goods originating in Iraq that are exported therefrom after 6 August 1990;

- prevent the sale or supply of all goods originating in Iraq that are exported therefrom after 6 August 1990;

- prevent the sale or supply of goods to Iraq;

- freeze Iraqi government assets;

- prevent all Canadians from entering into financial transactions with Iraqi interests;

- prohibit an operator of an aircraft registered in Canada from carrying goods to and from Iraq;

---

*   Copies of the legislation may be consulted in room S-3520.

0194   /...

- prohibit any person in Canada from operating an aircraft with the knowledge that it is intended that the aircraft concerned will be used to carry goods to and from Iraq;

- prohibit the overflight of Canada by any aircraft that is destined to land in Iraq, unless the aircraft was inspected and it was verified that no goods were being carried on board in contravention of the implementing measures adopted by Member States to give effect to United Nations Security Council resolutions 661 (1990) and 670 (1990); and

- prohibit the entry into Canadian ports of ships registered in Iraq that are or have been used in contravention of the measures against Iraq of United Nations Security Council resolutions 661 (1990) and 670 (1990), except in emergency situations to safeguard human life, and should any such Iraqi ships enter a Canadian port, order the detaining of such ships.

Section 8 of the UNIR provides that every person who contravenes any provision of the UNIR is guilty of an offence and liable to fines or/and imprisonment. Officers, directors or agents of a corporation that is subject to the UNIR are liable if they are involved in the commission of an offence by the corporation.

Subsection 3(2) of the United Nations Act provides that any goods, wares or merchandise dealt with contrary to any order or regulation made under its authority may be seized and detained and are liable to forfeiture at the instance of the Minister of Justice of Canada, on proceedings in the competent court.

Pursuant to section 9 of the UNIR, acts or things that would otherwise constitute an offence are not prohibited if the Secretary of State for External Affairs certifies in advance that:

"(a) the Security Council Resolutions do not intend that such acts or things be prohibited, or

(b) such acts or things have been approved by the United Nations Security Council or the Committee of the Security Council established by United Nations Security Council Resolution 661 (1990) of August 6, 1990."

On the basis of the decision of 22 March 1991, of the Committee of the Security Council, which made a general determination that humanitarian circumstances apply with respect to the entire civilian population of Iraq in all parts of Iraq's national territory and accordingly decided to authorize the supply of foodstuffs to Iraq on a simple notification procedure, the Secretary of State for External Affairs, pursuant to section 9 of the UNIR, on 27 March 1991, issued a General certificate authorizing the following acts with respect of donations of foodstuffs and medical supplies to Iraq: export, transport, shipment or transshipment, carriage by a Canadian ship, carriage by

0195 /...

an aircraft registered in Canada, or carriage by an aircraft operated over the territory of Canada, subject to the prior notification procedure. Since 27 March 1991, proposals for commercial sales of foodstuffs and medical supplies to Iraq are considered on a case-by-case basis. This applies to sales or supply of materials and supplies for essential civilian or humanitarian needs, and related financial transactions, as approved by the Committee under the simplified and accelerated "no-objections" procedure. This decision of the Committee was confirmed by paragraph 20 of resolution 687 (1991) of 3 April 1991.

0196

Security Council

Distr.
GENERAL

S/22923
12 August 1991

ORIGINAL: ENGLISH

NOTE VERBALE DATED 9 AUGUST 1991 FROM THE PERMANENT MISSION
OF BULGARIA TO THE UNITED NATIONS ADDRESSED TO THE
SECRETARY-GENERAL

The Permanent Representative of the Republic of Bulgaria to the United
Nations presents his compliments to the Secretary-General of the United
Nations, and with reference to the Secretary-General's note SCPC/7/91 (4-1) of
3 July 1991 related to Security Council resolution 700 (1991), has the honour
to transmit the following:

Bulgaria is abiding strictly by all resolutions of the Security Council
of the United Nations related to the Persian Gulf crisis and is firmly
adhering to the international economic sanctions against Iraq. The Bulgarian
Government has already undertaken concrete steps in this respect. The Council
of Ministers has issued two decrees (number 90 of 13 August 1991 and
number 104 of 22 October 1990) on halting trade, financial operations and
transportation links with Iraq mandatory for all Bulgarian organizations and
companies. The implementation of the provisions contained therein is
monitored by the competent State authorities.

Bulgaria had terminated the sale and supply of arms to Iraq even before
2 August 1990. In implementing the obligations for Member States under
resolutions 687 (1991) and 700 (1991), the Government of the Republic of
Bulgaria is currently preparing a decree that, after its adoption, would
implement in the country's legislation the principles enunciated in
paragraphs 24, 25 and 27 of Security Council resolution 687 (1991).

Bulgaria is convinced that the Security Council resolutions on the
situation between Iraq and Kuwait will make a substantial contribution to
strengthening security and stability in that part of the world, and is
prepared to actively assist in their implementation.

91-25957 2536h (E)

0197

Security Council

Distr.
GENERAL

S/22924
12 August 1991

ORIGINAL: ENGLISH

NOTE VERBALE DATED 9 AUGUST 1991 FROM THE PERMANENT
MISSION OF CYPRUS TO THE UNITED NATIONS ADDRESSED
TO THE SECRETARY-GENERAL

The Permanent Mission of the Republic of Cyprus to the United Nations
presents its compliments to the Secretary-General of the United Nations and
with reference to his Note No. SPC/7/91/(4-1) of 3 July 1991, has the honour
to transmit the following information:

(a) The Government of the Republic of Cyprus fully implements all
resolutions of the United Nations.

(b) In particular concerning Security Council resolutions 687 (1991) and
700 (1991) the Government prevents the sale or supply of arms and related
material, or the promotion or facilitation of such sale or supply to Iraq by
its nationals, or from its territory or using its flag vessels or aircraft as
called for in paragraph 24 of resolution 687 (1991) and as set out in the
guidelines of the Secretary-General approved by the Security Council in its
resolution 700 (1991).

(c) Resolution 700 (1991) of the Security Council, and the report of the
Secretary-General (S/22660) which contains the approved guidelines of the
Secretary-General to facilitate full implementation of paragraphs 24, 25 and
27 of Security Council resolution 687 (1991) have been brought to the
attention of the appropriate authorities of the Government of the Republic of
Cyprus.

91-26017 2537h (E)

0198

Security Council

Distr.
GENERAL

S/22935
13 August 1991
ENGLISH
ORIGINAL: SPANISH

NOTE VERBALE DATED 13 AUGUST 1991 FROM THE PERMANENT MISSION
OF COLOMBIA TO THE UNITED NATIONS ADDRESSED TO THE
SECRETARY-GENERAL

The Permanent Mission of Colombia to the United Nations presents its
compliments to the Secretary-General of the United Nations and, with reference
to document SCPC/7/91 (4-1) of 3 July 1991, wishes to state that the Republic
of Colombia, in keeping with its tradition of respect for the international
legal order, has faithfully implemented the provisions of the resolutions
adopted by the Security Council, particularly resolutions 687 (1991) and
700 (1991), relating to the situation between Iraq and Kuwait.

Colombia, which in its foreign policy endorses decisions that promote
disarmament, does not sell weapons or technology for their manufacture to Iraq
or any other country.

The Political Constitution of Colombia, which has been in force since
7 July 1991, stipulates in article 223 that: "Only the Government may
introduce and manufacture weapons, ammunition and explosives. No one may
possess them or bear them without the permission of the competent authority."

91-26182 2441c (E)

0199

UNITED NATIONS

Security Council

S

Distr.
GENERAL

S/22936
13 August 1991

ORIGINAL: ENGLISH

NOTE VERBALE DATED 13 AUGUST 1991 FROM THE PERMANENT
MISSION OF MALAYSIA TO THE UNITED NATIONS ADDRESSED
TO THE SECRETARY-GENERAL

    The Permanent Mission of Malaysia to the United Nations presents its
compliments to the Secretary-General of the United Nations and with reference
to the latter's Note of 3 July 1991, has the honour to inform the
Secretary-General that the Government of Malaysia has been observing the
prohibitions contained in resolution 687 (1991) and is satisfied that the laws
of Malaysia are adequate to ensure the compliance of those provisions.

    In accordance with the relevant Security Council resolutions, in
particular, resolutions 661 (1990) and 687 (1991), the Government of Malaysia
has not entered into any military contracts in any form with Iraq or its
agents.

91-26210 3190a (E)

0200

Security Council

Distr.
GENERAL

S/22938
14 August 1991
ENGLISH
ORIGINAL: SPANISH

NOTE VERBALE DATED 13 AUGUST 1991 FROM THE PERMANENT MISSION
OF MEXICO TO THE UNITED NATIONS ADDRESSED TO THE
SECRETARY-GENERAL

The Permanent Mission of Mexico to the United Nations presents its compliments to the Secretary-General of the United Nations and, with reference to the latter's note SCPC/7/91 of 3 July 1991, concerning Security Council resolution 700 (1991), has the honour to communicate the following information:

The Government of Mexico, seeking to discharge fully its obligations under the terms of paragraph 24 of Security Council resolution 687 (1991), has continued to implement scrupulously the measures adopted in accordance with Security Council resolution 661 (1991).

To this end, the Government of Mexico has maintained close communication and coordination between the Ministries of Foreign Affairs, Commerce, Transport and Communications, and Finance, as well as between other government offices, with a view to ensuring that the provisions of the Security Council resolutions are not violated.

Finally, it should also be noted in the context of paragraph 24 of resolution 687 (1991) that Mexico, in keeping with its traditional policy in support of general and complete disarmament, has no export weapons industry, nor does it promote or facilitate the sale or supply of arms or related matériel of any type. Likewise, Mexico neither promotes nor facilitates personnel or materials for training or technical support services relating to the design, development, manufacture, use, maintenance or support of any type of weapons or related materials.

0201

91-26314 2570e (E)

UNITED NATIONS

Security Council

S

Distr.
GENERAL

S/22949
15 August 1991

ORIGINAL: ENGLISH

NOTE VERBALE DATED 15 AUGUST 1991 FROM THE CHARGE D'AFFAIRES A.I.
OF THE PERMANENT MISSION OF SOUTH AFRICA TO THE UNITED NATIONS
ADDRESSED TO THE SECRETARY-GENERAL

The Chargé d'affaires a.i. of the Republic of South Africa to the United
Nations presents his compliments to the Secretary-General of the United
Nations and, with reference to the latter's Note SCPC/7/91 (4-1) dated
3 July 1991, has the honour to inform the Secretary-General that the
arrangements made to comply with Security Council resolution 661 (1990),
details of which were contained in the Permanent Representative's Note 8/3/2
over 9/1/7/3 of 30 November 1990, remain in force. These regulations will
also apply to the provisions of paragraph 24 of Security Council resolution
687 (1991).

Because the South African Government took a specific Cabinet decision on
22 August 1990 to abide by the Security Council decisions, regarding sanctions
against Iraq, these regulations will also be enforced until such time as the
Security Council changes its previous decisions in this regard.

91-26553 2645d (E)

0202

UNITED
NATIONS

S

Security Council

Distr.
GENERAL

S/22952
16 August 1991
ENGLISH
ORIGINAL: ARABIC

NOTE DATED 14 AUGUST 1991 FROM THE PERMANENT MISSION OF BAHRAIN
TO THE UNITED NATIONS ADDRESSED TO THE SECRETARY-GENERAL

The Permanent Mission of Bahrain to the United Nations presents its compliments to the Secretary-General and, with reference to his note No. SCPC/7/91 (4-1) of 3 July 1991 concerning the implementation of paragraph 24 of Security Council resolution 687 (1991) and of Security Council resolution 700 (1991), has the honour to state that Bahrain has adhered to the implementation of the boycott in all its forms and at all governmental and non-governmental levels and that it continues to adhere to its implementation up to the present moment. The boycott extends to the following:

1. Freezing of Iraqi deposits and of banking operations.

2. A halt to land, sea and air travel between the two countries.

3. Prohibition of importation from or exportation to Iraq.

4. Prohibition of all forms of technical cooperation.

UNITED
NATIONS

S

Security Council

Distr.
GENERAL

S/22964
20 August 1991

ORIGINAL: ENGLISH

NOTE VERBALE DATED 19 AUGUST 1991 FROM THE PERMANENT
REPRESENTATIVE OF THE ISLAMIC REPUBLIC OF IRAN TO THE
UNITED NATIONS ADDRESSED TO THE SECRETARY-GENERAL

The Permanent Representative of the Islamic Republic of Iran to the
United Nations presents his compliments to the Secretary-General of the United
Nations and with reference to the latter's note No. SPC/7/91(4-1) of
3 July 1991 has the honour to state the following:

The Government of the Islamic Republic of Iran has been observing the
relevant resolutions of the Security Council related to the Persian Gulf
crisis in particular those provisions contained in paragraph 24 of resolution
687 (1991). The executive orders of the Supreme National Security Council of
the Islamic Republic of Iran to ensure the full implementation of the relevant
provisions of resolution 661 (1990) as reflected in document S/AC.25/1990/38
continue to apply today and no decision has been made to cancel them.
Accordingly, the concerned authorities have been duly instructed to ensure the
full compliance with the prohibition set out in resolutions 661 (1990) and
687 (1991).

91-27037 2558h (E)

0204

외 무 부

종 별 :

번 호 : UNW-2244   일 시 : 91 0822 1830

수 신 : 장 관(국연,중동일,기정)

발 신 : 주 유엔 대사

제 목 : 걸프사태(이락특정무기폐기)

　　금 8.22 유엔측이 발표한 이락특정무기폐기 추진동향을 별첨송부함.

　　첨부:상기동향: UNW(F)-450 끝

　　(대사 노창희-국장)

국기국　　1차보　　중아국　　외정실　　안기부

UNW(刊)-450 10月11 18?°

(국면.중동원.기정)   NOTE FOR THE SPOKESMAN   5/10허

Special Commission Inspection Schedule Update

Thursday 22 August 1991

Here follows a comprehensive list of missions carried out by the Special Commission created by Resolution 687 to oversee the disarmament of Iraq. Some future dates are included.

Nuclear

15-21 May	1st inspection mission
22 June-3 July	2nd inspection mission
30 June-3 July	high-level mission (on denied access)
7-18 July	3rd inspection mission
27 July-10 August	4th inspection mission

Chemical

9-15 June	1st inspection mission (survey)
11-14 August	sp. mission (destruction techniques)
15-22 August	2nd inspection mission (precursors)
30 August-7 Sept	3rd inspection mission
30 August-5 Sept	4th inspection mission

Biological

2-8 August	1st inspection mission
20-27 September	2nd inspection mission

Ballistic missiles

30 June-7 July	1st inspection (and destruction)
18-20 July	2nd (surprise) inspection & destruct.
8-15 Aug	3rd mission (incl. "super gun")
5-12 September	4th inspection mission

Future missions

Nuclear: Will continue.

Chemical: "Super" mission to Muthanna site end September involving more than 70 inspectors.

Biological: Will continue.

Ballistic missiles: Fifth mission will include a closer inspection of the "super gun".

F. Eckhard

fg3-61

UNW-2244
훈녹

1-1

0206

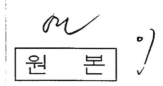

외 무 부

종 별 :

번 호 : UNW-2273 일 시 : 91 0823 2000

수 신 : 장 관(국연,중동일,기정)

발 신 : 주 유엔 대사

제 목 : 걸프사태(이락 화학무기 폐기)

　　유엔측 발표에 의하면, 유엔이락 화학무기 조사반이 지난 8.11-14 간 이락을 방문코 이란당국과 화학무기 폐기과정에의 이락참여 문제를 토의하였으며, 앞으로는 조사단계에서 폐기준비단계로 이행예정이라고함.

　　첨부:유엔측 발표내용: UNW(F)-457 끝

　　(대사 노창희-국장)

국기국　　1차보　　중아국　　외정실　　분석관　　안기부

PAGE 1

The following is issued by the Special Commission created Security
Council resolution 687.

UNW(FD)-457 /8/23 200
(국연. 중동일. 기정)
총/09

CW Destruction Mission to Iraq

Consistent with the requirement of resolution 687 (1991)
regarding the destruction, removal or otherwise rendering
harmless of Iraq's CW assets, a team of experts led by
Mr. J. Molander from the Special Commission visited Iraq on a
fact-finding mission 11-14 August to discuss with the Iraqi
authorities the possible options for direct Iraqi involvement in
a CW-destruction programme under appropriate Special Commission
control.

The discussions held in Baghdad 11-14 August, inclusive,
were based on a detailed analysis prepared by a panel of experts
which had met at UN Headquarters, and on the Iraqi offer of
9 June to carry out the process of destruction (document
S/22682). There were also short visits paid to the Muthanna
State Establishment and to a chlorination plant at Al Fallujah.

The subjects discussed in detail and on which expert views
were exchanged, included the interlinked topics of collection and
transport, defuzing and rendering munitions explosively harmless
and checking that munitions were defuzed and explosively inert;
breaching and draining of munitions; destruction of unfilled and
emptied munitions; destruction of CW agents and precursors.
Considerable progress was made in identifying potential Iraqi
contribution to all these aspects of the overall destruction
programme and in identifying the scope for direct Iraqi
participation in that programme. The discussions were carried
out in a positive atmosphere which undoubtedly contributed to the
progress made and the understanding achieved.

The Special Commission has, so far in the area of CW, given
priority to the survey, inspection and recording of Iraq's CW
assets. Besides continuing to inspect undeclared sites in order
to establish that all CW assets have been declared, the
Commission will now concentrate its inspection efforts at
declared sites with a view to preparing munitions and agents for
destruction.

22 August 1991

1—1

0208

분류기호 문서번호	중동일 720-	기 안 용 지 (720-2327)		시 행 상 특별취급	
보존기간	영구.준영구 10. 5. 3. 1	차 관		장 관	
수 신 처 보존기간					
시행일자	1991. 8. 28.				

보조기관	국 장	전결	협조기관	제1차관보 국제기구조약국장	문 서 통 제	
	심의관					
	과 장					
기안책임자		주 복 룡			발 송 인	

경 유		발신명의	
수 신	내부결재		
참 조			

제 목	대이라크 무기 공급 금지관련 각국의 조치사항 통보

1. UN 안보리는 대이라크 휴전 결의인 결의안 제687호(91.4.3)의

   제24조, 25조 및 27조에 의거, 각국이 이라크에 대하여 무기 및

   관련 물품을 공급치 않을 것을 준수토록 요구하고 있으며, 결의안

   제700호(91.6.17)는 이와 관련하여 각국이 취한 조치를 UN사무총장에

   통보하도록 결의한바 있습니다. (시한 : 91.8.1)

2. 상기와 관련, 91.8.20. 현재 45개국이 자국이 취한 조치와 관련된

   내용을 UN 사무총장에 통보해온바(미국, 소련은 상금 미통보),

   우리도 UN 대표부를 통하여 우리가 취한 조치 내용을 / 계속 . . .

더맑은 마음을, 더밝은 사회를, 더넓은 미래를

0209

별첨 문안으로 UN 사무총장에 통보토록 할것을 건의하오니 재가

하여 주시기 바랍니다.

첨 부 : 동 통보내용 문안(영문) 1부.   끝.

더맑은 마음을, 더밝은 사회를, 더넓은 미래를

0210

The Permanent Representative of the Republic of Korea to the
United Nations presents its compliments to the Secretary-General
of the United Nations and, with reference to his note SCPC/7/91
(4-1) of 3 July 1991, has the honour to inform him that the
Government of the Republic of Korea is abiding by Resolutions
687(1991) and 700(1991) concerning the prevention of the sale
or supply of arms and related material to Iraq or Iraqi
nationals and the competent authorities have also taken domestic
measures to ensure the implementation of the relevant provisions
of the said resolutions.

0211

UN 결의안 700호관련 자국조치사항 통보 국가 (91.8.현재)

가. <u>아 주(11)</u>

일본, 중국, 태국, 말레이지아, 싱가폴, 호주, 뉴질랜드, 인도,
파키스탄, 스리랑카, 미얀마

나. <u>미 주(7)</u>

카나다, 멕시코, 브라질, 아르헨티나, 콜롬비아, 칠레, 에쿠아돌

다. <u>구 주(22)</u>

영국, 프랑스, 독일, 이태리, 벨기에, 화란, 스페인, 아일랜드,
희랍, 오지리, 스웨덴, 노르웨이, 핀랜드, 교황청, 싸이프러스,
몰타, 리히텐슈타인, 유고, 체코, 헝가리, 불가리아, 터어키

라. <u>아.중동(5)</u>

이란, 바레인, 이스라엘, 탄자니아, 남아공

0212

별상1

무 정   28110- 1349   (503-9432)   1990.8.20.
수 신   수신처참조   무역 정책과.
제 목   대이라크 무역특별조치 실시

　　　　대외무역법 제4조의 규정에 의거 다음과 같이 무역에 관한 특별조치를
실시하니 관련업무 수행에 만전을 기하시기 바랍니다.
　　　　　　　　　　　　　　다　　음

　　1. 특별조치의 내용 : 다음의 경우는 수출.수입승인 중지

　　　　ㅇ 이라크 또는 쿠웨이트를 원산지 또는 선적항으로 하는 수입

　　　　ㅇ 이라크 또는 쿠웨이트를 도착항으로 하는 수출

　　2. 대상물품 : 한국통일상품분류(HSK) 고시품목 전체

　　3. 시행기간 : '90.8.22부터 상공부장관이 별도 통보하는 시기까지

　　4. 기 타

　　　　ㅇ 의약품등 인도적소요에 해당하는 물품에 대하여는 제1호 및
제2호에 불구하고 상공부장관의 허가를 얻어 수출승인할 수 있음.

　　　　ㅇ 이상 언급한 사항이외의 수출.수입에 관한 사항에 대하여는
원칙적으로 대외무역관리규정에 따르며, 필요시 상공부(무역정책과)에 문의하여
처리함. 끝.

　　　　　　　　　　상　　공　　부　　장　　관

수신처 : 외무부장관, 재무부장관, 농림수산부장관, 동력자원부장관, 건설부장관,
보건사회부장관, 교통부장관, 관세청장, 세관장, 산림청장, 수산청장, 수출
자유지역관리소장, 한국은행총재, 외국환은행장, 대한무역진흥공사장, 한국
무역협회장, 한국무역대리점협회장, 한국수출품구매업자협회장, 각수출입
조합장, 국방부장관.

접수일시	1990. 8.22	번호		결재 (공람)
처리과			23206	

0213

가. 조치형식

　　　ㅇ 상공부장관이 대외무역법 제4조에 의거 EL(Export License), IL
　　UUK-1401　900822 1733 DY
　　　(Import License) 발급권한이 위임되어 있는 외국환은행장에게

　　　동 발급중지 조치를 시달하고, 세관당국등 관계부처에 이를 통보

　　　* 대외무역법 4조

　　　　- 상공부장관은 무역상대국에 전쟁, 사변 또는 천재지변이

　　　　　있을시 수출, 수입의 제한 또는 금지에 관한 특별조치 가능

나. 조치내용

　　1) 수출·입 승인 중지

　　　ㅇ 이라크 또는 쿠웨이트를 원산지 또는 선적항으로 하는 수입승인 중지

　　　ㅇ 이라크 또는 쿠웨이트를 도착지로 하는 수출 승인 중지

　　2) 대상 품목

　　　ㅇ 전품목에 대해 수출·입 승인 중지

　　　　- 단, 의약품등 인도적 소요에 해당하는 물품에 대하여는 상공부

　　　　　장관의 허가를 얻어 수출승인 가능

　　3) 실시 시기

　　　ㅇ 90.8.22부터 상공부장관이 별도 통보하는 시기까지

3. 아국정부는 그간 소련, 중국등 공산권 국가 및 이란·이라크(교전국),
　　남아공등 19개 특수국가와의 교역통계는 대북한 관계, 외교적 고려등을
　　감안, 대외공표를 하지 않고 3급비밀로 분류하여 왔으나 최근 북방외교
　　진전, 이란·이라크 전 종결등 상황변화에 따라 남아공등 일부국가를
　　제외한 여타 특수국가와의 교역통계를 대외발표하도록 관세청에서 교역
　　통계관리제도 개선방안을 검토중에 있음. 끝.

예간: 90.12.31.까지　　　　　　　　　　　　　　　(통상국장 김삼훈)

0214

페만사태 관련 안보리 결의

결의안 표결일자	결 의 주 요 내 용	표결결과 (찬:반:기권)	결의번호
90.8.2.	ㅇ 이락의 쿠웨이트 침공 규탄 및 이락군의 무조건 철수 촉구	14:0:0	660 (1990)
8.6.	ㅇ 이락에 대한 광법위한 경제제재 조치 결정 - 안보이사회내에 제재위원회 설치 - 유엔비회원국 포함 모든국가의 661호 이행 촉구	13:0:2 (쿠바,예멘)	661
8.9.	ㅇ 이락의 쿠웨이트 합병 무효 간주 ㅇ 쿠웨이트 신정부 승인 금지	15:0:0	662
8.18.	ㅇ 이락,쿠웨이트내 제3국민들의 즉각 출국허용 요구 ㅇ 외국 공관폐쇄 철회 요구	15:0:0	664
8.25.	ㅇ 결의 661호 위반 선박에 대한 조치 권한 부여	13:0:2	665
9.13.	ㅇ 인도적 목적의 대이락 식품 수출 제한적 승인	13:0:2	665
9.16.	ㅇ 쿠웨이트주재 외국공관 침입 비난 ㅇ 외국공관원 즉시 석방 및 보호 요구	15:0:0	667
9.24.	ㅇ 대이락 제재조치에 따른 피해국 지원	15:0:0	669
9.25.	ㅇ 모든국가의 이락 및 쿠웨이트내 공항 이착륙 및 영공통과 불허 (인도적 식품 및 의약품운송 제외) ㅇ 모든국가에 의한 이락 국적선박 억류 허용	14:1:0 (쿠바)	670
10.29.	ㅇ 이락의 쿠웨이트 침공으로 인한 전쟁피해 및 재정적 손실에 대한 이락의 책임 규정 및 추궁	13:0:2 (쿠바,예멘)	674
11.28.	ㅇ 이락에 의한 쿠웨이트국민의 국적 말소기도 비난 ㅇ 쿠웨이트 인구센서스 기록의 유엔내 보존	미확인	677
11.29.	ㅇ 이락이 91.1.15한 상기 안보리 재결의를 이행치 않을 경우, 유엔 회원국에게 필요한 모든조치를 취할 수 있도록 허용	12:2:1 (쿠바,예멘) (중국)	678

- 686
0215 - 687

외   무   부

종   별 :

번   호 : UNW-2408   일   시 : 91 0903 1920

수   신 : 장 관(국연,중동일,국기,기정)

발   신 : 주 유엔 대사

제   목 : 걸프사태(이락 핵사찰)

  유엔 제4차 이락 핵사찰 (91.7.27-8.10) 결과 보고서가 금 9.3. 안보리 문서로 배포된 바, 동보고서중 요지부분을 발췌송부함.

  첨부:상기핵사찰 보고서: UNW(F)-498 끝

  (대사 노창희-국장)

UNW(FI)-49A 10903 1920
(국연. 중중일. 국기. 기정) 총2매

S/22986
English
Page 3

Enclosure

**REPORT ON THE FOURTH IAEA ON-SITE INSPECTION IN IRAQ
UNDER SECURITY COUNCIL RESOLUTION 687 (1991)**

27 July-10 August 1991

Salient Points

- The team was given full access to all designated sites, and the attitude of the Iraqi side continued to be as co-operative as in the course of the third inspection. Reticence was, however, noted as regards the disclosure of the procurement sources of equipment and material relevant to the centrifuge enrichment project. Deceptive behaviour was admitted in at least one instance in the course of the third inspection.

- Extensive information in response to intense questioning was gathered, and a large number of documents in the form of reports, detailed fabrication drawings and computer printout records of laboratory experiments were brought to Vienna for further analysis.

- On the first inspection day the Iraqi representative handed over to the team a list of nuclear materials which included items not previously declared. It confirmed the existence of a clandestine programme to i) manufacture several kilograms of uranium oxide fuel, ii) irradiate it in the IRT-5000 reactor and iii) reprocess the irradiated fuel in order to chemically separate gram amounts of plutonium.

- It is now certain that the Electro-Magnetic Isotope Separation (EMIS) approach to uranium enrichment was given priority and that the relevant project was fast-paced and had achieved the stage of initial industrial production at the Tarmiya establishment. The visit to several heavy mechanical production facilities used for the local fabrication of EMIS components indicated that their likely production rates were consistent with the Iraqi-stated amounts of EMIS equipment produced before the production facilities had been bombed. The production of uranium tetrachloride (EMIS feed material) would have been more or less sufficient to cover the needs of Tarmiya once the latter had reached full operation at the design capacity. The plan for Tarmiya was to bring on line a production facility of 90 separators which, with an average availability of 55%, could have produced 15 kg of highly enriched uranium (HEU) per annum using natural uranium as feed. An increase in separator availability, as a consequence of improvements in the systems, with a corresponding increase in the annual production of HEU, was deemed possible by the Iraqis.

- Iraq supplied the third inspection team with limited information on the magnitude of their centrifuge enrichment programme. A priority task of the fourth team was to obtain a more comprehensive picture of the Iraqi efforts in this area, including details of the overall plan and direction of the programme. The team was provided with an overall project plan showing key dates. According to this plan, following mechanical and functional trials on different models (1987-1991) a facility for centrifuge production would have started operation at the end of 1991. A 100-machine cascade would have been in operation in 1993 and a 500-machine cascade would have gone on stream in 1996. The team was able to visit the production facility of the Al Furat Project (the code name of this programme) at a site close to An Walid, 20 km south of Baghdad, a complex consisting of four buildings, two of them new. This complex had not suffered any attacks during the war, nor was it previously known as a nuclear-related site.

=UNW-24이
청먁

2-1

/...

0217

S/22986
English
Page 4

Although machine tools for manufacturing the centrifuges had not yet been installed (they had been procured but were dispersed to protect them against possible air attacks around the 25 July 1991 deadline), from the dimensions of this centrifuge production facility the team concluded that, once in full operation, the facility could easily have turned out 600 centrifuges per annum with the equipment already procured for this site.

- Extensive inspection work was carried out at the Al Jesira chemical production facility in the Mosul area, first designated by the Special Commission during the third inspection. This facility, which was heavily damaged by the bombing and by the salvaging-deception activities undertaken afterwards, housed the UO_2 and UCl_4 production lines and was the intended site for the production of UF_6 to feed the centrifuge enrichment project.

- No conclusive evidence was obtained as to the existence of weaponization activities.

2-2

0218

외 무 부

종 별 :

번 호 : UNW-2427   일 시 : 91 0904 1800

수 신 : 장 관(국연,중동일,국기,기정)

발 신 : 주 유엔 대사

제 목 : 걸프사태(안보리동향)

연: UNW-2347

1. BUBIYAN 섬 출돌사건

가. 케야르 사무총장은 유엔 이락.쿠웨이트 옵서버단 (UNIKOM) 활동 정기보고서를 안보리에 9.3.자로 제출해온바, 동보고서 (S/23000) 에 포함된 연호 BUBIYAN 섬 충돌사건 관련 내용을 별첨송부함.

나. 상기 보고서에 의하면 지난 8.28 오후 쿠웨이트 하안경비대가 이락어선 11척, 스피드보트 1척, 승선자 45명을 부비안섬앞 해상에서 나포하였으며, 동승선자 일부가 부비안섬에서 탄약등을 수거하였음은 확인되었으나, 부비안섬으로부터의 총격, 이락해군 스피드보트 출동, 부비안섬앞 보트잔해 발생경위 등에 대해서는 확인되지 않고있다함.

2. 이락 핵사찰

핵문제 관련 안보리의 이락 규탄결의 (707 호) 를 반박하는 A.HUSSEIN 이락외상의 8.28 자 사무총장앞 서한이 금 9.4. 안보리문서로 배포됨.(S/22998)

첨부:사무총장보고서 및 이락측 안보리문서:UNW(F)-499 끝

(대사 노창희-국장)

S/23000
English
Page 4

UNW(F)-499 0904 1800
(국연 중동일 국기 기정)   총504

13. In the afternoon of 28 August 1991, UNIKOM was informed by a Kuwaiti army liaison officer that there had been an incident involving firing between Iraqi and Kuwaiti personnel on, and in the vicinity of, the Kuwaiti island of Bubiyan, outside the DMZ. The incident has been the subject of communications addressed to the President of the Security Council by the Permanent Representative of Kuwait (S/22990) and by the Chargé d'affaires a.i. of the Permanent Mission of Iraq (S/22993).

14. UNIKOM has carried out an investigation, in the course of which Bubiyan Island was visited and some of the Kuwaiti military personnel directly involved, as well as some of the Iraqis taken into custody during the incident, were questioned by the investigating team. The UNIKOM team also visited the Al Faw peninsula in Iraq. The following is a summary of its findings:

(a) In the afternoon of 28 August 1991, a Kuwaiti Coast Guard detachment comprising 4 boats took custody of 11 Iraqi fishing boats and 1 speedboat in the waters off Bubiyan Island and of their crews, 45 persons in all. No one was taken from Bubiyan, and UNIKOM received no further information regarding earlier reports that some Iraqis had hidden on Bubiyan;

(b) According to its commander, the Kuwaiti detachment came under small arms fire from Ras al Qaid and Ras al Barshah on Bubiyan. The UNIKOM team was not able to find evidence of firing at those locations. There were no injuries and none of the vessels showed signs of having been hit;

(c) The crew of the speedboat and at least some of the crews of the fishing boats had collected ammunition and other items (e.g. military-style blankets) on Bubiyan. They stated that they had done so for financial gain. UNIKOM has had independent reports of trading in ammunition in southern Iraq. The UNIKOM team did not find, nor was it shown, evidence that there had been weapons on the Iraqi boats;

(d) A senior Kuwaiti army liaison officer stated that, during the incident on 28 August, 12 Iraqi navy speedboats left the Al Faw jetty to come to the assistance of the Iraqi boats off Bubiyan. The jetty mentioned by the Kuwaiti officer is the only marine facility that UNIKOM has observed on the southern shore of the Al Faw peninsula. It offers no protection and can be used only by small craft, which are grounded at low tide. The jetty is about 13 kilometres from UNIKOM observation post No. 6 and is visited by daily patrols from there. Those patrols have not, so far, observed any naval presence. Similarly, the UNIKOM personnel observing the access to the Khowr Abd Allah south of Umm Qasr had not observed any movement of Iraqi vessels;

(e) The UNIKOM team interviewed Kuwaiti airforce pilots, who stated that on the day of the incident, at 1710 hours local time and after the Coast Guard detachment had left the area with the captured vessels, they had engaged and sunk seven boats off Bubiyan. They did not know from where those boats had come. The UNIKOM team saw from the air the wrecks of two boats in the

#UNW-2427
철부물   5—1   /...

0220

S/23000
English
Page 5

vicinity of Ras al Qayd but was not able to establish their identity or when they had been sunk.

15.   Major-General Greindl and his staff are conscious of the implications of the incidents described in this report. They will continue to maintain a high level of vigilance in the performance of the tasks entrusted to them by the Security Council.

5-2

0221

S/22998
English
Page 2

Annex

Letter dated 28 August 1991 from the Minister for Foreign Affairs of Iraq addressed to the Secretary-General

I have the honour to refer to Security Council resolution 707 (1991).

The Government of Iraq considers that this resolution is unwarranted and that, like many of the other resolutions of the Council, it was adopted for motives based on the desire of a number of influential parties in the Security Council to harm Iraq and to contrive yet more pretexts for the non-implementation of the particular provisions of the Security Council resolutions from which Iraq may benefit by a lifting or mitigation of the unjust economic embargo imposed upon it. Iraq has fulfilled all of its obligations under the terms of resolution 687 (1991) in the manner requested by the inspection teams in general and the nuclear inspection teams in particular. It has done so by declaring all aspects of the Iraqi nuclear programme, whether in letters addressed to you or in those exchanged by the Chief of the Iraqi team and the Chiefs of the inspection teams that have visited Iraq. This has also been done in the seminars held, by answering all questions asked, and in the direct meetings held with those responsible for the nuclear programme and with research workers. This demonstrates the full cooperation that has been shown by the Iraqi authorities concerned.

For greater precision, we should like to state our view with regard to the provisions of the operative paragraphs of the Security Council resolution in question.

1.   With regard to paragraphs 1 and 2, in which Iraq is condemned twice in the same resolution, it must be said that Iraq has adhered to all of its undertakings under the terms of Security Council resolution 687 (1991). It has, moreover, complied with the safeguards agreement concluded with the International Atomic Energy Agency (IAEA). It has done so by means of the full disclosure of all aspects of the Iraqi nuclear programme and the measures it has taken on remedial action in implementation of the resolution adopted by the IAEA Board of Governors on 18 July 1991. We should like once more to ask the question we have addressed to IAEA on more than one occasion: what more is now required of us, after all the measures we have taken and all the information we have provided, so that Iraq may meet all of its obligations under the terms of the resolution?

2.   With regard to paragraph 3 (i) of resolution 707 (1991), Iraq has already provided full, final and complete disclosure, as required by resolution 687 (1991), of all aspects of its programmes. There are no programmes of this type, of any kind whatever, that Iraq has not declared.

3.   Since 28 June 1991, the inspection teams have noted no obstacle to their work in gaining access to any and all areas, facilities, equipment, records and means of transportation which they wish to inspect, as demanded in

5-3

/...

0222

paragraph 3 (ii). We should like, in this connection, to refer to the recent reports of the inspection teams, including that of the third nuclear inspection team contained in document GOV/INF/621 of 2 August 1991, in which reference is made to the full cooperation provided by the Iraqi side. We should like to ask once again: what site is there that a team has not been permitted to enter and inspect?

4.   With regard to paragraph 3 (iii), the Government of Iraq took the decision, as of 28 June 1991, to cease any movement or destruction of any material or equipment relating to Security Council resolution 687 (1991). With the arrival of the third nuclear inspection team, agreement was reached by the Chief of the team and his Iraqi counterpart on the movement of certain equipment, after it had been seen by the team, to an appropriate location so as to facilitate future monitoring and inspection by the inspection teams. Certain of these measures were taken under the supervision of members of the third team, and the fourth team once again verified them. Agreement was also reached with the Chief of the fourth team on the continued movement and assembly of those materials and equipment that the team had seen and recorded to the collection sites on which the two parties had agreed for the purpose of facilitating future inspections.

5.   Paragraph 3 (iv) refers to the concomitants of an issue which has become part of the past and which was over and done with even before the arrival of the third nuclear inspection team in the first week of July 1991. The third team examined all items and, together with the Iraqi side, undertook its removal to the locations agreed on. We therefore wish to ask what items are still outside the supervision of the inspection teams and to what were they denied access.

    We should be very grateful if you or the Special Committee would kindly inform us about such items as are referred to in paragraph 3 (iv). Since there were no such items, we wonder what were the grounds for including this paragraph in the resolution.

6.   With regard to paragraph 3 (v), Iraq has already given its opinion concerning aircraft flights. Although Iraq has no objections to that in principle, all that Iraq wishes to make clear, for its part, is that there are issues relating to administration, communications and logistics that must be taken into consideration in order to guarantee the safety of the aircraft and their crews and passengers and that Iraq is most concerned about that and hopes that the issue will be resolved by agreement and cooperation with the competent Iraqi authorities, in order to safeguard the security and safety of all.

7.   With regard to the halting of all nuclear activities of any kind, as referred to in paragraph 3 (vi), although this goes beyond the measures set forth in resolution 687 (1991), from the scientific and the practical viewpoints there is no longer any nuclear activity, even in the most elementary sense, following the comprehensive destruction of Iraqi nuclear locations - reactors, laboratories, materials and other. This is referred to

/...

5-4

0223

S/22998
English
Page 4

also in the report of the Director-General of the International Atomic Energy
Agency.

    I wish to point out that all the requirements of privileges and
immunities and travel facilities of the inspection teams and medical care for
them, referred to in paragraphs 3 (vii) and 3 (viii), have been made available
in full and to the furthest extent possible in the light of the economic
embargo imposed on Iraq. The recent reports of the inspection teams are the
best testimony to that.

8.   With regard to paragraph 5, Iraq reaffirms its full commitment to its
international undertakings, including the Non-Proliferation Treaty and the
Safeguards Agreement with the International Atomic Energy Agency.

    The preambular and operative paragraphs of resolution 707 (1991) are
based on the provisions of resolution 687 (1991), but it deliberately
overlooks the rights of Iraq set forth in resolution 687 (1991). In this
connection, we wish to inquire what is requested of Iraq, in order that it may
show even greater good will in demonstrating its compliance with Security
Council resolutions.

    We wish also to ask how long the Security Council will disregard the
rights of Iraq laid down in Security Council resolutions and when the
iniquitous economic embargo imposed on its people will be lifted.

                                    (Signed) Ahmad HUSSEIN
                                    Minister for Foreign Affairs
                                        of the Republic of Iraq
                                    Baghdad, 28 August 1991

                              5-5

                                                        0224

발 신 전 보

	분류번호	보존기간

번   호 : WUN-2566   910906 1900   종별 : _____

수   신 : 주   UN   대사. 총영사

발   신 : 장   관   (중동일)

제   목 : 대이락 무기공급 금지에 관한 조치사항 통보

대 : 주 국련 20313 - 654 (91.8.21)

표제관련, 우리의 조치내용을 아래와 같이 UN측에 통보바람.

THE PERMANENT REPRESENTATIVE OF THE REPUBLIC OF KOREA TO THE UNITED NATIONS
PRESENTS ITS COMPLIMENTS TO THE SECRETARY-GENERAL OF THE UNITED NATIONS AND,
WITH REFERENCE TO HIS NOTE SCPC/7/91 (4-1) OF 3 JULY 1991, HAS THE HONOUR TO
INFORM HIM THAT THE GOVERNMENT OF THE REPUBLIC OF KOREA IS ABIDING BY RESOLU-
TIONS 687(1991) AND 700(1991) CONCERNING THE PREVENTION OF THE SALE OR SUPPLY
OF ARMS AND RELATED MATERIAL TO IRAQ OR IRAQI NATIONALS AND THAT THE COMPETENT
AUTHORITIES HAVE ALSO TAKEN DOMESTIC MEASURES TO ENSURE THE IMPLEMENTATION
OF THE RELEVANT PROVISIONS OF THE SAID RESOLUTIONS.

(중동아프리카국장   이 해 순)

국제기구국장 : 통상국장

	보안통제	주

앙고재	91년9월6일 중동1과	기안자명 주		과 장 심의만	국 장 전결		차 관	장 관		외신과통제

주 국 련 대 표 부

주국련20313- **681**

수신　장관

참조　국제기구조약국장 , 중동아프리카국장

제목　이락무기공급금지 (안보리)

표제관련 안보리문서를 별첨과 같이 송부합니다.

첨 부 : 상기문서. 끝.

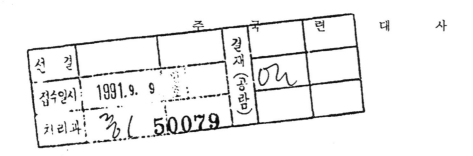

0226

Security Council

Distr.
GENERAL

S/22966
21 August 1991

ORIGINAL: ENGLISH

NOTE VERBALE DATED 20 AUGUST 1991 FROM THE PERMANENT
MISSION OF INDONESIA TO THE UNITED NATIONS ADDRESSED
TO THE SECRETARY-GENERAL

The Permanent Mission of the Republic of Indonesia to the United Nations presents its compliments to the Secretary-General of the United Nations and, with reference to his Note No. SCPC/7/91(4-1) of 3 July 1991, has the honour to inform the Secretary-General that the Government of the Republic of Indonesia strictly abides by the prohibitions against the sale or supply of arms to Iraq as contained in paragraph 24 of resolution 687 (1991).

91-27197   2561h (E)

0227

Security Council

Distr.
GENERAL

S/22969
22 August 1991

ORIGINAL: ENGLISH

NOTE VERBALE DATED 21 AUGUST 1991 FROM THE CHARGE D'AFFAIRES
OF THE PERMANENT MISSION OF DENMARK TO THE UNITED NATIONS
ADDRESSED TO THE SECRETARY-GENERAL

The Chargé d'affaires of the Permanent Mission of Denmark to the United Nations presents his compliments to the Secretary-General of the United Nations and has the honour, referring to paragraph 4 of Security Council resolution 700 (1991), to provide him with the following information.

Denmark's long-standing policies for export of arms and munitions are very restrictive. Therefore existing laws and regulations already met with the obligations and requirements of Security Council resolution 687 (1991) as regards the sale, supply or promotion of arms and related material to Iraq. In principle, arms exports from Denmark are prohibited and export licences are only granted after a close scrutiny by the authorities of each individual case. Parts of weapons as well as facilities for production of such parts are also covered by this legislation.

The Government of Denmark complies strictly with the arms embargoes agreed upon in the United Nations as adherence to these embargoes is one of the main criteria the Danish Government applies in its arms export policy. The legal basis for these criteria is the Arms Act (Law No. 529 of 11 December 1985, with subsequent amendments), which is administered by the Ministry of Justice, acting in close cooperation with the Ministry of Defence and the Ministry of Foreign Affairs.

Similarly, most other proscribed items and activities listed in the guidelines for prohibited categories of goods for export were also already covered by existing Danish legislation, in particular the regulation of 2 October 1987 with later amendments concerning export of certain goods, issued by the Ministry of Industry.

91-27408 2535i (E)   /...

0228

Furthermore, the European Community has enacted the following legislation
preventing trade by community members with Iraq which have direct effect in
Denmark:

-   EEC regulation 2340/90 of 8 August 1990, extended and amended by
    regulation 3155/90;

-   ECSC decision 90/414 of 8 August 1990.

Subsequently, the Danish legislation against trade and other commercial
contacts with Iraq, based on the resolutions of the United Nations as well as
the regulations and decisions adopted by the European Communities have been
embodied in an order dated 7 June 1991. This order provides for sanctions in
the form of imprisonment or fines in case of violation of the provisions. The
responsibility for the enforcement of this legislation lies largely with the
Ministry of Industry, which has the authority to issue export licences for all
types of goods except arms and related material. It is the duty of the
customs authorities to control at the time of export that the necessary
licences for export of certain goods are at hand.

0229

UNITED
NATIONS

Security Council

S

Distr.
GENERAL

S/22970
22 August 1991

ORIGINAL: ENGLISH

NOTE VERBALE DATED 21 AUGUST 1991 FROM THE PERMANENT
MISSION OF LEBANON TO THE UNITED NATIONS ADDRESSED
TO THE SECRETARY-GENERAL

The Permanent Mission of Lebanon to the United Nations presents its
compliments to the Secretary-General of the United Nations and, with reference
to his Note No. SCPC/F/91(4-1) of 3 July 1991, has the honour to inform him
that Lebanon has strictly complied with the relevant Security Council
resolutions, and with the guidelines annexed to the Secretary-General's report
(S/22660) approved by the Security Council in resolution 700 (1991).

91-27392 2465c (E)

0230

UNITED NATIONS

S

Security Council

Distr.
GENERAL

S/22973
23 August 1991
ENGLISH
ORIGINAL: FRENCH

NOTE VERBALE DATED 22 AUGUST 1991 FROM THE PERMANENT MISSION
OF THE LAO PEOPLE'S DEMOCRATIC REPUBLIC TO THE UNITED NATIONS
ADDRESSED TO THE SECRETARY-GENERAL

The Permanent Mission of the Lao People's Democratic Republic to the
United Nations presents its compliments to the Secretary-General and,
referring to his note SCPC/7/91/4-1 of 3 July 1991, has the honour to inform
him that the Government of the Lao People's Democratic Republic is strictly
complying with the prohibition against the sale or supply of weapons to Iraq
in implementation of the relevant Security Council resolutions.

UNITED
NATIONS

S

Security Council

Distr.
GENERAL

S/22976
26 August 1991

ORIGINAL: ENGLISH

NOTE VERBALE DATED 20 AUGUST 1991 FROM THE PERMANENT
REPRESENTATIVE OF POLAND TO THE UNITED NATIONS
ADDRESSED TO THE SECRETARY-GENERAL

The Permanent Representative of the Republic of Poland to the United
Nations presents his compliments to the Secretary-General of the United
Nations and, with reference to his note of 3 July 1991, has the honour to
inform him that the Republic of Poland, in full conformity with the relevant
Security Council resolutions, strictly abides by the prohibitions against the
sale or supply of arms to Iraq. All exports of arms and related material of
all types from the Republic of Poland are subject to a licence arrangement.
The competent authorities of the Republic of Poland will not issue a licence
that is contradictory to the Guidelines to Facilitate Full International
Implementation of paragraphs 24, 25 and 27 of Security Council resolution
687 (1991) approved by the Security Council in its resolution 700 (1991).

In connection with commercial relations with Iraq, the decree of the
Council of Ministers of the Republic of Poland of 13 August 1990 on the
prohibition against trade with Iraq is still in effect. The granting of an
exception to this prohibition is possible only in accordance with the
provisions of the decree of the Council of Ministers of the Republic of Poland
of 31 July 1991, adopted in accordance with the provisions of Security Council
resolution 687 (1991), for the export of foodstuffs or other commodities for
essential civilian needs subject to an individual export licence arrangement.

91-27627 2571h (E)

0232

Security Council

Distr.
GENERAL

S/22985
28 August 1991
ENGLISH
ORIGINAL: SPANISH

NOTE VERBALE DATED 23 AUGUST 1991 FROM THE PERMANENT MISSION OF
CUBA TO THE UNITED NATIONS ADDRESSED TO THE SECRETARY-GENERAL

The Permanent Mission of Cuba to the United Nations presents its
compliments to the Secretary-General and has the honour to inform him, in
response to the request received, that Cuba does not maintain any ties with
Iraq which contravene the provisions of paragraph 24 of Security Council
resolution 687 (1991).

91-27937 2581h (E)

0233

UNITED NATIONS

S

Security Council

Distr.
GENERAL

S/22989
28 August 1991
ENGLISH
ORIGINAL: ARABIC

NOTE VERBALE DATED 23 AUGUST 1991 FROM THE PERMANENT
REPRESENTATIVE OF JORDAN TO THE UNITED NATIONS
ADDRESSED TO THE SECRETARY-GENERAL

The Permanent Representative of the Hashemite Kingdom of Jordan presents his compliments to the Secretary-General of the United Nations and, with reference to his note No. SCPC/7/91 (4-1) dated 3 July 1991, has the honour to inform him that Jordan, in compliance with the principles of international law, respects and implements the resolutions of the United Nations, including those adopted by the Security Council. Accordingly, Jordan duly declared its compliance with Security Council resolution 661 (1990) by which the Council imposed sanctions on Iraq. The Jordanian Government informed the Secretary-General of the United Nations on 23 August 1991 of the measures it had taken at that time to implement the resolution. Those measures included the denial of all supplies of weapons and military equipment to Iraq. Those measures are still in force with regard to the related Security Council resolutions including resolutions 687 (1991) and 700 (1991).

The Permanent Representative of the Hashemite Kingdom of Jordan to the United Nations takes this opportunity to convey to the Secretary-General of the United Nations the assurances of his highest consideration.

91-28082   2472c (E)

0234

UNITED NATIONS

S

Security Council

Distr.
GENERAL

S/22994
30 August 1991

ORIGINAL: ENGLISH

NOTE VERBALE DATED 22 AUGUST 1991 FROM THE PERMANENT MISSION
OF THE UKRAINIAN SOVIET SOCIALIST REPUBLIC TO THE UNITED
NATIONS ADDRESSED TO THE SECRETARY-GENERAL

The Permanent Mission of the Ukrainian Soviet Socialist Republic to the United Nations presents its compliments to the Secretary-General of the United Nations and, with reference to the latter's note No. SCPC/7/91 (4-1), dated 3 July 1991, wishes to state that the Ukrainian SSR has been fully observing the provisions of the resolutions adopted by the Security Council, particularly resolutions 687 (1991) and 700 (1991), relating to the situation between Iraq and Kuwait.

91-28261   2838b (E)

0235

UNITED
NATIONS

S

 Security Council

Distr.
GENERAL

S/22995
30 August 1991

ORIGINAL: ENGLISH

NOTE VERBALE DATED 29 AUGUST 1991 FROM THE PERMANENT
REPRESENTATIVE OF THE PHILIPPINES TO THE UNITED
NATIONS ADDRESSED TO THE SECRETARY-GENERAL

The Permanent Representative of the Philippines to the United Nations
presents his compliments to the Secretary-General of the United Nations and,
with reference to his note No. SCPC/7/91(4-1) dated 3 July 1991, has the
honour to inform him that the Philippines implements the provisions of the
resolutions adopted by the Security Council relating to the situation between
Iraq and Kuwait, particularly resolutions 687 (1991) and 700 (1991).

91-28337   2586h (E)

0236

주 국 련 대 표 부

주국련 20313- **683**   1991. 9. 5.

수신 장 간

참조 국제기구조약국장, 중동아프리카국장

제목 유엔 이락 제4차 핵사찰 보고서 (안보리)

　　　표제 관련 안보리 문서를 별첨과 같이 송부합니다.

첨 부   상기 문서 .   끝 .

주　국　련　대　사

UNITED NATIONS

S

Security Council

Distr.
GENERAL

S/22986
28 August 1991

ORIGINAL: ENGLISH

NOTE BY THE SECRETARY-GENERAL

The Secretary-General has the honour to transmit to the members of the Security Council the attached communication which he has received from the Director-General of the International Atomic Energy Agency (IAEA).

91-28014 2596e (E)

/...

0238

<u>Annex</u>

<u>Letter dated 27 August 1991 from the Director-General of
the International Atomic Energy Agency addressed to the
Secretary-General</u>

Please find attached the report of the fourth IAEA inspection in Iraq under Security Council resolution 687 (1991). You may deem it appropriate to transmit the report to the members of the Security Council. I remain, of course, available with the Chief Inspector, Mr. David Kay, for any consultations you or the Council may wish to have.

(<u>Signed</u>) Hans BLIX

0239

/...

Enclosure

REPORT ON THE FOURTH IAEA ON-SITE INSPECTION IN IRAQ
UNDER SECURITY COUNCIL RESOLUTION 687 (1991)

27 July-10 August 1991

Salient Points

- The team was given full access to all designated sites, and the attitude of the Iraqi side continued to be as co-operative as in the course of the third inspection. Reticence was, however, noted as regards the disclosure of the procurement sources of equipment and material relevant to the centrifuge enrichment project. Deceptive behaviour was admitted in at least one instance in the course of the third inspection.

- Extensive information in response to intense questioning was gathered, and a large number of documents in the form of reports, detailed fabrication drawings and computer printout records of laboratory experiments were brought to Vienna for further analysis.

- On the first inspection day the Iraqi representative handed over to the team a list of nuclear materials which included items not previously declared. It confirmed the existence of a clandestine programme to i) manufacture several kilograms of uranium oxide fuel, ii) irradiate it in the IRT-5000 reactor and iii) reprocess the irradiated fuel in order to chemically separate gram amounts of plutonium.

- It is now certain that the Electro-Magnetic Isotope Separation (EMIS) approach to uranium enrichment was given priority and that the relevant project was fast-paced and had achieved the stage of initial industrial production at the Tarmiya establishment. The visit to several heavy mechanical production facilities used for the local fabrication of EMIS components indicated that their likely production rates were consistent with the Iraqi-stated amounts of EMIS equipment produced before the production facilities had been bombed. The production of uranium tetrachloride (EMIS feed material) would have been more or less sufficient to cover the needs of Tarmiya once the latter had reached full operation at the design capacity. The plan for Tarmiya was to bring on line a production facility of 90 separators which, with an average availability of 55%, could have produced 15 kg of highly enriched uranium (HEU) per annum using natural uranium as feed. An increase in separator availability, as a consequence of improvements in the systems, with a corresponding increase in the annual production of HEU, was deemed possible by the Iraqis.

- Iraq supplied the third inspection team with limited information on the magnitude of their centrifuge enrichment programme. A priority task of the fourth team was to obtain a more comprehensive picture of the Iraqi efforts in this area, including details of the overall plan and direction of the programme. The team was provided with an overall project plan showing key dates. According to this plan, following mechanical and functional trials on different models (1987-1991) a facility for centrifuge production would have started operation at the end of 1991. A 100-machine cascade would have been in operation in 1993 and a 500-machine cascade would have gone on stream in 1996. The team was able to visit the production facility of the Al Furat Project (the code name of this programme) at a site close to An Walid, 20 km south of Baghdad, a complex consisting of four buildings, two of them new. This complex had not suffered any attacks during the war, nor was it previously known as a nuclear-related site.

/...

0240

Although machine tools for manufacturing the centrifuges had not yet been installed (they had been procured but were dispersed to protect them against possible air attacks around the 25 July 1991 deadline), from the dimensions of this centrifuge production facility the team concluded that, once in full operation, the facility could easily have turned out 600 centrifuges per annum with the equipment already procured for this site.

- Extensive inspection work was carried out at the Al Jesira chemical production facility in the Mosul area, first designated by the Special Commission during the third inspection. This facility, which was heavily damaged by the bombing and by the salvaging-deception activities undertaken afterwards, housed the UO_2 and UCl_4 production lines and was the intended site for the production of UF_6 to feed the centrifuge enrichment project.

- No conclusive evidence was obtained as to the existence of weaponization activities.

Introduction

1. This report summarizes findings of the fourth inspection carried out by the IAEA under the terms of Security Council Resolution 687 (1991) with the assistance and co-operation of the Special Commission of the United Nations. The team consisted of 14 inspectors and 6 supporting staff, comprising 11 nationalities. It was headed by Mr. David Kay of the IAEA as Chief Inspector. The team arrived in Iraq on 27 July and started on-site activities on 28 July. The inspection ended on 10 August 1991, when the team departed for Bahrain. A total of 22 sites were inspected, 14 being visited for the first time - five of these 14 new sites were designated by the Special Commission.

2. In addition to follow-up activities arising from information gathered in the course of the third mission and to inspection of the new sites designated by the Special Commission, the following tasks were assigned to the fourth team:

   - Electro-Magnetic Isotope separation (EMIS) programme: to make a detailed assessment of the programme as a whole and an analysis of the capacity of local industries to produce process equipment, components and feed material;

   - Centrifuge enrichment programme: to obtain a more comprehensive picture of the programme, particularly with regard to machine component manufacturing, system (cascade) design and UF_6 feed preparation;

   - Weaponization activities: to verify the existence of activities relevant to the research and development, manufacturing and testing required in order to convert fissile material into a nuclear weapon.

3. In the morning of the first inspection day (28 July), the Iraqi representative submitted to the team a letter dated 27 July containing a list of nuclear material which included items not previously declared. The inspection programme had accordingly to be modified, in order to accommodate additional verifications.

4. No access problems were faced during the fourth inspection, and the attitude of the Iraqi representatives continued to be one of co-operation. As expected, the process of additional clarification and subsequent verification through detailed questioning by the team continued. The team's requests for information on procurement sources of specialized equipment were not met. A large number of samples were taken and a huge amount of documents and drawings obtained; their evaluation will require considerable time.

5. It became evident to the team that only high-level officials such as Dr. Jaffar are empowered to release information on sensitive matters. The same questions asked of other senior Iraqi officials produce untruthful answers. As this is greatly hindering the inspection process, complete frankness should be demanded - in the interest of both sides.

/...

0241

The Electro-Magnetic Isotope Separation (EMIS) Project

6. The mission of the team's EMIS experts was to provide as comprehensive a description as possible of the EMIS project and to assess the capability and product of that project.

Project Planning and Design

7. As clarified during the third inspection, the EMIS project was originated and directed by Dr. J.D. Jaffar. Dr. Jaffar is currently Vice-Chairman of the Iraqi Atomic Energy Commission (IAEC) and Deputy Minister of Industry and Minerals (MOI). In addition to the EMIS project, Dr. Jaffar now appears to have been in charge of the overall enrichment effort.

In several meetings with team members, Dr. Jaffar and others reiterated the principal reason for the project - i.e. the desire to create a domestic enrichment and nuclear fuel program, with consequent stimulation of a broad development of Iraq's industrial infrastructure. Dr. Jaffar claimed that the programme would eventually have been declared openly. There were persistent denials that the program had any weapons goal. However, Dr. Jaffar appeared to be aware of the implausibility of the denials [on several occasions openly prefacing his own remarks with the acknowledgement that the potential for making weapons material was obvious], but consistently refused to acknowledge that a weapons development intent had been central to the origin of the project.

It is now certain, however, that the EMIS project was fast-paced and that all of its components were of an industrial scale, which would have resulted in significant production of weapons-grade material.

The IAEC carried out necessary development work in physics and chemistry at its own sites. It enhanced the indigenous capabilities of Ministry of Industry (MOI) establishments for fabricating process components and, as necessary, provided design criteria - and awarded contracts - to foreign contractors for civil construction and non-process-specific components. As far as possible, the contracting process was used to upgrade local civil engineering practices as well.

According to MOI manufacturers, customers - principally the IAEC - supplied raw materials, special tooling, and design and production drawings and took back all drawings, acceptance reports and rejected items along with the accepted finished products. The manufacturers maintain that, as a result, they neither understood the program nor had any vision of future orders.

On the last day of the inspection, the Iraqis provided project planning, procurement, and design information that may permit more detailed evaluation of this process and the verification of Iraqi statements about total production of separators.

Research and Development Facilities and Accomplishments

8. According to Dr. Jaffar, work began on the EMIS project at Tuwaitha in 1982 as a result of the decision to abandon the reactor program after the Osirak bombing.

Separator development at Tuwaitha progressed through the construction and operation of several separators of different designs. In the first stage, a 400-mm [radius of beam curvature] isotope separator was built. It achieved a 1-mA current and permitted the testing of insulator and liner concepts.

0242   /...

In the second stage, a 500-mm and three 1000-mm separators were built and operated at Tuwaitha. These separators were used to test larger ion sources, multiple ion sources and a hexagonal liner design; control system and collector concepts were tested as well. Following on those efforts, the quad source of the 1200-mm system was designed for installation at Tarmiya, the magnet for the 600-mm Tarmiya machine was designed and built, and the double ion source and collector system for that separator were designed.

In parallel with separator development in Building 80 at Tuwaitha, chemical process development and operational support work was performed in Building 85; the process chemistry for converting UO_2 to UCl_4 was tested and the design criteria for the Al Jezira facility [i.e. the Mosul Production Facility] determined. The steps for recovering uranium from the separator pockets as UO_3 [and from the separator liners as UO_4] were developed as well. Until the Al Jezira UCl_4 production plant became operational, the preparation of feedstock for the Tarmiya testing operation was also performed at Tuwaitha.

As the Tarmiya facility became available, experienced operating and engineering staff were shifted from Tuwaitha. At the time of the 16/17 January bombing, the new staff at Tuwaitha had reportedly acquired considerable experience. The highest enrichments achieved were declared to have been 17% for gram quantities and 45% for milligram quantities. Progress reports submitted to the inspection team by the Iraqis and claimed to have been prepared during the actual operation of the Tuwaitha and Tarmiya facilities may -- if authenticated -- provide verification of the production. On the basis of very generous assumptions about the operation of prototype equipment, it was previously calculated that the Tuwaitha facility could have produced a maximum of 3 kg of enriched material during its probable operational period. Given the types of experiment which - it now appears - were carried out in Building 80, a much lower number is more probable.

Ministry of Industry Production Facilities

9. The team visited several mechanical production facilities declared during the third inspection, used for the indigenous fabrication of the magnets, vacuum chambers, ion sources and collector components of the separators. Among these facilities were the State Establishment for Heavy Engineering Equipment (SEHEE), Al Dura, Badr General Establishment, and three facilities grouped together as the Auqba Bin Nafi Establishment (Al Radwan, Al Ameer and Al Amin). Their capabilities before the Gulf conflict and their likely production rates are consistent with the Iraqi statements about amounts of EMIS equipment produced. However, until the Iraqi authorities comply with the repeated requests for the submission of production records, an independent check of this conclusion will not be possible.

The most impressive equipment were the 6m-diameter vertical turning machines at Al Radwan and Al Ameer that were used to produce the pole pieces for the Tarmiya separators.

The production of large and small separator components consumed 70% of the effort of Al Radwan and Al Ameer in the last year before the war. These facilities were nearly destroyed during the war and are at least 12-18 months away from being operable.

The production and integration of electrical systems remain less well understood than those of the mechanical systems. The electric equipment facility at Zaafarinyah Dijlah was capable of producing the necessary power supplies, but had been thoroughly sanitized by the time of the second inspection. The control computers, fibre optic links, and Computer Assisted Measurement and Control (CAMAC) equipment necessary for system integration and operation are not controlled items and are widely available. The Iraqis have submitted schematic designs and procurement records that should clarify the design and procurement sequences involved in building this equipment.

0243

/...

Feed Material Plants

10. Feed material for Tuwaitha operations and for the initial start-up of Tarmiya was provided by the chemical engineering laboratory at Tuwaitha (Building 85). Support for full-scale production work at Tarmiya - and potentially Ash Sharqat - was to come from the new feedstock plant at Al Jezira, near Mosul, where there were two separate plants - one for UO_2 production and one for UCl_4, the latter having two parallel lines.

According to the Iraqi authorities, the UO_2 plant was designed to produce 500 kg/day, began cold tests and precommissioning tests in July 1989 and began trial operation in November 1989; by the time of its destruction, in January 1991, it had produced, according to the Iraqi authorities, 96 t of UO_2, which had been transferred to the custody of the Ministry of Industry.

The UCl_4 plant's parallel lines were each designed to produce 150 kg/line/day. One line began precommissioning tests in February 1990 and continued in unstable trial operation until November 1990. The plant was declared by Iraq to have produced 1.2 t of UCl_4, which was released to the Ministry of Industry. The bombing and Iraq's subsequent salvaging efforts caused substantial destruction of the UCl_4 plant.

According to the Iraqi authorities, two additional processes were to have been added to the plant. A line had been designed to case the 1.5 kg cylindrical slugs of UCl_4 used in the separator ion sources. Dr. Jaffar disclosed that Al Jezira would have been the site for UF_6 production for the centrifuge program as well. It was claimed, however, that no detailed design work had been done by the time of the war.

Process Equipment and Facilities

11. The Tarmiya site was also revisited by this team. Because of the fact that further disclosures had been made by the Iraqi EMIS project personnel, a very thorough analysis of the whole site was made. The design details of the 1200 mm separators are now understood. Thanks to this design understanding - coupled with information obtained during discussions with the Iraqi operating staff, the results of isotopic analyses to be carried out in the next few weeks on samples taken from the few recovered ion sources, and submitted progress reports - it should soon be possible to verify the accuracy of the Iraqi-declared separative work in total.

The Iraqis had eight 1200mm separators in operation in Building 33 at Tarmiya, the declared initial operating dates ranged from 23 February 1990 to 10 September 1990, and this declared average availability was 15%. There was a single spare quad ion source for the eight separators. As the chemical facilities on-site had not yet been commissioned, the graphite collectors were returned to Tuwaitha for uranium recovery and the liners and sources were washed down for UCl_4 recovery in a temporary facility in building 54 at Tarmiya.

Each of the eight separators required a loading of 6 kg of UCl_4 at the start of each run and, according to Iraqi operating staff, achieved production operation on only 30% of the system vacuum cycles. In the light of discussions with the Iraqi authorities, the detailed process by which the separators were installed, debugged and improved seems credible.

A second line of 17 separators was being installed in Building 33 at Tarmiya at the time of the bombing. These separators were to incorporate improvements in liner design. Although the Iraqis were not specific on this point, it appears that the magnets, return iron, vacuum systems and power supplies were being installed at the time of the bombing. Ion sources and collectors were still in production according to Iraqi statements.

0244

/...

Building 245, designed to house the 600 mm separators, was incomplete in January 1991. A detailed description of how the twenty 600 mm separators were to be installed and a sketch of the design of the magnet system for these separators were provided. Dr. Jaffar subsequently released the design drawings of the dual ion source and collector systems to be used in their initial operation. Dr. Jaffar also indicated that a subsequent upgrade to four-source systems was considered possible. Six prototype magnets and vacuum chambers had been fabricated for the 600 mm system and six ion sources and collectors were being fabricated when the programme stopped.

Two chemical process buildings at Tarmiya were designed for the recovery of UCl_4 as UO_4 from liners. Building 57 was to service the 1200mm separators and Building 225 the 600 mm separators. The design batch size for Building 57 was $10m^3$ of HNO_3 wash solution per day, corresponding to the output of eight 1200 mm per day. The design batch size for Building 225 was $4m^3$ of solution per day, representing approximately the same capacity for the smaller separators. It should be noted that the design of process piping and vessels for Building 225 explicitly included criticality evaluations, indicating an intention to produce and handle HEU. Important in the discussion of the throughput criteria for these buildings was the admission that each was designed to handle the ultimate site capability and that a duplicate source and collector system would eventually be fabricated for each separator. That step, plus the installation of modified liners designed for quicker removal, raises the design availability for the separators from the Iraqi claim of 55%. The distribution of recovery functions between two buildings reinforces the conclusion that the production of HEU was a major design goal of the facility.

Building 46 at Tarmiya was designed for the batch recovery of uranium as UO_3 from collector pockets of the separators; enriched and depleted uranium from 1200 mm and 600 mm separators respectively would be recovered in four separate halls. The facility was sized for the ultimate site capacity.

The team carried out an inspection of Building 271, the separator support building. In this building, ion source and collector stores were kept, source and collector refurbishment was performed, vacuum checks and high-voltage tests were performed, and a universal co-ordinate machine (UCM) was used to verify the proper alignment of source and collector components in three dimensions. The thoroughness and scale of the industrialization of the Tarmiya site are evident from the use of bar coding and from the computerization of source and collector part ordering and inventory maintenance that were described during the inspection of this building.

The Tarmiya facility and its equipment were effectively destroyed by bombing and during subsequent dismantling and deception operations carried out by the Iraqis. The replica facility at Ash Sharqat was equally damaged.

12. It is possible - but by no means certain - that full production operation at Tarmiya might not have been achieved for another 18-36 months. The Iraqis claimed major design and operational failures at the Al Jezira facility that, if not promptly corrected, could have delayed adequate feedstock supply. They also claimed difficulties in the supply of graphite for collector pockets. Finally, there may have been human resource problems associated with these large facilities. What is clear from the quality and dedication of the people involved in this effort is that the problems would, at most, only have caused temporary delays.

In summary, the EMIS system being brought on line at Tarmiya alone could have produced 15 kg of HEU per annum (at 55% availability), and there was considerable upgrade potential that it is both prudent and reasonable to assume the Iraqis would have exploited.

0245   /...

<u>Verification and Reconciliation</u>

13. The Iraqis are still engaged in the recovery from desert disposal sites of the materials removed for concealment and destruction. They themselves have expressed concern about the difficulty of verifying their statements to the IAEA and the Special Commission. With the exception of major components such as magnets, coils, and backplates of vacuum boxes, verification of their statements remains incomplete. Four ion source assemblies have been recovered, but no significant fraction of the collector assemblies has been found. Some critical production equipment has been located, but the location of the coil winders has not yet been divulged. Given the nature of the dispersal and destruction operations which were carried out under the direction of the Iraqi military authorities, verification on the basis of production, acceptance and operating records may be necessary - but there will be a considerable element of uncertainty. At present, a data set consistent with the Iraqi declarations is available, but it has not been fully verified.

14. Major components of the EMIS system, such as magnets, coils and vacuum boxes, can be cut apart under supervision and released for salvage. Much of the multi-use equipment from Tarmiya and Ash Sharqat, such as transformers, switchgear, air-handling equipment and chillers, has already been removed from the site by the Iraqi authorities - for use, it is said, elsewhere in the Iraqi economy. What, if anything, remains can be either destroyed or released. Dies and coil-winding machines were used to produce unique process equipment, and their destruction will be required. The use of vertical turning machines capable of producing items larger than 3 m in diameter should be closely monitored.

The chemical production site at Al Jezira has been destroyed. Re-use of this site and of the sites at Tarmiya and Ash Sharqat should be for declared purposes and subject to inspection. The Iraqis have mentioned their intention to rebuild the Tuwaitha site for use in a regional, open research program. If this is done, close monitoring would be required.

The Gas Centrifuge Enrichment Project

15. During the third IAEA inspection, the Iraqis had declared that they had been conducting a gas centrifuge enrichment project but that it was second in priority to the EMIS project. They supplied the third inspection team with some centrifuge operating test data, but only on single-centrifuge machines. In addition, at the end of the third inspection visit they produced a small number of centrifuge components for inspection.

A priority task of the fourth inspection team was to obtain a much more comprehensive picture of the Iraqi gas centrifuge programme, including details of the overall plan and direction of the programme.

<u>Research and Development</u>

16. During visits by the fourth team to Tuwaitha and other establishments and at two seminars, Iraq reiterated their achievements with single-machine testing. They claimed to have carried out early testing during 1987 on an oil-type centrifuge (Model 1), an aluminum cylinder three inches in diameter employing oil-lubricated bearings. The tests were terminated when Iraq's magnetic/pivot bearing centrifuge (Model 2) became available.

This design is based on the Zippe Type Centrifuge. Two types of rotor were planned: an all-maraging-steel rotor with caps and baffles electron-beam-welded into place and a carbon-composite rotor cylinder with maraging steel caps and baffles held in place with epoxy resin. The main drawings of the rotating components and of the central feed and extraction pipes were supplied.

/...

0246

Iraq reiterated that only single-machine tests had been carried out in the mid-1988 to late 1990 period . A carbon rotor design speed of 60,000 RPM (456 m/sec wall speed) was achieved with two rotors, one in a mechanical test stand and one with UF6 gas in the process test stand. A Separative Work Output per machine of about 1.9 SWU/year was obtained, but with optimization they were expecting to achieve a 2.7 SWU/year output.

Details were given of the layout of the laboratory in Building 63 at Tuwaitha in which these experiments were declared to have been conducted, together with a description of the problems encountered. These problems suggest that the Iraqis' scientific understanding was still limited, with test work only just begun. The Iraqis also explained that, owing to limited UF_6 availability [a claim that contradicts repeated statements by Dr. Jaffar and others that they had no problem in meeting their UF_6 requirements], after the completion of a test run, including the mass-spectrometer analysis of product and tails concentration, they mixed the product and tails together to recreate the natural UF_6 feed material needed to continue the tests.

Gas Centrifuge Component Manufacture

17. The Iraqis restated that they had made the vacuum housings, the molecular pumps, the ball/pivot and numerous small components themselves at Badr and the State Enterprise for Heavy Equipment Engineering (SEHEE). These two companies had also joined together to build a factory capable of making all the components for the maraging steel (Model 2) centrifuge under the code name Al Furat Project. However, attempts to produce maraging steel cylinders of adequate quality by flow-forming were stated to have been unsuccessful. It was stated that a total of 25 pieces of 350 Grade maraging steel had been obtained (source unidentified). Of these, 19 were machined into preforms at the Nasser Engineering Establishment and the other six by a foreign company (again unidentified). Out of all these, only nine achieved the required tolerance and none was considered good enough for rotor assembly. Quite separately, ten carbon fiber cylinders had been procured from abroad (source unidentified); the two test centrifuges had been constructed from them.

The team prepared a list of the materials and items that are classed as sensitive, or essential, for centrifuge enrichment. Iraq was requested to indicate which items had been acquired abroad, the years of acquisition and the companies that had produced them. On the last day of the inspection Iraq presented its reply. Follow-up actions have been identified on the basis of this reply. Iraq did not meet the requirement of the fourth team that the sources of procurement be identified; in fact, it provided essentially useless information on this point.

The Al Furat Project

18. The Al Furat Project was at the construction stage at a location close to the Badr Engineering Complex, An Walid. The location was declared to have been the planned site for the serial production of gas centrifuges of a maraging steel design. The Iraqis stated that, in a small building designated B03, they had, prior to the outbreak of hostilities, flow-turned the maraging steel tubes and machined the vacuum casings and molecular pumps mentioned earlier. All equipment had been removed prior to the inspection.

The overall project objective was stated to have been to complete the civil construction and machine tool installation by mid-1991. However, all work was halted in August 1990. The Iraqi authorities declared that they had by then procured a number of manufacturing equipment essential to the program.

The machine tools at Badr and SEHEE had been dispersed around 25 July 1991 in an effort to hide them and protect them from possible air attacks. The team saw many such machines stored outdoors or in dirty warehouses. The machines were said to be unused for the most part.

0247   /...

Two indicators suggested otherwise: control consoles with hour meters all showed usage times greater than 100 hours, and many machines had chips caught in various places - in some cases despite cleaning. The machines were said to have been originally intended for use at the Al Furat plant.

Manufacturer's identification data and serial numbers had been defaced or cut off of all the higher-quality equipment. The Iraqis were unwilling to provide procurement data and to specify even the make of the machines.

The Al Furat site was to consist basically of four main buildings, two of them new:

- Building B00 was to be the workshop in which the machines were to be installed to manufacture caps and baffles. The machines were to be supplemented by the machine tools for the manufacture of the vacuum housings, molecular pumps, damper components, and other minor components. The building was divided into two temperature-controlled areas.

- The smaller Building B03 was to be converted into an incoming material store and preparation area.

- Building B02 was to be the flow-forming workshop for the manufacture of maraging steel tubes and for cleaning, galvanizing, painting and inspecting components as necessary.

- Building B01 was to be the rotor assembly and spin testing workshop, possibly with UF6 testing.

The two main buildings (B00 and B02) were large, measuring some 100m by 80m each. Clean-room technology of a very advanced design was incorporated into the project and was said by the Iraqis to be their first attempt at building to such strict design specifications.

Although the Iraqis claimed the target output in the first year of operation to be 200 machines from a single shift, it was concluded by the inspection team that the eventual workshop capability would have been far greater -- easily 600 machines/year from the equipment already available for this site.

The Iraqi authorities stated that in total the investment at the site would have been 11 million Iraqi dinars for construction and services, $30 million for imported equipment and materials for the buildings and services and, finally, $4.5 million for imported machine tools. It is impossible to verify local construction costs or to accurately assess claimed foreign procurement costs as long as the Iraqi authorities refuse to provide procurement records. The inspection team, having been denied such records, was of the general view that Iraq was understating the cost of this facility.

Detailed drawings of the complex were handed over to the inspection team.

0248

/...

Overall Project Plan

19. The Iraqis provided the inspection team with an overall project plan showing key dates. The highlights of the plan were:

Mid 87 - Late 89	Trials on Model 1 Centrifuge
Mid 88 - Mid 91	Trials on Model 2 Centrifuge
Late 89 - Mid 91	Construct Centrifuge Production Facility
Mid 91 - End 91	Trial Operation of the Production Facility
Early 91 - End 92	Design and Construct 100-Machine Cascade
End 92 - Mid 93	Install Centrifuges and Pipework
Mid 93	Commence Operation of 100-Machine Cascade
Mid 92 - Mid 95	Design and Construct 500-Machine Cascade
Early 95 - End 95	Install Centrifuges and Pipework
Early 96	Commence Operation of 500-Machine Cascade

After repeated questions, the Iraqi authorities identified the probable location of the 100-machine cascade as Building B01 at the Al Furat Centrifuge Production Facility.

Cascade Design

20. Cascade calculations had commenced for both a 36-centrifuge and a 102-centrifuge cascade. the aim being to enrich from natural uranium to 3.0% while stripping to 0.35%. These calculations, or at least the curves presented, indicate that the Iraqi scientists were still at an early stage of understanding.

Uranium Feed Preparation for Centrifuges

21. Information supplied by the Iraqis indicates that UF-4 production was initially a wet process. This was replaced by a gas phase system, based on fluorination of UO_2 in a rotating tube furnace with Freon 12.

Initially the team was told that UF_6 production was a laboratory scale batch tube furnace process using 2.5 times excess of F_2. Later it was told that the process was one with three furnaces and cold traps in series. This was said to be 100% efficient in fluorine. leaving an excess of UF_4. Iraqi scientists also said that they had developed their own fluorine production cells.

Technical Summation

22. The R & D test programme and cascade design as declared were at an early stage. Nevertheless, the Iraqi authorities were confident enough to press ahead with the construction of a large centrifuge production facility that was designed to a very high standard. Even though the only successful centrifuge trials declared to the inspection team had been carried out with carbon fibre overwrap cylinders, the Al Furat complex was being designed for maraging steel cylinder production - a technology which the Iraqis declared not to have mastered (see para.16). There was no evidence of any attempt to procure or put to work a carbon fibre rotor production line. This inconsistency has to be clarified.

The Iraqi authorities appeared very confident that they could circumvent export controls and obtain adequate quantities of 350 Grade maraging steel to enable them to manufacture all-maraging-steel rotors. The design of caps and baffles - and indeed of the centrifuge overall - leads to the conclusion that substantial help has been given by a person. or persons, with knowledge of an early Western-type centrifuge.

0249   /...

If used in cascade, between 1600 and 2000 centrifuges would be capable of producing 25kg/year of HEU enriched to 90% in uranium-235.

The conclusion reached on the basis of the equipment and information declared by Iraq and the inspections carried out by the team is that unless there is still deception of an inordinate magnitude taking place, the centrifuge enrichment programme was, at the time of the commencement of hostilities, second in priority to the EMIS programme. Also, the team is reasonably convinced that the centrifuge enrichment programme was receiving at least periodic -- and quite probably continuing - assistance from non-Iraqi sources. This assistance went beyond the supply of equipment and materials -- although this was substantial -- and very probably included continuing technical advice.

R & D activities for the centrifuge programme appear to have started later than those for the EMIS programme, but with assistance from abroad with both design and procurement -- which, in the team's opinion, Iraq certainly received -- and with a fairly large amount of skilled manpower and substantial financial resources being made available the intent was obvious. The programme was set upon a course to produce substantial numbers of centrifuges. The nature of the economics of this effort makes it impossible to draw any other conclusion than that the effort was for non-peaceful purposes. The programme would have reached its objectives with time. The plans set for the mid-1990s would most probably have been achieved once the capability to flow-turn and weld maraging steel had been acquired. While the damage incurred has set the programme back 2 to 3 years, the main know-how is still there.

Weaponization Activities

23. The fourth inspection team visited a number of facilities that had been identified, either through Special Commission designation or because of their general characteristics, as possible sites for nuclear weaponization activities.[1] Among the items shown and the information provided to it, the team found no direct evidence of an on-going weaponization programme. Dr. Jaffar stated that there had been no political decision by the Government of Iraq to proceed with nuclear explosive design and production and that any design activities that had occurred had been only individual exercises by interested scientists.

Whatever the intentions of the Government of Iraq, the team saw remarkable capabilities in relevant technologies -- much, however, in a state of only partial completeness.

There were significant inconsistencies and a lack of candor in the replies of individual facility managers. This increases the concern about the end-use of the technologies being developed, but by itself it is inconclusive.

One of the most visible weaponization activities is high explosive testing. The most suitable facility for this activity which came to the inspection team's attention was the firing bunker -- now heavily damaged -- belonging to the Hatheen Establishment at Al Musayyib, near the Al Atheer materials research center. The bunker appears to have been unfinished at the time of the Gulf hostilities, although it has clearly been used a few times for the crude testing of conventional explosives. It is capable of supporting significant physics experiments critical to nuclear weapons development, although no instrumentation of significance was seen. Some construction work is under way at this site despite the damage, and this suggests that such a facility has very high priority. Some development work could have been done at a less sophisticated site, but the team has not found any evidence of this.

0250

/...

Iraqi's uranium metallurgy technology is sophisticated and adequate for a weapons programme. A uranium metal reduction, casting and machining capability at Al Tuwaitha was developed - ostensibly - for an armor penetrator programme. The Al Atheer materials research center has all the capabilities necessary for applying the experience already gained in uranium metallurgy to a nuclear weapons programme if a decision to proceed in such a direction were to be made.

Up until the last day of the inspection, Iraq's high explosive production capability was claimed to be limited to RDX and melt-cast technologies, which are adequate for - but inconsistent with - an optimized nuclear weapon design; the team found no open relationship between the high explosive industry and the IAEC. Late on the last day of the inspection, the team was given the surprising information that "hundreds of tonnes of HMX" had been imported by Iraq and that the Iraqis had considerable experience in casting such material. This raised new questions concerning Iraq's capabilities and facilities and the credibility of previous Iraqi statements which -- because of the manner and timing of the release of the information by Iraq -- it was impossible to pursue adequately.

The team observed the fabrication of exploding bridge wire (EBW) detonators at Al Qa Qaa. Plausible, alternative explanations were given for the Iraqi interest in purchasing and using fire set components. Two experts at Al Qa Qaa have designed and tried to acquire components for firing sets for multi-EBW systems to be used in rocket motor stage separation, with 0.5 microsecond simultaneity. The testing and instrumentation reviewed by the team were crude.

In general, the team did not see instrumentation, diagnostics or experimental set-ups at vacant, damaged or partially finished facilities. This makes it very difficult to assess past performance or intent. What the team saw in the areas of quality control and diagnostics tended to be crude, go/no-go approaches. In response to specific queries, Iraq has now acknowledged the procurement of certain dual-use diagnostic instruments of potential relevance for weaponization.

Initiator science - including Po-210, Be, and deuterium-tritium reactions - was absent in what the team was able to observe. Dr. Jaffar acknowledged that Iraq has produced Po-210 in small quantities for steady-state neutron sources.

With only a very few exceptions, the people met on the sites were technicians, usually ill-equipped to answer questions. Most answers were vague and limited. In sharp contrast, the meetings with Dr. Jaffar were more productive because he had the authority to discuss sensitive subjects.

In general, Al Atheer and its companion facilities at Hatheen and Al Mutayyib constitute a complete and sufficient potential nuclear weapons laboratory and production facility within one common fence line. This combined facility is so big and so well equipped that it can clearly do much more than the limited non-weapons activities that the Iraqis claim as its purpose. It is certainly a top candidate for future monitoring.

Al Jesira Facility (Mosul Production Facility)

24. The Al-Jesira Facility (also known as the Mosul Production Facility) was first inspected, on the basis of a Special Commission designation, by the third inspection team. During that initial inspection, the facility -- not previously declared by the Iraqi authorities -- was stated to be a plant for the production of UO_2 and UCl_4. After the initial inspection, a number of

0251   /...

questions remained open, including questions about precise material flows into and from the facility and whether UF$_6$ was also produced there. Also, in their declaration of 27 July 1991 the Iraqis had stated that waste from this facility had contained 10 tonnes of uranium which had been moved to a nearby location. In an attempt to clarify these matters, it was decided to conduct an additional inspection of this facility; this inspection took place on 5-6 August 1991.

UO$_2$ Production Plant

25. Commissioning of the UO$_2$ plant was declared by the Iraqi authorities to have taken place in July 1989, full operation beginning in November 1989. The design capacity of the plant was declared to have been 500 kg of UO$_2$/day. It was further declared, however, that the plant was seldom able to operate at this rate and was only reaching operational stability at the time of the attack. The 10 tonnes of uranium that went to the liquid waste tanks (see para. 24) were cited as indicative of the problems being encountered.

Although the plant utilities building was heavily damaged, all services were identified. It was felt by the inspection team that they were reasonable for the plant as declared. The receipt and storage area of the plant had been totally removed, graded and covered with gravel by the Iraqis. The process area was collapsed in such a manner that it was clear that the bombing had been only partially responsible - the largest amount of damage being the result of post-attack deception efforts by the Iraqis themselves. The entire plant had been covered by approximately 1m^2 x 5cm sheets of styrofoam and this in turn covered with dirt. Gravel had been spread thickly around the entire plant, making sampling almost impossible. The general size of the plant seemed reasonable for its declared purpose.

UCl$_4$ Production Plant

Commissioning of the UCl$_4$ plant was said to have been in April 1990. Operational problems were said to have persisted from precommissioning, in February 1990 through to shutdown, in November 1990. It was claimed that actual operations lasted altogether only about two months and that during this period 1.2 tonne of UCl$_4$ was produced and shipped to the Ministry of Industry.

The design capacity of the UCl$_4$ plant was said to be 150 kg UCl$_4$/day/line. There were two lines, but only one was said to have been operational. Corrosion problems were declared to have been the major reason for production problems. In addition, volatility problems in the furnaces and problems with the chillers were said to have hindered operations.

The operators stated that the plant was the "only industrial UCl$_4$ supplier in Iraq"; they had no knowledge of who would use the UCl$_4$, they did not know what processes would require the UCl$_4$, they had never been visited by any staff of the IAEC; and they had no plans to expand production to include other uranium compounds. All of these statements by the operators were subsequently found to be false. It was declared that all UCl$_4$ was produced for and sent to the Ministry of Industry in Baghdad. However, all computer records of production, procurements and shipments were declared to have been stored, without backups, on a single personal computer that was destroyed in the bombing.

Relatively little damage was done by the bombing to the UCl$_4$ production plant; the purification (sublimation) area and the utilities suffered most. In the production area, the greatest damage was the result of post-bombing deception activities of the Iraqis themselves. The reception, laboratory and process areas had been cleared of all equipment, and the floors and lower walls had been painted; dirt had been thrown on top of the wet paint. The control room and offices suffered little damage, but all equipment and records had been removed. The computer was said to have been housed in a

/...

0252

different building and to have been destroyed. If there was indeed no on-line data acquisition at this plant, there would have had to be hard copies of the data. The team found the residues of several paper "camp fires" outside the building - an indication of pre-inspection document destruction. In subsequent discussions, the Iraqi authorities admitted that plans called for the on-site production of EMIS source slugs and a UF$_6$ production line to support the centrifuge programme.

Wastes from the UO$_2$ Plant

27. As earlier described, the Iraqis declared that wastes from the UO$_2$ plant contained 10 tonne [later stated to be 13 tonne] of uranium as a result of equipment design problems and operational errors: the wastes had been stored in two evaporative tanks. When the bombing started, the Iraqi authorities feared that these open tanks would be hit and cause an environmental problem. They therefore decided to transfer the solution (approximately 2500 m^3) by truck to a 5000-m^3 petroleum storage tank about 30 km from Al Jesira. This storage tank contained an unknown volume of kerosene. Although repeated attempts were made to gain a coherent explanation as to why the Iraqis felt the thick-walled, open evaporative tanks were more hazardous than an oil tank farm as a storage location, none was forthcoming. The most probable explanation -- and the one that fits the other large-scale deception efforts carried out at this plant - is that the wastes were moved in order to avoid detection of the real purpose of the plant within Iraq's undeclared uranium enrichment programme.

28. During the inspection, the waste tanks at Al Jesira were found to be about two-thirds full of water said to be for fire protection. There was evidence of solution spillage from the two evaporative tanks. Extensive pouring of new concrete around these tanks had occurred, so that sampling was fruitless. The petroleum storage tank posed sampling problems: the external valve intended for use in sampling could not be opened -- nor could it have been closed if forced open -- and internal baffles in the tank prevented deep sampling from the top.

In any case, the solution was inhomogenous and no capability existed for homogenizing it. The sample finally taken consisted primarily of kerosene and was not representative of the declared 10 tonne of uranium in the waste.

Nuclear-Material-Related Issues arising during the Fourth Inspection

29. The first IAEA Inspection Mission carried out pursuant to Security Council resolution 687 took place from 15 to 21 May 1991, the primary objective being to verify the accuracy and completeness of the declarations made by Iraq on 18 and 27 April 1991. The declarations did not mention previously exempted nuclear material, which included one irradiated fuel assembly of the IRT-type containing 1200 g of 10%-enriched uranium (initial values); exemption had been approved by the Agency on 11 May 1988.

At the insistence of the first inspection team, the Iraqis presented the previously exempted material, which - as a result of chemical reprocessing activities that they had carried out with the material - consisted of the chemically recovered uranium together with 2.3 g of plutonium separated from the irradiated fuel assembly and then purified. More importantly, the Iraqis declared that the exempted material had been subjected to "fuel reprocessing experiments". Exemption had been granted under Article 37 of INFCIRC/172 (the agreement between Iraq and the IAEA for the application of safeguards in connection with NPT), which limits the quantity of nuclear material that can be exempted from safeguards in a State.

0253   /...

On 27 July 1991 Iraq submitted to the fourth inspection team a list of nuclear material which included material not previously declared (Appendix 1); there were 20 separate items related to the Iraqi nuclear programme. The list was discussed with the Iraqis on 1 August.

Since the 7 July declaration it was apparent that Iraq had embarked on a clandestine programme to produce natural uranium fuel elements from undeclared nuclear material (UO$_2$) in the Experimental Reactor Fuel Fabrication Laboratory (ERFFL), to irradiate this fuel in the IRT-5000 reactor and subsequently to chemically process the irradiated fuel in the Radiochemical Laboratory, to which safeguard inspectors had no access. On 1 August the inspection team raised additional questions which were submitted to the Iraqis in writing on 2 August. A written reply was received on 6 August.

The following details relate to items No. 1, 2, 5, 10, 16 and 17 (see Appendix 1) of the 27 July declaration, which the team believes should be considered in any further assessment of Iraq's conduct in relation to its obligations under INFCIRC/172.

Item No. 1 (uranium metal)

Of the declared 27,000 kg of uranium metal declared on 7 July 1991 to have been imported from Brazil, 1000 kg had been converted to uranium metal for what was stated as use in a heavy bullet production programme.

Item No. 2 (3g of separated plutonium)

This plutonium had been recovered from irradiated natural uranium fuel elements within the framework of what was stated to have been an R&D programme related to "Pu extraction from spent fuel" in order to "to determine operational conditions for the manufacture of ceramic nuclear fuel which can be used in nuclear plants".

It was declared that three fuel elements (very similar to the EK-10 type but containing natural uranium oxide) had been manufactured between 10 December 1988 and 2 February 1989 at the Experimental Reactor Fuel Fabrication Laboratory (ERFFL). These fuel elements were stated to have been irradiated in the IRT-5000 as follows:

- One element: 22 days irradiation over 7 weeks (3 days/week) between February 1989 and April 1989; separated plutonium about 0.5g

- Two elements: 50 days irradiation between September 1989 and January 1990; separated plutonium about 2.2 grams

Irradiation had been performed using two different positions of the beryllium (Be) reflector in the IRT-5000 reactor core. According to available information, the irradiation was not continuous, i.e. the fuel elements could have been temporarily removed from their positions in the beryllium reflector in order to escape detection by safeguard inspectors. The IRT-5000 reactor had been regularly inspected twice a year.

The chemical processing of the three irradiated fuel elements and the purification of the separated plutonium were declared as having been carried out in Al Tuwaitha Building No. 9, the Radiochemical Laboratory (to which the safeguards inspectors had not had access), according to the following schedule:

- One element: between November 1989 and February 1990

- Two elements: between the beginning of February 1990 and July 1990

0254

/...

Item No. 5 (two irradiated fuel cells)

It was clarified in discussions with the Iraqi authorities that the terms "cell" and "element" are equivalent; basically the elements ("cells") are aluminium casings (shrouds) of the EK-10 type into which the zircaloy-cladded pins were loaded. Asked about the facility where the casings were produced, the Iraqis stated that the casings were taken from dummy fuel elements supplied by the USSR. However, the team believes that the manufacture of casings of this type would not have posed a major technical problem for Iraq.

The two elements ("cells") contain 7.9 kg of natural uranium in the form of UO_2 pellets; the UO_2 powder was stated as having been produced at the Mosul purification, and conversion plant; the uranium was said to have originated at the Al Qa'im facility (phosphate fertilizer complex).

The manufacturing facility for the pins was said to be the ERFFL, production being declared as having taken place in the period between 13 August 1989 and 17 November 1989.

Irradiation of these two elements is said to have been for a total of 37 days in the safeguarded IRT-5000 reactor during the period from mid-September 1990 to the first week of November 1990. At the time of the hostilities, the two elements had not yet been chemically reprocessed as planned. The Iraqis refused to answer repeated requests for the date of the removal of the two elements from the reactor core. They stated that, after removal from the core, the elements were put into a water-filled steel cylinder, placed on a truck prior to the first inspection mission then moved around in order to avoid detection by the first three inspection teams. The fourth team was told that during the first inspection this truck was within the boundaries of the Tuwaitha facility and that it moved as the inspectors moved. Immediately before the fourth team arrived, on 27 July 1991, the elements are said to have been placed at Location B, in an additional storage tank which had not been declared as such to previous teams. This must count as one of the most potentially dangerous deception activities encountered so far by the inspection teams. This information was received only on 6 August 1991. On 8 August 1991 the team visited Location B and found two storage tanks in addition to the previously declared 14 tanks. At the team's request they were both opened. One tank contained the two irradiated elements in a water-filled open steel cylinder. The other tank contained five irradiated beryllium elements from the IRT-5000 core; they were stored in a drum.

The storage tank with the two cells was given the number 15, photographs were taken and it was seals were applied using the procedure previously applied to tanks 1-14.

Item No. 10 (46 natural UO_2 experimental fuel rods)

These rods were made of UO_2 pellets in zircaloy cladding; production occurred at the ERFFL between 20 November 1990 and 30 December 1990. The total uranium contained is 11,000 g. The rods had not yet been irradiated and are currently stored at the "New Storage".

Item No. 16 (radioactive waste)

The Iraqis stated that this waste originated primarily from the spent fuel reprocessing activities performed in Building No. 9, where the three elements (item 2 above) were reprocessed. The liquid waste (HAW) had been diluted with low-activity waste (LAW) and subjected to concentration before bitumenization in Building No. 35 (Radioactive Waste Section) during the period February 1990 to May 1990.

Item No. 17 (UCl_4)

This type of nuclear material was already included in the 7 July 1991 declaration. The material was used in the EMIS programme, i.e. it was suitable for isotopic enrichment and had therefore reached the starting point of safeguards.

/...

0255

30. The 27 July 1991 declaration provided additional information that seems to the team to constitute evidence of Iraq's violations of existing safeguards provisions. However, of more immediate concern was the additional information which was obtained during question/answer sessions with the Iraqis and which relates to their sometimes reckless efforts to deceive safeguards inspectors and the inspection teams.

The team was particularly concerned by the fact that many Iraqi statements were not supported by any source "documentation" - production records of the fuel fabrication plant, nuclear material transfer records, reactor operation records, fuel history cards, etc. The Iraqi authorities claimed that these documents/records had been destroyed, but in the light of various observations (e.g. of empty but unburnt filing cabinets) the team does not consider this to be a credible explanation; moreover, one would have expected that, with a fuctioning national nuclear materials accounting system, the Iraqis would keep duplicates of relevant documents at the IAEC's establishments.

Therefore, the magnitude of Iraq's nuclear fuel manufacturing capability and the declared amount of irradiated and chemically processed irradiated fuel remain subject to a great deal of uncertainty.

Under any circumstances, however, Iraq should be required to provide the IAEA with a complete itemized inventory list of nuclear materials, which should indicate:

- the origins of all nuclear materials in Iraq's possession as of 3 April 1991;

- the places/facilities where the materials were produced or processed;

- their current location.

This would facilitate verifications of the accuracy and completeness of the various Iraqi declarations (18 and 27 April, 7 and 27 July).

The Iraqi Nuclear Program -- A Material Flow Perspective

31. The attached schematic chart with flow and inventory quantities represents accumulated information to date (19 August 1991). The flows and inventories are based on information acquired from:

1) The November 1990 IAEA inspection report;
2) Safeguards Information Treatment accounting printouts;
3) The 27 April 1991 Iraqi declaration;
4) The 7 July 1991 Iraqi declaration and follow-up reports;
5) The 27 July 1991 Iraqi declaration and follow-up reports; and
6) Discussion, briefing and seminar notes from IAEA inspection missions 3 and 4.

Much of the information on nuclear material provided by the Iraqis has been conflicting or incomplete. An effort has been made in preparing this schematic overview to evaluate the data, to identify areas of consistency and inconsistency, and to identify gaps in the information. Missing or questionable data will require follow-up actions. Further review is also needed by members of the last two inspection teams. Therefore, changes and/or corrections will be made as they prove necessary. The objective in preparing an overview of this type is to provide a framework for organizing and testing the information that is now becoming available. With such a framework it should become easier to detect erroneous data and gaps in our knowledge with regard to where nuclear material flowed in both the open and the clandestine parts of the programme. Following is a material balance summary corresponding to the attached schematic chart. All quantities refer to elemental uranium.

/...

0256

APPENDIX I

In response to the request of the International Inspection Team during the third Inspection visit, the table of nuclear material previously mentioned in the letter of the Iraqi Foreign Minister dated 7 July 1991 was rearranged in fulfilment of the promise of the Vice-President of the Iraqi Atomic Energy Commission (IAEC) to the International Inspection Team.

Ser. No.	Material	Weight	Remarks
1	Uranium metal	1 ton (approx)	
2	Plutonium (PuO$_2$ & solutions)	3 g (approx)	
3	ADU (ammonium di-uranate) & uranium oxides	50 g (approx) 70 g (approx)	Enriched at 10% (remains of the material exempted by Safeguards)
4	Uranium tetrafluoride	20 kg (approx)	
5	Irradiated fuel cell (element)		Two items
6	New Berillium cell (element)		One Item
7	Scrap UO$_4$		Eight barrels
8	UO$_2$ powder	2.5 tons (approx)	
9	Ventilation filter containing UO$_4$	100 kg	
10	Natural UO$_2$ fuel rods (experimental)		46 rods
11	ADU (natural uranium)	220 kg (approx)	
12	UO$_2$ (NO3)$_2$ powder (natural uranium)	400 g (approx)	Imported laboratory samples
13	U3O8 natural uranium	100 kg	
14	Plutonium	mgs (no figure)	Imported ampules
15	UO$_4$ in the form of liquid wastes from Al-Geslra laboratory	10 tons (approx)	
16	Radioactive wastes in the form of concrete containers (58 containers)		Radioactive wastes that do not contain nuclear material
17	Packages full of UCl$_4$ and plastic containers of UCl$_4$	150 kg (approx)	
18	Liquid wastes of natural uranium	6 kg (approx)	
19	U233	63 mgs	Imported
20	Depleted uranium	2 kg (approx)	Imported

Notes

1. All the above weights are approximate.

2. List of enriched and depleted uranium produced by the separators in Al Tuwaitha site were handed over to the Third Inspection Team on 18 July 1991.

/...

0257

APPENDIX II

IRAQ NUCLEAR PROGRAM

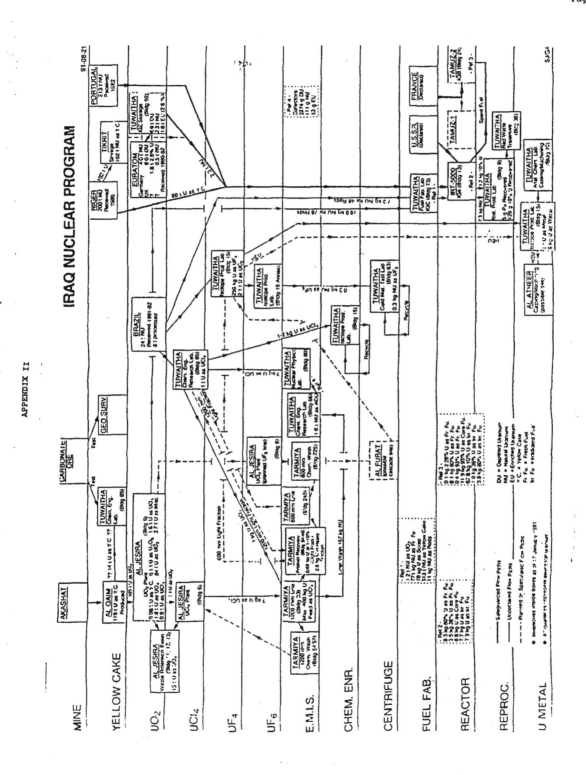

0258

외 무 부

종 별 :

번 호 : UNW-2477 일 시 : 91 0906 1720

수 신 : 장 관(중동일,국연,기정)

발 신 : 주 유엔 대사

제 목 : 걸프사태(대이락 무기 공급 금지)

　　　대: WUN-2566

　　1. 대호 내용을 금 9.4 자로 유엔측에 통보하였음을 보고함

　　2. 한편 금일 유엔측이 발표한 이락 특정 무기 폐기관련 유엔 대표단 파견내역을 별첨 송부함

　　　　첨부(FAX): 상기내역.끝

　　　　(대사 노창희-국장)

중아국　　　　　　　　1차보　　2차보　　국기국　　외정실　　분석관　　청와대
안기부

PAGE 1　　　　　　　　　　　　　　　　　　　　　　　91.09.07　　09:03 WI

　　　　　　　　　　　　　　　　　　　　　　　　　　외신 1과 통제관

UNW(F)-511 국연 *06 1720*
(중동일, 국연, 기정) 총 1대

NOTE FOR THE SPOKESMAN

Special Commission Inspection Schedule Update

Friday 6 September 1991

Here follows a comprehensive list of missions carried out to date by the Special Commission created to implement the disarmament provisions of Resolution 687.

Nuclear

15-21 May	1st inspection mission
22 June-3 July	2nd inspection mission
30 June-3 July	high-level mission (on denied access)
7-18 July	3rd inspection mission
27 July-10 August	4th inspection mission

Chemical

9-15 June	1st inspection mission (survey)
11-14 August	2nd mission (destruction techniques)
31 August-8 Sept	3rd inspection mission
31 August-5 Sept	4th mission (advance party--Muthanna)

Biological

2-8 August	1st inspection mission

Ballistic missiles

30 June-7 July	1st inspection (and destruction)
18-20 July	2nd (surprise) inspection & destruct.
8-15 Aug	3rd mission (incl. "super gun")
6-13 Sept	4th inspection (and destruction)

Future missions

Nuclear: 5th inspection mission mid-September.

Chemical: Large mission to Muthanna (over 50 inspectors for four weeks) beginning early October.

Biological: Will continue.

Ballistic missiles: Fifth mission to destroy the "super gun" late September.

F. Eckhard

fg3-82

\# *UNW-2477*
전부

/—/

0260

외 무 부

종 별 :

번 호 : UNW-2552 　　　　　　　　　일 시 : 91 0910 1830

수 신 : 장 관(중동일,연일,기정)

발 신 : 주 유엔 대사

제 목 : 걸프사태(대이락 무기 공급 금지)

　　대: WUN-2566

　　대호 아측 통보내용이 9.9 자 안보리 문서 (S/23016) 로 배포되었음을 보고함

　　첨부: FAX 안보리 문서(S/23016), UNW(F)-515 .끝

　　(대사 노창희-국장)

중아국　　1차보　　국기국　　외정실　　분석관　　안기부

PAGE 1　　　　　　　　　　　　　　　　　　　　91.09.11　　08:50 WG

　　　　　　　　　　　　　　　　　　　　　　외신 1과　통제관

**UNITED
NATIONS**

UNW(FI)-515 1991 1830
(중동일.면일.기정)   총 2 매

S

Security Council

Distr.
GENERAL

S/23016
9 September 1991

ORIGINAL: ENGLISH

NOTE BY THE SECRETARY-GENERAL

The attached note verbale, dated 6 September 1991, was addressed to the
Secretary-General by the Permanent Observer of the Republic of Korea to the
United Nations.

91-29009 2672j (E)   /...

#UNW-2552
첨부옥

2-1

0262

S/23016
English.
Page 2

<u>Annex</u>

<u>Note verbale dated 6 September 1991 from the Permanent
Observer of the Republic of Korea to the United Nations
addressed to the Secretary-General</u>

The Permanent Observer of the Republic of Korea to the United Nations
presents his compliments to the Secretary-General of the United Nations and,
with reference to his note dated 3 July 1991, has the honour to inform him
that the Government of the Republic of Korea is abiding by resolutions
687 (1991) and 700 (1991) concerning the prevention of the sale or supply of
arms and related material to Iraq or Iraqi nationals and that the competent
authorities have also taken domestic measures to ensure the implementation of
the relevant provisions of the said resolutions.

-----

2 - 2

0263

외 무 부

종 별 :

번 호 : UNW-2594

일 시 : 91 0911 1900

수 신 : 장 관(연일,중동일,기정)

발 신 : 주 유엔 대사

제 목 : 안보리동향

1. 유엔 이락 특정 무기폐기 특위(UNSCOM) 의 이락내 사찰활동과 관련 최근 이락측이 동사찰반 전용 헬기반입을 불허 (이락 헬기 이용요구) 함에따라 동 특위 R.EKEUS 위원장은 안보리 의장에게 이문제를 제기하여 온것으로 알려짐.(안보리결의 707 호 위반)

2. 안보리의장(불란서)은 본건관련 이사국들과 개별협의중인바, 보도에 의하면 이락기 이륙금지 및 무력사용 경고를 포함하는 안보리 결의안 추진도 검토중이라함.

3. 금 9.11 당관 원참사관이 불란서 J.SILVA 서기관에게 탐문한바에 의하면, 개별협의중 특기할 결과는 아직 없으며 곧 상임이사국 간 본건토의가 있을것이라고함.

4. 상기관련 동향 추보위계임.

첨부:NYT 사설, 기사 및 WP 기사:UNW(F)-519 끝

(대사 노창희-국장)

국기국	장관	차관	1차보	중아국	분석관	청와대	안기부

91.09.12 0 06

외신 2과 통 관 BS

0264

UNW(刊)-519 1091 1900
(연월. 중동원. 기점)
총 30개

#별첨

Keep the Cuffs on Iraq

Saddam Hussein would like to be free of international economic sanctions. But he isn't willing to meet the world's stated terms for lifting them: full compliance with the final United Nations cease-fire resolution. Instead the Iraqi dictator has tried to con world opinion by manipulating the hunger of millions of innocent Iraqi civilians.

The Security Council is obliged to address this very real human need. But it is also obliged to insist that Baghdad comply with the cease-fire resolution's arms control requirements and stop intimidating neighboring states and domestic dissidents.

Last month the Council attempted to deal honorably with the food problem. The original sanctions did not prohibit Iraq from purchasing necessary food. But by cutting off most Iraqi exports, the sanctions limited the money available to Iraq for food purchases.

So on Aug. 15 the Council authorized Baghdad to sell, under supervision, $1.6 billion worth of oil from its pipeline in Turkey. The proceeds would be deposited in a U.N.-controlled account. These revenues would then be used for approved food purchases and to meet Iraq's obligations to pay for war damages.

But so far, no oil has been sold. Baghdad refuses to go along with the Council plan, which it denounces as an unacceptable infringement of its sovereignty. It demands the right to sell more oil and control the proceeds more directly. Such stubbornness keeps the threat of mass hunger alive.

Now the Security Council is being asked to consider a report based on recommendations from Sadruddin Aga Khan, the Secretary General's main representative in Iraq. The report suggests increasing authorized oil sales by more than 50 percent, to $2.5 billion. It also suggests methods of U.N. supervision that Baghdad might regard as less threatening to its sovereignty. The motivation is humanitarian. But the report's approach would do far more harm than good.

It would ease the pressure on Iraq to comply with cease-fire obligations it continues to evade, like full disclosure of its weapons facilities. It would increase the danger of covert rearmament by letting more money, with fewer controls, pass through Baghdad's hands. And it would reward Iraq's manipulative tactics in a way likely to encourage fresh campaigns to weaken remaining sanctions.

There are better ways to feed starving Iraqis. Instead of indulging Iraq's demands for prematurely restoring full sovereignty, the United Nations could mount its own humanitarian relief operation, paid for out of frozen Iraqi funds abroad, or billed against future Iraqi oil revenues. If Baghdad refused to let U.N. relief workers enter its territory, it would fully bear the blame for any resulting suffering.

It's unfortunate that the world lacks effective ways to stop Saddam Hussein from victimizing his own people. But it has, at some cost in blood and treasure, imposed a set of requirements designed to keep him from ever again victimizing other countries. Undermining those requirements now in response to Iraqi intransigence would be an unforgivable mistake.

3-1

0265

Baghdad Requires Air Inspectors To Use Iraqi Copters, U.N. Says

By FRANK J. PRIAL
Special to The New York Times

UNITED NATIONS, Sept. 10 — Iraq has refused to allow United Nations inspectors to fly their planes over its territory, officials of the world organization said today.

As part of the United Nations-mandated cease-fire formally ending the Persian Gulf war, the Iraqis agreed to permit overflights by teams from the United Nations commission overseeing the destruction of Iraqi weapons. Germany contributed the use of three air force helicopters with crews and ground-support personnel.

After initially agreeing to the United Nations' use of the German aircraft, the Iraqis last week announced that United Nations personnel must be flown in Iraqi helicopters inside Iraq's boundaries, said Johan Molander, a spokesman for the inspectors. He said the United Nations officials had refused to comply.

"For both safety and other reasons, we would like to operate our own helicopters," Mr. Molander said. "We don't want to hear that we can't fly today because it's a Muslim holiday or because the crew is suddenly sick."

Inspections Without Preparation

To accomplish its work, he said, the commission must have independence. "It makes short-notice inspections shorter," he said.

The head of the commission, Rolf Ekeus, reported Iraq's about-face on Monday in a letter to the president of the Security Council. The Council discussed the matter briefly today.

A Western diplomat said that a recent flight in which United Nations inspectors used an Iraqi helicopter was aborted after the Iraqi pilot pretended that he was lost.

"The helicopter landed in the desert and took off again only after the pilot was threatened with disciplinary action," the diplomat said. "Shortly after they were airborne again, a door flew open on the helicopter. It raises serious questions about the quality of the Iraqi equipment."

Increasingly in recent weeks, the Iraqis have balked at provisions of the gulf war cease-fire agreement, which they accepted in April. Such provisions, they say, violate their nation's sovereignty. They especially object to restraints imposed in the proposed sale of Iraqi oil, under United Nations auspices, to raise money for food and medical supplies.

In another action today, United Nations officials near the Iraqi-Saudi Arabian border oversaw the return by the Iraqis of about 120,000 books and rare manuscripts taken from Kuwait's national library during the occupation.

The handover of the books and manuscripts near a Saudi town, Arar, was part of a schedule of such returns of Kuwaiti property that began with the return of 3,216 bars of gold bullion worth about $700 million.

3—2

U.N. Members Urge Use of Force
Against Iraq for Defying Resolution

By Trevor Rowe
Special to The Washington Post

UNITED NATIONS, Sept. 10—U.S., British and French diplomats here have urged their capitals to consider backing a tough new resolution that would authorize the use of military force to ground all Iraqi aircraft in response to Iraq's decision Sunday not to permit U.N. inspection helicopters to enter its airspace, according to a Western diplomatic source.

On Sunday, Iraq informed the United Nations that three helicopters intended for use by the Special Commission in charge of scrapping Baghdad's weapons of mass destruction would not be allowed to enter the country. Instead, Baghdad, citing safety concerns, offered to let the United Nations use Iraqi helicopters and crews, which would be familiar to Iraq's air traffic controllers.

Not only did the decision specifically contravene Resolution 707 authorizing the United Nations to use its own helicopters to inspect Iraqi weapon caches, according to diplomats, but it came immediately after technical details for such an arrangement had been agreed to by Iraqi and U.N. officials. "This defiance of U.N. Security Council resolutions is clearly unacceptable," State Department spokesman Richard Boucher said in Washington.

Western diplomats here feel that strong measures are called for as a result of what is viewed as an increasing number of Iraqi violations and continuing Iraqi "defiance." Soviet Ambassador Yuli Vorontsov warned Iraq of "serious consequences" if it failed to cooperate.

"This is a serious challenge to the council," said the Western diplomatic source, "We need to say to the Iraqis, 'You put anything up in the air and it will fall down. We'll decide what flies, we'll close you down, and let the U.N. operate.'"

The source, who spoke after an informal meeting of the Security Council, added that there was agreement among the U.S., British and French delegations here for a resolution permitting such action. He predicted that such a resolution, if introduced, would ultimately be adopted by a majority of Security Council members.

The diplomat said Iraq should be warned by the president of the council that it was in "blatant defiance." If Iraq failed to respond, then the council should adopt the resolution authorizing the grounding of all Iraqi aircraft.

The source said the United States, Britain and France, which are all permanent members of the Security Council, want to avoid another "hand-wringing" resolution that calls on Iraq to comply but lacks specific enforcement measures.

The source described a resolution authorizing force as the "ideal scenario." However, he cautioned that while the British, French and U.S. missions here favor strong action, military officials in the three capitals might have a different view. He added that no decision has been made in London, Paris or Washington. Pentagon spokesman Pete Williams said the United States would confer with other members of the Security Council on the issue; and it is not considering "unilateral" military action against Iraq, the Los Angeles Times reported.

Underlying the desire for strong action is the increasing conviction that if Iraq is not brought into line, the authority of the council will be perceived as eroding. "The resolutions are clear on what Iraq should do, and they're not doing it, and they're doing this in a deliberately provocative and outrageous manner," the source said.

Aside from not permitting the United Nations to use its own helicopters, Iraq has been criticized for welding together Scud missile-transporters the United Nations thought had been cut in half and rendered inoperative.

"We discovered the launchers had been welded together to facilitate transport. I don't think they could have been used . . . but it could have been a first step," said Johan Molander, the special adviser to the U.N. Special Commission.

Western diplomats also are concerned about Iraq's efforts to retain its old border with Kuwait despite a new one being defined by the United Nations. "They've pushed their posts into no man's land to where they shouldn't be," said the Western source.

"They should have kept back, but they've snuggled up front. When we ask why, they say, 'So we can retain the claim to the border as we see it exists,'" the source said.

3-3

0267

외 무 부

종 별 :

번 호 : UNW-2621 일 시 : 91 0912 1900

수 신 : 장 관(국연,중동일,기정)

발 신 : 주 유엔 대사

제 목 : 안보리 동향(이락 특정무기폐기 문제)

　　1.유엔 이락특정무기 폐기 특위 R. EKEUS위원장은 9.11 유엔 본부에서 기자회견을 갖고 연호 특위헬기 사용 문제와 관련, 사전통보 기간단축 불시 점검활동을 위해서는 이락측 헬기사용은 부적절 함을 <u>강조하였음</u>

　　2.또한 동 위원장은 특위에 대한 이락 협조문제와 관련 무기폐기 작업의 주요분야에서 <u>이락측의 협조가 미흡하다고 평</u>가하였음

　　3.본건 헬기 사용문제 (안보리 결의 707호위반)관련 9.13 안보리 비공식 협의가 개최될예정인바, 관련 동향 추보위 계임.끝

　　첨부(FAX)

　　1.NYT 지 기사(9.12)

　　2.WP 지 컬럼

　　UNW(F)-521

　　(대사 노창희-국장)

UNW(FT)-521 10912 19~
(국연. 중동일. 기계)   총2연

U.N. Says Iraq Is Stalling on Arms Destruction

By FRANK J. PRIAL
Special to The New York Times

UNITED NATIONS, Sept. 11 — The head of a special United Nations commission overseeing the destruction of Iraq's chemical, biological and nuclear arsenals asserted today that Iraq was continuing to delay and obstruct the commission's work.

"We cannot say Iraq has cooperated in any of the major areas, unfortunately," said the official, Rolf Ekeus.

Under terms of the cease-fire that ended the Persian Gulf war, Iraq agreed to the inspection and destruction of all its weapons of mass destruction and of all its sites for producing them in the future.

Mr. Ekeus said his inspectors had "made some progress," but still lacked a fundamental understanding of what he called Iraq's "master plan."

"We have lots of facts," he said. "I take it there must be an idea behind them, but we haven't been given that. Until we understand everything, we must not rest."

In the months since the war ended, Iraq has admitted to pursuing a three-pronged effort to produce enriched uranium and inspectors have discovered evidence of continuing chemical and biological warfare programs.

"How do all these activities fit together?" Mr. Ekeus said. He noted that Iraq had spent billions of dollars on a nuclear weapons program but continued to insist it was a program intended for peaceful purposes.

When pushed by the commission, Iraq has cooperated, to a small extent, in the search for chemical and biological weapons, said Johan Molander, a spokesman for the commission. But, he said, Iraq is concerned about the deteriorating stability of those weapons and would prefer to have them disarmed and destroyed.

As an example of Iraq's intransigeance, Mr. Ekeus said inspection teams found that the Iraqis had actu-

ally reassembled two Scud missile-launchers that had previously been dismantled as part of the cease-fire agreement. He also cited Iraq's refusal to permit the United Nations to use three German helicopters to ferry its teams around inside Iraqi territory. Calling the German helicopters "workhorses," he said they were essential to the task of carrying out unannounced investigations of hidden Iraqi weapons-production sites.

8,000 Pieces Destroyed

Iraq's United Nations representative, Abdul al-Anbari, took issue with Mr. Ekeus, saying: "I believe my Government has fully cooperated with the Special Commission. I am aware of Mr. Ekeus's statements and I find in them no specific facts that show we have not cooperated."

He said his country had turned down the Special Commission's request to be permitted to use German helicopters for overflights in Iran on security grounds.

"German aircraft, German pilots and German photographers could be used for German intelligence purposes," Mr. Anbari said, adding: "The U.N. has its own aircraft and its own crews. We would have no objection whatsoever to them."

Of 46,000 pieces of chemical ordnance, found by United Nations teams after the end of the war, 8,000 have been destroyed, Mr. Ekeus said. Most of the weapons contained nerve gas, he said, but some held mustard and tear gas.

He said the United Nations teams had destroyed 460 "major items" related to Iraq's ballistic missile pro-

grams, including 59 Scud and 9 Hussein al-Fahd missiles.

At the same time, he noted that Iraq had admitted acquiring some 800 missiles.

≠UNW-2621
청요

2-1

Jim Hoagland

Unfinished Business in the Gulf

The good news of the Soviet break-up and the bad news of a bitter U.S.-Israeli clash over loan guarantees and peace talks combine to produce one unrelentingly bad effect: America's current preoccupations buy valuable time for ex-Enemy Number One, Saddam Hussein. The Iraqi dictator breathes easier while American energies and attention are focused elsewhere.

The attrition strategy that the Bush administration adopted in May has proved vulnerable both to the rush of outside events and the strategy's internal contradictions. President Bush's middle course of military containment and economic isolation allows Saddam room to regain the initiative that had supposedly been taken from him forever with his expulsion from Kuwait.

Iraqi troops have mounted at least two raids behind the U.S.-dictated cease-fire line in the Kuwait theater to recover weapons in recent weeks. By going all the way to Bubiyan Island, as they did on Aug. 28, the Iraqis send the message that Saddam is returning to the regional intimidation business as the strong American position established by Operation Desert Storm erodes.

Saddam's fear of American retaliation has evidently lessened since July 26, when Washington let its deadline for a full disclosure and surrender of nuclear material pass without action, even though the Iraqis failed to comply.

Iraq now poses new obstacles by denying United Nations inspection teams the helicopters they need to hunt for hidden chemical weapons and nuclear facilities. The United States also did nothing when an Iraqi fixed-wing aircraft defied the order banning flights from Um Qasr airfield on the Kuwaiti frontier last month.

Saddam has also gone on the offensive in the north of Iraq, scuttling his autonomy talks with the Kurds and sending Republican Guard units back into the Kurdish town of Kirkuk.

Saddam's bid to renew his authority has drawn only a muted response from the Bush administration, which has understandably been riveted on the implosion of the Soviet Union.

But the concentration on the second Russian Revolution is only part of the reason for the White House's reluctance to respond with force to Iraqi transgressions. Bush's attrition strategy has shown itself to be difficult to implement, a fact that the administration is not eager to spotlight.

"Our experience shows that we could not be sure we would have gotten all the nuclear sites with new bombing raids," said one senior administration official. "So what would we have done after conducting a bombing raid at the end of July? Would we have announced that we had probably destroyed the nuclear sites we told the American people last winter we had already destroyed?"

The overselling of the military effectiveness of Desert Storm has returned to haunt Bush. So have Arab rivalries that were submerged during and just after Desert Storm but which resurfaced in the war's uncertain aftermath. The idea of a regional security force the United States wanted built around Egyptian and Syrian units has been quietly buried because of these differences.

Political change in Turkey also complicates U.S. military options. The new prime minister, Mesut Yilmaz, will be tempted to capitalize on a spreading feeling among Turks that Ankara did not get enough out of Washington and the European Community to justify its heavy investment in the coalition war on Iraq. One way of doing this would be to ask Western troops to leave their base near Iraqi Kurdistan.

Turkish agreement to the stationing of a mixed battalion of United States, French and British troops to deter new Iraqi atrocities against the Kurds expires at the end of this month.

There seems to be little enthusiasm within the administration for the difficult bargaining it may take to get Yilmaz to renew the small, militarily marginal "Poised Hammer" ground force for another three months. Saddam will proclaim its withdrawal as further proof that he was right when he said that he would outlast the Americans.

Bush and Israeli Prime Minister Yitzhak Shamir are bitterly fighting each other over peace talks and money rather than concentrating on the unfinished business of finishing off Saddam. Instead of checking the drift that has allowed Saddam to regroup, they allow him to slip further down the list of priorities.

This underestimates Saddam's capacity for surprise and villainy. He cannot be content simply to hunker down and survive. He built his regime on terror and force, and he must show he can still exercise both if he is to dominate Iraq and its neighborhood.

Saddam's own psychological and political needs drive him toward seeking an outcome in his contest with the Americans that will stand up to comparison with the record of his radical Iranian neighbors. He knows they destroyed Jimmy Carter's presidency and badly damaged that of Ronald Reagan.

As election season approaches, Saddam will find ways to remind George Bush and Americans of our unfinished business in the gulf.

2—2

관리 번호	91- 1085

외 무 부

종   별 :

번   호 : UNW-2674　　　　　　　　　　일   시 : 91 0913 2130

수   신 : 장관(연일,중동일,기정)

발   신 : 주 유엔 대사

제   목 : 안보리동향 (비공식협의)

　　안보리는 금 9.13 비공식 협의를 개최한바, 당관 원참사관이 관련 대표부들로 부터 탐문한 금일 협의 주요 결과를 아래 보고함.

　　1. 유엔 레바논 평화유지군(UNIFIL) 요원 피격사건

　　의장(불란서)이 사건경위, 조치현황에 관한 사무국측의 통보내용을 이사국들에게 설명하였으나, 특기할 그이상의 토의는 없었음.

　　2. 이락의 인도적 긴급수요와 관련한 석유수출 일부허용 결의안 이행에 관한 사무총장 보고서(S/23006)

　　다음주중 동 보고서 승인결의안 채택예정

　　3. 유엔 이락 특정무기 폐기특위(UNSCOM) 자체 헬기 사용 불허문제

　　본건을 이락의 중대한 안보리 결의(707 호) 위반행위로 보는 이사국들의 입장을 우선 의장이 이락측에 구두로 전달예정

　　4. 과테말라의 베리즈 승인조치

　　동 조치에 대한 이사국들의 환영의 뜻을 의장이 언론에 표명(에쿠아돌제외)끝

　　(대사 노창희-국장)

예고 : 1991. 12. 31 에 까지 고문에 의거 일반문서로 재분류됨

국기국 안기부	장관	차관	1차보	2차보	중아국	외정실	분석관	정와대

PAGE 1

　　　　　　　　　　　　　　　　　　　　91.09.14　　13:12

　　　　　　　　　　　　　　　　　　　외신 2과 통제관 BN

　　　　　　　　　　　　　　　　　　0271

원 본

1 (2)

외 무 부

종   별 :

번   호 : UNW-2697   일   시 : 91 0914 1700

수   신 : 장 관(연일,중동일,국기,기정)

발   신 : 주 유엔대사

제   목 : 걸프사태

유엔 이락 핵사찰결과 보고서(미발표)에 관한 금 9.15 자 NYT 지 기사 및 이락
구호문제에 관한 SADRUDDIN AGA KHAN 대표의 동지 기고문을 별첨송부함.끝

(대사 노창희-국장)

첨부 FAX,NYT 지 기사 및 기고문.끝

국기국   1차보   중아국   국기국   외정실   안기부

차관

PAGE 1   91.09.15   09:10 WH

외신 1과 통제관

0272

U.N. Says the Iraqis Could Have Devised A-Bombs in the 90's

By PAUL LEWIS
Special to The New York Times

UNITED NATIONS, Sept. 13 — The United Nations has concluded that President Saddam Hussein of Iraq could have possessed enough nuclear explosives to build at least two or three atomic weapons a year by the mid-1990's, if his secret production plants had not been destroyed by allied bombing during the Persian Gulf war.

The unpublished report, produced by United Nations inspectors responsible for finding and destroying Iraqi plants capable of producing nuclear weapons and material, also said that other countries provided Baghdad with substantial quantities of equipment and material for part of its nuclear program, and "very probably" sent experts to give continuing technical advice.

Since the start of the gulf crisis last year, there have been various estimates of Iraq's nuclear capacity and of the quantities of nuclear explosives it might possess.

The Iraqis, who maintain that their nuclear program was entirely peaceful, have admitted producing about a pound of slightly enriched uranium unsuitable for weapons use, in violation of their obligations under the Nuclear Nonproliferation Treaty. They have also admitted manufacturing a minute quantity of plutonium, which is also used in nuclear bombs, again in violation of international obligations.

But an Iraqi defector has been widely reported as telling American intelligence that the Baghdad Government has acquired about 80 or 90 pounds of highly enriched uranium, or enough for four or five weapons. In July, a Bush Administration official told Congress that Iraq probably had secretly enriched enough uranium to make at least one nuclear device.

The new United Nations report, summarizing the findings of the four nuclear inspections carried out so far, paints the most comprehensive picture yet available of Iraq's covert nuclear program and its potential. The report is expected to be published shortly as a Security Council document.

German Copters Sitting Idle

In a related development, the United Nations Security Council today warned Iraq in strong terms that it must cooperate more closely with inspectors in the future by allowing them to fly their own helicopters anywhere inside its borders as they search for secret nuclear plants.

Germany has lent the United Nations three helicopters and crews so that its inspectors can carry out spot checks at short notice anywhere in Iraq without being dependent on the Iraqi authorities for transportation.

But Iraq has so far refused to allow the helicopters, which are waiting in Turkey, to operate over its territory, saying this would violate its sovereignty.

The United States representative to the United Nations, Thomas R. Pickering, said that Iraq's attempt to deny the inspectors use of the German helicopters constituted "a very serious breach" of its obligations under Security Council Resolution 707. This authorizes the inspectors "to conduct both fixed-wing and helicopter flights throughout Iraq for all relevant purposes, including inspection, surveillance, aerial surveys, transportation and logistics without interference of any kind."

If Iraq does not comply fully, Mr. Pickering added, it will face "very serious consequences."

The Council's President, Jean-Bernard Mérimée, delivered what he termed "not an ultimatum, but a very serious warning" to Iraq's representative, Abdel Amir al-Anbari, telling him that Resolution 707 "has to be fully implemented."

Mr. Anbari said later that he was only a messenger and did not know "what will be the next step on the part of my Government or on the part of the Council."

Iraq's effort to prevent the inspectors from using the helicopters is the latest in a long series of attempts it has made to frustrate the Security Council's efforts to eliminate all its weapons of mass destruction. These efforts have included understating chemical weapons stocks, pretending it had no covert nuclear program at all, and denying any plans to develop biological weapons.

The United Nations inspectors, in their latest report, said Iraq had given priority to enriching uranium, using a method called electromagnetic separation. The United States employed this method when it built the first atomic bomb during World War II; it is now considered outdated.

The report said Iraq was planning to bring 90 such separators into production at its Tarmiya plant within 18 months and calculated that these would have produced about 30 pounds of highly enriched uranium a year — enough for at least one weapon. And Iraqi scientists acknowledged that they expected output to rise as more separators became available and they grew more expert at operating them.

In addition, the report said Iraq planned to produce more enriched uranium using the centrifugal method at a plant scheduled to start production at the end of this year.

Many More Centrifuges

Iraqi officials said they hoped to have 100 such centrifuges operating by 1993, rising to 500 by 1996.

The report also said that the Iraqis appeared to be planning a substantial expansion in centrifugal-enrichment operations because they had built an installation for making centrifuges at Furat, near Baghdad, capable of turning out at least 600 a year.

The United Nations inspectors noted that the plant, unlike most of Iraq's other nuclear sites, was never bombed by the allies during the gulf war because they did not know what its purpose was.

The inspectors said they had found no conclusive evidence so far that Iraq had actually decided to start designing and developing nuclear weapons — something its officials deny. But they cited several suspicious developments.

'Lack of Candor' Seen

They said Iraq already possessed "remarkable capabilities in relevant technologies — much, however, in a state of only partial completeness." Their report also noted "significant inconsistencies and a lack of candor in the replies of individual facility managers" to questions. And it said that this "increases concern about the end use of technologies being developed."

The report said that only on the final day of the visit were the inspectors told that Iraq had been importing "hundreds of tons" of a special explosive known as HMX, suitable for use as a nuclear trigger.

A new United Nations nuclear inspection team is scheduled to set out for Iraq on Saturday and another one is likely to go there in October.

Help Iraq Help Its People

By Sadruddin Aga Khan

GENEVA

The U.N. Security Council and Iraq are at a watershed in their relations. Upon their decisions depends the fate of Iraq's men, women and children, who should not continue to pay the price of a war they did not cause and of a peace that has turned increasingly bitter.

With food and medical supplies stretched to the limit, with power generation and water treatment deteriorating fast, a humanitarian crisis is looming. Means have to be devised to finance Iraq's essential civilian needs, which the Council has exempted from sanctions, from Iraq's own vast oil resources in a way that satisfies the international community.

The Security Council has never sought to deprive the Iraqi people of food and medical supplies. Last month, when the Council adopted Resolution 706, which authorized Iraq to sell $1.6 billion worth of its oil, it wanted the sales used exclusively toward this end and wanted the goods imported to be distributed equitably.

But it now appears that we risk seeing human lives and well-being sacrificed on the altar of politics. The Iraqi Government has expressed indignation over what it considers to be infringements of its sovereignty, particularly a U.N.-administered escrow account into which oil revenues would be paid. It has prepared the ground for a possible refusal to go along with "intrusive" arrangements for oil sales and monitoring the distribution of food and medical supplies. Bound as it may be by the Council's mandatory decisions, Baghdad still has its hands on the oil taps.

Sadruddin Aga Khan is the U.N. Secretary General's representative for humanitarian efforts in Iraq.

Iraq's position is a far cry from the growing international support for a "right of humanitarian intervention." It is hardly humanitarian that the authorities in Baghdad should arrogate to themselves the choice of disease and hunger over compliance with U.N. requirements. It is their sovereignty — but it is their people's starvation.

If Iraq decides not to sell its oil to finance purchases under the conditions the U.N. has set, the U.N. will not be able to avert a catastrophe. The relief operation we have carried out for months will be dwarfed by the magnitude of the crisis.

Our funds are well-nigh exhausted. And who will contribute more funds or unfreeze assets for essential needs if Iraq refuses to pump oil as directed? With no resources for food imports, Iraq will be confronted by massive malnutrition and hunger. With no money for medical supplies and for the power generation needed for water treatment, we will see today's first signs of fatal disease spiral into epidemics of staggering proportions.

While it may not be acceptable to speak of face-saving, Iraq should not be handed a pretext to reject the entire U.N. package as an unwarranted straitjacket, with the effect of paralyzing the U.N.'s humanitarian operation. Instead, with strict controls and monitoring arrangements, Iraq should be permitted to carry out the required purchase and distribution of imported goods; we intend under our current program to submit to the Council's sanctions committee proposals for using Iraq's own civilian aircraft to transport relief supplies and personnel.

The Council's ceiling of $1.6 billion should be raised by $900 million, to $2.5 billion, as Secretary General Javier Pérez de Cuéllar has recommended, to cover essential civilian needs. Revenues generated from the oil sales must be released rapidly to ease increasingly acute afflictions.

I believe humanitarian and political interests converge in meeting Iraq's essential and urgent needs. But whatever the perspective, let us be aware of what is at stake for that country's ill-starred, ill-served population. When winter comes, with an already destitute people facing a desolate land, with a lean harvest in sight and international relief committed elsewhere, recriminations over lost opportunities will be in vain. □

2-2

0274

외 무 부

종 별 :

번 호 : UNW-2733　　　　　　　　일 시 : 91 0916 1930

수 신 : 장관(연일,기정)

발 신 : 주 유엔 대사

제 목 : 안보리 동향(개발협의)

연:UNW-2594

1. 안보리는 금 9.16 의장(불란서)과 이사국간 개별 협의가 진행중인바, 당관 원 참사관이 관련 대표부들로부터 탐문한 협의동향은 다음과 같음

　가. 차기 사무총장 선출 절차문제(금일 협의개시, 현재 제기중인 사항)

　1)후보 명단 작성

　2)표결방식

　가)각후보에 대한 개발 부표

　나)상임이사국과 비상임이사국은 서로 다른 부표 용지 사용(상임이사국 거부권 적용)

　3)안보리 비공개회의에서 부표

　나. 유엔 이락 특정 무기 폐기 특위 헬기사용 문제

　이락측은 조건부(시간, 지역)유엔 헬기 사용 허용 용의를 표시하여 왔으나, 안보리 이사국들은 조건없는 사찰 활동 보장 원칙의 중요성 강조

　2. 한편 안보리 제재위는 대 이락 무기 공급금지 지침(안보리 결의 700 호)이행 보고서(S/23036)를 9.13 자로 안보리에 제출해온바, 동제재위에 제기된 본건 무기 공급금지 위반 사례는 아직 없었다고함

　3. 쿠웨이트및 제3 국 억류자 송환문제 관련 사무총장의 안보리 앞 보고서(S/23012)에 의하면 쿠웨이트는 국제적십자위원회(ICRC)에 미송환자 2,242 명 명단을 지난 9.9 제출하였음. 끝

　첨부:(FAX):UNW(F)-534

　1.CSC 지 기고문(사무총장 선출문제)

　2.NYT 지 W. SAFIRE 컬럼(9.23 부시 대통령 기조연설). 끝

국기국	장관	차관	1차보	2차보	외정실	분석관	청와대	안기부
				종아눙				

PAGE 1

(대사 노창희-국장대리)
예고:91.12.31 일반

91. 12. 31. 일반 /

0276

죵2124

UNW(F)-534
1 0916 1930
(변일, 기정)

The UN Labyrinth

By Richard C. Hottelet

THE United Nations Security Council today begins the process of choosing a new UN secretary-general. It hopes to send a name to the General Assembly for the formal appointment no later than Oct. 15. Secretary-General Pérez de Cuéllar's five-year term expires Dec. 31.

Given the expanded responsibilities and expectations now attached to this office, it is regarded as a fateful choice. In the absence of any prior screening, there is little time to decide. In fact, France and the Soviet Union have again been talking about persuading Pérez de Cuéllar to stay on for two more years. Africa has submitted an official list of six nominees. Several private citizens have nominated themselves. Dozens of other names have come up in speculation. Everyone wants some independent man or woman who can carry the political load and also tighten up a flabby, disjointed, and often wasteful UN administration. But thereby hangs a complex and contradictory tale.

The secretary general is the leader of what is called the UN system. This embraces the Secretariat with headquarters in New York, 14 specialized intergovernmental agencies, and approximately 150 bodies in the economic and social fields where some 80 percent of the UN's work is done. Altogether, the system employs some 50,000 officials and staff in roughly 620 foreign headquarters and field offices around the world, and spends anywhere from $4 billion to $6 billion a year. It seems impossible to pin down an exact figure.

On paper, all is well. The General Assembly, comprising the full UN membership (soon to be 166 states) is the supreme policy body setting the basic goals. The Economic and Social Council is charged by the UN Charter with recommending policy on international economic, social, cultural, educational, health, and human rights matters. (Just as the Security Council is given prime responsibility for the maintenance of international peace and security.) The secretary-general is to coordinate the whole in compliance with the Assembly's directives. In fact, the system is a patchwork shambles that has grown like Topsy for 45 years. An official study in 1969 called the UN's economic development aspect a "non-system," lacking a "central brain." Nothing has changed. Governments continue to demand greater coordination, rationalization, and economy; yet, the fault is in themselves. The UN, like any club, is no better than its members.

In the General Assembly, too much of the annual session's 150 point agenda has been described as obsolete, inactive, and overlapping. Debate covers the same ground in several forums. The Economic and Social Council, with 54 members and an amorphous jurisdiction, has no authority to make any UN-related body accept its guidelines. Specialized agencies, such as the International Labor Organization (ILO) and the International Telecommunications Union (ITU), are totally autonomous and do what they please.

Recently, the Assembly, in an act as astonishing as it was ineffectual, officially rebuked the ILO and the ITU for feathering their employee's nests in a time of fiscal stringency. Four bodies deal with world food. One of them, the Food and Agriculture Organization (FAO), is widely criticized as utterly mismanaged. The United States, in protest, has cut its contribution to the FAO budget; it has, for the same reason, left UNESCO, the UN Educational, Scientific and Cultural Organization. Economic development agencies fight over turf and together are at war with the UN Environmental Program in the classic conflict of green fields and smoking chimneys. Aid agencies jostled for a share of the action in the Kurdish refugee crisis.

THE secretary-general has no power to knock heads together. His efforts at coordination are routinely ignored. Even his management of his own bailiwick, the Secretariat, is undercut by the member states. In the Assembly, the majority sets up pork barrel programs intended to escape his control and restricts important personnel appointments. All demand jobs for their nationals – some qualified, some brothers-in-law.

The major powers, including the US, are thinking of saddling the next secretary general with a cluster of four top officials intended to relieve him of part of his burden but more likely, thereby, creating another clique of semi-autonomous bureaucrats. What all, including the small, developing countries, want is an honorable, competent, independent person – not too independent of them. The US calls for a "unitary UN," pulled together to overcome the confusion, waste, and redundancy of the present system but not enough, as Assistant Secretary of State John Bolton put it, to be "tightly orchestrated by a political majority in the General Assembly."

Lots of luck.

■ *Richard C. Hottelet is moderator of 'America and the World' on National Public Radio.*

7 –1

0277

WILLIAM SAFIRE
Bush at the U.N.

WASHINGTON

The moment has come for the President of the United States to step up to his obligation to form and articulate American foreign policy in the wake of the death of Communism and the breakup of the Soviet Union. The forum is the U.N. session opening this week in New York.

The need for a substantive speech, now scheduled for Monday Sept. 23, is all the more pressing because his last attempt — his dismaying "Chicken Kiev" speech in Ukraine on Aug. 1 — betrayed a misconceptual framework. That was the first address by a U.S. President that had to be followed by an op-ed article by his national security adviser to explain that what he said was not what he meant.

It came with ill grace for Mr. Bush to implicitly derogate his Presidential predecessors from Truman to Reagan, who waged and won the cold war, for having engaged Soviet leaders "in duels of eloquent bluff and bravado."

Worse was his dire warning to the peoples of Ukraine, the Baltics and other republics seeking independence from central Moscow rule that "Americans will not support those who seek independence in order to replace a far-off tyranny with a local despotism. They will not aid those who promote a suicidal nationalism based upon ethnic hatred."

That was to shore up the Gorbachev Communist centralizers against the likes of the Yeltsin separatists. Though Brent Scowcroft later insisted no pro-union purpose was intended, the plain truth was emphasized in another line: "America's first system of government — the Continental Congress — failed because the states were too suspicious of one another and the central government too weak to protect commerce and individual rights."

Came the putsch and its counter-coup, and the restive republics scrapped the centralism to create just the sort of loose articles of confederation Mr. Bush had instructed them were such a failure in our experience.

Small wonder Secretary of State Baker received such a lukewarm reception in the Baltic republics the other day. (The U.S., shamefully, was 39th to recognize their freedom, just after Mongolia.) The people knew their independence came despite the Bush Administration's historically wrongheaded support of Moscow central.

O.K., so the Bush foreign policy zigged while the world zagged, and the U.S. found itself sadly mispositioned on the central issue of our time. That was last month. This is now; time to abandon the old New World Order based on a Gemini hegemony and to set forward the new New World Order based on a high-flying eagle and a multipolar bear.

Can President Bush come up with a conceptual framework in the short time remaining? Yes, if he stops his frenetic travel and lectern-pounding to focus on his U.N. speech.

For openers, quote President Benjamin Harrison, who said in 1888: "We have no commission from God to police the world." Propose to intervene only to protect vital interests, as when an aggressor builds or buys nuclear weaponry. Invite world par-

Moment for his big speech.

ticipation in our space shield to safeguard everyone from nuclear blackmail or accidental missile launch.

State our intent to increase the momentum for freedom around the world, helping those who root out the Communists still lying in the weeds, creating financial magnets and laws to attract free-enterprise investments. Promise to use our economic retaliatory power to break tariff barriers and crush cartels.

Show how we will provide humanitarian aid in the spirit of our past generosity, expecting our prosperous trading partners to do the same, remembering that help toward self-help is the best help — no Marshall Plans or grandiose designs, especially when assets are wasted on standing armies and legions of spies.

A week is plenty of time to create the "Bush Doctrine." No State Department Pablum; no 15-minute package claiming leadership without being leaderly; no historic mistakes that call for op-ed clarification.

Take yellow-pad in hand, Mr. President, and show how America intends to participate in, rather than continue to observe, the sweep of history in the run-up to the millennium. By rising to this intellectual challenge, you will earn the world's attention at your next great forum, in Hawaii three months from now, aboard the battleship Missouri on the 50th anniversary of the attack on Pearl Harbor. □

0278

외 무 부

종 별 :

번 호 : UNW-2853   일 시 : 91 0919 2130

수 신 : 장 관(연일,중동일,미일,기정)

발 신 : 주 유엔 대사

제 목 : 겔프 사태

표제관련 금 9.19 NYT 지 사설및 기사를 별첨송부함.끝

첨부(NYT):NYT 지 사설및 기사.끝

(대사 노창희-국장)

(총3매)

UNW (F) - 5부   10919 2030

Measured Force on Iraq

President Bush has moved firmly but shrewdly to counter Saddam Hussein's persistent defiance of United Nations cease-fire resolutions. Yesterday he ordered American warplanes to prepare to escort U.N. helicopters should that be required to complete their arms inspection mission mandated by the Security Council.

The President has wisely resisted the temptation to bomb suspected weapons sites — an indiscriminate and probably futile approach. Instead, by backing up the U.N. mandate with an unmistakable threat of force, the President, in coordination with other Security Council members, reinforces respect for international law.

Mr. Hussein would be foolish to forget that Desert Storm was ended only on the basis of full compliance with U.N. resolutions requiring him to submit to full inspection and supervised destruction of his missiles along with any nuclear, biological or chemical weapons components.

The American planes are being made available to escort U.N. helicopters if Baghdad persists in obstructing their enforcement of these arms control provisions. The obstructions continue an Iraqi pattern of brazenly flouting cease-fire terms. These are not mere technical violations but a deliberate effort by Saddam Hussein to extract a psychological victory from the wreckage of military defeat.

Consider the record to date. Iraq has supplied inaccurate information about its missile stocks, enriched uranium supplies and chemical warheads. It refuses to acknowledge the existence of a biological warfare program that U.N. officials believe had reached at least the research stage. It has rewelded Scud missile launchers previously destroyed.

It has launched military incursions along the Kuwaiti border and fired weapons over the heads of U.N. inspectors seeking to visit a uranium enrichment facility. In the latest episode, it restricted helicopter inspections by imposing geographical, time and equipment limits on their flights.

Baghdad earlier this week began backpedaling on its helicopter restrictions, as it has done with other forms of non cooperation. Yesterday's deployment of U.S. warplanes is intended to add muscle to diplomatic pressures.

There remain two schools of thought at the U.N. on how to deal with Saddam Hussein. One would follow the old U.N. traditions of deference to sovereign leaders. Some diplomats even now look for ways for the Iraqi dictator to save face, by easing the Security Council's terms for oil sales, for example, or downplaying Iraqi cease-fire violations.

But world peace and security would be better served by the second approach — putting the needed muscle behind U.N. resolutions. Those resolutions, if carried out effectively, could form the basis for a new world order based on collective security and international law. President Bush does well to advance that no longer utopian cause.

첨부 UNW-2853   3-1

0280

U.S. WARNS IRAQIS IT MAY USE FORCE TO INSPECT ARMS

'PLENTY FED UP,' BUSH SAYS

He Authorizes American Planes to Provide Protection for U.N. Helicopter Flights

By ANDREW ROSENTHAL
Special to The New York Times

WASHINGTON, Sept. 18 — President Bush authorized American warplanes today to fly into Iraq to protect United Nations inspectors if President Saddam Hussein does not back down from tions of his military inspections diplomatic and intercom new threat of force, Mr. Bush said he was "plenty fed up" with Mr. Hussein's refusal of United Nations Security Iraqi leader not to test American resolve once again.

But the President, perhaps mindful of the volatile political backdrop to his actions as the United States tries to arrange a Middle East peace conference, told reporters during a visit to the Grand Canyon today that he was confident there would be no outbreak of war.

Missiles to Saudi Arabia

Mr. Bush said he was also sending a new supply of Patriot air defense missiles to Saudi Arabia and that the kingdom had given its assent to a new allied military operation, perhaps from its territory.

Mr. Bush said he was just doing some "prudent planning" on the strength of United Nations resolutions that he said permitted the further use of force to compel the destruction of Iraq's poison gases, Scud missiles and others. He said he had no specific plans for military action against Mr. Hussein.

better than to take on the United States of America," said Mr. Bush, whose words drew quick support from leading members of Congress.

Mr. Bush did not set a deadline for Iraqi compliance with the United Nations demand that its inspectors be allowed to fly into Iraq by helicopter. But it has been Mr. Bush's pattern in the last year to set deadlines and then follow with swift military action if they were not met, and officials said today that an ultimatum to Baghdad was under consideration.

Baghdad Eased Position

In the months since the war ended, the United States has implicitly threatened Iraq with the use of force as Baghdad balked at complying with a series of United Nations resolutions that established the cease-fire in the gulf and set the conditions for a permanent peace. Each time, Mr. Hussein backed down.

They said the United States had been on the verge of issuing an ultimatum when Iraq eased its stand on the helicopters somewhat over the weekend, saying it would agree to the inspection flights under conditions that were ican-led west of within or the American of the chief. Mr. Bush's actions today were a dramatic show of the West's determination to bend Baghdad to its will. Still, the move raised the specter of a renewed military action, after less than seven months of the uneasy peace that followed the Persian Gulf war.

U.S. Forces in Region

It also underscored the tenuous nature of the allied military victory over Iraq, which inflicted devastating damage on the Iraqi armed forces but left Mr. Hussein in power and set off armed conflict between Baghdad and ethnic and religious minorities in northern and southern Iraq.

A senior official traveling with Mr. American forces would additional

sent to Saudi Arabia within a day or two.

By tonight, there was no sign of any new deployment of American forces to the gulf region, where there are still about 36,000 American troops, along with about 60 warplanes in Saudi Arabia and more surface ships equipped with Tomahawk cruise missiles, which the United States used during the war against Iraq. American forces in Saudi Arabia were on a heightened state of alert today, Pentagon officials said.

'Plenty Fed Up'

administration officials, the White House plan was to prepare American fighters, along with British and French warplanes, to fly air cover for allied helicopters carrying United Nations inspectors and, if necessary, move to stop any Iraqi attack on the aircraft and then retaliate with strikes against Iraqi positions.

Mr. Bush said he was confident that American warplanes would not have to go into action in Iraq once again to force Mr. Hussein to permit the United Nations inspections. A senior official said, "This is not Desert Storm II."

But Mr. Bush said: "I'm plenty fed up. I think the man will see we are very serious about this."

Mr. Bush added: "There's no, you know, threats, there's just determination. That's all there is, firm determination that he will comply to the letter of the U.N. resolutions. And it's not just the United States, a lot of other countries feel this way too."

Asked if he could foresee a situation that would set off a new war, Mr. Bush said: "I don't think Saddam wants any of that. I don't think he does."

He paused and said, "I'm confident he doesn't. Absolutely confident."

lican who said down the ranks Rumor said Mr. Bush was taking "the appropriate precautions."

Referring to Mr. Hussein, the Senanyone much hope that he will choose the sane and sensible course — voluntary compliance with an agreement to which, let us not forget, Iraq did agree."

In a formal statement issued by the White House today and in a letter to the leaders of Congress that was delivered on Monday, Mr. Bush said he was basing his planning on United Nations Security Council Resolutions 687 and 707.

Under those resolutions, the White House said, "Iraq is obligated to eliminate its weapons of mass destruction and its ballistic missile capabilities. Special Commission and International Atomic Energy Agency inspection teams to verify Iraqi compliance."

The statement added that the inspectors must use helicopters to transport themselves around Iraq, but that Baghdad has refused to permit unfettered helicopter flights. At first, the Iraqis insisted that the United Nations teams had to fly on Iraqi helicopters manned permit some outside helicopter set strict conditions on their movements.

"This is a clear violation of U.N. Security Council Resolution 707, which permits the use of helicopters without condition."

3-2

Bush Rattles Saber: Will Iraq Flinch?

By R. W. APPLE Jr.
Special to The New York Times

WASHINGTON, Sept. 18 — By threatening to send American war planes back over Iraq, President Bush is hoping to make President Saddam Hussein retreat and permit unfettered United Nations inspections, but if he fails, he will face few major diplomatic or political risks in taking direct military action.

News Analysis

Administration officials and other experts expressed doubt today that a new American initiative would disrupt the Administration's plans for a Mideast peace conference next month. In any event, these plans have been menaced by other developments, including the dispute over loan guarantees for Israel.

At first, the President and his senior advisers made clear, United States fighter-bombers would merely escort United Nations helicopters on inspection trips, but if that did not work, Mr. Bush would have to try other means to fulfill his pledge to prevent Iraq from amassing a nuclear arsenal.

The President's problem is whether military action would change much. During the Persian Gulf war air raids failed to destroy several of Mr. Hussein's nuclear and chemical weapons sites, and there is no reason to expect that they would do a lot better now. Punitive air strikes to "teach Saddam a lesson," as one official called them, are unlikely to break a man unbroken by the crushing defeat that the allies inflicted on Mr. Hussein earlier this year.

Coalition Remains Intact

The allied coalition remains more or less intact. The British, the French and the Soviet Union, the three key European allies during the gulf war, signaled that they were on board again in comments today, and Secretary General Javier Pérez de Cuéllar of the United Nations did likewise. Saudi Arabia has agreed to provide bases in return for Patriot missiles.

"I think the man will see we are very serious about this," the President said of Mr. Hussein. "He's not going to question our resolve on this."

Former Secretary of State Alexander M. Haig Jr. noted that Mr. Hussein had often backed down. On other occasions, however, "He has shown that he is quite capable of taking a very dangerous line and walking straight into the lion's mouth," Mr. Haig said.

Mr. Hussein has clung to power despite his concession of defeat in the Persian Gulf war on Feb. 28. And since early this summer, he has put repeated roadblocks in the way of international teams sent to Baghdad to check whether he has carried out a United Nations resolution calling for the destruction of Iraqi installations for the making of chemical, biological and nuclear weapons.

The President is taking few risks in threatening military action.

Inspectors Are Obstructed

Just as he proclaimed his intention during the war of surviving to fight another day, whatever the allies threw at him, the Iraqi leader seems determined now to cling to as much of his weapons capacity as he can by outwitting the inspection teams.

Again and again, the Iraqis have withheld information or access, the United Nations has issued warnings, and Baghdad has yielded a bit of ground. But the inspectors charge that the Iraqis have continued to hide or destroy critical equipment and to take other steps to avoid full detection of their attempts to make weapons of mass destruction. One inspector has been shot at and others have been obstructed in attempts to stage surprise inspections.

"I have no indication that they are modifying their position so far," Mr. Pérez de Cuéllar said today.

A July 25 ultimatum issued by the United Nations produced no result. Washington talked about "military options" but did nothing when the deadline passed without action, and today's statements by Mr. Bush, six weeks later, constituted an attempt to restore credibility to his threats.

A Clear Field at Home

On the domestic political front, Mr. Bush appears to have a clear field. On the record, Democratic leaders said nothing critical of the President's saber rattling, and one of the party's leading foreign-affairs specialists commented privately, "It would be another low-risk, high-tech operation, and of course there's no longer any threat that these regional things will turn into superpower confrontations."

Those who have been critical of the President's decision to end the war when he did argue that the current difficulties demonstrate anew the costs of failing to break Mr. Hussein's power and drive him from office when the moment was ripe. But the Democrats are not prepared to make that a major theme.

Recent polls suggest that much of the American public wants to concentrate on domestic issues (and indeed Mr. Bush was doing so today on his Western trip when he paused at the Grand Canyon to warn Iraq once again). But few politicians of either party doubt that the President could quickly rally the country behind a new military effort to insure that Mr. Hussein does not equip himself with nuclear weapons.

The yellow ribbons are still on doorways around the country, suggesting that the surge of patriotism of nine months ago is not yet spent, and T-shirts inspred by the gulf war are still selling well. Mr. Bush has shown conclusively that he can quickly focus the country's attention on foreign affairs when he seeks to, and to change the terms of political discourse.

"Our problem," another prominent Democrat said, "is that we are in a period of instability abroad. We don't have any candidates with foreign-policy credentials, and every time something like this happens, you can almost see the voters running for shelter to the Republicans and George Bush."

3-3

0282

**UNITED
NATIONS**

S

Security Council

Distr.
GENERAL

S/22872/Rev.1
20 September 1991

ORIGINAL: ENGLISH

NOTE BY THE SECRETARY-GENERAL

The Secretary-General has the honour to transmit to the Security Council the attached revised plan for future ongoing monitoring and verification of Iraq's compliance with paragraph 12 of Part C of Security Council resolution 687 (1991) and with the requirements of paragraphs 3 and 5 of resolution 707 (1991) submitted by the Director-General of the International Atomic Energy Agency (IAEA).

PLAN FOR FUTURE ONGOING MONITORING AND VERIFICATION
OF IRAQ'S COMPLIANCE WITH
PARAGRAPH 12 OF PART C
OF SECURITY COUNCIL RESOLUTION 687 (1991)
AND WITH THE REQUIREMENTS OF PARAGRAPHS 3 AND 5
OF RESOLUTION 707 (1991)

**Submitted by the Director General
of the International Atomic Energy Agency**

0284

I. INTRODUCTION

1. In paragraph 13 of Security Council resolution 687 (1991), adopted on 3 April 1991, the Director General of the International Atomic Energy Agency (hereinafter referred to as the "IAEA" or "Agency") was requested by the Security Council to carry out immediate on-site inspection of Iraq's nuclear capabilities and to develop and carry out a plan for the destruction, removal or rendering harmless of items prohibited to Iraq under paragraph 12 of resolution 687. The Special Commission, established in accordance with paragraph 9 of resolution 687, was given a role in the nuclear area under resolution 687 of assisting and co-operating with the IAEA and designating sites to be inspected.

2. In paragraph 13 of resolution 687, the Director General of the IAEA was further requested - with the assistance and co-operation of the Special Commission - to submit to the Security Council for its approval a plan for future ongoing monitoring and verification of Iraq's compliance with its obligations under paragraph 12 of resolution 687.

3. The IAEA submitted to the Security Council for its approval on 29 July 1991 the plan referred to in paragraph 2 above. As the plan was originally developed while immediate on-site inspection was still ongoing, and while the plan for the destruction, removal or rendering harmless of proscribed items was still in an early stage of implementation, the plan was, as indicated therein, provisional in nature and subject to modification upon further direction from the Security Council and upon consideration of the results of the ongoing inspections.

4. As a consequence of the adoption by the Security Council on 15 August 1991 of resolution 707 (1991), and based on the results of the on-site inspections performed to date, the Director General of the IAEA now submits a revised plan (hereinafter referred to as "the plan") for approval by the Security Council.

0285

/...

5.   The plan incorporates the additional obligations of Iraq under resolution 707 and the corresponding monitoring and verification activities of the Agency.

6.   Although resolution 687 does not specify the party which should be assigned the responsibility for implementation of the plan, the Agency's extensive experience with inspection and verification activities in the nuclear field, which led to the Security Council's asking the Agency to take the lead during the first two phases under paragraph 12 of resolution 687, the need for continuity in the implementation of future measures, and the evident cost benefit of being able to draw on an existing infrastructure, suggest that the Agency be assigned the task of carrying out the plan. The plan was drafted accordingly. It is expected that the verification and monitoring activities will be administered and operated by a special unit in the IAEA Secretariat. For technical and practical reasons, the operation by the Agency, appropriately co-ordinated with the Special Commission or its successor, of field offices in Baghdad is also envisaged.

7.   In accordance with the Agency's mandate under resolutions 687 and 707, and as provided for in Articles IX and VII of the Agreement Governing the Relationship between the United Nations and the International Atomic Energy Agency(INFCIRC/11)[1], the Agency will report on the implementation of the plan to the Security Council.

_____

1) Article IX provides that the Agency "shall co-operate with the Security Council by furnishing to it at its request such information and assistance as may by required in the exercise of its responsibility for the maintenance or restoration of international peace and security."

Article VII provides inter alia that, "At the invitation of the Security Council, the Director General may attend its meetings to supply it with information or give it other assistance within the competence of the Agency."

0286

/...

8.   Resolution 707 obliges Iraq, *inter alia*, to "halt all nuclear activities of any kind, except for use of isotopes for medical, agricultural or industrial purposes, until the Security Council determines that Iraq is in full compliance with resolution 707 and with paragraphs 12 and 13 of resolution 687, and the IAEA determines that Iraq is in full compliance with its safeguards agreement with that Agency". So long as the proscriptions under resolution 707 remain operational, the Agency will secure the nuclear material, equipment and facilities which Iraq is allowed to keep and use under the terms of resolution 687 and verify that they are not used for any nuclear activity except as permitted under resolution 707. The Agency will also verify that nuclear material and isotopes are not produced indigenously by Iraq, and that isotopes held or imported by Iraq are used only for medical, agricultural or industrial purposes.

9.   The comprehensive sanctions established under Security Council resolution 661 (1991) for application by all States against Iraq, the prohibition against Iraq's acquisition of, and research and development related to, nuclear weapons and nuclear-weapons-usable material, as set out in paragraph 12 of resolution 687, and the prohibition in resolution 707 against all nuclear activities in Iraq except the use of isotopes for medical, agricultural or industrial purposes, all of which were imposed under Chapter VII of the Charter of the United Nations, carry with it the obligation of other States to respect the sanctions and prohibitions until such time as they are lifted by the Security Council and entails the acceptance of an obligation to report intended sales or supplies to Iraq of items not proscribed under resolution 687 or 707.

10.   This plan, and the annexes thereto, which constitute an integral part of the plan, will enter into force upon approval by the Security Council. It will govern all Agency activities in Iraq pursuant to resolutions 687 and 707. The duration of the plan, as well as the scope and content of the plan, remain subject to further decisions and directives of the Security Council.

11.   Security Council resolution 687 notes that the actions required of Iraq, including those relevant to nuclear weapons and nuclear-weapons-usable material, represent steps toward the goal of establishing in the Middle East a zone free from weapons of mass destruction. While the terms of any such zone agreement would have to be negotiated between the parties to the arrangement, some of the verification features envisaged in this plan may be of interest in future discussions about verification in such a zone.

/...

0287

II. THE PLAN

A. Relevant Decisions of the Security Council

12. In accordance with paragraph 12 of resolution 687, Iraq is obliged:

    - not to acquire or develop nuclear weapons or nuclear-weapons-usable material or any subsystems or components or any research, development, support or manufacturing facilities related to the above;

    - to submit to the Secretary-General and the Director General of the IAEA within 15 days of adoption of the resolution a declaration of the locations, amounts and types of items specified above;

    - to place all of its nuclear-weapons-usable materials under the exclusive control, for custody and removal, of the IAEA, with the assistance and cooperation of the Special Commission appointed by the Secretary-General in accordance with paragraph 9(b) of the resolution;

    - to accept, in accordance with the arrangements provided for in paragraph 13 of the resolution, urgent on-site inspection and the destruction, removal or rendering harmless, as appropriate, of such items; and

    - to accept the plan referred to in paragraph 13 for the future ongoing monitoring and verification of its compliance with these undertakings.

0288

/...

13. Pursuant to paragraph 13 of the resolution 687, the Director General of the International Atomic Energy Agency was requested, with the assistance and cooperation of the Special Commission:

- to carry out immediate on-site inspection of Iraq's nuclear capabilities based on Iraq's declarations and the designation of any additional locations by the Special Commission;

- to develop a plan for submission to the Security Council within forty-five days following adoption of the resolution calling for the destruction, removal, or rendering harmless as appropriate of the items proscribed under in paragraph 12 of the resolution, and to carry out the plan within forty-five days following its approval by the Security Council; and

- to develop a plan, taking into account the rights and obligations of Iraq under the Treaty on the Non-Proliferation of Nuclear Weapons of 1 July 1968, for the future ongoing monitoring and verification of Iraq's compliance with paragraph 12 of the resolution, including an inventory of all nuclear material in Iraq subject to the Agency's verification and inspections to confirm that Agency safeguards cover all relevant nuclear activities in Iraq, to be submitted to the Security Council for approval within 120 days of adoption of the resolution.

14. Under paragraph 3 of resolution 707, the Security Council demands that Iraq

- provide full, final and complete disclosure, as required by resolution 687 (1991), of all aspects of its programmes to develop weapons of mass destruction and ballistic missiles with a range greater than 150 km, and of all holdings of such weapons, their components and production facilities and locations, as well as all other nuclear programmes, including any which it claims are for purposes not related to nuclear-weapons-usable material, without further delay;

- allow the Special Commission, the IAEA and their Inspection Teams immediate, unconditional and unrestricted access to any and all areas, facilities, equipment, records and means of transportation which they wish to inspect;

0289   /...

- cease immediately any attempt to conceal, or any movement or destruction of any material or equipment relating to its nuclear, chemical or biological weapons or ballistic missile programmes, or material or equipment relating to its other nuclear activities without notification to and prior consent of the Special Commission;

- make available immediately to the Special Commission, the IAEA and their Inspection Teams any items to which they were previously denied access;

- allow the Special Commission, the IAEA and their Inspection Teams to conduct both fixed wing and helicopter flights throughout Iraq for all relevant purposes including inspection, surveillance, aerial surveys, transportation and logistics without interference of any kind and upon such terms and conditions as may be determined by the Special Commission, and to make full use of their own aircraft and such airfields in Iraq as they may determine are most appropriate for the work of the Commission;

- halt all nuclear activities of any kind, except for use of isotopes for medical, agricultural or industrial purposes until the Security Council determines that Iraq is in full compliance with this resolution and paragraphs 12 and 13 of resolution 687 (1991), and the IAEA determines that Iraq is in full compliance with its safeguards agreement with that Agency;

- ensure the complete implementation of the privileges, immunities and facilities of the representatives of the Special Commission and the IAEA in accordance with its previous undertakings and their complete safety and freedom of movement;

- immediately provide or facilitate the provision of any transportation, medical or logistical support requested by the Special Commission, the IAEA and their Inspection Teams;

- respond fully, completely and promptly to any questions or requests from the Special Commission, the IAEA and their Inspection Teams.

0290

/...

15. Paragraph 5 of resolution 707 further requires that the Government of Iraq forthwith comply fully and without delay with all its international obligations, including those set out in resolution 707, in resolution 687, in the Treaty on the Non-Proliferation of Nuclear Weapons of 1 July 1968 (NPT) and in its safeguards agreement with the IAEA (INFCIRC/172, 29 February 1972).

B. General Provisions

16. Iraq's obligations under paragraph 12 of resolution 687 and paragraph 3 of resolution 707 are broader in scope than the obligations which are undertaken under the Non-Proliferation Treaty and which are verified by the IAEA. While the approaches and techniques to be used under the present plan draw upon the Agency's safeguards experience, the scope and intensity of verification and monitoring under this plan are much greater in order to satisfy the requirements of Security Council resolutions 687 and 707 and to create confidence that the restrictions imposed upon Iraq in the nuclear field are actually complied with.

17. The safeguards agreement concluded with Iraq pursuant to the NPT shall continue to be in force. The verification activities pursuant to this plan will be carried out in a manner that takes into account the safeguards activities required under the safeguards agreement.

18. The activities under the plan for the future ongoing monitoring and verification of Iraq's compliance with paragraph 12 of resolution 687 and the nuclear aspects of paragraphs 3 and 5 of resolution 707 will be carried out with the assistance and co-operation of the Special Commission, or such other body as may be designated by the Security Council to carry out monitoring and verification activities relevant to Iraq's compliance with paragraph 10 of resolution 687 (chemical, biological and missile). The Agency will continue to provide information concerning the conduct and results of Agency inspections and related activities in order to assist the Special Commission in carrying out this task.

19. Financing of the verification and monitoring activities by the Agency in Iraq under the present plan will be secured by the United Nations.

0291   /...

C. Obligations of Iraq

20. Pursuant to its obligations as set forth in the relevant paragraphs of the Security Council resolutions quoted above, Iraq is

(a) prohibited under paragraph 12 of resolution 687 from acquiring or developing nuclear weapons or nuclear-weapons-usable material or any subsystems or components or any research, development, support or manufacturing facilities related thereto (see Annexes 1 and 3);

(b) required under paragraph 3 of resolution 707 to halt all nuclear activities of any kind except for use of isotopes for medical, agricultural or industrial purposes (see Annexes 1, 3 and 4); and

(c) required under paragraph 3 of resolution 707 to cease immediately any attempt to conceal, and any movement or destruction without notification to and prior consent of the Special Commission, of material or equipment relating to its nuclear weapons or other nuclear activities. This obligation is without prejudice to the obligation of Iraq to carry out, at the request of the Agency, the movement, destruction or rendering harmless of nuclear material, equipment or other items.

21. Iraq shall accept unconditionally all of the rights of the IAEA enumerated under section E of this plan. Iraq shall take no action to interfere with, impede, or obstruct the exercise of these rights by the Agency. Iraq shall take all measures which, in the view of the Agency, are necessary to facilitate the full exercise by the Agency of its rights under the plan, including, but not limited to:

(a) the designation of the Iraqi authority responsible for liaison with the Agency, and the name or names of the liaison officers within that authority who shall take the necessary measures to secure for the Agency the effective implementation of the Agency's rights laid down in the plan;

0292   /...

(b) notification to the Agency, immediately upon receipt of the name of the IAEA Chief Inspector for an inspection, of the name of the individual who will be the Iraqi Inspection Representative for the inspection;

(c) ensuring the safety and security of Agency personnel and property and the provision, upon request by the Agency, of appropriate escort, medical and other support personnel;

(d) the provision, at no cost to the Agency, of premises that may be necessary for the fulfillment of the Agency's functions in Iraq under the plan; and

(e) the acceptance of United Nations registration of means of transport on land, sea and in the air and United Nations licensing of the operator thereof.

22. Within 30 days of approval of the plan, Iraq shall provide to the Agency, and subsequently maintain current, information in accordance with Annex 2 on the following:

(a) an inventory of all nuclear material in Iraq, as defined in Annex 1;

(b) an inventory of all facilities, installations and sites in Iraq where nuclear activities of any kind, including but not limited to research facilities, laboratory-scale installations and pilot plants, have been or are carried out, or which are suitable for carrying out such activities;

(c) an inventory of all material, equipment and items in Iraq identified in Annex 3;

(d) an inventory of all isotopes in Iraq used for medical, agricultural or industrial applications as identified in Annex 4;

(e) information on existing and proposed programmes of nuclear activities in Iraq for the next five year period; and

0293 /...

(f) an inventory of all facilities, installations and sites in Iraq which are provided with any means of supply of electricity exceeding 10 MWe.

23. Iraq shall also provide to the Agency:

(a) complete design information for any planned nuclear facility or installation in Iraq 180 days before the start of construction of any such facility or installation;

(b) advance information on proposed imports and exports of any nuclear materials and isotopes, and non-nuclear material, equipment and items identified in Annexes 1, 3 and 4; and

(c) at the request of the Agency, any other information or data which the Agency requires to enable it to monitor Iraq's compliance with resolutions 687 and 707 or any other relevant Security Council resolutions.

24. Nothing in paragraphs 22 or 23 shall be construed as permitting activities, or the import, supply, sale or use of items, to the extent proscribed under Security Council resolutions 687 or 707 or any other relevant resolution of the Security Council.

25. Should Iraq require for use in an activity not prohibited under resolutions 687 and 707 any item in Iraq identified in Annex 3 as not proscribed under resolution 687, or require the importation into Iraq of isotopes for use in an activity identified in Annex 4, Iraq shall submit, prior to such use or import, respectively, a request to the Director General of the IAEA, specifying precisely the item and the quantities required, the facility, installation or site to be involved in activities with the item, the purpose of its use and the country of export of the isotopes. The Director General of the IAEA shall examine the request and, with the assistance and co-operation of the Special Commission or its successor, make a decision with regard to the disposition of the request, including any special arrangements which the Director General considers necessary.

0294

/...

26. Should Iraq require the importation for use in an activity not prohibited under resolution 687 or 707 of any item identified in Annex 3 as not proscribed under resolution 687, Iraq shall submit prior to import a request to the Committee established by the Security Council under paragraph 6 of resolution 661 (1991), or such other body designated by the Security Council for that purpose, through the Director General of the IAEA, specifying precisely the item and the quantities required, the facility, installation or site to be involved in activities with the item and the purpose of its use. The Director General of the IAEA, with the assistance and co-operation of the Special Commission, shall examine the request and make a recommendation to the Committee with regard to disposition of the request, including any special arrangements considered necessary.

27. At such time as, pursuant to paragraph 3(vi) of resolution 707, the Security Council determines that Iraq is in full compliance with resolution 707 and with paragraphs 12 and 13 of resolution 687 and the IAEA determines that Iraq is in full compliance with its safeguards agreement with the Agency, Iraq may seek to initiate nuclear activities which are not prohibited by resolution 687. To do so, Iraq shall submit a request to the Security Council specifying precisely the activity, the facility, installation or site where it is to be carried out, and the material or other items to be involved. In considering and examining the request, the Security Council may request the advice, assistance and co-operation of the IAEA and the Special Commission or its successor. Iraq shall not undertake any such nuclear activity until the Security Council has approved the activity.

D.   **Obligations of other States**

28. Paragraphs 24, 25 and 27 of Security Council resolution 687, _Inter alia,_ direct States not to provide to Iraq any of the items proscribed in paragraph 12 of that resolution.

0295

/...

29. Until such time as the Security Council and the IAEA make the determinations called for in paragraph 3 (vi) of resolution 707, States shall also be barred from supplying to Iraq any other nuclear material and any materials, equipment, facilities, other items or training which are especially designed or prepared for use in nuclear activities, except as related to the use of isotopes for medical, agricultural and industrial activities.

30. (a) States shall provide the Agency, 60 days in advance, with full and complete reporting of intended exports to Iraq of isotopes for medical, agricultural and industrial activities to the extent not prohibited by relevant Security Council resolutions as identified in Annex 4. States shall also provide the Agency, 60 days in advance, with full and complete reporting of intended exports to Iraq of any item identified in Annex 3 as not prohibited under resolution 687 for use in an activity not prohibited under resolutions 687 and 707. Transfers of items identified in Annexes 3 and 4 shall be subject to prior approval by the Agency in accordance with the provisions of paragraph 25 or 26, as appropriate.

(b) At such time as the constraints imposed by resolution 707 are lifted, States shall also provide the Agency, 60 days in advance with full and complete reporting of intended exports to Iraq of any item identified in Annex 3 as not prohibited under resolution 687, technological information, including training, and any other relevant items which could be used in nuclear activities not prohibited under resolution 687 (see Annex 1). Transfers of such items, information and training shall be subject to prior approval by the IAEA, and shall only be transferred for use in activities authorized by the Security Council under the provisions of paragraph 27.

0296

/...

E.   Rights of the IAEA

31. Without prejudice to the rights which the Agency has under the safeguards agreement with Iraq, under the Agreement on the Privileges and Immunities of the IAEA, and under the exchange of notes between the Secretary-General and the Foreign Minister of Iraq, which entered into force on 14 May 1991 and which applies to the Agency mutatis mutandis, the Agency shall have the following rights:

(a)   to carry out inspections, at any time and without hindrance, of any site, facility, area, location, activity, material or other item in Iraq upon designation by the Special Commission or its successor, or upon its own initiative. Iraq shall provide immediate and unimpeded access to, and shall take the measures necessary to enable inspectors to arrive at, the location where inspection activities are to be carried out by the time notified by the Agency;

(b)   to inspect any number of sites, facilities, areas, locations, activities, materials or items simultaneously or sequentially;

(c)   to conduct unannounced inspections and inspections upon short notice;

(d)   to secure any site, facility, area, location, activity, material or item to be inspected and prevent any material or other item from being taken to or from the site until the inspection is concluded;

(e)   to stop and inspect vehicles, ships, aircraft or any other means of transportation within Iraq. This also includes the right of the Agency to restrict and/or stop movement of suspected material, equipment or other items;

(f)   to inspect imports or exports of material and other items upon arrival or departure;

(g)   to establish special modes of monitoring and inspection, including prolonged or continuous presence of inspectors, use of instruments and other arrangements to facilitate monitoring and verification;

/...

0297

(h) to secure full and free access at any time to all sites, facilities, areas, locations, activities, material and other items, including documentation, all persons and all information which, in the Agency's judgement, may be necessary for its monitoring and verification activities. This includes unimpeded access to all nuclear material, facilities and installations, as well as equipment and non-nuclear material relevant to Iraq's undertakings, and all documentation related thereto;

(i) to request, receive, examine, retain, copy and remove any record, data and information, including documentation; to examine and photograph, including by videotaping, any activity or item; and to retain and move any item;

(j) to conduct interviews with any personnel at any site, facility, area or location under inspection, and with any Iraqi official;

(k) to install containment and surveillance equipment and other equipment and devices and to construct facilities for observation, testing, verification, monitoring and inspection activities;

(l) to verify inventories, and to take and analyze with its own instrumentation, or to request Iraq under the observation of Agency inspectors to take and/or analyze, samples, and to remove and export samples for off-site analysis;

(m) to mark, tag, or otherwise identify any material or other item;

(n) to use its own instrumentation to collect data during inspections and aerial overflights, including photographic, video, infrared and radar data.

32. The Agency shall also have the right:

(a) to unrestricted freedom of entry into and exit from Iraq, without delay or hindrance, of Agency officials and experts, property, supplies, equipment, including means of transport, and other items. No visas shall be required of such personnel travelling on a United Nations laissez-passer or certificate and possessing an inspection assignment document; Iraq shall ensure prompt issuance of visas of entry and exit for such personnel as may not possess a United Nations laissez-passer or certificate;

(b) to unrestricted freedom to move within Iraq, without advance notice, delay or hindrance of Agency officials and experts, property, supplies, equipment, including means of transportation, and other items. Iraq shall, at the request of the Agency, provide means of transportation, maps or other necessary information;

(c) to remove from Iraq any material and any other item, including documentation;

(d) to use its own means of transport, including fixed- and rotary-wing aircraft for overflights, throughout Iraq for all relevant purposes, including inspection, surveillance, transportation and/or logistics;

(e) to use airfields in Iraq for purposes determined by the Agency including landing, take-off, basing, maintenance, refueling and other support. Iraq shall secure priority clearance for aircraft used by the Agency;

(f) to communicate from any place within Iraq, and without censorship or other hindrance, by radio, satellite or other forms of communication and to connect with the IAEA and the United Nations by radio and satellite network, as well as by telephone, telegraph and other means of communication. Iraq shall, upon request of the Agency, provide appropriate means of communication;

0299   /...

(g) to use codes and receive papers, correspondence and other items by courier or sealed bags; and

(h) to fly the United Nations flag on premises and means of transport.

33. The Agency shall have the right to make its own arrangements to ensure the safety and security of its personnel and property and to take custody of any material or item.

F. National Implementation Measures

34. Iraq shall adopt the necessary measures to implement its obligations under resolutions 687 and 707, and other relevant Security Council resolutions, and the present plan, in particular to prohibit all natural and legal persons under Iraq's jurisdiction or control from undertaking anywhere any activity that is prohibited for Iraq by resolution 687 or 707, by other relevant Security Council resolutions or by the present plan. Iraq shall enact penal laws to secure enforcement of these prohibitions.

35. Iraq shall inform the IAEA of the legislative and administrative measures taken to implement resolutions 687 and 707, other relevant Security Council resolutions and the plan not later than 30 days after the approval by the Security Council of the plan and thereafter as determined by the IAEA.

G. Non-compliance

36. Should the IAEA discover any item, including documentation, that Iraq, under resolutions 687 or 707, is obliged to yield to the IAEA for destruction, removal or rendering harmless, the IAEA shall have the right to take it into

0300 /...

custody and shall provide for its disposal, as appropriate. Iraq shall retain no ownership interest in items to be destroyed, removed or rendered harmless pursuant to resolution 687 or the plan.

37. Should the IAEA discover any activity taking place in contravention of resolutions 687 or 707, it shall have the right to call upon Iraq to halt the activity and to prevent its recurrence. The IAEA shall also have the right to take any prohibited item involved into custody and shall provide for its disposal, as appropriate.

38. Findings by the IAEA that indicate that Iraq is not in compliance with its obligations under resolution 687 or 707 or the plan shall be brought to the attention of the Security Council.

39. Findings by the IAEA that Iraq is not in compliance with its obligations under the safeguards agreement between Iraq and the IAEA shall, in accordance with the safeguards agreement and the Statute of the Agency, be reported to the Security Council.

H. Reports

40. The IAEA shall, through the Secretary-General, report to the Security Council every six months, and at any other time the Security Council may request, on the implementation of the plan.

I. Revisions

41. The plan may only be revised by the Security Council. The IAEA may, however, after informing the Security Council, update and revise the Annexes in the light of information and experience gained in the course of the implementation of resolutions 687 and 707 and of the plan. The IAEA shall inform Iraq of any such change.

0301

/...

J. Entry Into Force and Duration

42. The present plan shall enter Into force Immediately upon Its approval by the Security Council. The duration of the plan shall be determined by the Security Council.

0302

/...

LIST OF ANNEXES

ANNEX 1   **DEFINITIONS**

ANNEX 2   **PROVISIONS RELATED TO INFORMATION REQUIREMENTS**

ANNEX 3   **LIST OF ITEMS TO BE REPORTED TO THE AGENCY**

ANNEX 4   **LIST OF NUCLEAR ACTIVITIES PERMITTED UNDER SECURITY
COUNCIL RESOLUTION 707**

0303

/...

ANNEX 1

DEFINITIONS

For the purposes of UN Security Council Resolutions 687 and 707, the following definitions will be adopted:

1. NUCLEAR MATERIAL

1.1 "Source material"
Uranium containing the mixture of isotopes occurring in nature; uranium depleted in the isotope 235; thorium; any of the foregoing in the form of metal, alloy, chemical compound or concentrate.

1.2 "Special fissionable material"
Plutonium-239; uranium-235; uranium-233; uranium enriched in the isotopes 235 or 233; any material containing one or more of the foregoing.

1.3 "Nuclear-weapon-usable material"
Nuclear material that can be used for the manufacture of nuclear explosive components without transmutation or further enrichment, such as plutonium containing less than 80% plutonium-238, uranium enriched to 20% uranium-235 and uranium-233 or more; any chemical compound or mixture of the foregoing. Plutonium, uranium-233 and uranium enriched to less than 20% uranium-235 contained in irradiated fuel do not fall into this category.

2. NUCLEAR ACTIVITIES

2.1 - 2.9 (inclusive) refer to activities prohibited under both Resolutions 687 and 707.

Any activity such as research and development, design, manufacturing, import of systems, equipment and components, pilot plant and plant construction, commissioning and operation, or utilization in one or more of the following:

0304

/...

2.1 Production of nuclear weapons

2.2 Production and any use of nuclear-weapon-usable material

2.3 Production of metals or alloys containing plutonium or uranium.

2.4 Weaponization
This covers the research, development, manufacturing and testing required to make nuclear explosives from special fissionable material.

2.5 Nuclear fuel fabrication using plutonium, uranium-233, uranium enriched to 20% or more in uranium-235.

2.6 Import, construction or use of research and power reactors of any kind utilizing uranium enriched to $\geq$ 20% in uranium-235, uranium-233, plutonium or MOX as a fuel or any reactor designed specifically for plutonium production. This includes critical and sub-critical assemblies.

2.7 Reprocessing of irradiated fuel
Including the use of hot cells and associated equipment

2.8 Enrichment of uranium in isotope 235 and any preparatory steps in this process, including the preparation of UCl_4 and UF_6.

2.9 Production and separation of the isotopes of plutonium, hydrogen, lithium and boron

2.10 - 2.18 (Inclusive) refer to activities, permitted under resolution 687 but prohibited under 707.

Any activity such as research and development, design, manufacturing, import of systems, equipment and components, pilot plant and plant construction, commissioning and operation, or utilization in one or more of the following:

2.10 Import, construction or use of research and power reactors of any type utilizing natural uranium or uranium enriched to less than 20% in uranium-235 as a fuel. This includes critical and sub-critical assemblies, but excludes reactors specifically designed for plutonium production.

2.11 Prospecting, mining or processing of ores containing uranium and/or thorium

2.12 Preparation of chemical compounds containing uranium enriched to less than 20 % in uranium-235 and thorium, excluding the preparation of UCl_4 and UF_6.

0305   /...

2.13 Nuclear fuel fabrication using natural uranium or uranium enriched to less than 20% in uranium·235.

2.14 Processing and disposal of radioactive wastes

2.15 Nuclear fusion experimental devices based on magnetic or inertial confinement, including diagnostics

2.16 Production of isotopes both radioactive and stable. The production of the isotopes of plutonium, hydrogen, lithium, boron and uranium is prohibited.

2.17 Import, construction and use of neutron sources, electron accelerators, particle accelerators, heavy ion accelerators

2.18 Research on radiation physics and chemistry and on the physical and chemical properties of isotopes except in area relevant to items 2.19, 2.20 and 2.21

2.19-2.21 (inclusive) refer to activities permitted under Resolution 707

2.19 Application of radiation and isotopes in food and agriculture

2.20 Applications of radiation and isotopes in medicine

2.21 Application of radiation and isotopes in industrial processes

0306

/...

ANNEX 2

PROVISIONS RELATED TO INFORMATION REQUIREMENTS

1.   The initial information under paragraph 22 of the plan to be submitted no later than 30 days after the adoption of the plan by the Security Council shall cover the period from 1 January 1989. Subsequent complete information shall be provided each 15 January and 15 July and shall cover the six-month period prior to the provision of the information.

2.   Whenever the information that Iraq is required to provide under paragraph 22 of the plan is equal to nil, Iraq shall provide nil returns and confirm this at monthly intervals.

3.   The inventory of nuclear material referred to in paragraph 22(a) of the plan shall include the quantity, form, compositon, location and current use of such material, including nuclear material containing uranium or thorium which has not reached the composition and purity suitable for fuel fabrication or for being isotopically enriched. For this purpose, the term "use" shall also include storage. The inventory shall be updated at monthly intervals.

4.   The information on facilities, installations or sites to be provided under the plan shall, for each facility, installation or site, include:

   (a)   the name of the facility, installation or site and of the owner, company or enterprise operating the facility, installation or site;

   (b)   the location of the facility, installation or site;

   (c)   a meaningful description of all types of activities at the facility, installation or site;

   (d)   the source(s) of the financing of the facility, installation or site and of its activities;

   (e)   the design of the facility, installation or site, including blueprints and photos as built;

   (f)   precise indication where material or other items, including equipment, specified in the plan or in Annexes are present, specifiying where applicable, building, room, place within the room;

   (g)   a detailed description of activities related to the material, other items, equipment or processes specified in the plan or in Annexes 3 and 4, including as applicable technical characteristics, material flow and process flow diagrams.

0307   /...

5.   The location of a facility, installation or site shall be specified by means of the address and a site diagram. Each diagram shall be drawn to scale and shall indicate the boundaries of the facility, installation or site, all road and rail entrances and exits, and all structures on the facility, installation or site, indicating their purpose. If the facility, installation or site is located within a larger complex, the diagram shall specify the exact location of the facility, installation or site within the complex. On each diagram, the geographic coordinates of a point within the facility, installation or site shall be specified to the nearest second.

6.   The inventory referred to in paragraph 22(c) of the plan on non-nuclear materials, equipment and items shall include specification of each item, including its packaging, the number and quantity of the item(s), and, where applicable, quantity, form and composition of such items, as well as the location and use (including storage) of all items on the inventory. The inventory shall be updated at monthly intervals.

7.   The information to be provided under paragraph 22(d) of the plan on the inventory of all types of isotopes used for medical, agricultural or industrial purposes shall, for each type of isotope, include the quantity, form, composition, location, list of facilities, installations or sites where produced and used (including storage), and the purpose for which used. The inventory shall be updated at monthly intervals.

8.   The information on the nuclear programme to be provided under paragraph 22(e) of the plan shall cover the subsequent five years. The information shall be updated on an annual basis, extending until such time as Agency activities under the plan cease. Any proposed change to that programme shall be notified to, and subject to approval by, the Agency before they are made.

9.   The information on each import or export to be provided under paragraph 23(b) of the plan shall include quantity, form, and composition of the material, a description of the equipment, and the origin, destination, point and time of entry into Iraq, and proposed use, of the item transferred. The information on imports and exports shall be provided at least 60 days before such transaction commences.

10.   Iraq shall notify:

(a)   any changes in the inventory referred to in paragraph 22 of the plan, one month in advance;

(b)   any changes to nuclear programme referred to in paragraph 22 of the plan, one year in advance;

0308   /...

(c)   complete description of the design information for any planned
       nuclear facility, installation or site or any planned modifications
       of any existing nuclear facility, installation or site, six months
       before the start of construction or modification of any such facility,
       installation or site;

11.   All information required under the plan should include the
       corresponding text in English.

0309

/...

ANNEX 3

LIST OF ITEMS TO BE REPORTED TO THE AGENCY

Security Council Resolution 707 demands that Iraq, _inter alia_, halt all nuclear activities of any kind, except for certain uses of isotopes, until the Security Council determines that Iraq is in full compliance with the provisions of Resolution 707 and paragraphs 12 and 13 of Resolution 687 and that the IAEA determines that Iraq is in full compliance with the provisions of its safeguards agreement with the IAEA. Once these determinations have been made affirmatively by the Security Council and by the IAEA, Iraq may seek to initiate the nuclear activities which are not prohibited by Resolution 687. Approval by the Security Council for Iraq to initiate one or more of these nuclear activities may necessitate a corresponding amendment to this list.

Items marked * are specifically prohibited to Iraq under Resolution 687; the others may be prohibited if they are used, or are to be used, in activities prohibited under Resolution 687.

1. **Source materials (see Annex 1, para. 1.1)**

2. **Special fissionable materials (see Annex 1, para. 1.2)**
   *Special fissionable materials which fall within the definition of nuclear-weapon-usable materials are prohibited.

*3. **Nuclear-weapon-usable materials (see Annex 1, para 1.3)**

4. **Equipment or materials referred to in Section 2 of Memorandum B of INFCIRC/209/Rev. 1 and in the Annex to INFCIRC/209/Rev. 1**
   *All items included in INFCIRC/209/Rev. 1 which are used for enrichment and reprocessing are prohibited. *Any item to be used in any activity listed in Items 2.1 to 2.9 of Annex 1 is also prohibited.

5. **EQUIPMENT AND MATERIALS USED IN URANIUM ENRICHMENT** Including

0310 /...

*5.1 Rotor fabrication and assembly equipment and bellows-forming mandrels and dies

(a) Rotor assembly equipment specially designed or prepared for assembly of gas centrifuge rotor tube sections, baffles, and end caps. Such equipment includes specially designed precision mandrels, clamps, and shrink fit machines.

(b) Rotor straightening equipment specially designed or prepared for alignment of gas centrifuge rotor tube sections to a common axis.

(c) Bellows-forming mandrels and dies, two-piece cylindrical with a single indented circumferential convolution bisected by the two halves.

*5.2 Centrifugal balancing machines
Centrifugal balancing machines, fixed or portable, horizontal or vertical.

*5.3 Filament winding machines
Filament winding machines in which the motions for positioning, wrapping, and winding fibers are coordinated and programmed in three or more axes, specially designed to fabricate composite structures or laminates from fibrous and filamentary materials and capable of winding cylindrical rotors.

*5.4 Centrifuge housing/recipients
Components to contain the rotor tube assembly of a centrifuge enrichment machine.

*5.5 Aluminium, high-strength tube
Cylindrical tubing in semifabricated or finished forms made of aluminium alloy

5.6 Fibrous and filamentary materials (high strength)
Fibrous and filamentary materials for use in composite structures

*5.7 Maraging steel
Maraging steel (high strength) with an ultimate tensile strength of 2.050×10^9 N/m^2 (300,000 psi) or more.

0311 /...

5.8   Titanium
Cylindrical tubing in semi-fabricated forms made of high-strength titanium alloys

5.9   Spin-forming and flow-forming machines specially designed or adapted for use with numerical or computer controls and specially designed parts and accessories therefor.

6.   CHLORINE TRIFLÚORIDE

7.   ELECTROLYTIC CELLS FOR FLUORINE PRODUCTION AND SPECIALLY DESIGNED PARTS AND ACCESSORIES THEREFORE

8.   MASS SPECTROMETERS FOR URANIUM HEXAFLUORIDE
Mass spectrometers for uranium hexafluoride as follows.

*8.1   Mass spectrometers, magnetic or quadruple:

8.1.1   Instruments having all of the following characteristics:
(a) Resolution of less than 1 atomic mass unit (amu) for molecular masses greater than 320 amu; and
(b) Electron-bombardment ionization source; and

8.1.2   Instruments having any of the following characteristics:
(a) Molecular beam ion sources;
(b) Ion source chambers constructed of or lined with nichrome or monel, or nickel plated;
(c) A collector system suitable for simultaneous collection of two or more isotopic species; and

0312

/...

*8.2 Sources for mass spectrometers having any of the following characteristics:

(a) Molecular beam source;

(b) Ion source chambers constructed of or lined with nichrome or monel, or nickel plated; or

(c) Sources for mass spectrometers designed especially for use with UF_6.

*9. URANIUM HEXAFLUORIDE-RESISTANT GAUGES

*10 URANIUM HEXAFLUORIDE-RESISTANT VALVES

Valves, with a bellows seal, wholly made of or lined with aluminium, nickel, or alloy containing nickel, either manually or automatically operated and specially designed parts or accessories therefore.

0313

/...

11 **LASERS AND EQUIPMENT CONTAINING LASERS AS FOLLOWS**

*(a) Copper vapor lasers with 40 W average output power;

(b) Argon ion lasers with greater than 40 W average output power;

(c) Nd: YAG lasers that can be frequency doubled and after doubling have an average power output at the doubled frequency greater than 40 W;

*(d) Tunable pulsed dye laser amplifiers and oscillators, except single-mode oscillators, with an average power greater than 30 W, a repetition rate greater than 1 kHz and a wavelength between 500 nm and 700 nm;

(e) Tunable pulsed single-mode dye oscillators capable of an average power greater than 1 W, a repetition rate greater than 1 kHz, a pulse width less than 100 ns, and a wavelength between 500 nm and 700 nm.

(f) Alexandrite lasers with a bandwidth of 0.005 nm or less, a repetition rate greater than 124 Hz, and an average output power greater than 30 W;

*(g) Pulsed carbon dioxide lasers with a repetition rate greater than 250 Hz, an average output power greater than 2.5 kW, and a pulse length less than 200 ns;

(h) Pulsed excimer lasers (XeD, XeCl, KrF) with a repetition rate greater than 250 Hz and an average output power greater than 500W;

*(i) Free electron lasers.

12 **PIPES, VALVES, FITTINGS**
*Pipes, valves, fittings, heat exchangers, or magnetic, electrostatic, or other collectors made of graphite or coated in graphite, yttrium, or yttrium compounds resistant to the heat and corrosion of uranium vapor.

*13 **RESINS AND ORGANIC COMPLEXING AGENTS CAPABLE OF SEPARATING ISOTOPES OF URANIUM**
Chemical exchange resin developed for the separation of isotopes of uranium and other fissile materials and organic complexing agents developed for the same purpose.

0314   /...

14   **SOLVENT EXTRACTION EQUIPMENT**
*Solvent extraction equipment suitable for use in the separation of uranium isotopes.

15   **ORDINARY AND SUPERCONDUCTING ELECTROMAGNETS**
Ordinary and superconducting electromagnets capable of creating magnetic fields of more than 2 teslas (20 kilogauss) as follows.

   (a) ordinary and solenoidal superconductive electromagnets of more than 300 mm inner diameter except such magnets shipped as integral parts of medical nuclear magnetic resonance (NMR) imaging systems.

   (b) ordinary and superconductive electromagnets with a diameter of 500 mm or greater except such magnets shipped as integral parts of NMR systems.

*16   **PROCESS CONTROL SYSTEMS FOR USE IN ENRICHMENT**
Process control systems configured for use in uranium enrichment, as follows:

   (a) Computer systems configured to read process variables, compute control levels, and automatically adjust process variables for such units;

   (b) Arrays of instrumentation for monitoring process variables such as temperature, pressure, pH, fluid level, and flow rate selected for specific production process and designed to operate in the hostile environment required by each process.

*17   **EQUIPMENT SPECIALLY DESIGNED FOR THE PREPARATION OF FEED MATERIALS FOR ENRICHMENT PROCESSES, INCLUDING THE PREPARATION OF UF_6 AND UCl_4.**

*18   **FEED MATERIALS FOR ENRICHMENT PROCESSES INCLUDING UF_6 AND UCl_4.**

0315

/...

NUCLEAR REACTORS, INCLUDING CRITICAL AND SUB-CRITICAL ASSEMBLIES, REACTOR EQUIPMENT AND MATERIALS

19 REACTOR SYSTEMS, SUB-SYSTEMS, EQUIPMENT AND COMPONENTS

19.1 Reactor vessels
Reactor vessels, including pressurized and unpressurized types.

19.2 Reactivity control mechanisms, devices and systems
Reactivity control mechanisms, devices and systems, including manual, electro-mechanical, hydraulic, pneumatic and chemical injection/removal-type systems.

19.3 Reactor process monitoring, measurement and control systems
Reactor process monitoring, measurement and control systems, sub-systems and components. All analog and digital process control computers and hydraulic and pneumatic process monitoring and control instruments and equipment.

19.4 Reactor fuel charging and discharging systems
Reactor fuel charging and discharging systems and equipment, including manual, electro-mechanical, hydraulic and pneumatic systems and components.

19.5 Calandrias
Calandrias, calandria tubes, pressure tubes and other fuel channel assemblies and components.

19.6 Primary and secondary heat transport and removal systems
Primary and secondary heat transport and removal systems, including steam generators, heat exchangers, coolant purification, coolant recovery, high and low pressure injection and circulating pumps, pressure relief devices and other pressure-retaining components especially designed, manufactured or prepared for use in such systems.

0316

/...

PLANTS AND EQUIPMENT USED IN REPROCESSING

*20 PROCESS CONTROL SYSTEMS FOR USE IN REPROCESSING

Process control systems configured for use in reprocessing, as follows:

(a) Computer systems configured to read process variables, compute control levels, and automatically adjust process variables for such units;

(b) Arrays of instrumentation for monitoring process variables such as temperature, pressure, pH, fluid level, and flow rate selected for the specific production process and designed to operate in the hostile environment required by each process.

*21 HOT CELLS AND ASSOCIATED EQUIPMENT

Hot cells and associated equipment for the handling and processing of irradiated fuel on any scale.

*22 OTHER EQUIPMENT FOR THE REPROCESSING OF IRRADIATED FUEL

Equipment for the reprocessing of irradiated fuel by methods other than solvent extraction, e.g., ion-exchange, fluoride volatility, pyrometallurgical.

*23 REPROCESSING WASTE TREATMENT

Plants and equipment for the treatment of wastes from reprocessing.

OTHER EQUIPMENT AND MATERIALS

24 Plants and equipment used for the following processes

(a) Prospecting for ores containing source materials;
(b) Mining of ores containing source materials;
(c) Separation of source material from ores and other naturally occurring materials to form concentrates;
(d) Preparation of metals, alloys, or any chemical compound containing source material or uranium enriched to less than 20% in uranium-235;
(e) Fabrication of source material or uranium enriched to less than 20% in uranium-235 into a form suitable for irradiation in a nuclear reactor;
(f) Treatment of wastes from mining, conversion and fabrication processes and plants.

0317   /...

25 Turning machines
*Turning machines (lathes) having one or more of the following characteristics:

(a) Vacuum chucks suitable for holding hemispherical parts;

(b) Machines installed within glove boxes.

26 High temperature furnaces
*Vacuum or controlled environment (inert gas) furnaces including induction, arc, plasma and electron beam furnaces, capable of operation above 700°C; and especially designed power supplies therefor.

*27 Crucibles resistant to liquid fissile metals
Crucibles made of materials resistant to liquid fissile metals and designed to avoid nuclear criticality.

28 Isostatic presses
Isostatic presses capable of achieving a maximum working pressure of 69 MPa or greater and specially designed dies and molds, components, accessories and controls and *specially designed software* therefor.

29 Beryllium
Beryllium as follows:

(a) Metal;

(b) Alloys containing more than 50% of beryllium by weight;

(c) Compounds containing beryllium;

(d) Manufactures thereof; and

(e) Waste and scrap;

except

(a) Metal windows for X-ray machines;

0318

/...

(b) Oxide shapes in fabricated or semi-fabricated forms specially designed for electronic component parts or as substrates for electronic circuits;

(c) Naturally-occuring compounds containing beryllium.

30 Calcium

High purity calcium containing both less than 0.1% by weight of impurities other than magnesium and less than 10 ppm (parts per million) of boron.

31 Lithium

*(a) Lithium enriched in lithium-6:

*(b) Facilities or specialized equipment for the separation of the lithium-6 isotope;

except

for use in thermoluminescence dosimetry.

32 Magnesium

High purity magnesium containing both less than 0.02% by weight of impurities other than calcium and less than 10 ppm (parts per million) of boron.

33 Tantalum

Tantalum sheet with a thickness of 2.5 mm or greater.

34 Plutonium, uranium-233 and enriched uranium contained in irradiated fuel.

35 Tungsten

Parts made of tungsten, tungsten carbide, or tungsten alloys (greater than 90% tungsten) having a mass greater than 20 kg;

except

parts specifically designed for use as weights or gamma-ray collimators.

36 Hafnium

Hafnium in any metallic, alloy or oxide form.

0319

/...

37 Boron
Boron and boron compounds and mixtures in which the boron-10 isotope is more than 20% of the total boron content.

IMPLOSION SYSTEMS DEVELOPMENT

*38 Hydrodynamic testing facilities
Hydrodynamic test facilities capable of handling the detonation of high explosive charges of 1 kg or greater and suitable for use of appropriate diagnostic instrumentation.

*39 Computers
Computer centers and networks using hydrodynamics codes, neutronic codes, and/or equation-of-state and nuclear data files.

40 Flash X-ray equipment
Flash X-ray generators or pulsed electron accelerators with peak energy of 500 keV or greater.

*41 Gun systems for large masses
Gun systems for accelerating large masses (greater than 5 kg) to low velocity using chemical propellants similar to those used in artillery, usually associated with timing, velocity, and other diagnostics.

*42 Shells, hollow spheres or portions thereof
Shells, hollow spheres, or portions of spheres made of high explosives or metals listed in 2 and molds for such parts.

43 Photographic equipment

*(a) Mechanical framing cameras with recording rates greater than 225,000 frames per second; streak cameras with writing speeds greater than 0.5 mm per microsecond; and parts and accessories thereof, including sznchronizing electronics specially designed for this purpose and rotor assemblies (including turbines, mirrors, and bearings).

0320

/...

*(b) Electronic streak cameras capable of 50 ns or less time resolution and framing cameras capable of 50 ns or less frame exposure time including single-frame cameras, and streak and framing tubes usable in such cameras.

*44 Transient recorders and/or digital oscilloscopes

Transient recorders and/or digital oscilloscopes using analog-to-digital conversion techniques capable of storing transients by sequentially sampling one-shot input signals at successive intervals of less than 20 nanoseconds (greater than 50 million samples per second), digitizing to 8 bits or greater resolution, and storing 256 or more samples.

45 Analog oscilloscopes and cameras

*(a) Analog oscilloscopes suitable for triggered single-sweep operation with a bandwidth greater than 250 MHz and associated oscilloscope cameras:

(b) Analog oscilloscopes in the 30-250 MHz range and associated oscilloscope cameras.

*46 Specialized equipment for hydrodynamic experiments

EXPLOSIVES AND RELATED EQUIPMENT

*47 Detonators and multipoint initiator systems

Detonators and multipoint initiation systems:

(a) Electrically driven explosive detonators of the types exploding bridge (EB), exploding bridgewire (EBW), slapper, or exploding foil initiators (EFI):

(b) Specially designed parts or bodies for any of the detonators described above; or

(c) Arrangements of multiple detonators designed to nearly simultaneously initiate an explosive surface from a single firing signal.

(d) explosive lenses designed to uniformly initiate the surface of a high-explosive charge.

0321 /...

*46 Firing sets and equivalent high-current pulsers (for controlled detonators)

(a) Explosive detonator firing sets designed to drive multiple controlled detonators covered under Item 4.1. above;

(b) Modular electrical pulse generators (pulsers) designed for portable, mobile, or rugged use (including xenon flashlamp drivers) having the following characteristics:

- capable of delivering their energy in less than 15 microseconds;

- having an output greater than 500 A; and

- having a rise time of less than 10 microseconds into loads of less than 5 ohms.

49 High explosives
High explosives including the following:

(a) Cyclotetramethylenetetranitramine (HMX);

(b) Cyclotrimethylenetrinitramine (RDX);

(c) Triaminotrinitrobenzene (TATB);

(d) Pentaerythritoltetranitrate (PETN),

except

when contained in pharmaceuticals;

(e) Hexanitrostilbene (HNS),

except

when contained in pharmaceuticals.

0322

/...

OTHERS

50 Neutron generator systems

* Neutron generator systems utilizing electrostatic acceleration to induce a tritium-deuterium nuclear reaction; and specially designed parts (including tubes) thereof.

*51 Tritium and tritium related plants, equipment, and materials

(a) Tritium, including compounds and mixtures containing tritium in which the ratio of tritium to hydrogen by atoms exceeds 1 part in 1000,

<u>except</u>

tritium in luminescent devices (e.g. safety devices installed in aircraft, watches, runway lights)

(b) Facilities or plants for the production, recovery, extraction, concentration, or handling of tritium, and equipment and materials suitable for use therein, including the following:

·· Tritium storage, separation, purification, and pumping systems using metal hydrides as the storage, pumping or purification medium;

— Pumps or compressors that are constructed without plastic parts and which are designed so that lubricating oils are not in contact with the process gas.

52 Deuterium and deuterium-related plants, equipment and materials

(a) Deuterium, including compounds and mixtures containing deuterium in which the ratio of deuterium to hydrogen by atoms exceeds 1 part in 5000.

(b) Facilities or plants for the production, recovery, extraction, concentration or handling of deuterium, and equipment and materials suitable for use therein

0323

/...

c) Compressors and blowers specially designed or prepared to be corrosion resistant to H_2S and having all of the following characteristics:

(i) An inlet operating pressure of 260 to 280 psi·gauge, with a differential pressure between outlet and inlet of approximately 30 psi;

(ii) a suction volume of 120,000 scfm;

(iii) capable of sustaining the above inlet pressure and suction volume in H_2S gas saturated with water vapor.

d) Specialized packings made of phosphor bronze mesh designed for use in vacuum distillation towers, suitable for use in separating heavy from light water.

53 Alpha sources

All alpha-emitting radionuclides and equipment containing alpha-emitting radionuclides meeting all of the following specification

(a) The radionuclides have an alpha half-life of 10 days or greater but less than 200 years;

(b) The radionuclides are contained in compounds or mixtures with a total alpha activity of 37 GBq per kilogram (1 curie per kilogram) or greater; and

(c) The radionuclides have a total alpha activity of 3.7 GBq (100 millicuries) or greater;

except

radionuclides in medical implant devices.

54 Photomultiplier tubes of the following descriptions:

a) An anode pulse rise time of less than 1 ns; or
b) Containing mircrochannel plate electron multipliers.

0324

/...

55 Capacitors with either of the following sets of characteristics:

A voltage rating greater than 1.4 kV having all of the following characteristics:

    1) Energy storage greater than 10 J;
    2) Capacitance greater than 0.5 μF; and
    3) Series inductance less than 50 nH;

or

A voltage rating greater than 750 V having both of the following characteristics:

    1) Capacitance greater than 0.25 μF; and
    2) Series inductance less than 10 nH.

56 High-purity (99.99%) bismuth with very low silver content (less than 10 parts per million)

57 "Robots" and specially designed robot controllers, and robot "end-effectors" having any of the following characteristics:

(a) Specially designed to comply with national safety standards applicable to explosive environments (for example, meeting electrical code ratings for explosive environments);

(b) Specially designed or rated as radiation hardened more than necessary to withstand normal industrial (i.e., non-nuclear industry) ionizing radiation.

58 Pulse amplifiers with gain greater than 6 decibels and with a baseband bandwidth greater than 500 megahertz (having the low frequency half-power point at less than 1 MHz and the high frequency half-power point at less than 1 MHz and the high frequency half-power point greater than 500 MHz) and output voltage greater than 2 volts into 55 ohms or less (this corresponds to an output greater than 16 dbm in a 50 ohm system).

0325

/...

59 Switching devices, as follows:

(a) Cold-cathode tubes (including gas krytron tubes and vacuum sprytron tubes), whether gas filled or not, operating similarly a spark gap, containing three or more electrodes, and having all of the following characteristics:

(1) Anode peak voltage rating of 2500 V or more;
(2) Anode peak current rating of 100 A or more; and
(3) Anode delay time of 10 microseconds or less;

(b) Triggered spark-gaps having an anode delay time of 15 microseconds or less and rated for a peak current of 500 A or more;

(c) Hydrogen/hydrogen-isotope thyratrons of ceramic-metal construction and rated for a peak current of 500 A or more.

60 Vibration test equipment using digital control techniques and feedback or closed loop test equipment and software therefore capable of vibrating a system at 10 g RMS or more between 20 Hz and 2000 Hz, imparting forces of 50 kN (11,250 lbs) or greater.

61 Electronic digital computers with a "composite theoretical performance" (CTP) of 12.5 million theoretical operations per second (Mtops) or greater except:

(a) Computers contained in or associated with other equipment or systems where the computers are essential for the operation of the other equipment or systems and the computers are not the principal element of the other equipment or systems, or

(b) Computers essential for medical applications and incorporated in equipment or systems designed or modified for an identifiable and dedicated medical applications.

62 Electronic equipment for time delay generation or time interval measurement:

(a) Digital time delay generators with a resolution of 500 nanoseconds or less over time intervals of 1 microsecond or greater;

(b) Multichannel (three or more) or modular time interval meters and chronometry equipment with time resolution less than 50 nanoseconds over time ranges greater than 1 microsecond.

0326   /...

ANNEX 4
LIST OF NUCLEAR ACTIVITIES PERMITTED
UNDER SECURITY COUNCIL RESOLUTION 707

The following peaceful applications of isotopes imported from other States after prior approval by the IAEA are permitted:

1. **AGRICULTURAL APPLICATIONS**

    1.1 **Soil fertility, irrigation and crop production**

    1.2 **Plant breeding and genetics**

    1.3 **Animal production and health**

    1.4 **Insect and pest control**

    1.5 **Food preservation**

    1.6 **Other uses as approved by the IAEA**

2. **INDUSTRIAL APPLICATIONS**

    2.1 **Radiography and other non-destructive testing methods**

    2.2 **Industrial process control and quality control**

    2.3 **Radiotracer applications in oil, chemical and metallurgical processes**

    2.4 **Development of water and mineral resources**

    2.5 **Industrial radiation processing**

    2.6 **Other uses as approved by the IAEA**

3. **MEDICAL APPLICATIONS**

    3.1 **Diagnostic and therapeutic medicine including dosimetry**

    3.2 **Radiotherapy by teletherapy and brachytherapy**

    3.3 **Nutrition and health-related environmental studies**

    3.4 **Other uses as approved by the IAEA**

0327

GLGL
o0348 ASI/AFP-BC03------
u i Iraq-U.N.-experts lead-i 09-24 0249
    Iraq detains U.N. experts again

    NEW YORK, United Nations, Sept 24 (AFP) - <u>Iraqi authorities detained U.N.
experts during an inspection in Baghdad Tuesday in the second such standoff in
as many days,</u> a senior State Department official said.
    The official, who spoke on condition of anonymity, said the Iraqis would
not allow the U.N. inspectors to remove documents from the site and were
demanding that they surrender a videotape.
    David Kay, the head of the U.N. inspection team in Baghdad, told Cable
News Network the 44-member group had been detained for more than five hours by
Iraqi security officials because they refused to hand over videotape and film.
    "We certainly don't feel we have freedom of movement," said Kay. "We're
surrounded by 60 Iraqi personnel in the middle of Baghdad with darkness only
about an hour away. It's not a very pleasant situation."
    He said the Iraqis had prevented the team from taking away documents
collected at the site and said they would not be allowed to leave until they
turned over their film and videotape.
    "They insisted that, in addition to the documents we had collected, that
all of our film and videotapes must be surrendered," said Kay. "We refused
that and have had negotiations off and on over the past five and a half hours
or so.
    "We have been told that unless we surrender the film and the videotape we
will not be allowed to leave the site," he said.

    David Kydd, the International Atomic Enery Agency (IAEA) spokesman in
Vienna, told CNN the Iraqis intervened after the inspectors had viewed
documents from personnel files at Iraq's Atomic Energy Agency.
    They were collecting documents he said were needed to monitor what
activities the Iraqis were engaged in.
    The experts were staying put until they received further instructions,
said Kydd, setting the stage for another confrontation with Iraq over its
nuclear program.
    Documents found Monday by the U.N. experts describing Iraq's program to
build nuclear weapons were seized by Iraqi authorities who detained the
inspectors for about 10 hours.
    Iraq said it returned the documents Tuesday, but Kydd in Vienna said most
of the documentation on its secret nuclear program was missing.
    In the CNN interview, Kydd said experts have been unable to determine
whether the nuclear weapons program described in the documents was ongoing,
saying that they were in Arabic and needed to be more closely scrutinized.
    He said that the experts had put together a picture of the Iraqi nuclear
program from information provided by Iraqi scientists, but that "the master
plan is something that had been missing."
    "We are now in documentary form seeing Iraqi interest in detonation of a
nuclear device," he said. "We have now seen such documentary evidence,
although we don't have material evidence or evidence that such detonation
occurred."
    jm/ak

    AFP 241344 GMT SEP 91
AFP 241345 GMT SEP 91

                              14   0328

유엔 조사단, 이라크 核무기 중합계획 발견

(유엔본부 AP=聯合) 이라크의 核시설에 대한 조사활동을 벌이다 이라크軍 병사들에 의해 억류된 유엔 조사단은 이라크의 핵무기 제조 중합계획에 관한 증거를 발견했다고 유엔의 한 고위관리가 24일 말했다.

이라크의 테러무기 해체를 관장하고 있는 유엔 특별 위원회의 롤프 에케우스 위원장은 이날 기자들로부터 "유엔 조사단이 이라크가 인근 국가들에 대한 核우위를 점하기 위해 마련한 핵무기 개발 중합계획을 발견했느냐"는 질문을 받자 이같이 대답하고 아울러 이 조사단은 외국기업들이 사담 후세인 이라크 대통령의 핵무기 개발 계획을 지원한 증거를 말해주는 문서도 발견했다고 덧붙였다.

에케우스 위원장은 그러나 어떤 기업 또는 어떤 국가가 이라크에 이같은 지원을 제공했는지는 밝히지 않았다.

한편 타리크 아지즈 이라크 副총리는 이날 바그다드에서 이라크 보안군에 의해 억류된 유엔 핵무기 조사단은 미국을 위한 스파이 활동을 벌였다고 주장했다.(끝)

15   0329

연합 H1-025 S06 외신(167)

안보리 이라크 영궁비행에 관한 최후 통첩
이라크에 전달

(유엔본부 로이터=聯合)유엔 안보리 의장은 24일 이라크는 앞으로 4시간안에 이라크내의 대량파괴무기 탐색을 위해 유엔 헬기가 무제한으로 이라크영궁 비행을 할 수 있는지 여부를 알리는 서한을 제출해야 한다고 경고했다.

9월 안보리의장인 프랑스의 장 베르나르 메리메氏는 그럼지 않을 경우에는 무력을 사용할 수 밖에 없을 것이라고 강조했다.(끝)

(YONHAP) 910925 0257 KST

0330

16

걸프戰 해군 작전태세 돌입

파시 "후세인 없는 한 제재 계속"

야혜 核査단 12시간 감금당해

美, 이라크에 최후통첩 검토

91. 9. 24 〈동아〉 4면

국기

외 무 부

종 별 :

번 호 : UNW-2996

일 시 : 91 0925 1930

수 신 : 장 관(연일,국기,중동일,미일,기정)

발 신 : 주 유엔 대사

제 목 : 안보리(걸프사태)

1. 유엔 이락 특정무기폐기 특위 (UNSCOM)헬기사용문제

가. 이락은 상기 헬기사용에 동의함을 9.24 자로 안보리 통보하여 왔음.(S/23064)

나. 한편 이락은 동사용 방식에 관하여는 이락과 특위가 합의해야 함을 제기해온바, 이와관련 안보리는 이락측의 상기 동의를 안보리결의 707 호의 조건없는 수락으로 간주하며, 본건특위 헬기사용에 따른 기술적인 사항은 특위가 정해 나갈것이라는 요지의 안보리 의장 성명을 동일 비공식 협의를 거쳐 발표하였음.

2. 유엔핵사찰반 억류사태

상기관련 안보리는 이락의 핵사찰 방해활동을 규탄하는 안보리의장 성명을 비공식 협의를 거쳐 9.24 발표하였음.

첨부 FAX:UNW(F)-560 :1. 이락의 UNSCOM 헬기사용동의 서한 및 안보리 의장성명

2. 핵사찰반 억류관련 안보리의장 성명, 이락측 안보리문서 및 사무총장 기자문답

3. NYT 지 기사.끝

(대사 노창희-국장대리)

국기국 안기부	차관	1차보	미주국	중아국	국기국	외정실	분석관	청와대

PAGE 1

91.09.26   09:38 WG

외신 1과 통제관

0332

UNW(유)-560   10925 1930,
(연월. 국가. 중동별. 미이. 기정) 총 6매 **S**

**UNITED
NATIONS**

 Security Council

Distr.
GENERAL

S/23064
24 September 1991
ENGLISH
ORIGINAL: ARABIC

LETTER DATED 24 SEPTEMBER 1991 FROM THE PERMANENT REPRESENTATIVE
OF IRAQ TO THE UNITED NATIONS ADDRESSED TO THE PRESIDENT OF THE
SECURITY COUNCIL

In follow-up to our meeting yesterday and on instructions from my
Government, I take pleasure in informing you that the Iraqi Government
consents to the use of helicopters by the United Nations inspection team for
the purpose of carrying out the tasks entrusted to it under resolution 687 and
other relevant resolutions, solely with a view to achieving the objectives set
out in the above-mentioned resolutions and in accordance with the modalities
to be agreed upon jointly by the Chairman of the Special Commission,
Mr. Ekeus, and the Iraqi side. It will then be possible for the helicopters
in question to enter Iraqi airspace and be received by the competent Iraqi
authorities.

I should be grateful if you would have the text of this letter circulated
as a document of the Security Council.

(Signed) Abdul Amir A. AL-ANBARI
Ambassador
Permanent Representative

91-31318 2597i (E)   6-1

UNW-2996 첨부

0333

United ⬡ Nations

Press Release

Department of Public Information • News Coverage Service • New York

SC/5308
IK/62
24 September 1991

SECURITY COUNCIL PRESIDENT TO ANSWER IRAQ'S LETTER ON HELICOPTER USE BY UN INSPECTION TEAMS

Following consultations of the Council, the President of the Security Council, Jean-Bernard P.H.P. Merimee (France), issued the following statement:

"The Iraqi Government has sent a letter to the Council on the use by the Special Commission of its own helicopters. I have been instructed to send to the Ambassador of Iraq a letter taking note of the answer that the Council considers as an unconditional acceptance of resolution 707 (1991).

"Technical modalities would be set up in the coming days by the Special Commission."

* *** *

6-2

4550P

0334

United 🌐 Nations

Press Release

Department of Public Information • News Coverage Service • New York

SC/5307
IK/61
24 September 1991

SECURITY COUNCIL DEMANDS IMMEDIATE RELEASE OF NUCLEAR INSPECTION TEAM
CURRENTLY DETAINED BY IRAQI AUTHORITIES

Following consultations of the Council, the President of the Security Council, Jean-Bernard Merimee (France), issued the following statement on behalf of the members of the Council:

"I have been mandated by the Council to make the four points that follow:

"First, the Council gives its full support to the Special Commission and to the inspection team currently present in Iraq which fulfil with exceptional dedication the tasks set out in the relevant resolutions of the Security Council; the Council reiterates that the Special Commission, acting under the authority of the Council, is the sole judge of the definition of the documents, sites or materials subject to inspection.

"Secondly, the Council expresses its strong condemnation of the way the Iraqi authorities have repeatedly prevented the inspectors from carrying out their duty. In particular, the Council considers unacceptable the fact that the inspectors are currently denied the possibility to leave freely the premises that they have inspected this morning.

"Thirdly, the Council demands that the inspection team be immediately allowed to leave the site where they are kept without any conditions and in particular that they can take with them all the documents they deem appropriate.

"Fourthly, the Council asks me to call upon the Ambassador of Iraq to convey to him its serious concerns."

* *** *

6-3

4551P

0335

**UNITED
NATIONS**

Security Council

Distr.
GENERAL

S/23065
24 September 1991
ENGLISH
ORIGINAL: ARABIC

LETTER DATED 24 SEPTEMBER 1991 FROM THE PERMANENT REPRESENTATIVE
OF IRAQ TO THE UNITED NATIONS ADDRESSED TO THE PRESIDENT OF THE
SECURITY COUNCIL

On instructions from my Government, I have the honour to transmit to you
the Iraqi Government's protest at the actions of the nuclear inspection team
currently in Baghdad, led by Mr. David Kay, which has exceeded its original
mandate by photocopying the personal files of industrial and metallurgical
personnel, including scientists and researchers. That activity is not within
the team's competence and, moreover, endangers the security of the personnel
concerned and their families, since the files in question contain details
concerning their private lives, as well as their private addresses and other
data entirely unrelated to section C of resolution 687. These actions by
Mr. Kay and his insistence on remaining inside the building where the personal
files of the personnel and researchers concerned are located, as well as
Mr. Kay's refusal to return the photocopies of the personal files that he made
improperly, are indicative of a form of conduct that appears to be motivated
by goals other than those of the United Nations and of the resolutions of the
Security Council - a form of conduct that is an obstacle to the implementation
of the above resolution and is prejudicial to the cooperative relationship
established in recent months between other United Nations inspection teams and
the competent Iraqi authorities.

I should be grateful if you would have the text of this letter circulated
as a document of the Security Council.

(Signed) Abdul Amir A. AL-ANBARI
Ambassador
Permanent Representative

91-31324 2676e (E)

6-4

0336

**REMARKS MADE BY THE SECRETARY-GENERAL UPON ENTERING THE
SECRETARIAT BUILDING ON WEDNESDAY 25 SEPTEMBER AT 9:20 A.M.**

Q.   Any comment on the inspectors being held in Iraq?

S-G   I hope that the Iraqis will decide to free our
      technicians as soon as possible.

Q.   Sir, at what point would you tell the UN inspectors to
      leave?

S-G   They have to hold for the time being. I will see the
      Foreign Minister of Iraq today and I want to make a new
      appeal to him. We are trying through diplomatic
      channels to obtain their freedom.

Q.   Do you have any indication that they might be in any
      danger?

S-G   Not so far. They are well fed and they have facilities
      but they have been in a bus for quite a long time. We
      will continue our efforts. At the same time, the
      Security Council is very vigilant.

Q.   Can you give us any indication of any likely release of
      an American hostage?

S-G   I hope, I hope very much but I cannot predict. We will
      continue our efforts on the spot and I hope that
      perhaps one (hostage) will be released before the end
      of the week. That is my hope. We are still working on
      the spot even if sometimes people forget about the
      United Nations efforts.

* * *

6-5

0337

By PAUL LEWIS
Special to The New York Times

UNITED NATIONS, Sept. 24 — The Security Council said today that Iraq had unconditionally agreed to allow international inspectors to fly their own helicopters in the country without hindrance as the inspectors search out and destroy President Saddam Hussein's weapons of mass destruction.

But the Council condemned as unacceptable Iraq's renewed detention of 44 United Nations inspectors taken into custody earlier today in Baghdad while they were copying documents related to Iraq's secret nuclear programs. The inspectors were still surrounded by Iraqi policemen and soldiers tonight.

The Council demanded the inspectors' immediate release and said they must be allowed to take with them "all the documents they deem appropriate."

Repeat of Monday's Events

The seizing of the United Nations team today followed Iraq's detention and then expulsion on Monday of the same inspectors from another building where they had been copying and removing secret plans for building nuclear weapons.

The new detention was also condemned by President Bush, though he stopped short of threatening Iraq or setting any deadline for the inspectors' release.

Mr. Bush, asked about reports that the United States, Britain and France were planning to give Iraq 48 hours to comply ully with the Council's demands or face renewed military action, told reporters: "No, we are not drawing any deadline. If I do, you'll know about it. I'll make it very, very clear."

The President today ordered American surface-to-air missiles sent to Saudi Arabia as a prelude to the deployment of about 50 combat aircraft, perhaps later this week, for escort operations inside Iraq. These American aircraft would fly along with the United Nations inspectors on their duties. [Page A14.]

Retreat From Hard Stance

The Iraqis, after having tried to attach unacceptable conditions to the use of helicopters by the inspectors, have now climbed down from that stance, sending the Council a letter today saying that the inspectors can fly the copters wherever they want in the country's airspace.

But Iraq's letter was not as explicit as the Council had wanted. As a result, it issued an additional statement saying it interprets the letter as "unconditional acceptance of Resolution 707," the provision giving the inspectors the right to use aircraft over Iraq without Government interference.

Britain's United Nations representa-

tive, Sir David Hannay, described the new detention of the inspectors as "a very serious situation" and said the Council will make an approach to the Iraqi Government at the highest level to insure that "this unacceptable behavior is brought to an end at the earliest moment."

But he termed Iraq's decision to allow the United Nations to fly its helicopters freely around the country "more hopeful news."

The United Nations' special commission supervising the aftermath of the Persian Gulf war is expected to test the Baghdad authorities' decision on helicopter use almost immediately by ordering its inspectors to start flying over the Iraqi desert to look for Scud missile sites and other banned military installations.

Still, the new and continuing detention of the inspectors from the Vienna-

The Iraqis again detain the entire team.

based International Atomic Energy Agency means that the Council remains on a collision course with Baghdad, diplomats say.

Britain's Foreign Secretary, Douglas Hurd, described the possibility of new military action against Iraq as being "in the background" for the moment. But he urged the United Nations to press ahead with its efforts to destroy Baghdad's most dangerous weapons, saying the inspectors' latest run-ins with the Iraqi authorities show that "the United Nations is getting into the guts of the Iraqi war machine."

Mr. Hurd said that if foreign forces were sent back into Iraq, British and French troops would be there alongside those of the United States.

Warning From French Envoy

Even if the United States and its allies start escorting the United Nations inspectors' helicopters, diplomats point out that this will not resolve the crisis over the inspectors' detention and the documents denied them.

The Security Council's President, Jean-Bernard Mérimée of France, told Baghdad's United Nations representative today that "it would be in Iraq's best interests" if it freed the inspectors

before the Security Council session tonight, warning that the situation was "deteriorating very fast."

The Council meeting began without any sign of change in the standoff in Baghdad, where the United Nations team was reported surrounded by about 60 Iraqi soldiers who were preventing its buses from leaving the building in central Baghdad that houses records of the Iraqi Atomic Energy Commission.

Process by Inspectors

The inspectors said they arrived at the building at 6 A.M. and began copying and removing records concerning personnel and the purchase of foreign supplies. They did this until 11 A.M., when the Iraqi authorities forced them out of the building and back into their buses, demanding that they hand over all their papers as well as a video recording they had made of the expulsion.

The inspectors said that when they refused, the Iraqis blocked the buses.

The inspectors were able to stay in contact with the outside world by means of the portable satellite phone that they take on their missions.

Officials of the nuclear agency said that the documents the inspectors removed from another building on Monday, before they were seized and then expelled, included highly incriminating designs for a nuclear trigger known as a shaped charge detonator.

"It shows conclusively that their nuclear intentions were not peaceful as they maintain," an official said.

Iraqi Official Is Defiant

In Baghdad, Deputy Prime Minister Tariq Aziz was quoted as saying that the team's American leader, David Kay, was a Central Intelligence Agency spy. He asserted that the inspectors were seeking personnel records of no concern to the United Nations.

Mr. Kay has worked for the International Atomic Energy Agency since 1983. As director of project evaluation in the department of technical cooperation, he is responsible for monitoring nuclear programs in more than 70 countries. He previously worked for the State Department as an assessor of United Nations programs in international narcotics control, nutrition and the safeguarding of nuclear material.

Mr. Kay said the accusation that he is a C.I.A. spy is "completely ridiculous and untrue."

Iraq's United Nations representative, Abdul Amir al-Anbari, told the Security Council today that the documents the inspectors want are "beyond the U.N.'s competence," adding, "We will not allow anybody to take them."

But Rolf Ekeus, the head of the Security Council's special commission, says he wants access to the Iraqi Atomic Energy Commission's personnel records in order to understand how Iraq's secret nuclear-weapons program is organized.

The United Nations experts also want to establish the names and professional qualifications of the top officials running the program so that they can interrogate them about their work. Such an examination might also show whether any foreign scientists were helping Iraq with its nuclear program.

The commission is also compiling a list of foreign governments and companies that helped Iraq develop its nuclear, chemical and biological weapons programs.

6—6

0338

외 무 부

종 별 :

번 호 : UNW-2998   일 시 : 91 0925 1930

수 신 : 장 관(연일,연이,중동일,미일,기정)

발 신 : 주 유엔 대사

제 목 : 유엔총회(각국 기조연설반응)

　　9.23-24 간 각국 기조연설 (아국연설 포함) 관련 NYT 사설및기사, WP 지 사설을
별첨 송부함.

　　첨부: UNW(F)-561 : NYT 사설및 기사, WP 지사설.끝

　　(대사 노창희-국장대리)

국기국	차관	1차보	미주국	중아국	국기국	외경실	문석관	정와대
안기부								

PAGE 1   91.09.26   09:39 WG
　　　　　　　　　　　　　　외신 1과 통제관
　　　　　　　　　　　　　　　　0339

UNW(F)-561 10925 19T   총40h
(연월 연이 중동일 미일 기서)

A Chance for Justice at the U.N.

A certain loftiness is customary from orators at the United Nations, and in any case President Bush, leader of Desert Storm, earned the right to recite the gains of freedom yesterday while aiming a blunt warning at an impenitent Saddam Hussein.

Yet he gave strong weight to an address thick with generalities by calling for the unconditional repeal of a notorious resolution about Zionism that may constitute the U.N.'s most unjust action. By voting for repeal, every member state can remove an obstacle to reconciling diplomacy.

In November 1975, the General Assembly formally stigmatized Zionism as a "form of racism and racial discrimination." No other declaration has spawned more ill will or done more to confirm Israel's distrust of the U.N. Yesterday Mr. Bush put the point simply: To equate Zionism with the intolerable sin of racism mocks U.N. claims to seek a just peace in the Middle East.

Whatever the Bush Administration's differences with Israel on loan guarantees or on settlements in occupied territories, on this Washington and Jerusalem can stand together. By moving to common ground, the President aims to drain the anger from arguments over legitimate differences.

The Zionist resolution was a malignant outgrowth of cold war rivalries. In 1948 the new state of Israel won immediate recognition in Washington and Moscow. By degrees, Soviet support turned into open hostility as Israel won wars and the Arabs lost territory. By 1971, Pravda was recklessly equating Zionism with racism; it even accused Jews of collaborating with Hitler. This slanderous campaign was taken up by nonaligned states, prodded by oil-producing sheikdoms.

By 1975, there were enough General Assembly votes to enact Resolution 3379. Leading the opposition was Daniel Patrick Moynihan, then chief U.S. envoy to the U.N. He has plainly described its disgraceful implications:

"While that resolution stands the U.N. is essentially on record as favoring the annihilation of a member state. For racism is the one public policy that can deprive a state of legitimacy — even legality — in the modern world. This is singularly the case with Israel, for it was founded to be a *Jewish* nation."

Zionism-is-racism remains code language for bigotry. The code has been eagerly taken up by Saddam Hussein. Though addressing problems of a very different nature, Mr. Bush aptly strikes a common chord in condemning both the Zionism resolution and Baghdad's refusal to allow U.N. inspection of Iraqi nuclear weapons.

Both affront the U.N. Charter's call upon nations to practice tolerance and live together in peace. By reaffirming that purpose, the President places himself on the honorable side of history.

Repeal the Zionism Resolution

PRESIDENT Bush's call for the United Nations General Assembly to repeal its resolution of 1975 equating Zionism with racism was at once interpreted as a friendly gesture to Israel at an otherwise tense moment in American-Israeli relations. It would be good if the Bush appeal did have the effect of reminding Israelis of Washington's continuing commitment and regard. Many Americans too would surely applaud a vigorous American effort to put repeal to a prompt vote and to smoke out states still reluctant to acknowledge their surrender to the prejudices of an earlier, darker day. That the Soviet Union—one of the original principal offenders—is now ready to renounce what its foreign minister yesterday called this "obnoxious" resolution bodes well for the count.

The Arab governments ought to be particularly ready to strike this sickening text, most of all those among them who profess to be champions of the Palestinians in whose name they gleefully whooped the resolution through. Any hesitation on their part can only be regarded as retrograde and out of keeping with current, rising standards of international discourse. To support keeping this resolution on the books will not fail to undermine the common ground on which the United States and most Arab states stood in the gulf war—a war in which Israel was on the same side as those Arab states and in which it played its own role of strategic discretion. Sanctioning repeal is a minimal contribution that others can expect Arabs to make to the Middle East peace process being organized now.

But it is not really Israel and either its longtime friends or its longtime adversaries that have the greatest interest in repeal. The true victim of this insupportable slur on a member nation's core legitimacy was the organization—the General Assembly—that enacted it. Passage of the Zionism resolution topped off a series of actions by which the one-nation, one-vote assembly forfeited its claim on the respect of decent people everywhere and sank into a slough of irrelevancy, which it is still trying to climb out of. It is the assembly that has the greatest reason now to repudiate this stain on its honor and utility. Mr. Bush put it very precisely: "This body cannot claim to seek peace and at the same time challenge Israel's right to exist."

UNW-2998 첨부   4-1

0340

By ANDREW ROSENTHAL
Special to The New York Times

UNITED NATIONS, Sept. 23 — President Bush called on the General Assembly today to repeal the 1975 resolution that equated Zionism with racism, telling the organization that it "cannot claim to seek peace" until the much-criticized document has been repudiated.

"We should take seriously the charter's pledge to practice tolerance and live together in peace with one another as good neighbors," Mr. Bush said in his fourth address to the assembly since he became President. He added that "Resolution 3379, the so-called Zionism-is-racism resolution, mocks this pledge and the principles upon which the United Nations was founded."

Mr. Bush had been expected to call for the resolution's repeal, a move that his Administration has been committed to for nearly two years but has delayed out of concern for other political imperatives, including the President's efforts last year to rally Arab support in the conflict with Iraq.

The President said repealing the measure now would promote the cause of peace in the Middle East, and his advisers are also counting on his appeal today to help heal the strain that has developed in his relations with Israel and the pro-Israel lobby in the United States over the issue of loan guarantees to Israel.

But Mr. Bush did not back up his call with any promise to lead the effort to repeal the resolution or any deadline for its repudiation.

American officials indicated that the United States was far from ready to put the repeal to a vote. The Assistant Secretary of State for International Affairs, John Bolton, said the United States believed that it had a majority in favor of repeal, but not a strong enough one for Washington to risk a vote now.

He added that the Soviet Union had not yet committed itself and that it was unclear how much support the United States had among the Arab countries.

In the 20-minute speech, Mr. Bush also renewed his oratorical assault on President Saddam Hussein of Iraq, calling once again for the Iraqi people to remove him from power and repeating the insistence that economic sanctions against Baghdad not be lifted as long as Mr. Hussein remains in power.

"Saddam continues to rebuild his weapons of mass destruction and subject the Iraqi people to brutal repressions," Mr. Bush said. "Its contempt for United Nations resolutions was first demonstrated back in August of 1990, and it continues even as I am speaking. His Government refuses to permit unconditional helicopter inspections and right now is refusing to allow U.N. inspectors to leave inspected premises with documents relating to an Iraqi nuclear-weapons program."

Mr. Bush's speech was delivered in markedly tepid tones and was interrupted for applause only once, when Mr. Bush praised the departing Secretary General, Javier Pérez de Cuéllar, who is leaving his post in December.

The address was the President's first chance to address the world community since the collapse of Soviet Communism, but he glossed over that monumental event in his remarks, which also touched only in the most general way on the Middle East process, the rebuilding of Eastern Europe's shattered economies and his continuing struggle with Iraq.

Mr. Bush singled out Cuba as a holdout against the tide of democracy that has swept Europe and Latin America in recent years, but he made no mention of China, with whom he has tried to maintain cordial relations, or other Communist regimes. His only reference to North Korea was to welcome the country as a new member of the General Assembly.

Mr. Bush condemned Mr. Hussein's efforts to thwart United Nations inspection and destruction of his nuclear, chemical and biological weapons and said the United States would not compromise on its demand that the United Nations be afforded unfettered access to weapons sites. But Mr. Bush did not say what he would do if Baghdad did not cooperate.

'Revival of History'

The bulk of the speech was devoted to a philosophical treatise on what Mr. Bush called "the resumption of history," a play on "The End of History," a magazine essay by Francis Fukuyama, a former State Department official, who argued in 1989 that the end of superpower competition removed the forces that had been driving modern history.

Mr. Bush countered by arguing that the end of East-West confrontation as it had existed since World War II instead offered a new era.

"Communism held history captive for years," Mr. Bush said. "This revival of history ushers in a new era, teeming with opportunities and perils.

"Now for the first time we have a real chance to fulfill the U.N. Charter's ambition of working to save succeeding generations from the scourge of war, to reaffirm faith in fundamental human rights, in the dignity and worth of the human person, in the equal rights of men and women in nations large and small."

He said that effort was challenged by the General Assembly's continued stand that Zionism is a form of racism, a position embodied in the resolution that was hotly opposed by the United States but has remained virtually without challenge on the floor of the Assembly for 16 years.

Change in Position

In December 1989, Vice President Dan Quayle committed the Bush Administration to work for the repeal of the resolution. But Mr. Bush did not call for its repudiation in his speech to the General Assembly last September, or in an appearance in March after the war with Iraq, out of fear of jeopardizing Arabs' support first for the war effort and then for postwar peacemaking.

Today, Mr. Bush said: "Zionism is not a policy. It is the idea that led to the creation of a home for the Jewish people in the state of Israel. And to equate Zionism with the intolerable sin of racism is to twist history and to forget the terrible plight of Jews in World War II and, indeed, throughout history. To equate Zionism with racism is to reject Israel itself, a member in good standing of the United Nations. This body cannot claim to seek peace and at the same time challenge Israel's right to exist."

Mr. Bush said the United Nations could spur peace in the Middle East by repealing the resolution.

Because of the Jewish holiday of Succoth, Israel's delegation had given advance notice that it would not attend the assembly session. Thus it was not present to hear Mr. Bush's plea to repeal the resolution.

In initial Arab reaction, the head of the Libyan delegation, Ali A. Treiki, faulted Mr. Bush for not calling as well for the right of the Palestinian people to a homeland.

Administration officials said Mr. Bush's main purpose in making the appeal was to smooth his efforts to schedule a Middle East peace conference next month. Israel has strongly objected to United Nations participation in the conference, in part because of the resolution on Zionism.

'Can Be Trusted as an Honest Broker'

But officials said Mr. Bush also was trying to smooth over the rift in American-Israeli relations produced by his demand that Israel's application for $10 billion in loan guarantees be delayed 120 days, until January, to avoid upsetting the efforts to convene an Arab-Israeli peace conference next month. "This shows our evenhandedness toward Israel and signals them that we can be trusted as an honest broker in the peace process to come," an official said.

It was part of a broader effort in recent days to make amends with American Jewish groups, nearly two weeks after the President had lashed out at supporters of Israel and their lobbyists on Capitol Hill for working in behalf of the loan guarantees. Last week, Mr. Bush wrote a conciliatory letter to Jewish leaders saying that his remarks were not intended to be pejorative.

4—2

Turning to Iraq and Mr. Hussein, Mr. Bush said: "It is the United States' view that we must keep the United Nations sanctions in place as long as he remains in power. And this also shows that we cannot compromise for a moment in seeing that Iraq destroys all its weapons of mass destruction and the means to deliver them."

'Dishonors the Iraqi People'

Mr. Bush said, as he has before, that he did not want to "punish the Iraqi people."

"Let me repeat," he said, "our argument has never been with the people of Iraq. It was and is with a brutal dictator whose arrogance dishonors the Iraqi people."

He said the United Nations effort against Iraq "has liberated Kuwait, and now it can lead to a just government in Iraq, and when it does, when it does, the Iraqi people can look forward to better lives, free at home, free to engage in a world beyond their borders."

As he expounded on his view of the coming century, Mr. Bush said: "The United States has no intention of striving for a pax Americana. However, we will remain engaged. We will not retreat and pull back into isolationism. We will offer friendship and leadership. And in short, we seek a pax universalis, built upon shared responsibilities and aspirations."

By JERRY GRAY
Special to The New York Times

UNITED NATIONS, Sept. 23 — In a speech before the General Assembly highlighted by his implicit criticism of the United States, the President of Brazil, Fernando Collor de Mello, said today that there was "an inescapable obligation" for nations to accept mandatory measures to protect the environment.

"Just as the question of development has yielded to other issues on the international agenda, I am concerned that the issue of the environment may also yield to other aspects of the day-to-day life of the world," said Mr. Collor, whose country is to be the site of the first Earth Summit in June.

The first day of general debate of the 46th General Assembly featured few surprises from the 14 speakers who went before the 166 member nations.

Foreign Minister Ali Akbar Velayati of Iran delivered a speech almost to-

Collor applies pressure on global warming.

tally devoted to discussion of the "New World Order." He ended his 30-minute speech with brief mentions of what he called the three major crises of the last several decades, the "Iraqi aggression" against Kuwait, Afghanistan and the issue of a Palestinian homeland.

Harking Back to the Environment

Iran has privately been at the center of efforts brokered by the United Nations to release Western hostages in Lebanon, but Mr. Velayati made no reference to that issue.

The speeches today were filled with prescriptions for peace and references to the "New World Order." But the environment was a recurring theme, from Mr. Collor's lightly veiled chastisement of the United States to an impassioned plea by President Bailey Olter of Micronesia to industrialized nations that use tiny South Pacific islands as dumping grounds.

"Our region cannot be considered by the larger nations as a convenient empty space for the disposal of toxic and hazardous waste and chemicals and radioactive materials," Mr. Olter said.

Leading off the speakers, Mr. Col-

lor's comments increased pressure on the United States to end its opposition to a series of proposals dealing with global warming and other environmental issues.

The third of five international meetings called to formulate a host of agreements to be voted on in Brazil at the Conference on Environment and Development ended last Friday in Nairobi, Kenya. The United States was still resisting efforts to set mandatory cuts in emissions of carbon dioxide. Scientists say carbon monoxide is the main manmade gas contributing to global warming.

Tracing the Responsibility

The European Community and Japan favor reducing carbon-dioxide emissions to the levels of last year by the year 2000. But the United States, the biggest producer of carbon dioxide, argues that too little is known about the warming threat to justify the costs of trying to adhere to mandatory limits.

In comments seemingly directed toward the United States, Mr. Collor said, "Lasting solutions to global problems require the commitment of the international community as a whole, each country according to its responsibility relating to the origin of these problems and to their management, as well as to its economic and technological capacity to overcome them."

The United States' objections could impede chances for a treaty at the meeting in Brazil. There are also other obstacles like demands by the United States and other developed nations for language to reduce the depletion of forests and waterways in many underdeveloped nations.

"The conference should not set the stage for grievances and recrimination," Mr. Collor said. "It should, on the contrary, provide the framework for mature and feasible proposals."

Mr. Collor, who said the Brazil meeting would allow a debate as broad and profound "as the political will of the participants will allow," was supported by New Zealand, whose Prime Minister, J. B. Bolger, said, "Next year's United Nations conference in Brazil will be the real test of our ability to cooperate in the endeavor to find the proper balance between development and environmental protection."

Other speakers included the Foreign Ministers of Angola, Australia, Burkina Faso, Iceland, Mexico, Norway and Sri Lanka.

4-3

0342

Soviets, at U.N., Back Bush's Call For Repeal of '75 Zionism Edi[ct]

South Korea Tells U.N. Of Hope for Unification

By JERRY GRAY
Special to The New York Times

UNITED NATIONS, Sept. 24 — President Roh Tae Woo of South Korea proposed a three-stage plan today for the reunification of his country with North Korea, conditioning such a move on North Korea's immediately abandoning its development of nuclear weapons and allowing international inspections.

A decades-long effort by North Korea and South Korea to join the United Nations ended in success last week when they became the 160th and 161st members. Today Mr. Roh became the first head of state from either country to address the General Assembly as a full member.

"Imperfect as it may be, the separate membership of the two Koreas in the United Nations is an important interim step on the road to national unification," Mr. Roh said. "It took the two Germanys 17 years to combine their U.N. seats. I sincerely hope that it

The plan singles out nuclear weapons as a central concern.

will not take as long for the two Korean seats to become one."

On a day when Mr. Roh lobbied for Korean reunification, the Soviet Foreign Minister, Boris D. Pankin, delivered a speech full of praise for the newly independent republics.

"Our country will never be the same," Mr. Pankin said. "Where an ossified empire once stood, a new union of free and truly sovereign nations bound together by common aspirations is being born. Democracy, human rights, openness toward each other and to the entire civilized world will be its main frame."

The Baltic countries of Lithuania, Latvia and Estonia joined the Marshall Islands, Micronesia, North Korea and South Korea as new members at the 46th General Assembly.

Mr. Roh, who previously addressed the General Assembly when South Korea held observer status, said that from his Government's view, reunification with North Korea hinged on three points, starting by replacing with a peace treaty the "fragile armistice"

that was signed to end the Korean War.

"We have been living under this unstable condition of neither peace nor war for the last four decades," the South Korean leader said.

Mr. Roh also proposed that for humanitarian reasons, the two nations should end "the period of disassociation," and begin to exchange goods and information and to allow their citizens to associate.

The final point of Mr. Roh's proposal centers on his Government's demand that North Korea "should immediately abandon the development of nuclear weapons, and submit, unconditionally, all of its nuclear-related materials and facilities to international inspection."

There was no official North Korean response. A representative of North Korea is scheduled to address the General Assembly Oct. 2.

Mr. Roh, in an interview this week, said his Government had evidence that North Korea was planning to develop nuclear weapons.

North Korea and South Korea are both signers of the Nuclear Non-Proliferation Treaty, but North Korea has refused to sign the safeguard agreement that would allow for on-site inspections.

Much of the speech by Japan's Foreign Minister, Taro Nakayama, dealt with relations with the Soviet Union and a dispute over a chain of islands going back to the end of World War II.

Mr. Nakayama said that Tokyo intended to begin direct negotiations with the Russian federated republic and its President, Boris N. Yeltsin, for the return of the Kurile Islands.

The Soviet Union took the islands, which form stepping stones from the north of Japan to the tip of the peninsula of the Russian republic, at the end of World War II and Tokyo's efforts to reclaim the Kuriles historically have centered on negotiations with the central Government of the Soviet Union.

"The weight of the negotiations now will be with Yeltsin, not Gorbachev," a Japanese diplomat said in an interview.

In a speech in Tokyo in January 1990, Mr. Yeltsin indicated that the territorial dispute was open for negotiation, but he gave little hope for a quick settlement.

Mr. Yeltsin outlined a plan that would take decades to complete and told his Japanese hosts that the final resolution of the problem would be left to the next generation.

UNITED NATIONS, Sept. 24 — The Soviet Foreign Minister, Boris D. Pankin, joined President Bush today in calling for the General Assembly to repeal its 1975 resolution equating Zionism with racism.

But Arab diplomats here and Arab-American organizations reacted coolly, saying that Mr. Bush's plea, in his address here on Monday, was a purely political gesture aimed at soothing his Administration's dispute with Israel.

"The whole thing is linked to the peace conference and other matters," an Arab diplomat said. "It cannot be treated separately."

Still, the Soviet and American appeals underscore a new confidence that the West, joined by the former members of the old Soviet bloc, could now repeal one of the General Assembly's most disputed resolutions.

'Legacy of the Ice Age'

In a wide-ranging speech promising a new Soviet committment to international cooperation, Mr. Pankin said the United Nations "should once and for all leave behind the legacy of the ice age, like the obnoxious resolution equating Zionism to racism."

The United States has opposed the resolution, adopted in 1975 at the urging of Arab and other third world nations, from the moment it was adopted. In recent years, as anti-Western sentiments here have moderated, it has sought its repeal.

Washington did not press the issue last year, however, because it feared upsetting the fragile alliance it was building against Iraq in the Persian Gulf.

Arab and other diplomats said it was unlikely that the United States would do so now, as it tries to muster support for a Middle East peace conference.

Arab and Muslim Comments

While the Israeli Foreign Minister, David Levy, said the President's call was "only natural," the Arab delegations here had no public response.

Iranian radio quoted President Hashemi Rafsanjani as saying that Mr. Bush was "trying to wipe off stains resulting from Israel's racism."

Clovis F. Maksoud, the former president of the Arab League who is now a professor at American University in Washington, said the President's decision to press for repeal was "a political sop to the Israelis" and "an insensitive rubbing it in to the Arabs" at a delicate moment in the peace process.

Albert Mokhiber, the president of the American-Arab Anti-Discrimination Committee, said there would be support for a repeal of the resolution if racism no longer existed in Israel. But he said, "The underlying reason for the original resolution not only exists, but exists in far greater dimensions."

4-4

Iraq Said to Yield on Nuclear Inspection

Baghdad Continues to Detain 44 Members of U.N. Team; Pentagon Orders Patriot Missiles Moved to Saudi Arabia

By John Lancaster and John M. Goshko
Washington Post Staff Writers

Facing threats of renewed U.S. military action, Iraq yesterday yielded to United Nations demands for unhindered access to its nuclear weapons facilities by helicopter inspection teams. But the international confrontation over the inspections continued as Iraqi troops detained a U.N. inspection team overnight in a Baghdad parking lot.

An Iraqi letter, delivered yesterday afternoon to the U.N. Security Council as it began closed-door consultations on the issue, gave "unconditional acceptance" of U.N. resolutions authorizing the helicopter-borne inspections, council President Jean-Bernard Merimee of France said.

At the same time, however, 44 U.N. inspectors remained surrounded by armed Iraqi troops outside the Baghdad office building where earlier they photographed documents relating to Iraq's nuclear program. The Iraqis, who charged that the American team leader was a CIA spy, told the inspectors they would not be allowed to leave until they had submitted to personal searches and turned over the materials they gathered.

Last night the Security Council demanded the release of the inspectors and the confiscated evidence. But as of dawn today Baghdad time, the team was still surrounded by Iraqi troops.

Before news of the Iraqi letter on the helicopters came yesterday, the Pentagon ordered the deployment to Saudi Arabia of 96 Patriot missiles and 1,200 U.S. Army troops from Germany to operate them, according to a Defense Department official.

It remained unclear last night how Washington would respond to the latest developments. Earlier yesterday, the Bush administration showed signs of hesitancy on whether and when to confront Iraq militarily.

Throughout the summer, the Bush administration, along with the United Nations, has charged Iraq with repeated interference in the U.N. inspections. Under Security Council resolutions related to the Persian Gulf War cease-fire last spring, U.N. inspectors are to locate and and destroy all of Iraq's weapons of mass destruction, including its nuclear, chemical and biological arsenals.

The helicopter issue arose early this month, when inspectors charged that they were unable, in the face of Iraqi efforts to relocate and conceal the weapons and related materials, to complete their mission with ground vehicles, and the United Nations authorized the use of helicopters to increase their mobility and ability to conduct surprise visits.

Iraqi then tried to impose conditions on how the helicopters could be used, leading to U.S. threats, backed by Britain and France, to provide military air protection for them. Faced with Iraq's continued intransigence, President Bush said he was "fed up" with Iraqi President Saddam Hussein, and it appeared that the United States was on the verge of military action.

On Sunday, French Ambassador Merimee, who holds the rotating Security Council presidency, began seeking to work out with Baghdad the language of a written response to the council's demand for unconditional freedom to make helicopter overflights of Iraqi territory. Late Monday, he said that Iraq had informed him a response was en route to New York.

But early yesterday, Iraq Ambassador to

See GULF, A21, Col. 1

3941-1

Sept. 25, 1991
WP

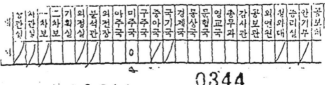

0344

GULF, From A1

the U.N. Abdul Amir Anbari said that he had no reply from Baghdad to offer, adding that one might be received within 48 hours.

Merimee said he told Anbari that was "unsatisfactory." While stipulating he was not issuing an "ultimatum," Marimee warned that it would be in "Iraq's best interest" if a reply was in hand by the time the Security Council began consultations last night about how to deal with Iraq's intransigence.

At the same time yesterday morning, however, Bush appeared to have pulled back from his implied threats, telling reporters traveling with him on a two-day visit to the United Nations that he was not inclined to set a deadline for Iraqi

"We feel quite strongly that the materials must not be turned over to the Iraqis."

— American inspector David Kay

compliance on the helicopters. He said he still wanted "to get a little more information, do a little more consultation" before taking further steps.

"You don't make decisions of this magnitude that could have an effect on human life without having all the information," Bush said.

Nevertheless, Bush said that Saddam should "not miscalculate" by continuing to interfere with the inspections.

A senior administration official traveling with Bush, who was due to return to Washington last night, said that Washington has continued consultations with Britain and France, and had spoken by telephone yesterday with French President Francois Mitterrand. Although both London and Paris had indicated they would support military protection of the helicopters, if necessary, they had been reluctant to imply any intention that full-scale military action against Iraq might be resumed.

As events continued to move quickly yesterday, the administration official said the emergence of the new issue of the detention of the 44 inspectors in Baghdad, and Saddam's "defiance and stalling" on the helicopters, "has thrown wrinkles into our planning that the president wants to consider in a more formal setting" where he can hear his senior aides offer their views on where the United States should go from here."

"We already had a lack of agreement before [yesterday's problems with the inspectors in Baghdad] happened," the official said in reference to infighting between the White House and the Defense Department over how strongly to respond to the helicopter impasse, "and now we have a plan that is behind the curve," the official said. "The president wants a timeout to think about this."

Yesterday's diplomatic maneuvering occurred on a day of high drama in Baghdad. That crisis began Monday, when the 44-member U.N. inspection team was detained for nearly 14 hours after it found secret documents that inspectors said proved Iraq had been developing nuclear weapons. The Iraqis forcibly confiscated the documents, but some were returned to the team yesterday.

But a new incident broke out early yesterday morning, when the inspectors went to another building where records of the Iraqi atomic energy commission are stored. Iraqi authorities appeared and demanded that the inspection be cut short and that the team turn over all confiscated materials. By nightfall, the surrounded inspectors had parked their vehicles in a protective circle and bedded down under the gaze of Iraqi troops.

The American leader of the team, David Kay, who is equipped with a portable telephone, said in a remarkable series of live interviews with Cable News Network and CBS News that the inspectors had photographed and videotaped documents detailing the extent of Iraq's weapons programs and efforts to buy nuclear materials abroad.

Kay, who said "we feel quite strongly that the materials must not be turned over to the Iraqis," described the team as "in quite high spirits." He said the inspectors were subsisting on watermelon, U.S. Army rations and water brought in by a U.N. colleague stationed elsewhere in the city.

At a news conference in Baghdad, Deputy Prime Minister Tariq Aziz accused Kay of working for the Central Intelligence Agency and behaving "like Rambo." A State Department spokesman dismissed the charge as "ridiculous."

Along with his government's letter on the helicopter issue, Anbari also delivered to the Security Council yesterday a letter of complaint from Baghdad about Kay's behavior, the Associated Press reported.

Last night, the council responded with a terse, four-point statement giving its "full support" to the team and demanding that it "be allowed to leave immediately" without conditions and with whatever documents it deemed necessary to take.

The statement insisted that "the [inspection] commission is the sole judge of the documents it needs to collect to carry out its work" under the council cease-fire resolutions. Anbari was instructed to inform his government of the council's "serious concerns" over the matter.

Lancaster reported from Washington and Goshko from the United Nations. Staff writer Ann Devroy, traveling with Bush, contributed to this report.

3941-2 (END)

Sept. 25, 1991
WP

0345

외　무　부

종　별 :

번　호 : UNW-3006　　　　　　　　　　일　시 : 91 0926 1500

수　신 : 장　관(연일,중동일,국기,기정)

발　신 : 주 유엔 대사

제　목 : 걸프사태(안보리동향)

　　1. 이락 A.HUSSEIN 외무장관은 걸프전중 미군이 이락군인들을 생매장 하였다는 최근 보도와 관련 동 진상조사를 위한 위원회 설치를 유엔사무총장에게 9.16 자 서한으로 요청하여 왔음.

　　2. 유엔이락 특정무기 폐기특위 (UNSCOM)헬기사용문지 관련 안보리 움직임. 특히 미.영.불의 특위활동 군지원 검토동향에 관해서는 별첨 금 9.18 자 NYT 지 참조바람.

　　첨부: UNW(F)-565 끝

　　(대사 노창희-국제기구국장대리)

UNW(FI)-565 1092-6 150N
(연월. 중동원. 국가. 기정)   총 1매

U.N. Considering a Troop Escort in Iraq

By PAUL LEWIS
Special to The New York Times

UNITED NATIONS, Sept. 17 — The United States, Britain and France are discussing sending military teams into Iraq to escort the United Nations inspectors looking for President Saddam Hussein's weapons of mass destruction if Baghdad's authorities continue trying to obstruct the search, diplomats here said today.

But the troops may not be needed because Iraq appeared tonight to be backing down in its quarrel with the Security Council, after its United Nations representative, Abdul Amir al-Anbari said he hoped that a complete agreement could be reached soon.

Mr. Anbari added that he believed the Security Council was acting "in an open-minded way and so are we," insisting that his Government was flexible and wanted a settlement.

He spoke after the representative of France, this month's Security Council President, rejected Iraq's latest attempt to limit the use of helicopters inside its territory by the United Nations inspectors.

Diplomats said the French delegate, Jean-Bernard Mérimée, told the Iraqi diplomat that the Security Council would not agree to a requirement that the inspectors refrain from taking aerial photographs, restrict their flights to western Iraq and limit searches to a maximum of two weeks as Baghdad officials had demanded.

Iraqi Observers Permitted

Earlier, the Iraqis had threatened to ban the inspectors from using any aircraft of their own inside the country. But on Monday, they softened their position and tried to place conditions on the helicopters' use instead.

Mr. Mérimée said the Council was ready to discuss the inspectors' plans for flights, and he indicated that Iraq could send officials in the United Nations helicopters to serve as guides and liaison officers. He also asked Iraq for a prompt written assurance that the copters, which Germany is lending to the inspectors, would be permitted to fly freely inside Iraq. The Council demanded this in Resolution 707, which says that they have the right to use their own aircraft for making searches.

Western diplomats also said they believed that Mr. Hussein's officials were backing away from a head-on confrontation with the Security Council over compliance with its terms on Iraqi conduct in the aftermath of the gulf war.

These include the destruction of all Iraqi nuclear, chemical and biological weapons, as well as ballistic missiles, by the United Nations inspectors. The inspectors are to be given complete freedom to perform this task.

But the three Western permanent members of the Security Council have discussed possible plans for providing air-force escorts for these teams and their helicopters if Iraq refused to let them operate freely.

This is considered preferable to military action because it could be presented as enforcing existing Security Council resolutions.

Supply of Heavy Water

A team of nuclear inspectors from the Vienna-based International Atomic Energy Agency is also in Iraq, trying to trace hundreds of pounds of a chemical substance called heavy water, which Iraq imported in the early 1980's, United Nations officials say.

Heavy water, or deuterium oxide, enables a reactor to produce the nuclear explosive plutonium from supplies of unenriched uranium.

The Iraqi imports of heavy water only came to the attention of the atomic energy agency after the supplier notified the special commission set up by the Security Council to oversee the destruction of Iraq's most dangerous weapons.

United Nations officials refused to name the supplier. But the only countries known to have heavy-water plants are Canada, China, India and Pakistan.

The commission today reported that a team of experts that left Iraq on Sept. 9 had begun transporting thousands of chemical weapons from their storage bases to a destruction site.

It also reported discovering about 6,000 containers filled with chemical agents for use in rockets. And it warned that some of the chemical weapons stocks it inspected were in a highly dangerous state, with bombs bursting open and lethal agents being released into the atmosphere.

UNW-3006
정부

1-1

외 무 부

관리 번호	91 ~1148

종 별 :

번 호 : UNW-3023

일 시 : 91 0926 2000

수 신 : 장 관(연일,중동일,아동,기정)

발 신 : 주 유엔 대사

제 목 : 안보리동향

　　1. 안보리는 금 9.26 이락의 유엔 핵사찰반 억류사태와 관련 비공식협의를 갖은바, 당관 원참사관이 관련 대표부로 부터 탐문한 금일 협의 주요결과는 다음과같음.

　　가. 이락측이 제의한 R.EKEUS 특위 의장의 이락 방문은 추진치 않기로 함.

　　나. 본건 사찰반의 억류해제 재촉구

　　다. 문제의 핵관련문서 등재에 대해서는 이의없음.

　　라. 이상사항을 안보리 의장이 이락측에 통보

　　2. 한편 명 9.27 캄보디아 문제관련 안보리회의 유엔옵서버단 파견에 따른 예산문제, 미측의 유보(의회와의 협의필요) 로 다음주로 연기될 가능성이 큰 것으로 알려짐.

　　첨부: 이락의 안보리의장앞 서한 및 NYT 기사:UNW(F)-568 끝

　　(대사 노창희-국장)

예고: 91.12.31. 까지 예고문에 의거 일반문서로 재분됨

국기국 안기부	장관	차관	1차보	2차보	아주국	중아국	분석관	청와대

PAGE 1

91.09.27　　09:26

외신 2과　통제관 BS

0348

25. 9. 91 첨부

UNSC(TI)-56 10926 2000
(단일. 중동원. 아동. 기침) 충 3매

On instructions from my Government, I have the honour to inform you as follows:

1.   With a view to solving the problem satisfactorily and avoiding any difficulties, Iraq wishes Mr. Rolf Ekeus to go to Baghdad so that we may discuss with him ways of remedying the current situation and so that the modalities for the use of the German helicopters may be considered.

2.   Should Mr. Ekeus not go to Baghdad within 48 hours, the Iraqi authorities insist that the Iraqi side and the inspection team jointly draw up a record of all the documents and photographs taken by the team before the team is authorized to remove anything whatsoever from the site.

3.   The Iraqi authorities do not and will not acknowledge any document or photograph that has not been entered in the record jointly drawn up by the two parties. Any allegation based on documents or photographs that have not been entered in the joint record will be indicative of a premeditated intention to prejudice Iraq's interests.

4.   Iraq once again strongly protests at the inspection team's actions, particularly those of the leader of the team, Mr. David Kay. Moreover, we reiterate what we have already indicated to Mr. Rolf Ekeus, namely, that the main source of the difficulties being encountered is the fact that inspection missions are entrusted to such a large number of United States nationals. These United States nationals simply implement the policies of their Government, which persists in violating both the letter and the spirit of the resolutions of the Security Council and imposes its hostile policies on the Iraqi leadersship.

    Please accept, Sir, etc.

SIGNED BY

PR

3-1

0349

The Bush-Hussein Duel

U.S. Aides Admit Iraq Is No Armed Threat But Say That Control Must Be Established

By ANDREW ROSENTHAL
Special to The New York Times

WASHINGTON, Sept. 25 — The showdown in a Baghdad parking lot between United Nations inspectors and Iraqi officials was less a struggle over a batch of documents than over who is calling the shots in Iraq in the Persian Gulf's unstable peace — George Bush or Saddam Hussein.

News Analysis

With Baghdad's new overture tonight to the United Nations, President Bush may have won the central gamble behind his strategy in the gulf. Administration officials have said they were betting that Mr. Hussein would back down and that Mr. Bush would never have to carry out his strongly implied threat of using military force.

Again Using U.N. Aegis

Clearly, Mr. Bush is driving the Western approach to the Iraqi President in the latest struggle although he is careful to do so in the name of the United Nations, as he has been throughout the last year.

The United States provided the intelligence that is leading the inspectors to increasingly sensitive Iraqi military installations in ways that Pentagon planners are fully aware will irk the Iraqis. Washington is supplying the technology for the inspectors to communicate with the outside world and thus turn their dispute into a public spectacle.

Like the recent tension over Iraq's refusal to permit the unfettered use of helicopters by the United Nations inspectors, the dispute over whether they may take documents out of Iraqi Government buildings narrowly sprang from efforts to carry out the Security Council resolutions that established a cease-fire in Iraq last spring.

It's More Complicated

But the motivations for the latest standoff between Mr. Bush and Mr. Hussein go well beyond the legalities of enforcing the resolutions or even removing Mr. Hussein's ability to develop nuclear weapons. American officials, including Gen. Colin L. Powell, Chairman of the Joint Chiefs of Staff, acknowledged today that is not any real threat — in the short term or even medium term.

Rather, the new tensions, and Mr. Bush's warnings of the possible use of force, demonstrate vividly that what exists in Iraq is not a permanent peace, but a continuation of the tenuous truce established after the allied ground offensive drove Iraqi forces from Kuwait.

That was only one of three major war objectives, set by the anti-Iraq coalition. Mr. Bush and his allies are still fighting — with little evident headway — to secure the two others: demolishing Iraq's ability to field a modern army that could threaten another neighbor and, perhaps more important to the President, eliminating Mr. Hussein as a political and military force in the Middle East.

The President would very much like to see Mr. Hussein ousted. He has said so at every opportunity, reaffirming in recent days that he will oppose the lifting of economic sanctions as long as Mr. Hussein is in power.

The President and his advisers continue to insist that they are not undertaking any open or covert effort to overthrow Mr. Hussein, although they would certainly deny any secret operation if one were under way. Washington has often turned to the Central Intelligence Agency and covert operations against a foreign government in circumstances similar to the current situation in the gulf, where other means, including open warfare, did not fully achieve American objectives.

"We're still not foolish enough to fall for the trap of changing the U.N. agenda to target any one individual," an Administration official said today.

Warning From the White House

What then does Mr. Bush hope to accomplish by keeping open the threat of possible new military action against Iraq? Clearly that is what the President was doing today by proceeding with deployment of Patriot missiles to Saudi Arabia, huddling in the Oval Office with General Powell and other advisers, and then putting out the word that his patience was wearing thin and that "all options are open."

Administration officials freely acknowledged that Mr. Hussein and his political power are a central target of current American policies in Iraq, which they hope will prevent him from dragging a political victory out of his military defeat and making, as one official put it, "a mockery" of the President's painstakingly wrought coalition.

"If you're going to build any kind of credibility for a new world order," another official said, "you've got to make people accountable to legal procedures, and Saddam's flouted every one."

Was the United States deliberately trying to increase tensions with Mr. Hussein as a way of provoking a military confrontation and giving itself an

3-

0350

excuse to resume the war, this time with more ambitious objectives?

Administration officials say no, and it is evident that the Pentagon is reluctant to take on another fight. General Powell has firmly established himself as a war planner who demands clear-cut military and political objectives and then does not move until he has more than enough reserve power to handle any contingency.

Some influential lawmakers, including Representative Les Aspin, Democrat of Wisconsin and chairman of the House Armed Services Committee, believe that Mr. Bush has backed down from the brink of military confrontation several times in recent weeks. "It looks like he's bending over backward to avoid it," Mr. Aspin said.

Various U.S. Objectives

Asked why Mr. Bush has been engaged in another test of wills with Mr. Hussein, Administration officials begin with the argument that they are simply trying to carry out the United Nations mandate to plumb the depths of Iraqi efforts to build a nuclear weapon, develop germ-warfare devices and stockpile poison gas for use in war — and then obliterate these programs.

Beyond that, officials said Mr. Bush is driven by complex political pressures, including his desire to hold together the anti-Iraq coalition, to maintain the United States' role as the enforcer of the peace in the Mideast as he seeks to drag the region's fractious people into a peace conference, and to maintain a strong American military presence as the agreement to keep a rapid-deployment force in southern Turkey nears its Sept. 30 expiration.

"The long-term threat is that the coalition could fragment and the sanctions against Iraq would simply fall by the wayside," an official said.

'Worst-Case Scenarios'

Another said: "Saddam's power is growing every day and the President cannot tolerate that. If he keeps solidifying this political power, and the coalition breaks up, then you're back to square one before the war. True, he won't be a real military threat to anyone for years. But you have to think in the long term and base your policy on

Building U.S. 'credibility for a new world order.'

worst-case scenarios, even if you don't believe they're going to happen."

Mr. Aspin argued that there are legitimate roles the United States military can play under these circumstances, saying: "First of all, sending the military in to escort inspectors could avoid the kind of standoff in the parking lot that you've got right now because you would have guys carrying guns to make sure they could leave with the documents. Of course, you'd have to have the backup there in case it turns into a firefight."

Mr. Bush, Mr. Aspin continued, "may have some further military role in mind "to leverage further cooperation by Saddam."

"Is there a military-target list or something else the military might do in order to put political pressure on the Iraqi Government?" he asked. "I wouldn't be surprised if they were looking at a list of targets. But the military would still want to know specifically what they were being assigned to do and what the measure of success would be, instead of just being drawn into some vague mission."

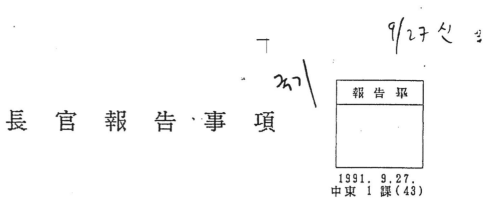
長官報告事項

報告果

1991. 9. 27.
中東 1 課 (43)

題 目 : UN의 對이라크 大量破壞 武器 査察 關聯 動向

> 　　　最近 美國은 이라크가 UN 安保理決議案 제687호, 특히 大量破壞 武器
> 廢棄 條項을 계속 違反해 온데 대하여 一部 同盟國과 함께 軍事攻擊 威脅등
> 强硬 態度를 취하고 있는바, 關聯 動向을 아래 報告 합니다.

1. 主要經過
    ○ UN은 이라크側 提出 核武器등 大量破壞 武器 明細書를 기초로 14회에
       걸쳐 調査團 派遣, 査察 實施
    ○ 그러나 이라크의 不誠實한 態度 및 義務 違反등 UN 事務總長의 指摘에
       따라 UN 安保理는 8.15. 이라크의 違反 糾彈 決議案 採擇(707호)
    ○ 9월초 이라크의 査察班 헬기사용 拒否 및 最近의 2차에 걸친 査察團員
       抑留問題등 發生

2. 美國 및 UN의 對應措置 및 이라크의 屈伏
    ○ 美國은 사우디에 美 軍事力을 增派中(패트리어트 미사일 100기 및
       操作要員등 兵力 1,300여명)
    ○ 9.11. UN 特別委 委員長은 記者會見에서 이라크의 非協助 姿勢 非難
    ○ 9.23. Bush 大統領은 UN 總會 演說을 통해 Saddam Hussein 政權이 査察班
       헬기 搬入을 拒否하고 査察班의 核計劃 關聯文書 保管所 接近을 禁止하고
       있다고 非難
    ○ 9.24. 安保理 議長은 이라크가 同日 17:00까지 UN 査察班 헬기의
       無制限 이라크 領空 飛行許容 書翰을 安保理에 提出토록 聲明發表
    ○ 9.24. 이라크는 安保理議長의 聲明發表直後 安保理에 UN의 査察活動을
       保障하는 書面確認書 提出

3. 言論對策 : 해당없음.

4. 關聯措置 : 우리의 對이락 關係는 追後報告　　　끝.

0352

<첨 부 1>

유엔의 대이라크 강제 핵사찰 실시

1. 대이라크 핵사찰 실시배경

o 91.4.N. 유엔안보리는 결의 제687호를 채택하여 이라크의 군비통제를 위한
  특별위원회(Special Commission)를 설치하고, 이라크내 핵무기 및 생화학
  무기 관련 정보 제공을 요청

  - 동 결의는 또한 대이라크 경제제재 조치 해제 이전에 이라크 보유 대량
    파괴무기 (핵무기, 생.화학무기)를 완전히 폐기토록 규정

o 이에 따라 IAEA 사찰관과 안보리 특별위원으로 구성된 핵사찰반이 이라크가
  제출한 핵물질 및 시설관련 정보를 바탕으로 91.5월부터 9월까지 6차례
  핵사찰을 실시

o 동 핵사찰은 이라크제제 안보리 결의에 의거한 사찰명령을 이라크가 수락
  함으로써 실시한것으로, IAEA 안전조치 규정상 특별사찰과 달리 무제한
  사찰권한을 행사하는 강제사찰임

2. 핵사찰 실시 내용

가. 제1차 핵사찰 (91.5.14-22)

o 91.4.27. 이라크가 제출한 핵관계 정보내용을 확인하기 위해 Al Tuwaitha
  핵연구 시설과 Tarmiya 지역내 핵시설을 사찰

o 사찰결과 고농축 우라늄(HEU)등의 핵물질 존재와 많은 핵시설 장비등이
  타지역으로 이전되었음이 확인되어, 사찰단은 이라크측에 이전된 핵시설
  장비의 완전한 리스트를 요청

- 1 -

0353

나. 제2차 핵사찰 (91.6.22-7.4)

　　o 제2차 사찰은 Tuwaitha 핵 연구시설외에 6개지역 핵시설에 대해 실시,
　　　이중 Al Ghraib와 Falluja 에서는 이라크 당국에 의해 사찰반의 접근이
　　　금지, 제한됨
　　　- 이에 따라 유엔 안보리는 의장성명을 통해 이라크의 사찰불응을
　　　　규탄한후, IAEA 사무국장, 특위위원장등의 고위급 대표단을 추가파견
　　　　함으로써 사찰을 재개

　　o 사찰결과 이라크가 전자 동위원소 분리기술(EMIS)을 사용한 우라늄
　　　농축 시설을 보유하고 있음을 확인
　　　- 이라크는 IAEA에 밝히지 않은 우라늄 농축 계획 일부가 있었음을
　　　　시인하고 91.7.7. 핵시설 장비 추가 리스트를 안보리에 제출

다. 제3차 핵사찰 (91.7.7-18)

　　o 91.7.7. 이라크 제출 추가 정보내용을 확인하기 위해 제3차 핵사찰을
　　　실시하였고, 7.12. 유엔 안보리는 이라크가 모든 핵개발 계획과 핵
　　　시설 물질을 공개할 것을 요구하면서 이에응하지 않으며 중대한 결과에
　　　직면할 것이라고 경고
　　　- 미국, 영국등은 이라크가 핵무기 개발내용을 완전 공개하지 않을경우
　　　　군사력 사용 재개 경고

　　o 91.7.18. IAEA는 특별이사회를 소집, 이라크가 IAEA와 체결한 핵 안전
　　　협정상의 의무 불이행을 규탄하고, 이라크 영토내 모든핵 물질을 IAEA
　　　감시하에 둘것을 촉구하는 결의 채택

- 2 -

0354

라. <u>제4차 핵사찰</u> (91.7.27-8.11)

　o 제4차 핵사찰반은 사찰결과 핵농축 및 재처리 시설 내용을 포함한 이라크
　　의 비밀핵개발 계획을 확인하고, 원심분리법을 이용한 고농축 우라늄(HEU)
　　생산 시설을 발견

　o 동 사찰결과, <u>91.8.15. 유엔안보리</u>는 이라크의 안보리 결의(687호) 불
　　이행을 규탄하고, 이라크가 동안보리 결의와 IAEA 안전조치 협정을 완전히
　　준수할때까지 모든 핵 활동을 중지할 것을 요구하는 <u>결의(707호)채택</u>

마. <u>제5,6차 핵사찰</u> (91.8,9월)

　o 상기 이라크의 의무 불이행규탄 안보리 결의(707호) 채택후, 유엔 사찰
　　반은 9월중 2회에 걸쳐 이라크내 핵 시설을 정밀 사찰하였으나, 이라크
　　측은 사찰반의 헬기사용거부 및 사찰단원을 억류하는등 사찰반의 활동을
　　계속 방해

　o 이에대해, 미국은 이라크에 군사력 사용재개를 경고하였고 이라크는
　　안보리 의장의 요청에 따라 유엔 사찰반 헬기의 무제한 이라크 영공
　　허용 서한을 9.24. 제출하고, 억류했던 사찰단원을 석방함

　o 상기사찰결과 이라크가 핵무기개발 계획하에 그간 핵농축은 물론 핵무기
　　운반체제, 핵탄두등을 개발하고 있었음이 밝혀짐
　　- 이라크가 다시 핵무기제조를 추진할 경우 <u>90년대중반까지 2-3개의</u>
　　　<u>핵무기를 생산할것</u> 으로 평가

- 3 -

0355

핵확산 방지조약(NPT)에 의한 핵 안전조치협정체결 과정

① 협정안 합의, 가서명
↓
② IAEA 이사회의 승인
↓
③ 협정서명
↓
④ 당사국의 비준
↓
⑤ 협정의 발효   ---   (NPT 가입후 18개월 이내)

⑥ 당사국은 사찰대상이 될 모든 핵물질에 대한 보고서를

   IAEA에 제출(최초 보고)   (협정발효후 30일이내)
↓
⑦ IAEA에 의한 보고내용 확인(수시사찰)
↓
⑧ 당사국이 기존 핵관련 시설에 대한 설계정보를 IAEA에 제출
↓
⑨ IAEA에 의한 설계정보 확인
↓
⑩ 보조 약정서 작성 . 발효   (협정발효후 90일이내)

↓

(일 반 사 찰 실 시)

0356

"이라크核 美·英등지원"

80년부터 기술제공… 사찰단 증거입수

英타임스紙보도

【런던＝元仁成특파원】유엔의 사찰을 거부하고있는 이라크의 핵무기제조시설인지 난80년부터 미국·영국·독일 등 선진국들이 기술과 설비를 제공해 건설된것이며 이라크에 억류돼있는 유엔핵무기사찰단은 지난25일 이같은 사실을 일쑤해주는 계약서를 입수했다고 영국의 더 타임스지가 27일 보도했다.

이 신문은 이라크에 핵무기제조관련기술과 설비를 제공한 나라는 미국·영국·프랑스·스위스·중국·브라질을 10여개국이나 되며 그중에서도 독일·스위스·영국의 기업들이 핵무기제조에 필요한 주요기술과 설비를 제공했다고 전했다.

기제조관련기술과 설비를 제공한 그들이 제공한 기용품수있는 것들이라고 밝혔으나 그들이 제공한 기용과 설비는 군사용으료사−했다.

美, 이라크에 武力위협 계속

安保理선 이라크提案 수용

【워싱턴AP＝聯合】조지·부시 美대통령은 26일 이라크내 대량살상무기 조사활용을 촉구한 유엔결의와 관련, 사어떤 조처라도 취할 태세를 갖추고 있다고 밝혔다.

美대통령은 이날 訪美중인 하산2세 모로코 국왕을 위한 만찬회에서 기자들로을 이라크측과 공동 작성을 위한 것을 허용한다면 유아직은 지켜볼 것이라고말 하는 것을 허용한다면 유엔사찰팀을 석방 하겠다는 이라크측 제의를 수락했

【워싱턴AP＝聯合】국제 원자력기구(IAE A)의 한관계자는 이들선 대량 살상무기 개발·후세인 이라크 대통령이 핵무기 개발계획을 알고도 이를 진정으로 이행하랴라

부시대통령은 이날 訪美

앞서 유엔측이 물수한 이라크 핵사찰팀들의 목크 핵계획관련 서류들의 목을 위한 만찬회에서 기자들록을 이라크측과 공동 작성하는 것을 허용한다면 유아직은 지켜볼 것이라고말 했다.

외 무 부

종   별 :

번   호 : UNW-3038

일   시 : 91 0927 1930

수   신 : 장 관(연일,중동일,미일,아동,기정)

발   신 : 주 유엔 대사

제   목 : 안보리동향

연:UNW-3023

1. 안보리의장 (불)은 9.26 유엔핵사찰 억류사태에 관한 연호 비공식 협의결과를 이락측에 통보하였으며, 금 9.27 현재 안보리의 특기할 관련 움직임은 없음.

2. 금일 오후 보도에 의하면, 상기 억류해제 , 핵관련문서목록 작업, 헬기사용방식에 관해 양측간에 합의가 이루어졌다고함.

3. 한편 캄보디아문제관련 안보리회의는 연호대로 다음주로 연기되었으며, 파리회의는 10 월말경 개최예정인 것으로 알려짐.

첨부:NYT 기사:UNW(F)-570 끝

(대사 노창희-국장)

예고:91.12.31. 까지

91. 12. 31. 인안

국기국 청와대	장관 안기부	차관	1차보	2차보	아주국	미주국	중아국	분석관

UNW(FH)-570   1-927 193-
(연법.중동일.미법.아동.기정)   총 2이

Getting the Goods on Iraq

One aim overrides all others in the confrontation between the U.N. and Saddam Hussein — halting Iraq's secret nuclear weapons program, which now appears far more extensive than previously suspected. The inspectors detained in Baghdad this week appear to have found much of the evidence needed to understand Iraq's effort and identify its outside suppliers.

From that information, analysts can figure out what's needed next to produce nuclear bombs. The significance of this data goes far to explain Mr. Hussein's crude interference. Through a deft combination of threats and restraint, the Bush Administration and its allies now appear poised to bring that evidence to the outside world.

The detention of 44 U.N. inspectors in a stifling Baghdad parking lot is only the latest, and probably not the last, Iraqi provocation. Iraq has lied about its weapons programs and stocks, threatened inspection teams and imposed crippling restrictions on helicopter reconnaissance flights.

President Bush's threats of force, coordinated with U.N. allies, have repeatedly compelled Baghdad to back down. But an actual resort to force, though it cannot be excluded, would have serious costs, well worth avoiding.

Saddam Hussein, at least, is gambling that renewed conflict would give him another shot at derailing the monumental Middle East peace conference scheduled to start next month. Of more direct relevance, air attacks on suspected weapons sites could, perversely, scatter evidence the U.N. inspectors want.

Israel's 1981 air raid on the Osirak reactor, like allied raids during the gulf war, set back but could not eliminate Iraq's nuclear program. Only inspections on the ground can fully detect and destroy enriched uranium supplies, illicit technologies and contraband imports of critical components.

Saddam Hussein deceived the world for years by hiding most of his nuclear program from International Atomic Energy Agency inspectors. In the wake of this deception, the entire international system of nuclear safeguards and inspections requires rethinking and toughening.

Despite Iraq's evasions, inspections remain the most reliable way to prevent nuclear proliferation. When faced with intentional cheating like Iraq's, inspectors need to be able to go where they choose without challenge or delay, and have full access to all evidence they find. Iraq's defeat paved the way for such inspections; subsequent Security Council resolutions authorized them.

It's now within the world's grasp to eliminate Iraq's arsenal of mass destruction weapons. Completing the job will require more resolute diplomacy. Pulling the trigger may be satisfying, but the task is to get the goods on Iraq.

#UNW-3038
첨부

2-1

0359

U.N. Accepts Iraq Proposal To Free Detained Inspectors

By PAUL LEWIS
Special to The New York Times

UNITED NATIONS, Sept. 26 — The United Nations Security Council today accepted Iraq's offer to release 44 United Nations nuclear inspectors if they sign a list of the secret documents regarding President Saddam Hussein's nuclear-weapons program that the inspectors plan to remove for analysis.

But the Council warned Iraq that this concession would not weaken its determination to see all of President Hussein's secret nuclear, chemical and biological weapons of mass destruction hunted down and destroyed.

It said the letter it is sending Iraq does not set a precedent for future inspections. It made clear Iraq has no right to veto removal of any of the documents by refusing to enter them on the inventory. And it rejected Iraqi charges that Americans are overrepresented on the teams it is sending to destroy President Hussein's most dangerous weapons under the terms of the Council's Persian Gulf war cease-fire resolution.

The key passage says the Council "has no objection to the immediate establishment in this particular case of a joint inventory, in the presence of Iraqi officials, enabling the inspection team to fulfill the responsibility entrusted to it by the Council."

Release Timetable Unknown

But the Council again condemned Iraq for detaining the inspectors since Tuesday and stated its "strong support" for the team and its work.

It remained unclear tonight when the inspectors, who were spending a third night of detention in buses and cars cordoned off by armed guards in a Baghdad parking lot, would be released.

The United Nations also said today that it would start using unarmed German helicopters Sunday in its search for Iraq's banned weapons of war, as Baghdad apparently agreed to earlier this week.

Iraq's agreement to these flights ended another dispute with Baghdad, which had banned such overflights. The United States, Britain and France had threatened to send armed helicopters and warplanes to escort the helicopters unless Iraq allowed them to fly wherever they wanted. In fact, plans were made to substitute American for German helicopters if Iraq did not consent to overflights because Germany said the law did not permit use of its forces in possible overseas combat zones.

New Letter From Baghdad

Tonight a new Iraqi letter arrived saying Rolf Ekeus, the Swedish ambassador and the chairman of the special commission charged with finding and destroying Iraq's most dangerous weapons, must go to Baghdad to work out arrangements for the aerial inspections before the helicopters are allowed to fly.

The Council decided to ignore this letter, assuming it to be a case of "crossed mail." But Britain's representative, Sir David Hannay, warned that if Iraq was trying again to block the inspectors, "the consequences will be very serious."

The special commission's first aerial mission, Mr. Ekeus said today, will hunt for secret Scud missile sites in the desert and arrange for the destruction of Iraq's "super-gun," a giant cannon capable of firing chemical or other shells hundreds of miles at targets as far away as Israel.

Iraq has already built one such gun with a 100-foot-long barrel and planned a second much larger weapon with a 300-foot barrel nearly three feet wide.

Despite the confusion caused by the new Iraqi letter, many diplomats said they still believed the crisis over the detained inspectors was near a solution, noting that it has followed the pattern of past stand-offs with Baghdad's first trying to obstruct the United Nations, then backing down under pressure.

A senior British official called it "part of series of obstructions by Iraq to stop the United Nations entering its sacred places."

The Soviet representative, Yuli M. Vorontsov, said he thought "we are now very close to the end of this unhappy incident."

The Council's latest quarrel with Baghdad began Monday when the Iraqi authorities expelled inspectors from a building where they were copying documents that showed Iraq was trying to design key parts for a nuclear bomb, including a detonating trigger.

The next day the same team was seized and detained while copying the personnel records of scientists working on Iraq's nuclear program and documents relating to foreign purchases of nuclear equipment.

2—2

The United Nations says it wants this information to help work out an overall picture of how Iraq's nuclear program is designed and what assistance it got from abroad.

While no one is sure how long it will take to prepare an inventory of the documents, western diplomats said they would not allow Iraq to draw out the process through bureaucratic quibbles in order to delay their release.

Iraq first appeared to be backing down in the crisis over the inspectors since Wednesday night when it sent the Council a letter inviting Mr. Ekeus to Baghdad for talks about the helicopters but saying that if he refused, Iraq and the inspection team must "jointly draw up a record of all documents and photographs taken by the team before the team is authorized to remove anything whatsoever from the site."

This was taken as implying that Iraq is now ready to let the inspectors depart with their copied documents, provided it gets a list of what they are taking.

In the letter Iraq also said it would regard any accusations against it based on undeclared documents as invalid.

It complained about the activities of the detained inspection team and its American leader, David Kay, and said that the attitude of the teams is influenced by anti-Iraqi prejudice rather than relevant Security Council resolutions.

Throughout this latest stand-off, diplomats say, the Council and its special commission have been anxious to avoid setting precedents that could allow Iraq to resist or obstruct their plans to destroy its present stocks of weapons and insure it does not acquire such weapons in the future.

COUNCIL'S RESPONSE

In reply to your letter dated 25 September 1991, I have the honor to inform you on behalf of the Security Council of the following:

1. The Council deplores Iraq's repeated violations of its obligations under resolutions 687 and 707 and reiterates its demand that the inspectors of the Special Commission, and the International Atomic Energy Agency be released immediately with all the material they hold. The Council has no objection to the immediate establishment in this particular case of a joint inventory, in the presence of Iraqi officials, enabling the inspection team to fulfill the responsibility entrusted to it by the Security Council.

2. Mr. Ekeus has already contacted your mission on the modalities and scheduling of the next inspection mission, which will use helicopters of the Special Commission.

3. The Council reaffirms its strong support for the items of the Special Commission and the International Atomic Energy Agency, whose members are highly conscious of their responsibilities as international civil servants and are performing difficult tasks with the full authority of the Security Council in accordance with the Charter of the United Nations.

0360

정 리 보 존 문 서 목 록

기록물종류	일반공문서철	등록번호	2012090043	등록일자	2012-09-03
분류번호	731.33	국가코드	IQ	보존기간	30년
명 칭	유엔안전보장이사회 이라크 대량살상무기 폐기 특별위원회, 1991. 전3권				
생 산 과	국제연합1과/중동1과	생산년도	1991~1991	담당그룹	
권 차 명	V.3 10-12월				
내용목차	★ UNSCOM: 유엔 이라크 대량살상무기 폐기 특별 위원회 ★ 10.11 이라크 대량살상무기 검증을 위한 유엔 사무총장 및 IAEA 사무총장 계획안 승인 결의안 채택(안보리 결의 715호) ★ 유엔 핵 조사단의 핵 사찰 실시 포함				

0001

외 무 부

종 별 :

번 호 : UNW-3120   일   시 : 91 1001 2200

수 신 : 장 관(연일,중동일,국기,기정)

발 신 : 주 유엔 대사

제 목 : 걸프사태

유엔 이락 핵사찰 동향에 관한 9.30 및 10.1. 자NYT 기사를 별첨송부함.

첨부:UNW(F)-594 끝

(대사 노창희-국장대리)

국기국	1차보	중아국	국기국	외정실	분석관	청와대	안기부

91.10.02   10:52 WG

외신 1과 룡제관

0002

UNWF-594 11:00 2200
초 2억

U.N. Officials See Mastermind in Charge of Iraq's Nuclear Effort

By PAUL LEWIS
Special to The New York Times

UNITED NATIONS, Sept. 30 — The United Nations officials charged with destroying Iraq's nuclear weapons sites are searching for an unidentified "mastermind" who they think had overall charge of President Saddam Hussein's secret nuclear weapons program, estimated to have cost $10 billion.

The conviction that there must have be an unknown top official, who could have been a foreigner, in command stems from their belief that none of the Iraqi scientists they have met so far appears to have a full grasp of the complex program that involved both production of enriched uranium explosive and attempts to design a weapon.

In particular, Jaafar Dhiah Jaafar, formally the No. 2 official on the Iraqi Atomic Energy Commission, appears to know only about the attempt to produce enriched uranium, officials say, while his superior, the head of the commission, is regarded as a figurehead.

A Special Commission set up by the United Nations Security Council to destroy Iraq's weapons of mass destruction has already established that the authorities in Baghdad were seeking to produce enriched uranium by three separate methods.

Its latest inspection team has also established that Iraq had some kind of a weapons development program under way by unearthing evidence that it was trying to design a nuclear detonation device.

But as yet no Iraqi official has been found with overall responsibility for both the enrichment and the weapons programs. "Personally I am rather convinced that there must be someone who links the enrichment and the design sides," said Rolf Ekeus of Sweden, the Special Commission's executive chairman.

[In New Orleans today President Bush, in terms starkly similar to those he used last year before the invasion of Iraq, warned that he would not tolerate Saddam Hussein defying the United Nations.

["Any aggression, any defiance of the United Nations resolutions now will not stand," Mr. Bush said at a fund-raiser for Gov. Buddy Roemer. "I am just as determined to see he does not succeed."]

The United Nations commission's inspectors, to test their theory, on an overall director, raided the Iraqi Atomic Energy Commission's records center last Tuesday and took away personnel files of many of the senior people working there. That raid led to their detention for four days by the Iraqi authorities.

The commission now wants its inspectors to track down these top Iraqi nuclear officials on the team's next visit to Baghdad.

Last week, the commission barred the team's American members from sending details of seized documents directly to the State Department instead of reporting only to the United Nations.

Mr. Ekeus said he sent a general order to the team to suspend all contacts with Washington on Wednesday after he discovered American members had been in direct contact with Washington by satellite phone. However, he denied reports that he had reprimanded them.

Most Were Americans

The team's leader, David Kay, is an American. He was accompanied on the mission by Robert L. Gallucci, the Special Commission's American deputy executive chairman. Altogether, 25 of the 44 team members were Americans, and they included Government scientists with practical experience in nuclear weapons design.

In particular, officials say that by sending reports directly to the United States Government, the Americans helped bolster the Iraqis' charge that Mr. Kay is a Central Intelligence Agency spy acting under cover of the Vienna-based International Atomic Energy Agency.

"We very firmly instructed them not to make such contacts but only to report to the Special Commission and the I.A.E.A.," Mr. Ekeus said today.

Commission officials say that the Americans argued that they were only trying to get the substance of confiscated material out of the country quickly for fear that the Iraqis would take it back by force.

At a news conference after the team's arrival in Bahrain today, Mr. Kay said that the inspectors had removed a total of 25,000 pages of documents dealing with Iraq's covert nuclear plans as well as 19 hours of videotape and 70 rolls of film used to photograph documents.

"I think we collected a lot of valuable information" on Iraq's secret nuclear program," he said, adding:

"You can't help but be impressed by the sophistication of it. You walk around those sites and you shake your head because they are far better than most I've seen."

He emphasized that the team had uncovered clear evidence, in the form of designs for building a nuclear detonating device, refuting Iraq's claim that it had no interest in developing a nuclear weapon.

"The emphasis was on uranium enrichment, virtually every known method," Mr. Kay said. "This for a country without a single power plant requiring enriched uranium. That is a major anomaly."

The team has also brought out records of nuclear material that Iraq purchased for its program from foreign countries and companies. While Mr. Kay refused to give details he said, "It would be very hard for me to understand, with some of the issues of supply, that they did not know they were going to be used in a nuclear program."

UNWF-3120
초 6

2-1

0003

Documents Said to Name Iraq Suppliers

By MICHAEL WINES
Special to The New York Times

WASHINGTON, Sept. 29 — Documents seized in Baghdad last week are yielding new details about Iraq's nuclear weapons program, including the names of Western companies that illegally supplied Baghdad with equipment and technology, international agency officials in Baghdad and Vienna said today.

The officials refused to release the names of the suppliers, and it was unclear when or if they might be made public. Nuclear arms experts said that assembling a list of smugglers of nuclear equipment and expertise would be a major achievement in the drive to dismantle Iraq's bomb-making capacity, and one United States official called it "a top priority."

But the papers have yet to resolve several important questions about the program's major focus — the manufacture of bomb-grade, or enriched uranium — that are causing concern among American nuclear experts, a Bush Administration official said in an interview today.

Is More Hidden?

Those experts question whether Iraq is still hiding an underground nuclear reactor that could be used to manufacture enriched uranium or plutonium, and whether another well-hidden installation has been built to refine enriched uranium from a uranium gas, the official said.

The official said the odds that Iraq has built either are believed to be fairly low. But United States analysts cannot dismiss the prospect, he said, in light of the recent discovery that Iraq had begun to make enriched uranium with huge electromagnetic separators, called calutrons, without being detected by foreign intelligence.

They also hope to learn whether Iraq has illegally bought low-grade uranium "feedstock" from foreign suppliers, an action that would have enabled scientists to speed the process of making weapons-grade uranium.

China is the most likely supplier of uranium feedstock, the official said, but the Chinese have denied any involvement in Iraq's nuclear program.

That official and other Bush Administration experts spoke on condition that they not be identified.

Few details of the papers seized in Baghdad have reached American officials, but Administration experts said today that they believe the broad outlines of the Iraqi program are now in hand. The documents are more likely to provide details of how the Iraqis bought technology and equipment for their bomb-making effort, how the effort was organized and controlled and what types of weapons Iraq scientists were contemplating.

5,000 Pages

The head of the International Atomic Energy Agency's inspection team in Baghdad, David Kay, told news agencies today that the 5,000 pages of Iraqi documents include "a considerable body of data" on Iraq's nuclear program, including its organization and its overseas procurement practices.

The inspection team, which was trapped in a Baghdad parking lot during a five-day dispute over the material, was to leave Iraq Monday. The documents are to be evaluated in Bahrain on Tuesday and Wednesday, an agency spokesman in Vienna told The Associated Press.

In Washington, a senior Bush Administration official said today that the documents identify not only companies, but also foreign governments that actively assisted the Iraqi nuclear program. The official, who spoke on condition that his name not be used, said he believes that the Administration will seek to make those names public.

A Washington expert on weapons proliferation, Gary Milhollin of the Wisconsin Project for Nuclear Arms Control, said that such a disclosure could deal a telling blow to weapons programs worldwide.

"That network is at the disposal of Iran, Libya, Pakistan and India still," he said, adding that "the best way to close it off is to make it public."

Officials of the United Nations special commission that is overseeing the dismantling of Iraq's nuclear program were said today to have many of the names of supplier companies. The United Nations will tell governments in the nations where those companies are based of the firms' activities.

2—2

0004

외 무 부

종   별 :

번   호 : UNW-3148

일   시 : 91 1002 2030

수   신 : 장관(연일,중동일,미중,기정)

발   신 : 주 유엔 대사

제   목 : 안보리(비공식협의)

안보리는 금 10.2. 오후 비공식협의를 개최한바, 당관 원참사관이 관련 대표부들 로부터 탐문한 동 협의결과를 아래보고함.

1. 이락 제재조치 정기심사

가. 안보리 휴전결의(687 호 본문 21 항) 상 안보리는 60 일마다 대 이락제재 조치 완화내지 해제여부를 심사하도록 되어있는바, 지난 6,8 월에 이어 금번 제 3 차 심사를 가짐.

나. 금일 협의시 특히 미,영,불,소련은 제재조치변경에 반대의견을 나타냈으며, 예멘이 인도적 문제를 제기한데 대해 동국들은 인도적 긴급 수요해결을 위해 안보리가 이락 원유수출을 일부 허용하는 조치를 이미 취하였음을 지적함.

다. 이에따라 안보리의장(인도)이 제재조치 유지 결론을 대외에 밝히기로 함. (동 발표문안 별첨참조)

2. 하이티 사태

안보리의장은 금일 온두라스 (중남미 제국 대표자격), 하이티 대사의 방문을 받았음을 이사국들에게 설명한바, 동 대사들에 의하면 현재 워싱톤 방문중인 J.B ARISTIDE 하이티 대통령이 안보리 이사국들에게 사태해결 지원을 호소하기 위해 당지를 금명간 방문할 가능성이 있다고함.

3. 금일 협의시 유엔 캄보디아 선발단(UNAMIC) 설치문제 토의를 위한 안보리 회의개최 계획(10.4. 경), 다음주 이락 특정무기 폐기문제와 관련한 UNSCOM, IAEA 보고서, 유엔 이락, 쿠웨이트 옵서버단(UNIKOM) 보고서 접수예정도 언급되었다고 함.

첨부:1. 안보리 의장명의 성명문안, 2. NYT,WP 지 사설:UNW(F)-598 끝

(대사 노창희-국장)

예고:91.12.31. 까지

91. 12. 31. 일반

국기국 청와대	장관 안기부	차관	1차보	2차보	미주국	중아국	외정실	분석관

PAGE 1

UNW(㈐)-598 11002 ──3o
총 244

#별첨

D R A F T

STATEMENT BY THE PRESIDENT OF THE SECURITY COUNCIL

The members of the Security Council held informal consultations on 2 October 1991 pursuant to paragraph 21 of resolution 687 (1991).

After hearing all the opinions expressed in the course of the consultations, the President of the Council concluded that there was no agreement that the necessary conditions existed for a modification of the régime established in paragraph 20 of resolution 687 (1991), as referred to in paragraph 21 of that resolution.

정부   2-1

0006

Haiti, by No Means Lost

The day of the dictator is truly over in the Americas, even if some Haitian military officers have yet to get the message. Their bloody ouster of President Jean-Bertrand Aristide, Haiti's first democratically elected leader, is an affront not only to the millions of Haitians who chose him, but to all Americans, North, South and Central.

The odds against a new military regime consolidating power in today's Haiti are long, and the strong response of the Bush Administration makes them longer still. Ambassador Alvin Adams helped negotiate President Aristide's safe evacuation to Venezuela. Then Washington, in coordination with France and Canada, moved quickly to ostracize the junta and deny it aid.

Just as it did when Soviet hard-liners seized Mikhail Gorbachev two months ago, the Administration acts as if the coup can and will be reversed. It insists that it will accept nothing less than restoration of the legitimate government and constitutional rule. Today foreign ministers from around the hemisphere are meeting in Washington, and they have extended a special invitation to President Aristide to join them.

To most Haitians, President Aristide is a hero whose charisma, courage and energy finally vanquished dictatorial rule. Just days ago he returned from a triumphant visit to New York, home of the largest Haitian community outside Haiti. In his seven months in office, he moved energetically against thugs from the old Duvalier regime. He bravely embraced fiscal austerity and cultivated excellent relations with the U.S.

But Mr. Aristide understood all too well that Haiti's old order had not yet accepted defeat. He repeatedly shuffled army commanders in an effort to insure loyalty. And, inexcusably, he encouraged mobs of fervent supporters to intimidate even law-abiding political opponents.

Now the army, perhaps in league with civilian Duvalierists, has struck back hard, inflicting hundreds of civilian casualties. Lamentably, President Aristide's own choice as army commander, Gen. Raoul Cedras, is deeply involved in the bloodbath. Even if the rebels can now be rolled back, the gulf between the army and other Haitians is sure to be dangerously widened.

That's a problem for the future. But the immediate priority is to restore constitutional rule and the legitimate government of President Aristide.

Haiti in Danger

HAITI'S government has once again been overthrown by violence, but this time it's different. This time the expelled president, Jean-Bertrand Aristide, had been elected under a democratic constitution. That makes it essential to reverse this coup and restore President Aristide to office. The Organization of American States, representing the 34 countries of this hemisphere, will meet today to consider how to do it.

It won't be simple. The coup seems not to have been the conventional sort organized by a handful of ambitious colonels. Reports from Haiti say that it was an uprising by enlisted men in which no officers were visible until it was over. Nor is it clear what political purpose it was supposed to serve. There are no signs that it was another attempt by the Duvalier family's supporters to restore their former despotism. To the contrary, one incitement may have been the rumors that President Aristide was forming a foreign-trained personal bodyguard that sounded to apprehensive Haitians like a recreation of the Duvaliers' strong-arm squad, the Ton-tons Macoutes.

It has to be said that President Aristide has been feeding an atmosphere of hysteria and violence that will make the restoration of democracy more difficult than it should be. He has suggested in public speeches that the lynch mob is the people's way of enforcing its will on public officials, and he has spoken of necklacing—the unspeakable practice of forcing a flaming tire drenched in gasoline over a person's head—as an acceptable threat to make officials respond to the mob. His idea of politics comes from Robespierre, not Jefferson. But if Haiti is ever to be a democracy, he will have to be restored. Since the country is now in a convulsion of panic and anarchy, that will take more than an airline ticket for him and a promise of foreign aid.

A peacekeeping force is going to be required. That is the first item that the OAS needs to consider. Many OAS countries have military forces capable of the job. Venezuela is a good friend of Haiti. Canada has French-speaking troops. Because the United States occupied Haiti for 19 years earlier in this century, it can't send soldiers. But it can support those who do.

Haiti needs a period of stability in which its desperate and frightened people can learn something about the government that they have adopted, as it begins to gain experience and public standing. Without an effective force in the country to preserve order, Haiti's democracy will be lost—and with it, the Haitian people's last hope for a decent life.

2 — 2

관리
번호 91 -1201

외 무 부

종   별 :

번   호 : UNW-3227   일   시 : 91 1007 1900

수   신 : 장 관(연일,중동일,국기,기정)

발   신 : 주 유엔 대사

제   목 : 안보리(비공식협의)

1. 안보리는 금 10.7 비공식협의를 개최한바, 당관 원참사관이 관련 대표부들로부터 탐문한 동협의 주요결과를 아래보고함.

가. 유엔 이락 쿠웨이트 옵서버단(UNIKOM)

1)안보리결의 689 호에 의하면 안보리는 UNIKOM 존속여부 및 방식문제를 매6 개월마다 심의하기로 되어있는바, 금일협의에서 유엔사무총장 권고대로 6 개월 더 유지키로 이사국들간에 합의가 이루어졌으며, 안보리 의장이 이를 사무총장에게 서면 통보키로 함.

2)한편 사무총장은 상기 안보리앞 권고에서 베두인존관습, 불법 양거래 (ILLEGAL SHEEP MARKET) 및 무기, 탄약수거목적의 월경사태가 양국간 국경마찰의 주원인이 되고있다고 지적하였으며, 비무장지대(DMZ) 내 이락경찰 초소 철거문제, 악천후시 관측용 전자장비 필요를 제기하였음.(S/23106)

나. 이락 대량 살상무기 폐기 검증계획(안)

1)안보리결의 687,707 호에 의거한 유엔사무총장 표제계획안 (S/22871/REV.1) 및 H.BLIX IAEA 사무총장 계획안(S/22872/REV.1) 이 안보리에 제출된바, 동 계획안을 승인하는 안보리 결의안이 추진될 예정임.

2)안보리는 10.8 경 유엔이락 핵사찰 제 6 진(핵관련 문서적발) 결과 보고를 IAEA 사무총장으로부터 청취할 가능성이 있다고 함.

다. 캄보디아 문제

유엔 캄보디아 선발단(UNAMIC) 설치를 승인하는 결의안 금주중 채택예정(UNW-3139 참조)

2. 금일 협의시 차기사무총장 선출문제도 토의되었으나, 현재 절차문제 협의단계 이며, 안보리의장이 이사국들과 개별협의를 계속해나갈 것이라고함.

국기국 안기부	장관	차관	1차보	중아국	국기국	외정실	분석관	청와대

(국가추천이 아닌 후보, 자국아닌 재 3 국의 추천 후보 처리문제)

3. 당초 91.9 월중 제출예정이었으나 그간 제출이 지연되어온 사이프러스 문제관련 사무총장보고서는 금주중 제출될 것으로 알려지고있음.

첨부:NYT 사설및 WSJ 지 기사:UNW(F)-609 끝

(대사 노창희-국장)

예고:91.12.31. 까지 고 에 외거 일반문서로 재분류

별첨

UNW(州)-609 11007 1900
(연일. 중동일. 국기 기정)   총204

The Right Choice for the U.N.

The revived prestige of the United Nations has spurred a lively race for its top job. Not since the U.N.'s founding have so many first-rate contenders vied for the post of Secretary General. The choice has to be made by Dec. 31, when Javier Pérez de Cuéllar's second five-year term expires.

There is one compelling choice in a generally excellent field: Egypt's Deputy Prime Minister, Dr. Boutros Boutros Ghali, a diplomat with warmth, vision and political savvy.

His biggest hurdle is the Security Council, whose five permanent members — the U.S., France, China, Britain and the Soviet Union — have to make a unanimous recommendation to the General Assembly. They are not, at the moment, united.

Preferring continuity to change, France and the Soviet Union have urged an extension of Mr. Pérez de Cuéllar's term. China maintains that it is Africa's turn to fill the top post. Britain and the U.S. have said little, though President Bush's firm farewell to the present Secretary General had a resounding air of finality.

So who will it be? Everybody's second choice appears to be Prince Sadruddin Aga Khan, a veteran U.N. diplomat. Longer shots include Norway's Prime Minister, Gro Harlem Brundtland, and Perh Gustaf Gyllenhamer of Sweden, the head of Volvo. But two Scandinavians have already filled the post, and a third seems an unlikely prospect. Costa Rica's Oscar Arias Sánchez, a Nobel laureate, is an even longer shot because a Latin American has already served for a decade.

Unable to agree on a single candidate, African nations offer six. They include a former Nigerian President, Gen. Olusegun Obasanjo; Zimbabwe's Finance Minister, Bernard Chidzero; and three lesser-known U.N. officials from Ghana, Sierra Leone and Cameroon. Mr. Ghali rounds out the list.

His claims transcend geography. Mr. Ghali was educated in Paris, and in sly deference to Gallic prejudice notes that even his English is French-accented. As Foreign Minister from 1977 until this year, he was a shaper of the Camp David accords that resulted in peace with Israel, and helped secure Arab support for the war against Iraq. The claim that at 68 he is too old ignores his vitality, which leaves his younger aides winded.

His most compelling qualification is that he speaks sensibly for a third-world constituency fearful of being marginalized by the end of the cold war. For poorer nations, the U.N. remains the only forum in which their collective voice can be heard.

If the Permanent Five ignore the third world's just claims for a greater say in the U.N., it would suggest that Mr. Bush's New World Order has no place for the powerless. The choice of Boutros Boutros Ghali would send a different, and happier, message.

2 —1

0010

Report Links Three German Companies To Iraq's Nuclear Weapons Program

By Frederick Kempe
Staff Reporter of The Wall Street Journal

BERLIN—A secret German Economics Ministry report names three German companies that have been "involved in Iraqi efforts to develop a nuclear capability."

German officials suspect that these companies, and perhaps others, may appear on lists of suppliers to Baghdad's nuclear weapons program now in the possession of U.N. officials, and that this could refocus U.S. attention on German assistance to Saddam Hussein at a time when Bonn has been stressing toughened export control laws and better enforcement efforts.

Officials in Bonn insist that the German companies were merely strands in a sophisticated web of Iraqi contacts around the world.

"Iraq isn't Libya," says a senior government official, referring to the role of Germany's Imhausen-Chemie G.m.b.H. as a contractor for Moammar Gadhafi's chemical weapons program. "It was relatively easy to get to Imhausen and prove his intentions. He built the [Libyan] plant, and he had to know what he was doing. But the Iraqis have been more refined. They have bought bits and pieces everywhere."

Gas Centrifuge Systems

The secret report, portions of which were obtained by The Wall Street Journal, was first prepared in late 1990, but German officials say its findings are still valid. The report names three German companies as well as engineers who formerly worked for a fourth. It focuses on the production of the Iraqi gas centrifuge systems, which are key elements in converting uranium ore to weapons material.

The report says Iraq "has been shown to have components and to a certain extent also system construction characteristics of different German gas centrifuge types."

It details the following:

• Two former employees of MAN Technologie AG, a subsidiary of MAN AG of Munich, are suspected to have played a central role in providing advanced knowhow for the building of a gas centrifuge plant. The report says one of the employees had access to construction plans for different centrifuge types during his time at MAN. After they left the company, both men spent considerable time in 1988 and 1989 in Iraq, where they are suspected of having worked as Iraqi intelligence and recruiting agents. "They attempted, without success, to recruit other centrifuge experts for Iraq," the report says. But the report adds that authorities couldn't prove the two were involved in illegal technology transfers.

• H & H Metalform G.m.b.H., a small company from the village of Drensteinfurt, delivered three advanced machine tools to Iraq during 1987 and 1988 that German government officials now believe were used as prototypes for production of gas centrifuges. Authorities issued export licenses for all three machines after assertions by H & H that they would be used for civilian purposes. When suspicions arose later, the company's records were seized. Its two partners are being investigated, but a company spokesman says that as late as June 1990, the last time the partners visited Iraq, its machinery hadn't even begun to operate and that it isn't suited to centrifuge production.

• Inwako G.m.b.H., the report says, is suspected of having arranged the circuitous delivery—without proper official approval—of ring magnets that are central to the gas centrifuge process. Inwako's owner was taken into custody and released, but an investigation is continuing. Inwako's lawyer, Volkmar Mehle, won't comment on whether ring magnets were sent but says his client had no knowledge that anything he was delivering required special licensing or would be used for weapons production.

• Export Union Duesseldorf G.m.b.H., the report says, was suspected of delivering a special grade of steel that may have been used in the nuclear weapons program. The initial charge was that the company improperly received approval for a steel shipment of a lower quality than was actually delivered. Since the report, prosecutors have focused on allegations that the steel was used to produce conventional delivery systems and not components for nuclear weapons production.

The company's acting director, Norbert Schax, says none of the steel delivered was suitable for weaponry. He says 90% of the initial order is still in stock, and he hopes prosecutors will soon confirm for themselves that Export Union didn't break any laws. No charges have been filed, but the investigation is continuing.

Spanning the Globe

A German official says the report only scratches the surface of a complex Iraqi nuclear program. Iraq's agents spanned the globe and diversified suppliers, partly in response to Israel's 1981 bombing of the Osiraq reactor at Tuwaitha, south of Baghdad. After that attack, Iraq sought a more easily concealed process.

One of the best leads German investigators have found has been the link between H & H and two Iraqi front companies that operated out of London, the Technology Development Group and Meed International. Both appear on contracts that H & H signed, copies of which were obtained by the Journal.

Worries about the links between H & H and Iraq prompted prosecutors in Karlsruhe to investigate one of the company's owners, Dietrich Hinze, on suspicion that he was an Iraqi intelligence agent. The case was dropped in 1989 for lack of evidence. Mr. Hinze says the company's activities abroad often brought him into contact with "business partners, who have other functions along with their business interests, possibly including intelligence work. Perhaps when one is seen together with such people, such suspicions can arise."

Middle East Hot-Rods

Peter Huetten, another owner-manager of H & H, denies links to Iraq's arms network. Pointing to a catalog of his products, he says, "The same machine that makes the sharp tip of this teapot can produce an anti-tank weapon." He says machinery he delivered to Iraq was designed to make customized aluminum wheels for Middle East hot-rods and wasn't precise enough for gas centrifuge production.

German officials raided H & H offices shortly after the Aug. 2, 1990, Iraqi invasion of Kuwait. Customs officials in Frankfurt had seized crates headed for Baghdad from H & H. The packing list read: "Parts for a Dairy Plant."

The contents, however, were high-quality steel components that were more suited to rocketry than milking machines. Also inside were a number of periodicals from the American Institute for Aeronautics and Astronautics—catalogs, a membership roster and product lists.

"Because nobody had ever heard of flying cows before, we decided to investigate," an Economics Ministry official says.

But Mr. Huetten says his workers were trying to save on postage by putting in documents that were intended for a Baghdad library, not the Iraqi War Ministry.

Iraq, With Foreign Help, Was Close to Nuclear Arms

By a Wall Street Journal Staff Reporter

VIENNA — Iraq's nuclear weapons program was supported by "broad-based international procurement efforts," according to United Nations inspectors returning from Baghdad.

Documents studied by the inspectors indicated that Iraq was testing a surface-to-surface missile as part of a sophisticated nuclear weapons program and was 12 to 18 months away from regular production of nuclear weapons materials, said David Kay, leader of the U.N. team that was detained for four days in a parking lot by Iraqis.

"The inspection team obtained conclusive evidence that the government of Iraq had a program for developing an implosive-type nuclear weapon," Mr. Kay said.

Among the 50,000 pages of documents taken by the inspectors are catalogs from foreign companies. Neither Mr. Kay nor officials from the International Atomic Energy Agency would identify any companies or give details of transactions, saying the catalogs and transactions were still being translated and studied. Hans Blix, IAEA director general, said the U.N. Security Council will decide whether company names will be made public.

Another IAEA official said some of the manufacturing facilities for Iraq's nuclear program involved machine tools produced only by Western companies. All identification plates and labels had been filed off by the Iraqis, he said.

A new team of U.N. inspectors headed for Iraq yesterday to make a detailed inventory of the country's main storage site for chemical weapons.

2-2

0011

원 본

외 무 부

종 별 :

번 호 : UNW-3259

일 시 : 91 1008 2030

수 신 : 장 관(연일,중동일,국기,기정)

발 신 : 주 유엔 대사

제 목 : 안보리(비공식협의)

1. 안보리는 금 10.8. 비공식협의를 갖고 H.BLIX IAEA 사무총장으로부터 대이락 핵사찰 특히 제 6 진 사찰 결과를 청취한바, 동보고 내용상세는 당관에서 입수한 별첨자료 참조바람.

2. 금일협의시 이사국들은 상금 은폐중인 핵설비여부, 이락 핵무기 개발진의 관리를 포함한 향후 이락핵개발 봉제대책에 관심을 나타냈으며, BLIX 총장은 이사국들의 질문에 대한 답변과정에서 이락이 걸프전 발발당시 핵무기 제조능력 획득을 12-18 개월정도 남겨놓은 상태였던 것으로 추정된다고 언급하였다고함.

3. 또한 BLIX 총장은 이락의 핵관련 거래기업 문제에 대하여는 동기업해당국에 개별봉보하는 방안을 검토중이라고 말한것으로 알려짐.

첨부:IAEA 총장의 안보리앞 보고내용 및 NYT 지 기사:UNW(F)-620 끝

(대사 노창희-국장)

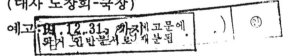

예고:91.12.31. 까지 재고문에 따라 일반문서로 재분류됨.

국기국   장관   차관   1차보   중아국   국기국   분석관   청와대   안기부

PAGE 1

Mr. President,

<u>Security Council resolution 687</u> did not foresee any reporting to
the Council on the results of the IAEA's immediate on-site inspection
of Iraq's nuclear activities. As I have the privilege today, for the
third time, of briefing the Council, it is mainly because the task of
mapping Iraq's nuclear activities has proved to be much larger and much
more arduous than expected.

Up to the present time the six teams sent to Iraq by the IAEA have
devoted over 2000 man-days to inspection tours to Iraq under the
direction of the Action Team in Vienna and our own laboratories have
devoted many man-months analysing samples taken in Iraq. Despite this
considerable effort and the uncovering and mapping of large nuclear
programmes we cannot report that we have yet mapped the total
programme.

One would have hoped that when explicitly accepting resolution
687, Iraq would have been determined fully and sincerely to comply with
the duty to declare "any research, development, support or
manufacturing facilities" related to nuclear weapons or
nuclear-weapons-usable material". Yet, it was only after the IAEA team
in dramatic circumstances obtained pictures revealing the EMIS
enrichment programme, that Iraq began to provide information about the
enrichment programmes. And although it would seem evident that

10-1

designing and experimenting for the production of nuclear weapons constitute "research and development" in the language of resolution 687, Iraq chose not to declare the activities which produced the documentary material discovered by the Agency team on 23 September. It would evidently save much time, effort and pain if Iraq took a new look at resolutions 687 and 707, decided to make a clean break with the past, declare all that there is to declare and co-operate with the IAEA in destroying, removing or rendering harmless what cannot be retained. On Friday last week - 4 October - I sent letter to the Foreign Minister of Iraq urging that such an attitude be at last taken.

Failing such an attitude the patient compilation of facts through mission after mission will continue. The seventh team will be on its way this week.

I should like to report today on the results of the fifth and sixth IAEA nuclear inspections, on some questions they have given rise to, on the plan submitted by the Agency for future ongoing monitoring and verification and on our work to prepare for the destruction, removal or rendering harmless of items which are in contravention of resolutions 687 and 707.

May I preface these remarks by telling the Council that the Board of Governors of the IAEA on 13 September concluded a second time that

/ 6 — 2

Iraq was in non-compliance with its nuclear non-proliferation obligations and the General Conference of the IAEA adopted a resolution to the same effect ~ GC(XXXV)/RES/568. These actions have been reported to the United Nations.

The fifth inspection team, consisting of 11 IAEA staff members and four non-IAEA experts, had an uneventful but productive visit, adding to our knowledge about the Iraqi nuclear programme. It had barely left Iraq when the sixth team went in and, in dramatic circumstances, during its first two days, uncovered documentary material showing, inter alia, that an advanced and sophisticated nuclear weapons programme was underway.

I shall not dwell on the violations by Iraqi authorities of the rights of the inspectors, e.g. in forcibly taking back documents, and in denying the inspectors freedom of movement. The Chief Inspector of the sixth team, Mr. David Kay, is with me and can answer any questions you may wish to put to him. The Council was itself very actively involved in protecting the security and release of the team. I should like to express the appreciation of the IAEA for the effective backing given to the team by the Security Council and the Chairman of the Special Commission.

The report is self-explanatory, but a few comments may be appropriate.

/ 0 — 3

This was the first time that a team went to examine documents in order to map the programme. The results show that the approach was amply justified. Although much documentation had been removed from the first inspection site before the inspectors arrived and although some documents and microfiches forcibly taken from the inspectors on Monday, 23 September were not returned to them, enough material remained to offer dramatic revelations.

The sixth inspection team had 45 members: 44 men and one woman. Owing to its special task of scanning documents in Arabic in search of evidence regarding the nuclear programme, the composition was somewhat special. There were three members from the IAEA: Mr. Kay and two Arab-speaking staff members with nuclear training. One member came from UNSCOM, namely its Deputy Executive Chairman, Mr. Robert Gallucci. The 41 other members were recruited from the outside, many from the United States, others from Australia, Canada, Germany, New Zealand, UK and other countries.

The next point I should like to make is that the report submitted to you through the Secretary-General is a first report. The results which were uncovered by scanning of documents and by the translation and analysis of some documents were such that a delay in reporting to the Council was not deemed acceptable. A vast amount of documentary material in Arabic is now collected and must be more closely scanned and, in part, translated and

/ ^ - 4

analysed. When this is done a full report will be drafted. We must also insist that Iraq provides relevant documents, including those which we have not succeeded in securing. I have been informed that the Chairman of the Special Commission during his visit in Baghdad a few days ago has transmitted such a request, on behalf of UNSCOM. This parallels my letter of 4 October to Iraq's Foreign Minister, which I mentioned a moment ago. I hope Iraq will fully and speedily respond to our respective requests by an additional declaration directed in accordance with Res. 687 to the Secretary-General and the Director General of the IAEA.

The key result of the sixth inspection is the uncovering of documents that show conclusively that Iraq was very well advanced in a programme to develop an implosion-type nuclear weapon and that links existed to a surface-to-surface missile project. Indeed, so advanced has the programme been deemed to be that the time needed to reach bomb-making capacity seems to have been determined by the time required for the enrichment activities rather than the weapons design activities. A significant document secured on 23 September and translated into English is now appended to the report of the sixth inspection. The document is available also in the Arabic original. I have requested that both the report and the appended document should be circulated as a Security Council document.

The sixth inspection has also found evidence of broad-based Iraqi international procurement efforts. It is quite possible - even

/0-5

0017

probable - that some of the procurement that has taken place, e.g. of sensitive equipment or material, has occurred in violation of laws of States from which the export originated. However, much, if not most of the procurement of which evidence will be available, will be found to pertain to equipment and material not subject to export controls anywhere. The material must therefore be handled responsibly. The IAEA and UNSCOM is consulting on guidelines for the handling of this documentary material and other such material that may be secured in Iraq. Some time will be needed simply for translation and analysis. As the inspections take place under a mandate from the Security Council, it goes without saying that any directive which the Council may adopt, would be followed.

Just as the evidence concerning a broad-based Iraqi international procurement programme raises questions regarding the effectiveness of various international efforts to prevent trade in nuclear-weapons relevant equipment, the uncovering of the undeclared facilities for uranium enrichment has led to public criticism of the safeguards system linked to the NPT, as presently organized.

The lessons from Iraq are almost written on the wall. No inspection system can blindly grope for undeclared facilities. In the case of Iraq information secured by Member States has been made available to the inspecting teams, thereby leading them with great success to sites requiring inspection.

16-6

At the request of the Board of Governors of the IAEA I am now preparing a proposal for a mechanism and a procedure in the IAEA through which Member States may make information available to a special secretariat unit in the IAEA regarding the possible existence of undeclared nuclear facilities in NPT States. If such information is deemed credible, the Secretariat may request a special inspection to verify it. Should the State in question decline such an inspection, the Board of Governors could, in the last instance, submit the matter to the Security Council. The inspectorate cannot force its way to an inspection and even the Board of Governors does not dispose of powerful sanctions. If enforcement were to be needed, the right to bring it about is vested in this Council.

In a world of accelerating nuclear disarmament and universal or near universal adherence to non-proliferation agreements, regional or global, it becomes even more important that confidence can be placed in the non-proliferation pledges. Truly effective verification is indispensible. The procedure and mechanism which I have described would draw on the vast nuclear inspection experience and capacity which exists in the IAEA - and which has been successfully used in Iraq. They would build on already existing rights of inspection under safeguards agreements and they could, in the last resort, be backed up by the Security Council.

10-7

C019

With your permission, I would like now to make a few comments on the IAEA's plan for the future ongoing monitoring and verification of nuclear activities in Iraq. A great deal of consultation has taken place between the Agency and UNSCOM to ensure that the two plans are consistent. The far-reaching provisions of Security Council resolutions 687 and 707 have necessitated correspondingly far-reaching rights for the monitoring and verification. Indeed, so long as it is not absolutely certain that immediate on-site verification has successfully uncovered and mapped all nuclear facilities, it will be vital to apply continuous extensive and intensive monitoring and verification.

On one minor point I should like to introduce a correction in the Agency's draft. In paragraph 18 it is stated that the "Agency will continue to provide information concerning the conduct and results of Agency inspections and related activities in order to assist the Special Commission in carrying out this task." It should be corrected to read "its tasks under resolution 687, in particular the task to designate sites for nuclear inspection." It is obviously especially important that results from nuclear inspections under Agency authority be fed back to the Commission to assist it in its task of making further designations.

The last point I should comment on is the duty of the IAEA under

10-A

OCT 08 '91 20:29 KOREAN MISSION

P.8

0020

resolution 687 to prepare for the destruction, removal or rendering harmless of items which Iraq is forbidden to retain under resolutions 687 and 707. In compliance with paragraph 13 of resolution 687 a plan was submitted to the Council on this matter on 16 May 1991 (document S/22615). In implementation of this plan, which we have assumed is acceptable to the Council, arrangements are underway for the removal from Iraq of its declared nuclear-weapons-usable material. I expect that the fresh fuel will be removed from Iraq within the next month and the irradiated fuel - provided that funds are available - toward the end of the year. Arrangements are also underway for the destruction under Agency supervision of equipment and material which is evidently and directly linked to the items prohibited under paragraph 12 of the Security Council resolution 687 (1991). This includes equipment such as that covered in the electromagnetic isotope separation programme, the centrifuge programme, weaponization activities, etc. Plans regarding destruction or rendering harmless of buildings of the facilities related to the programme may be submitted to the Council as a supplement to the Agency May plan.

One nuclear capacity that remains in Iraq are the many well-trained scientists and engineers, and this was part of the reason for the effort during the sixth inspection to identify the scientific and technical cadres involved in the clandestine Iraqi nuclear programme. However, it should be possible to ensure through close future ongoing monitoring of nuclear activities in Iraq that this wealth of talent and skill will be used only for peaceful purposes.

10-9

* * * * *

U.N. AIDES DISCOVER ATOM ARMS CENTER CONCEALED BY IRAQ

ONLY LIGHTLY HIT IN WAR

Survival of Plant Indicates That Allies Overrated Damage to Foe's Nuclear Potential

By PAUL LEWIS
Special to The New York Times

UNITED NATIONS, Oct. 7 — United Nations inspectors have discovered a complex of buildings that apparently served as the nerve center of President Saddam Hussein's covert nuclear weapons program but largely escaped allied attack during the Persian Gulf war.

In a report to the Security Council, United Nations inspectors sent to ferret out Mr. Hussein's nuclear plans said that on their most recent trip to Iraq they had found a top-secret document indicating that the hub of Iraq's weapons-development program was a scientific research installation called Al Atheer, about 40 miles south of Baghdad.

It was here, the report says, that Mr. Hussein planned "to design and produce a nuclear device," although Iraq has said the installation "had no nuclear connection."

Lightly Bombed in War

Previous inspection teams decided that Al Atheer was probably intended for the production of components for a nuclear weapon.

American and other allied intelligence agencies also apparently failed to spot the importance of this plant, officials say. It was only lightly bombed during the gulf war, with about 15 percent of its buildings hit, far fewer than at many other suspected nuclear sites that were almost completely destroyed.

The allies' failure to destroy this central nuclear installation in the air war against Iraq is a further indication that they underestimated the size of Iraq's nuclear program and overestimated the damage they had inflicted on it.

On Jan. 23, for instance, a week after the start of the air war, President Bush said, "Our pinpoint attacks have put Saddam out of the nuclear bomb-building business for a long time."

On different occasions in late January, Gen. H. Norman Schwarzkopf, the allied commander, said attacks had "destroyed all their nuclear-reactor facilities" and "neutralized their nuclear manufacturing capability."

The new report summarizes the preliminary findings of the sixth nuclear inspection visit that the Vienna-based International Atomic Energy Agency has made in Iraq under the terms of the Security Council's cease-fire agreement with Baghdad.

The report is based on a partial examination of more than 25,000 secret Iraqi documents, which the inspectors finally managed to remove from the country last month after twice being expelled from the sites where they were collecting material.

The whole team was then detained for 96 hours, held in a Baghdad parking lot in Iraq's most serious confrontation with the Security Council since the end of the war.

The report says the 44-member inspection team, which included American and British nuclear-weapon designers, "obtained conclusive evidence that the Government of Iraq had a program for developing an implosion-type nuclear weapon," which was code-named "Petrochemical Three."

Documents taken by the inspectors describe "nuclear weapons development experiments" involving, among other things, "neutron initiators, enriched uranium cores, reflectors, high explosive lenses and electronic firing sets."

One document says Iraq successfully produced nuclear weapons components out of natural uranium. But the Atomic Energy Agency inspectors have still not discovered whether Iraq's ambitious uranium-enrichment program had produced enough nuclear explosive "for an actual explosive device" by the time it was brought to a standstill by the allied raids.

The report also reveals that Iraqi scientists were working on a "surface-to-surface missile system — presumably the intended delivery system for their nuclear weapon."

Besides destroying only part of the Al Atheer plant, the allies failed even to attack a plant at Furat, outside Baghdad, where Iraq was secretly building uranium-enrichment centrifuges, because they did not know it was part of the weapons-development program. The plant's true purpose was discovered by the Atomic Energy Agency only after the end of the war.

Like earlier disclosures, the report to the Security Council does not identify any foreign companies or experts that helped Iraq with its nuclear ambitions. But it makes clear that the inspectors have gathered evidence of "substantial nuclear weapons-related procurement from foreign sources."

It says Iraq drew up lists of "approved suppliers whose products would meet the program's technical specification." But in making these foreign purchases, Iraq sometimes used "cover names" to disguise the products' destination. And many of the goods Iraq purchased abroad for its nuclear program were "multi-use items" with innocent applications.

The report also concludes that Dr. Jaffar Dhia Jaffar, the deputy director of Iraq's Atomic Energy Commission, probably had "the lead technical and administrative responsibility for the nuclear program as a whole, despite his repeated claims that no such program existed."

The United Nations had been looking for a missing "mastermind" with overall control of the uranium-enrichment and weapons-design program, largely because Dr. Jaffar, a British-trained Iraqi scientist, claimed he knew only about the enrichment side.

But on the basis of personnel records removed from Baghdad, the inspectors have now concluded Dr. Jaffar was, in effect, managing both the enrichment and the weapons-design program, although they do not rule out the idea that he may have been helped by unknown foreign scientists.

Finally, the report reveals that the first site raided by the inspectors last month was an installation identified as "the Nuclear Design Center," and that the second was the headquarters of the "Petrochemical Three" project.

Since neither site had been bombed by the allies, United Nations officials assume that the locations had only recently been discovered by Western intelligence services.

10-10

<첨 부 1>

유엔의 대이라크 핵사찰 실시배경 및 내용

1. 대이라크 핵사찰 실시배경

o 91.4.3. 유엔안보리는 결의 제687호를 채택하여 4.17. 이라크의 군비통제를
   위한 특별위원회(Special Commission)를 설치하고, 이라크내 핵무기 및 생
   화학 무기 관련 정보 제공을 요청
   - 동 결의는 또한 대이라크 경제제재 조치 해제 이전에 이라크 보유 대량
     파괴무기 (핵무기, 생.화학무기)를 완전히 폐기토록 규정
o 이에 따라 IAEA 사찰관과 안보리 특별위원으로 구성된 핵사찰반이 이라크가
   제출한 핵물질 및 시설관련 정보를 바탕으로 91.5월부터 9월까지 6차례
   핵사찰을 실시
o 동 핵사찰은 이라크제제 안보리 결의에 의거한 사찰명령을 이라크가 수락
   함으로써 실시한것으로, IAEA 안전조치 규정상 특별사찰과 달리 무제한
   사찰권한을 행사하는 강제사찰임

2. 핵사찰 실시 내용

가. 제1차 핵사찰 (91.5.14-22)

o 91.4.27. 이라크가 제출한 핵관계 정보내용을 확인하기 위해 Al Tuwaitha
   핵연구 시설과 Tarmiya 지역내 핵시설을 사찰
o 사찰결과 고농축 우라늄(HEU)등의 핵물질 존재와 많은 핵시설 장비등이
   타지역으로 이전되었음이 확인되어, 사찰단은 이라크측에 이전된 핵시설
   장비의 완전한 리스트를 요청

- 1 -

0023

나. 제2차 핵사찰 (91.6.22-7.4)

o 제2차 사찰은 Tuwaitha 핵 연구시설외에 6개지역 핵시설에 대해 실시,
이중 Al Ghraib와 Falluja 에서는 이라크 당국에 의해 사찰반의 접근이
금지, 제한됨
  - 이에 따라 유엔 안보리는 의장성명을 통해 이라크의 사찰불응을
    규탄한후, IAEA 사무국장, 특위위원장등의 고위급 대표단을 추가파견
    함으로써 사찰을 재개

o 사찰결과 이라크가 전자 동위원소 분리기술(EMIS)을 사용한 우라늄
농축 시설을 보유하고 있음을 확인
  - 이라크는 IAEA에 밝히지 않은 우라늄 농축 계획 일부가 있었음을
    시인하고 91.7.7. 핵시설 장비 추가 리스트를 안보리에 제출

다. 제3차 핵사찰 (91.7.7-18)

o 91.7.7. 이라크 제출 추가 정보내용을 확인하기 위해 제3차 핵사찰을
실시하였고, 7.12. 유엔 안보리는 이라크가 모든 핵개발 계획과 핵
시설 물질을 공개할 것을 요구하면서 이에응하지 않으며 중대한 결과에
직면할 것이라고 경고
  - 미국, 영국등은 이라크가 핵무기 개발내용을 완전 공개하지 않을경우
    군사력 사용 재개 경고

o 91.7.18.   IAEA는 특별이사회 를 소집, 이라크가 IAEA와 체결한 핵 안전
협정상의 의무 불이행을 규탄하고, 이라크 영토내 모든핵 물질을 IAEA
감시하에 둘것을 촉구하는 결의 채택

- 2 -

0024

라. 제4차 핵사찰 (91.7.27-8.11)

　　o 제4차 핵사찰반은 사찰결과 핵농축 및 재처리 시설 내용을 포함한 이라크
　　　의 비밀핵개발 계획을 확인하고, 원심분리법을 이용한 고농축 우라늄(HEU)
　　　생산 시설을 발견

　　o 동 사찰결과, 91.8.15. 유엔안보리 는 이라크의 안보리 결의(687호) 불
　　　이행을 규탄하고, 이라크가 동안보리 결의와 IAEA 안전조치 협정을 완전히
　　　준수할때까지 모든 핵 활동을 중지할 것을 요구하는 결의(707호)채택

마. 제5,6차 핵사찰 (91.8,9월)

　　o 상기 이라크의 의무 불이행규탄 안보리 결의(707호) 채택후, 유엔 사찰
　　　반은 9월중 2회에 걸쳐 이라크내 핵 시설을 정밀 사찰하였으나, 이라크
　　　측은 사찰반의 헬기사용거부 및 사찰단원을 억류하는등 사찰반의 활동을
　　　계속 방해

　　o 이에대해, 미국은 이라크에 군사력 사용재개를 경고하였고 이라크는
　　　안보리 의장의 요청에 따라 유엔 사찰반 헬기의 무제한 이라크 영공통과
　　　허용 서한을 9.24. 제출하고, 억류했던 사찰단원을 석방함

　　o 상기사찰결과 이라크가 핵무기개발 계획하에 그간 핵농축은 물론 핵무기
　　　운반체제, 핵탄두등을 개발하고 있었음이 밝혀짐
　　　- 이라크가 다시 핵무기제조를 추진할 경우 90년대중반까지 2-3개의
　　　　핵무기를 생산할것 으로 평가

　　o 91.10.11. 유엔 안보리는 6차 핵사찰 결과에 따라 이라크의 안보리 결의
　　　(687, 707호) 무조건 이행촉구 및 대이라크 핵사찰 무기한 실시를 결의
　　　(715호)

- 3 -

0025

<첨 부 2>

안보리 비공식 협의시 (91.10.8) IAEA 사무국장의
핵사찰 강화관련 보고내용

o 구체적 제안 내용

① IAEA 회원국들이 NPT 당사국내 미신고 핵시설의 존재 가능성에 관한 정보 를
   IAEA내 특별반(special secretariat unit)에 제출 할수 있는 장치(mechanism)
   와 절차(procedure)를 마련

② IAEA 사무국은 입수된 정보가 신빙성이 있다고 판단되는 경우 동 정보의
   사실여부 확인을 위해 특별사찰 을 실시

③ 문제의 당사국이 특별사찰 접수를 계속 거부할 경우 IAEA 이사회는 최후
   방법으로 동문제를 유엔 안보리에 제기
   - IAEA는 사찰을 강제할 수 있는 힘이 없기 때문에, 강제력이 필요한 경우
     이를 행사할수 있는 권한은 안보리만이 갖고 있음

o 세계적으로 군축이 가속화되고 NPT 체제가 보편화되고 있는 시점에서, NPT
  체제에 대한 신뢰 강화 가 중요하며, 이를 위해서는 효과적인 검증(effective
  verification) 이 필수적임

o 상기 특별사찰 강화제안 은 IAEA의 기존권능 과 이라크에 대해 성공적으로
  시행한 사찰 경험을 바탕으로 제기 한 것이며, 기본적으로 안전조치협정에 따라
  사찰을 실시하되 최후의 수단으로 안보리의 지원을 받을 수 있도록 하자는
  것임.   끝.

0026

외 무 부

원 본

암 호 수 신

종   별 :

번   호 : UNW-3274   일   시 : 91 1009 1930

수   신 : 장 관 (연일,중동일,국기,미일,기정)

발   신 : 주 유엔 대사

제   목 : 안보리 (걸프사태)

1. H.BLIX IAEA 사무총장 유엔 기자회견(북한 핵사찰 문제 언급포함)

가. BLIX 총장은 10.8. 이락 핵사찰관련 안보리 보고에 이어 유엔본부에서 기자회견을 가진바, 동 회견중 북한의 IAEA 사찰 거부문제에 관한 질문에 다음요지 답변함.

1)NPT 당사국인 북한은 IAEA 안전협정을 체결할 의무가 있음.

2)북한은 미국이 남한에서 핵무기를 철수하지 않는한 동 안전협정에 서명하지 않는다는 입장을 취했음.

3)최근 미국의 남한내 지상핵 미사일 철수결정으로 북한은 안전협정 용의를 표시했음.

나. BLIX 총장의 동일 기자회견중 여타 주요 언급사항은 다음과같음.

1)이락 수소탄 제조용 "LITHIUM 6 " 생산추진: 연간 100 키로그램 생산목표

2)NPT 사찰 체계 보완필요: 정보입수, 사찰권보장, 안보리지원

3)대이락 핵관련 품목 공급업체명단: 추후 책임있는 방식으로 처리

2. 이락 대량 살륙무기 봉제검증 대책

안보리는 본건관련 사무총장(UNSCOM), IAEA 계획안(S/22871/REV.1, S/22872/REV.1) 을 승인하는 결의안을 곧 채택할 것으로 관측되는바, 동 계획안에 의하면, 이락에 다음 봉제조치가 부과되게 됨. - (S) 7/5국

1)군사목적에 응용이 가능한 과학, 공업분야 활동 정기보고의무화: 6 개월마다 보고

2)각종 현황제출: 핵자재 및 설비 일정명세(30 일내), 향후 5 년간의 모든 핵관련 계획, 10 메가와트 초과 전기 공급이 가능한 시설명세, 무기제조에 사용가능한 설비, 화학품, 기타 자재현황

3)광범한 사찰활동 보장 (무제한 사찰실시)

국기국 분석관	장관 청와대	차관 안기부	1차보	2차보	미주국	중아국	국기국	외정실

PAGE 1

4)관련 위반자 처벌이 가능하도록 국내입법 조치

3. 이스라엘 전투기 이락영공 비행

가. 이락은 지난 10.4. 이스라엘 F-15 기 4 대가 시리아 상공으로부터 진입해와 이락 영공을 비행하다가 사우디 상공으로 날아갔음을 항의하는 안보리 문서를 10.7. 자로 배포함(S/23115)

나. 보도에 의하면 미국은 여사한 사례가 유엔의 대이락 특정무기 폐기추진에 장애가 될수 있음을 이스라엘에 강력히 경고하였다고 하며, 본건 이스라엘 전투기는 레바논, 요르단상공도 비행한 것으로 알려짐.

첨부:BLIX 총장 기자회견 요록중 북한언급부분:UNW(F)-625 끝

(대사 노창희-국장)

#별첨

To another query about North Korea's refusal to allow IAEA inspections, Mr. Blix replied that because that country was a member of the NPT, it was required to have a safeguards agreement with the Agency that would allow inspection. North Korea, however, had insisted that it would not sign the agreement unless the United States withdrew nuclear weapons from South Korea. With the recent United States decision to withdraw ground-based nuclear missiles from South Korea, Mr. Blix said he understood that North Korea had indicated its willingness to sign the agreement.

(총 104)

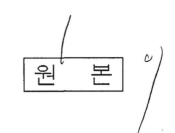

외 무 부

종   별 :

번   호 : UNW-3310   일   시 : 91 1011 2300

수   신 : 장관(연일,중동일,국기,기정)

발   신 : 주유엔대사

제   목 : 안보리회의(이락 대량살상무기통제 검증계획)

연:주국련 20313-740

1. 안보리는 금 10.11 공식회의(3012 차)를 갖고 이락 대량살상 무기통제 검증을 위한 유엔사무총장 및 IAEA 사무총장 계획안(S/22871/REV.1 , S/22872/REV.1)을 승인하는 결의안을 표결결과 만장일치(15:0:0)로 채택하였음.(안보리 결의 715 호)

2. 금일 표결에 앞서 이락은 민수용, 의료목적의 연구활동에 대한 영향, UNSCOM/IAEA/ 제재위의 이락 주권잠식기도, 유엔헌장과 기존안보리 결의수권범위 초과를 이유로 본건계획을 반대하는 발언을 하였으며, 이에대해 미.영은 그간 이락의 안보리 제결의 불이행사례, 민수용을 위장한 대량살상 무기개발 추진, 인도적,의료목적의 연구보호 조항포함을 들어 반박하였음.

3. 불란서는 표결후 발언을 통해 본계획의 중요성을 강조하면서 만장일치 채택을 평가하였음.

첨부:상기 결의안 및 NYT 지 기사: UNW(F)-640끝

(대사 노창희-국장)

국기국   1차보   중아국   국기국   외정실   청와대   안기부

PAGE 1   91.10.12   13:14 BU

외신 1과 통제관

0030

**UNITED
NATIONS**

*UNW(在)-640 11011 23:50
(연일.중동일.국기.기성) 총404*

  Security Council

PROVISIONAL

S/23134
10 October 1991

ORIGINAL: ENGLISH

(기5성)

Belgium, France, Romania, Union of Soviet Socialist
Republics, United Kingdom of Great Britain and
Northern Ireland and United States of America:
draft resolution

The Security Council,

Recalling its resolutions 687 (1991) of 3 April 1991 and 707 (1991) of
15 August 1991, and its other resolutions on this matter,

Recalling in particular that under resolution 687 (1991) the
Secretary-General and the Director General of the International Atomic Energy
Agency were requested to develop plans for future ongoing monitoring and
verification, and to submit them to the Security Council for approval,

Taking note of the report and note of the Secretary-General
(S/22871/Rev.1 and S/22872/Rev.1), transmitting the plans submitted by the
Secretary-General and the Director General of the International Atomic Energy
Agency,

Acting under Chapter VII of the Charter of the United Nations,

1.   Approves, in accordance with the provisions of resolutions
687 (1991), 707 (1991) and the present resolution, the plans submitted by the
Secretary-General and the Director General of the International Atomic Energy
Agency (S/22871/Rev.1 and S/22872/Rev.1);

2.   Decides that the Special Commission shall carry out the plan
submitted by the Secretary-General (S/22871/Rev.1), as well as continuing to
discharge its other responsibilities under resolutions 687 (1991), 699 (1991)
and 707 (1991) and performing such other functions as are conferred upon it
under the present resolution;

3.   Requests the Director General of the International Atomic Energy
Agency to carry out, with the assistance and cooperation of the Special
Commission, the plan submitted by him (S/22872/Rev.1) and to continue to
discharge his other responsibilities under resolutions 687 (1991), 699 (1991)
and 707 (1991);

3613E

*#UNW-3310
정약물*

4-1

0031

4. **Decides** that the Special Commission, in the exercise of its responsibilities as a subsidiary organ of the Security Council, shall:

(a) Continue to have the responsibility for designating additional locations for inspection and overflights;

(b) Continue to render assistance and cooperation to the Director General of the International Atomic Energy Agency, by providing him by mutual agreement with the necessary special expertise and logistical, informational and other operational support for the carrying out of the plan submitted by him;

(c) Perform such other functions, in cooperation in the nuclear field with the Director General of the International Atomic Energy Agency, as may be necessary to coordinate activities under the plans approved by the present resolution, including making use of commonly available services and information to the fullest extent possible, in order to achieve maximum efficiency and optimum use of resources;

5. **Demands** that Iraq meet unconditionally all its obligations under the plans approved by the present resolution and cooperate fully with the Special Commission and the Director General of the International Atomic Energy Agency in carrying out the plans;

6. **Decides** to encourage the maximum assistance, in cash and in kind, from all Member States to support the Special Commission and the Director General of the International Atomic Energy Agency in carrying out their activities under the plans approved by the present resolution, without prejudice to Iraq's liability for the full costs of such activities;

7. **Requests** the Committee established under resolution 661 (1990), the Special Commission and the Director General of the International Atomic Energy Agency to develop in cooperation a mechanism for monitoring any future sales or supplies by other countries to Iraq of items relevant to the implementation of section C of resolution 687 (1991) and other relevant resolutions, including the present resolution and the plans approved hereunder;

8. **Requests** the Secretary-General and the Director General of the International Atomic Energy Agency to submit to the Security Council reports on the implementation of the plans approved by the present resolution, when requested by the Security Council and in any event at least every six months after the adoption of this resolution;

9. **Decides** to remain seized of the matter.

4-2

0032

U.S. SAYS IT MISSED 2 A-PLANTS IN IRAQ

U.N. Team Evaluated Bases — One Was Hit Lightly and 2d Was Not Seen

By ERIC SCHMITT
Special to The New York Times

WASHINGTON, Oct. 9 — Allied intelligence failures and bad weather prevented American bombers from destroying two important Iraqi nuclear weapons installations during the Persian Gulf war, senior Pentagon officials said today. The centers survived the war virtually unscathed.

American planes destroyed some of the buildings at one of the industrial complexes, but only in the waning hours of the war, the officials said. They added that allied intelligence never identified the other site as part of President Saddam Hussein's weapons development program.

United Nations inspectors recently discovered that a nuclear research installation, Al Atheer, 40 miles south of Baghdad, suffered only minor damage. Another installation, Furat, closer to Baghdad, that was secretly building centrifuges for enriching uranium to weapons grade, was never hit. Many other known or suspected nuclear sites were heavily damaged or destroyed.

The latest United Nations discovery, coupled with earlier disclosures that other components of Iraq's nuclear program had survived attacks, underscores how the United States and its allies underestimated the size of Iraq's nuclear-weapons program and overstated the damage they inflicted during the air war.

'Intelligence Is Not Clairvoyant'

"We thought we had a reasonably good understanding based on information we had at the time," a senior Pentagon official said in an interview today. "Now we've learned we didn't have as good a picture as we should have. Intelligence is not clairvoyant, it's not perfect. You have to draw inferences and a lot of stuff is anecdotal."

High-ranking Pentagon officials acknowledge that the intelligence shortcomings on Iraq's nuclear programs raised serious concerns about the value of intelligence in determining the armaments of other potential enemies, including Libya and North Korea.

The lack of reliable informants inside Iraq's tightly controlled, highly compartmentalized nuclear program

Pentagon planners sought to explain why the Furat and Al Atheer nuclear installations escaped destruction in the gulf war.

greatly hindered precise targeting by allied air commanders.

The nuclear plant at Al Atheer is a good example. Known to American field commanders as Al Musaiyib, the complex consisted of a large open test area surrounded by protective walls, underground observation posts and an equipment-storage area. More than 30 installations were associated with the complex in a three-square-mile area, American intelligence findings showed.

The United States, however, did not link the complex with Iraq's nuclear program until a week before the war ended, a Pentagon official said. Poor weather prevented allied bombers from attacking five of the six buildings in the complex until the end of the war. Those buildings had the highest potential to support the Iraqi program, American intelligence had said.

United Nations inspectors later found that intelligence had picked the wrong buildings, failing to detect three others in the complex that were essential in assembling and testing components for a crude nuclear device.

"You can't bomb something you didn't know about," a senior Pentagon official said of the sites at Al Atheer and Furat.

During the war, intelligence officers and the air commanders used various methods, ranging from informants in Iraq to high-altitude reconnaissance photography to satellites, to detect buildings in industrial complexes that might have been weapons laboratories, storage areas or power plants.

Faced with picking out nuclear weapons plants inside industrial complexes as big as 20 square miles, American officers could often make only educated guesses about which buildings should be priority targets.

In contrast, American intelligence officials say that several Iraqi defectors since the war's end have given them much information about Baghdad's weapons-development program. The 25,000 secret Iraqi documents that United Nations inspectors finally managed to remove from the country last month resulted from a tip by one of the defectors, they said.

Bush Administration officials have conceded their surprise at the size of the Iraqi nuclear program, as revealed by the United Nations inspections. Pentagon officials, however, have refused to back away from President Bush's statement on Jan. 23, a week after the air war began, that allied attacks "have put Saddam out of the nuclear bomb-building business for a long time."

4-3   0033

U.N. Maps Plan to Nab Atomic Cheats

By PAUL LEWIS
Special to The New York Times

UNITED NATIONS, Oct. 10 — Stunned by Iraq's extensive violations of its pledge never to acquire nuclear weapons, the United Nations official charged with stopping the spread of such arms has asked government intelligence agencies to report suspected cheating by other countries and announced plans to check suspicious installations more agressively.

Hans Blix, the Director General of the Vienna-based International Atomic Energy Agency, which is charged with enforcing the 1970 Nuclear Nonproliferation Treaty, said in an interview that he wants governments to give him any evidence they have of other countries violating the treaty.

If the evidence seems credible, Dr. Blix said he planned for the first time to use his authority to order an inspection of the suspected site even though the country has not declared it as a nuclear installation or agreed to place it under I.A.E.A. safeguards.

Dr. Blix, who outlined his plan for strengthening the I.A.E.A.'s nuclear safeguards system to the United Nations Security Council in closed session on Tuesday, said he plans to set up a small secretariat attached to his office to assess the "credibility" of evidence that governments provide of nuclear cheating.

The secretariat is to guard against "frivolous" complaints and stop unfriendly countries from "harassing

I.A.E.A. will seek government help in finding treaty violators.

each other," he said. But if the evidence seems reasonable, he would then ask the I.A.E.A.'s 35-member Board of Governors, which represents a cross section of its membership, to authorize a spot check by agency inspectors.

Dr. Blix plans to present his detailed proposals in December to the I.A.E.A.'s board, which is expected to approve them at a meeting next February.

The head of the I.A.E.A. already has the power to order a "special inspection" of any site, even if it has not been declared as a peaceful nuclear installation and placed under agency safeguards. But this has never happened in the past and Dr. Blix said it would be "more prudent" for him to get backing from the Board of Governors first.

The country suspected of violating the nonproliferation treaty could still refuse the I.A.E.A. inspectors access. But this would imply it "has something to hide," he said. And the I.A.E.A. could then send the accusation to the Security Council, which has the power to order a compulsory search.

Under the treaty, 141 countries, including Iraq, have renounced nuclear weapons and agreed to place all their nuclear activities under I.A.E.A. safeguards, allowing agency inspectors regular access to them to insure they are not misused.

Iraq Evaded Treaty

While allowing the agency to inspect some of its nuclear plants, Iraq clandestinely developed a major nuclear weapons program without reporting its existence to the I.A.E.A. as required.

The proposed strengthening in the I.A.E.A.'s regular inspection system would still fall short of what the agency is currently doing in Iraq where the Security Council has ordered it to seek out and destroy all of President Saddam Hussein's "nuclear-weapons usable" material, going wherever necessary to carry out its task.

Not only would the I.A.E.A. have no automatic right of entry, but it could only order a special inspection in a country that has signed the nonproliferation treaty. Many countries suspected of clandestine nuclear activities, such as India, Pakistan and Israel, still have not signed the treaty.

The I.A.E.A. is also urging countries that export nuclear equipment and technology to press for an international register of such sales to keep track of the flow of potentially dangerous technology around the world.

Such a register would closely parallel the international register of arms sales that this year's United Nations General Assembly is expected to create later in its current session.

4—4

0034

UN安保理, 對이락 核武器 製造禁止 決議案 採擇

<1991>

1. UN安保理는 10.11 이락이 核武器를 제조할 수 없도록 이락의 核關聯産業
   을 禁止시키는 동시에 安保理가 필요로 할때 이락내 어느 장소에서나 無
   期限 核査察를 할 수 있는 權限을 부여하는 決議案(715號)을 滿場一致로
   채택했음.

2. 그간 UN의 對이락 核査察 관련 動向을 보면

   가. 걸프戰 停戰 決議案 687號(4.2)에 따라 현재까지 6차(5.15 - 21, 6. 22-
      7.3,   7.7 - 18, 7.27 - 8.10, 9.15 - 21, 9.22 - 30)에 걸쳐 核査察
      活動을 전개 하였으나

   나. 이락측이
      ○ 제2차 核査察團의 核物質 貯藏基地에 대한 出入을 沮止(6.23)하고 核
         物質 운반혐의 시설에 대한 寫眞撮影도 거부(6.28)한데 이어
      ○ 제6차 核査察團에 대해서도 동 査察團이 입수한 核關聯 文書搬出을
         거부코 一時 抑留(9.22 - 28)하는 등 査察活動을 방해함으로써 UN
         과의 지속적인 마찰을 야기해 왔으며

   다. 특히 최근 제6차 核査察團이 입수한 核關聯 文書와 資料를 분석한
      결과

31-23

0035

○ 이락이 100億弗을 투입한 核開發計劃을 바그다드南方 64㎞지점의 알 아티르 연구센터에서 推進하고 있는 가운데

○ 核武器用 농축 우라늄 製造는 물론 核起爆 裝置·운반용 地對地미사일 開發을 진행 (10.4 「케이」核査察 團長)하고 水素爆彈 製造에 이용되는 리튬-6 생산 계획을 진행 (10.8 「한스 블릭스」IAEA 事務局長)하고 있음이 밝혀진 바 있음.

3. 이번 UN安保理의 對이락 核武器 製造禁止 決議案 채택은

가. 이락이 水素爆彈까지 開發하고 있다는 사실이 입증되고 있으나 同國이 UN의 核査察 活動을 繼續 妨害·遲延시킴에 따라

나. IAEA등 核査察團에 대해 이락의 核을 무제한 査察할 수 있는 權限을 부여하여 이락의 核武器 제조를 근본적으로 封鎖하기 위한 것으로

다. 금후 UN의 對이락 核査察 活動을 보다 강력히 推進하는 계기를 이룰 것으로 보임.

31-24

0036

외 무 부

종 별 :

번 호 : UNW-3325

수 신 : 장 관(연일,중동일,국기,기정)

발 신 : 주 유엔 대사

제 목 : 이락 핵사찰(안보리)

일 시 : 91 1014 1930

H.BLIX IAEA 사무총장이 안보리에 제출해온 유엔 이락핵사찰 제6진 (91.9.22-30)
1차 보고서가 안보리문서로 금 10.14 배포된바, 동주요부분을 별첨송부함.

첨부:1. 핵사찰 6진 1차보고서(S/23122)(발췌)

2. NYT 지기사: UNW(F)-645 끝

(대사 노창희-국장)

S/23122
English
Page 3

Enclosure

First report on the sixth IAEA on-site inspection in Iraq
under Security Council resolution 687 (1991)
22-30 September 1991

Introduction

1.   The following report is based on a field analysis of documents obtained, photographed or seen during inspections of Iraqi establishments visited by the sixth IAEA inspection team. Most of the important documents were obtained, photographed or seen during visits to two establishments, the Nuclear Design Center and Petrochemical Three (PC-3) Headquarters, on 23 and 24 September 1991 respectively. The Appendix provides a chronology of activities.

2.   The documents obtained or photographed by the team are for the greater part in Arabic, and there has been limited time for scanning. Only a few documents - although some very important ones - have so far been completely translated. Accordingly, a follow-up report will be issued after a thorough analysis of all the documentary material removed from Iraq.

Summary

3.   The sixth IAEA inspection team obtained conclusive evidence that the Government of Iraq had a program for developing an implosion-type nuclear weapon, and it found documents linking this program - code-named "Petrochemical Three" (PC-3) - to Iraq's Ministry of Industry and Military Industrialization, the Iraqi Atomic Energy Commission (IAEC) and Iraq's Ministry of Defense. Documents were found showing that the nuclear weapons program was supported by broad-based international procurement efforts. Contrary to Iraq's claims of having only a peaceful nuclear program, the team found documents showing that Iraq had been working on the revision of a nuclear weapons design and one linking the IAEC to work on a surface-to-surface missile project - presumably the intended delivery system for their nuclear weapon.

PC-3 reports on Al Atheer

4.   On the basis largely of top-secret progress reports found on 23 September 1991, the team concludes that Iraq was engaged in a broad-based effort to design and develop an implosion-type nuclear weapon. The documents, which cover a period up to 31 May 1990, describe nuclear weapons development experiments involving - for example - neutron

/...

0038

S/23122
English
Page 4

neutron initiators, enriched-uranium cores, reflectors, high-explosive lenses and electronic firing
sets. One document points to Iraqi success in the machining of nuclear weapons components
from natural uranium, but it is not clear from the document whether Iraq had enough highly
enriched uranium for an actual explosive device.

5.   One document links the Al Qa Qaa High Explosives and Propellant Facility to the
program. Even more importantly, it shows clearly that nuclear weapons design work was
conducted at Al Atheer - a facility which Iraq claims to have had no nuclear connection. A
top-secret report states that the objective of the Al Atheer facility was to design and produce
a nuclear device. Previous teams carrying out inspections under Security Council resolution
687 concluded that the Al Atheer facility was most probably to be used for nuclear weapons
component production, high-explosive experiments and device assembly.

6.   The inspection team also found evidence of Iraqi work on sophisticated computer
codes used in the development of nuclear weapons, including one- and two-dimensional
hydrodynamic and neutronic models which simulate the behaviour of nuclear weapons as
they are being fired. Some of these sophisticated codes had been modified by Iraq before
being used at Al Atheer. The document states that, as of June 1990, the basic design for Iraq's
nuclear explosives device had gone through five modifications.

Additional evidence of intention to develop nuclear weapons

7.   The reports on Al Atheer appear to be the most important of those found in four boxes
full of classified Iraqi papers.[4/] The team also found a document suggesting the parallel
development of a missile delivery system for the ongoing nuclear weapons program; in the
document, the Ministry of Defense instructed the IAEC to postpone an experiment until after
surface-to-surface missile testing.

8.   Other documents contain evidence that since 1981 Iraq intended to produce enriched
uranium by methods other than electromagnetic isotope separation. Specifically, the
documents showed that Iraq explored gaseous diffusion and centrifuge enrichment techniques
as late as 1988 and as early as 1982, respectively. The documents included an IAEC-
accredited study in the field of nuclear implosion physics —another clear indication of nuclear
weapons development intentions.

[4/]   It should be recalled, however, that the Government of Iraq seized these boxes from
the inspection team on 23 September and has still not returned all of the documents
which were in them. Notes by the team on some of these documents indicate that
they contained additional information on the Iraqi nuclear weapons program.

7-2   /...

0039

Procurement activities

9.   On the basis of documents seen during the inspection, the team believes that Iraq conducted substantial nuclear-weapons-related procurement from foreign sources. Catalogues from numerous suppliers were found at the PC-3 Headquarters, many of them translated into Arabic. However, because of the team's hasty exit from this establishment before being detained in a parking lot, much information was lost. Although - as just indicated - the team believes that the procurement in question was in support of the nuclear weapons program, it must be stressed that most items will probably prove to have been innocuous, multi-use items for which export licences were not needed and/or which were dispatched before imposition of the United Nations trade embargo.

10.   From the documents seen it is evident that Iraq drew up lists of approved suppliers whose products would meet the program's technical specifications. On-site inspections of procured equipment and material have already shown that items supplied to the IAEC came from many countries.

11.   The team found evidence that, realizing that large-scale purchasing abroad could attract outside attention, the Iraqi authorities devised cover explanations for purchases. In this connection, a country-wide survey of the types and amounts of the equipment required for the civilian sector was recommended, the idea being that indigenously produced items should be used in the civilian sector, while high-quality imported items bearing the same general descriptions would be used for the clandestine nuclear weapons program.

12.   The team noted that the procurement of machinery had often been coupled with relevant on-the-spot training of Iraqi engineers by the manufacturer. In the case of machinery such as lathes and milling machines, test pieces had sometimes been ordered for the validation of technical specifications and computer numerical control software had sometimes been obtained.

13.   At the PC-3 Headquarters, the team found many volumes of documents related to procurement for the Iraqi nuclear weapons program. A number of cover names used by Iraq in its procurement activities have been identified, and it is expected that this number will grow as further procurement records are translated.

Administration of the nuclear weapons program

14.   From the documentation seen by it, the team concluded that the Iraqi nuclear weapons program was under the general control of the Ministry of Industry and Military Industrialization, with specific control assigned to PC-3. The team found numerous classified

7-3

/...

0040

S/23122
English
Page 6

communications with the IAEC heading and a sub-heading identifying PC-3, which confirms that some part of the IAEC was involved in the nuclear weapons program. In this connection it should be noted that the IAEC collaborated with the Iraqi Ministry of Defense on defense-related projects. The team has compiled a list of project activities to be followed up in the future.

15.   The PC-3 employee lists show that Dr. Jaffar Dhia Jaffar was a senior administrator for the program. Similar documentation shows that Dr. Jaffar was intimately linked to the uranium enrichment program. The team accordingly believes that Dr. Jaffar had the lead technical and administrative responsibility for the nuclear weapons program as a whole - despite his repeated claims that no such program existed.

Iraq's obstructing of inspectors

16.   Despite the success of the team in obtaining sensitive, classified documentation on Iraq's nuclear weapons program, one may never discover the true extent of that program. This is due partly to the fact that the Iraqi authorities confiscated documents collected on the first inspection day, despite strong protests by the team's Chief Inspector and the representative of the United Nations Special Commission (UNSCOM). Furthermore, it was obvious after reviewing the material returned to the team that some documents were missing. The team believes that, during the period of nearly seven hours before the return of the documents, the Iraqi authorities reviewed them, withholding the most sensitive ones. Although there might be other explanations, in the light of the continued attempts to conceal the true extent of Iraq's nuclear weapons program and of some very recent correspondence relevant to the programme found at one site, the question remains open whether Iraq has given up its nuclear weapons aspirations.

Continuing Iraqi non-compliance with Security Council resolutions

17.   On the basis of the above, it is concluded that the documents found by the team clearly demonstrate that the Government of Iraq is in violation of Security Council resolutions 687 and 707. This is underscored by the fact that Iraq detained the inspectors and confiscated documents which had been legitimately collected.

18.   Specifically, the following maybe noted:

-     Iraq had - despite its statements to the contrary - a complex, comprehensive nuclear weapons development program characterized by parallel approaches to fissile material production and by theoretical/experimental design work

7-4   /...

0041

-   Iraq still has substantial facilities which were part of the clandestine program and which have not been declared.

-   Iraq has removed significant documentary material and equipment from identified nuclear program sites - including some documentary material removed shortly before the arrival of the team.

19. Iraq has violated the privileges and immunities to which the inspectors were entitled:

-   It detained the team for five hours on the first inspection day.

-   It confiscated all documents collected by the team during the first inspection visit.

-   It interrupted access to the second inspection site before the team had completed its work.

-   It detained the team for 96 hours in the parking lot next to the second inspection site.

-   It opened official mail addressed to the team's Chief Inspector and to the UNSCOM representative.

20. From the evidence which the team has obtained and from the treatment of the team it is concluded that there was repeated and wilful non-compliance with Security Council resolutions 687 and 707 and violation of the UN/IAEA-specified privileges and immunities agreed to by the Government of Iraq.

7-5

/...

0042

Iraq Is Said to Have Hidden Nuclear Records From U.N.

By PAUL LEWIS
Special to The New York Times

By PAUL LEWIS
Special to The New York Times

UNITED NATIONS, Oct. 13 — Although the United Nations seized conclusive evidence of President Saddam Hussein's clandestine nuclear weapons program during a raid in Baghdad last month, Iraq managed to spirit away the bulk of its secret nuclear records only hours before inspectors arrived, according to officials involved in the case.

The officials said that the unnamed intelligence agency that located Iraq's top secret nuclear design center — presumably the Central Intelligence Agency — pressed the United Nations to make the raid "a matter of the highest urgency," apparently because it knew Iraq would soon try to move the incriminating material elsewhere.

But time was needed to assemble the 44-member team because it included nuclear-weapons designers specially borrowed from the United States and Britain. And by the time it arrived, at dawn on Sept. 23, the eight-story building opposite Baghdad's luxury Rashid Hotel had been hurriedly stripped of virtually everything it contained, apparently only hours before.

"They'd trashed the place inside," said Robert L. Gallucci, deputy chairman of the Special Commission ap-

Before the raid, an inspector says, Iraqis 'trashed' the building.

pointed by the Security Council to locate and destroy Iraq's most dangerous weapons and one of those who took part in the raid. "We even found a note saying all documents stored there were to be removed before any U.N. inspection," he added.

By removing the bulk of its records before the raid, officials say, Iraq may again have deprived the United Nations of the chance to once and for all get a complete overview of President Hussein's nuclear program.

The extent of what has been unearthed so far as well as Iraq's frenzied efforts to conceal whatever it could have already forced the Special Commission's experts to conclude that Baghdad may well have other unknown nuclear installations hidden away in the desert.

Its chairman, the Swedish diplomat Rolf Ekeus, says he can not exclude the possibility that Iraq may still possess a secret plutonium factory, as well as clandestine stocks of enriched uranium explosive, or that it might be experimenting with previously undisclosed enrichment methods like the nozzle technique.

Nevertheless, in their haste to save the building's secrets, Iraqi nuclear officials accidentally overlooked a rich cache of secret material stored in four steel trunks as well as enough other documents to fill several cardboard boxes and plastic bags and four cases of microfiches. For the Special Commission and the Vienna-based International Atomic Energy Agency, which shares responsibility for destroying Iraq's banned nuclear material, these overlooked documents were of the utmost value because they clinched the case the agencies had been trying to prove for months.

The documents established conclusively that in addition to clandestinely manufacturing enriched uranium, Iraq had embarked on a nuclear weapons development program and was trying to design nuclear triggers and other bomb components.

They also identified, for the first time, the Al Atheer installations on the Euphrates south of Baghdad as the nerve center of this weapons program. And they revealed that Iraq was planning to produce Lithium 6, a material used for boosting nuclear explosions up to thermonuclear strength.

'The Smoking Gun'

"It was a dream find for us because it gave us the smoking gun we wanted although the Iraqis thought they had cleared out the building," Dr. Gallucci says. "They were really quite upset at overlooking those secret documents" he adds.

And after examining some of the documents obtained in that raid, the Special Commission asked Iraq to surrender a new list of undeclared nuclear-related items, including fissile material, documents and equipment used in the weapons program, officials say. As yet Iraq has not replied.

Nevertheless Iraqi officials still got a chance to tamper with the material the inspectors found because they took the information back by force for several hours before eventually returning them. And the microfiches were never given back.

The day after the Sept. 23 raid on Iraq's nuclear documents center, the same team was arrested and detained for 92 hours in a parking lot after it raided the headquarters of another secret operation called Petrochemical Project 3, the code name for Iraq's nuclear weapon program.

On Friday the seventh United Nations nuclear inspection team arrived in Baghdad for an 11-day stay during which it is likely to investigate documentary evidence seized by the team

7-6

last month.

Although President Bush asserted in January that "our pinpoint attacks have put Saddam out of the bomb building business for a long time," it is already clear that allied bombers did not destroy vital nuclear installations during the Persian Gulf air war, including the Al Atheer site and a factory at Furat for building uranium enrichment centrifuges.

Iraq has confessed so far only to making a few grams of plutonium and about five pounds of lightly enriched uranium, which have no military significance. Last Friday the Security Council empowered the Special Commission to continue monitoring Iraq's

---

Iraq may have kept a plutonium factory.

---

industrial and scientific activites indefinitely to insure that Baghdad does not try to acquire new weapons of mass destruction.

The Special Commission, which is working with the International Atomic Energy Aagency on destroying Iraq's "weapons-usable" nuclear technology, is also charged by the Security Council with eliminating its chemical and biological weapons as well as its ballistic missiles.

With much of the 35,000 pages of mostly Arabic documents seized last month still untranslated, Commission officials are still reluctant to draw firm conclusions about President Saddam Hussein's covert nuclear weapons program. Nevertheless, there is widespread agreement among those who have examined the available material that Iraq appears to have embarked on a broad-based and diversified attempt to develop nuclear weapons in the late 1970's and early 1980's, exploring virtually every route and showing itself ready to spend colossal sums from its oil revenues.

Billions Spent

Iraq is estimated to have spent about $10 billion so far on its efforts to acquire a nuclear weapon. Besides the amount of money available to Iraq, several other factors may also have pushed the country toward a diversified approach. In 1981 Israel bombed Iraq's Osirak reactor, asserting that it was being used to produce plutonium explosive for a bomb, even though it was under international safeguards.

Another factor favoring diversification may have been Pakistan's success in producing highly enriched uranium using the centrifuge technique, according to weapons experts who spoke under condition of anonymity. Some of the technology found in Iraq's centrifuge enrichment machines resembles that developed by Britain, Germany and the Netherlands in their joint, Dutch-based Urenco commercial reactor fuel plant.

It has been widely reported that Pakistan acquired Urenco know-how for its nuclear program from a Pakistani scientist who had worked in the plant.

Experiments Acknowledged

In any event, Iraq has admitted experimenting unsuccessfully with chemical and gaseous diffusion techniques for producing enriched uranium suitable for weapons, as well as clandestinely making a minute quantity of plutonium in a research reactor officially under International Atomic Energy Agency safeguards.

"They may just have decided to follow the history of the Manhattan Project when the U.S. pursued every avenue towards enrichment at the same time," says one expert, referring to America's World War II atomic bomb program.

But in the end, experts say, Iraq concluded that its best hope lay in concentrating its effort on an obscure enrichment technique known as electro-magnetic isotopic separation as well as on the centrifuge process.

It remains possible that the electro-magnetic separation program and the centrifuge program were also intended to operate in harness rather than independently.

From reports of successful experiments with "flying plates" in the seized weapons design documents, experts have concluded that Iraq was trying to build the kind of implosion weapon the United States developed around 1948.

These bombs were smaller and more powerful than the implosion device dropped on Nagasaki, experts say, because they contained an "air gap" or empty space around the central core of nuclear material. This enables the trigger to squeeze the core more powerfully and increases the bomb's explosive force. J. Robert Oppenheimer, the father of the American atomic bomb, is credited with once defining the difference between the Nagasaki bomb and an "air gap" bomb as the difference between pressing a nail into a wall and hitting it with a hammer.

No Blueprint Yet

While many of the bomb components appear more up to date than those used by the United States 40 years ago, some Special Commission experts say that Iraq's weapons program appears less advanced than its drive to produce highly enriched uranium.

As yet no complete blueprint for the bomb itself has been found. And the designs for the nuclear trigger mechanism do not yet contain the safety features usually built into this mechanism to prevent accidental detonation, experts note.

The seized documents also reveal that Iraqi scientists were frequently stymied because complicated machinery they needed could not readily be obtained on the commercial market. One report lists flash X-ray and pulse power as well as special junction switches as "commercially unobtainable." These complaints suggest to some Western experts that Iraqi scientists were seeking to justify their inability to progress as quickly as the country's political leaders wanted.

7-7

0044

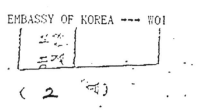

BOMBS AWAY

By Patrick Glynn

After several weeks of exhausting travel and tense confrontations with Iraqi authorities, U.N. inspectors have at last succeeded in laying bare Iraq's massive effort to evade the Nuclear Nonproliferation Treaty. On the basis of preliminary reports, the Iraqi effort appears breathtaking, clearly the largest circumvention of arms limitation provisions since Germany's violations of the Treaty of Versailles. Not that the world was unaware of Saddam Hussein's ambitions to attain the Bomb. Numerous warning signs during the 1980s—attempts by Iraqis to obtain illicit plutonium, materials for enrichment centrifuges, and even high-quality capacitors for triggering a nuclear weapon—had made Iraqi intentions clear. The question was how long it would take them to succeed. Before the Gulf war the U.S. intelligence community set the estimate at a reassuring five to ten years. Now that figure has been revised down to two. In short, the Gulf crisis may have been a closer shave than anyone imagined; had Saddam attacked later, or had the war for any reason been postponed, the West could well have faced a nuclear-armed Iraq.

How did Iraq, a signatory of the 1968 Nonproliferation Treaty, manage to get so close to a bomb while ostensibly remaining under the treaty's "safeguards"? The question is important because Iraq's success in evading the treaty raises the possibility of other states doing the same. And strengthening the "safeguards" administered by the International Atomic Energy Agency (IAEA)—in particular, a new suggestion for "special inspections" of suspected nuclear sites—won't likely solve the problem.

U.N. inspections of Iraq have dramatically exposed the inherent weaknesses of the IAEA system. Most obvious, inspections conducted by the Vienna-based international body charged with policing the Nonproliferation Treaty apply only to "declared" facilities involving special nuclear materials. Most, though not all, of Iraq's massive illicit bomb effort took place either at facilities outside the IAEA's legal jurisdiction or at potentially illegal, undeclared sites.

Production of an atom bomb involves the mating of two major activities, both of which, in Iraq's case, were far advanced. The first consists of the design and creation of a complicated detonation device, using conventional explosive—an activity not necessarily involving special nuclear materials and therefore not under IAEA jurisdiction. The Iraqis had undertaken a major effort to build such a detonation device at a facility known as al-Atheer, forty miles south of Baghdad. Unsuspected as the heart of the Iraqi bomb program, al-Atheer was only slightly damaged by allied bombing. Estimates vary of the success of the al-Atheer scientists in achieving a detonation design, though David Kay, head of the U.N. inspection team, has said Iraq achieved a "workable solution"—i.e., a basically practicable design on paper. The second activity needed to build a bomb is the production of enough weapons-grade or fissile material. This is what IAEA safeguards are specifically designed to prevent, and it's here that the system most clearly failed. The Iraqi effort to get fissile material involved a variety of facilities. The role of some of them in the bomb program was not understood. Others escaped detection and destruction entirely.

There are two alternative fuels for a bomb: plutonium, which is produced as a normal byproduct of "peaceful" reactor operation but which must be separated out by a chemical process (known as "reprocessing"); and enriched uranium, which is produced not by reactors but by costly, capital-intensive, and extremely time-consuming separation processes (known as "enrichment"). Back in the 1970s and early 1980s, the Iraqis sought to go the plutonium route. Then, after Israel bombed Iraq's Osirac reactor in 1981, Saddam's scientists turned clandestinely to enrichment—undertaken on a scale and with a method wholly unsuspected by nonproliferation experts.

Israel's decision to bomb the Osirac reactor is looking wiser by the day. In 1976 France sold Iraq a very large light-water research reactor to be constructed outside Baghdad. From a nonproliferation standpoint, the French-designed reactor posed two serious problems. First, it employed as its fuel highly enriched uranium—i.e., bomb-grade material. Second, as a big reactor it was capable of irradiating uranium to produce usable quantities of plutonium. In other words, operating such a reactor would by necessity have put large quantities of potentially weapons-grade materials in Iraqi hands.

At the time, the international community intended to rely on IAEA safeguards. As the Osirac reactor prepared to go on line, the IAEA readied an especially stringent regime. But that regime still probably wouldn't have stopped the Iraqis from getting a bomb. One major worry during the recent war, for example, was that the 27.5 pounds, or 12.5 kilograms, of highly enriched uranium that Iraq had purchased from France—technically under IAEA "safeguards"—would suddenly be diverted to use in a bomb. Imagine the headache with even larger reserves of fuel. The problem is that big reactors from which fuel can easily be removed are inherently not "safeguardable."

Set back by the Israeli attack and subsequently slowed by the war with Iran, the Iraqi nuclear program accelerated again in the late 1980s. Then the Iraqis turned mainly to enrichment to obtain fuel. Even before the recent Gulf war, it was known that Iraq had begun to procure materials—in particular high-quality miraging steel—to build uranium enrichment centrifuges. Nonetheless, a factory for assembling such centrifuges at Furat escaped detection and bombing during the war. Since the war, U.N. inspectors have uncovered another vast effort to enrich uranium using a process thought to be obsolete. This process, involving huge electromagnetic installations called "calutrons," was last known to be used during the Manhattan Project. U.N. inspectors discovered the remains of a massive calutron facility at Tarmiya and another pilot project at Tuwaitha. Targeted by allied bombers as a generally "suspicious facility," in the words of one official, the role of the massive Tarmiya installation, whether in the missile or nuclear program, wasn't understood. According to a State Department official, the discovery of the "incredibly inefficient" calutrons for enriching uranium came as a "big surprise." The calutron installations were part of a vast network of sites—many hardened, others shielded so as to avoid detection, some built as dummies—that made up Saddam's bomb program. The Iraqis also managed to produce three grams of plutonium—the one clear-cut violation but, because of the small quantities involved, militarily the least significant one.

In response to the Iraqi revelations, IAEA director Hans Blix has proposed requests for "special inspections" of suspect nuclear sites in member countries. Blix has called on intelligence agencies to share information and has asked for U.N. Security Council backing for IAEA requests. But the plan has several major snags. First, it needs approval of the IAEA's General Board, which may make inspection requests contingent on prior board approval. This could undercut any element of surprise and make the inspections meaningless. The present board includes not only proliferators such as India and Pakistan, but Cuba, Vietnam, and Iran. Second, such inspections will depend heavily on human intelligence, which, as Iraq showed, is usually in shortest supply where it is needed most. Even in the case of postwar Iraq, much of what we now know would not have been discovered without the help of a defector.

Does this mean we may face a widening proliferation threat? Probably. "If we didn't know Iraq had huge calutrons, then we don't know anything for sure," says Kathleen Bailey, former assistant director for nonproliferation at the Arms Control and Disarmament Agency. "There are lots of places I worry about—Iran, Libya, Egypt, Syria." One imminent threat, North Korea, has signed the Nonproliferation Treaty but deliberately delayed agreeing to "full-scope" safeguards and could have the bomb in as little as two to three years, according to a State Department official. India and Pakistan are assumed to have nuclear weapons, and everyone's now edgy about Algeria, which until recently was not even on the radar screen.

There's also concern about our allies. Israel has pursued a nuclear program largely out of concern that the Nonproliferation Treaty could not prevent the spread of mass-destruction weapons in its region—a well-founded fear, as events have shown. South Korea was persuaded to abandon its quest for the bomb in the late 1970s in exchange for extension of U.S. nuclear guarantees. But with the North Korean program proceeding apace and U.S. land- and sea-based tactical nuclear weapons scheduled for withdrawal under President Bush's recent disarmament initiative, South Koreans could conceivably re-evaluate. An atom bomb on the Korean peninsula, meanwhile, would likely put corresponding pressure on Japan.

Nonproliferation advocates frequently stress the virtues of disarmament by example. But not only is the U.S. moral example unlikely to inspire such leaders as Saddam Hussein to corresponding action, but retraction of American military power, including nuclear power, leaves U.S. allies exposed, widening the incentives to proliferate.

The solution? Most nonproliferation experts recommend a far greater strengthening of inspection powers than the IAEA is currently contemplating. Anthony Cordesman, aide to Senator John McCain, argues that radically more intrusive inspection—even surpassing the kind of inspection contemplated under the superpower START treaty—is essential not just in nuclear but in chemical and biological proliferation, where no safeguards exist at all. "You need rapid response. That means, in many cases, helicopters," notes Cordesman. That is the logical solution to the problem, but it's hardly politically feasible.

Short of sporadic Osirac-style bombings around the world, we're left with few options. One is to keep enough military power both to protect allies from countries seeking nuclear weapons and to discourage allied proliferation. We also need limited missile defenses to protect U.S. troops in the field and the American homeland from those less rational regimes that may be inherently undeterrable. It's indeed hard to miss the irony that at the very moment when the nuclear threat is diminishing from what used to be the Soviet Union, mass-destruction weapons are spreading everywhere else. The cold war may have ended, but the era of proliferation is only beginning.

PATRICK GLYNN is a resident scholar at the American Enterprise Institute.

4293-2 (END)

The New Republic
10/28/91

0046

U.N. Says Iraq Was Building H-Bomb and Bigger A-Bomb

By WILLIAM J. BROAD

Iraq's efforts to build a hydrogen bomb, described last week by the United Nations, were further along than generally believed and would also have sharply increased the destructiveness of its atomic bombs, according to weapons experts and United Nations documents.

Because hydrogen bombs can be hundreds or thousands of times more powerful than atomic bombs and vastly more destructive, some analysts expressed alarm about the recent disclosures. America's first hydrogen bomb, exploded in 1952, was about 700 times more forceful than the atomic bomb dropped on Hiroshima in August 1945.

Overall, the Iraqi bomb program was more ambitious, advanced and deadly than had previously been suspected, analysts said. A top former intelligence official said its enterprising nature and vast scale showed that the West's intelligence failure had been extensive.

Longer Work Was Seen

Before the Persian Gulf war, intelligence experts knew of Iraqi efforts to build an atomic bomb but made no mention of a hydrogen bomb program. Even those experts who rated Iraq's progress most highly assumed that it needed at least 2 years to begin production of crude warheads, while most others said it would take 5 to 10 years.

But from the evidence gathered by United Nations inspectors, it is now believed that Iraq could have been making atomic bombs in as little as a year.

Worse, Baghdad was apparently engaged in a broad effort to go down the thermonuclear road, producing not only hydrogen-bomb materials like lithium 6 but also computer software to predict the likelihood of thermonuclear reactions. In addition, it is now known that Iraq had acquired another key ingredient needed to unleash the latent thermonuclear forces of the atom. This is heavy water, or deuterium oxide, which United Nations officials say Iraq imported years ago.

Deuterium is a heavy form of hydrogen. When heavy water is mixed with lithium 6, the product is lithium 6 deuteride. This compound is the main component of hydrogen bombs. It undergoes nuclear fusion to give the bombs their fearsome power.

One Bomb Sets Off Another

Iraq would have probably needed several years to produce a hydrogen bomb, weapons scientists said. They noted that a prerequisite for any hydrogen bomb is an atomic bomb whose extraordinary heats act as a trigger.

But the weapons scientists added that Iraq's thermonuclear ambitions were also more immediate. Baghdad, they said, would have used small quantities of hydrogen-bomb fuel to triple or quadruple the explosive force of any atomic bomb.

Such "boosting," as it is known, is fairly easy to do. When lithium 6 is bombarded by subatomic neutrons in a nuclear reactor, it is converted into a form of heavy hydrogen called tritium. This is then added to the core of an atomic bomb, along with deuterium from heavy water.

Experts say this deuterium-tritium mixture can sharply improve the efficiency and resulting force of a chain reaction, transforming a crude atomic bomb into a weapon small enough and powerful enough to be suitable for delivery atop a missile.

United Nations officials have already disclosed that Iraq tested a surface-to-surface missile able to carry an atomic bomb as part of its program to develop nuclear weapons.

The explosive power of hydrogen bombs has no theoretical limit. And, weapons experts say, big ones are easier to build than small ones, conjuring up visions of Saddam Hussein with an arsenal of great power.

"It's really astonishing," said Dr. Theodore B. Taylor, a former designer of nuclear arms at the weapons laboratory at Los Alamos, N.M., the birthplace of the atomic and hydrogen bombs. "This shores up the idea that they had a very ambitious and extensive weapons program."

Scientist Expresses Fear

Leonard S. Spector, an expert on the spread of nuclear arms at the Carnegie Endowment for International Peace in Washington, called the whole episode alarming.

"Iraq clearly anticipated having a very big program that could graduate to hydrogen bombs," he said in an interview. "The Iraqi work wasn't sequential, as has been the case in lots of other places. They were doing everything in parallel."

United Nations officials had previously said that the International Atomic Energy Agency, a specialized agency based in Vienna, was trying to track down hundreds of pounds of heavy water that Iraq imported years ago. As a

Oct. 15, 1991
-- NYT

4299-1

Seeking a More Destructive Bomb

Evidence shows Iraq worked on thermonuclear reactions used to boost A-bombs and make H-bombs. The key in both cases is fusing deuterium and tritium, which are heavy forms of hydrogen.

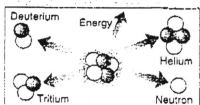

Deuterium | Energy
Tritium | Helium | Neutron

GETTING THE KEY INGREDIENTS

Deuterium is easily obtained from heavy water or deuterium oxide. With more difficulty, lithium 6, a silver-white metal, becomes tritium.

Reactor turns lithium 6 into tritium; it is mixed with deuterium at A-bomb's core. Resulting neutron bursts speed chain reaction to make bomb more powerful.

BOOSTED ATOMIC BOMB

Lithium 6 is mixed with deuterium. Showers of neutrons in exploding H-bombs turns lithium into tritium, which then fuses with deuterium, releasing huge burst of energy.

HYDROGEN BOMB

POTENTIALLY DESTROYED BY BLAST

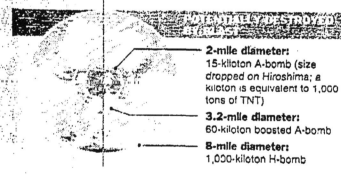

2-mile diameter:
15-kiloton A-bomb (size dropped on Hiroshima; a kiloton is equivalent to 1,000 tons of TNT)

3.2-mile diameter:
60-kiloton boosted A-bomb

8-mile diameter:
1,000-kiloton H-bomb

The New York Times

sign of hydrogen-bomb work, heavy water is ambiguous since it also has uses in nuclear reactors.

But a week ago today, David Kay, chief of the agency's inspection team in Iraq, told reporters that several of the documents his team had seized indicated that Iraq had already produced several pounds of lithium 6 and that another document referred to a plan to make about 220 pounds a year. Lithium 6 has no significant use other than in bomb manufacturing. This amount of lithium 6, Mr. Kay said, was enough to "raise real concern about weapons production."

Excess of Lithium 6

Several weapons experts, in interviews, said 220 pounds a year was probably more lithium 6 than was needed for simple boosting and suggested an intention by Baghdad to build hydrogen bombs.

For boosting, 220 pounds of lithium 6 could produce enough tritium for dozens to thousands of atomic bombs, depending on the power of the nuclear reactor used as a neutron source to turn it into tritium, Dr. Taylor said.

Experts estimate that the force of this hydrogen bomb would have been equal to somewhere between a million and 10 million tons of high explosives, depending on the bomb's design. The atomic bomb that destroyed Hiroshima had a strength equivalent to 15,000 tons of high explosives. The hydrogen bombs now atop American MX missiles have a force equal to 300,000 tons.

Lithium, soft and silver-white, is the lightest known metal — more abundant in the earth's crust than lead or tin, in nature. It occurs as a mixture of isotopes, with lithium 6 accounting for roughly 7 percent and lithium 7, roughly 93 percent of the deposits.

The aim in manufacturing weapons is to separate lithium 6 from that more prevalent isotope, a process that is said to be far easier than the separation of uranium isotopes.

Oct. 15, 1991
NYT

4299-2 (END)

0048

외 무 부

종 별 :

번 호 : UNW-3358   일 시 : 91 1016 1920

수 신 : 장 관(연일,중동일,기정)

발 신 : 주 유엔 대사

제 목 : 안보리(걸프사태)

1. 이락은 지난 10.4. 이스라엘 군용기 이락영공비행시 유엔 이락 대량살상무기 폐기특위 (UNSCOM) 헬기와 근접대오비행 (FLYING IN CLOSEMILITARY FORMATION) 함으로써이락이 필요한 방공대응조치를 취할수 없었다고 주장하면서 여사한 사례재발 경우유엔항공기와 승무원의 안전에 대해 책임을 질수 없다는 요지의 안보리 문서로 배포하였음. (S/23139)

2. 케야르 사무총장은 이락측 상기 주장에 대해 10.16 기자문답시 사실 무근이라는 반응을 보였음.

3. 한편 이락은 미국이 유엔특위와 사찰반을 대이락 첩보활동에 이용하고 있으며이렇게 입수한 제반정보를 이스라엘측에 넘겨주고 있음을 비난하는 안보리 문서를배포하였음. (S/23140)

첨부:사무총장 기자문답: UNW(F)-658 끝

(대사 노창희-국장)

국기국   1차보   중아국   외정실   분석관   정와대   안기부

PAGE 1   91.10.17   10:00 WG

외신 1과 롱제관

0049

UNW(舟)-658 11°ㅜ 1920
(연일.중동역.기정) 총 10매

REMARKS MADE BY THE SECRETARY-GENERAL UPON ENTERING THE SECRETARIAT BUILDING ON WEDNESDAY 16 OCTOBER 1991 AT 9:50 A.M.

Q. Regarding the Iraqi accusation that Israel is allowing its planes to use UN helicopters as a sort of shield to fly over Iraqi territory....

S-G As an accusation it is totally false and unjustified. There is no basis for saying such a thing.

Q. Have you been in touch with the people who are actually running the helicopters so that it is quite clear that this is not true?

S-G We have Ambassador Ekeus here and I am going to see him today but I am persuaded that this allegation is wrong.

Q. Have you heard anything from your representative in Lebanon about the hostages?

S-G Things are moving.

Q. We have heard that the people who are holding the hostages are asking for a guarantee.

S-G This is a matter which is extremely, extremely sensitive and that is why I have to refrain from any comment which could spoil the chances of getting some good results.

* * *

#UNW-3358
첨부

1—1

외 무 부

종 별 :

번 호 : GVW-2072   일 시 : 91 1021 1730

수 신 : 장관(국기,정안)

발 신 : 주 제네바 대사

제 목 : WHO 의 이라크내 생.화학무기 사찰.폐기활동

대: WGV-1422

대호, 안보리 결의 687 호(91.4.3)에 의거한 유엔특별위원회(UNSCOM)의 이라크내 핵.생.화학무기 및 미사일 폐기작업과 관련, 당관이 WHO 관계관으로 부터파악한 WHO 작업반의 이라크내 활동 내용을 아래 보고함.

1. WHO 작업반의 목적 및 파견 실적

가. WHO 의 이라크내 활동목적은 유엔특별위원회의 활동중 생.화학무기 사찰지역에 대한 공공보건(PUBLIC HEALTH) 상의 위해 유무 결정과 사찰단의 보건 예방에 있음.

나. 유엔 사무총장의 요청에 따라 WHO 사무총장은 상기 지원활동을 위해 지난 5 월 4 명의 WHO 전문가로 구성된 TASK FORCE 를 구성하고, 91.6 월 부터 9 월까지 4 차례에 걸쳐 유엔특별위원회의 일원으로 동 TASK FORCE 중 1-2 명을(WHO 작업반)파견한바 있음. (상세는 첨부 1 참조)

2. WHO 작업반 활동 내용

가. 화학무기 폐기작업반

0 91.6 월 중순과 91.8 월말 두차례에 걸쳐 화학무기 시설을 사찰지역 사찰대상 지역 숫자 및 이름등 WHO 작업반의 이라크내 활동 보고내용 대부분은 상금 공개가 어렵다함.

0 상기 시설중 바그다드로 부터 북동쪽으로 80 여 KM 떨어진 MUTHANNA 라는곳에서는 수천개의 화학무기가 발견되었다 함.

0 그러나, 동 시설에 가장 가까운 마을이 20 KM 나 떨어져있으며, 이곳에는별로 인구가 없으며 바람이 별로 불지 않는 점을 감안할때 인체에 대한 위해 가능성은 없다고 판단되었다함. (동 시설 운용요원에 대한 안전 교육은 WHO 작업반이 별도 실시했다함. 상세 내용 별첨 2 참조)

국기국 정와대	장관 안기부	차관	1차보	2차보	▬▬▬	외연원	외정실	분석관

PAGE 1

O MUTHANNA 에서 발견된 화학무기는 카나다와 소련의 장비를 지원받아 빠르면 91년말 부터 페기작업을 시작할 계획이라함.

　나. 생물무기 폐기 작업반

O 91.8 월초와 91.9 월 하순 두차례 작업반을 파견, 10 여개 시설을 사찰하였다함.

O SALAMAN PAK 등 작업반이 사찰한 지역에는 이라크가 생물무기 및 생산시설을 이미 제거 파괴한 상태였는바, 제거한 무기 및 시설등을 어디로 옮겼는지에대하여는 추후 사찰단을 파견, 조사할 계획이라함.

　3. 향후 활동 계획

안보리 결의 687 호에 의한 WHO 작업반 파견은 유엔의 파견 요청을 WHO 가 수락하는 형식을 취하므로, WHO 작업반 추가 파견문제는 지금 애기할 수 없으며 UN 과 협의 추진할 문제라함.

　4. 참고사항

WHO 관계관에 의하면, 상기 결의 687 호에 의거하여 유엔은 지금까지 연 442명의 19 개 사찰단을 파견하였으며 동 사찰단은 U.N, IAEA, WHO 대표외에 미국, 영국, 독일, 프랑스등 34 개국의 대표로 구성했다 함.

　첨부: 1: WHO AND UN RES.687

　2. UN PRESS RELEASE(IK/51/REV 1)

(GVW(F)-0433). 끝

(대사 박수길-국장)

예고: 91.12.31 에 예고문에 의거 일반문서로 재분류

PAGE 2

Note for the Record

WHO AND UN SECURITY COUNCIL RESOLUTION 687

Under the terms of UN Security Council Resolution 687, the Secretary-General set up a UN Special Commission (UNSCOM) to oversee the destruction of Iraq's weapons of mass destruction and Iraq's capability to manufacture the same. The Directors-General of WHO and the IAEA were also requested to assist in their specialized areas.

Therefore the Director-General of WHO appointed a Task Force consisting of 4 people to support UNSCOM in its work. These are:

Dr E. Smith, Promotion of Chemical Safety, WHO Geneva (for chemical disarmament)
Dr J. Woodall, Epidemiological Surveillance and Health Situation and Trend Assessment, WHO Geneva (for biological disarmament)
Dr J. Santesson, Swedish National Defense Research Establishment (for chemical disarmament)
Dr A. Bovallius, Swedish National Defense Research Establishment (for biological disarmament).

The Director-General also nominated:

Dr A. Saghafinia of Iran as medical officer to the first chemical weapons inspection team (CW1)
Dr M. Faessler, Swiss Army Atomic and Chemical Defence Centre, as WHO representative on the second biological weapons inspection team (BW2).

Inspections

WHO representatives have taken part in the following inspections as of 18 October 1991:

1. CW1 9-15 June 1991 - Dr Santesson as chemical weapons expert
                       - Dr Saghafinia as team medical officer

2. CW3 31 August - 8 September 1991 - Dr Santesson as Chief Inspector

3. BW1 2-8 August 1991 - Dr Bovallius as Deputy Chief Inspector

4. BW2 20 September - 3 October 1991 - Dr Faessler as process engineer.

The objective of WHO participation in these inspections is to determine whether a public health hazard exists at any of the inspected sites, and to safeguard the health of the inspectors.

To these ends, WHO has arranged the supply of anthrax vaccine to the inspectors, and of syringes containing nerve gas antidotes and of other appropriate medical supplies and eqipment.

3—1

United ⊕ Nations

Press Release

Department of Public Information • News Coverage Service • New York

IK/51/Rev.1*
18 September 1991

UNITED NATIONS SPECIAL COMMISSION CONDUCTS THIRD INSPECTION OF IRAQI CHEMICAL WEAPONS

A 26-member United Nations inspection team, headed by Dr. Johan Santesson of the World Health Organization (WHO), inspected chemical weapons sites declared by Iraq, as well as other sites, from 31 August to 9 September. The inspection report was submitted to the Executive Chairman of the United Nations Special Commission, Rolf Ekeus, last Friday.

The team visited three sites declared by Iraq as storage sites for chemical weapons, as well as five other sites or sub-sites not declared but considered by the Special Commission to be of possible interest in this connection.

The condition of the various munitions was examined. Samples were taken of the contents, which will be analyzed in Finland, Germany, Sweden, Switzerland and the United Kingdom.

The team inspected chemical warheads for the Al Hussein ballistic missile that were stored close to the main road between Baghdad and Samarra. Some of the warheads were filled with a nerve agent, and others with a starting material for the generation of a nerve agent. The warheads will be transported to the Muthanna State Establishment, near Samarra, for destruction.

The inspectors also viewed mustard-agent-filled bombs of two sizes that were stored at an airfield at Al Bakr. Some of the bombs had ruptured due to excess internal pressure and had released the mustard agent content. The area downwind of the storage site is not populated, thus the public was not at risk. Before the bombs can be transported, they must be vented to release the excess pressure.

(more)

* Revised to indicate in the headline that this was the third inspection team; the fourth team completed its inspection of Iraq's chemical weapon capabilities earlier.

4413P

Approximately 6,400 artillery projectiles filled with mustard agent were stored in the open at a chemical proving ground near Fallujah. The projectiles were in good condition and will be transported to the Muthanna State Establishment for destruction.

No undeclared filled chemical weapons were found by the inspection team. However, at one installation, about 6,000 undeclared containers for chemical warfare agents to be used in 122-millimetre rockets were found, and at another installation considerable quantities of tear gas munitions and devices were discovered, said by Iraq to be intended for training purposes.

* *** *

4413P

0055

외 무 부

종 별 :

번 호 : UNW-3447 일 시 : 91 1022 1900

수 신 : 장 관(연일,중동일,국기,기정)

발 신 : 주 유엔대사

제 목 : 안보리(걸프사태)

1. 유엔 이락 대량살상무기 폐기특위(UNSCOM)는 10.21-23 간 당지에서 R.EKEUS 의장주재로 제2차 본회의를 개최중인 바, 10.21에는 H.BLIX IAEA사무총장 보고도 청취하였으며, 작년 설립이래의 작업결과 점검이 금번회의의 주 목적이라고 함.

2. 한편 R.EKEUS 의장은 최근 이락방문 결과에 관해 10.23 안보리 비공식협의시 보고 예정이라고 하는 바, 관련사항 추보위계임.

첨부: NYT,WP 기사: UNW(F)-698 끝

(대사 노창희-국장)

국기국	1차보	중아국	국기국	외정실	분석관	정와대	안기부

UNW(市)-698 11022 1950
(연일. 중동일. 국가. 기점)   총2叶

U.N. Says Iraq Admits Research on Atomic Bombs

By PATRICK E. TYLER
Special to The New York Times

BAGHDAD, Iraq, Oct. 21 — The Iraqi authorities for the first time have admitted in a written declaration that they conducted research on building atomic bombs, the chief of the United Nations inspection team said here tonight.

Dimitri Perricos, the head of the seventh United Nations team to visit Iraq to supervise the disposal of Baghdad's weapons of mass destruction, said on the eve of his departure that the Iraqi authorities this week "made a declaration they had launched a research and study program on the weaponization process."

Mr. Perricos added that Baghdad had merely confirmed what a previous team discovered, "so in a way, this has been a proven thing now."

The previous team, led by David Kay, an American official of the International Atomic Energy Agency, seized large quantities of documents last month from the offices of the Iraqi atomic energy department. They showed that Iraqi scientists were actively pursuing a program to produce weapons-grade, highly enriched uranium and reprocessed plutonium for use in various nuclear weapons designs, officials said.

In addition, United Nations teams have found evidence that Iraq obtained from Western and other foreign suppliers technology to test various industrial processes that could lead to large-scale production of bomb-grade uranium by the mid-1990s.

But until this week, Iraqi officials continued to insist in their official statements that their nuclear program amounted to research into "peaceful" uses of atomic energy.

Mr. Perricos, speaking to reporters outside his hotel, said he would not discuss the contents of the Iraqi declaration, but he characterized its significance by saying, "It was the first time that they themselves admitted that they had research and studies launched into a program of what they say we call weaponization and what they say they call just research."

Referring to the Iraqis, Mr. Perricos said, "They, of course, insist that the whole program that they had was intended only to have them ready in case a political decision was taken" to go forward with a bomb program.

This formulation by the Iraqis may be an attempt to shield President Saddam Hussein and his Government from a charge of violating the Nuclear Nonproliferation Treaty of 1968, which the international agency is charged with enforcing. Iraq signed the treaty and thus forswore the development of nuclear weapons. It also agreed to open all of its nuclear installations to international inspection.

During this year's inspections, by United Nations teams searching for secret nuclear research laboratories and equipment, Iraqi press organizations have attacked the United Nations for applying a double standard to Iraq by failing to insist that Israel sign the nonproliferation treaty and open its nuclear weapons centers to international inspection.

Mr. Perricos declined to say when the next nuclear inspection team would arrive in Baghdad, but another United Nations official said Mr. Perricos would head the next team on Nov. 10. Another United Nations team will be responsible for disposing chemical weapons still here. A team of ballistics experts left last week after identifying and destroying a number of Scud missile sites.

The United Nations official added that Mr. Kay, whose inspection mission last month escalated into a four-day standoff with the Iraqi authorities in a Baghdad parking lot, had resigned his post at the International Atomic Energy Agency, which is based in Vienna, to take a new and unspecified job.

Mr. Perricos and his team arrived on Oct. 12 and conducted some "short-notice" inspections of weapons installations using German helicopters and crews. He said the team had destroyed some centrifuge equipment, which is used for enriching uranium, and some reprocessing equipment, which is used to separate usable uranium and plutonium isotopes for weapons production.

He also said the team was still in the midst of a "painstaking" collection and measuring process to catalogue and remove all of the nuclear fuel that had been purchased by Iraq.

#UNW-3447
첨부

2-1

U.N. Officials Are Asking How Iraq Imports Food Without Selling Off Oil

By Trevor Rowe
Special to The Washington Post

UNITED NATIONS, Oct. 21— U.N. officials say they are puzzled that Iraq has not found it necessary to sell oil or sought to use previously frozen funds to purchase food and medical supplies many predicted would be in "critical" need.

Instead, a senior U.N. official said, Iraq has requested and been given approval by the Security Council's sanctions committee to import "several million tons of food" without indicating where Baghdad got the funds to pay for it.

"We don't know how Iraq financed the import of food until now. Maybe he [President Saddam Hussein] has hidden assets," the U.N. official said. The United Nations did grant permission to import the food, the official added, but it does not know how much already has been delivered to Iraq.

Food and medical supplies are exempt under U.N. economic sanctions against Iraq, and Baghdad is not required to indicate how it intends to pay for those imports.

A Western diplomat said Iraq is believed to have imported up to 2 million tons of food in recent months. All of the food was part of new orders and unrelated to shipments contracted before the Persian Gulf War, he said, adding, "Where did they get the money?"

U.N. officials, including Secretary General Javier Perez de Cuellar, have repeatedly warned of serious food shortages and near-famine conditions in Iraq.

In response to this and warnings from humanitarian groups, the U.N. Security Council on Sept. 19 authorized Iraq to sell up to $1.6 billion in oil to buy medical supplies and food. About $900 million of this amount is slated for food and the rest is to pay for U.N. administration expenses and for a fund to compensate those who suffered as a result of Iraq's invasion of Kuwait.

However, Iraq has not sold its oil and argues that a U.N. mechanism set up to monitor oil sales and food distribution violates its sovereignty. "Iraqis will eat the earth rather than accept this, you can quote me," an Iraqi diplomat said.

U.N. sources said Iraq also has refused so far to make use of an estimated $340 million that had been frozen in the Bank for International Settlements.

The official said a number of countries and relief organizations have provided humanitarian aid to Iraq and helped to offset its food needs. He also said that overland shipments of oil products to Jordan were another source of money. But he said this accounted for only a small portion of the food imported so far.

The Iraqi denied his government had any "secret" source of money. He said the food imports were paid by the country's private sector. But a Western diplomat said, "This is far too big. It has to be government money, and it suggests they have plenty of hard currency around."

When asked where Iraq would get the money, the diplomat said, "Presumably their gold holdings, since they never told us the amount of their reserves."

The U.N. official said press reports and those sent by U.N. relief officials indicate that while "the food situation keeps slowly deteriorating," there are "no reports" of famine. "Market prices are soaring and rations are low, and we're surprised Iraq is not using its authorization to export oil."

Further delaying any possible petroleum exports is the fact that Iraq has yet to reach agreement with Turkey on use of Ankara's oil pipeline. But it is still unclear, even if that agreement is reached, that Baghdad will proceed to sell oil.

"Either this is a political ploy, or Iraq has other resources," said the U.N. official.

2 - 2

0058

관리
번호 91-1794

외 무 부

종 별 :

번 호 : UNW-3461   일 시 : 91 1023 1600

수 신 : 장관 (연일,중동일,국기,기정)

발 신 : 주 유엔 대사

제 목 : 안보리 (이락 대량살상무기 폐기문제)

1. 안보리는 10.23. 비공식 협의를 갖고 유엔 이락 대량살상무기 폐기특위 (UNSCOM) R.EKEUS 의장으로 부터 동인 이락방문 결과보고를 청취한후 당관 원참사관이 관련 대표부들로 부터 탐문한 동보고요지를 아래 보고함.

가. 이락당국은 특위 사찰반의 구성 및 사찰활동 과정에서 입수한 내용이 개별 정부에 유출되는 문제를 제기 (미국출신 반원 편중, 미국에 대한 제보사례를 거론하는 것으로 이해)

나. 특위 헬기사용 문제에 대해서는 이락측은 특위가 언제까지 헬기를 사용할 계획인지에 관심 표시

다. 유엔측 헬기가 이스라엘 군용기와 함께 이락상공을 비행하는 경우 유엔헬기 및 승무원의 안전을 책임질수 없다는 이락측 주장에 대해 EKEUS 의장은 본건 안전문제는 어느경우에나 이락측 책임임을 재강조 (J.PEREZ DE CUELLAR 사무총장도 같은입장을 이락당국에 통보한바 있음)

라. 이락 당국은 자국의 대량살상무기 개발계획 (수십억불 부입) 추진사실을 최초로 시인 (정책대안 예비를 위해 추진되어 왔다고 주장)

마. 이락측은 안보리 휴전결의 테두리 안에서 자위목적의 재래식 군사력은 계속 유지할 계획이라고 언급

2. 또한 금일 안보리 보고시 EKEUS 의장은 이락 대량살상무기 폐기 세부추진 문제와 관련 H.BLIX IAEA 사무총장과 계속 협의할 계획이며, 현지에서 파괴하는 것을 원칙으로 하되 핵연료와 같은 품목들은 수거조치 예정이라고 설명하였음. 동 의장은 군수, 민수 겸용 내지 다용도 품목에 대해서 이락측의 폐기면제 요청이 예상되나 여사한 요청에 대해서는 사안별로 신중히 검토하여 처리할 방침임을 언급함. (엄격한 기준 적용 시사) 전반적인 폐기작업 진도에 대해서 동의장은대상 파악의 단계는

국기국	장관	차관	1차보	중아국	국기국	외정실	분석관	정와대
안기부								

마무리 중이며, 특히 미사일 분야를 비롯하여 폐기실시 단계에서 큰진전이 이루어지고
있다고 평가하였음.

   3. 금일 협의시 특위의장 보고에 대하여 미.영. 소.불 은 특위측의 제반 관련
노력에 지지입장을 언급하였으며 특히 불란서는 이락의 대량살상무기 개발계획
시인내용 명세를 서면으로 정리해 줄것을 요망하였음. 반면 예멘은 지난 주말NYT 지에
보도될 이스라엘 핵무기개발 현황에 대해 우려를 언급하였다고 함. 끝

   (대사 노창희-국장)

   예고:91.12.31. 까지

일반문서로 재분류(1991. 12. 31 처)

PAGE 2

0060

대이라크 핵사찰 관련 IAEA 사무국장의 UN 사무총장앞 서한 및 관련 결의내용

91.10.17.   국제기구과

1. **IAEA 사무국장의 UN 사무총장 앞 서한 (91.9.27) 내용**

   o 91.9.12. **IAEA 이사회**는 91.7.18. 동 이사회가 채택한 이라크의 안전조치
     협정 의무이행촉구 결의(GOV/2532)사항을 재확인하면서, 동 내용을 **IAEA
     사무국장이 IAEA 헌장 12조에 의거 유엔 사무총장에게 보고할 것을 요청**
     - IAEA 헌장(12조 C호)와 유엔과 IAEA 관계에 관한 협정(16조)에 의하면 IAEA
       이사회는 안전조치 의무 불이행 내용을 유엔 안보리와 총회에 보고하도록
       되어 있음.
   o 또한 91.9.20. 제35차 IAEA 총회는 이라크의 안전조치의무 불이행 문제를
     총회 결의(GC(XXXV)/RES/995)로 채택하고, 동 내용을 유엔 사무총장에게
     보고토록 요청한 바 있음
   o 상기 의거 IAEA의 이라크 핵사찰 관련 조치 (결의채택)내용을 유엔안보리와 총회에 보고

2. **대이라크 핵사찰 관련 IAEA와 유엔 안보리 결의 내용**

   가. **IAEA 결의**

      1) **IAEA 이사회 결의** (91.7.18, GOV/2532)

         o 유엔 안보리 결의(687호, 91.4.3.)에 따라 이라크측이 제출한 핵물질
           관련 정보가 불충분하고, 3차에 걸친 핵사찰 결과 **이라크측이 관련
           정보를 계속 은폐**하고 있다고 IAEA 사무국장이 보고(GOV/2530)

         o 동 보고 내용에 따라 IAEA는 특별이사회를 소집, 아래 내용의 결의
           채택

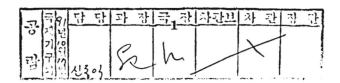

- 이라크 정부의 안전조치 협정의무 불이행 규탄

- 이라크 영토내 모든 핵물질을 IAEA 안전조치 감시하에 둘것을 촉구

- IAEA 사찰반의 활동을 간섭하는 행동을 중지할 것

- 동 내용을 IAEA 헌장 12조에 따라 유엔 안보리와 총회에 보고할 것

2) <u>IAEA 총회 결의</u> (91.9.20, GC(XXXV)/995)

o 상기 IAEA 7월 특별이사회 결의와 IAEA 이사회의 IAEA 총회 보고내용
에 따라 이라크의 안전조치협정 의무 불이행을 강력히 규탄하며,
이라크의 즉각적이고, 완전한 의무 이행을 촉구

o <u>IAEA 사무국장</u> 에게 이러한 IAEA 총회의 입장을 <u>유엔 사무총장에게</u>
<u>보고할 것을 요청</u> 함

나. 유엔 안보리 결의

1) 안보리 결의 687호(91.4.3, S/RES/687)

o 이라크의 핵, 생. 화학무기 및 미사일 파괴, 제거 확인 및 현장사찰
을 위한 <u>특별위원회(Special Commission)설치</u> 결정

o <u>이라크</u> 는 핵무기 사용물질, 개발시설 및 연구활동 관련 정보를
안보리결의(687호) 채택후 15일내 안보리와 IAEA에 제출, 모든 핵
물질과 시설을 특별위원회와 IAEA 감시하에 두고 <u>긴급현장사찰</u>
<u>(urgent on-site inspection)을 수락</u> 할 것

o <u>IAEA 사무국장</u> 에게 특별위원회의 도움을 받아 이라크가 신고한 핵
시설과 특별 위원회가 추가 지정한 장소에 대해 <u>즉각적인 현장사찰</u>
<u>(immediate on-site inspection)을 실시</u> 할 것과 <u>45일 이내</u>에 이라크
내 상기 <u>핵시설을 파괴</u> , 제거하기 위한 <u>계획서를 안보리에 제출</u> 할
것을 요청

o 또한 IAEA 사무국장에게 상기 계획서의 안보리 승인후 <u>45일 이내</u>
<u>동 계획을 이행</u> 하고, <u>향후 이라크가</u> 핵시설과 물질을 IAEA 안전조치

- 2 -

0062

하에 두고 IAEA의 검증과 사찰을 계속 받을 수 있도록 계획을 수립 할 것을 요청

2) 안보리 결의 707호 (91.8.15, S/RES/707)

o 이라크가 계속 안보리 및 IAEA 이사회의 결의를 이행하지 않고, 제4차 핵사찰 결과, 핵농축 및 재처리 시설을 포함한 이라크의 비밀 핵개발 계획이 밝혀 지자, 안보리는 대이라크 규탄 결의 채택

o 안보리 결의 707호 내용

- 이라크의 안보리 결의 687호 의무 위반 행위와 안전조치협정의무 불이행을 강력히 규탄

- 이라크 정부에 모든 핵개발 계획의 완전한 공개 와 IAEA 사찰반의 무조건적, 무제한 사찰허용 요구 (유엔 헬기의 이라크 영공 통과 허용 포함)

- 또한 안보리와 IAEA에 의해 이라크 정부가 안보리 결의와 안전조치 협정을 준수하고 있다고 판단될때까지 이라크는 의료, 농업 및 산업 목적을 제외한 모든 핵활동을 중단할 것을 요구

- 이라크는 안보리 결의 687호에 포함된 파괴 및 제거대상인 핵무기 및 시설에 대해 아무런 소유권리를 갖지 못함

3) 안보리 결의 715호 (91.10.11, S/RES/715)

o 제5,6차의 핵사찰 결과 이라크가 핵무기 개발계획하에 그간 핵농축은 물론, 핵폭발 장치, 운반장치까지 개발하고 있음이 밝혀 지자 안보리 는 대이라크 제재 결의 채택

o 안보리 결의 715호 내용

- 이라크 정부에 기존안보리 결의 내용 에 의한 의무 사항을 무조건 준수 할것과 IAEA와 안보리특위 활동에 완전히 협조할 것 을 요구

- 대 이라크 사찰 활동을 하고 있는 IAEA와 안보리특위 활동에 최대 한의 지원을 제공 함 (무기한, 무제한의 핵사찰 실시 권한 부여)

- 3 -

0063

다. IAEA의 유엔총회 연례보고서 제출

o IAEA 헌장 3조 B.4는 IAEA 활동에 관한 보고서를 매년 유엔 총회와 필요
  시 안보리에 제출하도록 되어 있음

o 이에 따라 IAEA는 매년 IAEA 년간 활동보고서를 유엔 총회에 제출, 총회
  가 결의 형식으로 동 보고서를 채택하여 왔음

o 91년 제46차 유엔 총회에서는 상기 대이라크 의무이행촉구 IAEA 총회
  결의 (GC(XXXV)/RES/995)를 IAEA 연례 보고서에 포함시켜 채택 시킬 예정

  채택결의에 언급한것을 검토중.

  끝.

- 4 -

발 신 전 보

분류번호	보존기간

번   호 : WGV-1422   911017 1854 FN   종별 : 암호송신

수   신 : 주 제네바   대사. 총영사

발   신 : 장   관 (국기)

제   목 : WHO의 대이라크 생화학무기 폐기

　　　1.　91.4.3. 유엔 안보리는 결의 687호를 채택하여 이라크의 핵, 생.화학

무기 및 미사일 파괴, 제거 확인 및 현장사찰을 위한 특별위원회를 구성하였으며

동 위원회는 현재 IAEA의 핵사찰팀과 함께 6차례의 사찰을 완료한 바 있음

　　　2.　상기 결의 의거 이라크의 생.화학무기(biological and chemical weapons)

폐기와 관련하여 WHO가 이라크에서 작업하고 있는 내용상세를 파악 보고 바람

　　　　　　　　　(World Federation of Proprietary Medicine Manufacturers)

　　　3.　한편 "세계대중약협회" 제10차 총회의 서울개최(10.16-18)를 계기로 보사부

장관 초청으로 방한(10.15-18)중인 나까지마 WHO 사무총장은 금 10.17(목) 본직을

예방한 자리에서 WHO가 작업반을 파견하여 이라크에서 생화학무기 폐기작업을 시작

하였다고 언급하였음을 첨기암　　　끝.

　　　　　　　　　　　　　(국제기구국장　문 동 석)

		보 안 통 제	윤

앙 고 재	91 년 10 월 17 일 국 기 과	기안자 성 명 (신동익)		과 장 윤		국 장		차 관	장 관 ㄴ	외신과통제

0065

"北韓 核사찰 강행해야"

유엔 이라크核조사단장 美상원서 증언

【워싱턴聯】 이라크 핵개발에 대한 유엔 조사단장인 데이비드 케인은 17일 美상원 외교위 증언에서 북한시리아등 핵무기 개발을 추구하고 있는 국가들로 핵사찰 필요가 있다고 말했다.

케인 단장은 유엔헌장7조는 安保理가 핵무기개발이 국제평화에 위협이 된다고 규정하면 국제원자력기구(IAEA)가 사찰을 시행하도록 되어 있다면서 "핵사찰이 이뤄지지 않고 있는 이유는 법적 권한이 없기 때문이 아니라 정치적 의지가 부족했기 때문"이라고 말했다.

계획이 국제 평화와 안보에 위협이 된다고 규정하면 국제원자력기구(IAEA)가 사찰을 시행하도록 되어 있다면서 "핵사찰이 이뤄지지 않고 있는 이유는 법적 권한이 없기 때문이 아니라 정치적 의지가 부족했기 때문"이라고 말했다.

케인 단장은 북한시리아등 일부 국가가 적극적으로 핵 개발을 하고 있는데 대한 핵확산방지책을 어떻게 조섭 바이든 의원의 질문에 대해 답변하면서 이같이 주장했다.

관리 번호	91- 1771

외 무 부

기
(사진요망)

종   별 :

번   호 : GVW-2072   일   시 : 91 1021 1730

수   신 : 장관(국기,정안)

발   신 : 주 제네바 대사

제   목 : WHO 의 이라크내 생.화학무기 사찰.폐기활동

대: WGV-1422

대호, 안보리 결의 687 호(91.4.3)에 의거한 유엔특별위원회(UNSCOM)의 이라크내 핵.생.화학무기 및 미사일 폐기작업과 관련, 당관이 WHO 관계관으로 부터파악한 WHO 작업반의 이라크내 활동 내용을 아래 보고함.

1. WHO 작업반의 목적 및 파견 실적

가. WHO 의 이라크내 활동목적은 유엔특별위원회의 활동중 생.화학무기 사찰지역에 대한 공공보건(PUBLIC HEALTH) 상의 위해 유무 결정과 사찰단의 보건 예방에 있음.

나. 유엔 사무총장의 요청에 따라 WHO 사무총장은 상기 지원활동을 위해 지난 5 월 4 명의 WHO 전문가로 구성된 TASK FORCE 를 구성하고, 91.6 월 부터 9 월까지 4 차례에 걸쳐 유엔특별위원회의 일원으로 동 TASK FORCE 중 1-2 명을(WHO 작업반)파견한바 있음.(상세는 첨부 1 참조)

2. WHO 작업반 활동 내용

가. 화학무기 폐기작업반

O 91.6 월 중순과 91.8 월말 두차례에 걸쳐 화학무기 시설을 사찰지역 사찰대상 지역 숫자 및 이름등 WHO 작업반의 이라크내 활동 보고내용 대부분은 상금 공개가 어렵다함.

O 상기 시설중 바그다드로 부터 북동쪽으로 80 여 KM 떨어진 MUTHANNA 라는곳에서는 수천개의 화학무기가 발견되었다 함.

O 그러나, 동 시설에 가장 가까운 마을이 20 KM 나 떨어져있으며, 이곳에는별로 인구가 없으며 바람이 별로 불지 않는 점을 감안할때 인체에 대한 위해 가능성은 없다고 판단되었다함. (동 시설 운용요원에 대한 안전 교육은 WHO 작업반이 별도 실시했다함. 상세 내용 별첨 2 참조)

국기국 정와대	장관 안기부	차관	1차보	2차보	■■■	외연원	외정실	분석관

91.10.22   07:38
외신 2과   통제관 BD

0067

O MUTHANNA 에서 발견된 화학무기는 카나다와 소련의 장비를 지원받아 빠르면 91 년말 부터 폐기작업을 시작할 계획이라함.

나. 생물무기 폐기 작업반

O 91.8 월초와 91.9 월 하순 두차례 작업반을 파견, 10 여개 시설을 사찰하였다함.

O SALAMAN PAK 등 작업반이 사찰한 지역에는 이라크가 생물무기 및 생산시설을 이미 제거 파괴한 상태였는바, 제거한 무기 및 시설등을 어디로 옮겼는지에대하여는 추후 사찰단을 파견, 조사할 계획이라함.

3. 향후 활동 계획

안보리 결의 687 호에 의한 WHO 작어반 파견은 유엔의 파견 요청을 WHO 가 수락하는 형식을 취하므로, WHO 작업반 추가 파견문제는 지금 애기할 수 없으며 UN 과 협의 추진할 문제라함.

4. 참고사항

WHO 관계관에 의하면, 상기 결의 687 호에 의거하여 유엔은 지금까지 연 442명의 19 개 사찰단을 파견하였으며 동 사찰단은 U.N, IAEA, WHO 대표외에 미국, 영국, 독일, 프랑스등 34 개국의 대표로 구성했다 함.

첨부: 1: WHO AND UN RES.687

2. UN PRESS RELEASE(IK/51/REV 1)

(GVW(F)-0433). 끝

(대사 박수길-국장)

예고:91.12.31. 까지

Note for the Record

WHO AND UN SECURITY COUNCIL, RESOLUTION 687

Under the terms of UN Security Council Resolution 687, the Secretary-General set up a UN Special Commission (UNSCOM) to oversee the destruction of Iraq's weapons of mass destruction and Iraq's capability to manufacture the same. The Directors-General of WHO and the IAEA were also requested to assist in their specialized areas.

Therefore the Director-General of WHO appointed a Task Force consisting of 4 people to support UNSCOM in its work. These are:

Dr E. Smith, Promotion of Chemical Safety, WHO Geneva (for chemical disarmament)
Dr J. Woodall, Epidemiological Surveillance and Health Situation and Trend Assessment, WHO Geneva (for biological disarmament)
Dr J. Santesson, Swedish National Defense Research Establishment (for chemical disarmament)
Dr A. Bovallius, Swedish National Defense Research Establishment (for biological disarmament).

The Director-General also nominated:

Dr A. Saghafinia of Iran as medical officer to the first chemical weapons inspection team (CW1)
Dr M. Faessler, Swiss Army Atomic and Chemical Defence Centre, as WHO representative on the second biological weapons inspection team (BW2).

Inspections

WHO representatives have taken part in the following inspections as of 18 October 1991:

1. CW1 9-15 June 1991 - Dr Santesson as chemical weapons expert
                        - Dr Saghafinia as team medical officer

2. CW3 31 August - 8 September 1991 - Dr Santesson as Chief Inspector

3. BW1 2-8 August 1991 - Dr Bovallius as Deputy Chief Inspector

4. BW2 20 September - 3 October 1991 - Dr Faessler as process engineer.

The objective of WHO participation in these inspections is to determine whether a public health hazard exists at any of the inspected sites, and to safeguard the health of the inspectors.

To these ends, WHO has arranged the supply of anthrax vaccine to the inspectors, and of syringes containing nerve gas antidotes and of other appropriate medical supplies and eqipment.

3—1

United Nations

Press Release

Department of Public Information • News Coverage Service • New York

IK/51/Rev.1*
18 September 1991

UNITED NATIONS SPECIAL COMMISSION CONDUCTS THIRD INSPECTION
OF IRAQI CHEMICAL WEAPONS

A 26-member United Nations inspection team, headed by Dr. Johan Santesson of the World Health Organization (WHO), inspected chemical weapons sites declared by Iraq, as well as other sites, from 31 August to 9 September. The inspection report was submitted to the Executive Chairman of the United Nations Special Commission, Rolf Ekeus, last Friday.

The team visited three sites declared by Iraq as storage sites for chemical weapons, as well as five other sites or sub-sites not declared but considered by the Special Commission to be of possible interest in this connection.

The condition of the various munitions was examined. Samples were taken of the contents, which will be analyzed in Finland, Germany, Sweden, Switzerland and the United Kingdom.

The team inspected chemical warheads for the Al Hussein ballistic missile that were stored close to the main road between Baghdad and Samarra. Some of the warheads were filled with a nerve agent, and others with a starting material for the generation of a nerve agent. The warheads will be transported to the Muthanna State Establishment, near Samarra, for destruction.

The inspectors also viewed mustard-agent-filled bombs of two sizes that were stored at an airfield at Al Bakr. Some of the bombs had ruptured due to excess internal pressure and had released the mustard agent content. The area downwind of the storage site is not populated, thus the public was not at risk. Before the bombs can be transported, they must be vented to release the excess pressure.

(more)

---

* Revised to indicate in the headline that this was the _third_ inspection team; the fourth team completed its inspection of Iraq's chemical weapon capabilities earlier.

4413P

0070

~ 2 ~   Press Release IK/51/Rev.1
18 September 1991

Approximately 6,400 artillery projectiles filled with mustard agent were stored in the open at a chemical proving ground near Fallujah. The projectiles were in good condition and will be transported to the Muthanna State Establishment for destruction.

No undeclared filled chemical weapons were found by the inspection team. However, at one installation, about 6,000 undeclared containers for chemical warfare agents to be used in 122-millimetre rockets were found, and at another installation considerable quantities of tear gas munitions and devices were discovered, said by Iraq to be intended for training purposes.

* *** *

4413P

3 — 3

0071

외 무 부

종 별 :

번 호 : UNW-3447   일 시 : 91 1022 1900

수 신 : 장 관(연일,중동일,국기,기정)

발 신 : 주 유엔대사

제 목 : 안보리(걸프사태)

1. 유엔 이락 대량살상무기 폐기특위(UNSCOM)는 10.21-23 간 당지에서 R.EKEUS 의장주재로 제2차 본회의를 개최중인 바, 10.21에는 H.BLIX IAEA사무총장 보고도 청취하였으며, 작년 설립이래의 작업결과 점검이 금번회의의 주 목적이라고 함.

2. 한편 R.EKEUS 의장은 최근 이락방문 결과에 관해 10.23 안보리 비공식협의시 보고 예정이라고 하는 바, 관련사항 추보위계임.

첨부: NYT,WP 기사: UNW(F)-698 끝

(대사 노창회-국장)

국기국	1차보	중아국	국기국	외정실	분석관	청와대	안기부

UNW(FR)-698 11022 1900
(연일·중동일·국가·기점) 총2매

U.N. Says Iraq Admits Research on Atomic Bombs

By PATRICK E. TYLER
Special to The New York Times

BAGHDAD, Iraq, Oct. 21 — The Iraqi authorities for the first time have admitted in a written declaration that they conducted research on building atomic bombs, the chief of the United Nations inspection team said here tonight.

Dimitri Perricos, the head of the seventh United Nations team to visit Iraq to supervise the disposal of Baghdad's weapons of mass destruction, said on the eve of his departure that the Iraqi authorities this week "made a declaration they had launched a research and study program on the weaponization process."

Mr. Perricos added that Baghdad had merely confirmed what a previous team discovered, "so in a way, this has been a proven thing now."

The previous team, led by David Kay, an American official of the International Atomic Energy Agency, seized large quantities of documents last month from the offices of the Iraqi atomic energy department. They showed that Iraqi scientists were actively pursuing a program to produce weapons-grade, highly enriched uranium and reprocessed plutonium for use in various nuclear weapons designs, officials said.

In addition, United Nations teams have found evidence that Iraq obtained from Western and other foreign suppliers technology to test various industrial processes that could lead to large-scale production of bomb-grade uranium by the mid-1990s.

But until this week, Iraqi officials continued to insist in their official statements that their nuclear program amounted to research into "peaceful" uses of atomic energy.

Mr. Perricos, speaking to reporters outside his hotel, said he would not discuss the contents of the Iraqi declaration, but he characterized its significance by saying, "It was the first time that they themselves admitted that they had research and studies launched into a program of what they say we call weaponization and what they say they call just research."

Referring to the Iraqis, Mr. Perricos said, "They, of course, insist that the whole program that they had was intended only to have them ready in case a political decision was taken" to go forward with a bomb program.

This formulation by the Iraqis may be an attempt to shield President Saddam Hussein and his Government from a charge of violating the Nuclear Nonproliferation Treaty of 1968, which the international agency is charged with enforcing. Iraq signed the treaty and thus forswore the development of nuclear weapons. It also agreed to open all of its nuclear installations to international inspection.

During this year's inspections by United Nations teams searching for secret nuclear research laboratories and equipment, Iraqi press organizations have attacked the United Nations for applying a double standard to Iraq by failing to insist that Israel sign the nonproliferation treaty and open its nuclear weapons centers to international inspection.

Mr. Perricos declined to say when the next nuclear inspection team would arrive in Baghdad, but another United Nations official said Mr. Perricos would head the next team on Nov. 10. Another United Nations team will be responsible for disposing chemical weapons still here. A team of ballistics experts left last week after identifying and destroying a number of Scud missile sites.

The United Nations official added that Mr. Kay, whose inspection mission last month escalated into a four-day standoff with the Iraqi authorities in a Baghdad parking lot, had resigned his post at the International Atomic Energy Agency, which is based in Vienna, to take a new and unspecified job.

Mr. Perricos and his team arrived on Oct. 12 and conducted some "short-notice" inspections of weapons installations using German helicopters and crews. He said the team had destroyed some centrifuge equipment, which is used for enriching uranium, and some reprocessing equipment, which is used to separate usable uranium and plutonium isotopes for weapons production.

He also said the team was still in the midst of a "painstaking" collection and measuring process to catalogue and remove all of the nuclear fuel that had been purchased by Iraq.

#UNW-3447
첨부
2-1

0073

U.N. Officials Are Asking How Iraq Imports Food Without Selling Off Oil

By Trevor Rowe
Special to The Washington Post

UNITED NATIONS, Oct. 21— U.N. officials say they are puzzled that Iraq has not found it necessary to sell oil or sought to use previously frozen funds to purchase food and medical supplies many predicted would be in "critical" need.

Instead, a senior U.N. official said, Iraq has requested and been given approval by the Security Council's sanctions committee to import "several million tons of food" without indicating where Baghdad got the funds to pay for it.

"We don't know how Iraq financed the import of food until now. Maybe he [President Saddam Hussein] has hidden assets," the U.N. official said. The United Nations did grant permission to import the food, the official added, but it does not know how much already has been delivered to Iraq.

Food and medical supplies are exempt under U.N. economic sanctions against Iraq, and Baghdad is not required to indicate how it intends to pay for those imports.

A Western diplomat said Iraq is believed to have imported up to 2 million tons of food in recent months. All of the food was part of new orders and unrelated to shipments contracted before the Persian Gulf War, he said, adding, "Where did they get the money?"

U.N. officials, including Secretary General Javier Perez de Cuellar, have repeatedly warned of serious food shortages and near-famine conditions in Iraq.

In response to this and warnings from humanitarian groups, the U.N. Security Council on Sept. 19 authorized Iraq to sell up to $1.6 billion in oil to buy medical supplies and food. About $900 million of this amount is slated for food and the rest is to pay for U.N. administration expenses and for a fund to compensate those who suffered as a result of Iraq's invasion of Kuwait.

However, Iraq has not sold its oil and argues that a U.N. mechanism set up to monitor oil sales and food distribution violates its sovereignty. "Iraqis will eat the earth rather than accept this, you can quote me," an Iraqi diplomat said.

U.N. sources said Iraq also has refused so far to make use of an estimated $340 million that had been frozen in the Bank for International Settlements.

The official said a number of countries and relief organizations have provided humanitarian aid to Iraq and helped to offset its food needs. He also said that overland shipments of oil products to Jordan were another source of money. But he said this accounted for only a small portion of the food imported so far.

The Iraqi denied his government had any "secret" source of money. He said the food imports were paid by the country's private sector. But a Western diplomat said, "This is far too big. It has to be government money, and it suggests they have plenty of hard currency around."

When asked where Iraq would get the money, the diplomat said, "Presumably their gold holdings, since they never told us the amount of their reserves."

The U.N. official said press reports and those sent by U.N. relief officials indicate that while "the food situation keeps slowly deteriorating," there are "no reports" of famine. "Market prices are soaring and rations are low, and we're surprised Iraq is not using its authorization to export oil."

Further delaying any possible petroleum exports is the fact that Iraq has yet to reach agreement with Turkey on use of Ankara's oil pipeline. But it is still unclear, even if that agreement is reached, that Baghdad will proceed to sell oil.

"Either this is a political ploy, or Iraq has other resources," said the U.N. official.

2—2

0074

외 무 부

종 별 :

번 호 : UNW-3501　　　　　　　　　　　일　시 : 91 1024 1900

수 신 : 장 관(연일,중동일,기정)

발 신 : 주 유엔대사

제 목 : 유엔 이락대량살상 무기 폐기특위(UNSCOM)

　　1. 표제 특위는 R.EKEUS 의장 주재로 10.21-23 간 유엔본부에서 비공개 회의를 개최한 바, 금번회의에서는 지난 6개월간의 특위 작업결과를 점검하는 한편, 향후 이락의 안보리 휴전결의 이행검증에 관련된 세부사항들을 토의하였다고 함.

　　2. EKEUS 의장은 유엔사무총장을 통해 안보리에 특위보고서를 제출예정이라고 함.

　　첨부:유엔측 보도자료: UNW(F)-717 끝

　　(대사 노창희-국장)

국기국	1차보	중아국	외정실	분석관	청와대	안기부

PAGE 1　　　　　　　　　　　　　　　　　　　　　91.10.25　　09:45 WH

　　　　　　　　　　　　　　　　　　　　　　　　　외신 1과 롱제관

　　　　　　　　　　　　　　　　　　　　　　　　　　　0075

UNSC(FP)-717 11:02 +9:00
(연밀·추둥멀·기겨)   총 204

PRESS RELEASE

SPECIAL COMMISSION HOLDS PLENARY SESSION 21-23 October

24 OCTOBER 1991

The Special Commission established by the Secretary-General in April to implement the requirements of section C of Security Council Resolution 687 (1991) met in closed session from 21 to 23 October.

The Special Commission discussed the progress achieved in the past six months towards the implementation of the requirement of section C of SCR 687 (1991) to destroy, remove or render harmless Iraq's weapons of mass destruction.

The Executive Chairman, Rolf Ekéus, reported that, together with the IAEA which has the lead responsibility for nuclear issues, the Special Commission has fielded 20 inspection teams, involving almost 300 individuals from 34 countries.

The progress on nuclear aspects has been reported in a number of documents presented to the Security Council by the Director-General of the IAEA.

On chemical weapons, it has been established that there are some 46,000 filled CW munitions, 79,000 unfilled CW munitions, over 600 tonnes of CW agents and some 3,000 tons of chemical precursors to be destroyed.

The destruction of ballistic missiles and related equipment has included 62 ballistic missiles, 18 fixed missile launch pads, 10 launchers, 11 dummy missiles, 32 ballistic missile warheads, 127 missiles storage support vehicles and a substantial amount of rocket fuel. Separately, an assembled 350 mm supergun has been rendered harmless, together with components for 350 and 1,000 mm superguns and one tonne of supergun propellant.

In the area of biological weapon capabilities, over 11 sites have been inspected. Conclusive evidence that Iraq was engaged in an advanced military biological research programme has been collected. No evidence of actual weaponization has been found but the inspections have provided a sound data base for future monitoring.

Among other matters, the Special Commission also discussed the details and implementation of the plans for future compliance submitted to and approved by the Security Council.

The Executive Chairman will shortly present a full report to the Secretary-General for presentation to the Security Council.

/...

#UNW-3501
첨부   24

2

The composition of the Special Commission is as follows:

Executive Chairman: Ambassador Rolf Ekéus (Sweden)
Deputy Executive Chairman: Dr. Robert Gallucci (USA)
Members: Mr. Paal Aas (Norway); Mr. Ken Adachi (Japan);
Mr. B.N.C. Agu (Nigeria); Mr. Andrzej Badek (Poland);
Mr. Bryan C. Barrass (United Kingdom); Mr. Peter von
Butler (Germany); Mr. Armando Caputo (Italy); Mr.
Ronald Cleminson (Canada); Mr. John Gee (Australia);
Mr. Helmut Hönig (Austria); Mr. B.A. Kuvshinnikov
(USSR); Mr. A.J.J. Ooms (the Netherlands); Ms. Marjatta
M. Rautio (Finland); Mr. Michel Saint Mleux (France);
Mr. Roberto Sanchez (Venezuela); Mr. B. Simandjuntak
(Indonesia); Mr. Miroslav Splino (Czech and Slovak
Federal Republic); Mr. Emile Vanden Bemden (Belgium);
and Mr. Yuan Renfeng (China).

#UNW-3501
전부

2-2

0077

외 무 부

종   별 :

번   호 : UNW-3538   일   시 : 91 1025

수   신 : 장 관(연일, 중동일,미일,기정)

발   신 : 주유엔대사

제   목 : 걸프사태

   표제사태관련 금 10.25 자 NYT 지 기사를 별첨송부함.

   첨부: UNW(F)-733 끝

   (대사 노창희-국장)

국기국	1차보	미주국	중아국	외정실	분석관	청와대	안기부

IRAQI OIL MINISTER REJECTS U.N. PLAN

Final Decision Not Yet Made on Exports to Cover Costs of Food and Medicine

By PATRICK E. TYLER
Special to The New York Times

BAGHDAD, Iraq, Oct. 24 — Iraq's Oil Minister said today that he had recommended that his Government reject a United Nations Security Council plan to allow the sale of $1.6 billion in Iraqi crude oil to finance the purchase of food and medicine.

The Oil Minister, Osama A. R. al-Hiti, charged in an interview that the terms laid down by the council's sanctions committee are "impractical" and "damaging" to Iraq's oil industry. He also said that the measures were an attempt by the United Nations to take away Iraq's control over its principal resource as a way to undermine President Saddam Hussein.

The sanctions committee developed the plan to allow limited oil sales to finance purchases of food and medicine while insuring that Iraq pays war reparations to Kuwait and cooperates with the destruction of its arsenal.

Mr. Hiti will not make the final decision on whether Iraq accepts the U.N. procedures, but he said there is no timetable for the Hussein Government to make the decision.

Pipeline Complications

Mr. Hiti said Iraq had made no recent attempt to determine whether its export pipeline through Turkey could be activated, although he added that Iraq is aware of reports that the pipeline could require months of cleaning after having sat idle since August 1990. He said his ministry was assured by Turkey that there were no obstacles to immediate resumption of pumping.

The United Nations procedures call for Iraq to pump crude oil to the Mediterranean terminal at Ceyhan, where United Nations personnel must approve contracts and every step of the sale and loading of oil. All proceeds would be paid into a U.N.-controlled fund to pay for closely monitored food shipments. Thirty percent will go toward reparations to Kuwait.

"The problems we will face without using this resolution are much easier than the problems we will face after using it," Mr. Hiti said. "It is like a spider web. Once you get into it, there is no end, and you will never be free from this."

Mr. Hiti said the U.N. procedures would prevent Iraq from concluding barter deals and pre-financing arrangements that were established with

lead to high pipeline costs with no assurance that further sales would be authorized.

Political Objections

Iraq's objections to the arrangements were as much political as technical, he said. "They are trying to change our Government, and it's not going to happen," he said."

Like other members of Mr. Hussein's Cabinet, Mr. Hiti expressed a strong determination to weather the tough conditions Iraq is suffering as a result of the restrictions imposed after the Persian Gulf war.

He said that after United Nations sanctions were lifted Iraq planned to nearly double its prewar production to 6 million barrels a day by 1995, a step that could require the Organization of Petroleum Exporting Countries to relinquish some quotas and markets to Iraq.

"I have put it forward to other OPEC members that Iraq reserves the right to ask for an extra quota to make up for those OPEC members who have gained from our situation," he said.

He asserted that with the lifting of sanctions, Iraq could return to exporting 1.25 million barrels per day "within a few days" and could reach its prewar export level by late 1992.

In a separate interview, Iraq's minister of industry, Amir H. al-Saadi, said that with the onset of cool weather in Iraq and with 70 percent of the country's power-consuming industries idle, his ministry would be able to provide ample electricity for some time.

But if United Nations sanctions continue into next spring with the return of searing daytime temperatures, he said

Gulf Nations Said to Be Committed to U.S. Allia:

By YOUSSEF M. IBRAHIM
Special to The New York Times

RIYADH, Saudi Arabia, Oct. 22 — Saudi Arabia and its allies on the Arabian Peninsula have emerged from the year-long Persian Gulf crisis persuaded that their security in the foreseeable future depends on closer military ties to the United States and a significant expansion in the size and armaments of their own military forces, senior Arab officials say.

These officials acknowledged that the elements of a broad security pact that will institutionalize these convictions are still being discussed with the United States, France and Britain, but they disputed reports in the United States that the Saudi Government has been dragging its feet in wrapping up an accord.

More than a dozen officials who discussed these plans here and in Bahrain said that the Saudis were firmly committed to a major component of the plan, a program to more than double the size of their armed forces to about 200,000 over the next five to seven years. One official said the intention was to "raise the threshold under which Saudi Arabia will call for help," as it did after the Iraqi invasion of Kuwait in August 1990.

More modest military buildups are planned for the other members of the Saudi-led Gulf Cooperation Council — a regional alliance that includes Kuwait, Oman, the United Arab Emirates, Bahrain and Qatar. The smaller countries will also make storage places available to position heavy American and perhaps European war materiel.

The officials said that the so-called "forward element" of the United States Central Command, now based in Tampa, Fla., will be stationed either in Oman or in the United Arab Emirates. Earlier reports had suggested that Bahrain, where there is now a small American naval service installation, was the primary candidate for this function.

Sensitivity on Foreign Troops

Foreign and Saudi officials said the United States had shown understanding for Saudi Arabia's wish not to have any large number of foreign troops on its soil, given the sensitivity of this issue among large segments of the Saudi population.

"The Saudis don't want any foreign troops stationed here, be they Arabs or non-Arabs," said a senior Gulf diplomat who has participated in negotiations on what he described as a "long-term security plan" for the Gulf region.

But the Saudi Government has denied recent reports that the Saudis had refused to accept additional American forces here to prepare for further military action against Iraq, should that be deemed necessary.

"Everything that is needed to undertake such action is in place," a senior envoy here said.

stone of their security, and indeed the security of all G.C.C. members."

Some United States officials in Washington have been described in recent press reports published as disturbed by the pace of negotiations with the Saudis and suggested that a dispute had arisen over the storage here of American military hardware. These reports also suggested that the United States has resisted Saudi requests for the purchase of weapons for an expanded Saudi Army.

But officials here, including Western as well as Arab diplomats, said these accounts were the product of what one senior envoy described as "narrowly focused" Pentagon views that failed to take into account wider considerations.

Several of those interviewed insisted that the United States and Saudi Arabia,

Stronger local defenses and firm ties to the West.

which are the principal parties in the talks, were agreed on the broad outlines of the security plan.

The official said that the still-evolving plan consists of three elements. One is that the six Gulf Cooperation Council countries will strengthen their defenses. This will be supplemented by agreements on the prepositioning of equipment and military cooperation between the six Gulf countries and the United States, France and possibly Britain. Finally the accords will be supplemented with a security agreement between the Gulf alliance and Egypt and Syria, which might be called upon to contribute "a symbolic" military persence in Kuwait.

Kuwait has already announced an agreement to station American troops and equipment there. The United Arab Emirates and Oman are formulating similar agreements. But the program to strenghten Gulf defenses will focus on Saudi Arabia, by far the largest country in the alliance.

A participant in strategy talks this summer between senior Saudi and United States military officials said it was decided "that they need the sort of defense that was established here by the Desert Shield operation which involved some 200,000 troops that can convincingly deter or stop an attacker, at least until help arrives."

One senior Arab official said that Saudi Arabia always assumed that it did not have the kind of enemies against whom it might have to marshal large numbers of troops. That, he said, is why it has always concentrated on having a strong air force but not a

The official said this Saudi thinking has now fundamentally changed. He said that while "Saudi Arabia agreed with the United States assessment" that it needed a force equivalent to the Desert Shield force within Saudi Arabia, such a force had to be Saudi and under total Saudi control.

'Confluence of Events'

The reason, he stressed, is that the "confluence of events" that resulted in the sending of American troops to Saudi Arabia may not be repeated.

"I am not sure," he said, "what would have happened, for instance, if Dukakis were the President of the United States. Would he have sent American forces here? Could we gamble on that?"

The officials, virtually all of whom spoke on condition that they not be identified, said that while the Saudi Air Force acquitted itself well in the Gulf war, the performance of the 38,000-man Saudi Army pointed to the need for a vast expansion in its size.

It was concluded that a military reserve system should be established, and that the Saudi National Guard, a 25,000-man force now largely charged with functions related to internal security, should be doubled or tripled. Similarly, the Saudi navy of 10,000 will have to expand to more effectively patrol both the Persian Gulf and the Red Sea.

Altogether the officials agreed that the Saudi forces should be increased over the next five to seven years to about 200,000, from the present total of about 90,000.

System of Recruitment

Saudi officials said they did not expect major difficulties in increasing their military recruitment, which has been based on quotas assigned to the country's various Bedouin tribes. Officials said that the system tended to exclude the country's rapidly growing urban population, and that tapping this group would yield the needed recruits.

Bigger problems were seen in raising the money to pay for the expansion. The senior diplomat estimated that the Saudis spent $65 billion during the Gulf crisis, and that they need time to find way to generate new funds as they have, by all accounts, nearly exhausted their once fabulous reserves which had reached a high of $80 billion in the late seventies.

"For the United States," a diplomat here explained, "the war was brief, inexpensive, perhaps even profitable. It has unified the American people and restored the prestige of the United States military. Here, the war was very ... deeply divisive particularly

0080

외 무 부

종 별 :

번 호 : UNW-3621

일 시 : 91 1031 2130

수 신 : 장 관(중동일,중동이,연일,기정)

발 신 : 주 유엔 대사

제 목 : 중동문제

1. 이스라엘은 지난 10.19-22 간 테헤란에서 개최된 '펠레스타인 인민의 회교혁명지원 을 위한 국제회의' 에서 H.RAFSANJANI 이란 대통령이 이스라엘에 대한 파병용의를 언급하였으며 KHAMENEI 지도자도 동회의개최에 앞서 이스라엘에 대한 성전(JIHAD)을 호소한바, 이는 이란측의 명백한 헌장위반행위 (무력사용 또는 사용위협금지)라고 주장하는 요지의 10.29 자유엔 사무총장앞 서한을 총회및 안보리문서로 배포하였음(A/46/605, S/23176)

2. 한편 유엔측은 91.9.20-10.30 간 제2차 이락생물무기 사찰결과를 금 10.21 발표한바, 동발표 내용을 별첨 송부함.

첨부:유엔이락 생물무기 사찰결과 발표 및 NYT지 기사: UNW(F)-757 끝

(대사 노창희-국장)

중아국	1차보	중아국	국기국	외정실	분석관	정와대	안기부	안기부

PAGE 1

91.11.01   13:12 WI

외신 1과 통제관

0081

Secon IN Biological Weapons Inspection Team
Concludes Mission to Ir

(delayed in transmission)

31 October 1991

In a second biological weapons inspection mission to Iraq, a team of United Nations experts did not find any biological weapons or facilities for filling weapons, but concluded that Iraq's research programme on biological agents for military purposes logically, would have included a plan for weapons development and production, possibly at a site not yet identified.

The small multinational team, led by Chief Inspector David Huxsoll (US), visited 10 different sites from 20 September to 3 October, four of them without advance notice. The sites, some of which had not been previously declared by Iraq, included vaccine production facilities, a pharmaceutical plant, research and development laboratories with fermentation capabilities and specially designed facilities for work with hazardous human and animal disease-causing agents.

Iraq had initially declared that it did not have a biological weapons programme. However, during the first UN inspection from 3 to 7 August, Iraqi authorities admitted to inspectors the existence of a research programme on biological agents for military purposes which was carried out at the Centre for Technical Research at Salman Pak, south of Baghdad. The Iraqis claimed that the research at that site was on a small scale, was limited to three agents, and that no other research sites existed. They further stated that they had since ceased all such activities and had never weaponized biological agents.

While the UN inspectors did not find evidence to directly contradict these claims, they identified a number of sites for which they would recommend future monitoring because of concern over dual-use. One of these, a facility at Al Hakam, located 45 kilometers southwest of Baghdad, consisted of an embryonic fermentation plant designated for development and production of single-cell protein, used primarily in animal feeds. Because of a potential link between this research and a biological weapons programme, the team recommended that the United Nations carry out on-going monitoring of activity at the site and prohibit the use of any human or animal pathogens there.

The team also concluded that three vaccine production facilities inspected had the capacity to produce sufficient quantities of biological agents to meet weapons requirements and that these too should be covered by the future compliance monitoring regime.

The inspection missions are organized by the United Nations Special Commission established to carry out the disarmament provisions of the cease-fire resolution between Iraq and Kuwait. Further biological weapons inspections are planned.

fg4-62   #UNW-3621

4-1

0082

How Sweet A Victory?

Bush Sees the War As Aid to His Goals

By R. W. APPLE Jr.
Special to The New York Times

MADRID, Oct. 30 — Many months after the event, George Bush and the United States today plucked the fruits of victory in the Persian Gulf war, but it is still much too early to predict how sweet they will prove to be.

Critics have suggested that the United States achieved far too little in the war, because Saddam Hussein was not overthrown, Iran remained as hostile and Kuwait as undemocratic as ever, and Saudi Arabia shed neither its isolation nor its archaic ways. Iraq was thrown out of Kuwait, some said, but very little else changed.

News Analysis

This morning it was clear that a very great deal had changed, even if most things remained shrouded in ambiguity and doubt as deep as the smog that blanketed Madrid. It was not only the energy and the diplomatic skills of Secretary of State James A. Baker 3d that created the remarkable tableau, with mortal enemies arranged around the same table, that Mr. Bush saw before him in the splendid Royal Palace this morning; all of his labors would have counted for very little without seismic shifts in the global order of things.

The Domestic Issue

So far, so good. But taking the next enormous steps toward lasting peace in the Middle East may require the deep personal involvement of Mr. Bush over many months, and that may lie beyond his domestic political reach.

Dramatic and momentous as the peace conference seems to Arabs and Israelis, as well as American Jews and Arab-Americans and foreign policy specialists all over the world, it seems distant to average Americans, an event unlikely to influence their own well-being directly. So Mr. Bush's undoubted triumph in bringing the talks into being may not earn him commensurate gains at home.

The situation is profoundly different from that which used to confront American policy makers and American voters as they looked toward the Middle East. No longer is there a threat that an Arab-Israeli conflict could escalate into a nuclear war between the United States and the Soviet Union. Though American politicians are not so impolitic as to say so, Israel is therefore much less of a strategic asset to the West than it used to be.

No longer is there an imminent threat of an oil embargo, with dire consequences for the world economy. Only the plight of the remaining American hostages touches most Americans deeply, and their number is slowly shrinking.

To many policy makers, the catastrophic situation in the Soviet Union, of which President Mikhail S. Gorbachev spoke so candidly today, and the emerging shape of Eastern and Western Europe, seem deserving of higher priority. To many voters — most of them, according to recent opinion polls — Mr. Bush seems far too inattentive to domestic economic problems.

As if to emphasize his intention to mind the store, he climbed back aboard Air Force One for the trip home without even waiting for the end of the first day's speeches here.

Facing a re-election campaign that will in a sense begin at a big Bush-Quayle fund-raiser in Texas later this week, faced with the growing conviction in the electorate that he spends too much time on foreign policy already, faced with growing evidence that further economic woes may lie ahead rather than the robust recovery he had hoped for, the President is seriously considering the curtailment of his trip to Asia and the Pacific next month.

From that perspective, it seems doubtful that Mr. Bush will want to put the Middle East at the top of his agenda, at least until next November has passed, in the way that Jimmy Carter focused intently on the peace process between Israel and Egypt in 1977 and 1978. And without sustained Presidential intervention, a decisive breakthrough in these talks may prove elusive.

Cold War Symbols

The end of the cold war was symbolized by the presence here of Mr. Gorbachev as a co-sponsor. The conflict between the Arabs and the Israelis, the Soviet leader acknowledged, "bears the heavy stamp of the so-called cold war, and it was not until an end was put to that, that ending this conflict became a tangible possibility."

But the United States won the cold war as well as the gulf war, so it was President Bush, and not Mr. Gorbachev, who spoke first today and who set out the general terms within which the peace talks will proceed.

The Soviet Union is no longer the protector of Syria, any more than it was the protector of Iraq. The United States is the only credible outside power in the region. The gulf war also changed the internal military balance, not only by removing Iraq from the equation, at least for the moment, but also by demonstrating that high-tech American weapons, more available to Israel than to the Arabs, again at least for the moment, were the future of warfare.

So Syria is here, and the Palestinians and the Jordanians — and because they are here, the Israelis did not feel

4-2

that they could stay away without suffering further erosion in their relations with Washington.

Saudi as an Observer

The Bush Administration was even able, in the end, to deliver Saudi Arabia to Madrid, with Prince Bandar bin Sultan, the Saudi Ambassador to Washington, flamboyantly garbed in the white robe of the desert, slipping into an observer's chair at the last moment. There could have been few more arresting demonstrations of his country's rapidly evolving regional role.

Mr. Bush sought to strike a balance in his address by endorsing the Arabs' demand for territorial concessions from Israel and at the same time defining "peace" in terms that delighted the Israelis. But the United States will have to play a less even-handed role than those comments implied if the conference is to succeed.

As Michael Mandelbaum of the Council on Foreign Relations pointed out, Israel "will be asked to give up a tangible security asset" — territory that it has occupied as a buffer against its enemies — "in exchange for something that is intangible and revocable; in effect, for a promise."

Only if the United States offers assurances of various kinds to Israel, many analysts believe, will Israeli public opinion propel the hard-line government of Prime Minister Yitzhak Shamir toward genuine bargaining. The President pledged today that if necessary Washington would "extend guarantees, provide technology and support, if that is what peace requires."

'Peace Is Possible'

Mr. Baker and others are ready, once the various participants have spelled out their positions in full, and especially if they reach an early deadlock, to try to inject some new ideas into the negotiations subtly, while at the same time carefully avoiding the elaboration of settlement plans that would only turn into targets for one side or the other to shoot down.

"We want to make them do the bargaining," a high-ranking American official said, "and we think each of them is sufficiently worried about looking like villains to the rest of the world to take this seriously."

"Peace is possible," Mr. Bush said, noting that France and Germany had become allies after a hundred years of war, and that the Soviet Union stood alongside the United States as a sponsor here despite the legacy of the cold war. Prime Minister Felipe González of Spain recalled how Christians, Jews and Arabs had lived together in harmony in this country until the Moors and the Jews were driven out in the year Christopher Columbus set sail.

It is a matter of mustering the will to try, a matter of taking chances, as Robert Schuman and Jean Monnet did in seeking European unity after World War II. One thing that could help to scatter the ghosts of distrust and hatred would be some sort of gesture from one side or the other, like President Anwar el-Sadat's trip to Israel in 1977, that would help to "break the fetters of the past," in Mr. Gorbachev's phrase. But there was no sign of that from either side today.

Instead, presented by the American organizers with an opportunity to fraternize during the 30 minutes that they waited in the marble hall for Mr. Bush and Mr. Gorbachev to arrive, the Arab delegates turned their backs on the Jews, and vice versa, except for the Egyptians, who have a special status. If the very convening of the conference was a good omen, the frostiness of the participants' demeanor constituted an offsetting note of pessimism.

4-3

0084

REPORT SAYS IRAN SEEKS ATOMIC ARMS

Some U.S. Officials Fear That Teheran's Nuclear Goals Are Underestimated

By ELAINE SCIOLINO
Special to The New York Times

WASHINGTON, Oct. 30 — In the wake of revelations by United Nations inspectors about Iraq's advanced nuclear weapons program, an American intelligence assessment has concluded that at least some of Iran's revolutionary leaders are intent on developing nuclear weapons.

The brief, cautiously worded assessment, contained in a broad, classified National Intelligence Estimate on Iran that is still subject to revision, also concludes that Iran's nuclear program is disorganized and only in an initial stage of development. Some Administration officials — as well as independent arms-control analysts — say they believe that the assessment underestimates the scope of Iranian intentions.

Since Iran-Iraq war ended in 1988, Iran's revolutionary leaders have actively sought nuclear-related technology from countries like China, India, Argentina, Pakistan and Germany.

Officials say they are most concerned about Iran's nuclear cooperation with China, which was formalized in June 1990 with an agreement to develop a small research reactor in the central Iranian city of Isfahan. Since then, China has sent a number of top scientists to Iran and has trained Iranian engineers and physicists.

'A Matter of Concern'

The Administration has also learned that Iran recently received a calutron, a crude device that can be used to enrich uranium, from Beijing.

The Administration consensus is that the calutron is one typically used for peaceful purposes, not readily adaptable to enriching uranium for use in nuclear weapons, and not like the calutrons built by Iraq that were clearly designed to enrich uranium. But another official expressed concern that Iran might be able to improve on and duplicate the calutron to eventually produce the hundreds needed to enrich uranium.

When asked about the Chinese-Iranian nuclear cooperation at a Senate Foreign Relations subcommittee hearing today, Richard H. Solomon, Assistant Secretary of State for East Asian and Pacific Affairs, said, "It is apparent that there is the sale of some nuclear-related technologies. There is something going on here. We have talked to the Chinese about it and will pursue it." He added, "It is a matter of concern."

Many of the details of Administration concern were first reported by the Washington Post today.

China's Reactor Denials

The State Department over the last few years has tried to dissuade governments from cooperating with Teheran on nuclear projects, and the issue is likely to be discussed if Secretary of State James A. Baker 3d visits Beijing as is tentatively planned next month.

Earlier this month, the Chinese Foreign Ministry denied as "groundless" press reports that China was building a nuclear reactor in Iran that was part of a secret weapons program.

Washington is also concerned about what one official called Iran's "shopping around" for a much larger nuclear reactor. One Iranian press report has suggested that Iran was seeking such technology from India.

And senior Administration officials said that in the past year Iranian officials met with Mirza Aslam Beg, then Pakistan's Chief of the Staff of the Army, who agreed to share technology, a plan that was quickly vetoed by Pakistan's civilian leadership.

A Right to Arms

In recent years, several Iranian officials have spoken openly about Iran's right to possess nuclear weapons. In a speech to the Revolutionary Guards in 1988, for example, President Hashemi Rafsanjani declared: "We should fully equip ourselves both in the offensive and defensive use of chemical, bacteriological and radiological weapons. From now on you should make use of the opportunity and perform the task." At other times, Mr. Rafsanjani has called for the complete prohibition and destruction of such weapons.

In an interview with the Persian daily Abrar last week, the Deputy President, Ataollah Mohajerani, said that all Muslim countries should be allowed to develop nuclear weapons if Israel remains a nuclear power. But he went further. "Israel should be totally deprived of its nuclear capacity," he said. "I mean, what has been done to Iraq in respect of its nuclear capacity should be done exactly to Israel."

Although some Iran experts interpreted Mr. Mohajerani's remarks as little more than anti-Israeli comments fueled by the peace talks in Madrid, they were unsettling to American policymakers who have sought to portray Iran's foreign policy as pragmatic.

Iran's nuclear program was launched in the 1960's by the Shah, Mohammed Reza Pahlevi, whose $30 billion plan envisaged 20 nuclear plants by the year 2000. Iran's only working nuclear reactor is a small American-built research facility on the campus of Teheran University.

Some Administration officials question why oil-producing Iran would need nuclear reactors and are worried that Iran's large bank of nuclear scientists, many of them leftovers from the era of the Shah, would be invaluable to a nuclear arms program.

Several officials and independent experts say they think Iran's nuclear threat is more serious than is portrayed in the intelligence assessment.

"There is no doubt that Iran is pursuing nuclear, chemical and biological weapons and seeking to obtain long-range missiles from North Korea and to develop them in Iran," said Anthony Cordesman, a military expert whose conclusions are included in his 1991 book, "Weapons of Mass Destruction in the Middle East."

4-4

외 무 부

종 별 :

번 호 : UNW-3635　　　　　　　　　　　일 시 : 91 1101 1800

수 신 : 장관(중동이,중동일,미일,아이,연일,기정)

발 신 : 주유엔대사

제 목 : 중동문제

　　1. 유엔이락 대량살상무기폐기특위 (UNSCOM) R.EKEUS 의장이 지난 10.21-23 간
개최된 동특위회의에 제출한 보고서가 금 11.1. 안보리문서로 배포된바, 동보고서는
파편 송부하였음.(주국련20313-848, S/23165)

　　2. 마드리드 회의관련 금 11.1. 지 사설,해설기사및 기고문을 별첨송부함.

　첨부 FAX:UNW(F)-762:

1. 상기 NYT사설,해설기사,기고문(머피 전 미국무부 차관보),

2. NYT 기고문(중동핵문제),

3. CSM 기사(중국의무기수출동향)끝

(대사 노창희-국장)

중아국 외정실	장관 분석관	차관 청와대	1차보 안기부	2차보	아주국	미주국	중아국	국기국

UNW(FI)-762 11/01 1800
총 504

Beyond Belligerency in Madrid

Of course the old belligerents, newly gathered in Madrid, spent yesterday restating familiar grievances. More hopeful and far more interesting were the doors left open for serious diplomacy by Israeli and Palestinian leaders. Both sides spoke with a dignity and seriousness befitting a tragic conflict, qualities grievously absent in the truculent posturing of the Syrian Foreign Minister, Farouk al-Sharaa.

Without reciprocal concessions there can be no enduring peace between Israel and its Arab neighbors. This imperative message was articulated Wednesday by Presidents Bush and Gorbachev, Madrid's co-sponsors. Yet Syria yesterday offered nothing more than a boilerplate assault on Zionism and a demand for the return of "every inch" of Arab land occupied by Israel since 1967 — thus staking a position in which any compromise might seem a sellout to unprepared Syrians.

•

Prime Minister Yitzhak Shamir, especially by contrast, sounded like a statesman. He pleaded the need for dialogue and accommodation, and spoke of Israel's yearning for peace. He said nothing about territorial compromises, which he and his party oppose, but called for the achievable: an agreement on interim self-government arrangements with Palestinians in the occupied territories.

The telltale word is "interim," meaning that the final status of these lands would be determined in the future. This was the formula agreed on at Camp David in 1978 but never realized. Recall that Mr. Shamir, then Speaker of the Israeli Parliament, joined with other hard-liners in rejecting the Camp David accord that brought peace with Egypt in return for Israel giving up the Sinai.

If Mr. Shamir has changed his stance, so have the Palestinians. Haidar Abdel-Shafi, who leads their delegation at Madrid, mostly avoided the ugly clichés of 40 years of bitterness. Without recrimination he described the torments of occupation and the anguish of the powerless. Tellingly, he expressed "solemn appreciation" to Israelis who came to the aid of Palestinians whose homes were being punitively demolished.

"We have marched together," he said, "often choking together in nondiscriminatory tear gas, all crying out in pain as the clubs descended on both Palestinian and Israeli alike. ... We once formed a human chain around Jerusalem, joining hands and calling for peace. Let us today form a moral chain around Madrid and continue that noble effort for peace and the promise of freedom."

Healing words like these mean far more than Syria's effusions or the failure of some Arabs and Israelis to shake hands in novel, and awkward, circumstances. Pessimists could find plenty of harsh language to dwell on from yesterday's transfixing performances. But the spirit of Mr. Abdel-Shafi's appeal augurs more hopefully for the direct talks expected soon to follow.

#UNW-3635
첨부   5-1

0087

New Talks, Old Ideas

Perennial Enemies Revert To Form

By THOMAS L. FRIEDMAN
Special to The New York Times

MADRID, Oct. 31 — The wildly conflicting and at times even insulting speeches which Israeli and Arab delegates exchanged today in Madrid raised some doubts about the thinking behind Washington's peace strategy:

News Analysis that if the parties can just be brought together for direct talks they will begin to shed hard-line positions and define common ground.

Today, left to talk to one another on their own without the firm hand of the United States defining the agenda and terms of reference, the Syrians, Israelis, Palestinians, Jordanians and Lebanese wandered from one minefield to another.

To be sure, no one expected Arabs and Israelis today to come into the Royal Palace and suddenly drop all of their previously held positions. But neither did anyone expect them to revert to some of the crudest, most archaic and unreconstructed arguments of the Arab-Israeli disputes.

Insults and Recriminations

There were lines in the speeches of Israel's Prime Minister, Yitzhak Shamir, and Syria's Foreign Minister, Farouk al-Sharaa, that have not been heard since campus debates between Arabs and Jews in the early 1960's. Not surprisingly, the Palestinian spokeswoman, Hanan Ashrawi, dismissed elements of Mr. Shamir's speech as "racist," while Israel's Deputy Foreign Minister, Benjamin Netanyahu, accused the Arabs of engaging in "vituperation, slander and condescension."

Jordan's Foreign Minister, Kamal Abu Jaber, resurrected the old argument that the Nazis are the ones who created Israel by driving all the Jews back to Palestine. Mr. Sharaa dredged up the canard that the real story of the Arab-Israeli conflict is not known in the West because extremist Jews control how it is recorded, and Mr. Shamir dusted off the old arguments about how Palestine was basically barren and empty until the Jews came back, implying that the Palestinian Arabs have no real claim to the land.

There was not a single new offer or gesture of reconciliation. Even old offers — such as explicit Palestinian recognition of Israel's right to exist, or Israeli statements that the Golan Heights were negotiable — were edited out by the speech writers.

Implications for U.S. Strategy

Such behavior would seem to have implications for how the Bush Administration conceives its role in this process, as well as for the timetable it has set for its own direct involvement.

President Bush declared on Wednesday that the United States will only serve as a "catalyst" to promote "direct negotiations" between the parties. The President added: "It will take time — time for the parties so long at war to learn to talk to one another, to listen to one another. Time to heal old wounds and build trust. In this quest, time need not be the enemy of progress."

But such an approach flies in the face of the history of American Middle East diplomacy as well as of today's reality. Even in the case of Egypt and Israel, whose peace negotiations were preceded by a dramatic gesture of reconciliation by President Anwar Sadat of Egypt, the United States was required to come in, not to promote direct talks but to prevent them from ending up in a diplomatic explosion.

Left to themselves, Mr. Sadat and the Israeli Prime Minister, Menachem Begin, clashed politically and personally. Had the United States not intervened to force Egypt and Israel to compromise, and to pave the way for that compromise with billions of dollars in American aid, there almost certainly never would have been a Camp David peace treaty.

Israeli Conditions

Bush Administration officials know this well. Their problem was that in order to persuade Mr. Shamir to come to the conference at all, they had to accede to his demand that the American-sponsored parley only be a ceremonial opening for separate, direct negotiations between Israel and Syria, Israel and Lebanon and Israel and the joint Jordanian-Palestinian delegation.

Mr. Shamir wanted the Americans out of these separate talks because he knows that the balance of power between Israel and its Arab negotiating partners, individually or collectively, is tilted in Israel's favor. Therefore, the only thing that would make the Arabs closer to equal was if the United States came in to assert long-held American positions about what would be fair solutions between Israel and her neighbors. The United States had to agree that as part of the invitation to this peace conference it would not publicize its interpretation of United Nations Security Council Resolution 242, which calls for an Israeli military withdrawal to "secure and recognized boundaries," because the American interpretation of that resolution corresponded with the Arab view that it requires Israel to trade land for peace.

What happened today, therefore, was inevitable. The Arabs and Israelis, finally unshackled from American constraints, weighed in with all of their most hard-line demands. When the United States mediates, it keeps to itself what Arabs and Israelis say to American diplomats about each other. With Mr. Baker sitting on the sidelines today, confined to the role of master of ceremonies, each side let loose a pent-up barrage of passion, rhetoric and rage.

Optimists' Views

American and Egyptian diplomats are dismissing today's venting of anger as a necessary phase of the negotiations, an enunciation of hard-line positions to be softened later in exchange for similar compromises from the other side. They may be right. But if Anwar Sadat had come to the Israeli Parliament in 1977 and given the same talk that the Syrian Foreign Minister gave today, there almost certainly never would have been enough political support in Israel for giving the Sinai back to Egypt in return for a peace treaty.

If this process is going to have the time that President Bush says it will need to ripen, it will need a support in the United States to sustain Washington's involvement and support for compromise in the countries themselves. Maybe it will come in time. But it certainly didn't start today.

Therein lies Mr. Baker's dilemma. He does not have an Anwar Sadat to work with in Israel, Lebanon, Jordan, Syria or the occupied territories. With no one to really change popular attitudes with a single bold gesture, he is trying to produce a Sadat-like effect through gradual, direct talks between these bitter foes. But if today's session is any guide, the more these leaders talk, the more at least some of them will clash.

Yet, if Mr. Baker intervenes too soon with American ideas in shuttle diplomacy — and he has detailed peace ideas in his pocket — the Israelis will argue that he is contradicting the terms of the process and destroying any hope for direct negotiations, and with it the popular change in attitudes that are supposed to be generated. His only hope may be that Israel will soon invite him to mediate. The Arabs would have had him start today.

5-2

0088

After Madrid, Time to Dig In

By Richard W. Murphy

With the Madrid conference ending today and Arab-Israeli bilateral talks about to begin, questions about the peace process trouble Americans.

Were the parties ready for Madrid? The Arabs and Israelis probably have not fully thought out their negotiating strategies for the next stage, but it is wrong to say they went to Madrid only because we dragged them there. They went also because they are tired of decades of conflict.

Arabs and Israelis alike resent the fact that years of confrontation have slowed their economic, social and political development. Many Israelis are concerned about the occupation of the territories, its effect on their building a democratic Jewish state and on their country's image abroad. Besides, the ending of the cold war has removed the incentive for Washington and Moscow to develop strategic alliances in the region. This has forced the parties, perhaps the Arabs more than the Israelis, to rethink their overall strategies.

Might the American efforts that brought them together have created a dynamic that could end up harming regional stability?

To suggest that Madrid may have set a course for war is nonsense. Whatever the outcome of the bilateral talks, there is no prospect of another war for many years. The disaster Saddam Hussein's adventuring brought Iraq reminded the Arabs and Israelis that the world will not tolerate efforts to resolve the region's rivalries militarily. Nonetheless, the military buildup continues and with it the potential for another war. Syria's purchases of Czech tanks and North Korean missiles are well-known. We can fairly assume that Israel will work to maintain its edge in nonconventional and conventional weapons.

How much more effort should America invest in behalf of an elusive Middle Eastern peace?

The U.S. and the Soviet Union will complete their formal roles as co-chairmen when the Madrid ceremonies end. To join the bilateral negotiations, both countries must be invited; such an invitation may come soon. Moscow's mediating energies will be limited. Even though Moscow retains influence in the region because of its long cooperation with Syria and the Palestinians, its contribution to the talks may well be simply good will. The burden of guiding the talks to some measurable success will fall to the U.S.

President Bush will have amply fulfilled his pledge to try to work out Arab-Israeli differences by pushing to convene the conference and start the bilateral talks. While popular at home, he faces mounting criticism for neglecting domestic policy. He surely knows that even if he appoints a special envoy to the talks, he will have to devote a substantial amount of time to the negotiating process. Would he find it worthwhile?

The developments that made possible this opening for U.S. diplomacy — the ending of the cold war and defeat of Iraq — ironically removed any readily apparent need for Washington to pursue an elusive Arab-Israeli peace. Still, the area remains volatile, and continuation of the Arab-Israeli conflict could eventually damage our friends and economic interests.

Even if Iran is serious about its threat to liquidate Israel, this threat can be controlled. The Egyptian-Israeli peace is cold, but it is not in either party's interest to let the treaty fall apart. Saudi Arabia is secure, and Kuwait will be back in full oil production within two years.

The basic reason for our continued role as the main mediator is that we have gotten in too far to get out. We will not be able to do the whole job, but no one can substitute for us. Our withdrawal would condemn the area to deteriorating security.

Richard W. Murphy was Assistant Secretary of State for Near Eastern and South Asian Affairs in the Reagan Administration.

5-3

0089

After Madrid, Time to Dig In

By Richard W. Murphy

With the Madrid conference ending today and Arab-Israeli bilateral talks about to begin, questions about the peace process trouble Americans.

Were the parties ready for Madrid? The Arabs and Israelis probably have not fully thought out their negotiating strategies for the next stage, but it is wrong to say they went to Madrid only because we dragged them there. They went also because they are tired of decades of conflict.

Arabs and Israelis alike resent the fact that years of confrontation have slowed their economic, social and political development. Many Israelis are concerned about the occupation of the territories, its effect on their building a democratic Jewish state and on their country's image abroad. Besides, the ending of the cold war has removed the incentive for Washington and Moscow to develop strategic alliances in the region. This has forced the parties, perhaps the Arabs more than the Israelis, to rethink their overall strategies.

Might the American efforts that brought them together have created a dynamic that could end up harming regional stability?

To suggest that Madrid may have set a course for war is nonsense. Whatever the outcome of the bilateral talks, there is no prospect of another war for many years. The disaster Saddam Hussein's adventuring brought Iraq reminded the Arabs and Israelis that the world will not tolerate efforts to resolve the region's rivalries militarily. Nonetheless, the military buildup continues and with it the potential for another war. Syria's purchases of Czech tanks and North Korean missiles are well-known. We can fairly assume that Israel will work to maintain its edge in nonconventional and conventional weapons.

How much more effort should America invest in behalf of an elusive Middle Eastern peace?

The U.S. and the Soviet Union will complete their formal roles as co-chairmen when the Madrid ceremonies end. To join the bilateral negotiations, both countries must be invited; such an invitation may come soon. Moscow's mediating energies will be limited. Even though Moscow retains influence in the region because of its long cooperation with Syria and the Palestinians, its contribution to the talks may well be simply good will. The burden of guiding the talks to some measurable success will fall to the U.S.

President Bush, will have amply fulfilled his pledge to try to work out Arab-Israeli differences by pushing to convene the conference and start the bilateral talks. While popular at home, he faces mounting criticism for neglecting domestic policy. He surely knows that even if he appoints a special envoy to the talks, he will have to devote a substantial amount of time to the negotiating process. Would he find it worthwhile?

The developments that made possible this opening for U.S. diplomacy — the ending of the cold war and defeat of Iraq — ironically removed any readily apparent need for Washington to pursue an elusive Arab-Israeli peace. Still, the area remains volatile, and continuation of the Arab-Israeli conflict could eventually damage our friends and economic interests.

Even if Iran is serious about its threat to liquidate Israel, this threat can be controlled. The Egyptian-Israeli peace is cold, but it is not in either party's interest to let the treaty fall apart. Saudi Arabia is secure, and Kuwait will be back in full oil production within two years.

The basic reason for our continued role as the main mediator is that we have gotten in too far to get out. We will not be able to do the whole job, but no one can substitute for us. Our withdrawal would condemn the area to deteriorating security.

Richard W. Murphy was Assistant Secretary of State for Near Eastern and South Asian Affairs in the Reagan Administration.

5-3

We Are Warned

Once more, a choice for the U.S.

Once more we have been clearly warned, and once more we have a choice.

We can accept the plain warning of mass murder to come and act to prevent it. Or we can say again that no man could be that evil, no nation could follow his madness, he is bluffing — and do nothing.

The first choice will mean that the major nations of the world will lose a profitable business — the death trade.

The other choice will mean that peace will not come for generations to one of the most important areas of the world, perhaps never. Quite likely hundreds of thousands will die as the result of our decision.

On April 5, 1990, those were the opening paragraphs of this column. Now they must be written again.

Until the eve of the Kuwait invasion, the West ignored the threats of extermination of his enemies screamed out by Saddam Hussein, as it had Hitler's for so long. Western companies and governments went on strengthening Saddam Hussein with credits, arms and the material and technology of chemical and nuclear missiles.

Hundreds of thousands may indeed have died — this time mostly his own countrymen. Only two things kept Saddam off schedule for nuclear delivery: the 1981 Israeli attack on his reactor and, a decade later, the decision by President Bush to stop him.

After the war, U.N. inspectors found that Iraq was not 5 to 10 years from nuclear weapons, as many specialists had told us, but a year or so. Before and even during the war, the West never knew the network of nuclear plants existed.

Now come the new warnings, loud, this time from Iran. A Deputy President said last week that all Muslim countries must have nuclear weapons and that exactly what was done to Iraq's nuclear capacity must be done to Israel's. Three years ago Iran's President had already issued instructions to develop "offensive and defensive chemical, biological and radiological weapons."

Listen to these men, as we should have listened to Saddam. These are not words but plans under way. The Washington Post prints a report, later confirmed, that U.S. intelligence believes Iran is aggressively trying to develop nuclear weapons and is getting help from Communist China.

William Triplett 2d, a senior staff member of the Senate Foreign Relations Committee, whose work against proliferation deserves a medal, writes that the Chinese contributed to Iraq's nuclear strength and are now building a nuclear plant for Algeria.

And what specialists dread most is rarely mentioned publicly: a nuclear bomb-building alliance among some Muslim nations aided by Communist China and North Korea. There is suspicion that Saddam Hussein helped Algeria — to scatter his nuclear potential as he scattered his planes.

An alliance between Iraq and Iran to build joint nuclear power against Israel is feasible and logical. Iraq has lots of nuclear experts now, but too many U.N. inspectors. Iran has some capacity, Chinese aid — and no inspectors.

Now comes the point where it is difficult to avoid screaming. The U.S. has the tools to fight the death trade but will not use them.

The way to fight is to publish the 450 or more names on the U.N. list of companies that supplied material and technologies to Iraq. Then, use Presidential power to expose all companies or countries continuing in the death trade — and ban them from U.S. export and import markets.

Mr. Bush will not do it — and last year vetoed legislation to mandate such action. "Leaders" of the Democratic Party collapsed. Some senators seem determined to keep fighting — among them John Glenn, Malcolm Wallop, Jesse Helms and Claiborne Pell.

But yesterday the House passed a bill from a subcommittee headed by Sam Gejdenson, a Connecticut Democrat, supposed to extend controls on export of relevant military technologies. The small, intellectually alert Center for Security Policy of Washington (another medal due) says the bill actually guts those controls. The subcommittee is heavily lobbied by the high-technology industries. Toby Roth, a Wisconsin Republican on the subcommittee, said candidly that "increasing exports and creating jobs are really the goal of the legislation."

And so on and so on. Once more America is making a choice. □

5 - 4

Chinese Vow Tested By Leader's Visit to Biggest Arms Buyers

By James L. Tyson
Staff writer of The Christian Science Monitor

HONG KONG

THE recent pledge by China to refrain from selling weapons in unstable regions is being put to the test with a visit by President Yang Shangkun to Pakistan and Iran, diplomats and analysts say.

The trip by Mr. Yang coincides with reports that China has sold Iran nuclear-weapons technology despite repeated Chinese assurances that it would not do so. Yang plans to leave Iran tomorrow for home. Military cooperation has likely been a central topic in Yang's talks with leaders from two of China's leading weapons customers, diplomats and foreign policy analysts say.

Ensuing arms deals would indicate whether China will follow rules for weapons exports that it endorsed Oct. 18 with the four other permanent members of the United Nations Security Council. The five powers pledged to refrain from weapons sales that would intensify conflicts or regional tensions.

Beijing denies reports of nuclear sales and is expected to sign the Nuclear Non-Proliferation Treaty soon. It is also considering an endorsement of the Missile Technology Control Regime, which sets limits on missiles capable of delivering nuclear warheads.

But weapons sales to Southwest Asia could prove irresistible. Such sales to Pakistan and Iran would help China win favor with Muslim leaders influential among Islamic fundamentalists in China's western region of Xinjiang.

"China's concern about unrest among its ethnic minorities is a main reason why it is keen to cultivate a friendly relationship with Islamic countries in Southwest Asia," says James Tang, professor of political science at the University of Hong Kong.

Also, weapons sales to Islamabad and Tehran would bring China hard currency. China's military craves such revenue because for years it has lacked money to buy the items on its long "wish list," the diplomats and analysts say.

Sophisticated hardware in any case is hard for China to obtain today. Moscow has shelved a sale of fighters to China since the failed right-wing coup; the West has banned arms sales to China since the crackdown on liberal activists in Beijing in June 1989.

"Both [Pakistan and Iran] are willing to pay top-dollar for basic military hardware and so they're natural partners for China," a Western diplomat says on condition of anonymity.

An offer of arms would help China acquire valuable weaponry from Iran: China hopes to obtain some of the Soviet-made MIG-29 and SU-25 fighters that Iraqi pilots flew to Iran during the Gulf war, diplomats say, quoting unconfirmed reports.

Arms sales would also help Beijing geopolitically: Pakistan has aligned with China to counterbalance India, its longtime rival, and Iran helps China in its attempt to contain United States influence in the Middle East, the diplomats and analysts say.

Pakistan is likely to be a ready buyer from China. Washington cut military and economic aid to Islamabad after it failed to give assurances that it was not developing nuclear weapons.

China manufactures heavy tanks in a joint project with Pakistan and is widely believed to be involved in a similar project producing jet fighter trainers. Beijing has provided Islamabad with an atomic bomb design and helped it to enrich uranium, according to Western intelligence reports.

China also has sold Iran a range of goods far broader than suggested by its well-publicized shipment of Silkworm missiles during the Iran-Iraq war, the diplomats say.

Beijing is helping Tehran build a nuclear reactor and negotiating to supply it with M-11 missiles, according to unconfirmed press reports. And China has sold Iran devices that enrich uranium to the level required for a nuclear bomb, according to recent reports quoting unnamed sources in the Bush administration.

Under the UN agreement, China is obliged to inform other members of the UN Security Council about the sale of major conventional weapons and certain missiles to Iran and other Middle Eastern countries. Nuclear weapons and ballistic missiles are not included in the agreement and sales to countries outside the Middle East such as Pakistan do not require such notification.

5-5

외 무 부

종 별 :

번 호 : UNW-3824

일 시 : 91 1112 2230

수 신 : 장 관(중동일,연일,기정)

발 신 : 주 유엔대사

제 목 : 걸프사태(안보리)

1. 쿠웨이트는 지난 10.10 이락어선 7척의 쿠웨이트 영해침범, 10.18 이락인 3명 쿠웨 이트월경(탄약류수거목적) 사례를 들면서 여사한 반복적인 쿠웨이트 침범사태의 책임은 이락당국에 있으며, 이락측이 안보리의 제반관련 결의 준수의사가 없음을 보여주는 것이라고 주장하는 요지의 안보리문서를 배포하였음. (S/23210)

2. 금 11.12.자 NYT 지는 유엔 이락화학무기 사찰반에 참여하고 있는 오지리 전문가를 인용, 동 사찰활동을 하는 과정에서 화학탄두가 장착된 다량의 유탄발사, 포탄, 폭탄류가 발견되었다고 보도함.

(이락측은 화학무기류 보유량을 4만개로 유엔측에 통보한바 있으나, 유엔사찰결과 10 만개에 이르는 것으로 밝혀짐.)

첨부: NYT 기사: UNW(F)-825 끝

(대사 노창희-국장)

중아국	장관	차관	1차보	국기국	외정실	분석관	청와대	안기부

PAGE 1

91.11.13 13:46 WH

외신 1과 통제관

0093

UNW(FI)-025   11/12 2230

총 104

Iraqi Weapons Had Chemical Warheads

By JOHN TAGLIABUE
Special to The New York Times

VIENNA, Nov. 11 — Austrian experts who recently returned from Iraq have said they found large numbers of Iraqi weapons outfitted with chemical warheads that could have been used in the Persian Gulf war.

They also said some of the weapons included Soviet-built Scud missiles. But they said that primitive ballistic technology and warheads that were unevenly filled with deadly liquid chemicals made it unlikely they could have been fired accurately, if at all.

The officials said they found large depots of rifle grenades, artillery shells and bombs with chemical warheads containing sarin, a deadly liquid substance that when distributed as an aerosol spray destroys the nervous system by stopping lung and heart muscles, and mustard gas, another poison gas more likely to incapacitate than to kill, which works similarly on contact with the skin.

The three officials, experts on chemical warfare protection from Austria's federal defense force who were part of a United Nations inspection team, said their last three-week tour, which ended Nov. 5, took them to storage sites reported by Iraq to the United Nations, one at Mosul north of Baghdad, a second west of the Iraqi capital, and a third in the south of Iraq near Basra.

Iraq has reported 40,000 chemical bombs and shells, but inspection has raised the figure to about 100,000, United Nations officials say. Roughly half have already been destroyed.

In an interview, the Austrians said most of the rifle grenades and 122-millimeter artillery shells they examined were outfitted with chemical warheads, often plastic containers with the deadly liquid chemical surrounding a so-called burster tube, a cylinder of TNT or other explosive that detonates on impact, sending the chemical content into the air.

The experts could not say how many Scuds were found in all. But they described Soviet technicians who examined the missiles as startled by the primitive workmanship. They said some experts believed that the missiles would have been destroyed by heat on re-entry into the atmosphere, had they been fired, while others believed that partly filled chemical warheads would probably have caused the kind of destabilization that occurs in half-filled oil tankers at sea, rendering the missiles useless.

There appeared to be no indication that the long-range missiles had ever been tested, the officials said. They said other weapons provided no clues as to why they were not deployed in the war.

The function of the United Nations inspection teams, usually about 25 experts from several countries, including the United States, is to take samples for testing and report the numbers, content and condition of the weapons and the plausibility of removing or destroying them. The Soviet Union and Canada have offered the use of mobile incinerators to destroy the weapons, United Nations officials said, but the technology is slow and costly.

United Nations experts returned to Iraq today to discuss with the Baghdad authorities the destruction of Iraq's chemical and nuclear weapons, Reuters reported. A nuclear team will return 78 rods of enriched uranium to its source, the Soviet Union.

UNW-3 024

첨부   1-1

0094

외 무 부

종 별 :

번 호 : UNW-3901　　　　　　　　　　일 시 : 91 1115 2000

수 신 : 장 관(중동일,연일,기정)

발 신 : 주 유엔대사

제 목 : 걸프사태(안보리)

이락 대량 살상무기 폐기관련 금 11.15. 유엔측발표 내용을 별첨 송부함.

1.유엔이락 대량살상 무기 폐기특위(UNSCOM)사찰활동 개요

2. IAEA, UNSCOM 의 이락 고농축 우라늄 수거

3. UNSCOM 화학무기 사찰반(10.22-11.2) 활동결과

첨부:상기자료: UNW(F)-850 끝

(대사 노창희-국장)

중아국	장관	1차보	국기국	외정실	분석관	정와대	안기부

NOTE FOR THE SPOKESMAN

죽주어   Special Commission Inspection Schedule Update

Friday 15 November 1991

Here follows a comprehensive list of missions carried out to date by the Special Commission, and where appropriate jointly with the IAEA, to implement the disarmament provisions of Resolution 687.

Nuclear

15-21 May	1st inspection mission
22 June-3 July	2nd inspection mission
30 June-3 July	(high-level mission on denied access)
7-18 July	3rd inspection mission
27 July-10 August	4th inspection mission
14-20 September	5th inspection mission
21-30 September	6th inspection mission (documents)
11-22 October	7th inspection mission
11-18 November	8th mission (fuel removal)

Chemical

9-15 June	1st inspection mission (survey)
11-14 August	2nd mission (destruction techniques)
31 August-8 Sept	3rd inspection mission
31 August-5 Sept	4th mission (advance party--Muthanna)
6 Oct-9 Nov	5th "super" mission (Muthanna)
22 Oct-2 Nov	6th mission (storage sites)
11-15 Nov	Fact-finding mission on destruction

Biological

2-8 August	1st inspection mission
20 Sept-3 Oct	2nd inspection mission

Ballistic missiles

30 June-7 July	1st inspection (and destruction)
18-20 July	2nd (surprise) inspection & destruct.
8-15 Aug	3rd mission (incl. "super gun")
6-13 Sept	4th inspection (and destruction)
1-9 Oct	5th insp. & dest. (incl. "super gun")

Future missions

Nuclear: Will continue.
Chemical: Will continue.
Biological: Joint biological/chemical inspection 18 Nov-1 Dec.
Ballistic missiles: Will continue.

F. Eckhard

fg3--85

#UNW-3901
첨부

3-1

P.1

IAEA

PRESS RELEASE

Removal of highly enriched uranium from Iraq

The first shipment of highly enriched uranium from Iraq in compliance with United Nations Security Council resolution 687 (1991) took place today, 15 November 1991. This morning a UN cargo flight loaded with 42 fuel elements from the IRT-5000 research reactor at Al Tuwaitha, containing a total of 6.6 kilograms of uranium-235, left Baghdad at 11:50 local time heading for Moscow. An International Atomic Energy Agency (IAEA) team, in co-operation with the Special Commission of the United Nations, supervised the shipment.

The airlift of the remaining quantities of non-irradiated highly enriched uranium will be completed next Sunday, 17 November 1991, when a second flight is planned. These quantities and also the fuel elements shipped out today belong to nuclear material which has been under IAEA safeguards from the time it was imported by Iraq.

The operation was arranged through a contract between the Ministry of Atomic Power and Industry of the USSR and the IAEA.

The highly enriched uranium will be processed at an appropriate facility in the USSR and returned to the IAEA after isotopic dilution.

3-2

PRESS RELEASE

Sixth Chemical Weapons Inspection, 22 October-2 November

A United Nations inspection team recently visited chemical weapons sites declared by Iraq in remote areas of the country and counted thousands of bombs, shells and warheads filled with lethal chemical agents, many of them damaged and leaking.

The 26-member team from 10 nations, headed by Dr. Bernhard Brunner (Switzerland), used UN helicopters to visit sites in the distant north, west and south of the country from 22 October to 2 November.

At a particularly hazardous storage site at Muhammadiyat, west of Baghdad, which had been heavily damaged by coalition bombing, leaking chemical munitions were scattered among thousands of unexploded conventional munitions, 122-millimetre rocket motors and other ordnance.

In the course of the inspection, the team counted about 2,000 bombs and 6,200 artillery shells filled with mustard agent, as well as several thousand 122-millimetre missile warheads filled with the nerve agent sarin. Many of the munitions were too heavily damaged to be moved, but those that could be safely transported will shortly be taken to the Muthanna State Establishment, near Samarra, where destruction of all of Iraq's chemical weapons will get under way early next year. Samples of the various chemical agents were taken for analysis to laboratories in France, Germany and Switzerland.

The mission was the sixth in a continuing series to assess Iraq's chemical weapons capability. It was organized by the Special Commission created by the UN Security Council to carry out the disarmament provisions of the Iraq-Kuwait cease-fire resolution, which calls for the elimination of Iraq's weapons of mass destruction.

* * *

fg4-82 Rev.1

제 7차 대이라크 핵사찰 결과및 향후 IAEA의 핵사찰 계획

. 91.11.19. 국제기구과

I. 안보리 결의 (687호)에 의한 제7차 대이라크 핵사찰 결과 (GOV/INF 1639, 91.11.13)

　　가. 사찰 실시기간 및 장소

　　　　: 1991.10.11-10.22, Al Atheer 지역등 18개 핵시설 장소

　　나. 사찰 목적

　　　　o 제6차 사찰 결과 밝혀진 이라크의 핵무기개발계획의 연구 및 실험범위

　　　　　평가

　　　　o 원심 분리 방법을 통한 이라크의 핵물질 농축기술 발전정도 조사

　　　　o 제5차 사찰결과 이라크내 새로 신고된 핵물질의 측정및 검증

　　다. 사찰 결과

　　　　o 91.9월 IAEA가 제6차 사찰시 발견한 이라크 핵개발 문서의 내용과 이에

　　　　　근거 IAEA가 내린 결론에 대해 <u>이라크 당국이 핵개발 사실을 인정</u>

　　　　　- Al Atheer 지역 연구소가 연구용 핵물질 생산뿐만 아니라 <u>핵무기개발</u>

　　　　　<u>연구를 위해 설립되었음을 인정</u>

　　　　o 핵무기 개발을 위해 이라크 당국은 <u>이라크 원자력위원회</u> (Iraqi Atomic

　　　　　Energy Commission)의 <u>조직</u> 을 구성하였고 <u>Petrochemical-3 (PC-3)</u> 라는 이름

　　　　　하에 <u>핵무기 개발 계획을 수립</u>

　　　　o 제7차 핵사찰에서는 이미 밝혀진 미신고 이라크 핵시설및 물질을 폐쇄,

　　　　　파괴하거나 통제하기 위한 사전단계로서 핵시설및 물질의 정확한 내용을 파악,

　　　　　구분하는 작업을 함.

공람	국제기구과 91년 11월 19일 신종영	담 당	과 장	국 장	차관보	차 관	장 관

0099

- 제5차 사찰시 검증하기 어려웠던 내용들을 계속 측정및 검증하여 <u>재고</u> <u>목록을 작성</u> (<u>수백 ton의 핵물질</u>에 해당)
- <u>36%의 농축 연료</u> 및 <u>93% 농축</u>(불란서 MTR-type) 방사능 연료는 측정을 마친후, <u>91.11월 중순까지는 이라크에서 반출</u>될 계획

Ⅱ. <u>안보리 결의(687,707호)에 의한 향후 대이라크 통제및 검증 계획</u> (GOV/INF/631,91.10.18)

1. 관련 안보리 결의 내용

   가. <u>안보리 결의 687호(91.4.3)</u>

   o 이라크는 핵무기나 핵무기에 사용될 물질 및 시설을 획득하거나 연구 계획을 개발하지 않음

   o 이라크내 모든 핵무기 사용물질을 IAEA의 감시하에 두고, IAEA와 특별 위원회의 현장 사찰을 수락할것

   o IAEA는 특별위원회와 협력, 이라크 핵시설에 대한 즉각적인 사찰을 수행하고 <u>45일내에 이라크내 핵시설을 파괴, 제거하기 위한 계획</u>을 안보리에 제출하며, 동보고서가 <u>안보리에 의해 채택된후 45일이내</u> <u>계획을 이행</u> 함.

   o IAEA는 이라크내 핵 활동과 관련하여 <u>향후 검증과 사찰을 위한 계획</u>을 동 결의(687호) 채택후 <u>120일 이내에 안보리에 제출</u> 함

   나. <u>안보리 결의 707호 (91.8.15)</u>

   o 이라크는 특별 위원회와 <u>IAEA가 사찰을 위해</u> 핵시설, 장소, 장비및 기록에 접근할수 있는 <u>무조건적이고 무제한의 권한을 인정</u> 해야 함.

   o 이라크는 핵 활동관련 비밀계획을 더이상 숨기지 말아야하며 사찰반이 사찰, 감시 및 조사를 위하여 비행기나 헬기로 <u>이라크 영공을 사찰</u> <u>하는 것을 허용</u> 해야 함.

   - 특별위원회와 IAEA 사찰관의 특권과 면제의 완전한 보장도 요구

   o 이라크는 안보리 결의 (687호) 내용을 완전히 이행 할때까지 <u>의료</u>, <u>농업이나 산업목적을 위한 동위원소 사용을 제외하고는 모든 핵 활동을</u> <u>중단</u> 해야 함.

- 2 -

0100

다. 기타관련 조항

　o 안보리결의에 의한 핵사찰외에도 <u>이라크 - IAEA간</u> 체결된 <u>안전조치협정</u>
　　(INFCIRC/172, 1972.2.29) 에 따라서도 <u>IAEA의 정기적 검증활동은 지속 됨</u>

　o IAEA는 상기 안보리 결의애따른 사찰정보를 계속 <u>특별위원회</u>에 제공하여
　　추가 핵사찰 장소를 지정받도록 하며, 향후 대이라크 사찰 활동에 따른
　　<s>경비는 유엔이 부담</s>
　　재정은 유엔에 의해 지원 받음

2. 향후 사찰계획에 따른 이라크와 여타회원국 의무

　가. <u>이라크의 의무</u>　(Obligations of Iraq)

　　o 이라크는 <u>IAEA 사찰 권한 행사를 간섭, 방해해서는 안됨.</u>
　　　- IAEA와의 연락 업무를 담당할 이라크 관리 지명
　　　- 사찰에 참여할 이라크측 사찰관을 임명, IAEA에 통보
　　　- IAEA 사찰관의 안전 보장과 적절한 보호 제공 및 이라크내 사찰 활동에
　　　　필요한 적절한 건물제공

　　o IAEA 사찰계획 수립후 30일이내에 이라크는 <u>아래관련 최신정보를 IAEA에 재출</u>
　　　- 이라크내 모든 핵물질재고, 시설 및 장소에 관한 정보
　　　　(10MW급 이상 발전시설 포함)
　　　- 의료, 농업, 산업 시설에 적용되는 이라크내 동위원소재고
　　　- 향후 5년간 이라크의 핵개발 계획에 관한 정보

　　o 이라크는 앞으로 아래사항에 관한 <u>추가 정보제출</u> 요구
　　　- 핵시설 건설 시작 180일전 핵시설 계획 관련 완전한 정보
　　　- 핵물질 및 동위원소의 수출·입 계획관련 사전 정보
　　　- 이라크의 안보리 결의 이행을 측정하는데 필요한 기타 정보

　　o <u>IAEA에 의해 이라크가 안보리 결의내용을 충실히 이행하고 있다고 결정</u> 될
　　　때, 이라크는 안보리결의(687호)에 의해 <u>금지되지 않은 핵활동을 재개</u> 할수
　　　있음
　　　- 안보리에의한 승인이 있을때까지 이라크는 모든 핵활동을 시도할수 없음

- 3 -

나. 기타 회원국들의 의무 (Obligations of other States)

  o 안보리와 IAEA에 의한 허가 결정이 날때까지, 기타 회원국들은 이라크에
    대한 어떠한 내용의 핵물질, 장비 및 시설등의 제공이 금지됨
    - 의료, 농업및 기타 산업활동을 위한 동위원소 사용은 제외
  o 안보리결의에 의해 허가된 의료,농업및 산업용 동위원소의 이라크에 대한
    수출시 회원국들은 60일이전에 IAEA에 완전한 관련정보를 제출 하여야 함
  o 이라크에 대한 제재조치(안보리 결의 707호)가 해제되더라도 모든 회원국
    들은 안보리결의 687호에 의해 금지되지 않은 핵활동에 사용될 관련 기술 및
    물질을 이라크에 제공시 60일이전에 IAEA에 완전한 관련 정보를 제출 하여야 함

다. IAEA의 권한 (Rights of the IAEA)

  o IAEA는 이라크와체결한 안전조치 협정 및 IAEA 특권및 면제 협정과 유엔사무
    총장 - 이라크 외무장관간 체결된 양해각서(1991.5.14)에 따라 아래와 같은
    권한을 향유
    - 이라크내 핵시설,장소,지역,활동및 물질등에의 접근시 어떠한 방해도 받지
      않고 사찰 수행
    - 사전 통보없이 (unannounced) 또는 임박해서 통보 (short notice)함으로써
      사찰실시 가능
    - 사찰받을 대상 장소,시설,위치,활동등을 확보하고 핵시설및 물질의 전용을
      방지
    - 이라크내 차량,선박,항공기등의 교통수단을 정지시켜 조사할수 있음
    - 핵물질및 시설의 수입및 수출관련 도착및 출발시 조사
    - 사찰관들이 필요시 언제라도 모든 핵시설, 물질및 지역을 사찰할수 있는
      권한 확보 등
  o IAEA는 사찰활동에 대해 아래와 같은 권한을 부여 받음
    - IAEA사찰관과 사찰장비의 이라크내 출입에 있어 무제한의 자유 보장
      (유엔 여권, 사찰수행증명서 소유자에 대해서는 입국 비자 불요

- 4 -

0102

- 이라크내 사찰관의 이동에 있어 완전한 자유 보장

- 이라크로부터 관련 물질및 문서등을 반출할수 있는 권한

- 사찰목적으로 사찰반이 이라크 전역에서 자신들의 모든 교통수단(비행기등)
  을 사용 할수 있는 권한

- 사찰목적으로 이라크내 모든 공항시설을 사용할수 있는 권한

- 사찰반이 이라크내 어느 장소에서도 검열이나 방해를 받지 않고 무전기 나
  인공위성을 통해 교신 하고 IAEA 및 UN본부와도 연락할수 있는 권한

- 사찰반이 사용하는 모든 시설과 차량에 유엔기를 부착할수 있는 권한

라. 이라크의 의무이행을 위한 조치와 불이행시 제재 조치

　　o 이라크 는 안보리 결의(687, 707호)에 의한 상기 의무와 향후 IAEA의 사찰계획
　　　이행을 위해 필요한 국내 입법및 행정조치를 취해 야하며, 향후 사찰계획의 안보리
　　　승인후 30일이내에 동 조치내용을 IAEA에 통보해야함

　　o 안보리 결의(687호)에 따라 파괴, 제거될 이라크내 핵시설및 물질에 대해
　　　이라크는 아무런 관할권이 없으며, IAEA는 이라크의 핵활동을 중지시켜 금지
　　　된 관련 핵물질이나 시설을 압수후 처분할수 있는 권한 보유

　　o 이라크의 상기 안보리 결의및 향후 사찰계획상 의무 불이행 이나 이라크-IAEA간
　　　안전조치협정상 의무 불이행사실이 밝혀지면 IAEA는 동내용을 안보리에 보고
　　　함

마. 보고및 효력 발생

　　o IAEA는 매6개월마다 유엔 사무총장을 통하여 안보리에 이라크 사찰관련 보고
　　　를 하며, 안보리는 사찰계획이행 상황 에대해 IAEA에 보고를 요청 할수 있음

　　o 향후 사찰계획은 안보리의 승인을 얻는 즉시 효력을 발생 하며, 계획 수행
　　　기간은 안보리에 의해 결정됨.　　끝.

- 5 -

0103

이라크, 이미 핵무기 보유 가능

外務部 情報狀況室
受信日時 91.11.28. 10:50

^U.N. Fears Iraq Could Already Have Nuclear Weapons<
^Eds: Updates with quotes from 2nd-ranking UN official, amount of
uranium needed for bomb<
^By PETER JAMES SPIELMANN<
^Associated Press Writer
    UNITED NATIONS (AP) _ A U.N. weapons expert, describing a
``worst case scenario,'' said Wednesday that Iraq could already have
nuclear weapons hidden away, based on the discovery of highly
enriched uranium during inspections.
    Derek Boothby, one of the experts on the U.N. Special Commission
that is getting rid of Iraq's weapons of mass destruction, said
there was no way of knowing whether or not Iraq might have nuclear
weapons hidden away.
    But he said the discovery of samples of weapons-grade uranium
enriched to 93 percent raised the possibility that Iraq possessed
nuclear weapons _ something the Baghdad government has denied.
    ``If the samples are verified, everybody in the whole world
should worry about it,'' said Dr. Robert Gallucci, the
second-ranking official on the commission.
    The commission previously disclosed the discovery of Iraqi
blueprints for a working nuclear weapon in searches of Iraqi
offices, and said Baghdad ran blast tests on components of the
weapon at a secret desert test range.
    The blueprints were for an implosion weapon, which is smaller
and lighter than a crude Hiroshima-style A-bomb, and which can be
fitted to a ballistic missile.
    U.N. experts had thought Iraq's slow and relatively
unsophisticated electromagnetic method for enriching uranium to
weapons-grade strength delayed its development of a nuclear weapon.
They had estimated it would have taken Iraq one to two years to
enrich enough uranium for a working weapon, if the Gulf War had not
disrupted its nuclear program.
    But the discovery of samples of the 93-percent pure enriched
uranium at Iraq's Al Tuwaitha main nuclear facility has prompted the
experts to revise their thinking.
    Inspectors from the U.N.'s International Atomic Energy Agency
discovered the uranium at the facility, located about 40 miles (64
kms) south of Baghdad, in October.
    ``The Iraqis deny ever acquiring or producing such material,''
the inspectors' report said. ``This important issue is still open
and under investigation.''
    More tests on the Tuwaitha samples are being conducted in France
to make sure they are accurate. Atomic sampling tests are normally
accurate but not foolproof, Boothby said.
    France and the Soviet Union, under IAEA auspices, had legally
supplied Baghdad with enriched uranium for a nuclear program Iraq
had described as peaceful.
^MORE

0104

Arms-Grade Uranium Believed Found in Iraq

Concern Arises About Progress on A-Bomb

By R. Jeffrey Smith
Washington Post Staff Writer

International inspectors probing Iraq's nuclear program recently discovered what appear to be traces of uranium capable of being used illicitly as the sparkplug for a nuclear weapon, according to U.S. and diplomatic officials.

The apparent discovery of unauthorized, highly enriched—or weapons-grade—uranium inside Iraq raises new concerns about the country's nuclear capabilities and may indicate that the regime of Iraqi President Saddam Hussein was closer to building a weapon than previously believed, the officials said.

Teams of experts for the International Atomic Energy Agency (IAEA) found the traces in samples taken from four sites within the Tuwaitha research complex near Baghdad during an inspection from Oct. 11 to Oct. 22, according to an IAEA report obtained by The Washington Post.

Experts previously had found a small quantity of less highly enriched uranium produced by Iraq as part of its secret research on nuclear weapons, but it was judged incapable of being used in a nuclear device. Baghdad has denied repeatedly that it had any more potent, weapons-grade uranium.

"This a source of concern and we should investigate it more," said Robert Gallucci, deputy chief of the U.N. Special Commission on Iraq, which is assisting in the nuclear inspections under a U.N. cease-fire resolution negotiated with the country last spring after the Persian Gulf War.

The inspectors' discovery was first reported in the United States last night by ABC News.

Gallucci said in a telephone interview that the discovery should be regarded as tentative because it requires additional scientific confirmation. He said the commission could not rule out the possibility that the samples were contaminated inadvertently by field personnel or by the laboratories in Austria and the United States where the samples were sent for analysis.

But the IAEA, which has some-times differed with the U.N. Special Commission on technical matters associated with the Iraq inspections, said without reservation in its report that "evidence of uranium enriched to 93 percent has persistently shown up" in the Tuwaitha samples.

The report was referring to detection of uranium consisting largely of a specific isotope, U-235, that is ideal for bomb-making, officials said. Natural uranium contains less than 1 percent U-235, and must be processed or "enriched" to remove other, less desirable elements for a weapons program—a central aim of the multibillion-dollar Iraqi effort uncovered in seven separate inspections.

The IAEA report said the agency's investigators had ruled out the possibility that the material was derived from nuclear reactor fuel provided to Iraq by France before the gulf war. That fuel also was enriched to 93 percent. Nor was it made in Iraq's massive calutron, or electromagnetic separation, program to enrich a quantity of uranium sufficient for at least one nuclear weapon, according to the report.

Gallucci said "it may mean, if the samples are good, that either Iraq had or has [an undiscovered] capability to enrich uranium to high levels or that Iraq acquired some quantity of high-enriched uranium" from another country.

"The source of this material remains an important open issue requiring further investigation," said the Vienna-based IAEA.

Officials said an unexpected feature of the samples—the presence of the isotope U-236—suggests the material was partly derived from a plant capable of reprocessing nuclear reactor fuel to make enriched uranium. Seven countries are believed by intelligence officials to have this capability: the United States, Soviet Union, Britain, France, China, India and Israel.

The officials also said that Iraq either secretly enriched the uranium to 93 percent by itself, or purchased the material from one of the nations believed to have such a capability: the United States, Soviet Union, Britain, France, China, Pakistan, or South Africa.

END

NOV. 26, 1991 WP

주 국 련 대 표 부

주국련20313ㄴ　　**972**　　　　　　　　　　　　　1991. 11. 29.

수신　장관

참조　국제기구국장, 중동아프리카국장

제목　유엔 이락핵사찰(제7차 사찰보고서)

　　　　표제관련 안보리 문서를 별첨과 같이 송부합니다.

　　첨　부 : 상기 문서(S/23215). 끝.

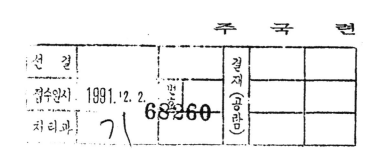

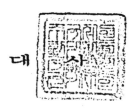

0106

Security Council

Distr.
GENERAL

S/23215
14 November 1991

ORIGINAL: ENGLISH

NOTE BY THE SECRETARY-GENERAL

The Secretary-General has the honour to transmit to the members of the Security Council the attached communication which he has received from the Director-General of the International Atomic Energy Agency (IAEA).

<u>Annex</u>

<u>Letter dated 12 November 1991 from the Director-General
of the International Atomic Energy Agency addressed to
the Secretary-General</u>

Please find attached the report of the seventh IAEA inspection in Iraq
under Security Council resolution 687 (1991). You may deem it appropriate to
transmit the report to the members of the Security Council. I remain, of
course, available with the Chief Inspector, Mr. Demetrius Perricos, for any
consultations you or the Council may wish to have.

(Signed) Hans BLIX

0108   /...

<u>Enclosure</u>

REPORT ON THE SEVENTH IAEA ON-SITE INSPECTION IN IRAQ
UNDER SECURITY COUNCIL RESOLUTION 687 (1991)

11 - 22 October 1991

SALIENT POINTS

- The existence of an Iraqi weaponization program has been acknowledged by the Iraqi authorities and confirmed; an organization chart has been obtained. Basic computations and high-explosive testing for component development had been carried out, but - if one takes the details provided by the Iraqi authorities as face value - a practical system for an implosion-type weapon had not yet been achieved.

- The Al Atheer site has been identified by the team as the prime development and testing site. The Al Qa Qaa site and the Al Hatteen High Explosive Test Site were, in the opinion of the team, also contributing to the program.

- The Iraqi authorities have admitted that buildings at the Al Atheer site were designed not only for general materials science research but also to meet the requirements of the weaponization program if a relevant political decision were taken.

- The validity of previous estimates of the extent of the centrifuge enrichment program has been further confirmed by this team, but no cascade or likely site was found. Iraq once again insisted that its entire uranium enrichment program has been declared.

- Feasibility studies on uranium enrichment by the gaseous diffusion method were admitted by the Iraqi authorities. These studies, which included laboratory work on diffusion barriers, were carried out from 1982 until 1987, when the program was phased out.

- Destruction or rendering harmless of centrifuge and EMIS components has started. All known equipment used in the manufacturing of centrifuge and EMIS components has been inspected and identified by means of IAEA seals with a view to future destruction or rendering harmless.

- The glove boxes associated with the clandestine production of approximately six grams of plutonium have been rendered harmless by having cement poured into them. The associated hot cells have been impaired by cutting of the manipulators. Further action is necessary to deal with the hot cells and other equipment.

- Some items of equipment were identified by means of IAEA seals pending a decision on their destruction or removal or the monitoring of their use.

0109

/...

- Measurements of the activity of the irradiated fuel in the IRT-5000 reactor and at storage location B continued. These measurements are intended to confirm the integrity of the fuel and the correctness of Iraqi statements regarding the extent of the irradiation to which the assemblies were subjected. Thirteen assemblies which were difficult to access have still to be verified.

- The two transport specialists who accompanied the team completed the initial preparations for the shipment of fresh fuel. This fuel will be removed from Iraq in the middle of November.

- The compilation of an inventory of the nuclear material (uranium concentrates and various uranium compounds, oxide powder etc.) accumulated at storage location C continued. This nuclear material, included in the lists attached to the Iraqi declarations made since 7 July 1991, consists of several hundred tons of nuclear material in many forms, scattered over several sites throughout Iraq. As a consequence of having been hurriedly removed for purposes of concealment from inspectors, in some cases the material is wrongly identified and the associated records are incomplete. This work will have to continue.

- Evidence of uranium enriched to 93% has persistently shown up in samples collected in and near Al Tuwaitha (at four different locations). This material is isotopically distinct from the 93%-enriched French fuel and is unlikely to be a product of the Iraqi enrichment program. The Iraqi authorities deny ever acquiring or producing such material. This important issue is still open and under investigation.

- Inspection visits were made to a number of new sites designated by the Special Commission, but only in the case of one site (Al Hadre) could the findings be related to a future use in the weaponization program.

0110

/...

INTRODUCTION

1. This report summarizes the findings of the seventh inspection carried out by the IAEA under Security Council Resolution 687 (1991) with the assistance and co-operation of the Special Commission of the United Nations. The inspection took place from 11 to 22 October 1991 and was headed by Mr. Demetrius Perricos of the IAEA as Chief Inspector. The team consisted of 26 inspectors and 13 supporting staff; it comprised 17 nationalities. During the inspection 18 sites and locations were visited. These are shown on the map of Iraq attached to this report.

    The objectives of the inspection were broadly

    -   to assess the extent of the Iraqi studies and experiments directed towards developing a nuclear weapon (referred to throughout this report as "weaponization").

    -   to further investigate the work done and progress made in enrichment, particularly by the centrifuge method.

    -   to continue the work of the fifth inspection team in measuring and verifying the declared nuclear material.

    Each of these three broad objectives was assigned to a separate group within the overall team, with a group leader responsible for co-ordination of the work within each group.

2. In the area of weaponization, a major clarification was obtained of the stage reached by Iraq. As a result of persistent investigation and questioning, the Iraqi authorities have now acknowledged that efforts had been under way to establish the design parameters and development work needed for a nuclear weapon. The acknowledgement is contained in a letter annexed to this report (Annex 1). The importance of this letter lies in its confirmation of the IAEA's conclusions and of the validity of the documents found during the sixth inspection, in September. The team believes that computations and experimental work had been carried out on a basic weapon model but had not yet yielded a workable production design. The studies and experiments had covered detonator initiation, the hydrodynamics of a compressed explosive system and basic explosive lens design, but they were still at an early stage.

3. Particularly important were the determination by the team and the admission by Iraq that the Al Atheer site was built not only as a materials production development site (as declared by Iraq; see letter in Annex 2) but also to serve the weaponization program once a decision was taken. This had been persistently denied by Iraq in the past.

0111   /...

4.   As a result of the findings relating to weaponization, the Iraqi authorities have now produced an organization chart of the Iraqi Atomic Energy Commission which includes the weapons program operation under the code name Petrochemical-3, PC-3 (Fig. 1). This confirms that there was a large, well organized program employing several thousand people. Iraq still insists, however, that the work was intended only to establish the technical basis for a political decision to proceed to a weapon and that the political decision had not been taken. Figure 2 shows the main facilities involved in the weaponization and the enrichment program.

5.   A primary focus of the inspection effort expended in Iraq thus far has been on identifying and characterizing the Iraqi uranium enrichment program, the goal being to understand it to the extent necessary in order to destroy it or render it harmless and to establish the basis for ongoing monitoring. With the completion of the seventh inspection, the team's opinion is that the emphasis of the inspection effort, as regards the Iraqi uranium enrichment program, should now move gradually from identification and characterization to monitoring. All known sites involved in enrichment R&D and component manufacture and production have been inspected. Process components generally consistent with the known extent of the enrichment program have been inventoried, and destruction has started. Similarly, component manufacturing equipment consistent with the known enrichment program deployment and plans has been identified and sealed for destruction or monitoring. Efforts by Iraq to hide the nature and extent of the enrichment program and some remaining inconsistencies leave open the possibility that the full Iraqi program has not been disclosed.

6.   The report of the fifth inspection team described the difficulties of adequately verifying the additional nuclear material declared by Iraq on 7 July and subsequently. This material was placed under seal by the third inspection team pending verification. The difficulties relate to the inadequate documentation, labelling and packing of the material, which is in the form of ore, uranium oxide and miscellaneous chemical compounds. These arise from the originally undeclared production of compounds such as uranium hexafluoride (UF_6) and uranium tetrachloride (UCl_4) which were used in clandestine enrichment development work. The seventh inspection team continued to compile an inventory of this material and to verify it. The demands of other activities, however, drastically reduced the inspection manpower available. It will therefore be necessary to continue with its work during subsequent inspections.

7.   As part of the task of monitoring the fresh and irradiated fuel kept in sealed storage in Iraq, it is necessary to periodically examine seals and in some cases to remeasure samples of the total fuel population. During this inspection, measurements were made of the 36%-enriched fuel and of the 93%-enriched French MTR-type irradiated fuel. It is expected that by the middle of November 1991 the fresh fuel will be removed from Iraq, reducing the task of periodic reverification. The two transport specialists attached to the team made the necessary initial preparations. Measurements were also made of some of the elements in the IRT-5000 reactor core and storage pond as part of the task of assessing the validity of the Iraqi declaration regarding irradiation.

0112

/...

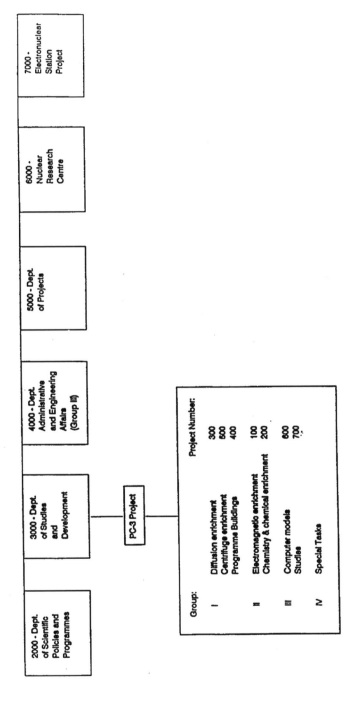

Figure 1

Iraqi Atomic Energy Commision
- 1000

/...

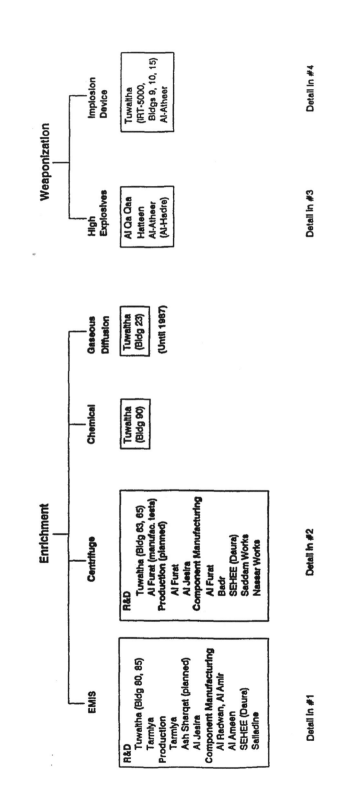

Figure 2

Main Facilities Involved in the Enrichment and Weaponization Programmes

8. The hot cells used to produce approximately six grams of plutonium clandestinely had previously been placed under seal. During this inspection these cells were impaired by cutting the working mechanisms of the manipulators. The glove boxes associated with this program had cement poured into them in order to render them useless.

9. Several samples taken in and around Al Tuwaitha indicate the presence of uranium enriched to approximately 93% in uranium-235. This material is isotopically distinct from the 93%-enriched French reactor fuel. Iraq strongly denies that it has or ever had such material. It is highly unlikely that this material is a product of the Iraqi uranium enrichment program. This important issue is still open and under investigation. Additional samples were taken for this purpose.

10. A feature of the seventh inspection was the large amount of correspondence between the Chief Inspector and the Iraqi counterpart while the team was in Iraq. The purpose of the many communications from the Chief Inspector was to unequivocally establish the Iraqi answers to key questions about the nuclear program. Experience has shown that oral questioning is insufficient for obtaining definitive statements and that very careful phrasing is required in order to convey precisely what is being asked. A full record of the correspondence is given in Annex 3.

0115

/...

THE IRAQI NUCLEAR WEAPONIZATION PROGRAM

11.   The seventh IAEA inspection mission has confirmed that for a number of years Iraq devoted considerable resources to a research and experimentation program of nuclear weaponization. One of the objectives of the seventh IAEA inspection was to assess the achievements of this program by analysing available documents found in Iraq during the sixth IAEA inspection and the results of previous inspections.

General design of the explosive device

12.   Within a general classification of nuclear weapon designs into three categories,

-   Gun type
-   Intermediary implosion type
-   Advanced implosion type

It can be concluded that the main effort of the program was concentrated on the second category.

In fact, no documentary evidence or experimental equipment which could be related to a gun-type design has been found or disclosed. The same applies to advanced implosion-type devices.

The production of lithium-6 may be considered indicative of an orientation towards "boosted" devices in the long term, and one may infer that Iraqi scientists intended to explore this concept at a later date.

Core geometry

13.   Progress reports on the PC-3 project (the code name for the Iraqi clandestine program) which are in the possession of the IAEA give a general description of the core geometry.

Several geometric configurations had been tested with hydrodynamic computer programs, in both mono- and bi-dimensional lattices. Some of these programs had been modified in Iraq for use on IBM PS/2-80 computers. The limitations of such computers are compensated by the fact that - as available literature indicates - comparable solutions have already been reached in experimentation. The same may be said for neutronic codes, which can provide acceptable results when the precision required for the yield value is not a fundamental design parameter.

0116

/...

Uranium metallurgy

14. It has been determined and documented that work covering the various phases of uranium metallurgy was conducted at Al Tuwaitha prior to the destruction of the relevant facilities. Buildings 10 and 15 were used for UF_4 production, uranium metal reduction and metal casting and machining (see Table 1 and Fig.3).

15. The IAEA inspection team confirmed, through documents and on-the-spot visual evidence, that the Al Atheer facility (fig. 4) was designed, _inter alia_, for large-scale uranium metallurgy. Induction furnaces, plasma coating machines, computer-controlled drills and lathes with recoverable chippings were identified in Buildings 50 ("casting"), 55 ("powder") and 84 ("carbide"). Smears and samples taken during the seventh inspection will indicate whether those facilities were used between July 1990 (date of completion of Building 55) and December 1990 (date when the facilities were evacuated prior to bombardment).

16. No assessment can yet be made concerning the amounts and types of weapons components (reflectors, tampers, flying plates, etc.), if any, which could have been produced at Al Atheer during that period. It can only be stated that the necessary knowledge and equipment for uranium metallurgy had been acquired. Most of the equipment, being dual-use in nature, has been put under seals by the seventh IAEA inspection team. The entire Al Atheer site, including the firing test bunker, deserves ongoing monitoring.

Explosive assembly

17. The Iraqi authorities declared at the end of the fourth inspection that they were in possession of large quantities (hundreds of tons) of HMX explosive. Part of it was used for filling aerial bombs. The remaining quantity (255 tons) was inventoried and put under IAEA seals in six storage bunkers at Al Qa Qaa by the seventh inspection team. It is obvious that, with such quantities available, the few tons necessary for a nuclear weaponization program did not represent a problem.

18. Two isostatic presses (hot and cold) suitable for shaping explosive charges and with sufficient capacity and and also various items of remote-controlled machining equipment with adequate cooling were located at Al Atheer. Should this equipment have been utilized, the possibility cannot be ruled out that some explosive structures were produced and are still being stored somewhere.

19. The fabrication of explosive "lenses" for experiments was mentioned in the PC3 progress reports. Two types of lenses seem to have been tested, probably at the Al Atheer "bunker", from March to May 1990: dual-explosive and flying-plate lenses. The experiments appear to have been limited to planar shock waves. However, it is prudent to assume that Iraqi scientists have a basic knowledge of the initiation of a spherical implosion.

0117   /...

0118

Table 1

Buildings involved in weaponization and enrichment

TUWAITHA

Building No	Description of Building	Activity
3	Administrative Building	Personal computers for hydrodynamic models
9	Chemical & Radiochemical Analysis Laboratory	Separation of Pu from exempted pins Separation of Pu from Irradiated pins Production of Po-210 sources
10	Chemical Analysis Laboratory	Production of U metal Melting and casting of metal uranium
10 annex	Nuclear Physics Department	
13	Research Reactor IRT-5000	Irradiation of EK-10 and EK-07 cassettes Irradiation of Bismuth for Po-210 production
15	Isotope Production Laboratory	Production of UF_4 and UF_6
16	Workshop	Initiator workshop
23	Laboratory Workshop Building	Gaseous Diffusion Enrichment Ceramic capacitor fabrication
24	Tamuz-2 zero Power Reactor Tamuz-2 Hot Cells	Storing of Irradiated cassettes Disassembling of cassettes Neutron measurements
35	Radioactive Waste Treatment Station (RWTS)	Handling of wastes from the Irradiation programme
63	Cold material testing laboratories	Gas centrifuge enrichment
66	Training Building	Initiator System Examination
73	Experimental Fuel Fabrication Laboratory	Manufacturing of EK-07
80	Nuclear Physics Laboratories	EMIS
82	Electronic Research Laboratories	Electronic systems
85	Chemical Research Laboratories	Production of yellow cake, UO_2 and UCL_4
90	Polymer chemistry Research Laboratory	Enrichment by solvent extraction and Ion exchange U-6 enrichment research

/...

Figure 3

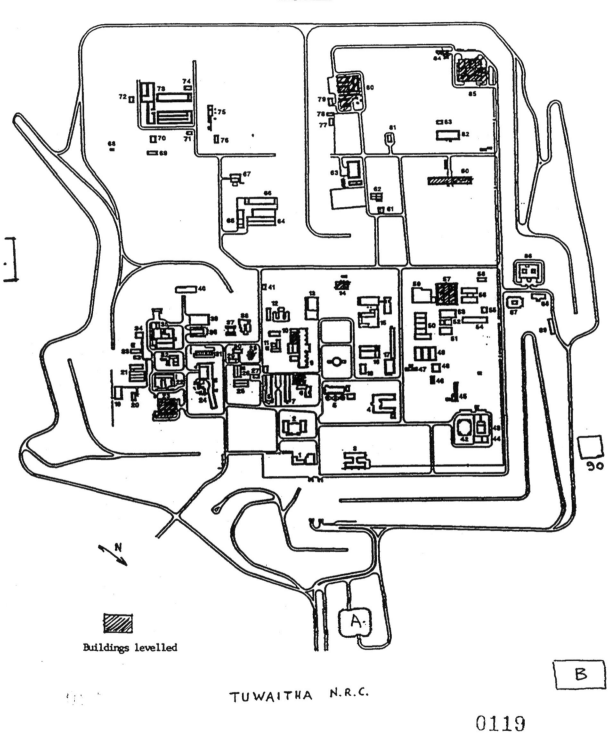

Buildings levelled

TUWAITHA N.R.C.

A·

B

0119

/...

Figure 4

AL ATHEER SITE

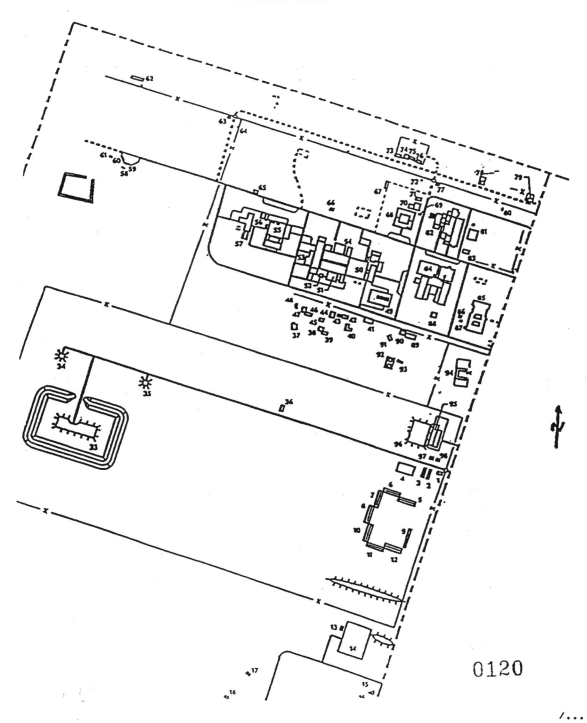

0120

/...

20.   Facilities for hydrodynamic studies and explosive testing exist at Al Atheer and Al Hadre. At Al Atheer, the "bunker" (under the authority of the Al Hatteen Establishment) has been visited several times by IAEA inspectors. It is overdesigned for its declared use. The existence of two high-speed streak cameras at Baghdad University (resolution 100 picoseconds) confirms that precise detonic experiments were possible. The Al Hadre site was a new site designated by the Special Commission. An open firing range for air-fuel bombs and fragmentation testing, it is a very suitable place for experimentation with entire explosive structures. The control bunker is equipped with electronic devices which appear overdesigned for their declared use.

It may be concluded that the explosive structure of an implosion-type device did not pose an insurmountable problem for Iraqi scientists. The facilities at Al Atheer and Al Hadre merit close ongoing monitoring.

Firing system

21.   The quality level attained in the firing system for nuclear weapons remains a question mark in the Iraqi program. In general, the results of IAEA inspections suggest that the local capabilities in electronics were not on a par with the competence in metallurgy, chemistry and detonics.

22.   The exploding bridge wire detonators (EBW) could not be imported, and were developed locally at Al Qa Qaa in the course of project 144. Documentary evidence links project 144 to the PC-3 program, although the Iraqi authorities had previously stated that EBW development was carried out to produce explosive bolts for the separation of two stages of a space rocket. The specifications were for simultaneity better than 0.5 microsecond. According to Iraqi statements, the experiment failed.

23.   The locally fabricated capacitors do not seem to possess the characteristics necessary for storing the energy required by the multiple detonator system specified in the project design. Two of these capacitors have been brought back to Vienna.

Neutronic initiator

24.   The initiator on which the Iraqi engineers were experimenting with a pneumatic cannon system is a polonium-beryllium internal source. Traces of polonium-210 have been found at Al Tuwaitha locations. Studies on alternative internal initiators, based on other alpha sources or on external initiators relying on intense plasma focus, are mentioned in Iraqi progress reports, but there is no indication that they had yet resulted in a workable solution.

Summmary of the present assessment of achievements

25.   To the best of the team's knowledge, based on Iraqi progress reports found and on the results of the IAEA inspections in the field, the status of the Iraqi work on the various pathways leading to nuclear weaponization is as shown in Figures 5 and 6; it can be summarized as follows:

0121   /...

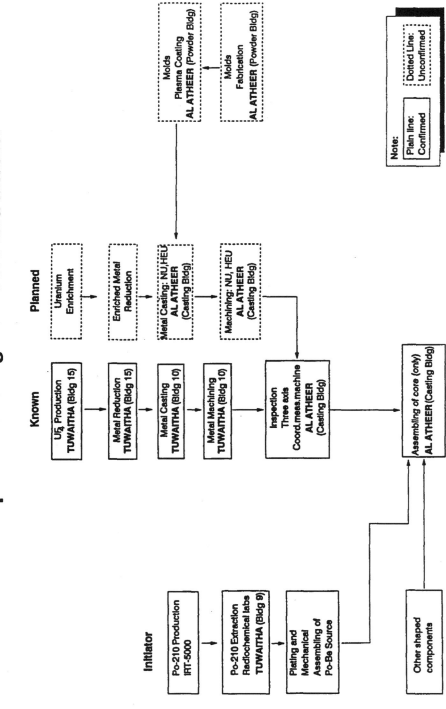

Figure 5

Weaponization Program - Core and Initiator

Figure 6

Weaponization Program - Explosives

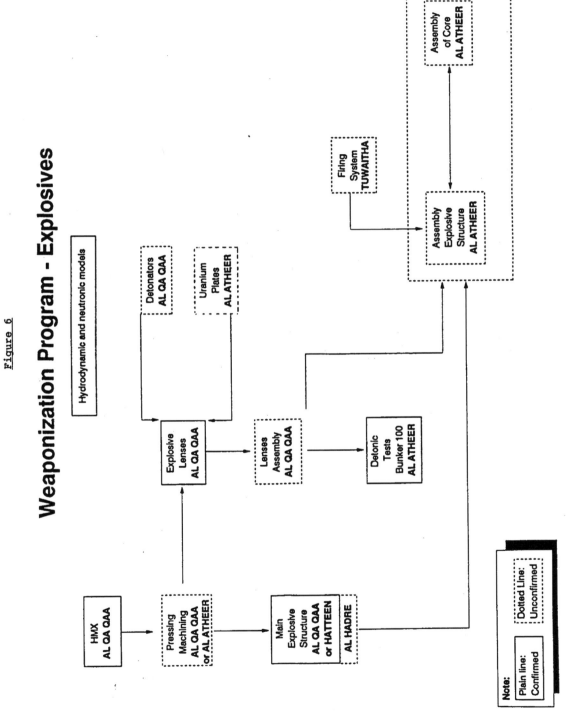

/...

Iraq has acknowledged that it was actively pursuing a research and development program with the goal of developing a "practical" design for a nuclear explosive. The explosive design type chosen by Iraq represents an intermediate-level technology that uses enriched uranium in an implosion system.

26.   The description of the nuclear-weapon design is incomplete. The main-charge high explosive was not addressed. However, the program as presented by the Iraqi authorities was a broad one encompassing all of the challenging features required - core, high-explosive lenses, detonators and firing system. The description of the design and of the work performed appears somewhat superficial in that it consists almost entirely of information that could be obtained through a literature search. Almost no information of a creative nature, results of detailed calculations or experimental results have been offered. The experiments as described were quite simple and the comments - if taken at face value - indicate that Iraq still had a long way to go.

27.   It is important to note that other options, involving both lower and higher technologies, were available. Given their thorough use of the literature, the Iraqi scientists were undoubtedly aware of these options. The lower-technology approach, a gun assembly type design, offers two significant advantages and one major disadvantage: the advantages are a much higher chance of success in a short time and much greater ease of concealing the design phase of the program; the disadvantage is the greater requirement for nuclear material as compared with the implosion design. Possibly the Iraqi scientists felt that their understanding of a gun-type weapon was such that, if the fissionable material became available, the nuclear explosive could be manufactured with a low-observability test program in a very short time. Furthermore, because the implosion design requires significantly more effort and time to develop, they chose to concentrate their efforts on a design which would give them potentially two options when the nuclear material became available.

28.   The Iraqi scientists appear to have been interested also in designs corresponding to technology levels higher than the "basic mechanism" implosion type. Work with lithium, particularly the enrichment of lithium-6, was probably associated with efforts to develop higher-level explosive technology, most likely as part of a continuing long-term program. The Iraqi authorities refer to "academic curiosity", "employment of chemists" and "medical products" as justifications for this effort, but it is noticeable that all documents on the subject are marked "top secret".

0124

/...

THE IRAQI URANIUM ENRICHMENT PROGRAM

29.   The Iraqi uranium enrichment program began in 1982, following the Osirak bombing. Work, at one time or another, on four uranium isotope separation technologies has been confirmed - primarily electromagnetic isotope separation (EMIS) and gas centrifuge enrichment.

30.   A large R&D effort covering all aspects of EMIS technology was carried out at the Al Tuwaitha Nuclear Research Center. Industrial-scale production facilities were being constructed at the Tarmiya and Ash Sharqat sites. Eight EMIS units were operating and additional units were being installed at Tarmiya at the time the facility was destroyed. Construction at the Ash Sharqat site continued up to the Gulf War. Most major buildings at both sites were heavily damaged, particularly at Ash Sharqat. The EMIS development and deployment was largely an indigenous effort.

31.   Serious development work on centrifuge enrichment began with single-machine (Model 1) trials in mid-1987. Design and performance testing was carried out at Al Tuwaitha. Work had progressed from a Beams type centrifuge to a Zippe type (Model 2) counter-current centrifuge by mid-1988. The centrifuge enrichment program was proceeding rapidly to industrial-scale centrifuge manufacture and deployment. A large manufacturing and testing facility was being constructed at Al Furat (Fig. 7) and all necessary manufacturing equipment (for centrifuges utilizing maraging steel rotor tubes) had been procured. This big jump from a very modest R&D program to large-scale industrialization was apparently made possible by substantial help from outside Iraq. Iraq had acquired the design and the basic manufacturing technology, but had not achieved full implementation at the time work stopped. Development work involving single-machine optimization trials (Model 2 with carbon rotor tubes obtained from abroad) proceeded concurrently with the efforts to master the production of maraging steel components. The manufacturing equipment intended for installation at Al Furat was adequate for the production of more than 2,000 centrifuges a year. The centrifuge enrichment program was definitely not an indigenous development effort. The decision to proceed with maraging steel rotors would have minimized the difficulties posed by export controls.

32.   R&D was also devoted to chemical exchange isotope separation and gaseous diffusion. Little remains of the Iraqi work on chemical exchange separation. The few reports describe results readily available in the open literature. Presentations by Iraqi scientists to inspection teams indicate that their work in this area had not progressed very far. The Iraqi scientists admit to a serious feasibility study (with some laboratory work on barrier material) of gaseous diffusion. Their conclusion was that Iraq lacked the industrial infrastructure necessary for large-scale deployment and abandoned the effort in mid-1987. There is no indication that Iraq pursued laser or jet nozzle enrichment technologies.

0125

/...

Figure 7

THE AL FURAT CENTRIFUGE PRODUCTION COMPLEX

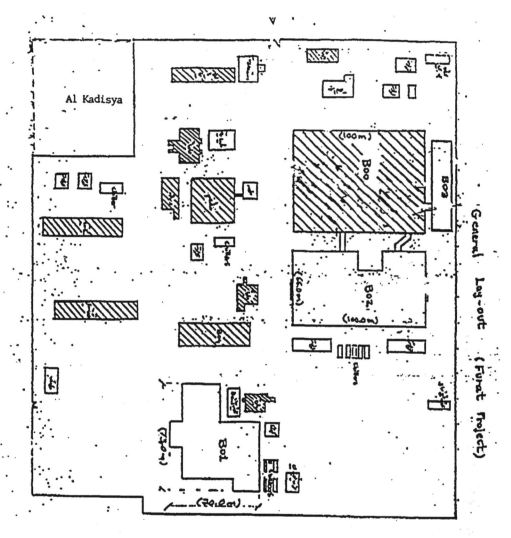

0126

/...

33. Schematics describing the R&D, manufacturing and production facilities for EMIS and centrifuge enrichment are given in Figures 8 and 9. A detailed description of the Iraqi uranium enrichment program is provided in Annex 4. The sites involved in EMIS development (Al Tuwaitha and Tarmiya), component manufacture (Al Radwan, Al Amir, Dijjla and SEHEE) and production (Tarmiya, Ash Sharqat and Al Jesira) have been identified. All facilities were badly damaged during the war. The conclusion of the third inspection team that the Ash Sharqat facility never operated has been confirmed.

34. Results from environmental samples taken at Tarmiya and in the vicinity of Buildings 80 and 85 at Al Tuwaitha (location of EMIS development work) are consistent with Iraqi declarations regarding the levels of enrichment obtained. However, environmental samples collected in other areas in and around Al Tuwaitha indicated the presence of 93%-enriched uranium with significant amounts of uranium-236. The source of this material remains an important open issue requiring further investigation, but it is highly unlikely that it resulted from Iraqi enrichment activities; the Iraqi authorities deny ever acquiring or producing such material.

35. EMIS components that were scattered about a number of sites around Baghdad have now been moved to a central location (Al Nafad) near Al Tuwaitha. The Iraqi declaration is consistent with the known extent of EMIS development and deployment. This declaration has been verified and all equipment not destroyed during the war has been either destroyed under the observation of the seventh team or marked for destruction when the means to destroy them have been found.

36. Manufacturing equipment used to produce EMIS components has been identified and marked with IAEA seals; it is destined for destruction or monitoring.

37. The known sites involved in centrifuge enrichment development (Al Tuwaitha), component manufacture and material production (Al Furat and Al Jesira) have been thoroughly inspected. The facilities at Al Tuwaitha and Al Jesira were destroyed; the Al Furat site was far from completion when work stopped.

38. All known centrifuge components have been either removed by the inspection team or destroyed. Manufacturing equipment consistent with the Iraqi program has been identified and marked with IAEA seals. Key equipment - such as a flow turning machine, electron beam and MIG welders, and oxidation furnaces - have been marked for destruction. The assessed extent of use of the equipment is considered to be generally consistent with Iraqi declarations.

39. Manufacturers of equipment and components have been identified for follow-up investigations.

40. All sites and equipment not destroyed are subject to monitoring. Past efforts by Iraq to hide the nature and extent of the enrichment program, the lack of firm procurement/project documentation and inconsistencies as regards quantities of centrifuge components declared contribute to the uncertainty as to whether the full Iraqi centrifuge enrichment program has been uncovered. Special short-notice inspections will continue to be carried out as part of the long-term monitoring regime. A number of follow-up activities for future inspection teams have been identified.

0127   /...

0128

Figure 8

Iraqi EMIS Programme

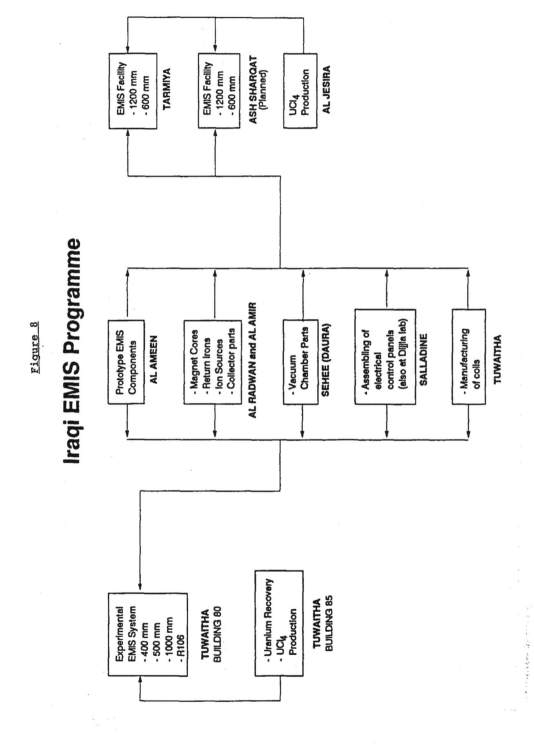

PRODUCTION
FACILITIES

MANUFACTURING
FACILITIES

R & D ACTIVITY

/...

Figure 9

Iraqi Centrifuge Enrichment Program

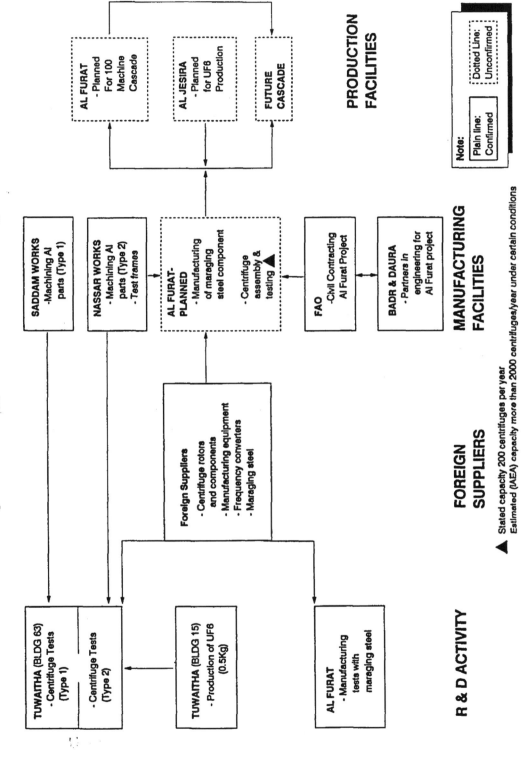

PRODUCTION FACILITIES

AL FURAT
- Planned For 100 Machine Cascade

AL JESIRA
- Planned for UF6 Production

FUTURE CASCADE

MANUFACTURING FACILITIES

SADDAM WORKS
- Machining Al parts (Type 1)

NASSAR WORKS
- Machining Al parts (Type 2)
- Test frames

AL FURAT-PLANNED
- Manufacturing of maraging steel component
- Centrifuge assembly & testing ▲

FAO
- Civil Contracting Al Furat Project

BADR & DAURA
- Partners in engineering for Al Furat project

FOREIGN SUPPLIERS

Foreign Suppliers
- Centrifuge rotors and components
- Manufacturing equipment
- Frequency converters
- Maraging steel

R & D ACTIVITY

TUWAITHA (BLDG 63)
- Centrifuge Tests (Type 1)
- Centrifuge Tests (Type 2)

TUWAITHA (BLDG 15)
- Production of UF6 (0.5Kg)

AL FURAT
- Manufacturing tests with maraging steel

Note:
Plain line: Confirmed
Dotted Line: Unconfirmed

▲ Stated capacity 200 centrifuges per year
Estimated (IAEA) capacity more than 2000 centrifuges/year under certain conditions

0129

/...

NUCLEAR MATERIAL VERIFICATION AND MEASUREMENT

Fuel elements

Fresh fuel at location A:

41.   The ten 36%-enriched EK 36-type rod cluster fuel elements were item-counted and reverified. Eight items were remeasured. One element was disassembled, and nine of the fifteen rods composing it were measured to check the internal consistency of their composition. All results are consistent with the Iraqi declaration.

In preparation for shipment, all storage drums were opened. The items were counted, the element support structures were rebuilt, and the elements were repackaged into eleven sealed drums. Some mechanical work was necessary to ensure that the drums were sound and safe for air transport. This material will be transported out of Iraq in mid-November.

One of the 2.2%-enriched rods (appr. 10 cm long) was moved to the "New Storage" and placed in a sealed cabinet. It was chosen as a standard for fuel measurement NDA work.

Irradiated fuel at location B:

42.   The thirty-two 93%-enriched French MTR-type lightly irradiated elements were reverified. Three of the six control elements were scanned along their lengths with a dose meter. The Iraqi side supplied diagrams of a typical Tamuz-2 reactor core configuration and a schematic drawing of the control elements. The measurement results are consistent with the Iraqi declaration. All seals were checked and eight were replaced. The previous inspection team had encountered measurement difficulties due to the low level of water in the storage tanks, and the Iraqi authorities had been asked to increase the level. This has now been done in seven tanks.

IRT-5000 reactor

43.   All fuel elements were counted and five were verified using a Ge-Li detector, including two which were declared to have been irradiated for only several hours. It was demonstrated that an element could now be removed from its storage position in the spent fuel pond without dust being raised in the water. This will enable the 13 previously inaccessible elements to be verified during a future inspection.

Beryllium (Be) inventory

44.   Seventeen Be assemblies and the Be central neutron trap have been declared as associated with the IRT-5000 reactor; 13 of the assemblies and the trap remain in the core, three assemblies are in the reactor storage racks and one (not irradiated) is

0130   /...

under seal in the "New Storage" cabinet. The items were counted and three were brought to the water surface for visual inspection and a dose measurement (< 100 mS/hr at 10 cm in air). Seven Be assemblies have been declared as associated with the Tamuz-2 reactor. They are in a barrel stored in pit 15 at location B. They were counted, and three were removed from the barrel and from their plastic wrapping for visual identification and dose rate measurements. A sample was taken from one of them. The barrel was sealed. The verification results so far are consistent with the Iraqi declaration.

Nuclear material in bulk form

45. A major objective of the IAEA inspections has been to physically verify all the bulk nuclear material in Iraq. However, most of this material (several hundred tons, mainly in powder form) had been clandestinely produced or imported. As a consequence of attempts to hide this material during the early inspections, the identifications on the containers and the associated paperwork are in some cases incorrect or incomplete. Moreover, during earlier attempts at clarification, complications arose as further declarations were made and new material provided.

These difficulties were commented on in earlier reports. The fifth inspection report in particular notes that it would require a full team working for at least a week to adequately verify the material and clarify the situation. Before the seventh inspection it was decided to attempt to verify all the material at storage location C (consisting of ore, yellow-cake, uranium oxide powders and scrap material from the enrichment process) and examine the associated records, and not to attempt to verify the material at sites other than Al Tuwaitha.

46. Table 2 summarizes the verification activities performed by the seventh team and includes the results obtained from verification by the third and fifth teams. The nuclear material flow chart in Figure 10 is based on information collected. Details of the bulk material verification are given in Annex 5.

A final conclusion about the amounts and categories of nuclear material presented in the different Iraqi declarations cannot be drawn until a full evaluation of the non-destructive and destructive analyses is performed. All material at location C has been left under seal.

ACTIVITIES RELATED TO PLUTONIUM PRODUCTION

47. The activities related to plutonium production at Al Tuwaitha were analysed. Four campaigns of one assembly each were processed in the hot cells of Building 9. The first campaign was for plutonium recovery from one exempt fuel element with an initial enrichment of 10% from the IRT-5000 reactor. The other three were for plutonium recovery from indigeneously produced Iraqi fuel elements. The fuel was manufactured in the fuel fabrication facility, Building 73. The natural uranium fuel elements were irradiated in the IRT-5000 reactor by removing a Be reflector and replacing it by a fuel element. The irradiated fuel elements were disassembled in the Tamuz-2 hot cell, and

0131   /...

0132

**7TH ON-SITE INSPECTION
LOCATION C**

Table 2

Summary of inspection results

UNSC 687

MATERIAL TYPE	ORIGIN Processing Site	PRESENTED TO TEAM TEAM No	DECLARED INVENTORY			VERIFIED INVENTORY VERIFICATION				LEFT UNDER SEAL Y/N
			No. of Items	Compound Weight (kg)	Element Weight (kg)	I	NDA	B	D	
Yellow Cake	Niger	1,3	430	135744	100200	430	156	55	18	Y
Cake	Portugal	1,3	915	286435	213015	915	321	121	44	Y
UO₂ Pellets	Previous Safeguards	4		28.10	23	1	1	1	1	Y
UO₃ 8 Powders		1,3				10	6	4	2	Y
UO₂ Powders		1	47	1350.7	1162	22	18	7	2	Y
UO₄ Powders		1				1	1	1	1	Y
Mixed Oxides		1				6	6	3	1	Y
UO₄ Slurry		4				8	8	8	2	Y
UO₄ Filters		4	37	·	50	37	·	·	1	Y
Liquid Waste	Brazil/ ALT. Bld 15	4	4	·	8	4	·	·	1	Y
UO₂ Powders	Brazil	3,4	227	22578	18643	227	48	227	10	Y
UF₆	Brazil/ ALT. Bld 15	3	1	0.465	0.312	1	1	1	1	Y
UF₄ Powders	Brazil/ ALT. Bld 15	1,3	5	359	233	5	4	4	3	Y
UCl₄	Brazil/ ALT. Bld 8/s	3,4	43	1520	957	43	41	25	9	Y

(Material types UO₂ Pellets through UCl₄ grouped under side label: N A T U R A L   U R A N I U M)

I = Item counting   B = Weighing   D = Sampling and analysis   NDA = Non-destructive analysis

*This table does not include the Nuclear Material present at Tikrit (138 tonnes compound weight of yellow cake of Niger origin, 3000 kg. compound weight of yellow cake produced at Al-Qaim and 2255 kg compound weight of UO₄ processed in Al-Mosul).

/...

Table 2 (continued)

UNSC 687

7TH ON-SITE INSPECTION
LOCATION C

MATERIAL TYPE	ORIGIN Processing Site	PRESENTED TO TEAM No	DECLARED INVENTORY			VERIFIED INVENTORY / VERIFICATION				LEFT UNDER SEAL Y/N
			No. of Items	Compound Weight (kg)	Element Weight (kg)	I	NDA	B	D	
NATURAL URANIUM U Metal	Brazil/ Al. T. BLD 1D	4	22	1000	1000	22	7	21	3	Y
ADU Powder	Brazil/ Al. T. BLD 85	3	31	1850	1357	31	-	3	1	Y
Liquid Recovery	Brazil/ Al. T. BLD 85	3	2	-	-	2	-	2	29	Y
ADU Powder		4	3	220	165	3	3	3	4	Y
UO4		3	2 samples	-	-	2	1	2	4	Y
NATURAL URANIUM U3O8	Al-Qaim/Al-Mosul	4	4	100	84	4	4	4	1	Y
UCL4		3	8	1207	780	5	8	8	3	Y
UO3 Powders		3	44*	2050	1701	8	8	8	12	Y
UO4 Powders Mixed		3				2	2	2	1	Y
Oxides						19	19	19	2	Y
UO2 Powders		3	409	96095	83883	409	307	97	41	Y
SCRAP	Al-Tuwaitha	3	1	-	-	1	-	1	1	Y

I = Item counting   B = Weighting   D = Sampling and analysis   NDA = Non-destructive analysis
* Rebatched and categorized during inspection

0133

/..

Figure 10

IRAQ'S NUCLEAR MATERIAL FLOW CHART

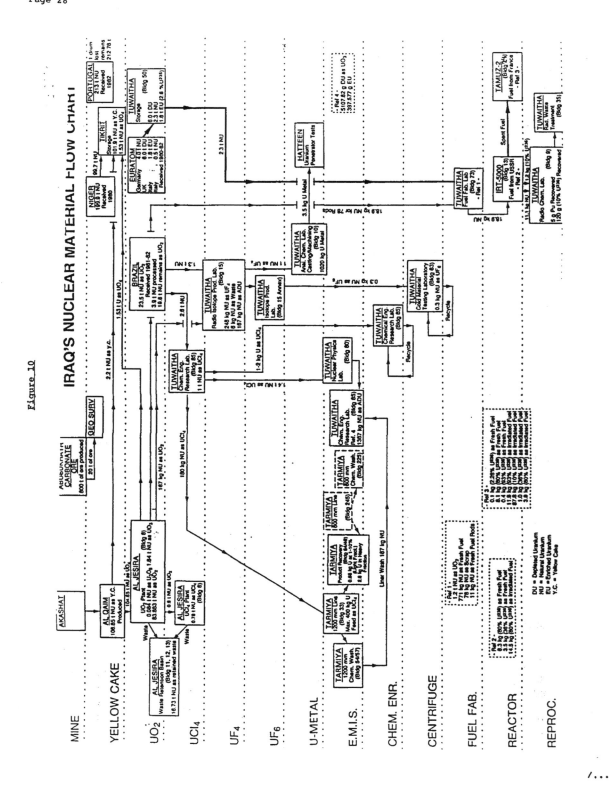

/...

individual fuel pins were transported to Laboratory C-1 in Building 9. Chopping and dissolving occurred in hot cell SC-1. Uranium and plutonium were separated from fission products in hot cell SC-3 in two banks of mixer-settlers with 16 cells in each bank. All zircaloy hulls from the three Iraqi fuel elements are stored in cans at the back of hot cell SC-2.

48. Uranium and plutonium were transferred from hot cell SC-3 to glove box GB 9, which contained the "accountability" and acid and valence adjust tanks. The solution was then pumped to glove-box GB 10, which contained two banks of mixer-settlers of 16 cells each for uranium-plutonium partitioning and plutonium recovery. Plutonium was batch-transferred to glove box GB 17 and concentrated using a heated mantle. No attempt was made to recover rare gases or iodine; they were vented to the atmosphere.

Waste from the exempted campaign was shipped to Building 35, where it was bitumenized. The bitumenized waste is stored in shielded casks in the waste storage building.

About 400 litres with 350 Ci of waste from the Iraqi campaigns is stored under Building 9 in two waste storage containers - one for aqueous and one for liquid waste. No attempt was made to recover neptunium from any of the four campaigns.

The campaigns were as follows:

3045EK10 exempted fuel	April 1988	2.26 g Pu
1st EK07 14 pins cassette	Nov 89 - Feb 90	0.506 g Pu
2nd 3rd EK07 (32 pins per cassette)	1 May 90 - 30 Jul 90	2.2 g Pu

The dissolving time was the bottleneck in the process; this suggests a maximum capacity of 60 g Pu/year without modification of the installation.

Plutonium-238 production

49. Microgram amounts of plutonium-238 had been produced from neptunium (Np^{237}) obtained commercially. The declared remaining neptunium is stored in two vials in glove box GB 4 of Laboratory C-2 in Building 9 and should be shipped by the next inspection team. The neptunium was irradiated in the IRT-5000 reactor. The plutonium-238 was reportedly recovered in glove box GB 2 of Laboratory C-2.

Polonium-210 production

50. Microgram amounts of polonium-210 had been prepared by irradiating bismuth in the IRT-5000 reactor. Several irradiations were performed from the end of 1988 to 1990, starting with gram quantities and working up to kilogram quantities. The polonium was recovered in glove boxes in the polonium laboratory on the second floor of Building 9. The laboratory was extensively damaged during the bombing and the glove boxes were broken. Four of the six declared boxes were removed and are now located in

0135 /...

a field near Al Tuwaitha. Three broken boxes were mildly and one severely alpha-contaminated.

The starting bismuth was 99.95% pure. No attempt was made to recover the bismuth. [The bismuth and polonium waste residue was placed in 15 or 16 drums in a bitumenized trench with a bitumen cover at the waste storage site]. Some surface alpha contamination is present at the site from the rupture of some drums during the bombing.

Lithium-6 production

51.   A laboratory for lithium-6 production existed in Building 90 but was completely destroyed during the bombing. The enrichment was performed by solvent extraction using crown ethers in a small-scale single rotating axial column. Approximately 0.5 - 1 kg of lithium passed through the column per annum. The highest single-stage enrichment factor was 1.03.

It was claimed that the lithium-6 work can be considered a continuation of work performed under an IAEA contract on the use of crown ethers for radiochemical separation for environmental purposes. A statement was made about the wish to continue the work in order to separate calcium isotopes for medical purposes.

None of the laboratory equipment is reported to exist and no files were produced, although requested. The office building connected to the facility was visited and, although all windows were damaged, all files should have survived. It was claimed that all files were destroyed by the bombing.

OTHER ACTIVITIES

Destruction of glove boxes and manipulators

52.   In Laboratory C-1 all cables for manipulators in hot cells SC-1, SC-2, SC-3 and JC-2 were destroyed. The manipulator parts are stored under seal in the manipulator repair shop along with the four previously sealed, unused manipulators. The room is sealed. All glove boxes (15 in total) in laboratories C-1 and C-2 were filled with cement to a depth of 5-10 cm. The new unused glove boxes in the decontamination laboratory, C-3, were disconnected and moved to Building 14 A. Laboratories C-1 and C-2 were sealed with wire and paper seals. Three manipulators and a periscope stored outside the Lama facility were removed to Building 14 A. In addition to the training manipulator from Building 35, all other undamaged manipulators in different buildings are under seal; the seals were verified.

A number of activities have been identified for follow-up.

Destruction of EMIS and Centrifuge Components

53.   A large amount of EMIS and centrifuge equipment was destroyed during the seventh inspection. A detailed inventory of the centrifuge components destroyed is provided

/...

0136

in Table 3. All known centrifuge components are now destroyed or were removed by the inspection team. Table 4 describe centrifuge-related items or manufacturing equipment destined for future destruction or monitoring. The full inventory of EMIS components, now stored at Al Nafad, is given in Annex 4. Most of this equipment was destroyed during the bombing or by the Iraqi military during its unsuccessful attempt to conceal the EMIS program. A few vacuum chambers were still fairly intact and were destroyed in the presence of the seventh team. The double-pole magnet cores, end pieces and portions of return iron have been inventoried and marked; they will be destroyed when the means to do so are found.

54. The following EMIS-related items were destroyed by having pieces cut out from each with a plasma torch:

1	1200 mm Vacuum Chamber Die
1	600 mm Vacuum Chamber Die
5	1200 mm Vacuum Chambers
2	600 mm Vacuum Chambers
1	106 mm System Chamber
2	Small Experimental Chambers
2	600 mm Vacuum Ducts
2	1200 mm Vacuum Ducts
19	Misc. 1200 and 600 mm Vacuum Chamber Cones

The following centrifuge-related items were destroyed using a large press or cutting-welding torches:

2	Centrifuge Test Jigs
2	Complete Oil Centrifuges
3	Oil Centrifuge Cylinders
7	Centrifuge Jackets
1	UF_6 Feeding System
5	Boxes of miscellaneous parts

Levelling of buildings at Al Tuwaitha

55. During the fifth IAEA inspection mission it was noted that a number of destroyed buildings at Al Tuwaitha had been levelled. The Iraqi authorities stated that this had been done because of the danger of their collapsing. The attached Al Tuwaitha site map indicates these buildings. The Iraqi authorities wish to level additional buildings for similar reasons, and their request is under consideration.

Activities at PC-3 Headquarters and the Nuclear Design Centre

56. During the sixth IAEA inspection mission, the team had applied IAEA seals to two safes and a metal cabinet at the Nuclear Design Centre and to a room at PC-3 Headquarters containing about 800 files with procurement, budget and training records.

0137 /...

Table 3

List of centrifuge components selected for immediate destruction

Stored in Warehouse 13b - Ash Shakyli (Al Tuwaitha)

Item	Quantity
Recipients with holes	4
Recipients with holes and pumps	2
Recipients without holes	1
Recipients of different design and 2 loose pieces	2
Top flanges	54
Top flange with damper	1
Test jigs	2
Set of piping with valves and vacuum circuit; components contained in a wooden crate	1
Aluminium cylinders for rotors - one with end caps	3
Maraging steel cylinders [2 full length & 3 shorter ones]	5
Molecular pumps	5
Carbon fibre cylinders	7
Scoop assembly (1 with manifold)	2
Tube (approx. 1 cm x 15 cm)	8
Inner magnet holder	28
Ring (approx. 1 cm OD)	107
Tube (approx. 1 cm x 45 cm) (scoop part)	19
Tube (approx. 1 cm x 30 cm) (scoop part)	18
Sensor holder	36
Lower bearing spacer	10
Upper damper spacer	6
Upper damper (3 cm Dia. x 6 cm)	8
Flange-spacer ring	4
Small sensor holder	6
Scoop assembly part (2 cm OD x 4 cm)	17
Scoop assembly part-tube (15 cm Dia x 7 cm)	27
U-cup upper damper part	5
K-F flange upper manifold part	6
Magnet outer holding ring (1.5 Dia x 6.5)	13
Washer (0.5 cm Dia x 4.5 cm)	29
Washer (0.4 cm Dia x 3 cm)	31
Scoop ring (3 cm Dia x 2 cm)	9
Lower bearing housing cover (5 cm Dia x 1.5 cm)	3
Ring (8 cm Dia x 1 cm)	1
Lower damper spacer	2

0138   /...

Table 3 (continued)

Item	Quantity
Ring (2 cm Dia x 1 cm)	4
Rocker arm	20
Pin for assembling (lower assembly) (0.3 cm Dia x 4 cm)	18
Spacer (0.6 cm x 0.2 cm)	55
Tubes for scoop assembly; Al (1 cm Dia x 84 cm)	10
Tubes for scoop assembly; Al (1 cm Dia x 74 cm)	20
Tubes for scoop assembly; Al (1.5 cm Dia x 35 cm)	23
Tubes for scoop assembly; Al (approx. 1.4 cm Dia x 50 cm)	5
Rings (10.5 cm OD x 1 cm) Motor coil	5
Cu scoop material (straight) (0.4/0.6 x 24 cm) (tapered)	20
Motor stator spacer (approx. 1.3 cm x 1.3 cm)	80
Tube (tails pipe for scoop assembly) (2.2 cm Dia x 20 cm)	22
Maraging steel rotor top cap	38
Carbon machine top baffle	7
Carbon machine top cap	10
Carbon machine bottom cap	1
Aluminium top rotating magnet holder (small)	13
Aluminium bottom damper skirt	76
Aluminium top rotating magnet holder (large)	6
Bottom damper housing	25
Spacer flange	16
Top damper housing	9
Bottom damper cover	14
Adjusting screw	21
Parts of scoop assembly	19
Pivot holder (brass)	18
Maraging steel top rotating magnet holder	41
Feed shroud	66
Feed input flange	47
Bottom bearing flange	22
Feed port	24
Top scoop holder	27
AlNiCo magnet holder	43
Part of top scoop	54
Bottom scoop boss	24
Washer	18
Top damper adjusting screw	60
Part of lower damper	30
AlNiCo magnets	84
CoSm magnets	49
Gas manifold	82
Transport shield for protection	1
Aluminium bottom flange	16

0139   /...

Table 4

Centrifuge-related items for future destruction
or monitoring

WAREHOUSE 13b, ASH SHAKYLI (AL TUWAITHA)

Item	Quantity
Valves (VAT & Nupro)	700
Oil (Fomblin) Vacuum pump oil - Krytox	100 Liters
Horizontal balancing machine	1
Vertical balancing machine	1
Frequency converters - Acomel	2
Assembly presses	2
Vacuum pumps - rotary	22

DAURA - STATE ENTERPRISE FOR HEAVY ENGINEERING EQUIPMENT

Item	Quantity
Flow turning machine	1
Mandrel	1
Expanding mandrel	1
Electron beam welding chamber and all associated apparatus	1
Oxidation furnaces and all associated apparatus	2
MIG welding equipment (for recipients)	1
Brazing furnace and associated apparatus	1
Heat treatment furnace and associated apparatus	1
CNC machines	3

BADER ENGINEERING SITE

Item	Quantity
CNC machines	10

0140

/...

The seventh IAEA team inspected these locations. The safes and the metal cabinet were found to be empty by the team after it had broken the seals. The files in the room at PC-3 Headquarters were all examined (approx. 10 000 pages of documents) and a selection of relevant procurement, budget and training documents was made. These documents were brought to Vienna and added to the documentation brought by the sixth team and awaiting further analysis. No problems from the Iraqi side were encountered.

The Al Kadisya State Establishment

57. The Al Furat site was originally a school for technicians. The training area (now designated as Building B00) had been reconfigured for the centrifuge manufacturing program. The remaining buildings are barracks and small support buildings. These buildings are unused. The north-east corner of the Al Furat site contains a separately fenced area (fig. 7). When the team requested access to this area for inspection purposes, the Iraqi authorities stated that the area belonged to another firm (the Al Kadisya State Establishment) and that a formal designation was required. This was quickly arranged, and the inspection proceeded. The area used to be part of the technician training centre that comprised the Al Furat site. The three larger buildings in this area are two barracks and a warehouse/storage building. The barracks are essentially untouched. Several rooms are being used as offices. The warehouse has been converted into a small machine shop used for some rudimentary robotics development work.

Uranium mine at Abu Sukhayr

58. This is an exploratory mine located approximately 25 km south-west of Najar. Prospecting started in September 1988 and ended at the end of 1990, when the mine was flooded by water from an aquifer. Twenty-five people were employed in all. The shaft was stated to be 75 m deep, with the galleries extending for 150 m, and the ore thickness 50 cm. Because of the flooding, it was not possible for the inspectors to enter the shaft to check these statements.

The total production during the time the shaft was in operation was stated to have been 800 tons of Marley limestone with an average uranium content of 150 ppm. The range varied from 80 to 800 ppm. Samples were taken from both crushed and uncrushed ore for analysis to verify this statement.

Apart from some 20 tons of ore stated to have been sent to the HQ organization ("General Establishment for Geological Survey and Prospecting"), all material extracted was on the site. The manager stated that drilling had been abandoned and that there was no intention to restart. The general appearance of the site supported this statement.

No records were available, it being claimed that everything in the administrative offices was destroyed following the war. The offices were portable cabins and caravans (trailers), which had clearly been completely wrecked.

The uranium content of the ore is two to three times higher than that of the ore at Akashat, which formed the feed to the uranium extraction plant to Al Qaim. It would probably be worthwhile for Iraq to carry out further exploration if a decision were taken in the future to resume nuclear activities.

0141   /...

ANNEX 1

IRAQI ATOMIC ENERGY COMMISSION

No:

Date: 14 October 1991

        With reference to your letter of 12 October 1991 concerning
what you call "weaponization", I wish – before responding to the
contents of that letter – to affirm the following facts:

1.   Iraq has officially confirmed the abandonment of its nuclear
programme, the latest such confirmation being contained in the
letter dated 10 October 1991 from Iraq's Minister of Foreign
Affairs addressed to the Director-General of the International
Atomic Energy Agency.

2.   There is no Iraqi political decision to manufacture nuclear
weapons.

3.   There is no Iraqi programme to produce nuclear weapons or
explosives.

4.   Al-Athir · Centre was designed to be a national materials
centre and represents the missing link in Iraqi industry and
technology.   The extent of the losses suffered by Iraqi industry
as a result of the problems concerning materials imported for
industrial purposes are no secret to anyone. However, the centre
could – at the same time – cover important aspects of the weapons
programme if such a thing were to be decided upon or desired.

5.   Various research and studies of the sort to which you refer
as "weaponization" have been carried out. The objective in
carrying out such research and studies was to establish the
practical; technical and scientific requirements for a programme
of this nature in the event that a political decision were to be
taken to proceed in that direction. The intention was that the
political leadership should be apprised of these requirements so
that it might consider them – together with the political
implications – and then take an appropriate decision on a topic
of such significance. We affirm that there was no political
decision – as of the the time when the 30-nation aggression was
launched against Iraq – to manufacture nuclear weapons or nuclear
explosives in any shape or form whatsoever.

Mr. Demetrius Perricos
Chief, 7th International Nuclear Inspection Team

                                                    0142

                                                        /...

6.   Al-Athir Centre was put into operation in approximately mid-1990.   From the outset and until the beginning of the aggression on the night of 16/17 January 1991, its activity revolved around matters of installation, organization and testing.   Furthermore, parts of the centre are still under construction and remain uncompleted, with civil works still in progress.   No scientific research, study or practical work had begun at the centre as of the beginning of the aggression on the night of 16/17 January 1991.

7.   Accordingly, none of the research and studies carried out – the questions concerning which will be answered by us – were performed at al-Athir Centre.

8.   In conclusion, we affirm once again that all the research and studies carried out and described by you as "weaponization" consist of laboratory-level research not designed to lead to the production of weapons.

     Please accept my respects.

                         (Signed) Dr. Abd al-Halim Ibrahim AL-HAJJAJ
                                 Head of the Iraqi Team

Enclosures: Answers to question 1

0143

/...

ANNEX 2

IRAQI ATOMIC ENERGY COMMISSION

No: 2300/920/177

Date: 21 October 1991

Further to our letter of 14/10/1991, I wish to add the following concerning Al-Athir Centre for Materials Production Development, in order to avoid any possible confusion and to ensure further clarification:

1.   All research and studies carried out under the heading of what you have decided to call "weaponization" were carried out by operational and technical teams belonging to Group IV of the project. All such activity was conducted at this Group's work-sites in Tuwaitha, apart from the plane lens experiments, which were conducted at the Hatteen Establishment explosives laboratory.

The intention was that the teams in this Group be returned to their original jobs, depending on area of specialization, after completing their specific task (to determine the operational, technical and scientific requirements for a weapons programme if a political decision should be taken to proceed). These teams would of course serve as the core for such a programme if it were decided to proceed in the future.

In 1990, this Group was given the code name "Al-Athir Plant".

The Group was headed by Dr. Khalid Ibrahim Sa'id.

0144

/...

2.   Al-Athir Centre for Materials Production Development is an entirely separate subject, bearing no relation to the work of this Group.   It was established to serve the country's industrial establishments, with the Ministry of Industry assuming responsibility for coordination and supervision.   Dr. Khalid Ibrahim Sa'id chaired the Centre's steering committee.

He, of course, ordered whatever he felt was necessary to meet the design requirements for the buildings which could serve the possible programme if a decision were to be taken to proceed in the future, including the possible use of Al-Athir Centre for such a programme, in addition to its fundamental uses.

In any event, Al-Athir Centre has not yet commenced operations of its current programme as a national materials centre.   It was definitely not used to carry out the research and studies which you refer to as "weaponization".

We hope that we have thus provided an adequate explanation of the separation between Al-Athir Centre and what you call "weaponization".

Yours sincerely,

(Signed) Abd al-Halim Ibrahim al-Hajjaj
Head of the Iraqi Team

Mr. Demetrius Perricos
Chief, Seventh International Nuclear Inspection Team

0145   /...

ANNEX 3

LIST OF DOCUMENTS AND DECLARATIONS SENT OR RECEIVED

7-1.   Mr. Perricos to Mr. Al Hajjaj on 911012 - requesting information on gaseous centrifuge enrichment, gaseous diffusion enrichment, laser isotope separation, chemical enrichment, reprocessing and plutonium production programs, and the general organization of the nuclear program.

7-2.   Mr. Perricos to Mr. Al Hajjaj on 911012 - requesting information on various aspects of the weaponization program.

7-3.   Mr. Perricos to Mr. Al Hajjaj on 911012 - referring to a meeting on 911012 and requesting additional information on the 93 % U-235 observed in some samples and providing lead questions about weaponization.

7-4.   Mr. Perricos to Mr. Al Hajjaj on 911012 - requesting a list of equipment collected at a location at Al Tuwaitha, indicating the origin of such equipment, and a schedule for the future movements of the equipment.

7-5.   Mr. Al Hajjaj to Mr. Perricos on 911013 - providing a list of the EMIS program equipment transferred to location T at Al Tuwaitha (Note: Upon inventory-taking some modifications to the list provided were made).

7-6.   Mr. Al Hajjaj to Mr. Perricos on 911012 - providing answers to some questions put by the fifth team on 910920 about mass spectrometers, electrochemical cells and mixer-settlers.

7-7.   Mr. Al Hajjaj to Mr. Perricos on 911014 - referring to paras 3 and 4 of letter of 911012 (item 7-1 above), concerning laser and chemical enrichment.

7-8.   Mr. Al Hajjaj to Mr. Perricos on 911014 - referring to enquiry of 911012 (item 7-3 above) regarding uranium enriched to 93 %.

7-9.   Mr. Al Hajjaj to Mr. Perricos on 911014 - referring to letter of 911012 (item 7-3 above), concerning the high-speed cameras and capacitors and providing a sample of such a capacitor.

7-10.   Mr. Al Hajjaj to Mr. Perricos on 911014 - referring to para.7 of letter of 911012 (items 7-1 and 7-2 above), concerning the organization of nuclear and weaponization program activities.

7-11.   Mr. Al Hajjaj to Mr. Perricos on 911015 - response to para.5, concerning fuel reprocessing and plutonium production, of letter of 911012 (item 7-1 above).

7-12.   Mr. Al Hajjaj to Mr. Perricos on 911015 - response to letter of 911012 (item 7-2 above), regarding project 144 and the HMX explosives.

7-13.   Mr. Al Hajjaj to Mr. Perricos on 911015 - response to the paras 1.1.1 to 1.2.5 of letter of 911012 (item 7-2 above), regarding weaponization.

0146

/...

7-14.   Mr. Al Hajjaj to Mr. Perricos on 911015 - response to paras.1 and 2, concerning the enrichment and the gaseous diffusion centrifuge method, of letter 911012 (item 7-1 above).

7-15.   Mr. Al Hajjaj to Mr. Perricos on 911015 - notifying, in response to letter of 911012 (item 7-4 above), the transfer of the equipment of the electromagnetic separation program from the destruction sites to the Al Tuwaitha site.

7-16.   Mr. Perricos to Mr. Al Hajjaj on 911016 - summarizing the points discussed at a meeting on 911015 (which included the availability of machines to cut the magnets of the EMIS program; the destruction of the dies used for the EMIS program magnets at Daura; the return of the microfilms and microfiches of the sixth inspection team; the presentation of the chemical enrichment columns; information regarding the buildings levelling operations at Al Tuwaitha; a list of the universities which have received the mass spectrometers; a list of the facilities which have received the graphite equipment; arrangements for a visit to the Saladdine establishment and the Abu Sukhayr mine; a list of the centrifuge parts to be destroyed; the destruction or rendering harmless of equipment in glove boxes and of certain manipulators; the further investigation of the import of maraging steel to Iraq; and a statement on the number of beryllium rods.

7-17.   Mr. Al Hajjaj to Mr. Perricos on 911016 - response to para.2, concerning the development of analytical tools, and para.3, concerning experimental programs, of letter of 901012 (item 7-2 above).

7-18.   Mr. Al Hajjaj to Mr. Perricos on 911016 - providing information on the inventory of beryllium rods in response to letter of 911016 (item 7-16 above).

7-19.   Mr. Perricos to Mr. Al Hajjaj on 911017 - stating that advance notification and agreement with the IAEA are required before the removal of any seals on items and/or material and/or the removal of items to other locations. The IAEA will provide a list of seals once the team returns to Vienna.

7-20.   Mr. Al Hajjaj to Mr. Perricos on 911017 - requesting copies of videofilms and photographs taken by the team at Al Atheer on 911016.

7-21.   Mr. Al Hajjaj to Mr. Perricos on 911017 - requesting copies of videofilms and photographs taken by the team at Al Hatteen on 911017.

7-22.   Mr. Al Hajjaj to Mr. Perricos - answers to questions 1 and 4, concerning material production, of letter of 911012 (item 7-2 above).

7-23.   Mr. Perricos to Mr. Al Hajjaj on 911019 - additional questions regarding matters connected with uranium enrichment (such as serial numbers on molecular pumps, strip chart in an oxidation furnace, the location of mandrels, the machine used for the preparation of groovings, the machine used for welding the ball to the needle, a request for the top and bottom bearings and the motor of the molecular pumps, and information on the manufacturer and technology of the motor and on the laboratory used for the diffusion research) arising out of the on-site inspection activities carried out on 911017.

0147   /...

7-24.   Mr. Perricos to Mr. Al Hajjaj on 911019 - requesting a discussion on the research on laser isotope separation (AVLIS and MLIS) in Iraq.

7-25.   Mr. Perricos to Mr. Al Hajjaj on 911019 - referring to letters of 911017 (items 7-20 and 7-21 above) and agreeing to provide a copy of relevant film and pictures later through the Iraqi Permanent Mission in Vienna.

7-26.   Mr. Perricos to Mr. Al Hajjaj on 911019 - requesting certain documents related to the inspection activities performed at Al Atheer, Al Qa Qaa and Al Hatteen and the second list of centrifuge-related items to be destroyed or rendered harmless.

7-27.   Mr. Perricos to Mr. Al Hajjaj on 911020 - requesting the production records of the Al Qaim and Ash Sharqat mines in the light of ore sample analysis results.

7-28.   Mr. Perricos to Mr. Al Hajjaj on 911020 - asking for additional information on: nuclear sources currently under IAEA paper seals at location C; UO_2 and UO_3 from Al Mosul; uranium solutions and powders from Building 85; uranium metal production; and tare weights of a UF_6 cylinder and the UO_2 drums from Al-Mosul.

7-29.   Mr. Al Hajjaj to Mr. Perricos on 911020 - answer to letter of 911017 (item 7-23 above), which had requested additional information on the enrichment program.

7-30.   Mr. Al Hajjaj to Mr. Perricos on 911019 - answer to paras 5 and 6 of letter of 911012 (item 7-2 above), concerning the facilities and equipment of the weaponization program.

7-31.   Mr. Al Hajjaj to Mr. Perricos on 911019 - answer to request of 911019 (item 7-26 above), with the Al Atheer equipment layout plan.

7-32.   Mr. Al Hajjaj to Mr. Perricos on 911019 - answer to para.7 of letter of 911012 (item 7-2 above), stating that information on weaponization is in the documents acquired by the sixth team on 910923 and 910924.

7-33.   Mr. Perricos to Mr. Al Hajjaj on 911021 - acknowledging receipt of plutonium solutions.

7-34.   Mr. Perricos to Mr. Al Hajjaj on 911021 - requesting: additional information about flying plates; the organization chart of PC3; a description of one- and two-dimensional codes; design specifications of the Al Hatteen bunker; a description of firing tests at the bunker between March and May 1990; a sketch of the explosive lenses used in the tests; sensors used for detonic tests; and information on sites where isostatic presses are located (referring to the meeting with Mr. Said on 911020).

7-35.   Mr. Perricos to Mr. Al Hajjaj on 911021 - requesting: additional information on imported beryllium, the return of uranium samples from Al Hatteen to Al Tuwaitha; a statement on the use of buildings at Al Atheer; information on the location of the ion sources of the Al Tuwaitha EMIS units; and information on the removal of equipment from and on the back-up role of Ash Sharqat.

7-36.   Mr. Gil-Ramos to Mr. Al-Saji on 911021 - asking for an explanation of the difference between the ICR and source documents for a UO2 shipment made on 820513.

/...

0148

7-37. Mr. Al Hajjaj to Mr. Perricos on 911020 - response to letter of 911010 (item 7-24 above), stating that there is no laser enrichment activity under way in Iraq.

7-38. Mr. Al Hajjaj to Mr. Perricos on 911021 - requesting the release of a "full" amount of HMX for civilian uses.

7-39. Iraqi Atomic Energy Commission, Annual report 1990.

7-40. Mr. Al Hajjaj to Mr. Perricos on 911021 - response to letter of 911020 (item 7-28 above), providing a list of radioactive sources stored at location C; giving information on the total production of UO_2 at Al Jesira, on UO_3 and UO_4 from the Al Jesira laboratory, on uranium solutions and powder from Al Tuwaitha Building 85, and on uranium metal; and stating tare weights of UF_6 cylinder and UO_2 drums.

7-41. Mr. Al Hajjaj to Mr. Perricos on 911021 - referring to machines sealed by the seventh on-site inspection team at the Badr General Installation and the General Installation for Heavy Equipment and to plans for using these machines for purposes of civilian production and construction, and asking for views regarding those plans.

7-42. Mr. Al Hajjaj to Mr. Perricos on 911021 - response to letter of 911021 (item 7-35 above), stating that after sending for destruction they have not been in a position to locate any of the ion sources and collectors, the transformers being moved from Ash Sharkat for use elsewhere, and that Ash Sharqat was selected as a substitute in mid-1988, and when the first Tarmiya separator was commissioned handed it over to the Ministry of Industry, and that there was no programme worked out to move equipment between Tarmiya and Ash Sharqat.

7-43. Mr. Al Hajjaj to Mr. Perricos on 911021 - response to letter of 911020 (item 7-27 above), providing information on production at Al Qaim.

7-44. Mr. Al Hajjaj to Mr. Perricos on 911021 - response to letter of 911021 (item 7-35 above), providing information on the use of beryllium.

7-45. Mr. Al Hajjaj to Mr. Perricos on 911021 - response to letter of 911021 (item 7-35 above), providing a list of buildings at Al Atheer, Al Hatteen and Balat Al Shohadaa.

7-46. Mr. Al Hajjaj to Mr. Perricos on 911021 - response to letter of 911019 (item 7-26 above), providing a plan of the Al Hatteen establishment.

7-47. Mr. Al Hajjaj to Mr. Perricos on 911021 - reponse to the third question on page 2 of letter of 911021 (item 7-35 above), reiterating that an answer was provided in letter of 910121.

7-48. Mr. Al Hajjaj to Mr. Perricos on 911021 - response to questions about presses at Al Atheer (items 7-2 above and 7-56 below).

7-49. Mr. Al Hajjaj to Mr. Perricos on 911021 - response to questions regarding the cameras used at Al Atheer, stating that the information was provided to the fourth inspection team in a letter dated 910809.

0149   /...

7-50. Mr. Al Hajjaj to Mr. Perricos on 911021 - response to letter of 911019 (item 7-31 above) providing the equipment layouts in the powder, casting and carbide buildings at Al-Atheer.

7-51. Mr. Al Hajjaj to Mr. Perricos on 911021 - response to letter of 911019 (item 7-26 above), providing information on the composition of the HMX used.

7-52. Mr. Al Hajjaj to Mr. Perricos on 911021 - reponse to questions 4 and 5 of letter dated 911019 (item 7-34 above), providing information on the design specifications of the bunker and a store.

7-53. Mr. Al Hajjaj to Mr. Perricos on 911021 - reponse to letter of 911017 (item 7-23 above), regarding the welding of the G1.3 cylinder and relevant oxidation process tests.

7-54. Mr. Al Hajjaj to Mr. Perricos on 911021 - response to letter of 911016 (item 7-16 above), providing a list of the buildings which have been or are to be removed from the Al Tuwaitha site.

7-55. Mr. Al Hajjaj to Mr. Perricos on 911021 - response to letter of 911016 (item 7-16 above), providing information on the destruction of EMIS equipment at Al Tuwaitha and Daura and stating that: the microfiches and films are still being sought; the chemical enrichment columns have been shown; the mass spectrometers are in the Chemistry Section of the IAEC; the graphite machining equipment has been moved to the Al Rabic plant; inspections were carried out at the Saladdine establishment and Abu Sukhayr; the centrifuge parts have been destroyed; destruction of the glove boxes has been carried out; and, regarding maraging steel, information was provided to the fourth team, but should the Agency have additional information, they would like to receive it for further investigation.

7-56. Mr. Perricos to Mr. Al Hajjaj on 911021 - asking for additional information on the design studies, basic design, lithium, detonators - exploding bridgewire system, hydrodynamic tests, and flash X-ray program.

7-57. Mr. Al Hajjaj to Mr. Perricos on 911021 - response to letter of 911021 (item 7-56 above), providing a report on the use of exploding bridgewires.

7-58. Mr. Al Hajjaj to Mr. Perricos on 911021 - response to letter of 911021 (item 7-56 above), providing a report on experiments with plane lenses.

7-59. Mr. Al Hajjaj to Mr. Perricos on 911021 - response to letter of 911021 (item 7-56 above), providing information on the one- and two-dimensional calculations, molecular calculations, neutronics calculations, and distortion and other calculations made.

0150

/..

Annex 4

The Iraqi Uranium Enrichment Program

The Electromagnetic Isotope Separation (EMIS) Process

1. The Iraqi EMIS project has been described at length in the full reports of the third and fourth inspection teams. The EMIS-related activities of the seventh inspection team consisted of:

    (a)   detailed inspection of the Ash Sharqat site;

    (b)   a verification of EMIS components that have been collected together at two sites near Al Tuwaitha (efforts to complete the destruction of EMIS components were initiated);

    (c)   the identification and sealing of manufacturing equipment used in the production of EMIS components.

    The Ash Sharqat site

2. The Ash Sharqat EMIS production site is located about 250 kilometers north of Baghdad. Development of the site began in 1988. According to Iraqi statements, the site was being developed as an alternative to Tarmiya (possibly for some of the activities located at Al Tuwaitha) at a time during the Iran-Iraq War when both the Al Tuwaitha and the Tarmiya site were seen as vulnerable to attack. The facilities at Ash Sharqat are a duplicate of the corresponding facilities at Tarmiya. Iraqi statements indicate that, after the end of the Iran-Iraq War (mid-1989), a decision was taken not to use the Ash Sharqat site for EMIS production.

3. The facilities at the Ash Sharqat site are distributed among three geographically separate locations. The separation was apparently necessary because of the relatively rough terrain. The locations are designated:

Location A	-	electrical and mechanical workshops
Location B	-	main production area
Location C	-	chemical recovery area

    The distance between the locations varies from 1 to 2 kilometers. The facilities were still under construction at the time of the Gulf War. The workshops at location A appear to have been essentially complete. The facilities at the other two locations were 80 - 90 % complete. Construction cranes were still in place at location C when the site was bombarded.

4. The inspection by the seventh team was the second inspection of this site (the first was by the third inspection team, in July 1991). The objectives of the seventh inspection team were: to confirm the judgement of the third team that this site never operated and that no EMIS equipment had been installed there; to complete the characterization of the site; and to discover the nature of the intensive work activity at and near the site since the time of the third inspection.

0151   /...

5. The Ash Sharqat site was extensively damaged during the Gulf War. Of the major buildings, only the mechanical workshop at location A survived relatively intact. The electrical workshop at location A, the main production hall and general utilities building at location B and the chemical recovery facilities at location C were damaged beyond recovery. It has been confirmed that this establishment never operated and that no EMIS equipment was ever installed there. The large amount of infrastructure equipment (transformers, switching gear, water treatment equipment, etc.) that was still in place at the time of the third inspection has been moved to an open storage area to the north and east of location B. The Iraqi authorities stated that this equipment is being made available to other companies in Iraq The equipment in the storage area was inventoried, but it is clear that many pieces of equipment observed by the third team have been removed from the site altogether. Several samples were taken in the main production and chemical recovery areas.

6. The Iraqi statement that by mid-1989 it had been decided not to use Ash Sharqat as an EMIS site appears credible: at that point in time the Iran-Iraq War was over, the Tarmiya site was nearing completion and Iraqi scientists were having some success with the centrifuge development work at Al Tuwaitha. However, there is no evidence at Ash Sharqat to support this statement: construction work at the site continued as planned; there is no indication that any of the facilities were being reconfigured for some other use; and the installation of infrastructure equipment (most with a 1990 manufacture date) suitable for EMIS but far in excess of the needs for the alternative uses described by the Iraqi authorities was obviously continuing up to the time when the site was attacked. The opinion of the inspection team is that Iraq remained committed to Ash Sharqat as a second EMIS site. The project designation 395 was observed in a number of places.

7. The inspection team also investigated several activities observed along the ridge that runs north-south at the eastern perimeter of the site. Some of these activities were connected with a large bunker located on the hillside due east of location B. It was discovered that the bunker provided access to a very large (approx. 3000 m^3) water storage tank buried in the hillside. The tank, which provides water for the Ash Sharqat facilities, is supplied by pipe from the Tigris river. Other activities included seismic testing connected with petroleum exploration along the ridge and the operation of a stone quarry, with the corresponding accumulation of spoil.

Verification of EMIS components

8. At the end of the third inspection, the Iraqi authorities were requested to move all EMIS equipment to a site in the vicinity of the Al Tuwaitha Nuclear Research Center. This has been done and a new declaration was presented to the seventh inspection team. Ion sources and collectors were presented at a location adjacent to the new dump site, just outside the Al Tuwaitha berm. The remaining equipment is about 3 km from Al Tuwaitha, at Al Nafad. The configuration of the Al Nafad storage site is indicated below.

0152

/...

VACUUM CHAMBERS
- 1200 mm
- 600 mm
- 1000, 500, 400 mm

POWER SUPPLIES
SWITCHING GEAR
DIFFUSION PUMPS

ACCESS ROAD, TUWAITHA →

DOUBLE POLE MAGNETS

- 1200 mm
- 600 mm
- R&D POLES

END PIECES
VERTICAL RETURN IRONS
MAGNET CARRIAGES

COPPER COILS
- 1200 mm
- 600 mm
- R&D POLES
POWER SUPPLIES
WINDING MACHINE

The Iraqi EMIS equipment declaration is presented in Tables 1 - 4. The presentation is organized according to where the equipment had been or was intended to be installed.

9. The Iraqi declaration is consistent with previous information regarding the installation of 1200-mm EMIS equipment at Tarmiya and of R&D equipment at Al Tuwaitha, except for the numbers of ion sources and collectors. The ion sources for the Tarmiya equipment seem reasonably complete, judging by previously established operation and production information, but only 50% of the collectors from the 1200-mm line A separators installed at Tarmiya can be clearly identified (the expected number of collector mounting flanges is present). No ion sources or collectors from the Al Tuwaitha development units have been declared. The quantity of 600-mm EMIS equipment was far greater than that seen by previous inspection teams. The horizontal return irons discovered at Tarmiya during the third inspection have not been moved to Al Nafad. Additional inspection results are summarized below.

(a) The Iraqi declaration describing the EMIS equipment at the Al Nafad and Al Tuwaitha sites has been verified. The extent of the declaration is generally consistent with the known extent of EMIS development and deployment.

0153   /...

(b)   Most of the equipment is destroyed. Any key pieces not visibly damaged beyond use (several vacuum chambers and the magnet pole pieces, end pieces and vertical return iron) were marked for destruction. Activities undertaken to destroy this equipment are described later in the report.

(c)   Some EMIS-related equipment - 40 diffusion pumps, a large amount of electrical equipment and a coil winding machine - are stored at the Al Nafad site. This equipment is not described in the Iraqi declaration. The coil winding machine is destroyed and the diffusion pumps and electrical equipment have been damaged.

(d)   Where it was evident that a collection pocket had been mounted, all sources and collector flanges were sampled. This equipment had been destroyed.

10.   The lack of ion sources and collectors from the Al Tuwaitha R&D units remains a concern. The Iraqi authorities indicated that they had been unable to find them and would continue to search. The question of possible EMIS recycling at Al Tuwaitha, necessary for reaching high enrichments, remains open.

EMIS component manufacturing equipment

11.   The manufacture of EMIS components was carried out at seven establishments. Their role in the manufacture of EMIS components and the status of the manufacturing equipment were as follows:

(a)   Al Radwan and Al Amir - These establishments were involved in the high-precision machining of magnet poles, return irons and various parts of the ion source and collector assemblies. Large-capacity turning and milling machines (5 at Al Radwan and 2 at Al Amir) were identified and sealed.

(b)   SEHEE (Daura) - Vacuum chambers for the 600-mm and 1200-mm system were manufactured at Daura. The dies utilized in the manufacturing of the chambers were sealed for identification and later destroyed (see Annex 1).

(c)   Al Tuwaitha and nearby location - The copper coil magnet windings were manufactured at these sites. The coil winding machine is destroyed, and the remnants are shown in the inspection team's inventory of the equipment at Al Nafad.

(d)   Salladine and Dijila - The assembly of electrical control panels from plans and parts supplied by the Iraqi Atomic Energy Commission was carried out at these sites. No special equipment was involved and nothing remains from the work at these locations. The Salladine plant was established in 1986 under license of a foreign company. Most of the work was with telephone and microwave communication equipment and radar for the Iraqi military.

(e)   Al Ameen - The facility at Al Ameen was involved in the manufacture of prototype EMIS components.

0154

/...

The Gas Centrifuge Enrichment Project

12. The centrifuge enrichment project started much later than the EMIS enrichment project. However, its potential had been recognized by the Iraqi authorities and the project was being pursued with equal vigour.

   The seventh IAEA inspection team can confirm that, as stated by previous inspection teams, Iraq was following two centrifuge development lines. These were both based on a Zippe type subcritical counter current centrifuge, one using a maraging steel cylinder, the other using a carbon fibre cylinder.

   Judging by the manufacturing equipment declared and inspected, the preferred line was the one using maraging steel. The equipment inspected represented everything necessary for mass-producing successful centrifuges. Much of this equipment had not been delivered before early 1990; indeed, some essential equipment was still in its delivery packing cases. Iraq had thus only just started to understand the manufacturing requirements for producing maraging steel cylinders of adequate quality and the necessary tolerances. Also, the means of centrifuge rotor assembly had not been completely mastered. It was therefore necessary to pursue the parallel development line based on a carbon fibre cylinder for single-machine optimization tests. The cylinders were purchased abroad, and rotor assembly was comparatively simple.

   From the components seen it is concluded that both lines were in the early stages of development, but it is highly likely they would have been successful. It is believed that lack of experience or manufacturing capability was partially overcome by significant advice from abroad.

13. After inspecting the Al Furat workshop complex and the declared machine tools, jigs and fixtures, it is the team's opinion that the output of the workshop would, in time, have been far greater than that declared by Iraq. Iraq claims that the complex was planned to produce 200 centrifuges a year. An ultimate production capability of 2000 or more centrifuges a year is more likely.

   At the time of the inspection, the buildings at Al Furat were devoid of services and equipment, with two of the four main buildings still in the early stages of construction. However, it was stated that one of the buildings had been used for a few months in late 1990 to produce components for development work.

14. A complete inventory of the declared components and equipment was made with the co-operation of the Iraqi authorities. Steps were then taken to destroy immediately the centrifuge components (with the exception of a few pieces removed as samples by the inspection team) and what remained of the R&D test stands. Associated equipment was sealed for future destruction or monitoring.

   Following destruction of the specially designed equipment and critical machine tools, Iraq will have difficulty in re-establishing the centrifuge project - provided that there is strict maintenance of export controls by the industrial nations backed up by regular monitoring by the IAEA of Iraq's nuclear industry.

0155 /...

However, since Iraq has not been forthcoming with procurement or project documentation and since there are marked anomalies as regards the numbers of individual components declared, it should be recognized that Iraq may still have an undisclosed program. It is therefore important that future inspection teams continue to press for the release by Iraq of all documentation relating to its centrifuge program and the associated procurement network.

Centrifuge development

15.   Initial investigations had been carried out on the flow turning and heat treatment parameters required for the manufacture of the maraging steel cylinder, although evidence of significant help from abroad is apparent. Iraq claims that it had not managed to weld the centrifuge end caps and baffles into the cylinder. The relevant declared equipment was still in its delivery packing cases, but an electron beam welder of sufficient capacity was among the equipment inspected at Al Tuwaitha. The Iraqi authorities stated that the cylinders produced during the last four months of 1990 were of inadequate quality or of unacceptable dimensions for centrifuge use and that all maraging steel centrifuge components had been built for laboratory-scale testing.

16.   They further stated that they had procured ten carbon fibre cylinders (the number remains to be confirmed) from abroad and that two centrifuges were assembled using them. The end caps and baffles for these were of maraging steel, and they differed from the components for the all-maraging-steel centrifuge only in the design of the external rim. One of the carbon-fibre-based centrifuges was run in a mechanical test stand, the other in a process test stand. The results were reported by the third and fourth inspection teams. It would appear that the centrifuge used in the process test stand broke down while being tested. The rotor seen by the third inspection team was badly damaged and the vacuum housing was scored in the area opposite the end caps. The rotor from the mechanical test stand remains and has been removed by the IAEA for analysis.

UF_6 Production

17.   Only 0.5 kg of UF_6 has been declared by Iraq. It was produced in building 15 at Al Tuwaitha. However, it was sufficient to enable single-machine testing to commence. The UF_6 was fed into the centrifuge and then collected as product and tails in cooled traps. After analysis of the isotopic content, the two streams were mixed together to recreate feed materials.

During the fourth inspection, Iraq informed the team that a UF_6 production facility was to be built eventually in the same building as the UCl_4 production facility at the Al Jesira plant.

0156

/...

Design

18. Both centrifuge development lines were based on the Zippe subcritical counter current centrifuge. For the maraging steel rotor, the end caps and baffles were to be welded into the cylinders; for the carbon fibre rotor, the end caps and baffles were to be held in place using epoxy resin. The rotor was supported on a hydrodynamic bottom bearing and held vertically by a top magnetic bearing. The rotor was driven by an axial hysterisis motor, the rotating element of which was the bottom end cap of the rotor itself.

The rotor was mounted in an aluminium vacuum housing with aluminium end flanges. The housing was mounted into the test stand by a large, centrally mounted collar welded to the housing. A molecular pump was fitted around the top end of the rotor.

Three concentric pipes are mounted centrally from the top flange. UF_6 feed material was fed into the centre of the rotor through one of these pipes. The product and tails were removed through the other two pipes, using 'pitot'-type copper scoops.

Centrifuge components and test facilities

19. The centrifuge components declared by Iraq and shown to the third inspection team remained in the Ash Shakyli warehouse. As promised, the Iraqi authorities had also moved into the warehouse the materials and items declared on the last day of the fourth inspection. After taking samples, the team made a complete, detailed inventory in co-operation with the Iraqi authorities. The inventory is provided in Annex 2. All the items were destroyed under observation of the seventh team.

Also, with the agreement of the Iraqi authorities, the two test stands and the process pipework from the separation test stand were also destroyed. Annex 2 provides a list of those items which were utilized in the R&D program but which have not yet been destroyed, including the high-frequency drive converters.

Manufacturing equipment

20. Visits were made to Badr and SEHEE, the two companies involved in the joint venture to construct a centrifuge manufacturing factory at Al Walid under the code designation "Al Furat project". The machine tools and equipment seen were, in the team's opinion, all that was necessary to commence centrifuge manufacture. Some of them were shown and some were declared on the last day of the mission. The list consists of:

- 11 CNC turning machines of various sizes.
- 2 CNC drilling/milling machines.
- 1 Flow turning machine with its associated mandrel and expanding mandrel.
- 1 Electron beam welding chamber.
- 1 Heat treatment furnace.
- 2 Oxydation furnaces.

0157 /...

- 1 Brazing furnace.
- 1 MIG welding jig.
- 2 Balancing machines (horizontal and vertical).
- 2 Presses.
- 5 High-speed grinding heads with 9 drive converters.

The Iraqi authorities said that the equipment for bottom bearing manufacture (photo table, ultra-violet source, lenses and grooving mask) were kept at Al Tuwaitha and destroyed in the bombing. No equipment was seen, and none for winding carbon fibre cylinders has been declared.

21. All the equipment was sealed, and a list was given to the Iraqi authorities of the equipment which is to be destroyed or monitored. It should be noted that manufacturer identification data had been removed from most of this equipment. Procurement information was still withheld, but it was noted that most of the equipment was dated 1989 or 1990. The experts identified the manufacturers of some equipment, and a list will be made available to relevant governments for further investigation.

22. A visit was also made to the Saddam Engineering Complex, which had been involved in the manufacturing of components for the Type 1 (Beams) centrifuge.

The Al Furat project

23. A visit was made to the Al Furat Centrifuge Manufacturing Complex, which is located close to the Badr Engineering Complex. No construction work has taken place since the fourth inspection team visited the site, early in August. The Iraqi statement regarding the use made of or planned for the four main buildings was as reported by the fourth inspection team.

The Iraqi authorities still claimed that the centrifuge output from the facility was planned to be 200 centrifuges a year starting from January 1992. However, they did concede that it could have been raised to about 400 centrifuges a year through the purchase of critical machine tools. There was sufficient space in the existing buildings to house such additional machine tools since the existing - and planned - buildings are oversized. Also, it was claimed that a reject rate of up to 70% was expected in the early phase of component production. Members of the inspection team with experience of centrifuge manufacturing facilities believe that the facility was quite adequate for producing over 2000 centrifuges a year with time.

The team was shown the area in Building B01 which could have been used for installation of a 100-machine cascade.

0158

/...

Chemical enrichment

24. The Iraqi work has been described in previous inspection reports. According to Iraqi declarations, laboratory-scale work on chemical enrichment involving both the ion-resin and the liquid-liquid process was carried out in Building 90 (located just outside the Al Tuwaitha berm). Iraqi scientists have given presentations about their chemical enrichment work to several inspection teams. The general assessment is that Iraq was not far along in its chemical enrichment work, having managed only to reproduce results reported in different publications.

25. There is very little available in the way of physical evidence or documentation to support (or contradict) the Iraqi declaration. Part of the chemical enrichment equipment is now stored in an outside compound near Building 90. The equipment inspected by the seventh inspection team consisted of:

8	jacketted glass columns (10 cm ID x 203 cm, 15 cm OD)
~10	glass columns (8 cm OD x 50 cm)
10	small rotary pumps
5	small stainless steel tanks
3	PTFE sieve plates for 8 cm diameter columns
3	stainless steel sieve plates for 8 cm diameter columns

The large jacketted columns were for ion exchange and the smaller ones for solvent extraction. Smear samples were taken. The diameter of the columns corresponds with information on the scale of the Iraqi chemical enrichment tests provided to the fourth inspection team. The small stainless steel tanks were declared to be for the conditioning of ion exchange resin. The pumps came from two different suppliers. Several showed a 1990 manufacture date.

26. The components inspected are only a part of two separate test rigs for studying the ion-resin and liquid-liquid processes. The space in Building 90 that Iraq states as having been devoted to chemical enrichment work is appropriate to much larger-scale activities than those described to the inspection teams.

It is noted that Building 90 at Al Tuwaitha was declared by the Iraqi authorities to be the location where research on lithium-6 enrichment was taking place.

Gaseous diffusion

27. Regarding work on gaseous diffusion enrichment, Iraq has stated that a theoretical/feasibility study, supported by a modest laboratory effort, was initiated in 1982 and stopped in 1987. The conclusion of the study was that Iraq lacked the infrastructure, both in scope and in materials, to implement the technology. The Iraqi authorities indicated that the sixth inspection team had documentation describing laboratory work on barrier materials, calculations regarding the enrichment process (cascade) and studies on the production of UF_6 gas. This has not yet been confirmed. The work on gaseous diffusion was carried out at Al Tuwaitha (Building 23).

0159

/...

Laser research

28. Iraq has declared that it never pursued uranium enrichment through laser isotope separation. Interviews with Iraqi scientists, sampling results and an inspection of lasers and laser-related equipment (relocated to Building 12 from Building 23) have disclosed no information that contradicts the declaration.

The research equipment in the laser laboratories included infrared, visible and ultraviolet lasers and additional equipment. The additional equipment (e.g., monochromators, oscilloscopes) appears to be consistent with the stated research activities.

0160

/...

Table 1

TABLE SHOWING RESEARCH AND DEVELOPMENT EQUIPMENT AT TUWAITHA

No.	Equipment	No. planned	No. present	Difference	Remarks
1	Half 500-mm-size separator including pole profile, pole face, return iron and coils	2	2	0	At Tuwaitha
2	500-mm-size vacuum chamber	1	1	0	At Tuwaitha
3	Half 1000-mm-size separator including pole profile, pole face, return iron and coils	1	1	0	At Tuwaitha
4	1000-mm-size pole face	5	5	0	At Tuwaitha (destroyed)
5	1000-mm-size return iron	5	5	0	At Tuwaitha (destroyed)
6	1000-mm-size coils	15	15	0	At Tuwaitha (destroyed)
7	1000-mm-size chambers	4	4	0	At Tuwaitha (destroyed), including one test chamber
8	106-system iron	2	2	0	At Tuwaitha (destroyed)
9	400-mm-size pole	6	6	0	At Tuwaitha (destroyed)
10	400-mm-size chamber	1	1	0	At Tuwaitha

0161

/...

Table 2

COMPONENTS OF 1200-SIZE SEPARATORS - FIRST LINE - TARMIYA

No.	Equipment	No. planned	No. present	Difference	Remarks
1	Double pole with double coil	9	9	0	
2	End pole	2	2	0	
3	Vertical return iron (bearing and pole)	2	2	0	
4	Vacuum chambers	8	8	0	At Al Nafad (Tuwaitha)
5	Quadruple sources	8	8	0	
6	Quadruple collectors	8	4	-4*	4 clearly distinguishable at Al Nafad (Tuwaitha) on 24/8/1991
7	Trolleys bearing double poles	9	9	0	At Al Nafad (Tuwaitha) on 24/8/1991
8	Vertical return iron	6	6	0	At Al Nafad (Tuwaitha)
9	Power injectors	59	59	0	Most smashed to pieces, at Al Nafad (Tuwaitha)

* 4 flanges without attachment + 1 rejected flange

0162

/...

Table 3

COMPONENTS OF 1200-SIZE SEPARATORS - SECOND LINE - TARMIYA

No.	Equipment	No. planned	No. present	Difference	Remarks
1	Double pole without coil	18	18	0	
2	Coils	33	41	8	At Tuwaitha on 25/8/1991 including some which failed and some which were not completed
3	End poles	2	2	0	
4	Vertical return iron (bearing end pole)	2	2	0	
5	Other vertical return iron	6	6	0	At Tuwaitha on 25/8/1991; one unmachined
6	Vacuum chambers	17	17	0	At Tuwaitha on 25/8/1991
7	Trolleys bearing double poles	18	18	0	
8	Sources	17	-	-	Under production
9	Collectors	17	-	-	Under production
10	Power injectors	67	67	0	At Tuwaitha on 25/8/1991

0163

/...

Table 4

COMPONENTS OF 600-SIZE SEPARATORS - TARMIYA

No.	Equipment	No. planned	No. present	Difference	Remarks
1	Double pole without coil	6	8	2	+ 2 unmachined
2	Coils	12	10	-2	8 uncompleted coils at Tuwaitha; 2 completed coils at Tuwaitha
3	Return iron	23	23	0	At Al Nafad (Tuwaitha)
4	Coil holders - binary discs	6	6	0	At Al Nafad (Tuwaitha)
5	End poles	2	2	0	At Al Nafad (Tuwaitha)
6	Vacuum chambers	6	6	0	6 at Tuwaitha (3 complete/3 destroyed): 3 evacuation systems at Tuwaitha
7	Sources	6	6	0	Under production: 5 source flanges at Al Nafad (Tuwaitha) and 1 source on 24/8/1991
8	Collectors	6	4*	-2	Under production: 3 collector flanges at Al Nafad (Tuwaitha) on 24/8/1991

* parts of one were widely scattered

0164

/...

Annex 5

Verification of Nuclear Material in Bulk Form

The following verifications were performed:

Yellow cake   Niger (100.2 tonnes U content, 430 drums)

1. All drums were counted. 156 drums were verified by non-destructive analysis attribute tests for gross and partial defects, 55 drums were weighed and 18 drums were sampled for destructive analysis.

Yellow cake   Portugal (213 tonnes U content, 916 drums)

2. Item counting was performed on 915 drums (1 drum containing 233 kg U was stated to have been lost during the war), 321 drums were verified by non-destructive analysis attribute tests for gross and partial defects, 121 drums were weighed and 44 drums were sampled for destructive analysis.

Natural uranium (previously under safeguards)

3. This includes:

    -   1 box containing 23 kg of UO_2 pellets. It was verified by item counting, weighing, non-destructive and destructive analysis.

    -   37 filters containing UO_4 with a declared weight of 50 kg U content. They were counted and sampled for NDA.

    -   Mixed uranium oxides. A total of 1162 kg U content in mixed oxides in 47 items were present at the facility during the November 1990 inspection. The following verifications were performed:

        -   10 items of U_3O_8 powder were counted, 6 of them were verified by non-destructive analysis attribute test for gross and partial defects, 4 of them were weighed and 2 sampled for destructive analysis.

        -   22 items containing UO_2 powder were counted, 18 of them verified by non-destructive analysis attribute test for gross and partial defects, 7 of them weighed and 2 sampled for destructive analysis.

        -   1 item containing UO_4 powder was counted, weighed and verified by non-destructive and destructive analysis.

0165   /...

- 6 items containing mixed uranium oxides were counted and verified by non-destructive analysis attribute test for gross and partial defects, 3 of them were weighed and 1 sampled for destructive analysis.

- 8 drums containing UO_4 slurry were counted, weighed and verified by non-destructive analysis attribute tests for gross and partial defects. In addition, 2 of them were sampled for destructive analysis. These drums were presented with the nuclear material covered by water, which was removed to allow adequate weighing.

UO_2 of Brazilian origin

4. In the declaration of 7 July 1991, the Iraqi authorities declared that they had received 27 tonnes of UO_2 and had processed 7 tonnes of it at Al Tuwaitha. The 20 tonnes of unprocessed UO_2, in 201 drums, were presented to the third team and left under seal at location D. During this seventh inspection this material was brought to location C. In addition, the Iraqi authorities presented natural UO_2 contained in 24 drums and 2 boxes. They declared that this material was part of the 7000 kg originally declared as processed at Al Tuwaitha. Therefore, at present there are 225 drums plus 2 boxes of UO_2 from Brazil, with a total declared weight of 22,578 kg UO_2 (19,642 kg U content).

5. This material was 100% item-counted and weighed. 48 items were verified by non-destructive analysis attribute tests for gross and partial defects, and 10 samples were taken for destructive analysis. The remaining 4422 kg UO_2 (3847 kg U content) processed at Al Tuwaitha were verified as follows:

Material processed in Building 10

- 22 boxes containing U metal (1 tonne U content) were item-counted, 21 were weighed (the remaining box contained small amounts of material as samples), 7 boxes were verified by non-destructive analysis and 3 samples were taken for destructive analysis.

Material processed in Building 15

- 1 cylinder of UF_6 containing 0.465 kg compound weight was weighed and verified by non-destructive and destructive analysis.

- 5 drums of UF_4 powder with an initial declared weight of 359 kg compound weight were counted, 4 of them were weighed (the remaining drum contained small amounts of samples in sample bottles), all of them were verified by non-destructive analysis and 3 were sampled for destructive analysis.

- 4 containers with liquid waste containing a total of 6 kg U content were item-counted and one sample was taken for destructive analysis.

0166

/...

Material processed in Building 85

- 42 drums of UCl$_4$ plus one drum containing plugs with a total declared weight of 1520 kg of compound material were counted, 25 of them were weighed, 41 were verified by non-destructive analysis and 9 were sampled for destructive analysis.

- 2 drums declared as containing recovered liquid were opened to verify their contents. Since this material belongs to the EMIS enrichment program, it was extensively sampled, 29 samples being taken for destructive analysis. It is estimated that there are around 50 liters in solution form plus around 40 kg in different solid forms in sample bottles.

- 27 drums containing smaller containers plus 4 stainless steel containers with a declared weight of 1850 kg of ADU compound - it was not possible to sort out this material owing to severe contamination in the area. However, during previous inspections 7 items were weighed and 2 sampled.

In order to finally assess the content of this material, all the drums should be emptied and their contents verified. This activity should be performed during the next inspection.

Material of Al Qaim origin

6. This includes the material produced by processing the yellow-cake from Al Qaim. A total of 164 tonnes of yellow-cake was declared as produced at Al Qaim; 3 tonnes are stored at Tikrit and the remaining 161 tonnes (as UO$_4$) were processed at Al Mosul and presented as follows:

- 1.53 tonnes of U content as (UO$_4$) were transferred to Tikrit in 9 drums.

- 409 drums with a total declared weight of 96,095 kg of UO$_2$ which had been presented to the third team were item-counted, 97 of them weighed, 307 verified by non-destructive analysis attribute tests for gross and partial defects and 41 of them sampled for destructive analysis.

- 6 drums were damaged and contained sand, which was removed to determine the amount of UO$_2$ present in them. After weighing, only one drum had less material than that declared in the itemized list provided by the Iraqi authorities.

- 8 process hoppers containing 1207 kg of UCl$_4$ were item-counted, weighed and verified by non-destructive analysis. In addition, 3 samples were taken for destructive analysis.

0167   /...

44 containers with a declared weight of 2050 kg of UO_3 were emptied to evaluate their content. It was found that they contained the following material:

- 2020 kg of UO_3. They were placed in 8 drums.
- 200 kg of mixed uranium oxides in 19 containers.
- 58 kg of UO_4 in 2 containers.

All of the above material was item-counted, weighed and verified by non-destructive analysis. In addition, 15 samples were taken for destructive analysis.

- 100 kg of U_3O_8 in 4 containers. These were item-counted, weighed and verified by non-destructive analysis; one sample was taken for destructive analysis.

- 220 kg of ADU, which was presented in 8 drums full of small containers. These containers were emptied into three drums. They were all counted, weighed and verified by non-destructive and destructive analysis.

- 2 drums containing samples of UO_4 were counted and weighed, and 4 samples were taken for destructive analysis.

Scrap

7.   1 drum of scrap was presented to the third team without declaration of its contents. It was weighed and sampled for destructive analysis.

0168

/...

0169

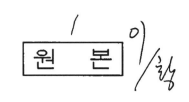

외 무 부

종   별 :

번   호 : UNW-4225   일   시 : 91 1205 2400

수   신 : 장 관(연일,중동일,국기,기정)

발   신 : 주 유엔대사

제   목 : 걸프사태(안보리)

　　1. 안보리 휴전결의(687 호) 및 후속결의(699 호)에 의거 R.EKEUS 유엔 이락 특위 (UNSCOM) 의장은 이락 대량파괴 무기폐기 이행관련 지난 10월 1차 보고서에 이어 2차보고서(S/23268)를 안보리에 제출해온 바, 동 보고서는 이락측의 비협조 및 방해활동이 계속 발견되고 있음을 지적하면서 이락에 대한 단호한 자세(RESOLUTE STANDS)견지를 강조하고 있음.

　　(핵, 생화학무기, 탄도미사일 및 장거리포, 행정분야별 상세 별첨참조)

　　2. 수단은 안보리의 대이락 경제조치 정기심사와 관련 동조치 해제를 호소하는 자국 청소년 단체(EXECUTIVE COMMITTEE OF SHABAB ATWATAN ORGANIZATION)의 안보리 의장앞 서한을 안보리문서로 배포하였음. (S/23266)

　　첨부:사무총장보고서(S/23268):UNW(F)-975 끝

　　(대사 노창희-국장)

국기국   장관   1차보   중아국   국기국   외정실   분석관   청와대   안기부

叫此(F)-975 11205 24 <=

종704

**INITED
IATIONS**

Security Council

Distr.
GENERAL

S/23268
4 December 1991

ORIGINAL: ENGLISH

LETTER DATED 4 DECEMBER 1991 FROM THE EXECUTIVE CHAIRMAN,
OFFICE OF THE SPECIAL COMMISSION ESTABLISHED BY THE
SECRETARY-GENERAL PURSUANT TO PARAGRAPH 9 (b) (i) OF
SECURITY COUNCIL RESOLUTION 687 (1991), ADDRESSED TO
THE SECRETARY-GENERAL

I have the honour to recall paragraph 3 of Security Council resolution 699 (1991) of 17 June 1991, which requests the Secretary-General to submit, every six months after the adoption of the resolution, progress reports on the implementation of the provisions of section C of resolution 687 (1991) relating to Iraq's weapons of mass destruction.

You will further recall that, on 25 October 1991, a first report by the Executive Chairman of the Special Commission established by the Secretary-General pursuant to paragraph 9 (b) (i) of Security Council resolution 687 (1991) was circulated on your instructions to the Security Council in document S/23165. This first report summarized all activities undertaken by the Special Commission and by the International Atomic Energy Agency (IAEA) in the implementation of section C of resolution 687 (1991) up to the middle of October 1991. Additionally, at the request of the Director-General of IAEA, the reports prepared by seven inspection teams led by the Agency have been circulated as Security Council documents (S/22788, S/22837, S/22986 and Corr.1, S/23112, S/23122 and S/23215). A report of the eighth IAEA-led inspection will be circulated in the course of December.

To comply with the provisions of paragraph 3 of Security Council resolution 699 (1991), I am transmitting herewith the text of a progress report which brings up to date the first report referred to in the previous paragraph.

I would be most grateful if you would circulate the attached second report as a document of the Security Council.

(Signed) Rolf EKÉUS
Executive Chairman
Office of the Special Commission

91-47303   2901d (E)   /...

#UNW-4225
천북

7-1

S/23268
English
Page 2

Annex

Second report by the Executive Chairman of the Special Commission established by the Secretary-General pursuant to paragraph 9 (b) (i) of Security Council resolution 687 (1991)

INTRODUCTION

1.   The present report by the Executive Chairman of the Special Commission established by the Secretary-General pursuant to paragraph 9 (b) (i) of Security Council resolution 687 (1991), covers the work of the Commission for the period from 15 October to 4 December 1991. This second report is confined to operational activities and matters directly pertinent thereto as these are the areas which need to be brought up to date to provide, together with the first report by the Executive Chairman (S/23165), a comprehensive picture of the establishment and functioning of the Special Committee since the adoption of Security Council resolutions 687 (1991) and 699 (1991).

ATTITUDE OF IRAQ

2.   The first report by the Executive Chairman contained, in paragraphs 16 to 19, a comprehensive account of the attitude of Iraq. In the period under review this attitude has not changed. In respect of sites and activities declared by Iraq and the issue of Iraq's participation in the destruction of chemical weapons, cooperation at the field level has been forthcoming. However, in respect of sites designated by the Special Commission, where the Commission and IAEA are acting on their own sources of information regarding possible clandestine conduct of proscribed activities, non-cooperation and obstruction continue to be encountered. There is thus no progress to report which would indicate a change of policy on the part of Iraq to one of candour, transparency and cooperation at all levels. As the Executive Chairman remarked in the first report, this is probably the one single element that could contribute most substantially to a timely and satisfactory implementation of the mandate of the Special Commission and of IAEA.

3.   The Special Commission has had to remain vigilant in the period under review to prevent implementation of measures proposed by Iraq which could impinge upon the facilities, privileges and immunities of the Commission and of IAEA in matters such as the taking into and out of Iraq of all necessary equipment, materials and other items required for inspections and the analysi of their results and the taking of photographs at sites under inspection. So far the strong position taken by the Commission and the Chief Inspectors involved seems to have been successful in preserving the rights concerned.

7-2

/.

0172

S/23268
English
Page 3

4.   With respect to ongoing monitoring and verification of Iraq's compliance with paragraphs 10 and 13 of Security Council resolution 687 (1991), the Special Commission has very recently received in New York from Iraq information which the Government states to be "the information required under resolution 687 (1991) that comes within the mandate of the Special Commission". Until the information is translated, the Commission cannot determine the extent to which it meets the substantive requirements of the Special Commission's and IAEA's plans for ongoing monitoring and verification (S/22871/Rev.1 and S/22872/Rev.1 and Corr.1) which were unanimously approved by the Security Council in its resolution 715 (1991), although it may be observed that certain procedural requirements laid down in the plans as to time-limits and languages of submission have not been met. If the Commission and IAEA are to be in a position to carry out their functions in connection with ongoing monitoring and verification, the Commission deems it to be of great importance that Iraq expressly recognize its obligations under the two plans and Security Council resolution 715 (1991). Such express recognition is still awaited.

NUCLEAR ISSUES

5.   Two more inspections were completed (IAEA 7/UNSCOM 19 and IAEA 8/UNSCOM 22), one each in October (11 to 22 October) and November (11 to 18 November), since the sixth nuclear inspection summarized in the previous report. In addition to the successful removal of unirradiated fuel from Iraq, the inspection teams focused much of their inspection activity on a number of sites associated with (a) Iraq's programme to design and develop the non-nuclear components of a nuclear weapon and (b) centrifuge component manufacture.

6.   Significantly, Iraq provided for the first time to the seventh nuclear inspection team formal though incomplete written acknowledgement of its nuclear weapons programme:

      "Various research and studies of the sort to which you refer as 'weaponization' have been carried out. The objective in carrying out such research and studies was to establish the practical, technical and scientific requirements for a programme of this nature in the event that a political decision were to be taken to proceed in that direction."

7.   The extensive and detailed documentation of the nuclear weapons programme that was obtained by the sixth inspection team, and its removal from Iraq only after that team's detainment in a parking lot for four days, preceded the Iraqi admission to the seventh team of having conducted research and studies on nuclear weapons. In fact, the seventh and eighth inspection teams visited designated facilities judged to be directly associated with the testing and development of the high-explosive components of the implosion system of a nuclear weapon. The characteristics of these facilities were considered inconsistent with Iraq's explanations of their purpose. Thus, Iraq's position that it conducted studies but had no programme to develop nuclear weapons is

7-3

/...

0173

S/23268
English
Page 4

inconsistent with both documents and inspection results that reveal a
well-funded and broadly based programme involving sophisticated facilities for
nuclear weapons development.

8. In the area of fissile material production, important questions put to
Iraq remain unanswered. While much of the electromagnetic isotope separation
(EMIS) equipment has been turned over for destruction, the critical collector
pockets which would permit confirmation of Iraq's assertions that only low
levels of enrichment were achieved have not been produced for analysis.
Substantial uncertainties also remain over the centrifuge programme where Iraq
has produced some but not all parts and materials, and failed to reveal the
sources of its supply of critical parts and materials. Even less information
has been produced by Iraq on their efforts in the diffusion and chemical
separation processes. All this is especially troubling in the light of
preliminary results of sampling accomplished at Al Tuwaitha, and noted in the
IAEA seventh inspection report (S/23215), that provide evidence of uranium
enriched to 93 per cent in the isotope U^{235}. Additional sampling was
undertaken by the seventh and eighth inspection teams. Analysis and further
investigation are clearly required.

9. Iraq's recent record in the nuclear area is consistent with, if less
dramatic than, its actions over the last six months that included the
concealment of evidence of plutonium separation, of uranium enrichment, and of
nuclear weapons development, of refusal to permit inspection teams to enter
some sites and exit others, and confiscation of documents from inspectors in
the course of an inspection. In sum, Iraq has not cooperated in the critical
area of nuclear-weapons-related activity and the Special Commission and IAEA
are some distance from achieving the transparency which is sought.

CHEMICAL AND BIOLOGICAL WEAPONS

10. Since the first report was prepared, two further chemical inspections
have been completed, one being the long and detailed inspection of the
Al Muthanna State Establishment (7 October to 8 November 1991) while the other
visited a series of declared chemical munitions storage sites (22 October to
2 November 1991). There has also been a combined chemical and biological
weapons inspection which visited (17 to 30 November 1991), at very short
notice, a number of sites designated by the Special Commission as being of
potential chemical weapons and/or biological weapons interest in addition to
revisiting the original site at Salman Pak.

11. The technically very successful inspection of Al Muthanna (UNSCOM 17)
compiled a comprehensive and detailed inventory of the site, including
facilities, munitions, agents, agent condition, precursors and intermediates.
Among the salient findings were the discovery of small quantities of the nerve
agents sec.butyl sarin, n-butyl sarin and ethyl sarin, although Iraq has
disputed the identification of the latter two agents. While the quantities
found were of no direct military significance, the relevance of the finding
lies in the fact that Iraq clearly had carried out research on nerve agents
other than those previously declared.

/...

0174

12. Although the mustard agent at Al Muthanna was generally of good quality (typically 90 per cent), the nerve agents were found to have undergone extensive degradation and the agent content was very low, generally below 10 per cent and in some cases below the 1 per cent level. This new information may have significant repercussions for the process finally selected for the destruction of the nerve agents as well as for the safety hazards likely to be encountered during destruction; both aspects will need further consideration.

13. In general, the findings of the inspection at Al Muthanna were in substantial agreement with Iraq's declaration, although in the case of the 122 mm rockets a precise and full count was not possible as the rockets generally were found to be in a very dangerous condition. Explosive demolition was considered to be the safest means of achieving their destruction since opening and draining operations would be particularly hazardous.

14. The inspection of the remaining declared storage sites (UNSCOM 20) was likewise a successful operation. All the declared sites, some of them distant from Baghdad and therefore requiring the use of United Nations helicopter transport, were inspected, the chemical weapons munitions verified, counted and recorded; where it was safe to transport the munitions to Al Muthanna the necessary instructions to this effect were given to Iraq. At Al-Tuz, Khamisiyah and Muhammadiyat numbers of munitions were discovered, including but not restricted to 122 mm rockets, which were considered to be in too unsafe a condition to move and for which a drilling and draining operation would be very hazardous. A recommendation was made on safety grounds that these items should be destroyed in situ by explosive demolition. In a few cases, due to extensive destruction by coalition bombing, it was not possible to observe and count all munitions; when the damage had been less extensive the number and types of munitions observed accorded well with the Iraqi declarations.

15. The combined chemical and biological weapons inspection (UNSCOM 21), except for the revisit to Salman Pak, concentrated on short notice inspection of undeclared sites designated by the Special Commission; some 13 sites were inspected.

16. The inspection was completed only very recently and the full official report is therefore not at present available. Field reporting, however, indicates that no chemical-or-biological-weapons-related activities were associated with any of the designated sites. In the course of the inspection a small sub-team was dispatched to Al Muthanna to witness an Iraqi experiment with a simulant to prove the use of the modified pilot plant for exploratory work on the destruction of nerve agents; this was successful.

17. Since the first report was prepared a small (4 person) mission has visited Iraq for detailed technical discussions (11 to 15 November 1991) with Iraqi counterparts on various of the issues related to the destruction of chemical weapons and agents, with particular emphasis on the direct

/...

7-5

S/23268
English
Page 6

involvement of Iraq in this process and on safety aspects. Issues discussed and on which the Special Commission team made recommendations included an Iraqi design for a mustard agent incinerator, the destruction of nerve agents by caustic hydrolysis, and the breaching and draining of munitions.

18. When, in the very near future, all the data compiled by UNSCOM 17 at the Al Muthanna State Establishment have been analysed, the Special Commission will have a very good understanding of Iraq's declared major primary chemical weapons site. Furthermore, the discussions on the destruction of chemical weapons and agents have resulted in a considerable improvement in technical understanding by both sides, particularly as regards the potential hazards involved in some operations and of the technologies potentially available for implementing the various destruction processes. Commencement of the destruction process early in 1992 can thus be confidently expected.

BALLISTIC MISSILES AND LONG-RANGE GUNS

19. With respect to ballistic missiles, by the end of 1991 two additional Special Commission ballistic missile inspections (UNSCOM 23 and UNSCOM 24) are expected to have been completed. To date, Special Commission inspection teams have, according to the latest revised data, supervised the destruction of 62 ballistic missiles, 18 fixed missile launch pads, 33 ballistic missile warheads, 127 missile storage support racks, a substantial amount of rocket fuel, an assembled 350 mm supergun, components of two 350 and two 1,000 mm superguns, and 1 tonne of supergun propellant.

20. So far, no information has come to light which clearly contradicts Iraq's disclosure of 5 July 1991 with respect to the status of its ballistic missile force. Nevertheless, the fact that Iraq continued to fire ballistic missiles throughout the Gulf war and still had a portion of its force following that war, despite what were, by all public accounts, the intensive efforts of coalition forces to find and destroy them, attests to the relative ease with which they could be concealed even in war. Special Commission inspection teams have found undeclared ballistic missile support equipment and noted Iraqi attempts to reuse previously destroyed missile transport vehicles.

21. The Special Commission is seeking further information, analysis of which may allow a more comprehensive understanding of this issue, and increase confidence in any assessments which may emerge. At the present time, however, as pointed out in the first report, important questions still remain unresolved, namely, whether Iraq continues to have any ballistic missiles in its possession, and its plans and progress in future ballistic missile development. The two ballistic missile inspections which are being undertaken this month should shed additional light on these questions.

7-6

/...

0.176

ADMINISTRATIVE ISSUES

22.   The administrative issues outlined in paragraphs 25 to 31 of the first report remain unresolved, most particularly the issue of financing.   The Special Commission is most grateful to record the receipt of additional voluntary contributions from Kuwait ($1,000,000) and Saudi Arabia ($1,730,000), which have enabled it to continue to function in the period under review.   However, the shortage of readily available funds will become critical early next year, particularly if the Special Commission and IAEA are to proceed with the very costly removal of the spent irradiated fuel from Iraq.

CONCLUDING OBSERVATIONS

23.   In the previous report, the full support of the Security Council, Governments, the Secretary-General and the Secretariat of the United Nations were identified as being of crucial importance in the carrying out of the mandate laid down in section C of Security Council resolution 687 (1991). This will certainly remain to be the case as the Special Commission and IAEA confront the difficult issues which will arise in connection with the destruction, removal or rendering harmless of Iraq's weapons of mass destruction and the facilities for their production and as the plans for ongoing monitoring and verification are put into full effect.   Experience to date has shown that results can be achieved only where resolute stands are taken in response to challenges by Iraq to the implementation of various aspects of the mandate of the Special Commission and IAEA.   Such resolute stands can be based only on the full support of the United Nations as a whole and its Member Governments in achieving all the basic objectives of section C of Security Council resolution 687 (1991).

7-7

0177

외 무 부

종 별 :

번 호 : UNW-4324

일 시 : 91 1212 2130

수 신 : 장 관(연일,중동일,기정)

발 신 : 주 유엔 대사

제 목 : 안보리(걸프사태)

1. 표제사태관련 안보리 이락제재위는 그간 대이락 무기공급금지 위반사례가 신고접수 된 것이 없음을 안보리에 통보하였음. (S/23279)

2. 유엔이락 특정무기특위 (UNSCOM)화학.생물무기 합동조사반 사찰결과를 별첨참조 바람.

첨부:안보리문서 및 UNSCOM 사찰결과(12.11):UNW(F)-1019 끝

(대사 노창희-국장)

국기국   1차보   중아국   외정실   분석관   정와대   안기부

PAGE 1

91.12.13   11:36 WG

외신 1과 통제관

0178

UNW(FI-1019 11212 2130
총 304

The first combined chemical and biological weapons inspection team to
Iraq has reported the discovery of chemical bomb-making equipment at a sugar
factory in Mosul, 350 kilometres north of Baghdad.

The United Nations inspectors found equipment from a bomb casing workshop
which, according to a June directive by the Special Commission on Iraqi
Disarmament, should have been moved to the Muthanna State Establishment for
destruction early next year. The items found were clearly intended for the
manufacture of aerial bombs for the delivery of chemical warfare agents.

In a press release today, the Special Commission said that the 18-member
United Nations expert team had inspected 16 sites throughout Iraq, looking for
evidence of undeclared chemical and biological weapons activity. The mission
was unique, it said, in that all designations were undeclared sites, and
concentrated on possible chemical or biological weapons storage sites, such as
airfield bunkers and ammunition depots. All inspections were carried out
without advance notice to the Iraqi side. The mission used United Nations
helicopters as a fast means of transport and for conducting aerial
reconnaissance.

The team further reported the discovery at an ammunition storage facility
west of Karbala of three undeclared SCUD transporter carriers, which had
apparently been discarded and overlooked. The Iraqis were directed to move
these carriers to Taji for future destruction.

On a number of occasions, the Special Commission says, the inspection
team was hindered when carrying out the inspection. However, following the
registering of an official protest by the Chief Inspector, the Iraqi
authorities concerned were cooperative for the remainder of the inspection.

#UNW-4324
첨부   3-1

0179

<u>Annex</u>

<u>Report of the Security Council Committee established by resolution
661 (1990) concerning the situation between Iraq and Kuwait
pursuant to paragraph 6, subparagraph (f) of the guidelines to
facilitate full international implementation of paragraphs 24, 25
and 27 of Security Council resolution 687 (1991)</u>

1.   The present report is submitted by the Security Council Committee
established by resolution 661 (1990) of 6 August 1990 concerning the situation
between Iraq and Kuwait in accordance with paragraph 6, subparagraph (f) of
the guidelines, 1/ for facilitating full international implementation of
paragraphs 24, 25 and 27 of Security Council resolution 687 (1991) of
3 April 1991 approved by Council resolution 700 (1991) of 17 June 1991.

2.   The first report of the Committee was submitted on 13 September 1991. 2/
Under paragraph 6, subparagraph (f) of the guidelines, the Committee is
required to report at 90-day intervals to the Security Council on the
implementation of the arms and related sanctions against Iraq contained in the
relevant resolutions of the Security Council.

3.   By paragraph 12 of the guidelines, all States are requested to report to
the Committee any information that may have come to their attention relating
to possible violations of the arms and related sanctions against Iraq
committed by other States or foreign nationals. During the period under
review, no information, as requested by paragraph 12 of the guidelines, has
been received by the Committee.

4.   In accordance with paragraphs 13 and 15 of the guidelines, all States and
international organizations ought to consult the Committee on the question of
whether certain items fall within the provisions of paragraph 24 of
resolution 687 (1991), as well as in cases relating to dual-use or
multiple-use items, i.e. items meant for civilian use but with potential for
diversion or conversion to military use. During the period under review, no
States or international organizations have consulted the Committee on these
questions.

5.   By paragraph 14 of the guidelines, international organizations are
requested to provide the Committee with any relevant information that may come
to their attention. In that connection, the Committee received a letter from
the Chairman of the Security Council Committee established by resolution
421 (1977) concerning the question of South Africa which the Committee
considered and took note of at its 52nd meeting held on 18 October 1991.

6.   In a note dated 2 October 1991, 3/ the President of the Security Council
published the text of the statement made to the media, on behalf of the
members of the Council. He stated that the members of the Council had held
informal consultations on 2 October 1991 pursuant to paragraph 21 of
resolution 687 (1991). After hearing all the opinions expressed in the course

3-2

/...

0180

of the consultations, the President of the Council concluded that there was no agreement that the necessary conditions existed for a modification of the regime established by paragraph 20 of resolution 687 (1991), as referred to in paragraph 21 of that resolution.

7.   Since the submission of the previous report of the Committee on 13 September 1991, 2/ no allegations of violations, particularly in connection with paragraph 24 of resolution 687 (1991), have been reported to the Committee, apart from the letter mentioned in paragraph 5 above.

8.   The Committee will continue its efforts to fulfil the mandate entrusted to it. The Committee recommends that the Secretary-General should send an early reminder to those States that have not yet replied in accordance with paragraph 4 of Security Council resolution 700 (1991) on measures they have instituted for meeting the obligations set out in paragraph 24 of Security Council resolution 687 (1991). 4/

Notes

1/   S/22660, annex.

2/   S/23036.

3/   S/23107.

4/   The States that have replied so far pursuant to paragraph 4 of Security Council resolution 700 (1991) are listed in the reports of the Secretary-General contained in documents S/22884, Add.1 and Add.2.

3-3

0181

발　신　전　보

	분류번호	보존기간

번　　호 : WUN-4339　911220 1759 ^{WH}종별 :

수　　신 : 주　　유엔　　대사. 총영사

발　　신 : 장　관　　(연일)

제　　목 : UNSCOM 보고서

　　　　　주한미대사관은 12.20(금) 91.12.4.자 UNSCOM의 제2차
　　　보고서와 함께 동 특별위원회의 지속적 활동을 지지하는 미국의
　　　입장을 표명한 문서를 수교해온 바, 동자료 별첨 FAX 송부하니
　　　업무에 참고바람.

　　　　첨　부 : 동 자료 1부.　끝.

　　　　　　　　　　　　　　　　　　　（국제기구국장　　　문동석）

0182

UNSCOM REPORT ON IRAQI COMPLIANCE WITH
SECTION C OF UNSCR 687

WUNF-0274   911220 1800   WH

FROM U.S. STATE DEPARTMENT:

-- WE COMMEND THIS REPORT TO YOUR ATTENTION AND FOR YOUR USE WITH YOUR PRESS AND PUBLIC. IT DEMONSTRATES BOTH THE REMARKABLE ACCOMPLISHMENTS MADE BY UNSCOM AND THE INTERNATIONAL ATOMIC ENERGY AGENCY, AND THE FACT THAT MUCH MORE REMAINS TO BE DONE BEFORE RESOLUTION 687 CAN BE SAID TO BE SUCCESSFULLY IMPLEMENTED.

-- OF PARTICULAR NOTE IS THE REPORT'S OBSERVATIONS OF IRAQ'S CONTINUED LACK OF COOPERATION AND EVEN OBSTRUCTION IN THE IMPLEMENTATION OF RESOLUTION 687.

-- A RELATED POINT IS THE REPORT'S COMMENT THAT IRAQ HAS YET TO ACCEPT ITS OBLIGATIONS UNDER RESOLUTION 715, WHICH CODIFIES UNSCOM'S AND IAEA'S LONG-TERM MONITORING PLANS. THE USG CONSIDERS THIS DISTURBING.

-- WE ALSO CALL YOUR ATTENTION TO THE REPORT'S CONCLUSION THAT IMPORTANT QUESTIONS REMAIN UNANSWERED, ESPECIALLY WITH REGARD TO NUCLEAR WEAPONS, BALLISTIC MISSILES, AND BIOLOGICAL WEAPONS.

-- FINALLY, THE REPORT DRAWS ATTENTION TO THE FINANCIAL DIFFICULTIES OF UNSCOM. AT PRESENT, THERE ARE NO FUNDS AVAILABLE TO CONTINUE UNSCOM'S ACTIVITIES INTO THE NEW YEAR.

-- THIS IS ESPECIALLY IMPORTANT BECAUSE WE BELIEVE IRAQ STILL MAINTAINS SOME FACILITIES, MATERIAL AND EQUIPMENT FOR WEAPONS OF MASS DESTRUCTION. SADDAM HAS NOT REVEALED ALL OF HIS WEAPONS YET. AS A RESULT, UNSCOM'S AND IAEA'S JOB IS NOT DONE YET. MORE CHALLENGE INSPECTIONS WILL BE NEEDED TO ENSURE THAT SADDAM IS NOT LEFT WITH A CLANDESTINE FORCE OF WEAPONS OF MASS DESTRUCTION FOR FUTURE USE.

-- RESOLUTION 687 GIVES UNSCOM AND IAEA THE MANDATE TO CONDUCT CHALLENGE INSPECTIONS, DESTRUCTION, AND LONG TERM MONITORING IN IRAQ INDEFINITELY. BOTH UNSCOM AND IAEA PLAN TO HAVE A PRESENCE IN IRAQ FOR THE FORESEEABLE FUTURE.

0183

-- THE USG -- LIKE MANY OTHER COUNTRIES -- CONTINUES TO
PROVIDE UNSCOM AND IAEA WITH INFORMATION TO ASSIST THIS
SEARCH, EXPERTS TO BE ON INSPECTION TEAMS, AND ANALYSIS
OF INSPECTION TEAM FINDINGS.

-- IT IS IMPORTANT THAT ALL COUNTRIES CONTINUE TO
SUPPORT IMPLEMENTATION OF RESOLUTION 687, DEMAND THAT
IRAQ BE FORTHCOMING ABOUT ITS WEAPONS PROGRAMS, DESTROY
IMMEDIATELY THE FACILITIES ALREADY DISCOVERED, AND
FORSWEAR FUTURE RECONSTITUTION OF THIS CAPABILITY.

4. BEGIN TEXT OF UNSCOM'S SECOND PROGRESS REPORT TO THE
UN SECURITY COUNCIL ON IMPLEMENTATION OF SECTION C OF
UNSCR 687, DATED DEC. 4 1991.

INTRODUCTION
----

1. THE PRESENT REPORT BY THE EXECUTIVE CHAIRMAN OF THE
SPECIAL COMMISSION ESTABLISHED BY THE SECRETARY-GENERAL
PURSUANT TO PARAGRAPH 9 (B) (I) OF SECURITY COUNCIL
RESOLUTION 687 (1991), COVERS THE WORK OF THE COMMISSION
FOR THE PERIOD FROM 15 OCTOBER TO 4 DECEMBER 1991. THIS
SECOND REPORT IS CONFINED TO OPERATIONAL ACTIVITIES AND
MATTERS DIRECTLY PERTINENT THERETO AS THESE ARE THE AREAS
WHICH NEED TO BE BROUGHT UP TO DATE TO PROVIDE, TOGETHER
WITH THE FIRST REPORT OF THE EXECUTIVE CHAIRMAN (S/23165),
A COMPREHENSIVE PICTURE OF THE ESTABLISHMENT AND
FUNCTIONING OF THE SPECIAL COMMITTEE SINCE THE ADOPTION OF
SECURITY COUNCIL RESOLUTIONS 687 (1991) AND 699 (1991).

ATTITUDE OF IRAQ
----

2. THE FIRST REPORT BY THE EXECUTIVE CHAIRMAN
CONTAINED, IN PARAGRAPHS 16 TO 19, A COMPREHENSIVE
ACCOUNT OF THE ATTITUDE OF IRAQ. IN THE PERIOD UNDER
REVIEW THIS ATTITUDE HAS NOT CHANGED. IN RESPECT OF
SITES AND ACTIVITIES DECLARED BY IRAQ AND THE ISSUE OF
IRAQ'S PARTICIPATION IN THE DESTRUCTION OF CHEMICAL

WEAPONS, COOPERATION AT THE FIELD LEVEL HAS BEEN
FORTHCOMING. HOWEVER, IN RESPECT OF SITES DESIGNATED BY
THE SPECIAL COMMISSION, WHERE THE COMMISSION AND IAEA ARE
ACTING ON THEIR OWN SOURCES OF INFORMATION REGARDING
POSSIBLE CLANDESTINE CONDUCT OF PROSCRIBED ACTIVITIES,
NON-COOPERATION AND OBSTRUCTION CONTINUE TO BE
ENCOUNTERED. THERE IS THUS NO PROGRESS TO REPORT WHICH
WOULD INDICATE A CHANGE IN POLICY ON THE PART OF IRAQ TO
ONE OF CANDOR, TRANSPARENCY AND COOPERATION AT ALL
LEVELS. AS THE EXECUTIVE CHAIRMAN REMARKED IN THE FIRST
REPORT, THIS IS PROBABLY THE ONE SINGLE ELEMENT THAT
COULD CONTRIBUTE MOST SUBSTANTIALLY TO A TIMELY AND
SATISFACTORY IMPLEMENTATION OF THE MANDATE OF THE SPECIAL
COMMISSION AND OF IAEA.

3.   THE SPECIAL COMMISSION HAS HAD TO REMAIN VIGILANT IN
THE PERIOD UNDER REVIEW TO PREVENT IMPLEMENTATION OF
MEASURES PROPOSED BY IRAQ WHICH COULD IMPINGE UPON THE
FACILITIES, PRIVILEGES AND IMMUNITIES OF THE COMMISSION
AND OF IAEA IN MATTERS SUCH AS THE TAKING INTO AND OUT OF
IRAQ OF ALL NECESSARY EQUIPMENT, MATERIALS AND OTHER
ITEMS REQUIRED FOR INSPECTIONS AND THE ANALYSIS OF THEIR
RESULTS AND THE TAKING OF PHOTOGRAPHS AT SITES UNDER
INSPECTION. SO FAR THE STRONG POSITION TAKEN BY THE
COMMISSION AND THE CHIEF INSPECTORS INVOLVED SEEMS TO
HAVE BEEN SUCCESSFUL IN PRESERVING THE RIGHTS CONCERNED.

4.   WITH RESPECT TO ONGOING MONITORING AND VERIFICATION
OF IRAQ'S COMPLIANCE WITH PARAGRAPHS 10 AND 13 OF
SECURITY COUNCIL RESOLUTION 687 (1991), THE SPECIAL
COMMISSION HAS VERY RECENTLY RECEIVED IN NEW YORK FROM
IRAQ WHICH THE GOVERNMENT STATES TO BE "THE INFORMATION
REQUIRED UNDER RESOLUTION 687 (1991) THAT COMES WITHIN
THE MANDATE OF THE SPECIAL COMMISSION". UNTIL THE
INFORMATION IS TRANSLATED, THE COMMISSION CANNOT
DETERMINE THE EXTENT TO WHICH IT MEETS THE SUBSTANTIVE
REQUIREMENTS OF THE SPECIAL COMMISSION'S AND IAEA'S PLANS
FOR ONGOING PLANNING AND VERIFICATION (S/22871/REV.1 AND
S/22872/REV.1 AND CORR.1) WHICH WERE UNANIMOUSLY APPROVED
BY THE SECURITY COUNCIL IN ITS RESOLUTION 715 (1991),
ALTHOUGH IT MAY BE OBSERVED THAT CERTAIN PROCEDURAL
REQUIREMENTS LAID DOWN IN THE PLANS AS TO TIME-LIMITS AND
LANGUAGES OF SUBMISSION HAVE NOT BEEN MET. IF THE
COMMISSION AND IAEA ARE TO BE IN A POSITION TO CARRY OUT
THEIR FUNCTIONS IN CONNECTION WITH ONGOING MONITORING AND

0185

VERIFICATION, THE COMMISSION DEEMS IT TO BE OF GREAT
IMPORTANCE THAT IRAQ EXPRESSLY RECOGNIZE ITS OBLIGATIONS
UNDER THE TWO PLANS AND SECURITY COUNCIL RESOLUTION 715
(1991). SUCH EXPRESS RECOGNITION IS STILL AWAITED.

NUCLEAR ISSUE
----

5.   TWO MORE INSPECTIONS WERE COMPLETED (IAEA 7/UNSCOM
19 AND IAEA 8/ UNSCOM 22), ONE EACH IN OCTOBER (11 TO 22)
AND NOVEMBER (11 TO 18), SINCE THE SIXTH NUCLEAR
INSPECTION SUMMARIZED IN THE PREVIOUS REPORT. IN
ADDITION TO THE SUCCESSFUL REMOVAL OF UNIRRADIATED FUEL
FROM IRAQ, THE INSPECTION TEAMS FOCUSED MOST OF THEIR
INSPECTION ACTIVITY ON A NUMBER OF SITES ASSOCIATED WITH
(A) IRAQ'S PROGRAM TO DESIGN AND DEVELOP THE NON-NUCLEAR
COMPONENTS OF A NUCLEAR WEAPON AND (B) CENTRIFUGE
COMPONENT MANUFACTURE.

6.   SIGNIFICANTLY, IRAQ PROVIDED FOR THE FIRST TIME TO
THE SEVENTH NUCLEAR INSPECTION TEAM FORMAL THOUGH
INCOMPLETE WRITTEN ACKNOWLEDGMENT OF ITS NUCLEAR WEAPONS
PROGRAM:

"VARIOUS RESEARCH AND STUDIES OF THE SORT TO WHICH
YOU REFER AS 'WEAPONIZATION' HAVE BEEN CARRIED OUT.
THE OBJECTIVE IN CARRYING OUT SUCH RESEARCH AND
STUDIES WAS TO ESTABLISH THE PRACTICAL, TECHNICAL,
AND SCIENTIFIC REQUIREMENTS FOR A PROGRAM OF THIS
NATURE IN THE EVENT THAT A POLITICAL DECISION WERE TO
BE TAKEN TO PROCEED IN THAT DIRECTION."

7.   THE EXTENSIVE AND DETAILED DOCUMENTATION OF THE
NUCLEAR WEAPONS PROGRAM THAT WAS OBTAINED BY THE SIXTH
INSPECTION TEAM, AND ITS REMOVAL FROM IRAQ ONLY AFTER
THAT TEAM'S DETAINMENT IN A PARKING LOT FOR FOUR DAYS,
PRECEDED THE IRAQI ADMISSION TO THE SEVENTH TEAM OF
HAVING CONDUCTED RESEARCH AND STUDIES ON NUCLEAR WEAPONS.
IN FACT, THE SEVENTH AND EIGHTH INSPECTION TEAMS VISITED
DESIGNATED FACILITIES JUDGED TO BE DIRECTLY ASSOCIATED
WITH THE TESTING AND DEVELOPMENT OF THE HIGH-EXPLOSIVE
COMPONENTS OF THE IMPLOSION SYSTEM OF A NUCLEAR WEAPON.
THE CHARACTERISTICS OF THESE FACILITIES WERE CONSIDERED
INCONSISTENT WITH IRAQ'S EXPLANATIONS OF THEIR PURPOSE.

0186

THUS, IRAQ'S POSITION THAT IT CONDUCTED STUDIES BUT HAD
NO PROGRAM TO DEVELOP NUCLEAR WEAPONS IS INCONSISTENT
WITH BOTH DOCUMENTS AND INSPECTION RESULTS THAT REVEAL A
WELL-FUNDED AND BROADLY-BASED PROGRAM INVOLVING
SOPHISTICATED FACILITIES FOR NUCLEAR WEAPONS
DEVELOPMENT.

8.   IN THE AREA OF FISSILE MATERIAL PRODUCTION,
IMPORTANT QUESTIONS PUT TO IRAQ REMAIN UNANSWERED. WHILE
MUCH OF THE ELECTROMAGNETIC ISOTOPE SEPARATION (EMIS)
EQUIPMENT HAS BEEN TURNED OVER FOR DESTRUCTION, THE
CRITICAL COLLECTOR POCKETS WHICH WOULD PERMIT
CONFIRMATION OF IRAQ'S ASSERTIONS THAT ONLY LOW LEVELS OF
ENRICHMENT WERE ACHIEVED HAVE NOT BEEN PRODUCED FOR
ANALYSIS. SUBSTANTIAL UNCERTAINTIES ALSO REMAIN OVER THE
CENTRIFUGE PROGRAM WHERE IRAQ HAS PRODUCED SOME BUT NOT
ALL PARTS AND MATERIALS. EVEN LESS INFORMATION HAS BEEN
PRODUCED BY IRAQ ON THEIR EFFORTS IN THE DIFFUSION AND
CHEMICAL SEPARATION PROCESSES. ALL THIS IS ESPECIALLY
TROUBLING IN THE LIGHT OF PRELIMINARY RESULTS OF SAMPLING
ACCOMPLISHED AT AL TUWAITHA, AND NOTED IN THE IAEA
SEVENTH INSPECTION REPORT (S/23215) THAT PROVIDE EVIDENCE
OF URANIUM ENRICHED TO 93 PER CENT IN THE ISOTOPE U 235.
ADDITIONAL SAMPLING WAS UNDERTAKEN BY THE SEVENTH AND
EIGHTH INSPECTION TEAMS. ANALYSIS AND FURTHER
INVESTIGATION ARE CLEARLY REQUIRED.

9.   IRAQ'S RECENT RECORD IN THE NUCLEAR AREA IS
CONSISTENT WITH, IF LESS DRAMATIC THAN, ITS ACTIONS OVER
THE LAST SIX MONTHS THAT INCLUDED THE CONCEALMENT OF
EVIDENCE OF PLUTONIUM SEPARATION, OR URANIUM ENRICHMENT,
AND OF NUCLEAR WEAPONS DEVELOPMENT, OF REFUSAL TO PERMIT
INSPECTION TO ENTER SOME SITES AND EXIT OTHERS, AND
CONFISCATION OF DOCUMENTS FROM INSPECTORS IN THE COURSE
OF AN INSPECTION. IN SUM, IRAQ HAS NOT COOPERATED IN THE
CRITICAL AREA OF NUCLEAR-WEAPONS-RELATED ACTIVITY AND THE
SPECIAL COMMISSION AND IAEA ARE SOME DISTANCE FROM
ACHIEVING THE TRANSPARENCY WHICH IS SOUGHT.

0187

CHEMICAL AND BIOLOGICAL WEAPONS
----

10. SINCE THE FIRST REPORT WAS PREPARED, TWO FURTHER
CHEMICAL INSPECTIONS HAVE BEEN COMPLETED, ONE BEING THE
LONG AND DETAILED INSPECTION OF THE AL MUTHANNA STATE
ESTABLISHMENT (7 OCTOBER TO NOVEMBER 1991) WHILE THE
OTHER VISITED A SERIES OF DECLARED CHEMICAL MUNITIONS
STORAGE SITES (22 OCTOBER TO 2 NOVEMBER 1991). THERE HAS
ALSO BEEN A COMBINED CHEMICAL AND BIOLOGICAL WEAPONS
INSPECTION WHICH VISITED (17 TO 30 NOVEMBER 1991), AT
VERY SHORT NOTICE, A NUMBER OF SITES DESIGNATED BY THE
SPECIAL COMMISSION AS BEING OF POTENTIAL CHEMICAL WEAPONS
AND/OR BIOLOGICAL WEAPONS INTEREST IN ADDITION TO
REVISITING THE ORIGINAL SITE AT SALMAN PAK.

11. THE TECHNICALLY VERY SUCCESSFUL INSPECTION OF AL
MUTHANNA (UNSCOM 17) COMPILED A COMPREHENSIVE AND
DETAILED INVENTORY OF THE SITE, INCLUDING FACILITIES,
MUNITIONS, AGENTS, AGENT CONDITION, PRECURSORS AND
INTERMEDIATES. AMONG THE SALIENT FINDINGS WERE THE
DISCOVERY OF SMALL QUANTITIES OF THE NERVE AGENTS
SEC-BUTYL, N-BUTYL SARIN AND ETHYL SARIN, ALTHOUGH IRAQ
HAS DISPUTED THE IDENTIFICATION OF THE LATTER TWO
AGENTS. WHILE THE QUANTITIES FOUND WERE OF NO DIRECT
MILITARY SIGNIFICANCE, THE RELEVANCE OF THE FINDING LIES
IN THE FACT THAT IRAQ CLEARLY HAD CARRIED OUT RESEARCH ON
NERVE AGENTS OTHER THAN THOSE PREVIOUSLY DECLARED.

12. ALTHOUGH THE MUSTARD AGENT AT AL MUTHANNA WAS
GENERALLY OF GOOD QUALITY (TYPICALLY 90 PER CENT), THE
NERVE AGENTS WERE FOUND TO HAVE UNDERGONE EXTENSIVE
DEGRADATION AND THE AGENT CONTENT WAS VERY LOW, GENERALLY
BELOW 10 PER CENT AND IN SOME CASES BELOW THE 1 PER CENT
LEVEL. THIS NEW INFORMATION MAY HAVE SIGNIFICANT
REPERCUSSIONS FOR THE PROCESS FINALLY SELECTED FOR THE
DESTRUCTION OF THE NERVE AGENTS AS WELL AS FOR THE SAFETY
HAZARDS LIKELY TO BE ENCOUNTERED DURING DESTRUCTION; BOTH
ASPECTS WILL NEED FURTHER CONSIDERATION.

0188

13. IN GENERAL, THE FINDINGS OF THE INSPECTION AT AL MUTHANNA WERE IN SUBSTANTIAL AGREEMENT WITH IRAQ'S DECLARATION, ALTHOUGH IN THE CASE OF THE 122 MM ROCKETS A PRECISE AND FULL COUNT WAS NOT POSSIBLE AS THE ROCKETS GENERALLY WERE FOUND TO BE IN A VERY DANGEROUS CONDITION. EXPLOSIVE DEMOLITION WAS CONSIDERED TO BE SAFEST MEANS OF ACHIEVING THEIR DESTRUCTION SINCE OPENING AND DRAINING OPERATIONS WOULD BE PARTICULARLY HAZARDOUS.

14. THE INSPECTION OF THE REMAINING DECLARED STORAGE SITES (UNSCOM 20) WAS LIKEWISE A SUCCESSFUL OPERATION. ALL OF THE DECLARED SITES, SOME OF THEM DISTANT FROM BAGHDAD AND THEREFORE REQUIRING THE USE OF UNITED NATIONS HELICOPTER TRANSPORT, WERE INSPECTED, THE CHEMICAL WEAPONS MUNITIONS VERIFIED, COUNTED AND RECORDED, WHERE IT WAS SAFE TO TRANSPORT THE MUNITIONS TO AL MUTHANNA THE NECESSARY INSTRUCTIONS TO THIS EFFECT WERE GIVEN TO IRAQ. AT AL-TUZ, KHAMISIYAH AND MUHAMMADIYAT NUMBERS OF MUNITIONS WERE DISCOVERED, INCLUDING BUT NOT RESTRICTED TO 122 MM ROCKETS, WHICH WERE CONSIDERED TO BE IN TOO UNSAFE A CONDITION TO MOVE AND FOR WHICH A DRILLING AND DRAINING OPERATION WOULD BE VERY HAZARDOUS. A RECOMMENDATION WAS MADE ON SAFETY GROUNDS THAT THESE ITEMS BE DESTROYED IN SITU BY EXPLOSIVE DEMOLITION. IN A FEW CASES, DUE TO EXTENSIVE DESTRUCTION BY COALITION BOMBING, IT WAS NOT POSSIBLE TO OBSERVE AND COUNT ALL MUNITIONS; WHEN THE DAMAGE HAD BEEN LESS EXTENSIVE THE NUMBERS AND TYPES OF WEAPONS OBSERVED ACCORDED WELL WITH THE IRAQI DECLARATIONS.

15. THE COMBINED CHEMICAL AND BIOLOGICAL WEAPONS INSPECTION (UNSCOM 21), EXCEPT FOR THE VISIT TO SALMAN PAK, CONCENTRATED ON SHORT NOTICE INSPECTION OF UNDECLARED SITES DESIGNATED BY THE SPECIAL COMMISSION; SOME 13 SITES WERE INSPECTED.

16. THE INSPECTION WAS COMPLETED ONLY VERY RECENTLY AND THE FULL OFFICIAL REPORT IS THEREFORE NOT AT PRESENT AVAILABLE. FIELD REPORTING, HOWEVER, INDICATES THAT NO CHEMICAL-OR-BIOLOGICAL-WEAPONS-RELATED ACTIVITIES WERE ASSOCIATED WITH ANY OF THE DESIGNATED SITES. IN THE COURSE OF THE INSPECTION, A SMALL SUB-TEAM WAS DISPATCHED TO AL MUTHANNA TO WITNESS AN IRAQI EXPERIMENT WITH A SIMULANT TO PROVE THE USE OF THE MODIFIED PILOT PLANT FOR EXPLORATORY WORK ON THE DESTRUCTION OF NERVE AGENTS; THIS WAS SUCCESSFUL.

0189

17. SINCE THE FIRST REPORT WAS PREPARED A SMALL (4 PERSON) MISSION HAS VISITED IRAQ FOR DETAILED TECHNICAL DISCUSSIONS (11 TO 15 NOVEMBER 1991) WITH IRAQI COUNTERPARTS ON VARIOUS OF THE ISSUES RELATED TO THE DESTRUCTION OF CHEMICAL WEAPONS AND AGENTS, WITH PARTICULAR EMPHASIS ON THE DIRECT INVOLVEMENT OF IRAQ IN THIS PROCESS AND ON SAFETY ASPECTS. ISSUES DISCUSSED AND ON WHICH THE SPECIAL COMMISSION TEAM MADE RECOMMENDATIONS INCLUDED AN IRAQI DESIGN FOR A MUSTARD AGENT INCINERATOR, THE DESTRUCTION OF NERVE AGENTS BY CAUSTIC HYDROLYSIS, AND THE BREACHING AND DRAINING OF MUNITIONS.

18. WHEN, IN THE VERY NEAR FUTURE, ALL THE DATA COMPILED BY UNSCOM 17 AT THE AL MUTHANNA STATE ESTABLISHMENT HAVE BEEN ANALYZED, THE SPECIAL COMMISSION WILL HAVE A VERY GOOD UNDERSTANDING OF IRAQ'S MAJOR PRIMARY CHEMICAL WEAPONS SITE. FURTHERMORE, THE DISCUSSIONS ON THE DESTRUCTION OF CHEMICAL WEAPONS AND AGENTS HAVE RESULTED IN A CONSIDERABLE IMPROVEMENT IN TECHNICAL UNDERSTANDING BY BOTH SIDES, PARTICULARLY AS REGARDS THE POTENTIAL HAZARDS INVOLVED IN SOME OPERATIONS AND OF TECHNOLOGIES POTENTIALLY AVAILABLE FOR IMPLEMENTING THE VARIOUS DESTRUCTION PROCESSES. COMMENCEMENT OF THE DESTRUCTION PROCESS EARLY IN 1992 CAN THUS BE CONFIDENTLY EXPECTED.

BALLISTIC MISSILES AND LONG RANGE GUNS
----

19. WITH RESPECT TO THE BALLISTIC MISSILES, BY THE END OF 1991 TWO ADDITIONAL SPECIAL COMMISSION BALLISTIC MISSILE INSPECTIONS (UNSCOM 23 AND UNSCOM 24) ARE EXPECTED TO HAVE BEEN COMPLETED. TO DATE SPECIAL COMMISSION INSPECTION TEAMS HAVE, ACCORDING TO THE LATEST REVISED DATA, SUPERVISED THE DESTRUCTION OF 62 BALLISTIC MISSILES, 18 FIXED MISSILE LAUNCH PADS, 33 BALLISTIC MISSILE WARHEADS, 127 MISSILE STORAGE SUPPORT RACKS, A SUBSTANTIAL AMOUNT OF ROCKET FUEL, AN ASSEMBLED 350 MM SUPERGUN, COMPONENTS OF TWO 350 AND TWO 1,000 MM SUPERGUNS, AND ONE TON OF SUPERGUN PROPELLANT.

20. SO FAR, NO INFORMATION HAS COME TO LIGHT WHICH CLEARLY CONTRADICTS IRAQ'S DISCLOSURE OF 5 JULY 1991 WITH RESPECT TO THE STATUS OF ITS BALLISTIC MISSILE FORCE. NEVERTHELESS, THE FACT THAT IRAQ CONTINUED TO FIRE

0190

BALLISTIC MISSILES THROUGHOUT THE GULF WAR AND STILL HAD
A PORTION OF ITS FORCE FOLLOWING THAT WAR, DESPITE WHAT
WERE, BY ALL PUBLIC ACCOUNTS, THE INTENSIVE EFFORTS OF
COALITION FORCES TO FIND AND DESTROY THEM, ATTESTS TO THE
RELATIVE EASE WITH WHICH THEY COULD BE CONCEALED EVEN IN
WAR. SPECIAL COMMISSION INSPECTION TEAMS HAVE FOUND
UNDECLARED BALLISTIC MISSILE SUPPORT EQUIPMENT AND NOTED
IRAQI ATTEMPTS TO REUSE PREVIOUSLY DESTROYED MISSILE
TRANSPORT VEHICLES.

21. THE SPECIAL COMMISSION IS SEEKING FURTHER
INFORMATION, ANALYSIS OF WHICH MAY ALLOW A MORE
COMPREHENSIVE UNDERSTANDING OF THIS ISSUE, AND INCREASE
CONFIDENCE IN ANY ASSESSMENTS WHICH MAY EMERGE. AT THE
PRESENT TIME, HOWEVER, AS POINTED OUT IN THE FIRST
REPORT, IMPORTANT QUESTIONS STILL REMAIN UNRESOLVED,
NAMELY, WHETHER IRAQ CONTINUES TO HAVE ANY BALLISTIC
MISSILES IN ITS POSSESSION, AND ITS PLANS AND PROGRESS IN
FUTURE BALLISTIC MISSILE DEVELOPMENT. THE TWO BALLISTIC
MISSILE INSPECTIONS WHICH ARE BEING UNDERTAKEN THIS MONTH
SHOULD SHED ADDITIONAL LIGHT ON THESE QUESTIONS.

ADMINISTRATIVE ISSUES
----

22. THE ADMINISTRATIVE ISSUES OUTLINED IN PARAGRAPHS 25
TO 31 OF THE FIRST REPORT REMAIN UNRESOLVED, MOST
PARTICULARLY THE ISSUE OF FINANCING. THE SPECIAL
COMMISSION IS MOST GRATEFUL TO RECORD THE RECEIPT OF
ADDITIONAL VOLUNTARY CONTRIBUTIONS FROM KUWAIT (1,000,000
US DOLLARS) AND SAUDI ARABIA (1,730,000 US DOLLARS)
WHICH HAVE ENABLED IT TO CONTINUE TO FUNCTION IN THE
PERIOD UNDER REVIEW. HOWEVER, THE SHORTAGE OF READILY
AVAILABLE FUNDS WILL BECOME CRITICAL EARLY NEXT YEAR,
PARTICULARLY IF THE SPECIAL COMMISSION AND IAEA ARE TO
PROCEED WITH THE VERY COSTLY REMOVAL OF SPENT IRRADIATED
FUEL FROM IRAQ.

0191

```
--------------------------
CONCLUDING OBSERVATIONS
--------------------------
```

23. IN THE PREVIOUS REPORT, THE FULL SUPPORT OF THE
SECURITY COUNCIL, GOVERNMENTS, THE SECRETARY-GENERAL AND
THE SECRETARIAT OF THE UNITED NATIONS WERE IDENTIFIED AS
BEING OF CRUCIAL IMPORTANCE IN THE CARRYING OUT OF THE
MANDATE LAID DOWN IN SECTION C OF SECURITY COUNCIL
RESOLUTION 687 (1991). THIS WILL CERTAINLY REMAIN TO BE
THE CASE AS THE SPECIAL COMMISSION AND IAEA CONFRONT THE
DIFFICULT ISSUES WHICH WILL ARISE IN CONNECTION WITH THE
DESTRUCTION, REMOVAL OR RENDERING HARMLESS OF IRAQ'S
WEAPONS OF MASS DESTRUCTION AND THE FACILITIES FOR THEIR
PRODUCTION AND AS THE PLANS FOR ONGOING MONITORING AND
VERIFICATION ARE PUT INTO FULL EFFECT. EXPERIENCE TO
DATE HAS SHOWN THAT RESULTS CAN BE ACHIEVED ONLY WHERE
RESOLUTE STANDS ARE TAKEN IN RESPONSE TO CHALLENGES BY
IRAQ TO THE IMPLEMENTATION OF VARIOUS ASPECTS OF THE
MANDATE OF THE SPECIAL COMMISSION AND IAEA. SUCH
RESOLUTE STANDS CAN BE BASED ONLY ON THE FULL SUPPORT OF
THE UNITED NATIONS AS A WHOLE AND ITS MEMBER GOVERNMENTS
IN ACHIEVING ALL THE BASIC OBJECTIVES OF SECTION C OF
SECURITY COUNCIL RESOLUTION 687 (1991).

0192

외 무 부

110-760 서울 종로구 세종로 77번지 / (02) 720-2334 / (02) 723-3505

문서번호 연일 2031-557

시행일자 1991.12.20.

수신 중동아국장

참조

선결			지시		
접수	일자시간		결재	어	
	번호		공람		
처리과		제1			
담당자					

제목 UNSCOM 보고서

　　　　주한 미대사관측은 12.20(금) UNSCOM의 제2차 보고서(91.12.4자)와 함께
동 특별위원회의 지속적 활동을 지지하는 미국의 입장을 표명한 별첨 문서를
전달해온 바, 업무에 참고하시기 바랍니다.

첨 부 : 동 자료 1부. 끝.

국 제 기 구 국 장

0193

외 무 부

110-760 서울 종로구 세종로 77번지 / (02) 720-2334 / (02) 723-3505

문서번호 연일 2031- 557

시행일자 1991.12.20.

(경유)

수신 중동아국장

참조

취급		장 관
보존		
국장	전결	〔서명〕
심의관		
과장	〔서명〕	
기안	이수택	협조

제목 UNSCOM 보고서

　　　주한 미대사관측은 12.20(금) UNSCOM의 제2차 보고서(91.12.4자)와 함께
동 특별위원회의 지속적 활동을 지지하는 미국의 입장을 표명한 별첨 문서를
전달해온 바, 업무에 참고하시기 바랍니다.

　　첨부 : 동 자료 1부. 끝.

〔수기: 사토: 공개 기록물〕

0194

UNSCOM REPORT ON IRAQI COMPLIANCE WITH
SECTION C OF UNSCR 687

FROM U.S. STATE DEPARTMENT:

-- WE COMMEND THIS REPORT TO YOUR ATTENTION AND FOR YOUR
USE WITH YOUR PRESS AND PUBLIC. IT DEMONSTRATES BOTH
THE REMARKABLE ACCOMPLISHMENTS MADE BY UNSCOM AND THE
INTERNATIONAL ATOMIC ENERGY AGENCY, AND THE FACT THAT
MUCH MORE REMAINS TO BE DONE BEFORE RESOLUTION 687 CAN BE
SAID TO BE SUCCESSFULLY IMPLEMENTED.

-- OF PARTICULAR NOTE IS THE REPORT'S OBSERVATIONS OF
IRAQ'S CONTINUED LACK OF COOPERATION AND EVEN OBSTRUCTION
IN THE IMPLEMENTATION OF RESOLUTION 687.

-- A RELATED POINT IS THE REPORT'S COMMENT THAT IRAQ HAS
YET TO ACCEPT ITS OBLIGATIONS UNDER RESOLUTION 715, WHICH
CODIFIES UNSCOM'S AND IAEA'S LONG-TERM MONITORING PLANS.
THE USG CONSIDERS THIS DISTURBING.

-- WE ALSO CALL YOUR ATTENTION TO THE REPORT'S
CONCLUSION THAT IMPORTANT QUESTIONS REMAIN UNANSWERED,
ESPECIALLY WITH REGARD TO NUCLEAR WEAPONS, BALLISTIC
MISSILES, AND BIOLOGICAL WEAPONS.

-- FINALLY, THE REPORT DRAWS ATTENTION TO THE FINANCIAL
DIFFICULTIES OF UNSCOM. AT PRESENT, THERE ARE NO FUNDS
AVAILABLE TO CONTINUE UNSCOM'S ACTIVITIES INTO THE NEW
YEAR.

-- THIS IS ESPECIALLY IMPORTANT BECAUSE WE BELIEVE IRAQ
STILL MAINTAINS SOME FACILITIES, MATERIAL AND EQUIPMENT
FOR WEAPONS OF MASS DESTRUCTION. SADDAM HAS NOT REVEALED
ALL OF HIS WEAPONS YET. AS A RESULT, UNSCOM'S AND IAEA'S
JOB IS NOT DONE YET. MORE CHALLENGE INSPECTIONS WILL BE
NEEDED TO ENSURE THAT SADDAM IS NOT LEFT WITH A
CLANDESTINE FORCE OF WEAPONS OF MASS DESTRUCTION FOR
FUTURE USE.

-- RESOLUTION 687 GIVES UNSCOM AND IAEA THE MANDATE TO
CONDUCT CHALLENGE INSPECTIONS, DESTRUCTION, AND LONG TERM
MONITORING IN IRAQ INDEFINITELY. BOTH UNSCOM AND IAEA
PLAN TO HAVE A PRESENCE IN IRAQ FOR THE FORESEEABLE
FUTURE.

0195

-- THE USG -- LIKE MANY OTHER COUNTRIES -- CONTINUES TO PROVIDE UNSCOM AND IAEA WITH INFORMATION TO ASSIST THIS SEARCH, EXPERTS TO BE ON INSPECTION TEAMS, AND ANALYSIS OF INSPECTION TEAM FINDINGS.

-- IT IS IMPORTANT THAT ALL COUNTRIES CONTINUE TO SUPPORT IMPLEMENTATION OF RESOLUTION 687, DEMAND THAT IRAQ BE FORTHCOMING ABOUT ITS WEAPONS PROGRAMS, DESTROY IMMEDIATELY THE FACILITIES ALREADY DISCOVERED, AND FORSWEAR FUTURE RECONSTITUTION OF THIS CAPABILITY.

4. BEGIN TEXT OF UNSCOM'S SECOND PROGRESS REPORT TO THE UN SECURITY COUNCIL ON IMPLEMENTATION OF SECTION C OF UNSCR 687, DATED DEC. 4 1991.

INTRODUCTION
----

1. THE PRESENT REPORT BY THE EXECUTIVE CHAIRMAN OF THE SPECIAL COMMISSION ESTABLISHED BY THE SECRETARY-GENERAL PURSUANT TO PARAGRAPH 9 (B) (I) OF SECURITY COUNCIL RESOLUTION 687 (1991), COVERS THE WORK OF THE COMMISSION FOR THE PERIOD FROM 15 OCTOBER TO 4 DECEMBER 1991. THIS SECOND REPORT IS CONFINED TO OPERATIONAL ACTIVITIES AND MATTERS DIRECTLY PERTINENT THERETO AS THESE ARE THE AREAS WHICH NEED TO BE BROUGHT UP TO DATE TO PROVIDE, TOGETHER WITH THE FIRST REPORT OF THE EXECUTIVE CHAIRMAN (S/23165), A COMPREHENSIVE PICTURE OF THE ESTABLISHMENT AND FUNCTIONING OF THE SPECIAL COMMITTEE SINCE THE ADOPTION OF SECURITY COUNCIL RESOLUTIONS 687 (1991) AND 699 (1991).

ATTITUDE OF IRAQ
----

2. THE FIRST REPORT BY THE EXECUTIVE CHAIRMAN CONTAINED, IN PARAGRAPHS 16 TO 19, A COMPREHENSIVE ACCOUNT OF THE ATTITUDE OF IRAQ. IN THE PERIOD UNDER REVIEW THIS ATTITUDE HAS NOT CHANGED. IN RESPECT OF SITES AND ACTIVITIES DECLARED BY IRAQ AND THE ISSUE OF IRAQ'S PARTICIPATION IN THE DESTRUCTION OF CHEMICAL

0196

WEAPONS, COOPERATION AT THE FIELD LEVEL HAS BEEN
FORTHCOMING. HOWEVER, IN RESPECT OF SITES DESIGNATED BY
THE SPECIAL COMMISSION, WHERE THE COMMISSION AND IAEA ARE
ACTING ON THEIR OWN SOURCES OF INFORMATION REGARDING
POSSIBLE CLANDESTINE CONDUCT OF PROSCRIBED ACTIVITIES,
NON-COOPERATION AND OBSTRUCTION CONTINUE TO BE
ENCOUNTERED. THERE IS THUS NO PROGRESS TO REPORT WHICH
WOULD INDICATE A CHANGE IN POLICY ON THE PART OF IRAQ TO
ONE OF CANDOR, TRANSPARENCY AND COOPERATION AT ALL
LEVELS. AS THE EXECUTIVE CHAIRMAN REMARKED IN THE FIRST
REPORT, THIS IS PROBABLY THE ONE SINGLE ELEMENT THAT
COULD CONTRIBUTE MOST SUBSTANTIALLY TO A TIMELY AND
SATISFACTORY IMPLEMENTATION OF THE MANDATE OF THE SPECIAL
COMMISSION AND OF IAEA.

3.   THE SPECIAL COMMISSION HAS HAD TO REMAIN VIGILANT IN
THE PERIOD UNDER REVIEW TO PREVENT IMPLEMENTATION OF
MEASURES PROPOSED BY IRAQ WHICH COULD IMPINGE UPON THE
FACILITIES, PRIVILEGES AND IMMUNITIES OF THE COMMISSION
AND OF IAEA IN MATTERS SUCH AS THE TAKING INTO AND OUT OF
IRAQ OF ALL NECESSARY EQUIPMENT, MATERIALS AND OTHER
ITEMS REQUIRED FOR INSPECTIONS AND THE ANALYSIS OF THEIR
RESULTS AND THE TAKING OF PHOTOGRAPHS AT SITES UNDER
INSPECTION. SO FAR THE STRONG POSITION TAKEN BY THE
COMMISSION AND THE CHIEF INSPECTORS INVOLVED SEEMS TO
HAVE BEEN SUCCESSFUL IN PRESERVING THE RIGHTS CONCERNED.

4.   WITH RESPECT TO ONGOING MONITORING AND VERIFICATION
OF IRAQ'S COMPLIANCE WITH PARAGRAPHS 10 AND 13 OF
SECURITY COUNCIL RESOLUTION 687 (1991), THE SPECIAL
COMMISSION HAS VERY RECENTLY RECEIVED IN NEW YORK FROM
IRAQ WHICH THE GOVERNMENT STATES TO BE "THE INFORMATION
REQUIRED UNDER RESOLUTION 687 (1991) THAT COMES WITHIN
THE MANDATE OF THE SPECIAL COMMISSION". UNTIL THE
INFORMATION IS TRANSLATED, THE COMMISSION CANNOT
DETERMINE THE EXTENT TO WHICH IT MEETS THE SUBSTANTIVE
REQUIREMENTS OF THE SPECIAL COMMISSION'S AND IAEA'S PLANS
FOR ONGOING PLANNING AND VERIFICATION (S/22871/REV.1 AND
S/22872/REV.1 AND CORR.1) WHICH WERE UNANIMOUSLY APPROVED
BY THE SECURITY COUNCIL IN ITS RESOLUTION 715 (1991),
ALTHOUGH IT MAY BE OBSERVED THAT CERTAIN PROCEDURAL
REQUIREMENTS LAID DOWN IN THE PLANS AS TO TIME-LIMITS AND
LANGUAGES OF SUBMISSION HAVE NOT BEEN MET. IF THE
COMMISSION AND IAEA ARE TO BE IN A POSITION TO CARRY OUT
THEIR FUNCTIONS IN CONNECTION WITH ONGOING MONITORING AND

0197

VERIFICATION, THE COMMISSION DEEMS IT TO BE OF GREAT
IMPORTANCE THAT IRAQ EXPRESSLY RECOGNIZE ITS OBLIGATIONS
UNDER THE TWO PLANS AND SECURITY COUNCIL RESOLUTION 715
(1991). SUCH EXPRESS RECOGNITION IS STILL AWAITED.

NUCLEAR ISSUE
----

5. TWO MORE INSPECTIONS WERE COMPLETED (IAEA 7/UNSCOM
19 AND IAEA 8/ UNSCOM 22), ONE EACH IN OCTOBER (11 TO 22)
AND NOVEMBER (11 TO 18), SINCE THE SIXTH NUCLEAR
INSPECTION SUMMARIZED IN THE PREVIOUS REPORT. IN
ADDITION TO THE SUCCESSFUL REMOVAL OF UNIRRADIATED FUEL
FROM IRAQ, THE INSPECTION TEAMS FOCUSED MOST OF THEIR
INSPECTION ACTIVITY ON A NUMBER OF SITES ASSOCIATED WITH
(A) IRAQ'S PROGRAM TO DESIGN AND DEVELOP THE NON-NUCLEAR
COMPONENTS OF A NUCLEAR WEAPON AND (B) CENTRIFUGE
COMPONENT MANUFACTURE.

6. SIGNIFICANTLY, IRAQ PROVIDED FOR THE FIRST TIME TO
THE SEVENTH NUCLEAR INSPECTION TEAM FORMAL THOUGH
INCOMPLETE WRITTEN ACKNOWLEDGMENT OF ITS NUCLEAR WEAPONS
PROGRAM:

"VARIOUS RESEARCH AND STUDIES OF THE SORT TO WHICH
YOU REFER AS 'WEAPONIZATION' HAVE BEEN CARRIED OUT.
THE OBJECTIVE IN CARRYING OUT SUCH RESEARCH AND
STUDIES WAS TO ESTABLISH THE PRACTICAL, TECHNICAL,
AND SCIENTIFIC REQUIREMENTS FOR A PROGRAM OF THIS
NATURE IN THE EVENT THAT A POLITICAL DECISION WERE TO
BE TAKEN TO PROCEED IN THAT DIRECTION."

7. THE EXTENSIVE AND DETAILED DOCUMENTATION OF THE
NUCLEAR WEAPONS PROGRAM THAT WAS OBTAINED BY THE SIXTH
INSPECTION TEAM, AND ITS REMOVAL FROM IRAQ ONLY AFTER
THAT TEAM'S DETAINMENT IN A PARKING LOT FOR FOUR DAYS,
PRECEDED THE IRAQI ADMISSION TO THE SEVENTH TEAM OF
HAVING CONDUCTED RESEARCH AND STUDIES ON NUCLEAR WEAPONS.
IN FACT, THE SEVENTH AND EIGHTH INSPECTION TEAMS VISITED
DESIGNATED FACILITIES JUDGED TO BE DIRECTLY ASSOCIATED
WITH THE TESTING AND DEVELOPMENT OF THE HIGH-EXPLOSIVE
COMPONENTS OF THE IMPLOSION SYSTEM OF A NUCLEAR WEAPON.
THE CHARACTERISTICS OF THESE FACILITIES WERE CONSIDERED
INCONSISTENT WITH IRAQ'S EXPLANATIONS OF THEIR PURPOSE.

0198

THUS, IRAQ'S POSITION THAT IT CONDUCTED STUDIES BUT HAD NO PROGRAM TO DEVELOP NUCLEAR WEAPONS IS INCONSISTENT WITH BOTH DOCUMENTS AND INSPECTION RESULTS THAT REVEAL A WELL-FUNDED AND BROADLY-BASED PROGRAM INVOLVING SOPHISTICATED FACILITIES FOR NUCLEAR WEAPONS DEVELOPMENT.

8.   IN THE AREA OF FISSILE MATERIAL PRODUCTION, IMPORTANT QUESTIONS PUT TO IRAQ REMAIN UNANSWERED. WHILE MUCH OF THE ELECTROMAGNETIC ISOTOPE SEPARATION (EMIS) EQUIPMENT HAS BEEN TURNED OVER FOR DESTRUCTION, THE CRITICAL COLLECTOR POCKETS WHICH WOULD PERMIT CONFIRMATION OF IRAQ'S ASSERTIONS THAT ONLY LOW LEVELS OF ENRICHMENT WERE ACHIEVED HAVE NOT BEEN PRODUCED FOR ANALYSIS. SUBSTANTIAL UNCERTAINTIES ALSO REMAIN OVER THE CENTRIFUGE PROGRAM WHERE IRAQ HAS PRODUCED SOME BUT NOT ALL PARTS AND MATERIALS. EVEN LESS INFORMATION HAS BEEN PRODUCED BY IRAQ ON THEIR EFFORTS IN THE DIFFUSION AND CHEMICAL SEPARATION PROCESSES. ALL THIS IS ESPECIALLY TROUBLING IN THE LIGHT OF PRELIMINARY RESULTS OF SAMPLING ACCOMPLISHED AT AL TUWAITHA, AND NOTED IN THE IAEA SEVENTH INSPECTION REPORT (S/23215) THAT PROVIDE EVIDENCE OF URANIUM ENRICHED TO 93 PER CENT IN THE ISOTOPE U 235. ADDITIONAL SAMPLING WAS UNDERTAKEN BY THE SEVENTH AND EIGHTH INSPECTION TEAMS. ANALYSIS AND FURTHER INVESTIGATION ARE CLEARLY REQUIRED.

9.   IRAQ'S RECENT RECORD IN THE NUCLEAR AREA IS CONSISTENT WITH, IF LESS DRAMATIC THAN, ITS ACTIONS OVER THE LAST SIX MONTHS THAT INCLUDED THE CONCEALMENT OF EVIDENCE OF PLUTONIUM SEPARATION, OR URANIUM ENRICHMENT, AND OF NUCLEAR WEAPONS DEVELOPMENT, OF REFUSAL TO PERMIT INSPECTION TO ENTER SOME SITES AND EXIT OTHERS, AND CONFISCATION OF DOCUMENTS FROM INSPECTORS IN THE COURSE OF AN INSPECTION. IN SUM, IRAQ HAS NOT COOPERATED IN THE CRITICAL AREA OF NUCLEAR-WEAPONS-RELATED ACTIVITY AND THE SPECIAL COMMISSION AND IAEA ARE SOME DISTANCE FROM ACHIEVING THE TRANSPARENCY WHICH IS SOUGHT.

C199

CHEMICAL AND BIOLOGICAL WEAPONS

10. SINCE THE FIRST REPORT WAS PREPARED, TWO FURTHER CHEMICAL INSPECTIONS HAVE BEEN COMPLETED, ONE BEING THE LONG AND DETAILED INSPECTION OF THE AL MUTHANNA STATE ESTABLISHMENT (7 OCTOBER TO NOVEMBER 1991) WHILE THE OTHER VISITED A SERIES OF DECLARED CHEMICAL MUNITIONS STORAGE SITES (22 OCTOBER TO 2 NOVEMBER 1991). THERE HAS ALSO BEEN A COMBINED CHEMICAL AND BIOLOGICAL WEAPONS INSPECTION WHICH VISITED (17 TO 30 NOVEMBER 1991), AT VERY SHORT NOTICE, A NUMBER OF SITES DESIGNATED BY THE SPECIAL COMMISSION AS BEING OF POTENTIAL CHEMICAL WEAPONS AND/OR BIOLOGICAL WEAPONS INTEREST IN ADDITION TO REVISITING THE ORIGINAL SITE AT SALMAN PAK.

11. THE TECHNICALLY VERY SUCCESSFUL INSPECTION OF AL MUTHANNA (UNSCOM 17) COMPILED A COMPREHENSIVE AND DETAILED INVENTORY OF THE SITE, INCLUDING FACILITIES, MUNITIONS, AGENTS, AGENT CONDITION, PRECURSORS AND INTERMEDIATES. AMONG THE SALIENT FINDINGS WERE THE DISCOVERY OF SMALL QUANTITIES OF THE NERVE AGENTS SEC-BUTYL, N-BUTYL SARIN AND ETHYL SARIN, ALTHOUGH IRAQ HAS DISPUTED THE IDENTIFICATION OF THE LATTER TWO AGENTS. WHILE THE QUANTITIES FOUND WERE OF NO DIRECT MILITARY SIGNIFICANCE, THE RELEVANCE OF THE FINDING LIES IN THE FACT THAT IRAQ CLEARLY HAD CARRIED OUT RESEARCH ON NERVE AGENTS OTHER THAN THOSE PREVIOUSLY DECLARED.

12. ALTHOUGH THE MUSTARD AGENT AT AL MUTHANNA WAS GENERALLY OF GOOD QUALITY (TYPICALLY 90 PER CENT), THE NERVE AGENTS WERE FOUND TO HAVE UNDERGONE EXTENSIVE DEGRADATION AND THE AGENT CONTENT WAS VERY LOW, GENERALLY BELOW 10 PER CENT AND IN SOME CASES BELOW THE 1 PER CENT LEVEL. THIS NEW INFORMATION MAY HAVE SIGNIFICANT REPERCUSSIONS FOR THE PROCESS FINALLY SELECTED FOR THE DESTRUCTION OF THE NERVE AGENTS AS WELL AS FOR THE SAFETY HAZARDS LIKELY TO BE ENCOUNTERED DURING DESTRUCTION; BOTH ASPECTS WILL NEED FURTHER CONSIDERATION.

0200

13. IN GENERAL, THE FINDINGS OF THE INSPECTION AT AL MUTHANNA WERE IN SUBSTANTIAL AGREEMENT WITH IRAQ'S DECLARATION, ALTHOUGH IN THE CASE OF THE 122 MM ROCKETS A PRECISE AND FULL COUNT WAS NOT POSSIBLE AS THE ROCKETS GENERALLY WERE FOUND TO BE IN A VERY DANGEROUS CONDITION. EXPLOSIVE DEMOLITION WAS CONSIDERED TO BE SAFEST MEANS OF ACHIEVING THEIR DESTRUCTION SINCE OPENING AND DRAINING OPERATIONS WOULD BE PARTICULARLY HAZARDOUS.

14. THE INSPECTION OF THE REMAINING DECLARED STORAGE SITES (UNSCOM 20) WAS LIKEWISE A SUCCESSFUL OPERATION. ALL OF THE DECLARED SITES, SOME OF THEM DISTANT FROM BAGHDAD AND THEREFORE REQUIRING THE USE OF UNITED NATIONS HELICOPTER TRANSPORT, WERE INSPECTED, THE CHEMICAL WEAPONS MUNITIONS VERIFIED, COUNTED AND RECORDED, WHERE IT WAS SAFE TO TRANSPORT THE MUNITIONS TO AL MUTHANNA THE NECESSARY INSTRUCTIONS TO THIS EFFECT WERE GIVEN TO IRAQ. AT AL-TUZ, KHAMISIYAH AND MUHAMMADIYAT NUMBERS OF MUNITIONS WERE DISCOVERED, INCLUDING BUT NOT RESTRICTED TO 122 MM ROCKETS, WHICH WERE CONSIDERED TO BE IN TOO UNSAFE A CONDITION TO MOVE AND FOR WHICH A DRILLING AND DRAINING OPERATION WOULD BE VERY HAZARDOUS. A RECOMMENDATION WAS MADE ON SAFETY GROUNDS THAT THESE ITEMS BE DESTROYED IN SITU BY EXPLOSIVE DEMOLITION. IN A FEW CASES, DUE TO EXTENSIVE DESTRUCTION BY COALITION BOMBING, IT WAS NOT POSSIBLE TO OBSERVE AND COUNT ALL MUNITIONS; WHEN THE DAMAGE HAD BEEN LESS EXTENSIVE THE NUMBERS AND TYPES OF WEAPONS OBSERVED ACCORDED WELL WITH THE IRAQI DECLARATIONS.

15. THE COMBINED CHEMICAL AND BIOLOGICAL WEAPONS INSPECTION (UNSCOM 21), EXCEPT FOR THE VISIT TO SALMAN PAK, CONCENTRATED ON SHORT NOTICE INSPECTION OF UNDECLARED SITES DESIGNATED BY THE SPECIAL COMMISSION; SOME 13 SITES WERE INSPECTED.

16. THE INSPECTION WAS COMPLETED ONLY VERY RECENTLY AND THE FULL OFFICIAL REPORT IS THEREFORE NOT AT PRESENT AVAILABLE. FIELD REPORTING, HOWEVER, INDICATES THAT NO CHEMICAL-OR-BIOLOGICAL-WEAPONS-RELATED ACTIVITIES WERE ASSOCIATED WITH ANY OF THE DESIGNATED SITES. IN THE COURSE OF THE INSPECTION, A SMALL SUB-TEAM WAS DISPATCHED TO AL MUTHANNA TO WITNESS AN IRAQI EXPERIMENT WITH A SIMULANT TO PROVE THE USE OF THE MODIFIED PILOT PLANT FOR EXPLORATORY WORK ON THE DESTRUCTION OF NERVE AGENTS; THIS WAS SUCCESSFUL.

0201

17. SINCE THE FIRST REPORT WAS PREPARED A SMALL (4 PERSON) MISSION HAS VISITED IRAQ FOR DETAILED TECHNICAL DISCUSSIONS (11 TO 15 NOVEMBER 1991) WITH IRAQI COUNTERPARTS ON VARIOUS OF THE ISSUES RELATED TO THE DESTRUCTION OF CHEMICAL WEAPONS AND AGENTS, WITH PARTICULAR EMPHASIS ON THE DIRECT INVOLVEMENT OF IRAQ IN THIS PROCESS AND ON SAFETY ASPECTS. ISSUES DISCUSSED AND ON WHICH THE SPECIAL COMMISSION TEAM MADE RECOMMENDATIONS INCLUDED AN IRAQI DESIGN FOR A MUSTARD AGENT INCINERATOR, THE DESTRUCTION OF NERVE AGENTS BY CAUSTIC HYDROLYSIS, AND THE BREACHING AND DRAINING OF MUNITIONS.

18. WHEN, IN THE VERY NEAR FUTURE, ALL THE DATA COMPILED BY UNSCOM 17 AT THE AL MUTHANNA STATE ESTABLISHMENT HAVE BEEN ANALYZED, THE SPECIAL COMMISSION WILL HAVE A VERY GOOD UNDERSTANDING OF IRAQ'S MAJOR PRIMARY CHEMICAL WEAPONS SITE. FURTHERMORE, THE DISCUSSIONS ON THE DESTRUCTION OF CHEMICAL WEAPONS AND AGENTS HAVE RESULTED IN A CONSIDERABLE IMPROVEMENT IN TECHNICAL UNDERSTANDING BY BOTH SIDES, PARTICULARLY AS REGARDS THE POTENTIAL HAZARDS INVOLVED IN SOME OPERATIONS AND OF TECHNOLOGIES POTENTIALLY AVAILABLE FOR IMPLEMENTING THE VARIOUS DESTRUCTION PROCESSES. COMMENCEMENT OF THE DESTRUCTION PROCESS EARLY IN 1992 CAN THUS BE CONFIDENTLY EXPECTED.

BALLISTIC MISSILES AND LONG RANGE GUNS
---

19. WITH RESPECT TO THE BALLISTIC MISSILES, BY THE END OF 1991 TWO ADDITIONAL SPECIAL COMMISSION BALLISTIC MISSILE INSPECTIONS (UNSCOM 23 AND UNSCOM 24) ARE EXPECTED TO HAVE BEEN COMPLETED. TO DATE SPECIAL COMMISSION INSPECTION TEAMS HAVE, ACCORDING TO THE LATEST REVISED DATA, SUPERVISED THE DESTRUCTION OF 62 BALLISTIC MISSILES, 18 FIXED MISSILE LAUNCH PADS, 33 BALLISTIC MISSILE WARHEADS, 127 MISSILE STORAGE SUPPORT RACKS, A SUBSTANTIAL AMOUNT OF ROCKET FUEL, AN ASSEMBLED 350 MM SUPERGUN, COMPONENTS OF TWO 350 AND TWO 1,000 MM SUPERGUNS, AND ONE TON OF SUPERGUN PROPELLANT.

20. SO FAR, NO INFORMATION HAS COME TO LIGHT WHICH CLEARLY CONTRADICTS IRAQ'S DISCLOSURE OF 5 JULY 1991 WITH RESPECT TO THE STATUS OF ITS BALLISTIC MISSILE FORCE. NEVERTHELESS, THE FACT THAT IRAQ CONTINUED TO FIRE

0202

BALLISTIC MISSILES THROUGHOUT THE GULF WAR AND STILL HAD
A PORTION OF ITS FORCE FOLLOWING THAT WAR, DESPITE WHAT
WERE, BY ALL PUBLIC ACCOUNTS, THE INTENSIVE EFFORTS OF
COALITION FORCES TO FIND AND DESTROY THEM, ATTESTS TO THE
RELATIVE EASE WITH WHICH THEY COULD BE CONCEALED EVEN IN
WAR. SPECIAL COMMISSION INSPECTION TEAMS HAVE FOUND
UNDECLARED BALLISTIC MISSILE SUPPORT EQUIPMENT AND NOTED
IRAQI ATTEMPTS TO REUSE PREVIOUSLY DESTROYED MISSILE
TRANSPORT VEHICLES.

21. THE SPECIAL COMMISSION IS SEEKING FURTHER
INFORMATION, ANALYSIS OF WHICH MAY ALLOW A MORE
COMPREHENSIVE UNDERSTANDING OF THIS ISSUE, AND INCREASE
CONFIDENCE IN ANY ASSESSMENTS WHICH MAY EMERGE. AT THE
PRESENT TIME, HOWEVER, AS POINTED OUT IN THE FIRST
REPORT, IMPORTANT QUESTIONS STILL REMAIN UNRESOLVED,
NAMELY, WHETHER IRAQ CONTINUES TO HAVE ANY BALLISTIC
MISSILES IN ITS POSSESSION, AND ITS PLANS AND PROGRESS IN
FUTURE BALLISTIC MISSILE DEVELOPMENT. THE TWO BALLISTIC
MISSILE INSPECTIONS WHICH ARE BEING UNDERTAKEN THIS MONTH
SHOULD SHED ADDITIONAL LIGHT ON THESE QUESTIONS.

ADMINISTRATIVE ISSUES
----

22. THE ADMINISTRATIVE ISSUES OUTLINED IN PARAGRAPHS 25
TO 31 OF THE FIRST REPORT REMAIN UNRESOLVED, MOST
PARTICULARLY THE ISSUE OF FINANCING. THE SPECIAL
COMMISSION IS MOST GRATEFUL TO RECORD THE RECEIPT OF
ADDITIONAL VOLUNTARY CONTRIBUTIONS FROM KUWAIT (1,000,000
US DOLLARS) AND SAUDI ARABIA (1,730,000 US DOLLARS)
WHICH HAVE ENABLED IT TO CONTINUE TO FUNCTION IN THE
PERIOD UNDER REVIEW. HOWEVER, THE SHORTAGE OF READILY
AVAILABLE FUNDS WILL BECOME CRITICAL EARLY NEXT YEAR,
PARTICULARLY IF THE SPECIAL COMMISSION AND IAEA ARE TO
PROCEED WITH THE VERY COSTLY REMOVAL OF SPENT IRRADIATED
FUEL FROM IRAQ.

0203

```
---------------------------
```
CONCLUDING OBSERVATIONS
```
---------------------------
```

23.   IN THE PREVIOUS REPORT, THE FULL SUPPORT OF THE
SECURITY COUNCIL, GOVERNMENTS, THE SECRETARY-GENERAL AND
THE SECRETARIAT OF THE UNITED NATIONS WERE IDENTIFIED AS
BEING OF CRUCIAL IMPORTANCE IN THE CARRYING OUT OF THE
MANDATE LAID DOWN IN SECTION C OF SECURITY COUNCIL
RESOLUTION 687 (1991).   THIS WILL CERTAINLY REMAIN TO BE
THE CASE AS THE SPECIAL COMMISSION AND IAEA CONFRONT THE
DIFFICULT ISSUES WHICH WILL ARISE IN CONNECTION WITH THE
DESTRUCTION, REMOVAL OR RENDERING HARMLESS OF IRAQ'S
WEAPONS OF MASS DESTRUCTION AND THE FACILITIES FOR THEIR
PRODUCTION AND AS THE PLANS FOR ONGOING MONITORING AND
VERIFICATION ARE PUT INTO FULL EFFECT.   EXPERIENCE TO
DATE HAS SHOWN THAT RESULTS CAN BE ACHIEVED ONLY WHERE
RESOLUTE STANDS ARE TAKEN IN RESPONSE TO CHALLENGES BY
IRAQ TO THE IMPLEMENTATION OF VARIOUS ASPECTS OF THE
MANDATE OF THE SPECIAL COMMISSION AND IAEA.   SUCH
RESOLUTE STANDS CAN BE BASED ONLY ON THE FULL SUPPORT OF
THE UNITED NATIONS AS A WHOLE AND ITS MEMBER GOVERNMENTS
IN ACHIEVING ALL THE BASIC OBJECTIVES OF SECTION C OF
SECURITY COUNCIL RESOLUTION 687 (1991).

0204

CONSIDERATION OF GOV PAPERS ON "SPECIAL INSPECTIONS" AND "DESIGN INFORMATION" AT THE DECEMBER 1991 BOARD OF GOVERNORS MEETING

GENERAL

RECENT REVELATIONS REGARDING IRAQ'S MASSIVE, COVERT NUCLEAR WEAPONS PROGRAM HAVE GENERATED CONSIDERABLE INTEREST IN STRENGTHENING THE IAEA'S SAFEGUARDS SYSTEM. ON OCTOBER 23. THE IAEA SECRETARIAT DISTRIBUTED TO GOVERNMENTS REPRESENTED ON THE BOARD OF GOVERNORS THE TEXTS OF TWO PAPERS WHICH ARE BEING PUT IN FINAL FORM FOR DISTRIBUTION AS BOARD DOCUMENTS. THE PAPERS ARE INTENDED TO MOVE FORWARD THE PROCESS OF STRENGTHENING THE AGENCY'S SAFEGUARDS SYSTEM.

THE PAPERS DEAL WITH SPECIAL INSPECTIONS AND DESIGN INFORMATION UNDER INFCIRC/153 AND OTHER COMPREHENSIVE SAFEGUARDS AGREEMENTS. THESE ARE TWO RELATED ASPECTS TO THE NEED TO ENSURE THAT IAEA SAFEGUARDS DEVELOP THE CAPABILITY TO IDENTIFY NUCLEAR ACTIVITIES UNDERTAKEN OUTSIDE REQUIRED SAFEGUARDS BY PARTIES TO COMPREHENSIVE SAFEGUARDS AGREEMENTS OUTSIDE REQUIRED SAFEGUARDS.

THE UNITED STATES SUPPORTS THE RECOMMENDATIONS OF THE TWO IAEA SECRETARIAT PAPERS, AND BELIEVES IT IMPORTANT THAT THESE RECOMMENDATIONS BE ADOPTED AT THE UPCOMING DECEMBER IAEA BOARD OF GOVERNORS MEETING.

ACTION AT THE DECEMBER 1991 BOARD

THE DECEMBER BOARD SHOULD AND WILL GIVE FULL CONSIDERATION TO TECHNICAL ASSISTANCE PROSPECTS, AS IS CUSTOMARY, AND THIS WILL BE THE LEAD ITEM ON THE AGENDA. HOWEVER, THE IMPORTANCE OF DEALING WITH TECHNICAL ASSISTANCE IS NOT A JUSTIFICATION FOR LIMITING THE MEETING TO TECHNICAL ASSISTANCE AND CANNOT TAKE PRECEDENCE OVER THE NORMAL RULES CONTAINED IN PART V OF THE BOARD'S RULES OF PROCEDURE, PARTICULARLY RULE 15(C), WHICH ALLOWS ANY MEMBER TO REQUEST ITEMS ON THE AGENDA, AND 15(F), WHICH ALLOWS THE DIRECTOR GENERAL TO ADD ITEMS.

IAEA SAFEGUARDS ARE NOW AT A CRITICAL JUNCTURE AND UNDER INTENSE PUBLIC AND GOVERNMENTAL SCRUTINY. THE DIRECTOR GENERAL HAS BROUGHT FORWARD CONCRETE PROPOSALS TO ADDRESS THESE CONCERNS. FAILURE EVEN TO CONSIDER SAFEGUARDS-RELATED ISSUES AT AN IAEA BOARD MEETING WOULD NOT BE UNDERSTOOD BY THE PUBLIC OR GOVERNMENTS AND COULD SUBJECT THE AGENCY TO SERIOUS CRITICISM.

0205

THE U.S. HAS URGED COMPREHENSIVE REVIEW OF SAFEGUARDS
ISSUES IN THE WAKE OF IRAQ. THIS REVIEW BEGAN IN FACT AT THE
FEBRUARY 1991 MEETING OF THE BOARD AT WHICH TIME THE DIRECTOR
GENERAL BROUGHT THESE AND OTHER ISSUES TO THE BOARD'S ATTENTION
AND IDENTIFIED POSSIBLE SOLUTIONS. THE REVIEW HAS CONTINUED
SINCE THEN ON THE BASIS OF TWO SECRETARIAT PAPERS, GOV/INF/613
AND ADD. 1, AND WITH DISCUSSIONS AT BOTH THE JUNE AND THE
SEPTEMBER BOARDS. CONSIDERATION OF THESE TWO RELATED
SAFEGUARDS PROPOSALS, THE NEED FOR WHICH IS ALREADY WIDELY
APPRECIATED, IS PART OF AND NOT AN EXCEPTION TO THE CONCEPT OF
A COMPREHENSIVE REVIEW. IT IS NEITHER NECESSARY NOR DESIRABLE
TO DELAY THESE PROPOSALS TO THE FEBRUARY BOARD AND THEREBY TRY
TO COMPRESS ALL BOARD ACTIONS ON STRENGTHENING SAFEGUARDS INTO
A SINGLE BOARD MEETING.

THE FIRST INSPECTION UNDER UN SECURITY COUNCIL RESOLUTION
687, WHICH PROVIDED THE FIRST EVIDENCE OF ILLICIT, UNDECLARED
NUCLEAR ACTIVITIES IN IRAQ, TOOK PLACE IN MAY 15-21. WITH SIX
MONTHS HAVING ELAPSED, IT IS NOW CLEARLY INCUMBENT ON THE
AGENCY TO DEMONSTRATE CONCRETE PROGRESS, AS THE SECRETARIAT
PAPER ON SPECIAL INSPECTIONS COGENTLY STATES. INABILITY OF THE
AGENCY TO ACT ON THESE PROPOSALS, INVOLVING THE USE OF
AUTHORITY IT ALREADY POSSESSES, AFTER THIS MUCH TIME WILL RAISE
QUESTIONS ABOUT THE IAEA'S DETERMINATION TO DISCHARGE ITS
SAFEGUARDS RESPONSIBILITIES.

SPECIAL INSPECTIONS

THE PAPER ON SPECIAL INSPECTIONS INDICATES THAT THE IAEA
DIRECTOR GENERAL WILL REQUEST A SPECIAL INSPECTION WHEN HE HAS
REASON TO BELIEVE THAT UNDECLARED NUCLEAR ACTIVITIES ARE TAKING
PLACE IN A STATE WITH A COMPREHENSIVE SAFEGUARDS AGREEMENT.
THE PAPER EXPLAINS THAT A SMALL IAEA UNIT WILL BE CREATED TO
RECEIVE AND ASSESS INFORMATION (BOTH EXTERNAL, INCLUDING
NATIONAL INTELLIGENCE, AND INTERNALLY-GENERATED MATERIAL)
POINTING TO POSSIBLE UNDECLARED ACTIVITY. IF UNDECLARED
ACTIVITY IS CONFIRMED, THE IAEA WOULD MAKE A FINDING OF
NON-COMPLIANCE AND REFER THE MATTER TO THE UN SECURITY COUNCIL
FOR ACTION. THE PAPER ASKS ONLY THAT THE BOARD TAKE NOTE OF
THE APPROACH.

THE PAPER STRESSES THAT THE IAEA ALREADY POSSESSES AUTHORITY
UNDER ITS COMPREHENSIVE SAFEGUARD AGREEMENTS TO FOLLOW THIS
APPROACH AND CONDUCT SPECIAL INSPECTIONS OF UNDECLARED
FACILITIES, LOCATIONS, AND MATERIAL.

AN EXHAUSTIVE REVIEW OF THE NEGOTIATING HISTORY OF
INFCIRC/153, CARRIED OUT BY THE UNITED STATES GOVERNMENT
ESTABLISHES CONCLUSIVELY THAT THE IAEA POSSESSES THE AUTHORITY

0206

TO CALL FOR AND CONDUCT SPECIAL INSPECTIONS OF UNDECLARED
ACTIVITIES AND FACILITIES. THIS REVIEW WAS CONDUCTED IN 1984
AND, THUS IS NOT INFLUENCED IN ANY WAY BY RECENT IRAQI
EXPERIENCES. THIS CONCLUSION IS FULLY SHARED BY THE IAEA LEGAL
STAFF AND THE DIRECTOR GENERAL.

KEY POINTS IN OUR LEGAL ANALYSIS OF THE QUESTION ARE
PARAGRAPH 2 OF INFCIRC/153, WHICH GIVES THE IAEA THE "RIGHT AND
OBLIGATION" TO APPLY SAFEGUARDS TO ALL NUCLEAR MATERIAL IN ALL
PEACEFUL NUCLEAR ACTIVITIES, AND THE NEGOTIATING HISTORY WHICH
ESTABLISHES THAT DURING THE DEVELOPMENT OF INFCIRC/153 EFFORTS
TO LIMIT SAFEGUARDS TO DECLARED ACTIVITIES WERE MADE AND WERE
REJECTED. THE COMPLETE ABSENCE FROM INFCIRC/153 OF THE TERMS
"DECLARED" AND "UNDECLARED" IS NOT ACCIDENTAL AND CLEARLY
CONFIRMS THAT NO DISTINCTION IN SAFEGUARDS RIGHTS IN RESPECT TO
THESE CATEGORIES WAS MADE OR INTENDED.

SPECIAL INSPECTIONS TO DEAL WITH THE POSSIBILITY OF
UNDECLARED NUCLEAR ACTIVITIES WILL LIKELY TAKE PLACE VERY
INFREQUENTLY. WHILE THERE MAY BE OTHER APPROPRIATE USES OF
SPECIAL INSPECTIONS, THE UNITED STATES DOES NOT SUPPORT THE
CONCEPT OF FREQUENT CONDUCT OF SPECIAL INSPECTIONS SIMPLY TO
REDUCE THE POLITICAL PROFILE OF THIS MECHANISM. NO AMOUNT OF
NON-ADVERSARIAL SPECIAL INSPECTION WILL CHANGE THE ATTITUDE OF
A NON-COMPLYING STATE FACING AN AGENCY REQUEST FOR A SPECIAL
INSPECTION TO CONFIRM SUSPECTED UNDECLARED ACTIVITY.

IT IS IMPOSSIBLE AT THIS BEGINNING STAGE OF THE INITIATIVE
ON SPECIAL INSPECTIONS TO REACH ANY REALISTIC OR PRACTICAL
CONCLUSION REGARDING THEIR FINANCING. FEW CASES CALLING FOR
SPECIAL INSPECTIONS CAN BE EXPECTED TO ARISE, AND THE INITIAL
INSPECTIONS, IF ANY, TO CONFIRM WHETHER OR NOT SUSPECTED
ACTIVITY EXISTS COULD BE STRAIGHTFORWARD AND NOT RESOURCE
INTENSIVE. FOLLOW-ON ACTION, HOWEVER, TO DETERMINE THE FULL
EXTENT OF NON-COMPLIANCE COULD BE QUITE COSTLY, AS IN IRAQ, BUT
THIS WOULD BE AN EXTRAORDINARY ACTION WHOSE COSTS CANNOT BE
FORECAST AND WHOSE FINANCING WOULD HAVE TO BE HANDLED ON AN AD
HOC BASIS.

DESIGN INFORMATION

THE SECRETARIAT PAPER ON DESIGN INFORMATION INDICATES
THAT, UNDER COMPREHENSIVE SAFEGUARDS AGREEMENTS, THE IAEA WILL
REQUEST DESIGN INFORMATION ON NUCLEAR FACILITIES AS SOON AS A
DECISION TO CONSTRUCT IS MADE. UP-DATED DESIGN INFORMATION
WILL THEN BE SUBMITTED AT VARIOUS STAGES OF FACILITY
CONSTRUCTION AND WILL BE VERIFIED BY IAEA VISITS TO
FACILITIES. SHUT-DOWN FACILITIES WILL ALSO BE VISITED TO
ENSURE OPERATIONS ARE NOT RESUMED.

0207

SINCE COMPREHENSIVE SAFEGUARDS AGREEMENTS ALREADY REQUIRE STATES TO SUBMIT DESIGN INFORMATION "AS EARLY AS POSSIBLE," IAEA POSSESSES THE AUTHORITY FOR THIS APPROACH AS WELL. HOWEVER, SINCE SUBSIDIARY ARRANGEMENTS GENERALLY SPECIFY THAT DESIGN INFORMATION NEED NOT BE SUBMITTED UNTIL 180 DAYS PRIOR TO OPERATION, THE BOARD IS ASKED TO "CALL UPON" STATES TO AGREE TO AMENDMENTS TO SUBSIDIARIES TO PROVIDE FOR EARLY SUBMISSION AND TO PROVIDE INFORMATION VOLUNTARILY PENDING AMENDMENTS.

BY IMPLICATION BUT NOT EXPLICITLY, IAEA WOULD TAKE SIMILAR ACTION IN RELATION TO NON-COMPLIANCE WITH DESIGN INFORMATION REQUIREMENTS AS IN CONNECTION WITH SPECIAL INSPECTIONS; THAT IS, IF THE IAEA HAS REASON TO BELIEVE THAT A FACILITY IS UNDER CONSTRUCTION ON WHICH DESIGN INFORMATION HAS NOT BEEN SUBMITTED, THE INFORMATION WILL BE REQUESTED AND, IF THE INFORMATION IS NOT FORTHCOMING, A FINDING OF NON-COMPLIANCE WILL BE MADE.

ONE OF THE CONCERNS WHICH HAS ARISEN FROM THE GENERAL EXPERIENCES OF IRAQ IS THE LACK OF TIMELY IAEA KNOWLEDGE OF NEW NUCLEAR ACTIVITIES. THE ABSENCE OF ANY ARRANGEMENTS FOR NOTIFYING THE IAEA OF A STATE'S INTENTION TO BEGIN A NEW NUCLEAR ACTIVITY AND RATHER OUTDATED ARRANGEMENTS FOR PROVIDING DESIGN INFORMATION ON NEW FACILITIES HAVE CONTRIBUTED TO THIS PROBLEM.

IN HIS STATEMENT AT THE FEBRUARY 1991 IAEA BOARD MEETING THE DIRECTOR GENERAL REFERRED TO THE QUESTION OF TIMELY DESIGN INFORMATION FOR NEW INSTALLATIONS. HE CITED THE IMPORTANCE OF SUCH INFORMATION IN RESPECT TO THE CONFIDENCE OF MEMBER STATES IN THE SAFEGUARDS SYSTEM AND TO TAKING SAFEGUARDS INTO ACCOUNT IN THE DESIGN OF NEW FACILITIES.

WE SHARE THE DIRECTOR GENERAL'S CONCERNS AND BELIEVE THAT NOW IS AN OPPORTUNE TIME FOR POSITIVE BOARD ACTION TO REMEDY THE SITUATION AND SUPPORT THE BOARD ACTION RECOMMENDED IN THE SECRETARIAT PAPER.

THE SECRETARIAT PAPER INCLUDES AN ADDITIONAL POINT ON THE NEED OF THE IAEA TO BE ABLE TO CONFIRM PERIODICALLY THE CONTINUED VALIDITY OF DESIGN INFORMATION ON WHICH SAFEGUARDS CONCLUSIONS DEPEND. THE SECRETARIAT PROPOSES THAT THIS CONFIRMATION BE ACHIEVED THROUGH REGULAR VERIFICATION OF THE RELEVANT DESIGN INFORMATION AT APPROPRIATE INTERVALS. WE SUPPORT FULLY THIS IMPORTANT POINT.

0208

외교문서 비밀해제: 걸프 사태 23
걸프 사태 유엔안전보장이사회 동향 6

초판인쇄 2024년 03월 15일
초판발행 2024년 03월 15일

지은이 한국학술정보(주)
펴낸이 채종준
펴낸곳 한국학술정보(주)
주 소 경기도 파주시 회동길 230(문발동)
전 화 031-908-3181(대표)
팩 스 031-908-3189
홈페이지 http://ebook.kstudy.com
E-mail 출판사업부 publish@kstudy.com
등 록 제일산-115호(2000. 6. 19)

ISBN   979-11-6983-983-9 94340
       979-11-6983-960-0 94340 (set)